1993

Instructional
Design

Instructional Design

Patricia L. Smith
Tillman J. Ragan

The University of Oklahoma

Merrill, an imprint of Macmillan Publishing Company
New York

Maxwell Macmillan Canada
Toronto

Maxwell Macmillan International
New York   Oxford   Singapore   Sydney

Editor: Linda Sullivan
Production Supervisor: Proof Positive/Farrowlyne Associates, Inc.
Production Manager: Aliza Greenblatt
Text and Cover Designer: Proof Positive/Farrowlyne Associates, Inc.

This book was set in Times by Carlisle Communications, Ltd., and printed and bound by Book Press.
The cover was printed by Phoenix Color Corp.

Macmillan Publishing Company
866 Third Avenue, New York, New York 10022

Macmillan Publishing Company is part of the
Maxwell Communication Group of Companies.

Maxwell Macmillan Canada, Inc.
1200 Eglinton Avenue East
Suite 200
Don Mills, Ontario M3C 3N1

Library of Congress Cataloging-in-Publication Data

Smith, Patricia L.
    Instructional design / Patricia L. Smith, Tillman J. Ragan
        p.   cm.
    Includes bibliographical references and index.
    ISBN 0-675-21262-6
    1. Instructional systems—Design.   I. Ragan, Tillman J.
    II. Title.
    LB1028.38.S65   1992
    371.3'078 — dc20
                                                    92-31790
                                                    CIP

Printing: 1 2 3 4 5 6 7   Year: 3 4 5 6 7 8 9

To our spouses, without whose constant support, encouragement, and patience this work would not have been possible.

preface

The strongest motivation to write this book came from the questions of our students and other professionals in the field. Some of these questions pertained to changing media capabilities, while others involved the need to speed up the design process. Many questions were the result of the enrichment of theoretical bases contributing to our field. The most urgent questions were in the area of designing instructional strategies. These questions are a product of what we call "the empty box syndrome." In most models or procedures for instructional design, front-end analysis is followed with the procedural step of "design the instructional strategy." Many of our current and former students as well as professional designers report that the information provided in traditional texts is insufficient for individuals to learn how to complete this step. Hence, eight of the seventeen chapters in this text (Chapters 6–13) address the design of instructional strategies. The chapters use Gagné's types of learning outcomes as a framework for designing strategies appropriate to particular types of learning. We have also related these strategies to Bloom's taxonomy and Anderson's division of learning into declarative and procedural components.

Our treatment of instructional strategies is based more heavily on a cognitive psychology theoretical base than most texts; this reflects the paradigm shift in the field of instructional design and instructional technology that many scholars in the field have noted. We hope to provide the young field of instructional psychology with clear descriptions of some prescriptive relationships between the external facilitation of learning, which we call *instruction*, and the internal cognitions that lead to learning.

We have also provided a balanced treatment of both supplantive instructional strategies—in which much cognitive processing is supported or prompted by the instruction—and more generative strategies (such as exploratory learning strategies) in which learners provide more of the instructional events for themselves. A significant difference between our work and traditional instructional design texts is the expansion and rewording of Gagné's events of instruction to reflect both learner-initiated processing and instruction-supplied processing.

Our text also emphasizes the contributions of cognitive psychology to instructional design. For example, Chapter 3 (which addresses learner characteristics) underscores the paramount role that the learner plays in the learning act. The text contains many examples that indicate the impact cognitive psychology has had on our field, such as the following: (1) the process for analyzing the cognitive information processing of tasks during task analysis; (2) the discussion of how assessment items may be written to elicit information about the underlying "understanding" of a subject matter; and (3) the use of think-aloud protocols in formative evaluation.

While we have accommodated the paradigm shift from previous views of systems and behaviorist concepts, we have not "thrown out the baby with the bathwater." For example, we have retained the general procedural systems model of instructional design and the specification of targeted outcomes prior to the design of instruction. Reasoned and validated theoretical eclecticism has been a key strength of our field because no single theoretical base provides complete prescriptive principles for the entire design process.

This text is appropriate for all students of instructional design: practicing professionals such as teachers and professors, instructional designers, or training and development professionals; and college students, including graduate students in instructional technology, instructional design and development, instructional media, or educational and instructional psychology. It is also a challenging and comprehensive text for undergraduates who are studying instructional media or teacher education, and other students who will be creating, revising, and implementing systematic instruction. This text would be especially helpful for public education applications due to the current focus on "outcomes-based education" and other movements to improve education by creating logical relationships among instructional goals, activities, assessment, and evaluation. We have supplied examples involving public education, training, and informal education contexts so that readers will not only see how instructional design principles apply within their own environments, but also how they apply in less familiar arenas.

Text Features

Several instructional features that we have found to enhance the learning of instructional design are included in the text:

- In our discussions of the application of critical principles, we have provided many **examples** and some much-needed **nonexamples**. Some of these examples are presented in a narrative form, which promotes students' interest and comprehension.
- One unusual feature of the text is the **Extended Example** for the design of components in an instructional photography course. This section appears at the end of Chapters 2–16, and it exemplifies the major principles presented in each chapter. It has been our experience that while learners benefit from the diversity of short examples within each chapter, they also greatly benefit from seeing the instructional design for one content unfold across the entire instructional design process.
- **Exercises** are embedded within the chapters so that students can monitor their learning as they progress through the chapter. We base the exams that we give our own students on the item specifications from which these Exercises were derived. (Model answers to these Exercises may be obtained from the authors.)

- The text also contains **graphic summaries** that readers can use to organize the content and take notes.
- Finally, many chapters contain **Job Aids**, which summarize the information that learners must obtain and the decisions that they must make to complete each phase of the instructional design process. We expect that learners, instructors, and practicing designers will adapt these Job Aids to more closely match the particular instructional design problems that they encounter.

We envision this text being used in at least four general ways. First of all, it can be used as a beginning instructional design text for a course in which the goals would be the application of individual concepts and principles presented in the text. (The Exercises would be very helpful for students and instructors using the book in this context.) Secondly, the book might be employed in an advanced instructional design course that reviews prerequisite concepts and principles and utilizes the text as a guide for development of an instructional design product. The text could also be used in a manner that ambitiously combines the first two methods described. This is how we use the text in *our* classrooms. Finally, this text might be read as a handbook for practicing instructional designers.

Acknowledgments

We are indebted to our esteemed former professors and colleagues for their ground-breaking scholarship, especially L. J. Briggs, W. Dick, R. M. Gagné, J. Keller, and W. Wager. After writing this text, we more fully realize that we "stand on the shoulders" of our predecessors! We are grateful for the thoughtful questions of our students in EDTE 6163; without their conviction that "the story isn't finished yet," we never would have completed such an enormous five-year project. We are also indebted to the students in this same class for their formative feedback of iterations of the text over the past four years. We must specifically mention Tom Bergman and Mary Beth Smith, who provided us with detailed written feedback over an entire semester. We gratefully acknowledge the insightful and scholarly comments of our reviewers: Brock Allen, San Diego State University; John Belland, Ohio State University; Barry Bratton, University of Iowa; Carol Carrier, University of Minnesota at Minneapolis; Doris Dale, Southern Illinois University at Carbondale; Philip Doughty, Syracuse University; James Farmer, Jr., University of Illinois at Urbana-Champaign; Gary Ferrington, University of Oregon; Barbara Grabowski, Pennsylvania State University; Robert Gray, East Texas State University; Karen Medsker, Marymount University; Tim Newby, Purdue University; Albert Pautler, Jr., SUNY Buffalo; Taher Razik, SUNY Buffalo; Landra Rezabek, Florida State University; and Paul Welliver, Pennsylvania State University. Finally, we acknowledge the guidance and careful attention to our manuscript provided by Linda Sullivan, editor, Macmillan Publishing Company, and Bobby Reed of Proof Positive/Farrowlyne Associates.

Patricia L. Smith
Tillman J. Ragan
The University of Oklahoma
September 1992

Author Biographies

Patricia Smith is an associate professor in the Instructional Psychology and Technology program at The University of Oklahoma. She received her Ph.D. in Instructional Systems from Florida State University in 1982. Smith is the author of two books and numerous journal articles on computer-based instruction and instructional design. She has been on the board of directors of the Research and Theory Division and the Division of Instructional Development of AECT. Other positions include being cochair of the Professors of Instructional Design Technology conference in 1992 and president of the Instructional Technology Special Interest Group of AERA in 1993. Her area of research and teaching is instructional design, particularly the design of organizational strategies, the design of print-based instruction, and instructional feedback.

Tillman J. Ragan is a professor in the Instructional Psychology and Technology program at The University of Oklahoma. He received his Ph.D. in Instructional Technology from Syracuse University in 1970. Ragan is the author of five books and numerous articles on instructional technology, and he is a columnist for *Educational Technology* magazine. He has served on many committees and has held the titles of president of the Research and Theory Division of AECT, vice-president of IVLA, and cochair of the Professors of Instructional Design Technology conference in 1992. His area of research and teaching is instructional technology, with specific interests in learner characteristics, visual literacy, and applications of computer technology to instruction.

brief contents

contents

Introduction to Instructional Design

one

Chapter Objectives

At the conclusion of this chapter you should be able to do the following:

- Define *instructional design.*

- Define *instruction,* distinguish it from related terms (such as *education, training,* and *teaching*), and when given descriptions of educational activities, determine which of these are instruction.

- Identify and describe the three major phases of the instructional design process, and when given descriptions and instructional design activities, identify which phase is being employed.

- Describe at least four major assumptions of instructional design and discuss how these assumptions relate to your own philosophy of education.

- Describe advantages of using instructional design.

- State why it is important that instructional designers know the theory bases associated with their field.

- Define and describe the concept and purpose of *theory.*

- Describe each of the major theory bases and the ways in which they have contributed to instructional design practices.

- Given a description of a learning situation, describe how learning occurs according to information processing theory.

Introduction

Fourth-grade teacher Dora Brady is sitting at her desk after school, looking at the scores that her class made on the long-division quiz she gave today. She is reviewing the students' performance in her mind and recalling how she taught the students. She is working on new ways to teach the kids. She is drawing upon her knowledge of something called *instructional design* in her thinking.

Dick Montiville is in conference with three coworkers at Amalgamated Airlines. Mr. Montiville and his team are figuring out the exact nature of the learning that aircrew members need in order to improve the safety of the company's flights. The areas of required learning have already been established, and now the team is breaking those learning tasks down into the components and prerequisites. Montiville and his team are using some techniques from instructional design to guide their work.

Fay Hartman and William Burke are in charge of evaluating the new textbook series in organic chemistry being developed by MacBurdick Publishers. The series is intended to capture the market in its subject area, and principles of instructional design were used in many phases of the project, including the evaluation work of Hartman and Burke.

What Does *Instructional Design* Mean?

The term **instructional design** refers to the systematic process of translating principles of learning and instruction into plans for instructional materials and activities. An instructional designer is somewhat like an engineer. Both plan their works based upon principles that have been successful in the past—the engineer on the laws of physics, and the designer on basic principles of instruction and learning. Both try to design things that are not only functional but also attractive or appealing to the user of the product. Both the engineer and instructional designer have established problem-solving procedures that they use to guide them in making decisions about their designs.

Through this systematic process both the engineer and the instructional designer plan out what the finished product will be like. Both write specifications (plans) for the products, but they do not necessarily translate their specifications into an actual product. They often hand their plans to someone who specializes in production (a building contractor, in the case of an engineer, and a media production specialist in the case of the instructional designer) to develop the product. This holds true for many instructional designers. However, some designers—for instance designers with production skills, such as computer programming, video production, or development of print materials—may themselves translate their specifications into the final instructional material. Classroom teachers typically implement their own plans. In any event, the designer does not begin the production until the specifications are completed.

Careful, systematic planning is particularly important when the medium of instruction is something other than a teacher. Good teachers have the ability to adjust instruction "on the spot" according to the learners' needs. When the instructional medium is not so immediately adaptable (as with printed materials, videotaped materials, and computer-based instruction), having a design that is based upon principles of instruction is even more important. Any oversights that were made in the design of these instructional materials cannot be easily remedied because the instruction is being delivered via instructional media. Therefore, individuals who develop instructional materials (particularly people in the field of instructional technology) are the most consistent users of instructional design procedures and principles.

In order to understand the term *instructional design* more clearly, we will review the meanings of *instruction* and *design*.

What Is Instruction?

Instruction is the delivery of information and activities that facilitate learners' attainment of intended, specific learning goals. In other words, instruction is the conduct of activities that are focused on learners learning specific things. For example, a teacher or trainer may wish to help learners use a particular kind of computer software to solve a certain set of problems. The instructional designer will develop materials and activities that are intended to prepare the learners to use the software effectively. Every learning experience that is developed is focused toward a particular goal. In addition to having effective instruction as a goal, designers also wish to create instruction that is efficient (requiring the least time and cost necessary) and appealing.

Terms such as *education, training,* and *teaching* are often used interchangeably with *instruction*. However, in this text we will make some fine distinctions among these terms. Certainly, these distinctions may not be made in the same way among all individuals in the field of education, or even in the field of instructional design. However, we have found these definitions helpful in laying the framework for this text. Figure 1.1 illustrates the relationships between these terms.

We will use the term **education** very broadly to describe all those experiences in which people learn. Many of these experiences are unplanned, incidental, and informal. For example, many people learn to drive a car in city traffic through a trial and error process involving many harried morning trips. The driver learns, so these experiences can be considered part of his general education; however, no one has specifically arranged this learning experience so that he can learn well, quickly, and with a minimum of frustration. It would be possible to create a series of particular experiences (perhaps using videotapes and city maps) that would be specifically focused on preparing one to navigate city traffic easily. We would call the delivery of these focused educational experiences **instruction.**

So, all instruction is part of education because all instruction consists of experiences leading to learning. But not all education is instruction because many learning experiences that could be considered education are not specifically developed and delivered to ensure effective, efficient, and appealing experiences leading toward particular learning goals.

We generally use the term **training** to refer to those instructional experiences that are focused upon individuals acquiring very specific skills that they will normally apply almost immediately. For example, many instructional experiences in vocational education classes can be considered training. The students learn skills, specifically focused toward job competencies, which they will use almost immediately. Much instruction in business, military, and government settings can be termed *train-*

ing because the experiences are directed toward preparing learners with specific on-the-job skills. In addition, the instruction in certain special education classes is "training" because the learning experiences have been developed to provide students with life-skills, such as counting change, which we anticipate they will use almost immediately.

Not all instruction can be considered "training," however. For instance, in military education programs, learners may be provided with some general instruction in math and reading. These learning experiences can be termed *instruction* because the lessons were developed with some specific goals in mind, such as a certain level of proficiency in reading and mathematics. However, these skills are often not directed toward a specific job task, nor is there anticipation of immediate impact upon a specific job task. The influence on job performance is anticipated to be more diffuse throughout job responsibilities and outside job tasks. Therefore, in our terminology, these learning experiences would not be termed *training*.

Of all the terms, *teaching* and *instruction* may be most often used interchangeably. In this text, we will use the term **teaching** to refer to those learning experiences in which the instructional message is delivered by a human being—not a videotape, textbook, or computer program—but a live teacher. Instruction, then, includes all teaching and other learning experiences in which the instructional message is conveyed by other forms of media. As you will discover later, one of the primary tenets of instructional design is that a live teacher is not essential to all instruction.

As Figure 1.1 shows, not all teaching is considered to be instruction. There are occasions in an educational environment in which a teacher does not focus learning experiences toward a specific learning goal. On these occasions, teachers may provide many learning activities, and during these activities learning goals may emerge, often from the learners themselves as they encounter the activities. For example, some preschool education falls within this category, such as instances in which learners are provided with a variety of manipulative materials that they can use to pursue many problems. These pursuits might lead to various learning outcomes, not all of which have been specifically anticipated by the teacher.

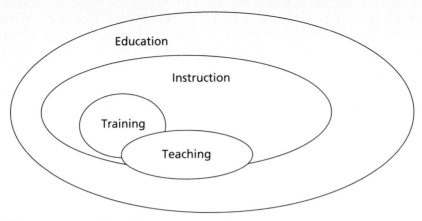

Figure 1.1: Relationships Among Terms Associated with Instruction

In summary, in this text we will consider *instruction* to be a subset of *education*. The term *training* will be considered a subset of *instruction*. In some cases *teaching* will be considered instruction, and in others it will fit the more general category of education but will not have the specific focus that characterizes instruction. We will concentrate, in this text, on the design and development of information presentation and activities that are directed toward specific learning outcomes. This text focuses on instruction.

What Is Design?

Many fields use the term *design* as part of their title; examples include interior design, architectural design, and industrial design. The term **design** implies a systematic planning process prior to the development of something or the execution of some plan in order to solve a problem. Design is distinguished from other forms of planning by the level of precision, care, and expertise that is employed in the planning process. Designers employ a high level of precision, care, and expertise in the systematic planning of a project because they perceive that poor planning can result in serious consequences, such as misuse of time and other resources, even in loss of life. Specifically, instructional designers fear that poor instructional planning can result in poor, inefficient, and unmotivated learning—a consequence that can have serious long-term effects.

Design involves the consideration of many factors that may affect or be affected by the execution of the plan. For example, interior designers must consider the purpose and level of use of a facility, the anticipated traffic patterns, and the type of people who will be using the facility. They must consider the engineer's plans, such as the location and strength of walls. They must follow laws and regulations with regard to accessibility and safety. If they do not consider all these factors and how they interrelate, the designers risk creating a work or living space that is unusable.

Designers of instruction also consider the factors that can affect the success of instruction. Throughout this text, we will address the factors that instructional designers must consider prior to writing, producing, or delivering even one word of instruction.

Creativity also has a role in design. Novice designers sometimes have the impression that doing design work is a "cut-and-dried" activity. This is not the case. For example, if one were to give several architects the same conditions—site, materials, and purpose—the plans for the structures that they would create would vary radically. Some would be highly imaginative and innovative, while some might be more mundane and standard. All the designs may "work" in the sense that when executed the buildings would remain standing and serve their purpose. However, some imaginative and ingenious structures may inspire awe, while more mundane structures may be totally forgettable.

Just as the design of the architect benefits from creativity and imagination, so do the designs of the instructional designer. There is a critical need for imagination and ingenuity in the design of instruction. This text contains rules for designing instruction that will "work." Students of instructional design must interject imagination and ingenuity to make instruction inspiring and memorable.

Another key aspect of instructional design is its extensive and demanding nature. Experienced designers (not to mention novices) frequently express concern about the time and effort that they can expend when applying what is currently known about designing efficient, effective, and appealing instruction. Clearly, there is enough of a "technology" undergirding the design process that a casual approach to either learning or application of skills in instructional design will not do it justice. However, those who are beginning their study of instructional design should know that once the concepts and principles of instructional design are learned, they can be appropriately applied with a wide range of effort, precision, and formality. Even classroom teachers in public schools (who by virtue of their teaching loads do not generally have time to engage in instructional design in a full-blown fashion) can significantly improve the effectiveness of their teaching by applying instructional design principles in an informal fashion. They may choose to apply design principles mentally and document little, if any, of their thinking on paper. Of course, in instructional design classes learners are asked to document their thought processes so that the instructor can evaluate them and provide remediation where necessary. In many contexts—particularly those situations in which teams work together on a design project or scenarios in which legal liability for the quality of the design is a key issue—a hard-copy documentation of the design process may be essential.

Recent developments in the field are specifically directed at reducing the time and effort required by the instructional design process. We review a number of these "fast-track" approaches to instructional design in the final chapter of this text.

*T*he Instructional Design Process

Another way to define *instructional design* is to describe the process involved in the systematic planning of instruction. At the most basic level, the instructional designer's job is to answer three major questions (Mager, 1984):

1. Where are we going? (What are the objectives of the instruction?)
2. How will we get there? (What is the instructional strategy and the instructional medium?)
3. How will we know when we have arrived? (What should our tests look like? How will we evaluate and revise the instructional materials?)

These three questions can be stated as major phases that an instructional designer completes during the design and development process:

1. Perform an instructional analysis to determine "where we're going."
2. Develop an instructional strategy to determine "how we'll get there."
3. Develop and conduct evaluation to determine "how we'll know when we're there."

These three steps form the foundation of the approach to instructional design[1] that this book describes. We will expand on these three phases throughout the text.

An Overview of the Design Process: Designing Training for Digital-Magic Repair Persons

The purpose of this textbook is to help students learn the procedures for designing instructional materials, and the following section will provide an overview of the entire process. We will describe how designers might prepare a system of instructional materials to train individuals to repair the fictitious Digital-Magic stereophonic, 3-D television system that will soon be marketed across the United States.

Analysis. During this phase the designers will learn as much as they can about the environment in

---

[1] We use the term *instructional design* to refer to the entire process of design, development, implementation, and revision of instruction. The term *instructional development* is a related term, and if it were not so awkward, we might refer to the process as *instructional design and development*. Some aspects, particularly production, would seem to fit more easily under a term like *development* than *design*. Since the term *instructional design* is currently the most widely used of the choices available, we will use it in this text.

which the learners (repair persons) will be trained, about the learners themselves, and about the repair tasks for which the learners must be prepared. The designer will ask many questions of the managers and supervisors in the Digital-Magic company, the developers of the new television system, those who have provided training for repair persons in the past, and of the learners themselves. They will analyze the learning task itself, asking what learners must know or be able to do in order to learn to make repairs. The designers will want the answers to questions such as the following:

1. Will the learners be brought together in a central location or will they be trained in their own work environments?
2. How much time is available for training?
3. Will it be possible for the learners to have access to the new television systems to work with as they learn about them?
4. How do learners feel about the training? What sorts of incentives to learn will they be given?
5. What kinds of people are the prospective learners? What interests them? What kinds of educational backgrounds do they have?
6. What do the learners already know that will help them learn the new information or skills?
7. What are the skills and knowledge that the learners must acquire in order to make the repairs on the new system? Do they need to know only the technical procedures of repair or do they also need to know the conceptual or theoretical *whys* of the procedures?
8. How should the learners' achievement of the objectives be assessed? Is a pencil-and-paper test adequate? Should learners be assessed on actually repairing a Digital-Magic television set? Can this performance be simulated?

Selecting the Instructional Strategy. During this phase, the designers determine the way that instructional material relating to repair of the television sets should be presented. They also decide which learning activities the learners should be asked to complete. In addition, the designers determine what sequence the steps of instruction should follow. They choose the medium or media that will deliver the instruction. This is the stage in which the designers will determine exactly how instruction will take place.

Some of the questions that designers would answer in this phase are the following:

1. What kinds of content must be learned by the students? In what size segments should the content be presented? Should information be presented, or should the content be embedded within an activity?

2. What activities should the learners engage in? What role will learners' activities have? Will they supplement essentially informational presentations, or will they be the primary means of learning? Should learners answer written questions? Should they practice troubleshooting problems on the actual equipment? For what topics (if any) will reading be an appropriate learning activity? What topics will require viewing demonstrations and visual examples? Are discussions needed?

3. In what sequence should instruction proceed? Should a "discovery" sequence be followed, or should an "expository" approach be used? If expository, what sequence of presentation should be employed?

4. What media are most appropriate for the delivery of instruction? Should learners see a live demonstration of repair procedures, a videotaped presentation, or an interactive video presentation? Or should they read about it in a text or workbook? Or should they use both? Should the students have a job performance aid (such as a manual) available to them for reference?

5. What groupings should learners be placed in for learning? Should they study independently, in a small group, or in a large group?

Evaluation. When designing evaluation, the designers plan an approach for evaluating the instructional materials to determine what kinds of changes need to be made in them. So, at Digital-Magic, some of the questions that may be asked include the following:

1. Is the content accurate? Have there been design changes in the Digital-Magic television sets since the instruction was originally developed?
2. What learners should use the materials in order to get information to guide revisions? How

should we conduct these tryouts? Should the sample be large or small? Should students be observed one at a time or in groups?

3. What questions should be answered in order to determine problems in the instruction?
4. What revisions should be made in the instruction?

When we use the term **evaluation** it will often be in reference to the broad topic including both assessment of learners and evaluation of the instruction. When we are talking about evaluation of students' learning, we will generally use the term **assessment** instead of the more familiar but often misleading term *tests* (see Chapter 5). Frequently we use the term *evaluation* in the context of evaluating the instruction itself; the terms *formative evaluation* and *summative evaluation* will be used in this fashion (see Chapter 16).

The Digital-Magic Story: A Postmortem. The instructional designers at Digital-Magic did a good job of instructional design. The training system for repair persons was highly effective and efficient. Not only did the student technicians learn what they needed to learn, but they also enjoyed the process and developed a good attitude about their work. It was a good thing, too, because the new television set was very popular in the market, and the first 10,000 Digital-Magic televisions that were manufactured had a faulty part in them. The well-trained service technicians fixed the problems, and as time passed they acquired the reputation of being excellent repair persons.

Congruence Among the Phases of Instructional Design

Instructional designers insist on creating instruction in which the objectives, the instructional strategy, and the evaluation all match. By "match," we mean that the strategy (instructional method) that is used is appropriate for the learning task (objectives) and that the tests measure how well the learners have achieved the learning task (assessment).

For example, let's say you are an instructional designer now, and that you are working on the design of instruction in which students will learn to classify objects as either transparent, translucent, or opaque. **Learning tasks** are the things we want students to learn, so being able to classify objects

as either transparent, translucent, or opaque is the learning task, and this particular learning task involves *concept learning*. The idea of "matching" learning tasks and instructional strategy means that you would select an instructional strategy that is appropriate for learning about concepts; you would ensure that students were given several examples and nonexamples of the concepts to be taught. To match evaluation with the learning task and instructional strategy, you would devise your test to determine whether students have learned the concepts by asking them to classify objects as either transparent, translucent, or opaque. In this instruction, the objective—to learn the concepts of "transparent," "translucent," and "opaque"—the presentation of information and learning activities, and the assessment are congruent with one another. In other words, they match.

This consistency between intent and action is seen in other approaches to the improvement of education. In the specialties of curriculum development and teaching methods, the idea of "curriculum alignment" is another reflection of congruence between objectives, instruction, and assessment.

Instructional Design Models

To answer the questions "Where are we going? How will we get there?" and "How will we know when we've arrived?" the designer goes through a three stage process: analysis, strategy development, and evaluation. These three stages are the essence of what is often called **instructional design models.** Andrews and Goodson (1980) have described 40 such models for systematic design of instruction. In this text we will recommend a simple model of design (see Figure 1.2). It is similar to the design models suggested by Dick and Carey (1985), and Davis, Alexander, and Yelon (1974).

You will notice in Figure 1.2 that we have listed the steps of design within each major phase of design in a particular sequence. In general, designers follow this sequence; however, particular circumstances may cause a designer to modify the sequence of design steps. Many times the steps within a particular phase may occur concurrently.

Note that the fourth step, the writing of test items, occurs within the analysis phase, immediately after analyzing the learning task. This sequence may

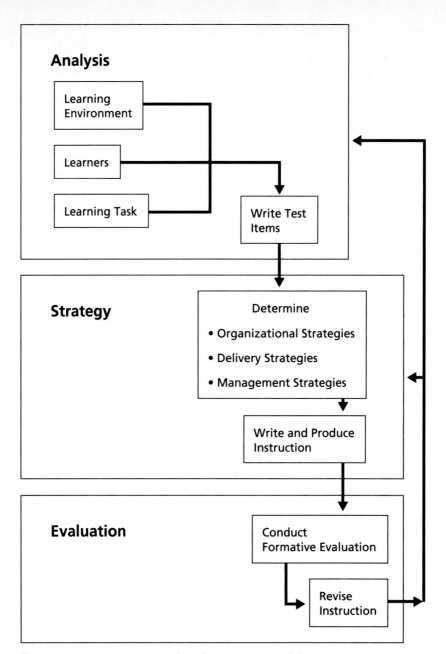

Figure 1.2: An Instructional Design Process Model

seem unusual to you at first glance, particularly if you are accustomed to designing tests after delivering instruction. There is a good reason for this sequencing, which we will discuss in the chapter on assessment.

You will notice that revision of instruction is considered part of the evaluation process. This is the point where most of the revisions take place—after learners have tried out the instruction. However, revision may occur during the analysis or strategy stages as well. Design (somewhat like the branches of the U.S. government) contains a series of "checks and balances." Many decisions made early in the design process may have to be modified as decisions are made and information is acquired in later steps. For example, instructional objectives may have to be modified when designers realize that they cannot create reliable and valid evaluation to assess their objectives. This constant revision during design makes the instructional product, such as a workbook, videotape, or piece of software, a much more effective and efficient form of instruction.

Assumptions Underlying Instructional Design

There are a number of assumptions underlying the process of instructional design. Novice designers should encounter these assumptions in an explicitly stated form. Although they may not totally agree with the assumptions (and often design excellent instruction without this agreement), novice designers can find the design process more meaningful when these assumptions are made explicit. Below are some of the most critical assumptions:

1. In order to design instruction, the designer must have a clear idea of what the learner should learn as a result of the instruction.
2. The "best" instruction is that which is effective (facilitates learners' acquisition of the prescribed knowledge and skills), efficient (requires the least possible amount of time necessary for learners to achieve the objectives), and appealing (motivates and interests learners, encouraging them to persevere in the learning task).

3. Students may learn from many different media: A "live teacher" is not always essential for instruction.
4. There are principles of instruction that apply across all age groups and all content areas. Here is an example: Students must participate actively, interacting mentally as well as physically with material to be learned.
5. Evaluation should include the evaluation of the instruction as well as the evaluation of the learner's performance. Information from the evaluation of instruction should be used to revise the instruction in order to make it more efficient, effective, and appealing.
6. Learners should be evaluated in terms of how nearly they achieve the instructional objectives rather than how they "stack up" against their fellow students.
7. There should be a congruence among objectives, learning activities, and assessment. The objective should be the driving force behind decisions about activities and assessment.

These assumptions will be alluded to and further explained throughout this text.

Advantages of Using Systematic Instructional Design

For those involved in developing instruction there are a number of advantages to using a systematic process. The following is a list of some of the advantages of systematic instructional design:

1. *Encourages advocacy of the learner.* To a very large degree, the learner is the focus of instruction. Designers spend a great deal of effort during the beginning stages of a design project trying to find out about the learner. Information about learners should take precedence over other factors that might drive design decisions, including the content itself. Often the designer is not a content expert. In their constant querying of a subject matter expert for clarification, designers are standing in the place of the learner, trying to obtain information to make the content clearer to the learner.

2. *Supports effective, efficient, and appealing instruction.* All of these factors are considered

indicators for success. The process of design itself focuses on effective instruction. Efficiency is particularly facilitated by the process of instructional analysis in which any unnecessary content is eliminated. The consideration of the learner and the concentration on designing appropriate strategies promotes the appeal of instruction. The process of formative evaluation provides the opportunity to revise instruction to make it more effective, efficient, and appealing.

3. *Supports coordination among designers, developers, and those who will implement the instruction.* The systematic process and resulting written documentation allow for communication and coordination among individuals involved in designing, producing, and delivering instruction. It allows for common language and general procedure. The written plans (objectives, description of target audience, and analysis of task) and the written products that are results of instructional design efforts assist the process of review and revision of work in progress in a coordinated team effort.

4. *Facilitates diffusion/dissemination/adoption.* Because the products of systematic instructional design are in fact physical "products," they may be duplicated, distributed, and used in the field. In addition, due to the consideration and use of information about the learners and setting, products will have a high likelihood of being practical, workable, and acceptable solutions to the instructional problems that they are designed to solve.

5. *Supports development for alternate delivery systems.* Much of the work that goes into an instructional design project is independent of the specific form that the finished product takes (such as print, computer, or video). The front-end analysis and consideration of instructional strategies will be valid beginning points for projects that employ delivery systems other than that which the original project used.

6. *Facilitates congruence among objectives, activities, and assessment.* The systematic approach to instructional design helps ensure that what is

taught is what is needed for learners to achieve stated goals for learning, and that evaluation will be accurate and appropriate.

*L*imitations of Systematic Instructional Design

Instructional design does have limits of applicability; it's not the solution to all the ills and problems of education and training, nor is it the only method for creating education. In particular, instructional design has more limited applicability to educational experiences in which learning outcomes cannot be identified in advance (i.e., non-instructional education). In such cases, because there is no "lead time" to the education, there is limited opportunity to apply many of the principles and procedures of instructional design. An example of such a situation might be an advanced graduate class or other educational situations in which the learners have exceptional prior knowledge of the content; these students would have well-developed cognitive strategies and be required to identify the outcomes of the course, devise the educational strategies, and assess their learning themselves. If a teacher is available in this situation, a skilled instructor might be able to process information rapidly enough so that as learners identify goals and devise strategies, the instructor could make suggestions for better or alternative strategies. In such a case the teacher's knowledge of instructional design may be very helpful in her consultant role; however, she may not have time to employ much of the instructional design process and principles. In a situation without pre-specified learning outcomes, if a teacher is not available, then the responsibility for structuring the learning experience rests totally on the learners, and their success depends on their own cognitive strategies, prior knowledge, and motivation. The educational system in such a case may attempt to provide informational resources to the learners; but without pre-specified outcomes, it is highly probable that they will incorrectly guess the resources that are needed.

Many educational problems are not amenable to instructional design. We will discuss solutions, such as management, policy, and incentives, that are not instructional solutions in Chapter 2. Instructional design is not intended to take the place of expertise in particular teaching methods for individual subject areas (although instructional design can be a helpful undergirding for such methods).

*E*xercises A

1. What activities other than those of an engineer are similar to the role of an instructional designer? Describe these similarities in your own words.

2. The following is a description of the design procedures that an instructional designer is conducting. Identify by writing on the line beside the description which phase— analysis (A), strategy development (SD), or evaluation (E)—the designer is completing.

   _____ a. The designer determines that the prospective learners are able to read (on the average) at the ninth-grade reading level.

   _____ b. The designer decides to use a simulation method as part of training a department store's customer service representatives.

   _____ c. The designer determines what the learners need to know in order to learn to balance chemical equations.

   _____ d. After a tryout of the prototype of a computer based instruction (CBI) lesson on writing instructional objectives, the designer adds additional practice items on identifying the "conditions" of an objective.

   _____ e. The designer writes test items to assess whether learners have achieved the objectives of a CBI lesson.

3. Which of the following activities would be termed *education, instruction, training,* and/ or *teaching*? Circle the term or terms that apply.

   a. The teacher presents a lesson in which she hopes that the learners will learn the difference between polygons and nonpolygons. She has carefully planned activities in which she will present examples and nonexamples of polygons and will help students determine the differences. She will test the students at the end of instruction to confirm that they have learned to identify those geometric figures that are polygons.

   education   instruction
   teaching   training

   b. The instructional designer for a large corporation has developed a print-based instructional package for managers who are involved in hiring to prepare them to follow legal practices during the hiring process. The learning materials inform them of the rules and show them examples and nonexamples of the rules' application. The tests provide a copy of an interview dialog between a manager and a potential employee. The learners must indicate whether all laws were followed. If they were not followed, learners must identify which laws were broken and what should have been said to avoid breaking the law.

   education   instruction
   teaching   training

   c. A television documentary presents information on types of whales, where whales live, what whales do, what whales eat, and the history of whales. Viewers tend to remember and learn different things from the program depending upon what they already knew and their interests.

   education   instruction
   teaching   training

4. To what degree do you agree or disagree with the assumptions that underlie the process of instructional design? In addition to these assumptions, what assumptions might other people subscribe to concerning the improvement of education and training? (You may include some assumptions that are contrary to the assumptions underlying instructional design.)

*I*nterim Summary

One of the reasons that the quality of much instructional material is poor is because it is not carefully planned. Instructional design procedures offer a process for the systematic planning of instruction that may improve the effectiveness of the materials. The design procedure follows the phases of analysis, strategy development, and evaluation. The components of instruction—objectives, learning activities, and test items—which are the products of the design process, should be congruent with each other. Design is an interactive process involving revisions of decisions based upon later decisions or learners' performance data.

Before you begin actually designing and producing your own materials, you will learn in the following chapters a few of the fundamental principles and procedures of instructional design. Figure 1.3 summarizes the major points in this chapter thus far.

Instructional Design Is. . .

the systematic process of translating principles of learning and instruction into specifications for instructional materials and activities.

Instruction Is. . .

the development and delivery of information and activities that are created to facilitate attainment of intended, specific learning goals.

Related terms. . .

Education: all experiences in which people learn.

Training: instruction focused toward acquisition of specific skills that will be used immediately.

Teaching: instruction delivered by a person.

Three Phases of the Instructional Design Process. . .

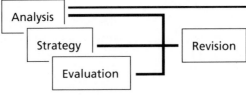

Analysis

Strategy

Evaluation

Revision

Figure 1.3: Interim Summary Diagram for Chapter 1

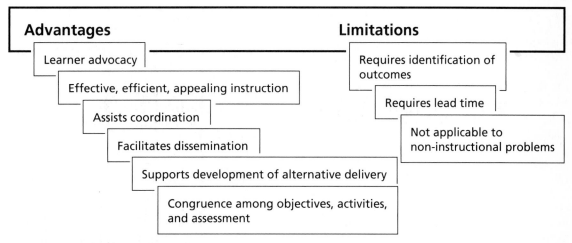

Some Assumptions and Values. . .

Knowledge of intended learning outcomes

Effectiveness, efficiency, and appeal

Live teacher not always necessary

Similar principles across content and ages

Instruction can be improved by evaluating its effects

Advantages

Learner advocacy

Effective, efficient, appealing instruction

Assists coordination

Facilitates dissemination

Supports development of alternative delivery

Congruence among objectives, activities, and assessment

Limitations

Requires identification of outcomes

Requires lead time

Not applicable to non-instructional problems

Figure 1.3: Continued

Why Discuss Theory in an Instructional Design Text?

Instructional design is an applied, decision-oriented field. So why include information on theory, particularly so early in the text? We have three major reasons for including this material. The first one is a matter of academic integrity. We feel that it is imperative that writers in our field acknowledge the bases of their conclusions and recommendations. The suggestions in this text are not just our studied opinions, nor are they based upon experiences with ''what works.'' They are based upon theories that have been substantiated and modified upon the basis of empirical research. Second, these theories have definitely shaped the directions of instructional design. Your awareness of these theories may give you the historical insight to understand why certain areas have been emphasized in this field. The theory bases are the common ground that we share with other professionals in the field. Third, these theories allow designers to explain why they make the decisions they do. Sometimes, designers must justify or even defend their decisions to clients or students. Theory can provide a rationale for many of our actions.

Most importantly, these theories are the source of principles from which many of the prescriptions for design arise. We will be referencing these theory bases throughout the book, particularly in the chapters on instructional strategies. Your knowledge of these theories is imperative. We suggest prescriptions and techniques for doing design work that is based upon the conditions (learners and context) and desired learning outcomes (tasks). However, you will face situations that have conditions or outcomes not covered by this text. Or you may try our suggestions and find that they don't work. In such situations you must reflect upon what you know to develop your own prescriptions for instruction. If you are knowledgeable of the theory bases available to you, you can make intelligent and reasoned decisions in such situations.

This chapter only points to the theories that have formed the basis of instructional design. It is an introductory treatment and is not intended to represent a sufficient background of theory for professional instructional designers. We recommend that the education of instructional designers include as many courses in learning theory and instructional theory as possible. In addition, it should also include as much reading as possible about the other historical theory bases and emerging theory bases related to this field.

What Is a Theory?

A **theory** is an organized set of statements that allow us to explain, predict, or control events. The theories from which instructional design draws are of two kinds—descriptive theory and prescriptive theory. **Descriptive** theory describes phenomena as they are hypothesized to exist. Many learning theories are descriptive: They describe how learning occurs. **Prescriptive** theories prescribe actions to take that will lead to certain results. Instructional theories are basically prescriptive in nature: They suggest that if instruction includes certain features, it will lead to certain types and amounts of learning.

*M*ajor Theory Bases Contributing to Instructional Design

Instructional design has drawn from many theory bases. However, the major theories that have contributed to instructional design are general systems theory, communication theory, theories of learning, and theories of instruction.

General Systems Theory

We see the influence of general systems theory in many of the models of instructional design and even in some theories and models of individual learning. In Andrews and Goodson's (1980) article reviewing models of instructional design, 70 percent of the models employed some elements of systems theory. The information-processing model used as a basis for some learning theories that will be described later in the chapter looks at the individual as a system that processes information from the environment. Central to this theory is the concept of a "system." A **system** is often defined as "a set of interrelated and interacting parts that work together toward some common goal." Systems exist naturally, such as the human body, the solar system, and the atom. Systems are also contrived, as in human-made systems, such as a business organization, the heating-cooling unit of a house, and a school system. Systems are set within a supra-system. For example, a school system is part of the larger system of the community. In turn, a system may have sub-systems comprising it. A school district contains individual schools, which operate as separate systems. Each of these sub-systems, or components, serves a purpose and is viewed as interdependent upon each other sub-system. Therefore, a change in one component will cause a change in its interdependent components.

In the following chapters, we will describe the procedures followed to examine the supra-systems in which a particular learning system operates. For example, in the analysis phase of design, we examine the supra-system in which the target learners exist, in order to develop instruction that can be implemented in the system. Such an examination of the learning context is critical because as changes in one system affect all components within the system as well as the supra-system in which it is found, it is critical that the effects of new instruction are anticipated and considered.

The environment also places constraints upon the system, limiting its goals and its inputs. We see the evidence of the interaction with the supra-system in public schooling. Many of the recent, large-scale changes in public education are a result of society's evaluation that when the "products" of public education (the learners) are returned to the system (society), their performance is inadequate (feedback). Therefore, substantial revisions are made in some of the inputs and resources, such as changes in teachers' education and funding changes, as well as in the processes of education.

We see evidence of this process of feedback and revision within most systematic design models. As we have noted, most models employ an evaluation and revision cycle. New instruction is "tried out" on a limited basis. The performance and attitudes of students and teachers/trainers provide information that leads to revisions in the instruction before it is fully implemented for all target learners.

Systems Tools.   One contribution that systems theory has made is tools for planning and problem solving, which grew out of applying systems theory in real-world situations. Two systems tools that are now in widespread use in many walks of life are flowcharts and critical path techniques such as PERT. Flowcharts were originally developed by computer scientists as a tool to assist in planning and representing computer programs. However, the utility of the flowchart as a tool for representing procedures of all kinds soon became recognized, and people now use flowcharts to represent everything from results of task analysis to instructional design models. Critical path techniques are project management tools that assist a manager or team in determining how long a complex project will take to complete and in ensuring that the project is completed on schedule.

Another major outgrowth of general systems theory has been the **systems approach.** When applied to a field of study or domain of human enterprise, systems thinking and tools result in an approach. The systems approach in education is a major contributing theoretical perspective to instructional design. Briggs (1977) defined the systems approach in education as "an integrated plan of operation of all components (sub-systems) of a system, designed to solve a problem or meet a need" (p. 6). So within the instructional design processes the system is a set of components (or steps) of a plan that have as their purpose the solution of a particular learning problem or need. The four common components of an instructional design model—analysis, strategy design (synthesis), evaluation, and revision—are common to systems approaches in many disciplines and very similar to a generalized model of problem solving applied in many settings.

Some individuals find the application of a systems approach to human endeavors to be mechanistic and cold. We tend to disagree. We find the systematic approach to be a way to find order and sense in endeavors that may appear chaotic. Use of the systems approach does not preclude creativity or the employment of human values by creative and sensitive designers.

Communication Theory

Communication theories have had a strong impact on the field of instructional design. This impact is particularly seen in decisions made during media selection and in the writing and production of instruction. While there is much that can be learned from such theories, most of them were developed to predict or explain events involved in information exchange or persuasion, not instruction. Instruction typically has as its goal the expansion of learners' cognitive structures, which are long lasting and transferrable. Therefore, instructional designers must carefully consider the value of these theories in the light of the goals of instruction.

One of the contributions of communications theory is a model of how information is communicated from one person to another. The communication model that is most often used by designers is the Schramm (1956) model (see Figure 1.4).

Note how the model incorporates a concept called **feedback,** which points out that for communication to occur, not only must a message be sent but there must also be a response by the receiver. This response alters subsequent messages from the original sender. The model also emphasizes the role of humans in encoding and decoding the message. In addition, the model gives an indication that factors may influence how the message is encoded and how it is decoded; these factors are all influenced by the sender's and receiver's respective fields of experience. In other words, the way the message is portrayed by the sender and interpreted by the receiver is strongly influenced by their prior experiences. Finally, it also emphasizes that the message may be distorted by noise. In instruction, the instructional message may be distorted by competing stimuli or poor quality transmission, two examples of noise.

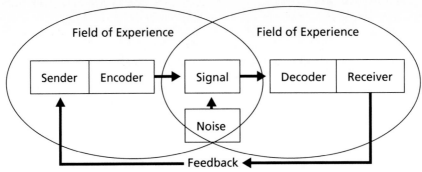

Figure 1.4: An Adaptation of Schramm's Communication Model
Source: Schramm (1956).

A number of considerations within instructional design methodology arise from communication theories. For example, the analysis of the learners that we discuss in Chapter 3 is an effort to understand the target learners' prior experiences, interests, and motivations so that the sender (instructional designer, teacher, or trainer) can understand the receivers' (learners') field of experience. The more the fields overlap, the greater the understanding of the message. The feedback loop substantiates the need for responses from and interaction with learners during instruction. These responses allow the teacher, trainer, or other instructional medium to adapt to the level of understanding of the learner. In addition, the formative evaluation step in instructional design procedures provides feedback about the effectiveness of the instructional message and thus allows the designer to make appropriate revisions in the instructional message.

Other theories and research surrounding communication theory contribute substantially to the field of instructional design. The major categories of this research address the following issues: the characteristics of various media as channels for the instructional message (discussed in Chapter 14) and the capabilities of the learners to decode instructional messages (discussed in Chapter 3).

Learning Theories

Promoting learning is what instructional design is all about. Therefore, instructional designers are very interested in learning theories, those theories that attempt to describe, explain, and predict learn-

ing. It is probably helpful at this time to define what is commonly meant by **learning.** R. Gagné defines learning as a "change in human disposition or capability that persists over a period of time and is not simply ascribable to processes of growth" (1985, p. 2). Mayer (1982) elaborates on this concept in his definition of learning:

"Learning" is the relatively permanent change in a person's knowledge or behavior due to experience. This definition has three components: (1) the duration of the change is long-term rather than short-term; (2) the locus of the change is the content and structure of knowledge in memory or the behavior of the learner; (3) the cause of the change is the learner's experience in the environment rather than fatigue, motivation, drugs, physical condition, or physiological intervention. (p. 1040)

According to this definition, has a person who has successfully followed the directions for assembling a swing set learned something? Not necessarily. The individual may have simply performed each step without trying to remember or understand any aspects of the process. There may be no lasting change in the individual's memory, nor change in ability to assemble objects in the future. Conversely, the individual may have acquired a new understanding of how certain types of pieces fit together, new knowledge in selecting an appropriate tool for a particular task, or new ability to manipulate a tool. This learning may be noted in the individual's ability to perform future assembly tasks more rapidly or with more aptitude. In such a case, we would say that learning has occurred.

As you recall from a previous discussion in this chapter, learning theories are chiefly descriptive. They describe how learning takes place. They are not necessarily prescriptive (i.e., they do not suggest what kinds of instructional intervention should support learning). Two major categories of learning theory that have influenced instructional design procedures and decisions are behavioral learning theories and cognitive learning theories.

Behavioral Learning Theories

The predominant school of thought in learning theory for the first half of the twentieth century has been labeled *behaviorism*. The behaviorist view of psychology had its beginnings in the late nineteenth century and in the first decade of this century with Ivan Pavlov's ''classical conditioning.'' Other important research includes E. L. Thorndike's work that culminated in his ''laws of learning,'' and J. B. Watson's articulation and formation of the behaviorist movement. B. F. Skinner's work on ''operant conditioning'' in the 1940s and 50s marked the maturation of the movement. Although some research on learning was being pursued from perspectives other than behaviorism during this time, the dominance of the behaviorist view, particularly in the United States, was almost complete during the first half of this century. Behaviorism's most visible influence on instructional design today is seen in some of the steps and techniques that we include in the design process, such as specification of behavioral objectives, development of performance-based assessments, and evaluation and field testing of instructional packages.

The behaviorist view held that the only things about human learning worth studying are those that can be observed. Behaviorists did not conjecture about thinking processes, mental states, and other unobservable phenomena. Rather, they concentrated on the observable **behavior** of organisms. At first, it may appear that a behaviorist view would be so limiting as to make it absurd. However, even though our current interests go beyond the strict limitations of the behaviorists, the behaviorist view has spawned the research and theory of many important phenomena of learning. Much of what was learned by the behaviorists appears to still be relevant to instructional designers today.

Behavioral theory emphasizes the importance of the environment on learning. According to behaviorism, learning has occurred when learners evidence the appropriate response to a particular stimulus. It is the importance of this connection or association between stimulus and response that characterizes behavioral theory. Behavioral theories explain the development of this association as being the result of learners receiving the appropriate reinforcement when the appropriate response is given to a particular stimulus.

An influential outgrowth of behaviorism, specifically of Skinner's work, was programmed instruction. Although programmed instruction did not revolutionize education as many thought it would at its introduction, its legacy has been significant. Innovations that were a part of programmed instruction include the use of behavioral or performance objectives, delivery of instruction through an instrument, and development of the materials through an empirical test of their effectiveness.

As is so often the case, the real significance of programmed instruction was not recognized until long after intense interest in it had passed. During the heyday of programmed instruction, controversies and debates raged over the two major formats in use: linear and branching. The linear format was an outgrowth of Skinner's work in learning theory, and the branching type had no particular theoretic foundation. The arguments between the two camps revolved about such concerns as the use of small steps in instructional presentation, the form of the learner's response (constructed responses versus selected responses), the kind and amount of feedback given, and the style of instruction. The camps also debated whether or not allowance should be made for student errors. Now that the dust has settled and research data are in and digested, we find that these questions are generally on factors that make little or no difference in learning, particularly as embodied in one or the other of the two programmed instruction formats. But the innovations of use of performance objectives, use of instructional instruments, and empirical evaluation of materials under development are all major building blocks in the principles of instructional design. They have had an enormous impact on education and training.

Cognitive Learning Theories

Currently cognitive learning theories are the dominant theoretical influence on instructional design practice. Schuell (1986) cites Bartlett's and Tolman's work in the 1930s and verbal learning research in the 1960s as the roots of cognitive learning theory. Cognitive learning theory places much more emphasis on factors within the learner and less emphasis on factors within the environment than behavioral theories. Schuell credits five major ways that cognitive psychology has influenced learning theory:

(a) the view of learning as an active, constructive process; (b) the presence of high-level processes in learning; (c) the cumulative nature of learning and the corresponding role played by prior knowledge; (d) concern for the way knowledge is represented and organized in memory; and (e) concern for analyzing learning tasks and performance in terms of the cognitive processes that are involved. (p. 415)

Clearly, cognitive learning theory focuses on the cognitive structures and processes that mediate between instructional stimuli and learning responses. In attending to these structures and processes, the importance of the learner as an active participant in the learning process takes on great importance. The learner is viewed as constructing meaning from instruction, rather than meaning residing alone within instruction. Therefore, cognitive learning theories attempt to explain learning in terms of cognitive processes and structures that are hypothesized to operate within the learner.

One of the most influential contributions from cognitive learning theory to instructional design practice is information-processing theory. Most current cognitive learning theorists advocate a theory (actually a set of theories) called **information processing.** Information-processing theories, in strong contrast to behavioral theories, describe learning as a series of transformations of information (i.e., processing) through a series of postulated structures within the brain. These structures currently are merely hypothesized and utilized to explain learning processes. To date, brain research has not identified specific locations of these particular structures. Atkinson and Shiffrin (1968) were the first to model this information processing.

R. Gagné's (1988) elaboration of this model illustrates the structures and processes of information processing (see Figure 1.5).

Sensory Register and Selective Perception. We receive information from our environment through our sensory receptors, our senses. The sensations are converted to electrochemical messages and sent to the brain where these impulses are stored very briefly (approximately one quarter of a second [Sperling, 1960]) in a structure, or a cluster of structures, labeled the **sensory register.** Perceptions of many environmental stimuli enter this register, but very few receive the attention, sometimes termed **selective perception,** to be further processed within the brain. The unattended stimuli receive no further consideration. Without such a process, we would be overwhelmed by the multitude of environmental stimuli we encounter in every instant. Our prior experience, including our expectancies, influence the stimuli to which we attend. For example, you may have noticed how easily you overhear your own name in a conversation at a party, or how easily you can find your name in an extensive list.

Short-Term Memory. Information to which attention has been paid passes into a structure called **short-term memory,** sometimes called *working memory.* This structure is characterized by its limited capacity, in terms of amount of information that it can retain (seven plus or minus two units of information [Miller, 1956]), and its short duration, in terms of the limited amount of time that information can be retained here (10 seconds [Murdock, 1961] to 20 seconds [R. Gagné, 1985]). Short-term memory has been likened to a desk top or a work bench, which is where everything actually happens but which can only hold a finite amount on its surface. Working memory is also similar to the RAM memory of a computer, which is certainly limited in size, but within which everything must at least momentarily reside to be processed.

As you can see from the bidirectional arrows in Figure 1.5, there is continuous transfer of information between long-term and working memory. Information is brought out of long-term memory into working memory (retrieval) in order to make sense out of new, incoming information. Not all information that enters working memory is trans-

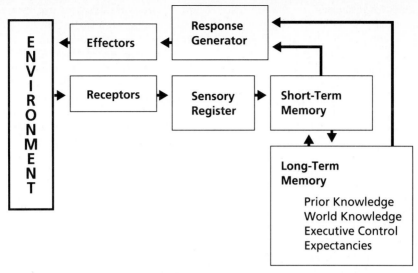

Figure 1.5: An Information-Processing Model of Learning and Memory
Source: Adapted from Gagné & Driscoll (1988). Reprinted with permission of Allyn & Bacon.

ferred to long-term memory. We have all experienced such a drop-out of information when we have retained a phone number only long enough to be able to redial it. We can keep that information in working memory longer than 10 to 20 seconds by rehearsing or repeating it. However, such a process would be an impossible method to retain all the information we need. Therefore, information is transferred, or encoded, into long-term memory.

Encoding and Long-Term Memory. Transfer of information into **long-term memory** is the most critical process of all the information processing to those who are interested in learning. A critical characteristic of information that is stored into long-term memory is that it must be meaningful. Non-meaningful information cannot be stored into long-term memory. In order for information to be meaningful, it must be integrated with related prior knowledge (i.e., information that is already stored in long-term memory). We can store fairly nonsensical information in long-term memory if we artificially make it meaningful. For example, we can remember a phone number by making it meaningful. A number like 799-2779 can be remembered by noticing the relationship of the numbers 7, 2, and 9, with the repetition of the nines in the first set

of numbers and the sevens in the second set. Likewise, we may try to "learn" (store in long-term memory) someone's name by connecting it with the interests or physical appearance of the person.

Organization is also a critical characteristic. Most theorists suggest that information is stored in non-random patterns. They generally conjecture that information is stored within memory in networks of propositions, ideas, or concepts that are connected with relationships (Anderson & Bower, 1973; Kintsch, 1972). The richness of these relationships and the adequacy of the organization will influence how available the stored information is for retrieval and use. In addition, some theorists believe that images may be stored as images in long-term memory (Paivio, 1971).

A third characteristic of long-term memory is its relatively unlimited capacity and permanency. Unlike working memory, long-term memory's capacity is theoretically open-ended and its duration may last a lifetime. While in learning we may experience a feeling of being "overloaded," this is due to the overloading of working memory or a difficulty in retrieving relevant prior knowledge with which to integrate it, rather than a saturation of long-term memory. And, while we may be unable to retrieve information stored in long-term memory, this may not mean that it has been lost from memory, but rather that the cues or strategies we are using are inappropriate. We have all experienced the inability to retrieve a person's name on one occasion, only to find that we could retrieve it on a later occasion.

Long-term memory is composed of propositions (and, perhaps, images) of a number of kinds. Certainly, information related to particular contents or experiences is stored there. In addition, executive control strategies, which are cognitive or learning strategies that influence how we manipulate information, are stored in long-term memory. Also, affective memories, including expectancies regarding learning experiences, are stored there. All of these memories influence all the stages of information processing. For example, our prior knowledge of a particular content, our expectancies regarding the goal and relevance of a lesson, and the strategies that we have learned to approach a particular content all influence that which we choose to "selectively attend to" in a lesson on that particular content.

Retrieval and Response Generator.   As we described earlier, memories of relevant information are retrieved from long-term memory into working memory to allow us to understand incoming information and in order to integrate the new information with the old. In some cases, this information is simply recoded in its enriched form and restored in long-term memory. In other cases, in addition to this recoding and storage, people may act upon the information by speaking or writing an answer, manipulating objects, or any of a number of other physical responses. The form, organization, and sequence of the response is determined by the response generator. This information is sent to the effectors, muscles, nerves, and glands, which in turn act and affect the environment.

A number of theorists have elaborated and expanded upon the processes and structures in information processing, particularly as they apply to learning. In contrast to the gestalt psychologists who primarily concerned themselves with the initial stages of information processing, recently cognitive learning theorists have concentrated primarily upon the later stages of information processing. Specifically, they have conjectured upon the structures and processes surrounding encoding

information into long-term memory from working memory and retrieval of information from long-term memory into working memory.

Cognitive psychology is the set of learning theories that is most influential in instructional design today. While the systematic approach to instructional design, which evolved from systems theory and materials development in the behavioral tradition, still influences the steps that we follow in conducting instructional design, a great deal of *how* we conduct each step is influenced by cognitive psychology. We will briefly review how each of the phases of design (analysis, strategy development, and evaluation) is affected by cognitive psychology.

The analysis phase involves analysis of the learner, the task, and the context. What is included in the analysis of the learner and the task has been influenced by cognitive psychology. The analysis of the context is much more strongly influenced by systems theory and by sociological theories, such as principles regarding the dissemination and diffusion of innovations.

As you might expect, with the shift from behavioral to cognitive theory bases, the attention given to the analysis of the learner has grown. The learner plays the constructive role according to cognitive theory. Therefore, in order to provide learners with instruction from which they can build, designers must acquire knowledge about the learners' prior knowledge and the organization of that knowledge. In addition, knowledge of the learners' general aptitudes in terms of processing skills is becoming increasingly sought by designers. As you will see in Chapter 3, designers also draw from cognitive and social development theories for other learner characteristics, such as attitudes, motivations, attributions, and interests that should be analyzed due to their strong influence on learning.

One of the points where cognitive psychology has had its strongest influence is in the way that an instructional task is analyzed. In the past, a task was analyzed by noting the observable behaviors that had to be completed to do a particular task. This procedure has been, at the least, supplemented by attention to the mental tasks required in order to perform the observable tasks. This type of analysis is called an *information-processing analysis* or a *cognitive task analysis*. Some designers may even analyze the difference between the ways novices and various levels of experts complete the mental and physical tasks in order to understand the levels of expertise that can be learned. This emphasis on the cognitive as well as the performance aspects of the task is reflected in the types of goals and objectives that are developed. Attention is given within objectives to tapping the "understanding" underlying a performance. For example, it is not uncommon to find objectives that ask learners to explain the reasoning processes behind their performance.

The development of the **instructional strategy** is the area in which cognitive psychology, including gestalt psychology, has its greatest influence. Instructional designers draw upon the conclusions of cognitive psychologists' research to infer principles for design. Where no conclusive findings exist, designers draw upon theories themselves to infer instructional treatments that may support particular learning outcomes. Gestalt psychology, in particular, influences the techniques used in instructional message display (the way information is arranged on a page or screen). The chapters on strategy development in this text contain many references to this influential research and theory.

The two aspects of evaluation—evaluation of the learners' performance and evaluation of the instruction—are both influenced by cognitive psychology. For example, evaluation may include test forms that solicit information on the learners' reasoning, in congruence with objectives that reflect an interest in the learners' acquiring understanding. Evaluation of instruction, particularly of instruction that includes materials, may include the use of techniques such as "read-think-aloud" protocols (Smith & Wedman, 1988) in formative evaluation. This procedure allows the designer to obtain information about the internal processing of learners as they interact with the instruction.

We have merely described a few of the influences that cognitive psychology has had and continues to have on instructional design practice. For a more comprehensive review we suggest that you review articles by Bonner (1988), Di Vesta and Rieber (1987), Low (1981), and Wildman (1981).

In the next section, we will discuss instructional theories. These theories themselves have developed from cognitive learning theory.

Instructional Theories

Of all theory bases, instructional theories are those that instructional designers draw from most directly. Bruner (1966) is usually credited with being the first to describe the characteristics of instructional theory. More recently, Gagné and Dick (1983) described instructional theories as follows:

Theories of instruction attempt to relate specified events comprising instruction to learning processes and learning outcomes, drawing upon knowledge generated by learning research and theory. Often instructional theories are prescriptive in the sense that they attempt to identify conditions of instruction which will optimize learning, retention, and learning transfer....To be classified as theories, these formulations may be expected, at a minimum, to provide a rational description of causal relationships between procedures used to teach and their behavioral consequences in enhanced human performance. (p. 264)

Although none of the theories is complete for all types of learning and all kinds of learners, many of the theories do attempt to prescribe the characteristics of instruction that will support learning. These theories are quite different from learning theories that describe how learning occurs, without attention to features in the learner's environment that might facilitate this learning. In contrast, instructional theories explicitly address which and how features of the environment should be arranged to intentionally promote learning.

As an example, we will describe one general instruction theory—Bloom's Model of Mastery Learning. In addition, many other instructional theories will be described throughout the text, including Gagné's theory on conditions of learning, Reigeluth's Elaboration Model, Collins' Theory of Inquiry Teaching, and Keller's ARCs Model of Motivation.

Bloom's (1971) most influential contribution to the field of instructional design is the proposition that the "normal curve" should not be the model of outcomes of instruction that we expect. According to Bloom, the normal curve, with a few students learning very well, some learning well, some learning less well, many learning medially, some learning poorly, and a few learning very poorly, is what we might expect to occur *without* the intervention of instruction. It is what we would expect if students were to learn totally on their own, with aptitude (and, perhaps, perseverance) being the only factors influencing learning. However, instruction should be the promoter of performance. Its very purpose should be to support learners at points where their own native aptitudes or attitudes might infringe on learning. Hence, Bloom contends the following:

Most students (perhaps more than 90 percent) can master what we have to teach them, and it is the task of instruction to find the means which will enable them to master the subject under consideration. (p. 51)

Bloom has proceeded, through the years, to investigate variables within learners and instruction that can be altered to promote "mastery learning" for almost all learners. He has identified two learner characteristics, cognitive entry behaviors and affective entry behaviors, and quality of instruction as factors that can be altered to promote mastery learning (Bloom, 1976). In his discussion of cognitive entry behaviors he supports the identification of specific task prerequisites within instruction. If entry skills are missing, he suggests a number of ways to ameliorate the situation. With regard to affective entry behaviors, Bloom asserts that learners "vary in what they are emotionally prepared to learn as expressed in their interests, attitudes, and self-views" (p. 74). While he feels that these affective characteristics may be difficult to change, he asserts that quality instruction that promotes successful learning experiences and ensures that the learner finds reward in successful experiences will aid in promoting a positive affect toward learning.

Finally, Bloom discusses features of quality instruction that can promote mastery among most learners. He describes four features of quality instruction: cues, participation, reinforcement, and feedback/correctives. Cues are communications to the learner as to the requirements of the learning task and how to go about meeting these requirements. Participation involves covert or overt active practice with the learning task. Bloom suggests that reinforcement, whether positive or negative, should be given to learners by teachers, peers, or other adults to indicate approval of positive learning performance and disapproval of poor performance. Feedback and corrective procedures follow participation or interaction by the learner. They may include "alternative cues or additional time and practice" (p. 125).

Bloom's model of mastery learning has had a strong impact upon instructional design practice, indeed upon its fundamental philosophy. The goal of instructional design is to develop instruction from which the majority of students learn very well. For instance, it is very common to have a designer trying to design and revise instruction to an 80/80 criterion (at least 80 percent of the learners achieve at least 80 percent of the objectives). Although mastery learning models generally incorporate instructional design practices, the reverse is not always true. Not all instructional programs created with instructional design principles and procedures are predicated on a mastery model. An instructional system that adheres to a mastery model sets a minimum level of competence for all, or most, students. The system is developed to provide the remediation and reevaluation necessary to bring learners to this level of competence and has developed a scheme for grading that accommodates the mastery model. Instructional systems may use instructional design principles and procedures, but due to infeasibility or alternate philosophies, choose not to employ a mastery model.

The instructional theories included in this text are not exhaustive. There are a number of other theories that might be included. We attempted to select for inclusion in this text those theories that have had or that we expect to have the greatest impact in the field. Refer to Reigeluth's texts on instructional design theories (1983, 1987) and Gagné and Dick's review article of instructional psychology (1983) for additional information in this area.

*E*xercises B

1. In your own words, explain why it is important for instructional designers to be able to describe and explain the theory bases of their field.

2. Describe the major differences between behavioral and cognitive learning theories.
3. Describe how each of the major theory bases has contributed to instructional design practice.
   a. Systems theory
   b. Communication theory
   c. Learning theory
   d. Instructional theory
4. Ted is sitting in class listening to his teacher explain the difference between the concepts "liberal" and "conservative." Using the model of information processing described in this chapter, explain how this information flows through Ted's cognitive processes and structures. Give particular attention to the processes of selective perception, encoding, and retrieval.

Summary

The major theory bases that have contributed to the field of instructional design are systems theory, communication theory, learning theory, and instructional theory. Systems theory has contributed some of the procedures and tools of instructional design, as well as the perspective of education involving interdependent elements. Communication theory has provided principles for constructing visual and verbal messages. Over the years, learning theory has continued to clarify how humans learn. Instructional theory suggests the conditions in the learning situation that can facilitate learning.

While this chapter does not exhaustively cover the theories and theory bases that have contributed to instructional design, it is our goal that as you read subsequent chapters you are able to relate assertions and principles that are stated to their particular theory bases. We also hope that we have pointed you toward additional sources of information to which you may refer throughout your career. Figure 1.6 summarizes key points in this chapter.

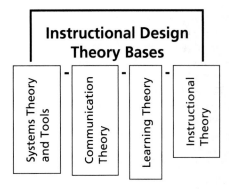

Figure 1.6: Summary Diagram for Chapter 1

Readings and References

Anderson, J. R., & Bower, G. H. (1973). *Human associative memory.* Washington, D.C.: V. H. Winston.

Andrews, D. H., & Goodson, L. A. (1980). A comparative analysis of models of instructional design. *Journal of Instructional Development, 3,* 2–16.

Atkinson, R. C., & Shiffrin, R. M. (1968). Human memory: A proposed system and its control processes. In K. W. Spence & J. T. Spence (Eds.), *The psychology of learning and motivation, Vol. 2.* New York: Academic Press.

Bloom, B. S. (1971). Learning for mastery. In B. S. Bloom, J. T. Hastings, & G. F. Madaus (Eds.), *Handbook on formative and summative evaluation of student learning.* New York: McGraw-Hill.

Bloom, B. S. (1976). *Human characteristics and school learning.* New York: McGraw-Hill.

Bonner, J. (1988). Implications of cognitive theory for instructional design: Revisited. *Educational Communication and Technology Journal, 36,* 3–14.

Briggs, L. J. (Ed.). (1977). *Instructional design: Principles and applications*. Englewood Cliffs, NJ: Educational Technology Publications.

Britton, B. K., Westbrook, R. D., & Holdredge, T. S. (1978). Reading and cognitive capacity usage: Effects of text difficulty. *Journal of Experimental Psychology: Human Learning and Memory, 4,* 582–591.

Bruner, J. S. (1966). *Toward a theory of instruction*. Cambridge, MA: Harvard University Press.

Davis, R. H., Alexander, L. T., & Yelon, S. L. (1974). *Learning system design*. New York: McGraw-Hill.

Di Vesta, F. J., & Rieber, L. P. (1987). Characteristics of cognitive engineering: The next generation of instructional systems. *Educational Communications and Technology Journal, 35,* 213–230.

Dick, W., & Carey, L. (1985). *The systematic design of instruction*. Glenview, IL: Scott, Foresman.

Gagné, R. M. (1985). *The conditions of learning* (4th ed.). New York: Holt, Rinehart, & Winston.

Gagné, R. M., & Dick, W. (1983). Instructional psychology. *Annual Review of Psychology, 34,* 261–295.

Gagné, R., & Driscoll, M. (1988). *Essentials of learning for instruction* (2nd ed.). Englewood Cliffs, NJ: Prentice Hall.

Heinich, R., Molenda, M., & Russell, J. D. (1989). *Instructional media and the new technologies of instruction*. New York: Macmillan.

Kerr, S. T. (1983). Inside the black box: Making design decisions for instruction. *British Journal of Educational Technology, 14,* 45–58.

Kintsch, W. (1972). Notes on the structure of semantic memory. In E. Tulving & W. Donaldson (Eds.), *Organization of memory*. New York: Academic Press.

Low, W. C. (1981). Changes in instructional development: The aftermath of an information processing takeover in psychology. *Journal of Instructional Development, 4,* 10–18.

Mager, R. F. (1984). *Preparing instructional objectives* (2nd ed.). Belmont, CA: Fearon-Pitman.

Mayer, R. E. (1982). Learning. In H. E. Mitzel (Ed.), *Encyclopedia of educational research*. New York: The Free Press.

Miller, G. A. (1956). The magical number seven, plus or minus two: Some limits on our capacity for processing information. *Psychological Review, 63,* 81–97.

Murdock, B. B. (1961). The retention of individual items. *Journal of Experimental Psychology, 62,* 618–625.

Paivio, A. U. (1971). *Imagery and verbal processes*. New York: Holt, Rinehart, & Winston.

Reigeluth, C. M. (Ed.). (1983). *Instructional design theories and models*. Hillsdale, NJ: Lawrence Erlbaum.

Reigeluth, C. M. (Ed.). (1987). *Instructional theories in action*. Englewood Cliffs, NJ: Erlbaum.

Schramm, W. (1956). Procedures and effects of mass communication. In N. B. Henry (Ed.), *Mass media and education,* NSSE Yearbook 53, 116. Chicago: University of Chicago Press.

Schuell, T. J. (1986). Cognitive conceptions of learning. *Review of Educational Research, 56,* 411–436.

Smith, P. L., & Wedman, J. F. (1988). Read-think-aloud protocols: A new data-source for formative evaluation. *Performance Improvement Quarterly, 1,* 13–22.

Sperling, G. A. (1960). The information available in brief visual presentation. *Psychological Monographs, 74,* Whole No. 498.

Wildman, T. M. (1981, July). Cognitive theory and the design of instruction. *Educational Technology,* 14–20.

Instructional Analysis: Analyzing the Learning Context

two

Chapter Objectives

At the conclusion of this chapter you should be able to do the following:

- Describe the purposes of the analysis phase of the design process and list the three components that are analyzed in this phase.

- Describe the purpose of an analysis of the instructional context.

- Describe the purpose of a needs assessment, the conditions that might require a needs assessment, and the steps in a needs assessment procedure.

- Describe factors that should be analyzed in the learning environment and discuss why these factors should be considered.

- When given an instructional situation, describe the procedures you would follow and questions you would ask in conducting an analysis of the instructional context.

Overview of Analysis Phase of Design

Consider this episode involving a fictitious small educational software company, First Try Software, Inc. The five employees of First Try sank their savings into the company. As their first software development project, they decided to produce a computer-based package on fractions to market to public schools throughout the country. Its name was *Fraction Fever*. They spent hundreds of hours in developing novel instructional games to help students learn all about fractions. They used the ALVIRA microcomputer system, a new system with exceptional capability in display and memory capacity. They used clever input formats like a light pen and a graphics tablet. They used color to highlight the parts of the display that learners should focus upon. They laid out the screen in an attractive 80-column format. They paid a team of programmers a lot of money to code the instruction in the most sophisticated language. They invested the remainder of their resources in slick packaging and lots of advertising.

Much to the developers' surprise and disappointment, *Fraction Fever* didn't sell. A few months later they attended a regional computer conference and spoke to some teachers to whom they loaned their fractions package in return for the teachers' evaluation and reports about the software.

What information did they gain from the teachers' comments?

- The novel approach that they used to teach fractions was contrary to the popular math educational theory of the day.
- Teachers especially enjoyed teaching fractions with a hands-on approach, and they felt that this approach was successful.
- Few schools had the ALVIRA system; most had Apples or IBMs. They also found that of the few ALVIRA systems in use in schools, most did not have color monitors, input devices like graphics tablets and light pens, or 80-column display capabilities.
- In schools where *Fraction Fever* could be used, teachers reported that the students learned a lot about the rules of the games in the software but very little about fractions.

- Many students were unable to use the software because the developers had assumed that they were skilled in determining the least common denominator, and many students were not competent in this skill.
- Some students reported that the games were too cute and that the characters used in the games were insulting.

First Try had learned a painful lesson about instructional design: Instructional designers must become clever investigators, examining the characteristics of the potential users, the learning environments, the perceived need for the instruction, and the instructional task before investing time and resources in the costly production of instructional materials.

Of course few software companies make all the mistakes that First Try made. But many developers, trainers, and teachers, to their sorrow, have failed to "do their homework" in analyzing the learning system with sufficient detail. This chapter and the following two chapters will discuss some factors that developers of instruction, whether they are developing materials for their own classrooms or for national distribution, should consider. This stage of development is sometimes called *front-end analysis*. During front-end analysis, designers analyze three basic components: the instructional context, the prospective learners, and the learning task.

Although many people develop instruction without front-end analysis and begrudge the time investment that such an analysis takes, we have found that investing time and thought early in the design process saves time, cost, and frustration in the end. This investment allows one to design and develop instructional materials that teach what is really critical, in a way that the materials can be actually used by the intended learners in their learning environment.

Front-end analysis may seem like wasted effort to instructional materials developers who are in a hurry to get their products out as soon as possible. In training environments, there is always a rush to make training available to employees because time delays often mean loss of revenue. Developers of commercial educational materials may be fearful that other developers will "scoop" their ideas and put a competing product on the market before their product is out. So they take shortcuts where they can, and that often happens to be at the analysis stage. Teachers may give little attention to front-end analysis because they must prepare so much instruction with little time for planning. There are, however, sufficient instances (like the First Try scenario) in which much time and money have been invested in preparing instruction without front-end analysis, and the resulting product was (1) unacceptable to the teachers/trainers; (2) not suitable for the available equipment; or (3) not capable of meeting a real instructional need. In these situations, the instruction is not implemented.

Analyzing the Learning Context

The analysis of the learning context involves two steps: (1) the substantiation of a need for instruction in a certain content area, and (2) a description of the learning environment in which the instructional product will be used.

The first step is often called a **needs analysis** or **needs assessment.** Designers conduct this phase to determine that there actually is a need for new instruction to be developed. Those who omit this step risk developing instruction that may be unnecessary or inappropriate. Describing the context involves determining the characteristics of the environment or context in which the instruction will be used. Designers who omit this step may find themselves designing instruction that simply cannot be implemented in the environment in which they are expecting to implement it.

Determining Instructional Needs

Designers often conduct a needs assessment to find out whether instruction should be designed. This step arises out of developers' desire, for efficiency's sake, to adhere to the adage "If it ain't broke, don't fix it." Violations of this principle are common in the development of instructional materials: The instruction that is already available in a subject matter for a particular group of students and in a particular setting is effective, efficient, and appealing. It is generally a mistake to invest in the de-

velopment of new instructional materials for topics that students are learning well with existing cost-effective instruction.

Or in other cases, if there seems to be no compelling argument that students learn a particular skill or information (e.g., there is no subsequent learning task or future job task that seems to require the acquisition of skill or knowledge now), it may be a waste of precious resources to develop instruction directed toward teaching this skill or knowledge. In both cases, there is no clear indication that more instruction needs to be designed.

For teachers or trainers who are designing instruction for their own classrooms, a needs assessment can be rather informal but is nonetheless important. At the most basic level, such needs assessment can be directed at determining what portions of the curriculum involve learning tasks with which, year after year, a large number of students experience difficulty in learning and for which no readily available instructional solution exists. For designers who are creating instruction to be used in a less immediate environment, such as designing software to be used by fourth-graders across the state or employees in offices across the country, a more formal needs assessment is in order.

When Should a Needs Assessment Be Conducted?

One can determine whether a formal needs assessment is necessary by answering the following six questions. The first is "Are there learning goals that are not being met by our students?"

The learning goals for an instructional system may come from curriculum guides or states' mandates in public schools, from certification or licensing requirements for vocational or professional schools, and from job and task analyses in training units. Identification of gaps between these learning goals and actual learners' performance may be determined in a formal, standardized testing program, in a systematic observation of on-the-job performance, or from informal assessment of students' performances. If there are learning goals that are not being reached by an acceptable percentage of the students, then these goals are possible candidates for the development of instruction.

The second question is "Is existing instruction being delivered efficiently?"

There are occasions in educational and training environments when learning goals are being reached by an acceptable percentage of the learners but with a Herculean effort on the part of teachers/trainers and/or learners. For example, in an educational setting, teachers may spend many hours outside of class individually tutoring learners who have fallen behind or who are ahead of the pace of most learners. Or, in training environments, learners may spend exorbitant hours outside of class to compensate for inadequate or inappropriate instruction. Instruction that requires the expending of effort, time, and other resources beyond that needed by alternate or revised instruction can be considered inefficient. Inefficient instruction often indicates that an alternate form of instructional delivery is appropriate, such as computers, video, or another alternative medium.

The third question is "Is instruction unappealing, and therefore, impeding the motivation, interest, and perseverance of learners?"

If learners are unmotivated and uninterested in the instruction, their perseverance in the learning task and pleasure in learning, in general, may be substantially reduced. This attitude can influence not only immediate learning but also have repercussions in future learning experiences; therefore, this situation may require a needs assessment that investigates the source of the disinterest and lack of motivation.

One should also ask, "Is instruction for unreached learning goals being presented already?"

If instruction for unreached goals is already being delivered, then the first thing that should be considered is a revision of the current instruction. If this appears to be impossible, perhaps because the current delivery system is not capable of adequately presenting the instruction, then development of new instructional materials may be considered.

Another question is "Should new learning goals be added to the curriculum?"

Occasionally new learning goals must be added to the curriculum for a number of reasons. For example, in businesses, new responsibilities may be added to a job description. In educational institutions changes in educational philosophies or pressures from interest groups may cause new learning goals to be added to the curriculum. In industry, new equipment may be purchased that employees must be taught to operate. In governmental agencies, new laws may be passed that must be implemented. In such cases, new instruction often must be created "from scratch."

The sixth question is "Has there been a change in the composition of the learner population?"

Often a change in the composition of the learner population signals that a needs assessment is required. For example, the addition of many Vietnamese students into some school populations during the 1970s stimulated needs assessments to determine what skills and knowledge goals needed to be added to the public school systems' curricula. A change in the composition of the personnel entering the armed services with the inception of all-volunteer induction policies may have instigated a needs assessment to determine what changes in basic skills instruction might be required with the new population of service personnel.

How Do You Conduct a Needs Assessment?

The purpose of a needs assessment is to determine whether there is a gap between "what ought to be" (what learners should know or be able to do) and "what is" (what learners are currently able to do) and then to determine which of these gaps should be addressed with the design and development of new instruction. This determination can be conducted very formally following a model of needs assessment by a school system or very informally by a classroom teacher who mentally reviews the progress of the learners in his class.

Several books and many articles have been written about how to conduct a needs assessment. Most of these descriptions contain the following steps in their models of needs assessment:

1. *List the goals of the instructional system.* In other words, one should first determine "what ought to be" (what must learners be able to do or know at the end of their instruction). These goals can be for a lesson, unit, course, semester, year, or several years. These descriptions of "what ought to be" are called **learning goals.** In public schools, quite often committees of community members, educators, and students are

involved in determining these goals. Some states have involved individuals statewide in prescribing goals for students in specific contents for particular grade levels.

In businesses and other environments the identification of learning goals may involve interviewing and observing persons who are expert in performing skills that learners must learn. It may involve key personnel in management describing the type of knowledge or skill that they wish their employees to possess. It may involve employees describing the skills and knowledge they feel they must possess to adequately perform their jobs.

2. *Determine how well the identified goals are already being achieved.* Once a learning system has identified what learners within that system must know or be able to do, the next step is to determine how well the learners in the system are already reaching these goals. The reason for this step is obvious: If learners are learning well with the instruction that they are receiving, there is no need to design and develop new instruction. Of course, very rarely do we find this ideal state of affairs. Most often we find that there are certain goals that are not adequately being achieved by at least a portion of the learning population.

The current level of achievement of instructional goals can be determined through the use of paper-and-pencil tests, observations of individuals completing tasks on-the-job or in simulated situations, learners' self-assessments, or evaluation of products of learners, such as error rates and reports from quality control sections. Of course, combinations of several of these assessment techniques would probably render the most reliable estimate of the current level of performance of instructional goals.

3. *Determine the gaps between "what is" and "what should be."* In other words, identify the gap between what learners should be able to do and what they are currently able to do for each of the identified goals. This gap is often stated in percentages, such as this: "All of the students should be able to make correct change when given a bill of ten dollars or less and the cost of the purchase. Only 67 percent of the students

were able to do this. There are 33 percent of the students who are unable to reach this goal."

For some goals this gap is easily seen. For instance, if a business has added a new instructional goal to its curriculum for employees, such as being able to correctly apply a new business policy, one might assume that the gap is 100 percent; that is, none of the employees currently knows how to apply the policy. Or when new employees enter the business, one can assume that there are considerable gaps between what they must know and what they do know. One should be cautious with making assumptions of this nature; when learners haven't had instruction on something, assuming they do not know it can be dangerous. As you will recall from the discussion in Chapter 1, people learn from many different situations, only some of which involve formal education. One can confirm an assumption of prior knowledge with some of the techniques we have discussed. Otherwise, one might waste much energy designing instruction for goals that learners have already attained.

4. *Prioritize gaps according to agreed-upon criteria.* Quite often, especially when working with many goals, such as an entire curriculum for a grade level or level of employees, there will be many gaps between what learners should be able to do and what they are currently able to do. Often it is impossible to attend to all of these gaps immediately. A teacher, school system, or business organization must determine which of the gaps are most critical and attend to those gaps first. There are several criteria that decision makers can use in determining which gaps to attend to first. These criteria might include the following:

- The size of the gap, attending to the biggest gaps first
- The importance of the goal, working on the goals that are most critical first
- The number of students affected, choosing those gaps that affect the most students first
- The consequences of not meeting the goal, selecting those gaps that have the most serious consequences if the gaps are not closed first
- The probability of reducing the gap, attending to the gaps that have the greatest probability of being closed with the available resources first

5. *Determine which gaps are instructional needs and which are most appropriate for design and development of instruction.* One of the biggest mistakes that designers, teachers, and educators make is assuming that instruction is the solution to all performance problems. In other words, they are determining a solution (instruction) before completely analyzing the problem (that learners are not performing well on some task). This leap can lead to investing both instructional and learners' resources and time into instruction that may not be required. There are many reasons that learners may not perform well, only one of which is that they do not know how to do something.

For example, a school system may find that first-graders in a certain school (or perhaps a group of schools) are performing very poorly on standardized tests in reading. Without investigating the problem carefully, the school district might assume that the reading instruction is poor and requires revision, either in approach or in delivery. However, if the members of the needs assessment team investigated a little farther, they might discover that the students in question have an extremely high absenteeism rate—27 percent. Therefore, it may not be that reading instruction is poor; it may be that students are simply not present in the classroom often enough to learn. The absenteeism problem must be attended to before any changes in the instruction should be instigated.

Similar performance problems that are not due to poor instruction can be observed in the business world. An employer might observe that employees are completing work tasks very slowly. He might assume that this slow rate of completion is due to employees not knowing how to complete the job quickly, and he might begin developing a training program. Further investigation might reveal, however, that this is not a training problem. It could be that employees are not motivated to work quickly or well. Perhaps there are hidden rewards for working slowly, such as the approval of other employees, or punishments for completing work quickly, such as being given more or distasteful tasks when work is completed.

Instructional designers should not immediately assume that poor performance in learning tasks implies a need to correct or revise instruction. Often this is the case, and instruction *is* required. However, as you can see there are additional reasons why learners may not perform well. The designer must become a detective who delays determination that instruction is the solution to a performance problem until the problem has been thoroughly investigated. This investigation is often conducted in tandem with the needs assessment through the development of a thorough description of the instructional environment and, as will be described in the following chapters, an analysis of the learners and the instructional task.

Describing the Learning Environment

The second phase in analysis of the learning context is a description of the learning system. As in the case of the needs assessment described above, if you are designing instruction for your own class, this description can be rather informal but is nevertheless important. If you are designing instruction for a more distant or larger environment, it is more difficult to describe the learning system but of even greater importance. The primary task at this point is to think about the "system" in which the instructional product will be placed. This "instructional system" is composed of all factors that affect and are affected by the learning that takes place: learners (which we will discuss in the next section), instructional materials, the teacher/trainer, instructional equipment (such as microcomputers, slide viewers, video, and so forth), the instructional facilities, and the community or organization.

A designer is often wise to consider, beyond the immediate learning system, the larger learning system into which the classroom environment belongs, such as the local or state school system or the business organization in which training is to be conducted. An in-depth investigation into what the environment is like where an instructional product will be used helps to ensure that the product will, indeed, be used in that environment. For example, if you are designing computer-based instruction to be used as training material in a business, it is important that you know how many and what kind of microcomputers are available for instructional purposes, where the computers are located, as well as how the trainer feels about computer-based instruction.

Here are some of the questions that you may wish to ask about the learning environment when contemplating developing instructional materials.

1. *What are characteristics of the teachers/ trainers who will be using these materials?*

- What are the interests and preferences of the teachers/trainers? How do they see their roles in the classroom?
- How do the teachers/trainers in the learning environments feel about having instruction delivered via media or other nontraditional methods?

Some teachers and trainers may find certain forms of instruction, such as computer tutorials, unacceptable because they take over the role of disseminator of information that teachers particularly enjoy or view as their main function. Teachers in specific content areas may feel that a particular medium is an inappropriate form of instruction for their particular content. In these cases, even the best instructional material may not be adopted because it conflicts with what the potential adopters view as the appropriate role of instructional materials.

- Do teachers/trainers like to use media-based instruction for the central portion of instruction in a particular content area? Or do they plan to use media-based instruction for remediation, enrichment, or review? What experience have teachers/trainers had with individualized learning systems?

Whether it is from limited hardware availability or from teachers' perceptions of their roles, media that is designed to be the primary deliverer of instruction may not be adoptable in some learning environments. In other environments, due to problems with availability of teachers with the necessary expertise or due to the variability of learners' backgrounds, it may be necessary that the mediated materials be the primary deliverer of instruction, at least for particular units of instruction. Whatever the case, developers must have some idea of how the software can and will

be used in the instructional environment. Teachers and trainers who have positive experiences with individualized learning systems will probably feel more comfortable using alternative forms of instruction as the primary instructional delivery system.

- What is the level of experience of the teachers/ trainers with the content, learners, and teaching in general?

The more inexperienced teachers and trainers are with the content, the learners, or teaching, in general, the more they may benefit from structure and organization within the materials. In addition, the school system and organization must have this information in order to plan the training that instructors and teachers will require in order to use new instructional materials effectively.

2. *Are there existing curricula into which this piece of instruction must fit? If so, what is the philosophy, strategy, or theory used in these materials? If a particular approach is used to teach a specific content, for instance reading, then in order to be compatible and integratable into the curriculum, material should be developed that utilizes this theory or philosophy. There may be occasions when instruction that portrays an alternate philosophy or theory may be appropriate, but developers should be aware that this is what they are doing.*

3. *What hardware is commonly available in the potential learning environments? Are there video playback machines, and what are their formats (U-Matic, VHS, Beta, etc.)? Are microcomputers available? If so, what kind, how many, and in what configurations? What about slide or overhead projectors? What software and other materials are available?* One of the biggest impediments to utilization of mediated instruction seems to be hardware availability. To assure that instruction is usable by the projected learning environments, developers should conduct surveys that indicate what hardware is available. In the First Try example, the developers of computer-based materials emphasized critical cues in their materials in color. Many public schools only

have green screen or black and white display capability with their microcomputers because color monitors are often three times as expensive as monochromes. If First Try employees had investigated the learning environment, they might have chosen a different feature, such as using inverse lettering, to provide emphasis.

Designers sometimes assume that the computer software they are accustomed to using is available everywhere. Even the most commonplace productivity software, such as a particular word processing package or database, may be different at another site.

4. *What are the characteristics of the classes and facilities that will use the new instruction?* The size and location of facilities and classes can affect the way instructional materials should be developed and what they should include. Obviously, a designer planning instruction in high school chemistry must consider the lab facilities, equipment, and materials that are generally available in high schools. When designing a course to prepare workers to interview anxious potential clients, the designer must consider whether facilities and room are available to spread out into role-playing and discussion groups. A more subtle factor to consider is class climate. Are learners more accustomed to being information receivers or active learners? Are they accustomed to working cooperatively in groups or individually? These factors may have a substantial effect on what instructional techniques a designer may choose or how much preparation or training the designer must build into the instruction to prepare learners to use an unfamiliar technique.

5. *What are the characteristics of the school system or organization in which the new instruction will take place?* Here again, the designer becomes something of a detective, investigating the beliefs of the organization in terms of the roles and expectations of the learners, the teachers/trainers, and the management. What does the school system or the organization see as its primary mission? How does the proposed instruction relate to the mission of the organization? Who are the primary decision makers in the organization? The risk in not considering these

factors is designing instruction that runs contrary to organizational beliefs. There is also the risk of not considering the input of critical individuals in the organization. The ultimate effect of this is the designing of instruction that cannot be implemented into the existing system.

6. *What is the philosophy and what are the taboos of the larger community in which the organization or school system exists?* Often, this is not a critical issue. However, due to the powerful consequences of *not* considering these issues in certain circumstances, it is worth the time to consider the larger system into which the instruction will be placed. For instance, developers of science curricula have learned to consider the established beliefs of the community when designing instruction that touches on Darwinism. Business organizations must consider reigning political and economic attitudes when designing instruction on labor relations.

We have barely touched on some of the factors within the learning environment that should be considered when designing instruction. You will probably be able to generate some additional factors that influence the design of instruction for your particular circumstances. Tessmer (1990) provides an extensive discussion of ''environment analysis.'' What is critical is that you consider instruction as a system in which many factors are interrelated. Changing one factor—instruction—will affect other factors. To create instruction that can be used in the learning system, it is important that you consider these effects as you design the instruction. This will save you from rude surprises like those First Try received. Following is an example of how a state educational system examined instructional needs and the learning environment as it considered the design of a physics curriculum.

*E*xample of Validation of Need and Analysis of Learning Environment

The mythical state of Corona has many small rural school districts. A problem identified among these small districts, as well as in many of the larger ones, is a lack of teachers who are qualified to teach advanced high school science courses, particularly physics. The Corona State Education Agency is investigating the possibility of delivering this instruction via a series of videotapes. A task force has been created to investigate the learning environments into which this instruction might be implemented to help determine the feasibility of video as a delivery system. Following are some of the questions they asked and the answers they found.

1. *Are there learning goals in advanced high school physics not currently being met in school districts in the state?* Surveys of high school math teachers, administrators, current and graduated students, and parents of current and graduated students indicate a dissatisfaction with advanced science instruction in high schools in 80 percent of smaller school districts and 45 percent of larger school districts. Standardized test scores on advanced placement tests in science indicate that only 20 percent of the state's students who take these exams receive advanced placement credit. In other words, the instruction is inadequate to prepare students to pass advanced placement exams.

2. *Is instruction already offered in this area or is it a new learning goal?* A survey of school districts found that 90 percent of the larger school districts and 50 percent of the smaller districts offer courses in physics. In the larger districts, 65 percent of the high schools in the district offer the advanced courses. In the smaller districts, 35 percent of the high schools in the districts offer these courses. The schools that do not offer the courses list lack of teacher expertise and small numbers of students interested in the courses as reasons for not offering them. In general, acquisition of skills and knowledge in physics seems to be a learning goal that is espoused by most school districts and for which many school districts offer instruction. However, this instruction is by no means available in all high schools.

3. *Is existing instruction delivered efficiently?* In many of the smaller school districts offering physics courses, classes contain ten or fewer stu-

dents. Teachers in these courses report that they spend much time in remedial instruction because students often enter the class with insufficient math or science background to learn successfully from available instructional materials on physics. Therefore instruction seems to be inefficient in terms of the expending of teachers' resources.

4. *Does the learning context seem to require the particular capabilities of a particular medium?* This question will be answered in more detail later in design decisions but it does seem initially that the diversity of the student population and the lack of qualified teachers suggest video as a potential solution to the instructional problem. Many of the topics of advanced physics cannot be studied in laboratory experiments in high schools and must be simulated. Video can simulate reality but is rather limited in providing opportunities for feedback or other learner interaction with the material being presented. Additional materials such as lab supplies, print-based instruction, and computer software could be developed and integrated with the video lessons to provide demonstrations of principles, active student practice, and corrective feedback.

5. *What is the existing philosophy, strategy, or theory behind the current physics curriculum?* Surveys of existing physics curriculum materials, physics teachers, and physics education specialists indicate that there seem to be two divergent philosophies with regard to physics education. One school of thought feels that the goals of physics education should be that learners are able to remember and apply the concepts and principles of physics. The other school of thought feels that the goal of physics education should be that learners acquire the skills of a scientist: to identify and define researchable problems and to conduct experimentation. Some physics educators feel that both sets of goals may be achieved in the same curriculum. The majority of physics teachers in Corona feel that the primary goal of physics education should be that learners can remember and apply the concepts and principles of physics. The ability to conduct experimentation is a secondary goal. However, most teachers support the hands-on experimentation available

in a physics lab in which learners directly experience and "prove" established physics principles.

This finding suggests that either (1) the instructional program be designed to achieve the current goals of physics instruction or (2) strategies be planned to convince teachers of the importance of alternate goals.

6. *What types and quantities of hardware are available in Corona school districts?* Surveys of school districts in Corona indicate that 95 percent of the larger school districts and 80 percent of the smaller school districts have an adequate number of video playback machines in their high schools. Of these, 70 percent are VHS machines and 30 percent are Beta players. In addition, 95 percent of the larger school districts and 90 percent of the smaller districts have some microcomputers available for supplemental instructional uses (50 percent IBM or IBM compatible, 30 percent Apple II family, 20 percent other).

The results of this survey suggest that although the school districts are, in general, limited in the availability of hardware, both video and computer hardware is available in most schools. In addition, the survey suggests that there is a diversity of hardware available in the districts. This finding suggests that the instructional materials must be developed in forms that will accommodate this diversity. (Duplication of videotapes in both VHS and Beta formats is not much of a problem, but provision of computer software for the major brands of computers may be somewhat difficult.)

7. *Do teachers/administrators plan to use mediated instruction as the primary deliverer of instruction? What experiences have the teachers had with individualized delivery systems?* Some of the physics instructors have had experience teaching with some of the individualized learning systems developed during the 1960s. When questioned, many of the teachers liked the idea of individualized systems but found the management of such systems onerous. A survey indicated that many teachers feel that the primary source of instruction must be the teacher and that instructional materials can only serve supplemental functions. The survey revealed that some

teachers supported the use of mediated instruction but they did not see how this might be feasible with the hardware limitations that they have in their schools.

The implications of such findings are threefold. First of all, teachers may be open to a video/computer combination as a way to deliver individualized instruction, particularly if the system makes evaluation of student products, prescription of future lessons, and management and reporting of student records easy. Secondly, some teachers may feel that using video as the primary delivery system is antithetical to the role of a teacher. In this case, either programs must be developed that support the role of the teacher, or teachers must be educated to accept a different role and to perceive instruction as something that can be delivered via a variety of media. Lastly, if the instructional video/computer products are developed to be the primary sources of instruction, then developers must identify what constitutes an adequate amount of hardware in a classroom and suggest management techniques for teachers to employ with assignment of students.

Working with an Expert

How do you find out all of the information that you must know about the context, learner, and instructional task? In each case you will locate individuals who have experience, knowledge, and expertise in one or more of these areas. An expert may be very well informed about the learning environment, its organization, the curriculum, and so on. An expert may have taught or worked with learners who are similar to the target audience. An individual may be expert in completing the task(s) represented by the instructional goal. Sometimes an individual may be expert in all of these areas. Instructional designers must form a relationship with such experts and interview them in a way that provides complete and accurate information. Often, experts have not been in such a role before and it is the designers' responsibility to get the information they need. At the end of this chapter are several references that are invaluable when planning to work with an expert. We will describe some rudimentary suggestions for a first meeting with an expert.

Before the First Meeting

1. Learn about the expert. Determine the expert's area of expertise. Does the expert know the content? The learners? The context? All three? What is the length and degree of the expert's experience? What common experiences do the designer and expert have?

2. Do your "homework" on background information. Read as much documentation as possible about the organization, the learners, and the content. Are there documents available from recent self-studies? Is there a written profile of the learners? What is written about the content?

3. Develop a written project description for the expert. In as simple terms as possible, write down your understanding of the project. What are the deliverables? What is the time line? Who is the audience and what is the scope of the context?

4. Find sample products to use as examples. Show example deliverables that are similar to your project. Explain what the differences will be for your project.

5. Develop a written set of questions. Determine what specific information you need to obtain from the expert. How should you organize your questions? What is a logical sequence? What language will convey your needs most clearly? Which are the priority questions?

6. Plan how to take notes. Decide how you can obtain the most complete record of the expert's responses. Can you record them with videotape or audiotape? What is the best form for your written notes?

During the First Meeting

1. Establish rapport. Ask some general questions about the expert. Listen to the replies. Respond positively to information given. Try to identify common experiences. Be professional but warm.

2. Share expectations. Determine why the expert believes she is there. Explain why you think the expert is there and in general what kinds of information you require. Communicate how much of the expert's time is required. Discuss any terminology that you will consistently use and explain your meaning. Determine discrepancies in use of terms and negotiate their meanings for the project.

3. Develop a communication plan. Provide a way that you can be reached via phone, fax, or electronic mail. Identify the times when it is easiest to contact you directly. Solicit the same information from the expert. Preview when communications or other meetings may be necessary. Obtain a general overview of the expert's schedule in coming months.

4. Gather information. Use questions to guide your interview. Be sensitive to cues in responses that lead to new questions. Be open to volunteered information. On any sensitive issues provide as much anonymity as possible. Obtain written information that answers any questions.

After the First Meeting

1. Consolidate notes. Integrate information obtained in written materials, notes, and tapes.

2. Determine gaps and inconsistencies. Once information is integrated, ascertain what information is incomplete. Locate information that appears to be contradictory.

3. Arrange to gather missing information. Determine whether gaps and inconsistencies must be addressed in face-to-face, written, or oral form. Gather missing information.

4. Plan the next meeting. Decide whether an additional meeting is required and identify what the direction and scope of this meeting will be. Begin a list of questions for this meeting.

*E*xercises

1. In your own words, describe the purposes of the analysis phase of the design process, and list the three components that are analyzed in this phase.
2. In your own words, describe the purpose of an analysis of the learning environment.
3. In your own words, describe the following: (1) the purpose of a needs assessment, (2) the conditions that might require a needs assessment, and (3) the steps in a needs assessment procedure.
4. In your own words, describe factors that should be analyzed in the learning environment, and discuss why these factors should be considered.

5. Suppose you were on an instructional development team that was developing materials to be used in adult basic education classes. The course that you are considering delivering via mediated instruction would cover financial issues. The goal is that students will learn about managing checking and savings accounts, paying bills, and managing credit accounts. What would you want to know about the instructional need and the learning environment before you begin actually designing instruction? How would you go about answering these questions?

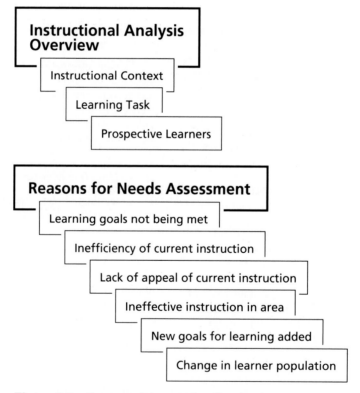

Figure 2.1: Summary Diagram for Chapter 2

Summary

This chapter was the first of three that address instructional analysis, describing the analysis of the learning context. In subsequent chapters we will take a look at analysis of learners and analysis of learning tasks. Analysis of instructional context involves needs assessment and a description of the environment in which instruction will take place. Figure 2.1 summarizes key points in this chapter.

Needs assessments can be initiated for any of a number of reasons, including learning goals not being met given current instruction, current instruction being inefficient, current instruction being unappealing, lack of instruction in a given area, new goals being added to the curriculum, and changes in the learner population.

Needs assessments can be accomplished through a five-step process:

1. Describe the learning goals of the current instructional system.
2. Evaluate achievement of goals in the current system.
3. Describe the gaps between what is desired and what is accomplished.
4. Set priorities for action.
5. Determine what needs are instructional needs, and of those needs that are instructional, determine what ones are appropriate for resolution through design and development of instruction.

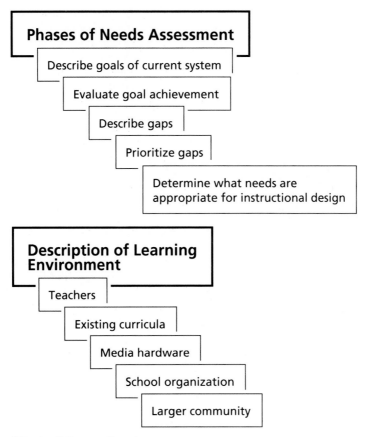

Figure 2.1: *continued*

Analysis of the learning environment involves looking at existing conditions that surround and support instruction, including teachers, existing curricula, instructional media equipment available, school or training organization, and factors in the larger community.

Job Aid

You can use the following job aid to help you analyze the context of the learning environment for an instructional design project at the course level. This analysis may involve citing information that is currently available to you, plus planning to obtain information that is not currently available to you.

Establishing or Validating the Instructional Need

1. Goal identification:
    Are instructional goals currently identified for this course?

    Yes

    - Who developed them and when were they developed?
    - How and when were these goals last validated?
    - Are there circumstances that suggest that these goals may no longer be valid?
    - What are the procedures that you would use to validate these goals?
    - Are the statements of these goals available to you?

    Yes

    Attach them to this form.

    No

    Where can a statement of these goals be obtained?

    No

    Move to step 2.

2. Goal development
    - Who should be involved in the development of instructional goals for this course?
    - What procedures would you use to get these people to help you identify relevant goals?
    - How would you validate that these goals are the critical ones?
    - What is the desirable level of attainment of these goals?

3. Gap identification
    - What is the level of attainment of the goals of those learners completing the course? (If this information is not currently available, what procedures would you follow in determining the answer to this question?)
    - What is the level of attainment of the goals of those learners before they enter the course? (If this information is not currently available, what procedures would you followin determining the answer to this question?)
    - Is there evidence that the course is necessary?
    - Is there evidence that the goals are being reached to the desirable level as a result of instruction?

    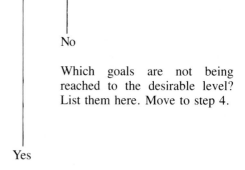

    No

    Which goals are not being reached to the desirable level? List them here. Move to step 4.

    Yes

    Is there evidence that this is being achieved with suitable levels of efficiency in terms of time, costs, interest, and motivation? (If this information is not currently available, what procedures would you follow in determining the answer to this question?)

| No

Which goals seem to be related to inefficient or unappealing instruction? List them here. Move to step 4.

Yes

Conclude the needs assessment here.

4. Prioritize goals
   - Which individuals should be involved in prioritizing the unreached goals?
   - What criteria should be used in prioritizing the unreached goals?
   - Using these criteria, list the goals in order of importance.
5. Instructional needs
   - Of the prioritized goals, which currently are not included in instruction? Of these goals, which appear to be reachable via instruction? Explain why.
   - Of the prioritized goals, which currently are included in instruction? What evidence do you have that these are instructional needs?

- Is there evidence that these gaps are due to noninstructional problems? Explain this evidence. In cases where sufficient information is currently unavailable, describe how you would go about obtaining the information.

Analyzing the Learning Environment

1. Describe the teachers or trainers for the course in terms of range of experience, interests, backgrounds, and preferences.
2. Describe the existing curricula (scope and sequence) into which this course fits. Include the philosophy, strategies, or theories underlying this curricula.
3. Describe the instructional hardware that is currently available.
4. Describe the classes and facilities that will use the course.
5. Describe the school or organization in which the learning will take place. Attach any organizational charts to this form. Include a description of the way decisions are made regarding the selection of instructional materials.
6. Describe the community in which the school or organization resides. Specifically identify any characteristics that might influence the acceptability of the instruction in this content area.

Extended Example

In the remaining chapters of this text, we will follow the design and development of one course through each of the phases of the instructional design process. The course being developed is titled Photography Basics, an introductory course for beginning graduate students in the instructional technology programs of universities.

Instructional Need

The need for such a course was determined by a committee composed of the instructional technology faculty, a group of former students, and employers of graduates. The committee conducted an analysis of existing courses in the curriculum and an analysis of the skill requirements of graduates of the program. It also examined existing statements of needed competencies for instructional technologists (those produced by organizations such as the National Society for Performance and Instruction, the Association for Educational Communications and Technology, and the Association for Training and Development).

The current curriculum has no course in basic photography, although it does contain courses in television and interactive video production, which involve knowledge of composition of visuals with a camera and camera operation. Knowledge of certain basics in photography are prerequisite knowledge for video production skills. The instructors of these courses must spend valuable class time teaching these basics to students who do not have these skills when they enter the class. When a basics of photography pretest was given to 24 students at the beginning of the introductory video production course, the average score obtained was 23 (total possible score 100), with a standard deviation of 8.4 and a range of 2 to 89. The instructor of the video production course has suggested that some type of course to cover these prerequisites be developed. While there are existing courses on campus, both in art and journalism, these courses contain additional content unnecessary and potentially confusing to the instructional technology student.

A survey of graduates of the instructional technology program from the past three years indicates that 25 percent of the graduates reported using some photography skills (including video production, or supervising that production) in the past year. Seventy percent of the graduates reported a desire for more basic knowledge in photography. The employers of graduates reported they felt that graduates occasionally opted for other media when photographs or slides might be more appropriate. They suggested that this might be due to graduates' lack of experience with photography.

Although there are no statements of goals for this particular course produced by an official group, goals for such a course have been developed by a number of course developers in trade and technical schools, informal learning situations, community schools, other college courses, and other instructional technology programs. These existing goal statements might be obtained from these organizations and revised for the context of an instructional technology course.

Learning Environment

1. *Teachers for the course: range of experience, interests, backgrounds, preferences.* Instructors for this course will range from full professors with training to adjunct instructors. Most will have doctorates in instructional technology or related fields, although some adjuncts may have a master's degree in an area other than instructional technology. They will range in experience from over 20 years of college teaching to no prior teaching experience. Rarely will a course be offered by more than one faculty member.

The majority of instructors will have an instructional technology background, including preferences for objective-based instruction and systematically produced instruction. They will generally favor the use of media-based instructional supports. Most will have a preference for viewing their courses as preparing students with specific, job-related competencies. The photographic skill background among instructors will range from those who are professionally skilled to "vacation photographers" who may be very limited in experience and lack some of the basics themselves. Some instructors may feel they possess adequate technical skills but feel uncomfortable with the perceived "artistic" demands of photography.

2. *Existing curricula (scope and sequence) into which this course fits. Include the philosophy, strategies, or theories underlying this curricula.* This course will fit within both a master's and doctoral program. (It might also be taken as an elective by non-majors.) The instructional technology program has a core set of courses that involves an introduction to the field, a basic instructional design course, a basic media course, and an introductory learning theory course. Then students may take design and production courses that focus on particular media as well as advanced design and learning theory courses. This course will be an advanced production course that will be prerequisite to video production courses. Course offerings already utilize all available personnel and time slots. Alternate delivery systems that are not instructor-intensive or time-bound might be considered.

Within the instructional technology program there is a strong orientation toward objective-based, criterion-referenced instruction that prepares the student with specific skills. Generally, the validity of these skills is determined through their applicability to job-related skills. However, also within the philosophy of graduate-level courses is the acquisition of the theory that underlies these skills, the understanding of why particular decisions are appropriate, and the ability to move beyond the specific skills acquired based upon this understanding.

3. *Instructional hardware that is currently available.* The instructional technology program has microcomputers available for instructional purposes. However, few of these are state-of-the-art systems. Macintosh computers and IBM-compatible hardware are available. Most likely, there is no existing soft-

ware available for teaching photography. The program has overhead projectors, slide projectors, and video playback (VHS, predominantly) units available.

4. *Classes and facilities that will use the course.* Classes will generally be less than 30 students, with the typical class averaging 15 to 20. Classrooms will most generally be generic college classrooms with either tables and movable chairs or movable desks. Developers should not count on classes having a classroom in which materials may be left out or be referred to outside of class hours. A serious consideration is that the program does not have darkroom facilities available. (Occasionally, alternate darkroom facilities may be located.) Instruction must take this possibility into consideration, perhaps with alternate or optional units available. With regard to class climate, attitudes may vary. The program allows part-time students. Part-time students often are unable or unwilling to work cooperatively on projects. Students will be taking the course relatively early in their graduate careers and therefore may not know each other very well.

5. *School or organization in which the learning will take place.* The course will be given in a university that includes graduate programs in instructional technology. This program is situated within the College of Education. As this course occurs within the College of Education, specific application of course content to public education must be made apparent. Applications to training environments and other non-public education environments may not be viewed as central to the mission of the college. The program varies from three to five faculty members. Decision making with regard to course offerings and course content is totally within the program itself. However, funding and staffing decisions necessary to implement these decisions are often made at the department or college level.

6. *Community in which the school or organization resides.* The university that offers this graduate program is in a sizable town near a large city. Often, there are opportunities within the school or business community to apply course content to real-life instructional problems. It is unlikely that community mores or taboos would affect decisions regarding course content or delivery.

Readings and References

Becker, J. M., & Hahn, C. L. (1977). *Wingspread workbook for educational change.* Boulder, CO: Social Science Educational Consortium.

Bratton, B. (1979–80). The instructional development specialist as consultant. *Journal of Instructional Development, 3*(2), 2–8.

Briggs, L. J. (Ed.) (1977). *Instructional design: Principles and applications.* Englewood Cliffs, NJ: Educational Technology.

Briggs, L. J., & Wager, W. W. (1981). *Handbook of procedures for the design of instruction,* 2nd Edition. Englewood Cliffs, NJ: Educational Technology.

Davis, R. H., Alexander, L. T., & Yelon, S. L. (1974). *Learning system design.* New York: McGraw-Hill.

Dick, W., & Carey, L. (1985). *The systematic design of instruction,* 2nd Edition. Glenview, IL: Scott, Foresman.

Greer, M. (1992). *ID project management.* Englewood Cliffs, NJ: Educational Technology Publications.

Havelock, R. J. (1973). *The change agent's guide to innovation in education.* Englewood Cliffs, NJ: Educational Technology.

Kaufman, R., & English, F. W. (1979). *Needs assessment: Concept and application.* Englewood Cliffs, NJ: Educational Technology Publications.

Leitzman, D. F., Walter, S., Earle, R.S., & Myers, C. (1979). Contracting for instructional development. *Journal of Instructional Development, 3*(2), 23–28.

Rossett, A. (1988). *Training needs assessment.* Englewood Cliffs, NJ: Educational Technology Publications.

Tessmer, M. (1990). Environment analysis: A neglected stage of instructional design. *Educational Technology Research & Development, 38*(1), 55–64.

Instructional Analysis: Analyzing the Learners

three

Chapter Objectives

At the conclusion of this chapter you should be able to do the following:

- Describe the stable and changing similarities and differences among learners.

- Describe the categories of cognitive characteristics that should be considered in designing instruction.

- Describe the difference between general characteristics and specific prior knowledge of a learner population.

- Describe some instructional strategy variables that may be influenced by learner characteristics and explain how different learner characteristics may influence how the variables are implemented.

- Describe sources of information about learner characteristics of a particular audience.

- When given a description of a situation, list questions regarding learner characteristics that you would wish to know before designing instruction, as well as techniques and procedures you would use to find the answers to these questions.

Overview of Learner Analysis

You will remember in our sad story of the First Try company that the instructional software was unsuccessful for many reasons. Two of these reasons had to do with the knowledge and perceptions of the learners that the instructional designers had not anticipated: (1) Many students were unable to use the software because the developers had assumed that they were skilled in determining least common denominator, and many students were not competent in this skill; and (2) some students reported that the games were too cute and that the characters used in the games were insulting.

The designers had not "done their homework" in analyzing the characteristics of the learners that they anticipated using the instruction, usually termed the **target audience** or **target population.** It is critical for designers to consider their target audiences, as this knowledge will be important in designing instruction that is effective and interesting to the learners. As in earlier analyses, if you are designing instruction for your own students, this stage will be relatively easy but is nonetheless critical and should not be overlooked. Analyzing learners who are remote, such as the merchandise managers in a nationwide department store chain, can be quite a challenging task. Sometimes designers must ask a lot of questions before they get an adequate profile of their audience.

The danger in not analyzing the characteristics of an audience is assuming that all learners are alike. An even more common error is assuming that the learners are like the designers. This means that we tend to explain things the way we will understand them, use examples that are familiar to us, and use instructional techniques that work well for us. This hidden form of ethnocentrism can play havoc with the design of instruction. For one thing, we are generally familiar with, or quickly become familiar with, the content for which we are designing. We are tempted when designing instruction to inadequately explain some things and overexplain others. In addition, this ethnocentrism may limit the effectiveness of the examples we select. For example, one designer who was creating instruction on heart-healthy menus was embarrassed during evaluation of her materials to find that there were no references to foods that Hispanic populations commonly include in their daily menus. We

need to consciously examine the diversity and commonalties of the target audience so that we can design appropriate and effective instruction for them.

It is critical that you create instruction with a particular audience in mind, rather than centering design around the content and then searching for an audience for which it is appropriate. In the latter case, you could find that you have created instruction that is appropriate for *no one.*

There are occasions when you may find yourself developing instruction that is appropriate for more than one audience. In such a case, it is of value to identify the **primary audience** and the **secondary audience** and describe each audience as completely as possible. Later in the design process, you may have to make decisions that focus on the primary audience.

A caution is needed here. Novice instructional designers often find themselves describing the characteristics that they hope their learners have, rather than the actual characteristics of their target audience. Carrying this approach to its extreme, you could find yourself designing instruction for an audience that doesn't exist at all! You can detect this faulty thinking in your written descriptions: "Learners *ought* to be motivated to learn this skill" or "Learners *should* have a reading level of at least sixth grade." In the next chapter you will learn to identify the skill and knowledge that learners must obtain in order to reach an instructional goal; however, during learner analysis you should not be thinking of what learners should be like or what they need to know, but what they *are* like and what they *do* know.

Similarities and Differences Among Learners

What things are important to know about the people for whom we will be designing particular instruction? Although each learner is a unique individual, possessing a complexity that defies complete description, there is a finite and manageable array of human characteristics, which are useful to instructional designers. The importance of understanding these characteristics is demonstrated by the requirements for courses such as Human

Learning and Human Development (in programs in which people are studying to be instructional designers). And, although the knowledge that psychologists have amassed about the characteristics of humans is formidable indeed, to provide an overview of this area we can organize the relevant characteristics into four major classes. On the following pages we will look at this classification scheme, the characteristics that are contained within it, and implications of these characteristics for instructional designers.

Taking a look at human characteristics from within a framework can be helpful in organizing the knowledge about learners that has been developed over the years. Although some information about a particular target group of learners and about the individuals within that group can be gained by casual or unsupported observation, a great deal of information about learners that we can consider in the design of instruction does not come directly from studying learners in a particular target audience. Rather, it comes from the instructional designer's knowledge about human characteristics, applied to a specific target audience of learners.

To begin with, we can consider two broad types of human characteristics: individual differences *between* people and similarities *among* people. Some schools of thought in education have emphasized individual differences, ignoring the important ways in which people are alike. In fact, both similarities and differences are important. As we shall see, a great deal of work has been done by psychologists and other researchers in providing useful descriptions of both similarities and differences. Individual differences are aspects of human form, function, and experience about which people are more characterized by their variation than by their sameness. These individual difference factors include intelligence, aptitudes, cognitive styles, hemispheric lateralization, developmental state, and prior learning. Similarities, on the other hand, are aspects that are characterized by a sameness among people rather than a difference, even though relatively insignificant differences do exist. These similarities include sensory capacities, information-processing capabilities and limits, and developmental processes (not states but the dynamics and process aspects of development), including intellectual, physical, psychosocial, and language development.

In addition to similarities and differences, we can consider whether a characteristic exhibits *change* over time or remains relatively *stable* over time. Some human characteristics, such as information-processing limits and intelligence, are more or less stable over time. People from childhood through mature adulthood may change very little in some ways and, even though some change can be observed, stability is part of the characteristic in question. Other characteristics are notable for their quality of change. The most notable of these characteristics are development (both the process of development and the developmental states or stages themselves) and learning. Both development and learning are constantly changing for all people.

The result of considering similarities among people and differences between them, along with changing and stable characteristics, is a matrix of four categories of human characteristics (see Figure 3.1):

1. Stable similarities—similarities among people that are relatively unchanging over time
2. Stable differences—differences between people that are relatively unchanging over time
3. Changing similarities—similarities among people that change over time
4. Changing differences—differences among people that change over time

Stable Similarities

There are many obvious stable similarities among learners that have very little to do with most instructional design decisions, such as where the lungs and ears are located. Another stable similarity may be seen in response to classical conditioning. As is widely known, classical or Pavlovian conditioning consists of a stimulus substitution (Hilgard & Bower, 1965, pp. 46–48). For instructional designers, this sort of learning is learning only in a narrow, technical sense—Pavlov's dogs did not learn to do anything new, only to produce a pre-existing involuntary response (salivation) in the presence of a substitute stimulus (the sound of a bell ringing).

One stable similarity among people that is more useful to instructional design is that of **sensory capacities.** Although people vary in their

	Similarities	**Differences**
Stable	• Sensory Capacities • Information Processing • Types and Conditions of Learning	• Intelligence Quotient • Cognitive Styles • Psychosocial Traits • Gender, Ethnicity, and Racial Group

Changing	Development Processes
	
	• Intellectual
	• Language
	• Psychosocial
	• Moral
		• Development State
		
		• Prior Learning
		  • General
		  • Specific

Figure 3.1: Four Categories of Learner Characteristics

eyesight, hearing, tactile sensitivity, and so forth, human sensory capacities and perceptual responses are more alike than they are different. The human sense of hearing, for example, is amazingly sensitive on the one hand, but it is terribly limited compared to that of a dog. And, although eagles or hawks could do it if they knew how, no person is able to read typewritten material with unaided vision from 200 feet away. There are capabilities and limitations for all of our senses. In addition, the perceptual mechanisms, as illustrated by common optical illusions, are well known and shared by us all.

For instructional designers, knowledge of sensory and perceptual characteristics becomes important when attempting to fully involve the senses in learning. The success of an audiovisual presentation, interactive educational game, activity package, or simulation trainer will often rely upon appropriate visual detail, use of color, auditory characteristics, and so forth. The more ambitious one becomes in such treatments, the more critical a knowledge of perception and the characteristics of sense modalities becomes. But even in more mundane situations, knowledge of sensory and perceptual characteristics is helpful. All of us have had enough experience with presentations that had inadequate illumination levels, low contrast, and

microscopic image size to know that decisions about such matters are easy to misjudge. And a knowledge of the selective nature of perception would assist in the attention-focusing and maintenance qualities of many a text and lecture.

In addition to sensory characteristics, characteristics associated with human **information processing** are also stable similarities that can be of assistance to instructional designers (see Chapter 1 for a description of information processing). Whether one is discussing the capacity to make discrete judgments about a single stimulus (Miller, 1956), capacity for temporary storage of isolated, non-meaningful units of information (Miller, 1956), processing multi-sensory simultaneous inputs as studied by Broadbent (1958), or Paivio's (1971) work in encoding and memory of visual and verbal information, capabilities and limits are found that do not vary with intelligence, college major, or even age.

The limits imposed by information-processing characteristics are real, and they are a commonplace source of learning problems in schools and training settings. Information overload, confusion, and inability to keep up with material being presented are typical student learning problems caused by ignoring human information-processing characteristics.

Knowledge of information-processing characteristics can not only help the designer avoid problems caused by limits in processing capability but can also help the designer find solutions to processing-based problems. For example, remembering isolated, non-meaningful bits of information can be made easier by chunking individual units into groups, with each group of bits becoming a single set of information. Or, the limits of short-term memory may be bypassed altogether through calling upon alternative processing capabilities such as visualization or mnemonic techniques.

Although it is not typical to think of the **types of learning** as a human characteristic, it is a fundamental fact that people are more or less alike in how they acquire different sorts of learnings (such as verbal information, concepts, rules, and problem solving). Robert Gagné (1985) developed a synthesis of the various psychologically distinguishable products of learning. Gagné pointed out that once we know that a person is going to learn, for example, a concept, we know that certain conditions *must* exist both within the learner and external to the learner for that learning to take place. These **conditions of learning,** which are themselves a similarity among people, do not vary between people, or even between subject areas. The psychological conditions for learning a concept in mathematics are identical to the conditions for learning a concept in grammar. (For more information on types of learning, see Chapter 4. For more information on conditions of learning, see Chapters 6 through 13, in which instructional strategy recommendations for different types of learning are presented.)

The principles on which instructional design is based, particularly instructional strategy, are largely drawn from a knowledge of the similarities among learners—not only Gagné's work but also human information-processing and sensory characteristics. It is upon these principles that much of this text is based.

Stable Differences

A number of factors that vary among individual learners remain relatively stable over time. Designers of instruction can accommodate these factors by either (1) making sure that a single instructional treatment can accommodate learners across the range of differences or (2) creating several instructional treatments, each of which is adjusted to a narrowed range of characteristic (e.g., "tracks" for high, average, and low ability learners; different instructional strategies for learners with different backgrounds or aptitudes; and so forth).

Intelligence quotient (I.Q.) is a stable difference among people that is fundamentally related to learning from instruction. I.Q. is best defined as "aptitude for school learning." Although there is some disagreement among the experts in this area, all would agree that I.Q. is not a measure of some global, qualitative factor such as "good brains." Intelligence testing has acquired some vigorous critics, and the accusations made are not entirely groundless. The worst abuses resulting from uses of I.Q. information have come from making inappropriate use of individual students' I.Q. test scores, and the harm done has generally rested upon the "good brains" conception of I.Q. and blanket judgements made and communicated to students based on I.Q. test scores. However, as just noted, I.Q. is a fundamental aptitude factor and can contain information about individuals that is very helpful to the design of optimally effective instruction for them. From I.Q. test scores a designer may make good inferences about a number of factors that *are* related to learning from instruction, including cognitive strategies available and amount of general prior knowledge available to build upon. Snow and Lohman (1984) make just this distinction in describing "general ability," which is an analogous concept to I.Q. They state that general ability has two components: crystalized ability and fluid ability. Crystalized ability reflects the skill acquired from past experience with similar tasks. Fluid ability is the creative adaptation of skills to novel tasks.

I.Q. indices may help predict which students will (1) need more/fewer examples, (2) be able to interpret analogies, (3) require more/less learning time, (4) need more/less practice, (5) have positive/negative attitudes toward learning, or (6) persevere in learning for short/long periods of time.

The issue of stability should be briefly noted here. I.Q., as well as other cognitively-based stable differences, is not a factor for which we claim absolute immutability when we classify it as a "stable" characteristic. We know that the scores

Style Dimension	Key Investigator(s)	Primary Measures
Field Independent / Dependent Cognitive Style	Witkin et al.	Rod & Frame, Group Embedded Figures
Leveling/Sharpening Cognitive Controls	Klein Santostephano	L/S Wagon Test (child) L/S House Test (adult)
Impulsive/Reflective Cognitive Tempo	Kagan	Matching Familiar Figures
Visual/Haptic Perceptual Style	Lowenfeld & Brittain	Successive Perception Test—I

Figure 3.2: Some Cognitive Styles and Their Measures

an individual makes on I.Q. tests can vary over the years, and that, in fact, with specially enriched (or deprived) environments, an individual's I.Q. scores can be seen to gradually and slowly increase (or decline) over time. However, for I.Q. as well as the other stable differences discussed below, there remains an important tendency toward stability over time and a dogged resistance to predictable change through intervention. In the final analysis, even though change may be observed in it, I.Q. is more characterized by stability than by change.

Another type of stable individual difference can be seen in the ways that people receive and process information. These differences are variously called cognitive styles, cognitive controls, cognitive tempo, and perceptual styles. We will refer to them collectively here as **cognitive styles.** Terms that are also frequently used interchangeably with *cognitive styles* and bear important distinctions are factors called *learning styles.* We will discuss learning styles separately from cognitive styles due to important differences between them.

A good deal is known about a variety of processing-style differences. In an extensive review, Ragan and associates (1979) found eleven style dimensions that have potential usefulness to the design of technical training. Of these, four styles, field independent/dependent cognitive style (Witkin et al., 1977), leveling/sharpening cognitive controls (Klein, 1951; Santostephano, 1978), impulsive/reflective cognitive tempo (Kagan, 1966), and visual/haptic perceptual style (Lowenfeld

& Brittain, 1970), seem to have the most potential utility to instructional design. Key points about each of these four style dimensions are presented in summary form in Figure 3.2.

Cognitive styles are useful to instructional designers because they provide information about individual differences from a cognitive and information-processing standpoint. Information about a learner's cognitive style can provide insight into not only whether an individual is likely to be able to perform well or poorly on a particular learning task but also why. Information from cognitive style measures is relevant only when considered with regard to particular learning tasks.

For example, if an individual is "field dependent," it does not mean that the individual learns all things well or poorly, or even that the individual learns all things in a particular way that is different from other people. It does mean, however, that if the learning task involves isolating and manipulating a detail from within a complex embedding field, it is likely that field dependent people would need more help from instruction to perform the task successfully than would field independent people. Such tasks would include the following: learning to find particular elements in complex electronic circuit diagrams; learning to determine from a printed diagram or pattern where different fabric layers are supposed to go in complex junctions found in sewing a suit; or learning to quickly find and extract information from an instrument in a complicated instrument panel in a cockpit.

Objective: Given an AN/PSM-6 multimeter and a resistor, measure the resistance to the nearest graduation.

(1) AN/PSM-6 ohmmeter function

(2) Resistance measurements

Analysis: This objective requires knowledge of the correct use of the AN/PSM-6 multimeter. Learning to use this piece of equipment could be related to cognitive style because the equipment is complex in terms of the visual field of stimuli it presents. Since the multimeter comprises a complex visual array, discrimination and analysis of its components might be made easier for field dependent, haptic, constricted field control, and impulsive students through the use of visual and verbal attention-focusing and cueing techniques as each component is discussed. One alternative might be to begin instruction with a progressive series of illustrations of the multimeter, gradually building up its elements in an increasingly complex visual field, explaining the function and operation of elements as they are added. Then instruction could proceed with the real item.

Figure 3.3: Example Analysis of a Training Objective from United States Air Force Course
Source: Ausburn, Ausburn, & Ragan (1980), page 37, Weapons Mechanic, Course #3ABR46230-2,-3,-4.

Performance of these same tasks would also be influenced by differences in the leveling/sharpening and visual/haptic dimensions, with people who are relative "sharpeners" and "visual" being much like the field independent people, and those who are relative "levelers" and "haptic" responding similarly to field dependent people (Ausburn, Ausburn, & Ragan, 1980). The impulsive/reflective cognitive tempo most specifically affects tasks requiring learners to select choices from among multiple alternatives. Thus, if the learning task presented multiple options, such as being able to match a logic diagram to given Boolean expressions (AND, OR, NOT, NAND, NOR), the impulsive learner may quickly select an incorrect match, as contrasted with a reflective learner who considers all alternatives before making a choice. Figure 3.3 presents an example analysis of a training objective from a cognitive-style standpoint.

Information about learners' cognitive processes (whether from an individual difference standpoint, as is the case with cognitive styles, or from a similarity standpoint, as in the case of perception and information processing as noted earlier) is valuable information to instructional designers.

Cognitive styles can be differentiated from other constructs with which they are frequently confused by the specificity with which cognitive styles may be applied. In the case of learning styles and so called "educational cognitive styles," applicability of information about learners is presumed to be of equal utility regardless of learning task. In such formulations, an individual may be diagnosed as being, for example, a "visual learner," an "auditory learner," or a "horizontal learner." The "horizontal learner," for example, is said to learn best when lying down (rather than sitting or standing, presumably), and the superiority of the prone position for learning is assumed regardless of the skill or topic being learned. The difficulty in substantiating the validity of the styles, as well as the apparent freewheeling generation and application of these styles to any and all situations, leads us to recommend viewing learning styles with extreme caution. While information about an individual's learning style may be helpful to that individual in regulating her own learning within a learning situation, this information is not typically sufficiently prescriptive to aid instructional designers in making design decisions.

Locus of control is a personality variable associated with an individual's perception of the source of major life influences and is frequently associated with "style" variables (Lefcourt, 1976). The primary measure used for locus of control is the Rotter I/E Scale, which is a paper-and-pencil instrument that yields a score reflecting the extent to which an individual reflects "internal" or "external" locus of control. An individual with a predominantly internal locus of control would perceive the major influences on life to be from within the person—perseverance, effort, one's own actions, and so forth. An individual with a relatively external locus of control, on the other hand, perceives major influences to come from outside one's self—luck, what the other person does, the boss, and so forth. Of all the "styles" discussed here, locus of control presents the greatest amount of change (in the "change vs. stable" classification). Individuals can experience major changes in their locus of control depending upon life circumstances, and they can experience small changes from morning to evening.

Determining what has been conscientiously developed and what has not been so developed is particularly important in the cognitive-style and learning-style areas. The line is not always easy to see between worthwhile and pointless formulations. In making your own investigations, look for information about the theoretic construct behind the style, validity and reliability of instruments used to measure, evidence of the independence of styles from one another, independence of the style from general measures of aptitude and intelligence, and the breadth of application claimed.

Psychosocial Traits. Three personality characteristics can also be viewed as stable differences among learners: trait anxiety, trait locus of control, and academic self-concept. These personality characteristics are not the only personality constructs that we could consider; however, all three are particularly helpful for the instructional designer to utilize. A trait characteristic is a characteristic that tends to be stable over time in contrast with a related characteristic that is changing. For example, an individual would be described as high on trait anxiety if that individual has a tendency to be generally anxious, regardless of the circumstances. Spielberger (1972) has developed an instrument, the Manifest Anxiety Scale (MAS), to determine an individual's level of trait anxiety (as

well as the changing characteristic of state anxiety). Although at or above a certain level, anxiety can inhibit learning, various instructional accommodations, such as frequent feedback, clear specification of expectations, and overlearning, can minimize the negative influence of anxiety on learning.

Locus of control, described earlier as a style, can also be considered a psychosocial trait. Locus of control is expressed as varying tendencies to be "internal" or "external" in one's perceptions of the primary source of influence in life events. For example, to attribute a recent promotion on the job to hard work and persistence would be consistent with internal locus of control, whereas attribution of the event to good fortune or the influence of other people would be consistent with external locus of control. Or, a failure to achieve a goal would be likely to be associated with lack of sufficient effort or ability from an internal locus of control standpoint, whereas the external standpoint would tend to attribute the failure to something like bad luck, "the system," or some other cause external to one's self. As noted above, locus of control can change in an individual. In addition, however, many people tend to attribute a persistent leaning toward "internal-ness" or "external-ness" over time as a personality *trait*. For these individuals, some adaptation can be made to instruction to promote greater learning. One instructional manipulation that can accommodate differences in locus of control is the amount of structure built into a lesson. Whereas extreme "internals" learn best in a relatively unstructured learning environment, extreme "externals" appear to require more structure.

A third, similar characteristic is academic self-concept. Although a person's assessment of academic ability may vary by circumstance, it is often the case that after a surprisingly short time in schooling learners have developed a generalized image of themselves as learners. If this image is positive it will promote a positive attitude toward learning and perseverance in learning tasks. If academic self-image is negative, it can seriously impede learning. Instructional adaptation to poor academic self-concepts is similar to strategies to assist highly anxious learners.

You may be thinking that anxiety, locus of control, and academic self-concept may vary depending upon the circumstance, in addition to being

ing stable characteristics. This is true. We will discuss these characteristics as "state" characteristics in the section on changing differences.

Gender, Ethnicity, and Racial Group.   Three additional stable differences may be considered when designing instruction: gender, ethnicity, and racial group identification. One must be cautious in reflecting upon why these three factors might be considered when analyzing the learner population. We consider these differences *not* because members of one gender or racial group process information differently, but because members of a gender, ethnic, or racial group tend to have common experiences due to their group membership that may be quite different from those had by members of other groups. Designers should consider these group memberships in their learner analyses to ensure that as they design instruction they include contexts and examples that are relevant and comprehensible to members of all groups represented in the target audience. Regardless of particular ethnic considerations, all learners will come from a culture. Cultural factors are important, whether the situation is a multicultural one or not.

Changing Similarities

A number of physiological similarities exist that change over time but which are not of any particular significance to instructional design. The "startle response" in infants is an example of this sort of characteristic. All neurologically normal newborn infants wave their arms in a particular way when they are unweighted (quickly lowered). The particulars of this reflex go away in a short period of time and probably form the neurological basis for a more localized response that soon develops: facial manifestations of surprise. The startle response serves to illustrate the category of characteristic that we are considering here—a characteristic that changes over time but which we share as a similarity among us.

More relevant characteristics in the changing similarity category can be seen in **development processes.** People are continuously changing in their development, but the process or dynamics of development is more or less the same for everyone. In other words, if a particular developmental

theory is valid, it will produce some degree of predictability in the changes to which it addresses itself. The stages in Piaget's **intellectual development** theory provide an example of a changing similarity (Inhelder & Piaget, 1958). These stages of development are sensorimotor, preoperational, concrete operations, and formal operations. Briefly, the sensorimotor period extends from birth to approximately 18 months. During this period senses and motor abilities develop rapidly; however, development of language and other cognitive maturation is less apparent. During the preoperational period (approximately ages 18 months to 7 years) children learn to reason and problem-solve. However, children at this age are not bothered by inconsistencies in their reasoning, nor are they able to view a problem from another person's perspective. During the stage of concrete operations (approximately ages 7 to 12), learners acquire such skills as classification, seriation (ordering), reversal of operations, reciprocity, and identity. Learners at this stage of development can think logically but require concrete objects to support this thought process. The stage of formal operations extends from approximately 12 years of age and on. Learners at this stage can think abstractly and mentally manipulate symbols without requiring concrete supports.

The work of Piaget and his followers has aided educators in understanding what kinds of cognitive operations are involved in outcomes that involve abstract thinking. In addition, Piaget's ideas about how people come to acquire capabilities for certain kinds of abstract thought have been used to suggest generative, inquiry-oriented instructional strategies for helping people achieve these capabilities (Renner et al., 1976).

Although knowledge of these approximate stages of mental development is helpful to designers as they consider a target audience, it is important that these stages are viewed as guidelines rather than immutable absolutes. These stages are the periods through which learners pass without substantial intervention (i.e., instruction). Case (1978, 1985) has developed a theory of instruction that particularly focuses on teaching cognitive strategies (executive control processes) to children. Case's work draws from the theory bases of Piaget's work in intellectual development, Bruner's theory of instruction (1966), Newell and Simon's studies of problem solving (1972), and information-processing theory. Case's model of instruction involves working at the "cutting edge" of a child's developmental level to enhance the development of the strategies needed for the next level of development. In contrast to Piaget's theory and more in concert with Bruner's theory, Case employs a procedure for direct instruction of cognitive strategies. Case suggests that instruction promotes development.

Like intellectual development, the dynamics of **language development**—probably a subset of intellectual development—reflect a process of change that is, in many respects, the same for all people, no matter what person or language is in question, with the exception of major language dysfunctions or disabilities. One view of language development that underscores the similarity dimension is that of Chomsky (1965). In general, Chomsky's theory holds that a propensity or talent for the structure of language is in a sense "wired-in" to human brains. His theory was in part stimulated by the observation of children learning to speak. Chomsky found that there are many kinds of errors that you would think a child would make when learning to speak. However, there are syntactical-logical errors of various sorts that are simply never made, regardless of the language being learned. Apparently, changes that occur over time in the facility and use of language are enabled and governed by common attributes that all persons possess.

Other developmental theories are similarly illustrative of changing similarities. The dynamics of **psychosocial** and **personality development** have been treated by Freud, Maslow, Erikson, and others. If we look at the dynamics or change processes that major personality theories propose, we see ways in which people change that lend some degree of predictability to their behavior. Perhaps the most commonly applied of these theories in training settings is Maslow's "hierarchy of needs" (Maslow, 1954). In its simplest form, the Maslow needs hierarchy describes types of human needs: (1) physiological needs, (2) safety needs, (3) love and belonging needs, (4) esteem needs, and (5) the self-actualization need. These needs are proposed to operate in a sequential, hierarchical fashion. If a person is extremely hungry (a physi-

ological need), considerations for safety will be secondary. If you expect truly creative behavior (an aspect of human functioning that resides at the self-actualization level) it will not be likely to occur if there are major frustrations at the lower levels of need. Although Maslow's is the most familiar, other approaches that lend insight into individual growth provide insights into changing similarities that instructional designers can take into consideration.

Erikson (1968) has described an eight-stage model of psychosocial development. He describes each stage in terms of the psychosocial crisis that must be dealt with during this period.

1. *Trust vs. Mistrust*. During infancy, the attentions and comfort provided by the infant's mother are the focus of the infant's life. Being an infant under the care of a loving parent generates a capacity for trust, but the times that the parent cannot or will not satisfy needs (Mommy can't always be there) produce frustration and mistrust.

2. *Autonomy vs. Shame*. As a toddler, the child first acquires mobility, producing a sense of being able to do something. At the same age, learning the existence and control of elimination of waste and other bodily functions generally involves a degree of shame.

3. *Initiative vs. Guilt*. During early childhood, with development of language and improved thinking and motor skills, the child begins to be able to take the initiative (let's do this; I want to wear that shirt; and so forth). First experiences with guilt come from knowledge of having done wrong things.

4. *Competence vs. Inferiority.* During middle childhood, roughly corresponding to Piaget's period of concrete operations, the child acquires many important skills—not only the fundamentals of school learning such as reading, writing, and arithmetic, but also fine motor and athletic skills that give the child a new sense of competence. Yet, when the child looks at adults, the child sees a fundamental inferiority to them in skills, size, and authority.

5. *Identity vs. Identity Confusion.* During adolescence, the sense of one's self as an adult begins to form, but the new identity is a confusing one.

6. *Intimacy vs. Isolation.* During young adulthood, a typical pattern is to experience intimate relationships and learn how to handle intimacy, while at the same time experiencing isolation as a product of being out on one's own for the first time.

7. *Generativity vs. Stagnation.* During adulthood people have mature powers to be creative contributors and can learn to channel and direct their capabilities to productive ends, while at the same time feeling the pull toward complacency and self-satisfaction.

8. *Integrity vs. Despair.* As an aging adult, the individual has the potential to achieve an ego integrity impossible at a younger age (due to a rich life of learning and experience), while dealing with the knowledge that death is unavoidable and near.

A number of characteristics of interest to the designer are associated with learners' level of psychosocial growth. In general, individuals in the same cohort tend to have similar interests, motivations, relationships to peers, feelings toward authority, and role models. Of course, the characteristics will vary some within an age group, but there are more similarities than differences. Designers should consider these characteristics when selecting examples, creating relevancy statements, and making grouping decisions. These characteristics are particularly important when designing attitude lessons and when designing the motivational aspects of a lesson. The review of a good text on human development for the particular age group of your target audience will aid you in learning these general characteristics.

Another facet of personality development is **moral development.** Kohlberg (1969) has suggested that people generally develop in their morality through stages. The preconventional morality stage includes an egocentric period, in which people suppress their own desires only because of the fear of punishment, and a reciprocity period, in which members do kindnesses only out of an agreement to get something in return.

The conventional morality stage is the next stage, characterized by an initial phase of behaving morally in order to please an authority figure or in a sense of doing one's duty. This phase involves a legalistic and rote adherence to laws (in the extreme) to maintain order. Most intermediate elementary, middle school, and some high school students fall within the conventional morality stage.

Kohlberg's final stage of moral development is postconventional, or principled, morality. The initial phase in this stage is characterized by viewing laws as means to ends, a set of social contracts, and the view that certain social values may take precedence over the law. The final phase describes individuals whose behavior is guided by universal principles such as human dignity and fairness. Kohlberg tends to describe this phase by "best examples" such as Ghandi and Martin Luther King (see a discussion of the best example technique for teaching concepts in Chapter 8). These individuals characterized the values they possessed. (See Chapter 12, the discussion of Krathwohl's taxonomy of affective objectives, for more information on characterization of values.) During high school and young adulthood many learners move into the stage of principled morality, although many adults do not develop into this stage.

An understanding of the stages of moral development can be quite helpful to designers, particularly as they design for attitude objectives, design instructional management strategies, or design instruction in psychosocial content areas.

Changing similarities are those learner characteristics that are developmental: They appear to develop in a predictable pattern over time. Knowledge of these phases is useful to a designer when designing instruction for a target population, many of whom will be similar in their level of cognitive, language, psychosocial, and moral development. It is useful for the designer to analyze the population along these dimensions because it will provide some sense of the similarities among the population and therefore some sense of how examples and contents may be cast.

It is important to interpret these stages as being flexible, permeable, and open to advancement through instruction. It is not uncommon to find educators who adhere to developmental theories so inflexibly that they believe learners to be impervious to change as a result of instruction. Such individuals will oppose teaching certain concepts and principles because they perceive the learners of a particular stage to be developmentally "not ready." This position is particularly true of those who strictly adhere to theories of intellectual development. Instructional designers tend to believe that developmental states are mutable; that is, they are changed "naturally" through the cumulative effect of incidental learning, and therefore can be advanced intentionally through instruction of the right sort. This instruction involves determining learners' current state of prior knowledge and identifying prerequisite knowledge that must be learned for a learner to move on to the next stage of "development." Case (1972) has successfully employed these tactics in advancing learners through stages of intellectual development. We will discuss the process of prerequisite analysis in the next chapter.

Changing Differences

Among the many differences between people that change over time are physical features such as weight, strength, stamina, and details of physical appearance. These particular changing differences, ones that are such blatantly obvious differences between people, are among the least useful to an instructional designer. However, there are several areas of changing differences for which a target audience should be analyzed: values and beliefs, personality states, developmental stages, and levels of prior knowledge.

Although some values, beliefs, motivations, and interests may devolve from the psychosocial and moral stages of development (of which several stages may be represented in a population), many of these affective dimensions may vary among individuals due to their own unique experiences. If the designer is creating instruction for a national or international population, it is clear that these affective characteristics may vary greatly based on cultural mores. In order to make learning relevant and meaningful, it is important for the designer to obtain information on these values, beliefs, and interests. It may be that it will be impossible to always accommodate this variety in instruction,

but at least the knowledgeable designer can actively avoid offending those who hold these values and beliefs.

You will remember in the section on stable differences we mentioned three trait characteristics: anxiety, locus of control, and academic self-concept. These factors can also be "states" that change among individuals depending upon the circumstance. For example, an individual who has a low trait anxiety and a high academic self-concept may have a high *state* anxiety and a low academic self-concept when encountering highly unfamiliar or complex content. A person who is normally very internal in terms of locus of control may become very external when in an unfamiliar or threatening learning environment. Measurement instruments to assess anxiety, locus of control, and academic self-concept have been revised so that they can be used to determine learners' states at a particular point in time. Designers may consider using these instruments to assess the target audience if they suspect that the context or the content (learning task) may negatively affect these states. If these states are found to be sufficiently extreme, so as to negatively affect learning performance, then, as mentioned in the section on stable differences, certain instructional strategy techniques can be used to accommodate them.

Developmental theories, the dynamics of which were noted earlier as examples of similarities among people, also tend to contain descriptions of people at various states or stages that they may achieve. These **developmental states** or **stages,** which are described within developmental theories, are examples of changing differences. Although individuals in a target audience, particularly if they are of similar age, will tend to be at a similar developmental stage, it is quite possible that learners may fall into two or even more stages. And, as the year goes by, a teacher will be able to observe many children changing in this regard, moving from one stage to another. Typically, developmental states or stages are seen to be age-related but not age-bound; therefore, there is a tendency to move upward in a developmental sequence, but the change itself varies with the individual and is not inevitable.

An example of a developmental theory offering a perspective on a changing difference that is useful to instructional designers may be seen in the stages of intellectual development as identified by Piaget, which reflect an increasing capacity to engage in certain kinds of abstract thought. At the formal operations stage, for example, the individual can isolate and deal with the variables contained in abstract problems in which multiple propositions are present and in interaction. Research in intellectual development has demonstrated fairly clearly that a large proportion of adults, including college students, have not achieved this frequently assumed capability, even though it is believed to be within the potential of practically everyone (Phillips, 1969, pp. 169–170). An instructional designer who neglects to consider factors such as these can make fundamental errors in assuming that learners will be able to benefit from instruction that is impossible for some of them to comprehend.

Another view holds that an individual's evolving capabilities are the results of **prior learning,** rather than development. Although people who work from the prior learning perspective do not deny the validity of the developmental view, they believe there is a greater amount of specific help for the instructional designer in looking at major capabilities not as representatives of stages of development but rather as reflections of accumulated learning. As instructional designers, if we view a major capability that we wish to teach (such as the ability to solve a particular type of problem) as the reflection of accumulated learning, then we are led to ask the question "What learnings are accumulated to reach this capability?" We call these learnings *prior learning*—specific, lower-level learnings that are prerequisite to achieving a capability of a higher order, such as an intellectual skill. (Specific prior learning is discussed in the following section.) Another result of prior learning is general world knowledge. Every person has a storehouse of knowledge, which varies with age, culture, and many other factors, and can be called **general world knowledge.** Although general world knowledge is not used in the same way as specific prior learning, it is an essential element upon which meaningfulness of instruction depends.

One type of prior knowledge that is relevant to instructional designers is learners' levels of "visual literacy." Dondis (1973) has defined **visual literacy** as "the ability to manipulate symbols in visual format for thinking and communicating" (p. 22). Learner factors that have been postulated to influence ability to decode visuals are age, experience, culture, and training. Learners' ability to decode visual messages increases with age. For example, Saiet (1978) found that children develop the ability to decode visual elements that convey motion over time. Individuals who have not had much experience with visuals, such as learners in non-literate cultures, may have difficulty interpreting commonly used visual conventions. For example, learners who have not experienced many visuals may be confused by an elephant in the background of a visual being smaller than a human in the foreground (Hudson, 1960). Culture also influences learners' ability to decode visual messages. Bagby (1957) found that learners do not even "see" (notice) visuals that do not have meaning in their culture. There is evidence that visual decoding skills can be taught (Dondis, 1973). One method used is to provide opportunities for learners to develop their own visuals, utilizing the conventions they find in visuals around them.

Specific Prior Learning

The most important factor for a designer to consider about the audience is specific prior learning. Thus, instructional designers must ask many questions about the target audience members: Do they have some background knowledge or skills that will help them learn the current task? Will the instructor have to fill in this background knowledge for some of the students? Is there a wide variation in background knowledge among prospective learners? Do some of the prospective learners already have some of the skills and knowledge that the instructor plans to teach?

For example, if the designer is creating materials on operating a 35mm camera, he will need to obtain as much information as possible on what the targeted learners already know about cameras, film, the effect of light on film, the composition of a good photograph, the processing of film, and so on. It is also important to consider prior knowledge not directly related to photography that may be critical to students' learning the new information. For example, do they have prior experience and knowledge of art that will serve as important background information that can be built on?

Sometimes designers acquire this information from actually testing representative students from the target audience. Sometimes they question the trainers/teachers that work with the target audience. Sometimes they cautiously base their assumptions about prior knowledge on information about the instruction that the learners have had in the past. Remember, these assumptions should be made with caution. The fact that a learner has taken a course in Algebra I does not necessarily mean that she has all the knowledge she needs to begin Algebra II. Just because something has been taught does not mean that it has been learned. In addition, some of the student's knowledge and skill may have been forgotten, or some of the information might not have been included in Algebra I that the designer is assuming was included. In any case, the more designers know about the relevant knowledge and skills that the learners already have, the more effective and efficient they can make the instruction.

An Outline of Learner Characteristics

The following list contains the major characteristics that should be used in a target audience description. We have recategorized them from the changing/stable, similarities/differences system because we have found that while it is easier to conceptualize learners using that system, it is easier to analyze them with the following system. Depending upon the instructional task, some characteristics may be more critical than others. For an individual design project, it is unlikely that all factors will be included in the learner analysis.

1. Cognitive Characteristics
   - General aptitudes
   - Specific aptitudes
   - Developmental level, such as Piaget's levels of cognitive development
   - Language development level
   - Reading level
   - Level of visual literacy, ability to gain information from graphics
   - Cognitive processing styles—preferred and most effective
   - Cognitive and learning strategies
   - General world knowledge
   - Specific content knowledge
2. Psychosocial Characteristics
   - Interests
   - Motivations
   - Motivations to learn
   - Attitude toward subject matter
   - Attitude toward learning
   - Academic self-concept
   - Anxiety level
   - Beliefs
   - Attribution of success, i.e., locus of control
   - Relationships to peers
   - Feelings toward authority
   - Tendencies toward cooperation or competition
   - Moral development, such as Kohlberg's stages of moral development
   - Socioeconomic background
   - Racial/ethnic background, affiliations
   - Job position, rank
   - Role models
3. Physiological Characteristics
   - Sensory perception, such as visual, auditory, tactile, and olfactory acuity
   - General health, which may influence tendency toward fatigue as well as many other health-related factors
   - Age

Of course, the designer may not consider all of these characteristics for all learning tasks and all audiences. For example, physiological characteristics may be very important for geriatric audiences but of little importance for general public school audiences. In general, the designer should collect a great deal of information because often when one is conducting a learner analysis one is not aware of information that will be critical later in the design process.

Information on learner characteristics may help the designer to create effective, efficient, and interesting instructional materials. For instance, knowledge about the learners' socioeconomic and ethnic background and regional location may help the designer determine their interests and, consequently, select examples and contexts that make the instruction relevant and interesting. The designer may also wish to obtain information on students' interest in the content area and their interest in learning in general.

Assessing Learner Characteristics

How do designers find out about the general characteristics of the target audience? If the designers are developing for their own classrooms, they can observe, talk to, and assess their learners to determine their characteristics. Even then they may wish to conduct some additional research to find out more about the learners. But suppose a designer is developing instruction to be used by learners whom he has never met. How can information about this audience be obtained? Here are some of the things that designers can do:

* Interview teachers, trainers, and other educators who work with the target audience.
* Interview and/or observe members of the target audience.
* Have members of the target audience complete surveys that provide information about their backgrounds and interests.
* Have members of the target audience complete assessment instruments that provide information about cognitive strategies, processing styles, and preferred instructional delivery modes.
* Examine job descriptions and personnel profiles of organization.
* Read texts and articles about particular age groups and developmental levels that provide information on their interests, social development, and physical characteristics.
* Read texts and articles that discuss the interests and motivations of individuals with particular socioeconomic, ethnic, or racial backgrounds.

To avoid stereotyping members of a particular target audience, the designer should use several of these sources of information to describe the diversity as well as the similarities of the members.

Implications of Learner Characteristics for Design

A careful consideration of the general characteristics of the target audience when designing instruction may be what elevates a mundane segment of instruction into compelling, imaginative, and memorable instruction. These factors are considered when the the designer determines what information and instructional techniques, which we call *strategies,* will be used in the instruction. Following is a beginning list of instructional strategy factors that are directly related to learner characteristics. These information and instructional techniques that may be varied according to learner characteristics:

* Speed of presentation (pace)
* Number of successful experiences learners should have in practice
* Types of statements to convince students of the relevancy of the instruction
* Techniques for gaining and focusing attention and the frequency of use of these techniques
* Context of examples and practice items
* Amount of structure and organization
* Medium/media of instruction
* Level of concreteness/abstraction
* Grouping of students
* Size of instructional chunks
* Response mode (written, oral, etc.)
* Number and difficulty of examples and practice
* Type of feedback given after practice items
* Level of learner control
* Reading level
* Vocabulary and terminology used
* Amount and types of reinforcement
* Amount of time allowed for instruction
* Amount and type of learning guidance, cues, and prompts provided

When designers conduct the learner analysis and begin writing a description of the learners, it is important that they include some of the implications that these characteristics have for the design of the instruction. Occasionally these implications are very apparent; occasionally they require a lot of thought and research to determine how to adjust the instruction to learner characteristics. The following example describes the characteristics of a target audience and discusses some of the implications of these characteristics for the design of instruction.

An Example of a Learner Analysis

In this example, the target audience is computer hardware service professionals who are to be trained to repair the SX-7, a new mainframe computer from MetaCom Corporation (a fictitious computer manufacturer), and to train customers to operate the computer.

The Target Audience

The approximately 400 service professionals (SPs) who must be trained to repair the MetaCom SX-7 range in age from 23 to 52. Seventy percent of the SPs are male, and 30 percent are female. Forty percent of the SPs have been repairing systems for ten years or more (30 percent for five to ten years, and 20 percent for two to five years). Consequently, the majority of SPs have had considerable experience in repairing complex mainframe systems. Sixty percent of the SPs have two or more years of college education, the majority in electrical engineering and mathematics programs. Thirty percent of the SPs attended technical schools and received training in electronics. On the average, these employees have received 150 hours of on-the-job and classroom training while working with MetaCom. This instruction has centered on repair of mainframe systems and peripherals (printers, disk systems, and so on), electronic circuit analysis and fault-trace procedures, time management, and customer training.

When tested, the reading levels of these SPs ranged from tenth grade to over twelfth grade level. The SPs scored exceptionally well on exam questions requiring them to interpret complex diagrams and charts. This skill is perhaps a result of their on-the-job requirements to use schematics.

The SPs have received, on the average, 40 hours of computer-based-training (CBT) in their regional offices. All SPs have received some training via computer. They are somewhat ambivalent about this instruction. They like it because it al-

lows them to remain at home or near home during training, rather than having to go to a central location for instruction. However, many of the SPs find this CBT boring. Many SPs say they would prefer hands-on training on the new systems rather than CBT. On CBT lessons that allow learners to control the selection of content and the pace of instruction, evaluation indicates that the majority of learners tend to speed through instruction without interacting with sufficient examples and practice exercises before testing. Hence, test performance on this type of instruction tends to be low when using CBT that allows a high level of learner control. SPs generally prefer instruction from a lecturer, followed with hands-on practice on a real mainframe. The credibility of the lecturer is extremely important in obtaining the SP's attention and motivation.

Interest assessments indicate that the learners are unusually analytical and skilled at quantitative skills. In addition, aptitude assessments, surveys, and on-the-job observations indicate the SPs have a greater-than-average difficulty in establishing interpersonal relationships. This is of some concern as the SP's job entails an element of sales and a large amount of customer training.

The majority of the SPs report a higher-than-average level of job satisfaction. The factors that the learners identify as contributing most to this level of satisfaction are job security, the challenge of troubleshooting malfunctioning equipment, and relationships with long-term customers.

Implications for Design

The characteristics of the MetaCom service professionals have implications for the design of CBT training for their use. The SPs possess a considerable level of background knowledge and expertise upon which the designers can build. Instruction on the new system can center around how this system differs from previous, similar systems. A CBT delivery system may be appropriate as the learners are able to learn from textual and graphic information. The CBT system will be more popular with learners if designers incorporate strategies that simulate hands-on, on-the-job activities (perhaps with interactive video). The designers will probably wish to restrict the level of learner control over content and pace of instruction. This can be achieved by using pretests or responses to practice exercises embedded in the instruction.

The designers may want to provide for some small group instruction so that SPs can practice, perhaps through role-playing, the human interactions required in training a customer to use the new system. The designers could use experienced and credible lecturers for some of the content. They may wish to reserve this costly medium for skills that are particularly difficult to learn, such as the interpersonal skills.

*E*xercises

1. Describe the four categories of characteristics that should be considered in designing instruction. List four particular characteristics that might be described under each of these major categories.

2. In your own words, describe the difference between general characteristics and specific prior knowledge of a learner population.

3. List and describe at least seven instructional strategy variables that may be influenced by learner characteristics.

4. Suppose you were a member of the task force that is investigating the possibility of a mediated physics program in Corona (review this scenario in the section on analyzing the learning environment). What information would you wish to know about the high school students who will receive this mediated physics program? List the questions that you would ask. Tell how you would go about finding the answers to your questions.

Summary

Learner characteristics are an important aspect of instructional design. The four major categories of learner characteristics are cognitive (general and specific), physiological, affective, and social. Cognitive characteristics have these dimensions: similarities/differences and changing/stable. The four dimensions of cognitive characteristics each possess different qualities and implications for instructional designers.

Specific prior knowledge is generally the most important single learner characteristic to consider. Figure 3.4 summarizes key points in this chapter.

Job Aid

Complete the following form to organize your description of the learners for the instruction of any project. If it is clear that knowledge of a particular characteristic is not important to this particular project, write *NA* beside the characteristic. If information regarding a particular, relevant characteristic is not available to you currently, specify how you would go about obtaining this information. Add to this list any characteristics (or design implications) that may be unique to your particular population.

1. Cognitive Characteristics
   a. General Characteristics
      - General aptitudes
      - Specific aptitudes
      - Developmental level, such as Piaget's levels of cognitive development
      - Language development level
      - Reading level
      - Level of visual literacy, ability to gain information from graphics
      - Cognitive processing styles—preferred and most effective
      - Cognitive and learning strategies
      - General world knowledge
   b. Specific prior knowledge

2. Physiological Characteristics
   - Sensory perception
   - General health
   - Age

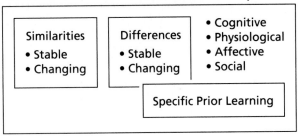

Kinds of Learner Characteristics

Similarities	Differences	• Cognitive
• Stable	• Stable	• Physiological
• Changing	• Changing	• Affective
		• Social

Specific Prior Learning

Implications for Instructional Design

- pace
- practice
- relevance statements
- attention
- context of examples
- context of practice items
- structure

- medium
- concreteness/abstraction
- grouping
- chunking
- response mode
- number of examples
- amount of practice

- feedback
- learner control
- reading level
- vocabulary
- reinforcement
- time
- learning guidance

Figure 3.4: Summary Diagram for Chapter 3

3. Affective Characteristics
   - Interests
   - Motivation
   - Motivations to learn
   - Attitude toward subject matter
   - Attitude toward learning
   - Perceptions of and experience with specific forms of mediation
   - Academic self-concept
   - Anxiety level
   - Beliefs
   - Attribution of success, i.e., locus of control

4. Social characteristics
   - Relationships to peers
   - Feelings toward authority
   - Tendencies toward cooperation or competition
   - Moral development, such as Kohlberg's stages of moral development
   - Socioeconomic background
   - Racial/ethnic background, affiliations
   - Role models

Extended Example

The following is a continuation of our extended example of the design of a course, Photography Basics, for graduate-level instructional technology students.

1. Cognitive Characteristics
   a. General

In general, members of this audience are above average in intelligence. By the time they reach this advanced level of education, they have developed highly sophisticated study strategies and skills, although this may vary significantly among individual students. With the advent of computer-based instruction and the addition of computer-related courses in instructional technology programs, many students have developed extremely high quantitative and analytical skills. This trend is sometimes related to a commensurate lowering of verbal ability skills among the graduate students. The learners typically read at least at the college level.

Many of the learners are considerably less visually literate than they are verbally literate. That is, while they are able to "read" visual images at least as well as members of the general population, they are in general not particularly skilled in producing visual images, or even consciously aware of how visual messages are conveyed. Of course, this characteristic is highly variable among the audience. In fact, some students are attracted to the field because of their interest in visual message design.

In general, the learners are at the formal operations level of reasoning. However, with unfamiliar content they tend to profit from concrete referents to ease this reasoning. With regard to cognitive style, the visual/haptic style may have some relevance to the particular content and skills in this course. It could be anticipated that approximately 15 to 25 percent of the population could be considered "haptic" (i.e., to have difficulty remembering visual images accurately).

Artistic talent is as evenly distributed in this group as in the general population. Therefore, it can be anticipated that few members of the audience will possess exceptional artistic talent. This may make learning some elements of composition more difficult, or at least, less intuitive. It may also be anticipated that this "lack of talent" may influence the learners' perceptions and attitudes in learning some photography concepts.

   b. Specific Prior Knowledge

The learners vary in their experiences with photography. There will be some learners who have extremely limited experience. They may not have operated a camera in which settings must be adjusted, much less have prior knowledge of the variations in film and the selection of lenses. On the other hand, there may be a few learners in each course who have had more experience with photography than the instructor. However, most likely none of the students will have learned about the application of photography from the perspective of developing instructional materials.

The learners will possess certain general world knowledge that will be helpful in learning photography skills and concepts, such as knowledge of fractions, perception of lightness and darkness, estimating distances, and concepts of duration and intensity.

2. Physiological Characteristics

The learners generally range in age from mid twenties to fifties, with the majority of the students in their thirties. Most programs are about equally divided among females and males. The only physiological characteristic that might have an important impact in learning the photography content is color blindness.

3. Affective Characteristics

Most learners enter instructional technology programs to facilitate a job change. There are also those learners who have entered the program to acquire skills and knowledge to enable them to perform better in their current job. Of course, to a varying degree, the learners also simply wish to know more about the content. Many of the learners are from public education jobs or other social services, such as social work and other helping professions (with approximately half of the learners coming from public education jobs). So, many are motivated to learn in order to contribute more to society. There is also a large number of learners who wish to move into positions in which they can receive more monetary rewards. Many individuals from the business environment have entered the programs as a means of moving into public education. Many students work full-time day jobs and attend night school. Consequently, learners are often tired and distracted in classes. They also find it difficult to commit more time than the specific class time to on-campus activities.

In general, learners will have a positive attitude toward the content and toward learning photography: It is very pragmatic and hands-on. They will be able to see relevance to their immediate lives, as well as implications for their ability to perform jobs in future positions as instructional technologists. Some learners may be somewhat unmotivated in learning photography, as they may perceive the medium as being ''low tech'' compared to media such as computers and interactive video. Some learners may perceive the content as requiring artistic talent and may be somewhat apprehensive in taking the course.

The learners generally will have a positive attitude toward learning and academics. Since attending graduate school is voluntary and most schools are fairly selective, students will be eager to learn and motivated to perform.

Although they are entering the field of instructional technology, many will not have had experiences in learning from media other than teachers, other students, transparencies, blackboards, and texts. They tend to think, ''If it didn't come out of a teacher's mouth, it hasn't been taught.'' They may not have acquired strategies of learning from many media, although it is anticipated that they will be more eager than members from the general graduate population to acquire these strategies.

Learners typically are fairly anxious about learning in graduate school and are highly motivated to make high grades. Some students may be somewhat intimidated by the equipment and paraphernalia associated with photography. Some may have had unsuccessful experiences in taking photographs in the past.

While most of the students are typically very internal in locus of control in their professional lives (ascribing success or failure to their own efforts rather than to some external force), they often become external in their initial experiences in graduate school.

4. Social Characteristics

As this will be a fairly early course in the curriculum, so the learners will be more independent and less cooperative than they may be in later classes. They are generally very interpersonally capable and comfortable in social situations. Since they are adult learners from highly responsible jobs, they often view themselves as equal in status with the instructor and capable of making substantial and relevant contributions to the course. The learners are from a variety of socioeconomic and ethnic backgrounds. Many programs have a high percentage of their populations from other countries, particularly from Asian and Middle Eastern countries. Those learners from these international environments are often uncomfortable in the egalitarian, social environments typical of most graduate classes.

The learners are typically more liberal in perspective than members of the surrounding community. Often their role models are intellectuals or socially active personalities.

5. Design Implications
   a. The variability in specific prior knowledge of the content is an important factor. The designers may wish to consider some type of modularized, self-paced delivery system so learners can begin at the appropriate point in instruction.
   b. The perception of photography requiring artistic skill may inhibit learners' attitudes, and consequently, their learning. The instruction should provide early successful experiences. It should also emphasize that the content is very rule-based and that rules can be learned by everyone.
   c. Learners will be tired and distracted in class. The class should have many hands-on activities, with frequent changes in pace and activity.

d. Since most learners work full time, outside class assignments (when possible) should be designed so that they can be completed at the learners' homes or workplaces, and within the learners' own weekly time frame.

e. Instruction on visual message design should be included in the content. The instructor should not anticipate that students possess this prior knowledge.

f. If alternative and unfamiliar media are used, students should be instructed on strategies to utilize in learning from these unfamiliar media. International students may require additional instruction on how to learn from a typical U.S. graduate class.

g. If cooperative projects are required, students should receive some guidelines and instruction on how to work effectively in groups.

Readings and References

Ausburn, F. B., Ausburn, L. J., & Ragan, T. J. (1980). *Task analysis schema based on cognitive style and supplantational instructional design with application to an Air Force training course.* AFHRL TR 79-59, Brooks AFB, Texas: Air Force Human Resources Laboratory.

Bagby, J. W. (1957). A cross-cultural study of perceptual predominance in binocular rivalry. *Journal of Abnormal and Social Psychology, 54,* 331–334.

Broadbent, D. E. (1958). *Perception and communication.* New York: Pergamon.

Bruner, J. S. (1966). *Toward a theory of instruction.* Cambridge, MA: Harvard University Press.

Case, R. (1972). Validation of a neo-Piagetian mental capacity construct. *Journal of Experimental Child Psychology, 14,* 287–302.

Case, R. (1978). A developmentally based theory and technology of instruction. *Review of Educational Research, 48,* 439–463.

Case, R. (1985). *Intellectual development: Birth to adulthood.* Orlando: Academic Press.

Chomsky, N. (1965). *Aspects of the theory of syntax.* Cambridge: The M.I.T. Press.

Cronbach, L. J., & Snow, R. E. (1977). *Aptitudes and instructional methods: A handbook for research on interactions.* New York: Irvington.

Dondis, D. A. (1973). *A primer of visual literacy.* Cambridge: Massachusetts Institute of Technology.

Erikson, E. (1968). *Identity: Youth in crises.* New York: Norton.

Gagné, R. M. (1985). *The conditions of learning,* 3rd Edition. New York: Holt, Rinehart, & Winston.

Hilgard, E. R., & Bower, G. H. (1965). *Theories of learning,* (3rd Ed.). New York: Appleton-Century-Crofts.

Hudson, W. (1960). Pictorial depth perception in sub-cultural groups in Africa. *Journal of Social Psychology, 52,* 183–208.

Inhelder, B., & Piaget, J. (1958). *The growth of logical thinking.* New York: Basic Books.

Kagan, J. (1966). "Reflection-impulsivity: The generality and dynamics of conceptual tempo," *Journal of Abnormal Psychology, 71,* 17–24.

Klein, G. (1951). "The personal world through perception," in R. R. & G. V. Ramsey (Eds.), *Perception: An approach to personality.* New York: Ronald Press.

Kohlberg, L. (1969). Stage and sequence: The cognitive-developmental approach to socialization. In D. Goslin (Ed.), *Handbook of socialization theory and research.* Chicago: Rand McNally.

Lefcourt, H. M. (1976). *Locus of control: Current trends in theory and research.* Hillsdale, NJ: Erlbaum.

Lowenfeld, V., & Brittain, W. L. (1970). *Creative and mental growth.* New York: Macmillan.

Maslow, A. H. (1954). *Motivation and personality.* New York: Harper & Row.

Miller, G. A. (1956). "The magical number 7, plus or minus two: Some limits on our capacity for processing information," *Psychological Review, 63,* 81–97.

Newell, A., & Simon, H. A. (1972). *Human problem solving.* Englewood Cliffs, NJ: Prentice-Hall.

Paivio, A. (1971). *Imagery and verbal processes.* New York: Holt, Rinehart & Winston.

Phillips, J. L., Jr. (1969). *The origins of the intellect: Piaget's theory.* San Francisco: Freeman.

Ragan, T. J., Back, K. T., Stansell, V., Ausburn, L. J., Ausburn, F. B., Butler, P. A., & Burkett, J. R. (1979). *Cognitive styles: A review of the literature.* AFHRL-TR-78-90-I. Brooks AFB, Texas: Air Force Human Resources Laboratory.

Renner, J. W., Stafford, D. G., Lawson, A. E., McKinnon, J. W., Friot, F. E., & Kellog, D. H. (1976). *Research, teaching and learning with the Piaget model.* Norman, OK.: University of Oklahoma Press.

Saiet, R. A. (1978). *Children's understanding of implied motion cues.* (Doctoral dissertation, Indiana University, 1978). *Dissertation Abstracts International, 39,* 09A.

Santostephano, S. G. (1978). *A biodevelopmental approach to clinical child psychology.* New York: Wiley.

Snow, R. E. (1977). "Individual differences and instructional theory," *Educational Researcher, 6*(10), 11–15.

Snow, R. E. & Lohman, D. F. (1984). Toward a theory of cognitive aptitude for learning from instruction. *Journal of Educational Psychology, 76* (3), 347–376.

Spielberger, C. D. (Ed.) (1972) *Anxiety: Current trends in theory and research.* New York: Academic Press.

Sternberg, R. J. (1980, September). Factor theories of intelligence are all right, almost. *Educational Researcher,* 6–18.

Vernon, M. D. (1971). *The Psychology of perception,* (2nd Ed.). Baltimore: Penguin.

Witkin, H. A., Moore, C. A., Goodenough, D. R., & Cox, P. W. (1977). "Field-dependent and field-independent cognitive styles and their educational implications," *Review of Educational Research, 47,* 1–64.

Instructional Analysis: Analyzing the Learning Task

four

Chapter Objectives

At the conclusion of this chapter, you should be able to do the following:

- Recognize and write an appropriate instructional goal.

- Conduct an information-processing analysis of an instructional goal.

- Conduct a prerequisite analysis of an information-processing analysis.

- Define, give examples of, recognize examples of, and describe the differences between different types of learning.

- Recognize and write appropriate performance objectives.

- When given a gap statement, conduct a complete instructional task analysis.

Overview of Analysis of the Learning Task

At the completion of a needs assessment (described in Chapter 2) the designer has a list of "gap statements," which reflect what learners currently are unable to do. These are not in a form upon which one can begin designing instruction. The process of task analysis transforms gap statements into a form that can be used to guide subsequent design. Designers expend a great deal of effort in obtaining as clear a description and as thorough an analysis as possible of the learning task.

The primary steps in performing a learning task analysis are as follows:

1. Write an instructional goal.
2. Determine the types of learning of the goal.
3. Conduct an information-processing analysis of that goal.
4. Conduct a prerequisite analysis and determine the type of learning of the prerequisites.
5. Write performance objectives for the instructional goal and each of the prerequisites.

The final product of the learning task analysis is a list of objectives that explicitly describe what the learners should know or be able to do at the completion of instruction and the prerequisite skills and knowledge that learners will need in order to achieve that objective.

Why should one complete such an analysis? Recall that in the First Try fiasco presented in Chapter 2, one of the problems that the designers found out too late was that many students were unable to use the software because the developers had assumed that they were skilled in determining least common denominator and many students were not competent in this skill.

As we noted in Chapter 3, the First Try designers did not complete a learner analysis to determine what the learners were like and what specific prior knowledge they possessed. They may have also failed to analyze the learning task — calculating with fractions — to determine what learners actually need to know in order to solve such problems. Apparently, they failed to include instruction on determining the least common denominator, or write any notice in the teacher's manual accompanying the software that this skill was a prerequisite. Had they conducted a learning task analysis they would have identified what the prerequisites for the instructional task were.

In conducting a learning task analysis, we determine what content needs to be included in a segment of instruction for learners to achieve the instructional goal. Traditionally, this content has been determined by the following: (1) including what has always been taught on the subject in the past (what is included in texts or reference materials on the subject); (2) trial-and-error (teaching learners a certain amount and then adding more information as confusions arise); (3) following the structure of the content (for example, organizing and including information in science topics according to "systems"). These traditional approaches may provide some good information about the content to be included in a lesson. However, designers do not start at this point because the traditional approach to determining content has two pitfalls. The designer may include deadwood, and she may fail to include prerequisite information.

Deadwood is information that is not essential or especially supportive in learning an instructional goal. Deadwood is often included in instruction when a content expert writes the instruction. The expert may include information that is nice to know or especially interesting to him, but may not be essential to the learning task. Deadwood is a problem because it detracts from the central learning task; it may even confuse a learner who is encountering a particular learning goal for the first time. Deadwood is also a problem because including it in instruction may waste precious instructional time that could be better spent presenting information or practice that is focused toward the instructional goal.

The second problem with the traditional approach is that it may fail to identify critical **prerequisite information and skills.** The traditional, content-centered approach typically does not look at the content from the novice's perspective but from the expert's perspective. Experts may not be able to remember all the things that they needed to learn or know to learn the instructional goal. They may, therefore, fail to include critical prerequisite information in the instruction.

Writing Instructional Goals

After conducting a needs assessment, the designer has a list of instructional gaps that need to be filled, such as "learners need to be able to read at the fifth-grade level," or "learners need to be able to repair a broken VCR." To have these gap statements in a form in which we can continue with their analysis, we write them as instructional goals. **Instructional goals** are statements of what learners should be able to do at the conclusion of instruction. These can be lesson goals, unit goals, or course goals. At this point, we are not making decisions as to which of our goals are lesson, unit, or course. We are intent on converting our gap statements into clear descriptions of what learners should know or be able to do after instruction.

We say the goals are stated in *performance terms* because they describe what performances learners will demonstrate—what observable things they must be able to do—to show they have learned. We use performance-based terms because we need statements in this form to have a clear idea of what learners are to learn, so that we can continue with other steps in the design process. Without these clear statements, completion of the other stages of instructional task analysis and other phases of the design process cannot take place. The following statements (EX 1 and EX 2) are examples of an instructional goal for a lesson:

- EX 1: When given a broken VCR with one of four possible malfunctions, the learner will be able to locate the malfunction and repair it.
- EX 2: When given relevant information and the purpose of a business letter, the learner will be able to write an appropriate business letter.

The following two statements are *not* appropriate goal statements:

- EX 3: Given a malfunctioning VCR, the learners will understand how to repair it.
- EX 4: When given a videotape lesson, the learner will watch a demonstration of VCR repair.

EX 3 is a poor example of an instructional goal because it does not tell what the learners would do to demonstrate that they "understand."

Do they need to be able to explain how to repair a VCR? Do they need to be able to recognize the parts and functions of a VCR? Do they need to be able to actually fix a VCR? Depending upon what is meant by *understand,* the instruction would be designed in quite different ways. The designer must have a more precise knowledge of the intent of the goal. If you are creating instruction based upon a needs assessment conducted by someone other than yourself, you may have to discuss the intent of the gap statements with those individuals who contributed to the needs assessment.

EX 4 is a poor example because it does not describe what learners should be able to do *after* instruction. It describes a learning activity that the learner will complete while learning. At this point, the designer is not ready to make decisions yet about *how* to teach; she is still trying to determine *what* to teach. Remember, a goal describes what learners should be able to do after instruction.

Those readers who are familiar with performance statements may wonder how instructional goals differ from instructional objectives. Both are written in performance terms, describing what learners should be able to do after a segment of instruction. However, instructional goals are generally more inclusive and less precise than instructional objectives. We generally do not write an instructional goal for a segment smaller than a lesson. However, a lesson may contain many objectives that must be learned to achieve the lesson goal. We may convert an instructional goal, which describes the outcome of a lesson, into a more precise form: a lesson objective. We will return to this distinction between goals and objectives later in the chapter when we discuss objectives.

*E*xercises A

Which of the following goals are stated in performance terms? Rewrite those not stated in performance terms so that they give a clearer description of exactly what the learners should be able to do or know at the conclusion of instruction.

1. Students will hear lectures and attend discussions on future trends in technology, philosophy, and business.

2. The student can select examples of the concept *conservative* (in the political dichotomy liberal vs. conservative) from a list of examples and nonexamples.
3. The student will understand the procedure for applying for welfare.
4. The student will administer an allergy injection following techniques for sterility.
5. The student can compute the mean, range, and standard deviation of a series of ten numbers.
6. The student has acquired the ability to deal with angry parents.

*D*etermining Types of Learning

After you have written an instructional goal for a course, unit, or lesson, it is valuable to identify the type of learning outcome the goal represents. Identifying the type of learning helps one to determine how to break down the learning goal into its component parts. Later this will provide clues as to how to teach and assess the goal.

Some learning tasks are substantially different from others in terms of the amount of effort required in learning, in the kinds of learning conditions that support their learning, and in the ways to test for their achievement. For instance, learning to recite the Prologue to Chaucer's *Canterbury Tales* seems to be a qualitatively different task from learning to prove a geometric theorem.

The learning task of memorizing requires attention and perseverance but seems to require a minimum of mental effort. The conditions that support this kind of learning are breaking the task up into smaller pieces, memorizing one piece at a time, putting all the pieces together, and then practicing recital of the entire poem. Prompting from a friend or teacher may help. Understanding what the poem means may help memorizing it but is not absolutely essential. Practice and repetition over a period of time improve the chances that the poem will be remembered.

In contrast, learning to prove geometric theorems requires a different kind of mental effort. A student must keep many rules or laws in mind at one time, select from the available rules those that appear most appropriate in a particular proof, and

decide in which sequence these rules should be applied. Unlike with the memorizing task, which is always the same, with each different proof the appropriate rules and sequences will vary. Students may be guided in their learning by being reminded of appropriate rules and by being given many practice exercises with feedback as to whether their answers are correct or incorrect. This learning outcome is not tested by having students prove a theorem they have already proved but by having them prove previously unencountered problems.

Bloom's work (Bloom, et al., 1956) describes these differences among types of learning with a taxonomy of objectives in the cognitive domain: recall, comprehension, application, analysis, synthesis, and evaluation. This categorization is often useful in lesson planning, especially in encouraging teachers to aim their objectives, when appropriate, toward higher order, more mentally demanding outcomes. Another excellent task analysis system was developed by M. David Merrill (Merrill, 1983) and describes tasks in terms of the intersection of two dimensions—content and performance level. Merrill identifies types of content as facts, concepts, procedures, and principles. These outcomes are similar to four of Robert Gagné's categories. Merrill then crosses each of these content outcomes with three levels of performance that he suggests learners may demonstrate within each content category: remember, use, and find. Merrill's system is in wide use by instructional designers. However, we find the categorization system developed by Robert M. Gagné to be the most fundamental, most widely used, and of most utility in designing instructional materials. We will use Gagné's system throughout this text as our foundation for learning task analysis. Once you have learned the Gagné system, it is not difficult to transfer to other systems.

R. Gagné (1985) has divided possible learning outcomes into five large categories or "domains": verbal information (or declarative knowledge), intellectual skills, cognitive strategies, attitudes, and psychomotor skills. Most learning objectives can be classified into these categories. Gagné conjectures that the type of mental processing required for achieving outcomes in each category is qualitatively different from the mental activities required in other categories. Hence, the types of instructional support (the instructional strategy) needed in each category will be substantially different, also. The bulk of Gagné's *The Conditions of Learning* (1985) describes these categories of human learning outcomes and the instructional "conditions" that support learning in each of these categories. We will describe each of these categories and the types of objectives that fit in each category because we believe that thinking of instructional goals in such a way can be most profitable in aiding the identification of prerequisite objectives, designing effective instructional strategies, and designing appropriate tests.

Gagné's Types of Learning Outcomes

Verbal Information. The learning task mentioned earlier, memorizing the Prologue to Chaucer's *Canterbury Tales,* can be classified as a verbal information learning task. Verbal information objectives require a learner to recall in verbatim, paraphrased, or summarized form facts, lists, names, or organized information. Learners are not required to apply the knowledge that they have acquired but merely to recall or recognize it. Verbal information learning is analogous to Anderson's (1976) **declarative knowledge,** which is sometimes described as "knowing that" something is the case (E. Gagné, 1985). It is also comparable to Bloom's (1956) levels of *recall* and *understanding*. Examples of verbal information objectives include the following:

- Write the names of at least three types of synthetic fabric.
- Recite the multiplication table for the number 7.
- In your own words, summarize the three steps that you must follow in converting a BASIC file into a DOS 3.3 text file.

Instructional materials that allow students to practice their multiplication facts most likely have a verbal information objective. So does instruction that helps children to practice their spelling words.

Verbal information (or declarative knowledge) objectives have received a lot of "bad press" in recent years. We agree that the majority of instructional objectives in a lesson or unit should not be in this category. Schooling or training that starts and stops at recall of facts and memorization of lists falls far short of students' needs. However, knowing verbal information helps students learn higher-order, more complex objectives. For instance, the ability to recall multiplication facts aids students in solving quadratic equations, and the ability to spell correctly aids students in composing essays. In other words, recall of verbal information can be a suitable objective if it leads to more complex learning outcomes, such as intellectual skills.

Intellectual Skills. Intellectual skill outcomes are the predominant objectives of instruction in both school and training settings. Intellectual skills are typified by the application of rules to previously unencountered examples. This type of learning outcome differs from verbal information objectives because students learn how to not only recall, but also to apply other instances not encountered during instruction. Anderson (1976) described this type of learning as *procedural knowledge*. E. Gagné (1985) distinguished it from declarative knowledge: Procedural knowledge is "knowing how," and declarative knowledge is "knowing that." Intellectual skills are analogous to Bloom's (1956) levels of application, analysis, synthesis, and evaluation.

The objective of proving a geometric theorem is an intellectual skill objective because students learn how to respond to a *class* of problems, not just individual problems that they have been taught to solve. There are a number of subcategories of intellectual skills that we will discuss briefly below.

When learners learn to differentiate between two stimuli—whether the stimuli are visual, auditory, tactile, olfactory, or gustatory—they have learned to make **discriminations.** A lot of the learning of very young children falls into this category. They learn to discriminate between Mother's and all others' faces. They learn that a square block will fit into a square hole and not a round hole. People learn to make discriminations in later life, too. When learning a foreign language we learn to distinguish the differences between sounds that we have not had to distinguish before. While cooking, we learn to discriminate when there is too much or not enough spice in the food. Some early childhood instructional materials teach discriminations, asking children to tell whether two things are alike or different. For instance, a workbook may ask a student to mark a figure that is the same as another figure that is given. Discriminations are fundamental to learning; however, we rarely teach them by themselves in school or training environments because discriminations are simply the ability to tell whether things are alike or different, not the ability to recognize these things as members of a large class of entities with a particular name. That ability is what the next level, concepts, is all about.

The acquisition of **concepts** helps the learner to simplify the world. Rather than having to respond to each thing in the world as different, he can respond to things as members of groups. For instance, when encountering a large metal object with glass windows and four rubber tires, we can think "Oh, yes, this is a car. I can expect it to move fast, cost a lot, and need gasoline." We do not have to figure out for ourselves that each individual car goes fast, costs a lot, and needs gasoline. We do not even need to have ever seen a particular kind of car before to know that it is a car. Grouping things into categories makes us more efficient thinkers.

It is helpful to think of two kinds of concepts as learning outcomes: concrete concepts and defined concepts (R. Gagné, 1985). The ability to classify things into categories by their physical characteristics—whether visual, auditory, tactile, olfactory, or gustatory—is the ability to identify **concrete concepts.** Concrete concept learning differs from discrimination learning in that if learners have acquired a concrete concept they can identify examples of that concept. For example, if a child were able to match one oak leaf with another oak leaf when they were placed alongside a maple leaf, the child would be exhibiting the ability to make discriminations. However, you could teach a child this discrimination and the child might still be unable to tell you what kind of leaf you are pointing to when you point to an oak leaf while out in the woods. If the child said, "That's an oak leaf" when you point to an oak leaf (one the child has not seen before), you can be fairly certain that she has learned the concept "oak leaf." The child who can identify pictures that represent a square, a circle, or a rectangle has learned some concrete concepts. The chemistry student who can identify the odor of hydrogen sulfide has also acquired a concrete concept. A lesson that teaches students to recognize trapezoids, parallelograms, hexagons,

and octagons is giving instruction in concrete concepts. Another example is a music instructional package that helps students learn to recognize major and minor chords auditorially.

There are many abstract "things" in the world that cannot be classified by their physical characteristics. For instance, we say that a book is a "who-done-it mystery" if it has certain characteristics: (1) usually it is fiction, (2) early on in the book some heinous act is committed against an individual or individuals, (3) a number of characters in the book have the opportunity to commit this act, (4) the remainder of the book is taken up with trying to either make the case that each individual had a reason to commit the act or narrowing down the possibilities to one, and (5) quite often, in the end, the actual perpetrator of the crime is a surprise (not necessarily the butler, but sometimes). We really cannot tell whether it is a mystery by the physical characteristics of the book itself; we must read it to determine whether it has the attributes detailed above. In other words, we must determine whether the book matches the *definition* of a "who-done-it mystery."

Concepts that are classified by whether they match a definition or a list of characteristics are known as **defined concepts.** The terms *democracy, Marxism,* and *anarchy* are defined concepts, as are the terms *acid* and *base* to a chemist (who defines acid and base in terms of Ph level).

Students must be able to do more than simply state the definition of a concept for us to be able to say that they have learned a defined concept. Learners who have acquired defined concepts are able to classify previously unencountered examples and nonexamples of the concepts. An instructional package that teaches students to determine whether a teacher's reaction to a student's actions can be described as "negative reinforcement," "positive reinforcement," or "punishment" is providing instruction on defined concepts. Every content area has its own set of concepts that a learner must be able to use to go onto more complex learning tasks, such as rule using.

Much of our lives are "rule-governed": We avoid touching hot things because we know they will burn us; we follow certain prescribed steps when planting a vegetable garden; we look both ways before crossing a street because we know that failure to do so can lead to accidents. Much of learning is composed of learning **rules** or **principles.** Instruction in math, science, and social sciences is filled with rule and principle outcomes. There are two general categories of rules: relational rules and procedural rules.

Relational rules can typically be expressed in the form of "if-then" statements:

- If gas is heated, then it expands.
- If demand goes up, then supply goes up.
- If the subject is plural, then the plural form of the verb is used.

These examples are all relational rules. Relational rules help us to predict, explain, or control circumstances in our environment by describing either natural or volitional responses to those circumstances. For instance, we might say that learners have acquired the rule "If gas is heated, then it expands" if they can (1) predict what will happen to a filled balloon that is left in a hot car all afternoon, (2) explain why a filled balloon shrinks when left in the freezer, or (3) tell how to fix a balloon of a certain size so that it will fit through a ring that it currently will not fit through.

Procedural rules, on the other hand, tell us in what order certain steps should be taken. Much math instruction is directed at the learning of procedural rules. For example, the process for calculating an average is a procedural rule: First, you find the sum of the individual numbers, and then you divide by the number of individual numbers. Training in vocational, business, military, and industrial settings often includes outcomes that are procedural rules, teaching learners how to do certain portions of their jobs.

Instruction that helps students learn to complete math calculations has a rule-learning objective. Instruction that teaches students how to explain, predict, or control economics using the principle of supply and demand instructs on relational rules.

Many times, as in the case of students' proving geometric theorems, learners must select from a number of possible rules, whether relational or procedural, and apply those rules in a unique sequence and combination to solve a previously unencountered problem. We call this kind of learning **higher-order rule learning.** R. Gagné (1985) also calls this type of learning "problem solving."

Once learners have acquired higher-order rules, they may apply them to similar types of problems. Nursing students acquire higher-order rules when they learn to write nursing-care plans for patients who have a unique set of physical problems, medications, and other treatments. Graduate students learn higher-order rules when they determine a methodology to utilize to research a specific question. Students of marketing who plan an advertising campaign for a particular product are acquiring higher-order rules. Developing the design plans for a new restaurant is the application of higher-order rules for an interior design student.

Finally, notice that intellectual skills build on each other; that is, they are hierarchical. Learners must be able to make discriminations among objects before they can identify concrete concepts. They must have acquired the concepts that are used in rules. And, they must have acquired the rules they will combine in unique ways to create higher-order rules. This hierarchical arrangement of learning tasks is a great help to us when we are analyzing a learning task. For example, if our terminal objective is a rule, then we must examine that rule for concepts that the learners must know in order to learn the rule.

Cognitive Strategies. Students use cognitive strategies to manage their own learning. Sometimes these are referred to as **learning strategies** (Weinstein & Mayer, 1986) or "learning how to learn." For instance, most of us have learned particular strategies that we use to study a textbook. We may, for example, skim through the chapter, read the headings and the summary, and then closely read the text. Cognitive strategies support learning in other domains. They are particularly evident when students are completing problem-solving tasks. Some cognitive strategies are effective across content and across domains. Students often "discover" these strategies; until recently they were rarely directly taught in public schools.

Weinstein and Mayer (1986) categorize these strategies into eight major categories. Rehearsal strategies are used for (1) basic learning tasks and (2) complex learning tasks that aid in selection of information to be recalled and enhance retention of that information. Elaboration strategies are used for (3) basic learning tasks and (4) complex learning tasks that tie new information to prior knowledge. Organizational strategies are used for (5) basic learning tasks and (6) complex tasks that select information to be retained and define the relationships among this information so that it may be integrated into memory. Comprehension monitoring strategies are sometimes referred to as (7) metacognition, or ''students' knowledge about their own cognitive processes and their ability to control these processes by organizing, monitoring, and modifying them as a function of learning outcomes'' (Weinstein & Mayer, p. 323). Affective strategies are (8) those strategies that learners use to ''focus attention, maintain concentration, manage performance anxiety, establish and maintain motivation, and manage time effectively'' (p. 324).

Attitudes. Like cognitive strategies, attitudes influence learning across content and domains. An **attitude** is a mental state that predisposes a learner to choose to behave in a certain way (R. Gagné, 1985). Gagné describes attitudes as having cognitive, affective, and behavioral components that interact. Attitudes influence the choices that learners make. For instance, an individual's dislike of math may cause him to choose to avoid all courses that contain a math component. A child who loves animals may choose to purchase a pet. Certainly attitudes play a strong role in learners' motivation to initiate and persevere in learning.

Instruction in attitudes in schools and training settings is often subtle and indirect. As a matter of fact, we are often hard-pressed to intentionally design components into our instruction that can influence attitudes. Very few instructional materials attempt intentional instruction in attitude change or attitude formation. However, materials used by agencies such as the American Heart Association, American Cancer Association, and many other health and welfare groups have strong attitude components.

This is not to say that instruction cannot be designed for attitudes and other learning outcomes in the affective domain. Simulation games in which a learner is actually playing a role are powerful tools for influencing learners' attitudes. Films, especially when used with discussion, can be used to influence deeply held beliefs and attitudes, as demonstrated by research on the ''Why We Fight'' film series produced during the World War II by the noted director Frank Capra.

Finally, the way in which instruction is conducted inevitably generates attitudes about the material being learned, whether there are affective objectives in the content or not. For example, the constant feedback, reinforcement, and instruction adapted to an individual's level of proficiency that is possible in a well-developed individualized system of learning may positively influence learners toward the content being taught and toward learning in general.

Psychomotor Skills.   Coordinated muscular movements that are typified by smoothness and precise timing are called **psychomotor skills** (R. Gagné, 1985). We learn a lot of motor skills in our early lives: grasping, crawling, walking, and drawing. These early skills become automatic with enough practice. In later years we may choose to acquire other psychomotor skills, such as typing on a keyboard, playing tennis, or water-skiing. Although psychomotor skills have a visible muscular component, they are also dependent on a cognitive component, usually a procedural rule that organizes the kind and sequence of actions. When we are learning a psychomotor skill, this procedure is very much in evidence. For instance, a novice tennis player when confronted with an approaching ball may be heard repeating to herself, ''side to net, eye on ball, racket back, step into the ball, follow through.'' Eventually, with sufficient practice, this procedure becomes automatic, and the player stops verbalizing the steps. Instruction may be designed to teach the rules related to motor skills; however, psychomotor skills must be physically practiced to be learned.

Exercises B

Given below are some instructional goal statements. Decide which category the goals represent: verbal information, discrimination, concrete concept, defined concept, rule (principle), problem solving, cognitive strategy, psychomotor, or attitude.

1. The student must be able to select the beakers from a set of laboratory equipment.
2. The learner must be able to type 60 words per minute.

3. The student teacher must choose to utilize positive reinforcement rather than punishment.
4. The student must select the appropriate pronoun so that the noun (referent) and pronoun agree in number.
5. The student must select curtains that match the color of the carpet.
6. The student must list all fifty states and their capital cities.
7. When given a series of poems, the learner must tell which ones are examples of haiku.
8. The student must tell the date of the Norman invasion of Britain.
9. The learner must locate the source of a malfunctioning printer.
10. The student must invent a way to remember people's names.
11. The learner must convert a number from standard notation (16,301) to scientific notation (1.6301×10^4).

Conducting an Information-Processing Analysis

Whether you are designing a course, unit, or lesson, once you have identified the instructional goal and determined what type of learning outcome it is, you will find an analysis of the goal a useful tool in determining the needed content of that instruction. This goal analysis involves two stages: (1) an information-processing analysis of the goal and (2) a prerequisite analysis of the steps identified in the information-processing analysis. Although this is not the only approach to "decomposing" the task (sometimes called task analysis), it seems to be the easiest, most straightforward approach to take.

Why is it necessary to analyze the goal? To have effective instruction, you will want to ensure that students are provided with the opportunity to learn everything they must learn to achieve that goal (the superordinate objective of the lesson). In other words, there are some prerequisite skills and knowledge that the students must acquire. At the same time, to have efficient instruction, you will not want students to learn something in the lesson that is irrelevant to the instructional task. How can you determine what should be included in the instruction and what can be left out? Conducting an

information-processing analysis (Briggs, 1977; Dick & Carey, 1985) is the first step in "decomposing" or breaking down the goal into its prerequisites, identifying what the students need to learn to attain the goal.

In conducting an information-processing analysis one asks, "What are the mental and/or physical steps that someone must go through in order to complete this learning task?" We call this an information-processing analysis because it describes the sequential mental processes that the learner might go through in completing the goal. Suppose our lesson goal were the following:

Given a topic in the area of "instruction" and the resources of a college or university library, the learner will be able to locate journal articles relevant to that topic.

We might identify the following 11 steps that someone who knew how to complete the goal (an expert) might go through:

1. Locate the ERIC thesaurus (a book containing the key words used to classify materials that are held in the *Educational Resources Information Clearinghouse*).
2. Determine a related descriptor from the thesaurus.
3. Locate the most recent cumulative CIJE *(Current Index of Journals in Education)*.
4. Find the descriptor in the CIJE (under which will be listed journal article titles that relate to the descriptor).
5. Read through the journal titles and select possible articles.
6. Locate and read the abstracts of the possible articles.
7. Select the most appropriate articles and write down the citations.
8. Locate the journal names in the library holdings index, and write down the call numbers of the journals.
9. Locate the journal volumes.
10. Locate the articles, read them, and determine if they are appropriate.
11. Photocopy the articles.

Of course, depending upon the library, its resources, its holdings, and the preferences of the learners, these steps might vary. However, if we've done a good job of performing the learning environment and learner analyses, we will have clues as to what these resources and preferences might be.

How can we determine what the information-processing steps are for a particular goal? One of the simplest and most often-used techniques is to simply mentally review the steps that one might go through in completing the task. And often, that is exactly what we do if time is short or the task is simple. However, as we discussed in Chapter 3, it is not a good idea to assume that all individuals will go about things the same way we do. Following is a procedure you might follow to determine these information-processing steps.

1. *Read and gather as much information as possible about the task and content implied by the goal.* This will allow you to familiarize yourself with common terminology and help you begin to understand what is involved in the skill. You may begin to develop a list of questions about this knowledge or skill, such as "How does someone know when to do that?" or "What does this term mean?" For example, if our task is learning how to solder we would read all that we could about soldering. We might even begin a rudimentary information-processing analysis on what we think a person does and thinks as she completes a soldering task. Then we would create a list of questions, things we would like to ask subject matter experts.

2. *Convert the goal into a representative "test" question.* For example, for the library problem mentioned we might write the question "If you were asked to use the university library to find three articles on 'feedback in instruction,' what would you do?" Or, for the soldering task, we might ask, "What do you do when you solder two things together?" For verbal information goals, the question might be to explain the verbal information to the designers: "Explain the periods of art history."

3. *Give the problem to several individuals who know how to complete the task and do one of the following:*

- Observe them completing the task and ask them to talk aloud about their thought processes as they complete the task. Ask them to describe how and why they are making the decisions they make.
- Observe them completing the task and write down or videotape the steps they go through.
- Have the individuals complete the task and ask them to write down the steps they went through.
- Ask the individuals to write down the steps they would go through if they were asked to complete the task.

The first two techniques listed will give you the most information because people who are experts often forget how they do things. Many actions and thoughts become automatic. However, it may not be feasible to actually observe individuals in action. In this case, the other approaches listed will also provide you with information that you can use in writing the information-processing analysis. The first technique (which asks experts to think aloud as they complete a task) has much promise because it allows us insights into information and cognitive processes that the expert is utilizing that may not be observable. It is helpful to complete this process with more than one expert, as people can develop some idiosyncratic ways of addressing a problem.

4. *Review the written steps or replay a video-tape of the expert completing the task and ask questions about the process.* During this process you can ask for clarification or elaboration. Many of your questions will be aimed at trying to find out the unobservable cognitive knowledge that underlies the expert's behavior. You should ask, "What? When? Where? How? Why? Why? Why?" Some of the questions we might ask our soldering expert include the following:

- How do you know that you need to solder? When? Why?
- When wouldn't you use solder?
- Can you solder all metals?
- Do you always solder the same way? Why not? What other ways can you do it? When would you use other techniques?
- How do you know how much insulation to strip off the wire?
- Why did you twist the wires together like that?

- How do you know if it's a good solder joint? What might you have done if it hadn't been a good joint?
- Does everyone do this the same way you do?

5. *If more than one expert is used in steps 3 and 4, identify common steps and decision points used by the experts in steps 3 and 4.* In other words, locate the commonalities in the process that the experts followed. It may be advantageous if you do this with the group as a whole, because you may find the group together arriving at a consensus of the process that is best. If you complete this step with a group of experts, you will often find that there is individual disagreement as to how a task is performed. Making note of the disagreements will help you find decision points in the cognitive procedure (points at which experts assess the characteristics of the particular task and, based upon these characteristics, take alternative routes in completing the task). You should make note of these decision points and alternative routes.

6. *Identify the shortest, least complex path for completing the task, noting factors that require this simpler path.* For example, the shortest, least complex path for completing the library task is listed in the eleven steps on the previous page. It assumes that a descriptor for the topic could be easily found, that the descriptor was included in the most recent CIJE, that some of the abstracts appeared to be appropriate for the topic, etc. Circumstances in which these assumptions are incorrect would require additional steps to deal with the complexity of the situation. In addition, the task could be made simpler, with an automated (computer-based) system that could search the databases for articles based upon key words. However, this path would require some additional steps (and prerequisite knowledge) that the manual search would not require. In the soldering example, one might ask the question "What do you do to solder two objects together?" The expert may respond, "What are the objects?" Different processes are used to solder different materials together, as well as different types of objects. Soldering two copper wires together is a more simple and common process, so this could be the "simple" path.

(See Scandura, 1983, for more information on path analysis.) In some of the disagreements that the experts have in step 5, you may find they describe very complex paths with many decision points. Often you may find, upon inquiry, that these very complex paths are used only under rare circumstances. There may be one, more commonly used information-processing path that occurs in the majority of occasions. This information-processing path should be described first, as it is probably the one you will design for first. In noting these alternative scenarios that make a task more or less complex, you may find that you are able to refine your instructional goal, gaining a clearer idea of your intentions.

7. *Note factors that may require a more complex path or more steps (these may indicate decision points).* As described above, the more complex path for the library example would include some situations in which information could not be found. The complex path would indicate an "if-then" plan. Here is an example: "If you cannot find a descriptor for the topic, then locate by hand one article about the topic and work backwards through the article and the CIJE, finding the descriptors that CIJE used for that particular article." Note the factors that make a more difficult or simpler path, and try to obtain some information about the frequency of occurrence of the more complex solutions. You may wish to analyze and describe a number of these paths, or only the most simple ones, depending upon the level of proficiency that the learner must have in order to apply that learning.

8. *Select the circumstances, simpler or more complex paths, that best match the intentions of your goal.* Often, we wish to teach learners to complete the simpler path. Later we may return to the learning task and explain circumstances that might require a more complex procedure and teach learners to complete that more complex procedure. (See a discussion of this technique in Chapter 9 on designing instructional strategies for procedural rules.)

9. *List the steps and decision points appropriate to your goal.* Whether it is the steps determined

in the less complex path identified in step 4 or the more complex paths identified in step 5, list those steps in sequential order. There should be from 3 to 12 steps in the information-processing analysis. This may be accomplished by making sure the steps are comparable in size and that a similar amount of mental effort seems to be required for each step; consolidating some steps and breaking up others can help you achieve a reasonable step size and number of steps.

10. *Confirm the analysis with other experts*. If time permits, it is a good practice to give the original question (step 1) and the steps from the information-processing analysis to another group of experts and ask the experts to review, confirm, or revise the analysis.

A note of caution is in order with regard to writing information-processing analyses. Occasionally, novice designers make the error of writing an analysis of how one might *teach* toward the goal. Remember, we are not yet making any decisions about how we will teach or instruct. We are still working on obtaining a clear description of *what* the learner must learn to do. We are describing how someone who already knows how to do the learning task goes about doing that task. We are breaking it into its component parts so that we can identify what the learner must learn. A key aspect of instructional design is that we delay making decisions about *how* to instruct until we have a very clear idea of *what* it is we are going to teach.

The development of an information-processing analysis is iterative. In other words, you will find yourself revising and revising the analysis as you gain a better perspective of the learning goal itself. Often the information-processing analysis is revised even at the point of writing objectives and test items. Rather than being a source of frustration, the analysis should be an encouragement. You will be gaining a clearer and clearer picture of the actual cognitive requirements of the task and, hence, will be able to create much more effective and efficient instruction. Another encouraging fact is that there are many "correct" ways to represent an information-processing analysis. This process is not like solving a math problem in which there is

only one answer. There is not just one "right" answer because generally there are many ways that experts address a learning task. Remember, you are trying to identify one, workable information-processing procedure.

*E*xample Analyses

We have found that information-processing analyses for particular categories of learning outcomes tend to have some similar characteristics. Therefore, we have included examples of information-processing analyses for the major types of learning outcomes. We will begin with learning outcomes in the intellectual skills domain. (Since discriminations are so seldom taught in public school and training environments—and their analyses look quite similar to concepts—we have chosen to omit that analysis from the examples.)

Concept Learning. Basically, applying a concept involves determining whether a particular instance is an example of that concept. This involves comparing the characteristics of the instance with the defining attributes of the concept. (See the first two sections of Chapter 8 if this idea is unclear to you.) The procedure might be slightly modified if the instructional goal were to create an original example of a concept, rather than recognizing examples of a given concept. Concept learning involves (1) recalling the critical attributes of a concept and (2) sequentially comparing attributes of an instance to attributes of the concept. (If the instance does not have the required attributes, then it is not an example of the concept.)

Suppose the instructional goal were that the learner could identify which of a number of figures is a rhombus (see Figure 4.1). We might find through interviews or observation that "experts" use the following information-processing procedure:

1. Recall the characteristics of a rhombus. (Many experts do this unconsciously.)
2. Determine if the figure is a polygon. If yes, continue on to step 3. If no, go to step 6.
3. Determine if the figure is a parallelogram. If yes, continue on to step 4. If no, go to step 6.

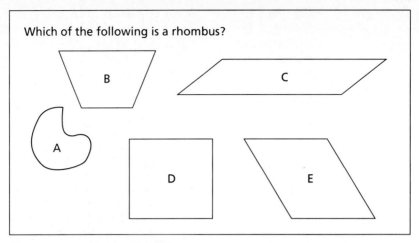

Which of the following is a rhombus?

B

C

A

D

E

Figure 4.1: Concept Example

4. Determine if the figure's sides are equilateral. If yes, continue on to step 5. If no, go to step 6.
5. Determine if the figure's angles are oblique. If yes, it is a rhombus. If no, go to step 6.
6. The figure is not a rhombus.

You will note that the defining attributes of the concept "rhombus" are that (1) it is a polygon, (2) it is a parallelogram, (3) it has equilateral sides, and (4) it has oblique angles. Experts might vary as to the order in which they checked the attributes against the characteristics of the figure; however, they would probably agree on the most efficient order to follow. Considering the most inclusive attribute first (i.e., polygon) would be most efficient with this example. We could also show this information-processing analysis in graphic form (See Figure 4.2).

Relational Rule. Applying a relational rule involves doing the following:

• Determine which concepts or variables are involved.
• Determine the rule or principle that relates those concepts or principles.
• Recall the rule or principle.
• Determine which concept or variable has varied and the direction or magnitude of its variation.
• Determine which concept or variable has been affected.

• Then determine the magnitude and direction of the effect on the affected concept or variable.
• Confirm that the value is reasonable.

(If the idea of "relational rule" is still a bit unclear to you, you may wish to read the first two sections in Chapter 9, which further explain relational rules.)

For example, an instructional goal in which a learner could apply Boyle's law (When the temperature remains constant, the volume of a confined gas varies inversely as its pressure) might be represented in the following question:

A piston is placed in a cylinder that has a volume of 150 cubic inches and is pushed into the cylinder until the enclosed air is compressed to 50 cubic inches. If the pressure of the air at the beginning was 15 pounds per square inch, what is the pressure of the trapped air?

We might find through interviews or observation that "experts" use the following information-processing procedure:

1. Determine the variables in the problem (air pressure and volume of gas).
2. Determine the relational rule that states the relationship of these variables (Boyle's law).
3. Recall Boyle's law.
4. Determine which variable (pressure or volume) has varied.

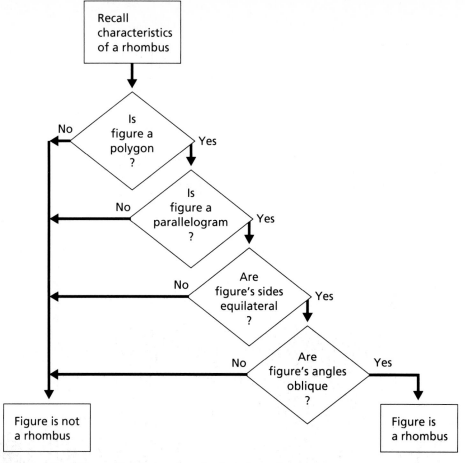

Figure 4.2: Information-Processing Analysis for a Concept

5. Determine the direction and magnitude of the variation (how much greater or less).
6. Determine which variable (pressure or volume) will be affected.
7. Determine the direction and magnitude of the effect (by placing values into the equation stating the relationship).
8. Confirm that the value is reasonable.

We can also present this information-processing analysis graphically (see Figure 4.3).

Procedural Rule. Instructional goals that are procedural rules are the easiest goals upon which to conduct an instructional analysis. Generally, application of procedural rules involves these steps:

- Determine whether a particular procedural rule is applicable.
- Recall the steps of the procedural rule.
- Apply the steps in order, with decision steps if required.
- Confirm that the end result is reasonable.

(If the idea of ''procedural rule'' is somewhat unclear to you, review the first two sections in Chapter 9, which refer to procedural rules.)

For example, a procedural instructional goal might be that learners are able to apply the Fry Readability Graph to determine the reading level of some printed material. The information-processing analysis for such a goal might follow this pattern (see the nine steps on page 79):

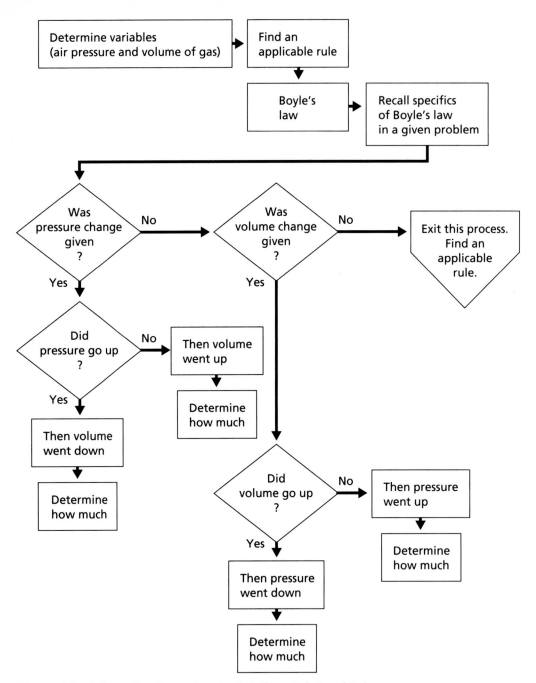

Figure 4.3: Information-Processing Analysis for a Relational Rule

1. Determine if application of the Fry Readability Graph is appropriate to the reading material.
2. Recall the steps in the procedure.
3. Select representative passages.
4. Calculate the number of sentences for each 100-word passage.
5. Determine the number of syllables in each passage.
6. Determine the average number of sentences and average number of syllables.
7. Locate the intersection of average number of sentences and average number of syllables on the graph.

8. Read grade level from graph.
9. Confirm that value is reasonable (check answer).

This information processing analysis is graphically represented in Figure 4.4.

More complex procedural rules may have subprocedures based upon decision steps. These decision steps would involve determining which set of conditions exist. Such an information-processing analysis would have yes/no decision points with branches of different operations following each side of the decision.

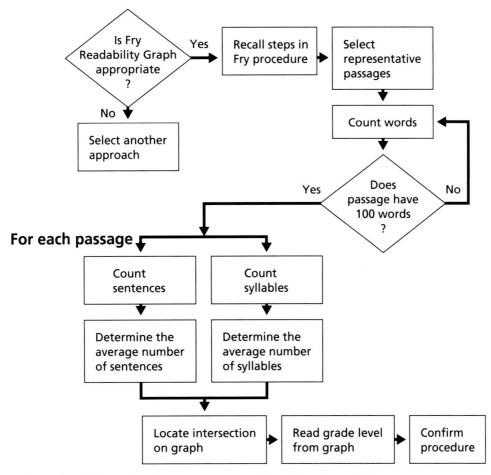

Figure 4.4: Information-Processing Analysis for a Procedural Rule

Higher-Order Rules (Problem Solving). Information-processing analyses for higher-order rules generally include the following major procedural steps:

- Determine the knowns, the givens.
- Determine the unknowns, the problem.
- Determine the relational rules that relate the knowns and unknowns in the situation.
- Determine the procedural rules that determine the application of the relational rules.
- Apply the procedural rules and the ''nested'' relational rules.
- Confirm that the problem is solved; unknowns are determined.

(If the idea of problem-solving skills is unclear to you, you might want to review the first two sections in Chapter 10.)

An example of the application of higher-order rules would be the development of a nursing-care plan for a patient. The nurse would be given a history of the patient, the patient's current symptoms, and the doctor's diagnosis and prescription. This information-processing analysis is described as follows:

- Assess patient's status.
- Analyze data collected.
- Determine nursing diagnosis.
- Develop plan of care.
- Implement care.
- Evaluate care.

This analysis could be represented graphically (see Figure 4.5).

Generally, course and unit instructional goals are higher-order rules or combinations of higher-order rules. Lesson goals, on the other hand, more often involve concept and rule learning that are required to acquire higher-order rules.

Verbal Information/Declarative Knowledge.
Verbal information-processing analyses are in some ways quite different from intellectual skills analyses. The sequence of application of information is often not so critical in verbal information analyses as with intellectual skills. More important is how an expert organizes the verbal information into meaningful, memorable segments. These relationships may be represented graphically in many ways, such as webs, networks, or maps. (You may wish to review verbal information skills and the varieties of graphic representation in Chapter 7.) An example of such an analysis might be developed for an instructional goal in which the learner would learn to summarize the characteristics, composers, and a chronology of the major periods of music history. Of course, as the goal involves knowledge of chronology, sequence does somewhat enter into the information-processing

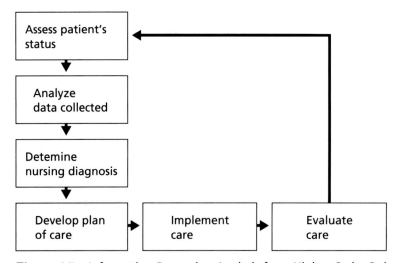

Figure 4.5: Information-Processing Analysis for a Higher-Order Rule

analysis of this goal. An instructional analysis for this goal might have the following pattern:

- Recall major periods in music.
- Describe Renaissance music characteristics.
- Describe Baroque music characteristics.
- Describe Classical music characteristics.
- Describe Romantic music characteristics.
- Describe Contemporary music characteristics.

A graphic representation of the analysis is provided in Figure 4.6.

Attitudes.   Although attitudes are seldom a major instructional goal, they frequently play an important role in courses, units, and lessons. Information-processing analysis of attitude objectives has not been researched a great deal. We suggest that such an analysis include the following:

- Evaluate the situation, and consider possible courses of action.
- Determine which course of action is valued.
- Choose that course of action.
- Perform that course of action.

The analysis is represented graphically in Figure 4.7.

An example for this type of analysis might be the attitude goal ''the learner will choose to solve class disputes in a nonviolent way.'' Here are the steps:

- Evaluate the dispute, and consider possible courses of action.
- Determine that nonviolent solution is valued.
- Choose nonviolent behavior.
- Behave in a nonviolent manner.

The steps are graphically represented in Figure 4.8.

Psychomotor Learning.   An information-processing analysis for a psychomotor task is very similar to an analysis for a procedural rule. It usually involves the following:

- Determine whether a particular psychomotor action is required (although this may be automatic).
- Recall the steps of the procedure (although this may be unconscious).

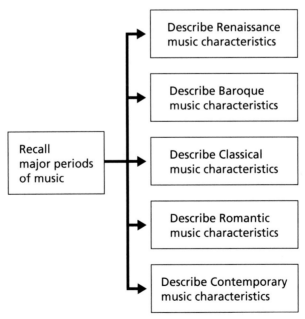

Figure 4.6: Information-Processing Analysis for Verbal Information

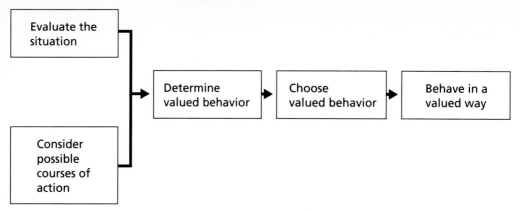

Figure 4.7: General Information-Processing Analysis for Attitudes

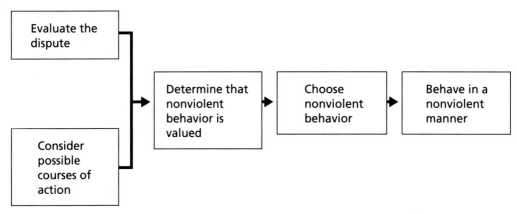

Figure 4.8: Information-Processing Analysis for Nonviolent Dispute Resolution

• Execute the steps of the psychomotor procedure in order, with decision steps and consequent actions, if required.
• Confirm that the steps have been correctly applied.

(You may wish to review psychomotor learning in Chapter 13.)

An example of a psychomotor information-processing analysis for the instructional goal of completing a tennis serve could be as follows:

• Determine that this is an appropriate moment for a serve.
• Mentally review the steps in executing a serve.
• Position self in appropriate court and location on court.

• Orient self to net.
• Determine desirable trajectory of ball.
• Execute ball toss.
• Execute racquet swing.
• Contact ball.
• Step forward.
• Follow through.
• Confirm correct execution of serve.

Figure 4.9 presents a graphic representation of this information-processing analysis.

You will notice that this analysis resembles the analysis of a procedural rule. Indeed, the procedural rule is the ''psycho-'' portion of the psychomotor skill. The precision and timing of the execution of these steps is the ''-motor'' part of the

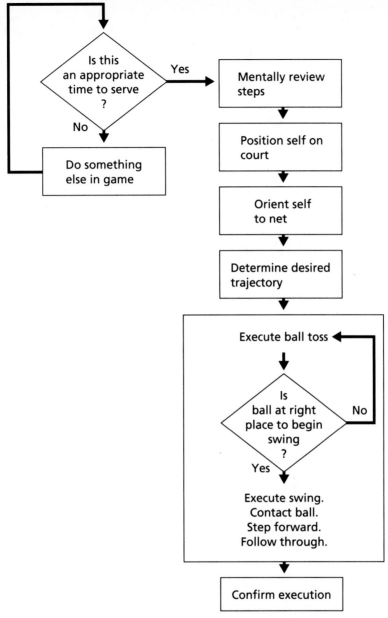

Figure 4.9: Psychomotor Skill Information-Processing Analysis

psychomotor skill. As with procedural rules, the information-processing analysis for psychomotor skills may be more complex if alternative sub-procedures are invoked, depending upon which set of conditions exists. For example, when returning a tennis serve, different procedures are followed depending upon whether the serve comes to the left, to the right, or straight-on to the player.

Cognitive Strategies. The information-processing analysis of a cognitive strategy outcome resembles that of a problem-solving analysis. Typically, the steps in applying a cognitive strategy involve the following:

- Determine the characteristics and requirements of the learning task.
- Select or invent strategies appropriate for the task.
- Select the optimum strategy.
- Apply strategy.
- Evaluate effectiveness of strategy.
- If effective, continue using strategy; if ineffective, return to first step.

(You may wish to review cognitive strategies in Chapter 11.)

An example of a cognitive strategy is the use of a text structure application strategy that can be used to aid the selection, encoding, and retrieval of pertinent information from a selection of expository prose. One way to represent application of this strategy would be with the following steps.

- Is this a reading task? If yes, continue; if no, select another strategy.
- Is the selection continuous prose? If yes, continue; if no, select another strategy.
- Is the selection expository prose? If yes, continue; if no, select another strategy.
- Is the purpose to recall main ideas and details? If yes, continue; if no, select another strategy.
- Examine main overviews, summaries, and topic sentences for statements of structural organization or cue words for structure.
- Determine overarching structure for entire selection. (Note: These structures are typically cause-effect, time-order, problem-solution, comparison/contrast, or description.)
- Predict main ideas and supporting details based upon prior knowledge and structure.
- Read selection.
- Examine secondary overviews, summaries, and topic sentences for statements of structural organization or cue words for structure.
- Determine secondary structures.
- Review and take notes utilizing overarching structures and sub-structures.
- Assess whether comprehension is adequate for the situation. If yes, end; if no, return to step 1.

A graphic representation of this analysis is provided in Figure 4.10.

*E*xercises C

Complete an instructional analysis on one of the following instructional goals:

1. Look for a book on a certain topic in the library.
2. Change the oil in a car.
3. Find the average of five numbers.

*C*onducting a Prerequisite Analysis

Once you have decomposed the instructional goal into its information-processing tasks, you have made much progress in determining what the content of the instruction must be. You have already determined much of what learners will need to know how to do to complete the goal. The next step in decomposing the task is called **prerequisite analysis.** You will look at each one of the steps in the information-processing analysis and ask, "What must the learner know or be able to do to achieve this step?" You will continue to ask this question until each step has been broken down into everything the students must know to achieve the instructional goal. You cease analysis when it can be assumed that *all* the students have the described knowledge and skills. This process is often called "top down" analysis, as you are starting at the top of analysis with the most superordinate task, which will be broken down into smaller prerequisite tasks and knowledge.

For example, to determine the content for this book, we started with the goal that you learn to systematically produce simple instruction. We decomposed that goal into the steps identified in the model for design that we presented in the first chapter (a procedural rule). Then we examined each step in the model and asked, "What must the learner know or be able to do to complete this step of the process?"

Example Prerequisite Analysis: Locating Journal Articles on a Topic

Let's trace the process of prerequisite analysis by using the first step of information processing from the previous library example. For the task of locating journal articles on the topic "instruction"

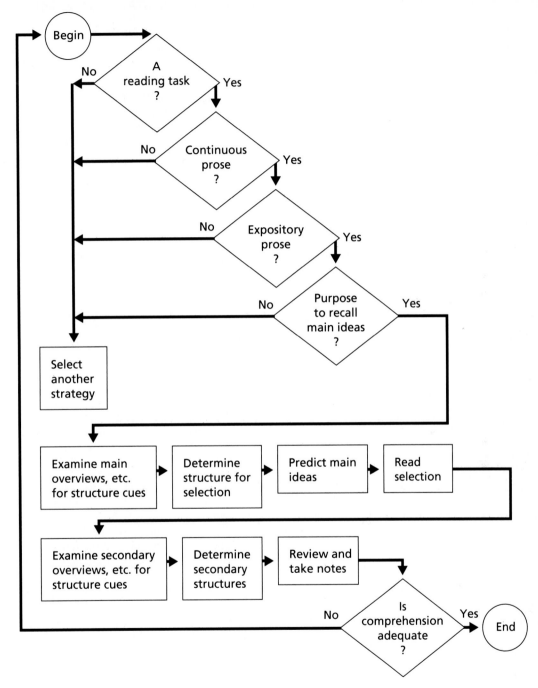

Figure 4.10: Cognitive Strategy Information-Processing Analysis

given the resources of a college or university library, we determined the first step to be as follows:

1. Locate the ERIC thesaurus. If we were to conduct a prerequisite analysis on this first step, we would find that to locate the ERIC thesaurus the learner must do the following:

- Know what ERIC means and its purpose
- Know what a thesaurus is and its purpose
- Know what an ERIC thesaurus looks like and where to locate it
- Know what the term *reference* means with regard to library usage
- Be able to locate reference books in the library

We might break down any of these prerequisites into its prerequisites. For example, the step "know what a thesaurus is and its purpose" requires that the learner understand the concept "synonym." We would examine other prerequisites for step 1 to see if we could identify any additional prerequisites. When finished, step 1 might look like this:

1. Locate the ERIC thesaurus. The learner must do the following:

- Know what ERIC means and its purpose
- Know what a thesaurus is and its purpose (understand concept of "synonym")
- Know what an ERIC thesaurus looks like and where to locate it
- Know what the term *reference* means with regard to library usage
- Be able to locate reference books in the library (know the layout of the library)

Further developed, the prerequisite analysis of the library example would look like this:

1. Locate the ERIC thesaurus.
   - Know what ERIC means and its purpose
   - Know what a thesaurus is and its purpose (understand concept of "synonym")
   - Know what an ERIC thesaurus looks like and where to locate it
   - Know what the term *reference* means with regard to library usage
   - Be able to locate reference books in the library (know the layout of the library)

2. Determine a related descriptor from the thesaurus.
3. Locate the most recent cumulative CIJE.
4. Find the descriptor in the CIJE.
5. Read through the article titles and select possible articles.
6. Locate and read the abstracts of the possible articles.
7. Select the most appropriate articles and write down the citations.
8. Locate the journal names in the library holdings index, and write down the call numbers of the journals.
9. Locate the journal volumes.
10. Locate the articles, read them, and determine if they are appropriate.
11. Photocopy the articles.

A graphic representation of this prerequisite analysis is presented in Figure 4.11. Due to space limitations, we have presented only a portion of this graphic analysis.

Because a prerequisite analysis is rather complex, we'll provide you with one more example.

Example Prerequisite Analysis for the Concept "Rhombus"

1. Recall the characteristics of a rhombus. (Many experts do this unconsciously.)
   - Be able to list the four major attributes of a rhombus (polygon, parallelogram, equilateral sides, and oblique angles).

2. Determine if figure is a polygon. If yes, continue on to step 3; if no, go to step 6.
   - Be able to recognize examples of a polygon.
   - Be able to define a polygon (although the ability to define this and the following definitions may not be absolutely prerequisite).
   - Be able to recognize examples of geometric figures.
   - Be able to define geometric figures.
   - Be able to recognize examples of plane figures.
   - Be able to define plane figures.
   - Be able to recognize examples of closed figures.

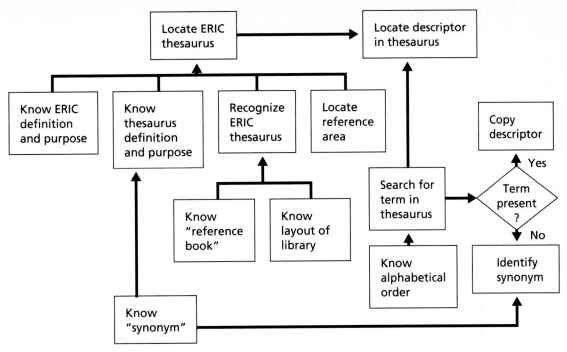

Figure 4.11: Prerequisite Analysis: Finding a Journal Article Using ERIC

- Be able to define closed figures.
- Be able to recognize straight-sided figures.
- Be able to define straight-sided figures.
- Be able to recognize examples of figures.
- Be able to define *figure*.

(The relative subordination of prerequisites to other prerequisites is indicated by indentions.)

3. Determine if the figure is a parallelogram. If yes, continue on to step 4; if no, go to step 6.
   - Be able to recognize examples of a parallelogram.
   - Be able to define a parallelogram.
   - Be able to recognize examples of a quadrilateral.
   - Be able to define the concept "quadrilateral."
   - Be able to recognize examples of "side."
   - Be able to recognize examples of "angle."
   - Be able to determine if sides in a figure are parallel.

- Be able to identify sides of a figure.
- Be able to define the concept of "parallel."

4. Determine if the figure's sides are equilateral. If yes, continue on to step 5; if no, go to step 6.
   - Be able to recognize examples of figures with equilateral sides.
   - Be able to define *equilateral*.
   - Be able to recognize examples of the concept "side."
   - Be able to recognize examples of the concept "equal sides."
   - Be able to define *equal* in the geometric sense.

5. Determine if the figure's angles are oblique. If yes, *it is a rhombus*; if no, go to step 6.
   - Be able to recognize examples of figures with oblique angles.
   - Be able to define *oblique angle*.
   - Be able to define/explain *degree,* as in an angle.

- Be able to estimate degrees in an angle.
- Be able to recognize examples of angles.

6. The figure is not a rhombus.

This prerequisite analysis is represented graphically in Figures 4.12 and 4.13.

The boxes containing skills in Figure 4.14 are the prerequisites that must be acquired before the learner can acquire the concept diagrammed in Figure 4.13. A skill that is listed below a second skill is prerequisite to it. Where physically possible we have listed verbal information knowledge (e.g., "list the characteristics of polygon") to the side of a skill to which it contributes, rather than below it. This is because often (technically speaking) verbal information is helpful but not prerequisite to intellectual skills (R. Gagné, 1985).

After a review of the characteristics of the learners, the designer may determine that the learners already possess some of the skills and knowledge listed, particularly those listed at the bottom of the hierarchy (at the bottom of the graph). As you can see these are the skills and knowledge that are the most simple (e.g., recognizing sides of a figure). If the designer has a strong reason to assume that the learners already possess some of these simple skills and knowledge, he may indicate this by labeling it as an entry skill on the prose list or drawing it below a dotted line, marked "entry level skills," on the graphic.

Once the prerequisites (including both the information-processing steps and the prerequisites for these steps) of an instructional goal have been identified, these outcomes can be converted into performance objectives. Before we discuss the development of performance objectives, it would be a good idea to look at the terms we will use when talking about objectives.

Some terms that we will use in the context of objectives are *terminal objective, enabling objective, prerequisites,* and *entry skills. Terminal objectives* are the more precise statements of instructional goals. Whereas the intent for learning of a lesson or module of instruction may be expressed by one instructional goal, there may be more than one terminal objective for the module or lesson. Terminal objectives are the skills and knowledge we want learners to achieve as a product of instruction. *Enabling objectives* are the sub-objectives, the knowledge or skills that enable the learner to

learn to do the terminal objective. The elements that your information-processing and prerequisite analyses reveal are the material out of which you will develop enabling objectives. *Prerequisites,* a term which we have already used, are the building blocks of a learning task. So enabling objectives are also prerequisites. *Entry skills* are another kind of prerequisite, specifically referring to skills and knowledge that the learner brings to instruction. Entry skills are "prerequisites" in the everyday usage of the term: things you must know before you are qualified to begin a class or other form of instruction.

*E*xercises D

1. Below is an information-processing analysis of the instructional goal "the learner will be able to divide two fractions."

- Determine whether the situation requires the use of a procedural rule.
- Recall the steps in the procedure.
- Write the problem horizontally.
- Convert whole numbers or mixed fractions to fractions.
- Invert second fraction.
- Multiply two fractions.
- Reduce resulting term to lowest terms.
- Confirm that process was applied correctly.

Conduct a prerequisite analysis of each of these steps. If you do not know the proper mathematical terms, provide examples of what you mean.

2. Conduct an instructional analysis (both information-processing and prerequisite analysis) to determine the prerequisite skills that learners must acquire in order to subtract one three-digit number from another.

*W*riting Performance Objectives

Now that you have identified the prerequisites for a learning goal and have begun to think about what type of learning each prerequisite represents, you are ready to convert each of these prerequisite statements and the goal statement into more precise, concrete, and performance terms. You will be

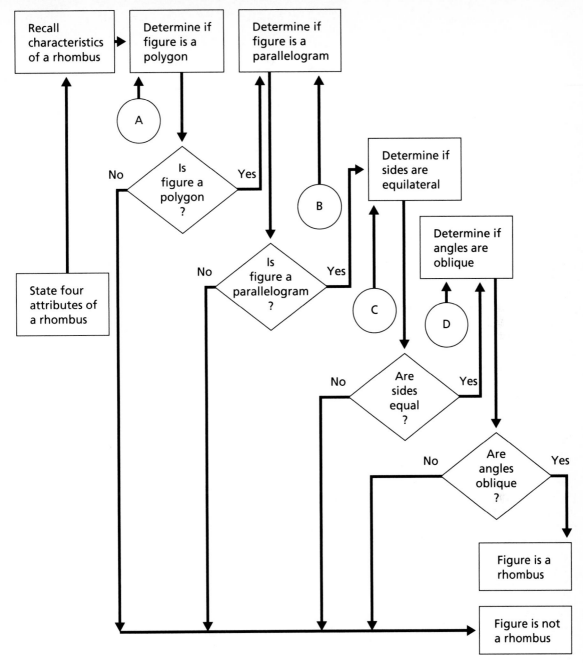

Figure 4.12: Part 1 of a Prerequisite Analysis of the Concept "Rhombus"

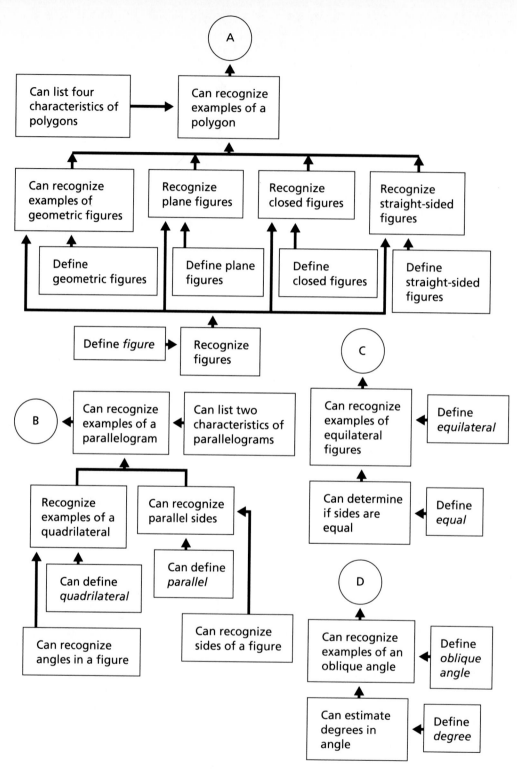

Figure 4.13: Part 2 of a Prerequisite Analysis of the Concept "Rhombus"

converting prerequisite statements and the goal statement into performance objectives. As we stated earlier, the precision and concreteness of this type of objective allows us to have a complete perspective of "where we are going."

A **performance objective** is a statement that tells what learners should be able to do when they have completed a segment of instruction. What learners "do" must be observable so that the learners know that they have learned and what they have learned. In addition, it is important for both teachers and instructional designers to know precisely what learning is intended. Whether it is to write down if an object is translucent, transparent, or opaque when given a series of objects or whether it is to become able to design and develop effective instruction, it is critical that objectives be specified.

Nebulous objectives like "the learners will be aware of metric measurements," or "the learner will understand the importance of the three branches of the U.S. government" do not give much guidance to the designer as to what the learners should actually know about converting to the metric system or about the three branches of government. Performance objectives give much more direction as to what learners actually need to learn to do:

- Given a series of English measurements of length, weight or volume, the learners can convert them to their metric equivalents.
- The learners will be able to summarize the functions of each of the branches of the U.S. government and explain the "checks and balances" among the branches.

A second common problem in stating objectives (as with writing instructional goals) is that designers sometimes write the objective to describe the learning activities that the students will be involved in, rather than what the students should be able to do when they finish these activities. For example, in a unit on ecology a designer might inappropriately state the objective as a learning activity: "The learners will play a simulation game in which they experience the interactions of variables in the ecosystem." The designer should instead state the terminal objective of the lesson: "When given a description of an ecosystem, the learner will be able to identify potential sources of pollution and suggest methods to control or eliminate the pollution."

Objectives are valuable to all members of the learning system. They aid the designer since they provide a focus of the instruction, guiding the designer in making decisions about what content should be included, what strategy should be used, and how students should be evaluated. The specification of clear objectives is especially critical when a number of individuals—such as designers, content experts, graphic artists, and programmers—are working together to produce instruction. In these situations, performance objectives serve as a concrete focus of communication.

Objectives stated in performance terms are also beneficial when stated in the documentation of instructional guides. They aid the potential adopters of the system—teachers or trainers, and school administrators or training directors—in making decisions as to whether the material is suitable for helping the learners achieve the learning goals of the particular learning system. When expressed to students during instruction, objectives help them focus their efforts and conduct periodic assessments of their own learning.

One common problem with instructional material is designers' failure to utilize performance objectives. Often it is impossible to determine the purpose of the instruction even after going through the complete instructional materials. If the objectives are not listed in the instruction, in the documentation that accompanies the instruction, or, at the very least, inferable from the instruction itself, the potential user has a very good reason to seek out better-designed instruction. Certainly as you develop instruction, you will want to have a clear idea of what you would wish the learners to learn from your instruction before you begin writing.

How to Write Performance Objectives

Objectives can be written at the lesson level, the course level, or various intermediate levels such as units, blocks, or chapters. There are many different forms of objectives that can give equally precise and concrete descriptions of learning outcomes. We will demonstrate how to write the simplest form: three-component objectives, as first described by Robert Mager (1962).

Three-component objectives are verbal statements of learning outcomes that include three parts:

- A description of the terminal behavior or performance
- A description of the conditions of demonstration of that behavior
- A description of the performance statement or criterion

The most critical part of a performance objective is the description of the terminal behavior. The statement of the **terminal behavior** includes a description of the performance that the learner can show that will demonstrate that he has learned. The terminal behavior statement includes action verbs such as *select, identify, list, solve, repair*, and *write*.

As with instructional goals, you should avoid using terms that fail to communicate the intent of the objective. Some of these ambiguous terms are *understand, be aware of, appreciate*, and *become familiar with*.

Here are some examples of the terminal behavior description:

- Circle the polygons.
- Underline the verbs.
- List the steps in the instructional design process.
- Locate and repair the problem.
- Write a performance objective.

The description of the **conditions of demonstration** is the second most critical part of a performance objective. This component of the objective describes the tools or information that the learners will be given when they demonstrate their learning. Often this component is at the beginning of the objective statement. It usually begins with the word *given:*

- *Given 10 drawings of geometric figures,* circle the polygons.
- *Given a paragraph,* underline the verbs.
- List the steps in the instructional design process
- *Given a malfunctioning VCR,* locate and repair the problem.
- *Given an instructional goal,* write a performance objective (for it).

As you can see, we took the terminal behaviors from earlier in this section and added appropriate conditions statements that describe what stimulus, or material, will be presented to the learners when they demonstrate the behavior. You will notice that the third objective does not contain a conditions statement. There are occasions, particularly with verbal information objectives, when no conditions are necessary: Learners will be given no tools or information when asked to demonstrate their learning. Novice instructional designers sometimes include the phrase *after instruction* in the statement of conditions of performance. This is an unnecessary statement within an instructional objective, and it should be avoided.

The final component of a three-component objective is a description of the **performance standards** or **criteria.** This statement describes how well the learner must perform for you to say the learner has achieved the objective. These standards (Mager, 1963) may refer to the following:

- Accuracy, e.g., "student's answer must be within $+/-$ 3 degrees"
- Number of errors, e.g., "with three mistakes or fewer"
- Number of correct responses, e.g., "with at least 80 percent correct"
- Time, e.g., "in 12 minutes or less"
- Consistent with an established standard, e.g., "in the order listed in the text"
- Consistent with a stated standard, e.g., "that includes the following three descriptors: plane, closed, and straight-line figure"
- Consequences, e.g., "so that the customer walks away satisfied"

The following examples complete the objectives that we have been developing in this section:

- Given ten drawings of geometric figures, circle *all* of the polygons.
- Given a paragraph, underline *at least 90 percent* of the verbs.
- List *at least six* of the steps in the instructional design process *in the correct order.*
- Given a malfunctioning VCR, locate and repair the problem *so that the VCR functions correctly.*

- Given an instructional goal, write a performance objective (for it) *that includes a description of terminal behavior, conditions, and the standard.*

An alternate approach to writing the criterion (especially in cases in which the criterion will be stated in terms of how many items must be correct out of a total number of items) is to delay writing the criterion until you write the assessment item specifications related to that objective. We actually prefer this approach as the idea of a standard or criterion fits more neatly into the concept of assessment than in statement of purpose. You may find that you, too, prefer to write the conditions and performance statement in the objective and place the criterion in your assessment item specifications (see Chapter 5).

Examples of Performance Objectives for Various Learning Outcomes

In the following section we have included a discussion and examples of objectives for each of the major categories of learning outcomes.

Verbal Information. Verbal information objectives need to reflect whether learning will be recognition (choosing from options) or recall, verbatim or paraphrased, and listed or summarized. Examples of verbal information objectives follow:

1. Given a list of 20 chemical elements and their symbols in random order, the learner will match the element name with the symbol. At least 18 of these matches must be correct.

2. Without referral to any references and within 20 minutes, the learner will summarize the principal protections to individual liberties provided under the Bill of Rights. The learner must describe at least five of the "rights" accurately, as per the textbook.

3. Upon request, the learner will define in her own words *instructional technology.* This definition should include at least one of the following key phrases: "process and product," "solving instructional problems," or "setting up external events to support intentional outcomes." The definition should not limit itself to such things as "using media or hardware in instruction."

4. Upon request, the learner can list and give a brief description in his own words of at least six instructional delivery systems.

Concepts. Concept objectives should reflect the learners' ability to classify and label ideas, objects, and events as examples/nonexamples of a concept. They may require that the learner state how/why such classification was made.

Examples of concept objectives follow:

1. Given a verbal description of the designer/developer's activities, the learner will be able to label each activity according to the phase of instructional design/development that is being conducted. All labels must be correct.

2. Given pictures of 12 geometric figures, some of which are polygons, the learner should be able to circle those that are polygons. She should correctly identify at least 10 of these. In addition, the learner must state why she made the distinction that she did. This explanation should be couched in an explanation of how this figure does/does not represent the three key attributes of polygons. At least 8 of these explanations must be correct.

3. Given directions to list examples not included in instruction, the learner will list four novel examples of the concept "transparent." At least three of these examples should not be those included in instruction. All examples should contain the key attributes of the concept; that is, that both light and images can be seen through the object.

Rules. Rule objectives should reflect the intention that the learner can use the rule to predict, explain, or control something, or successfully complete a procedure defined by a procedural rule. The objectives may require that learners explain their application of the rule. Occasionally, objectives may ask students to recognize whether a rule was correctly or incorrectly applied and tell why or why not.

Examples of rule objectives follow:

1. Given 10 descriptions of diffusion/dissemination problems, the learner can state at least one principle for each that was violated and its source as the D/D problem. Then he can state in his own words what should have been done in each case to avoid the problem or what could be done now to remedy the problem. At least 8 of these must be correct in all three areas— identification of the rule, source of the problem, and what could be done differently.

2. Given 15 multiplication problems in which the multiplier is a decimal with one, two, or three decimal places, the learner can solve at least 12 of them correctly.

3. Given an aperture and shutter setting for a 35mm camera, the learner can give at least five correct equivalent settings.

Problem-Solving. Problem solving objectives should reflect the requirement that the learner do the following:

- Assess the problem situation.
- Determine which rules are applicable.
- Synthesize these rules to solve a particular problem.

Examples of problem-solving objectives follow:

1. Given the desired output of a computer program that requires the use of conditional statements, print statements, loops, and assignment of value, the learner will be able to generate the program lines to get this output. The program should run without any "bugs" and should yield the output described in the problem statement.

2. Given a list of computers in education references and a word-processing program, the learner can generate a word-processed, 3–5 page paper on educational applications of computers in her subject area. The product should achieve at least 70 points when assessed with the checklist that is attached.

3. Given three descriptions of aperture, shutter speed settings, and film type that lend a correct

exposure for a particular situation and descriptions of a change in the environment (such as change in light intensity or motion of subject), the learner will be able to determine what change in settings is required to yield a correct exposure in each of the situations.

Psychomotor Skills. Psychomotor objectives should reflect what "new" muscular activities are required. The standards often reflect time or speed, or consequences or number of times the learner must correctly execute the motions.

An example of a psychomotor skill objective follows:

Given a level parallel parking spot along a curb with two poles 15 feet apart and a manual transmission car, the learner can parallel park the car between the two poles within 3 minutes without bumping either pole.

Attitude. Attitude objectives must reflect what the learner must do to demonstrate acquisition of an attitude. They may also require that the learner tell why the performance is important. Lesser "levels of directness" may be used, which require the learner to simulate (either in writing or in role-playing) demonstration of the desired attitude.

An example of an attitude objective follows: Between September and October the learner will increase the frequency of actions that indicate that he is operating under the principle that it is better to solve disagreements nonviolently.

Cognitive Strategies. Cognitive strategy objectives require that the learner do the following:

- Assess the learning task.
- Select (or invent) a strategy appropriate to the task.
- Apply the strategy.
- Assess the success of the strategy.
- Modify the strategy if it is not effective.

An example of a cognitive strategy objective follows:

Given an expository prose passage in which the requirement is that the learner recall main ideas and details, the learner will apply the text structure strategy as evidenced by notes reflecting the content structure of the passage.

*E*xercises E

1. In the following objectives, underline the words that give a description of the conditions, circle the statement of the terminal behavior, and draw a box around the part of the sentence that gives the performance standards.

- Given a level parallel parking spot along a curb with two poles 15 feet apart and a manual transmission car, the learner can parallel park the car between the two poles within 3 minutes without bumping either pole.
- Given a list of computers in education references and a word-processing program, the learner can generate a word-processed, 3–5 page paper on educational applications of computers in her subject area. The product should achieve at least 70 points when assessed with the checklist that is attached.
- Given 15 multiplication problems in which the multiplier is a decimal with one, two, or three decimal places, the learner can solve at least 12 of them correctly.
- Given pictures of 12 geometric figures, some of which are polygons, the learner should be able to circle those that are polygons. He should

correctly identify at least 10 of these. In addition, the learner must state why he made the distinction that he did. This explanation should be couched in an explanation of how this figure does/does not represent the three key attributes of polygons. At least 8 of these explanations must be correct.

2. Below are statements of instructional goals. Rewrite them as performance objectives.

- The student can select examples of the concept "conservative" (in the political dichotomy of *liberal* vs. *conservative*) from a list of examples and nonexamples.
- The student will administer an allergy injection following techniques for sterility.
- The student can compute the mean, range, and standard deviation of a series of ten numbers.

3. Following is an instructional goal. Conduct a complete instructional analysis (information-processing analysis and prerequisite analysis) including steps in the information processing analysis as performance objectives. The goal is "The learner will be able to subtract one two-digit number from a second two-digit number."

Summary

The output of the front-end analysis stage of design is a clear description of the learning environment, the learners, and the learning task. The learning task has been clearly specified in terms of both terminal objectives and, through an instructional analysis, enabling objectives. These objectives have been classified according to the types of learning outcomes required, in our case according to Gagné's learning outcomes taxonomy. This clear delineation of environment, learner, and task will enable the designer to design an instructional package that can and will be implemented in the targeted learning environment. The instructional analysis, specification of the performance objectives, and categorization of the learning outcomes assist the designer in selecting the appropriate instructional strategy and appropriate evaluation items and procedures. Figure 4.14 summarizes key points in this chapter.

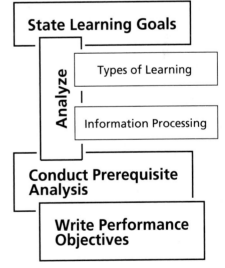

Figure 4.14: Summary Diagram for Chapter 4

Job Aid

1. Write the instructional goal of the course, unit, or lesson in performance terms. (Remember, you may omit the standards at this time.)
2. What kind of learning outcome does this goal represent?
3. List the 3–12 information-processing steps that an expert would use in completing this goal. (Remember you can write a representative test question to guide this analysis.)
4. (Optional) Represent the information-processing analysis graphically.
5. For each step in the information-processing analysis, indicate the prerequisites.
6. (Optional) Represent the prerequisite analysis in graphic form.
7. Write a performance objective for the instructional goal, each step in the information-processing analysis, and each prerequisite in your instructional analysis.

Extended Example

This section continues the instructional design of the course Photography Basics.

1. *Instructional Goal.* Given the prose text for instructional materials, the learner will be able to generate photographs to accompany the prose that are well-composed, focused, and correctly exposed.

2. *Type of Learning Outcome.* This is a higher-order rule (problem solving) goal because it requires the selection and use of many principles and rules in order to get an appropriate, well-composed, focused, and correctly exposed photograph. It has an overarching, sequenced procedure that must be followed in applying these rules.

3. *Information Processing Analysis.* The information-processing analysis starts with the expert determining what kinds of photographs will be produced, and the analysis ends with the expert taking the photographs (see Figure 4.15).

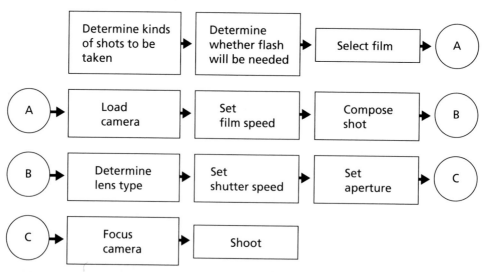

Figure 4.15: Information-Processing Analysis of the Procedure

4. *Prerequisite Analysis.* Lack of space prohibits our providing the prerequisite analysis of all steps in the information-processing analysis. For example purposes, we have provided a prerequisite analysis of the step "select appropriate shutter speed" in Figure 4.16.

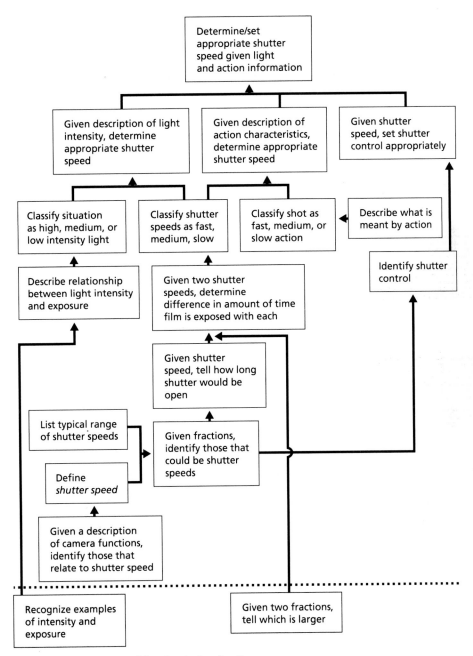

Figure 4.16: Prerequisite Analysis of a Step

5. *Performance Objectives.* For example purposes, we will provide the performance objectives for the section on shutter speed.

Terminal Objective

Given a description of (1) the intensity of the light in a given situation, (2) the action, and (3) how the image should appear, the learner will be able to set the shutter speed so that the photograph will be correctly exposed and focused.

Objective 1. Given a description of the light intensity conditions and a selection of four possible shutter speeds, the learner will be able to select the appropriate shutter speed so that the image would be correctly exposed.

Objective 2. Given the action characteristics of the subject of the photo (still, moving quickly, etc.), the desired ''effect'' of the photo (clearly focused, background blurred etc.), and a selection of four possible shutter speeds, the learner will be able to select the appropriate shutter speed so that the image will appear as desired.

Objective 3. Given a 35mm camera and a set of three shutter speed settings, the learner will be able to physically set the shutter control to each of three settings correctly.

Objective 4. Given the descriptions of the light intensity conditions in four situations, the learner will be able to classify the situations as high, medium, or low intensity light. At least three of the four classifications must be correct.

Objective 5. Given six descriptions of the action of the subject in a potential shot, the learner can correctly classify the actions as fast, medium, slow, or still in at least four of the six situations.

Objective 6. Given six shutter speeds, the learner can classify them as fast, medium, or slow speeds.

Objective 7. Given three line drawings of three different models of 35mm cameras, the learner can correctly circle the shutter control on all three of the drawings.

Objective 8. In the student's own words, the learner can explain the relationship between light intensity and exposure of the film to light. (The explanation should include the rule that the greater the intensity of light, the shorter the period of time that the film must be exposed to light.)

Objective 9. Given four sets of shutter speeds, the learner can determine the difference in the amount of time the film would be exposed to light in each situation. At least three of the four calculations must be correct.

Objective 10. Given a list of 10 shutter speeds, the learner will be able to correctly tell the amount of time that the film will be exposed to light for all 10 settings.

Objective 11. In the student's own words, the learner can define or describe the term *action* as it applies to photography. (The definition should include that *action* is the amount of movement of the subject in a photograph.)

Objective 12. Given a list of 15 fractions, the learner will correctly identify all of those that are shutter speed settings for a 35mm camera.

Objective 13. The learner will list all of the settings in a typical range of shutter speed settings for a 35mm camera. This list should include at least 10 settings. None of the settings included should be incorrect.

Objective 14. In the student's own words, the learner can define *shutter speed*. (The definition should include that *shutter speed* is a setting that determines the length of time that the shutter remains open, and consequently, the length of time that the film is exposed to light.)

Objective 15. Given a list of functions that different controls and structures of the camera provide, the learner will be able to identify those two functions that are provided by the shutter.

Objective 16 (entry-level skill). Given four sets of two fractions, the learner will be able to identify which of the two fractions is larger. All four answers must be correct.

Objective 17 (entry-level skill). Given four descriptions of lighting situations, two of which typify the concept of "change of intensity of light" and two of which typify the concept of "change in duration of light," the learner can classify all four of the situations correctly.

Readings and References

Anderson, J. R. (1976). *Language, memory, and thought.* Hillsdale, NJ: Lawrence Erlbaum Associates.

Bloom, B. S., Englehart, M. D., Furst, E. J., Hill, W. H., & Krathwohl, D. R. (1956). *Taxonomy of educational objectives: Handbook I, cognitive domain.* New York: McKay.

Briggs, L. J. (Ed.). (1977). *Instruction design: Principles and applications.* Englewood Cliffs, NJ: Educational Technology Publications.

Carlisle, K. E. (1986). *Analyzing jobs and tasks.* Englewood Cliffs, NJ: Educational Technology Publications.

Dick, W., & Carey, L. (1990). *The systematic design of instruction* (3rd ed.). Glenview, IL: Scott, Foresman, and Co.

Gagné, E. D. (1985). *The cognitive psychology of school learning.* Boston: Little, Brown, and Company.

Gagné, R. M. (1985). *The conditions of learning,* 4th edition. New York: Holt, Rinehart & Winston.

Jonassen, D. H., & Hannum, W. H. (1986). Analysis of task analysis procedures. *Journal of Instructional Development, 9,* 2–12.

Mager, R. F. (1962). *Preparing instructional objectives.* Palo Alto, CA: Fearon.

Merrill, M. D. (1983). Component display theory. In C. M. Reigeluth (Ed.), *Instructional design theories and models.* Hillsdale, NJ: Lawrence Erlbaum.

Merrill, P. F. (1987). Job and task analysis. In R. M. Gagné (Ed.) *Instructional technology: Foundations* (pp. 143–174). Hillsdale, NJ: Erlbaum.

Rossett, A. (1988). *Training needs assessment.* Englewood Cliffs, NJ: Educational Technology Publications.

Scandura, J. M. (1983). Instructional strategies based on the structural learning theory. In C. M. Reigeluth (Ed.), *Instructional design theories and models.* Hillsdale, NJ: Lawrence Erlbaum.

Weinstein, C. F., & Mayer, R. F. (1986) The teaching of learning strategies. In M. C. Wittrock (Ed.). *Handbook of research on teaching,* 3rd edition. New York: Macmillan.

Assessing Learner Performance

five

Chapter Objectives

At the conclusion of this chapter you should be able to do the following:

- Given descriptions of assessment situations, determine the appropriate model—norm referenced or criterion referenced—to guide the development of assessments.

- Given a completed learning task analysis, identify which objectives would appear on entry skills assessment, pre-assessment, and post-assessment.

- Given descriptions of types of assessment—simulation, observation, or written test—describe trade-offs among validity, reliability, and practicality.

- Write production and recognition items for objectives of different types of learning.

- Identify which of several possible assessment items are valid assessments of objectives for various types of learning.

- Given an objective, write appropriate item specifications, and write five assessment items (if appropriate) that are congruent with the item specs.

- Write an appropriate assessment instrument blueprint that includes test length, description of content domain, proportionality, directions and administration procedures, type and number of measures, scoring methods, weighting of items, and criterion level/cutoff score.

- Evaluate sample assessment items according to the characteristics of "good" assessment instruments and guidelines for that type of item, suggesting revisions where appropriate.

Overview of Assessment of Learners' Performance

Jim Evans just concluded teaching a workshop for trainers in state governmental agencies on creating effective visuals. He had some admirable objectives for his workshop, such as the following:

- Given a description of the audience characteristics, purposes of the presentation, and source materials, the learner will be able to develop a transparency master that incorporates the principles of visual design and good lettering.
- Given a description of the audience characteristics, purposes of the presentation, and a handout developed for a presentation, the learner will be able to evaluate the handout based upon the principles of visual design, effective lettering, and appropriate use of the medium and suggest revisions.

Jim conducted only one assessment in the class, at the conclusion of the workshop. He administered a 50-item test with items such as this:

Which of the following is not a characteristic of the design element "surface"?
a. texture
b. color
c. value
d. form

Another test item was "List and discuss the eight principles of visual design."

Some of the learners performed unexpectedly poorly on the test, and the mandated instructor evaluation forms at the end of the class contained statements such as the following:

"I don't think the test was fair."

"I knew most of the stuff that the instructor taught. It wasn't very challenging."

"There were a lot of times that I was lost. The instructor assumed that I already knew some things that I didn't know."

However, despite these negative comments, Jim was pleased to see that when he plotted the learners' scores, they formed a normal or "bell" curve.

Despite his reaching this distribution of scores, Jim has problems with his own instruction. Specifically, his evaluation procedures and assumptions may be quite inappropriate considering his objectives and the purposes for his evaluation. What problems do you notice with his procedures and approach? In this chapter we will address many of the issues related to assessment within an instructional design context.

Purposes of Evaluation

As Mager (1962) stated, the question that instructional designers must ask in addition to "Where are we going?" and "How will we get there?" is "How do we know when we're there?" Planning for evaluation allows us to determine "how we know when we're there." Evaluation serves two purposes in instructional design: to assess individual students' performances and to provide information about what kinds of revisions are needed in the instructional materials. So there are actually two kinds of "getting there" that we must determine during evaluation. The first question is that of assessing whether individual learners are "getting there" (i.e., after instruction they can demonstrate the performance described in the objectives). That is the focus of this chapter. The second aspect of evaluation is determining how well the instruction "works." In other words, is the instruction effective, efficient, and appealing? And if it is not working well, what changes need to be made? This type of evaluation is the focus of Chapter 16.

Sequencing of Evaluation Design Stage

We have chosen to talk about assessment of students' performance at this point in the text because we want to use the structure of (1) analysis, (2) develop strategy, and (3) evaluation as an organizational pattern. Clearly, assessment of student performance fits into the last stage—evaluation. However, it is important for you to know that, in actuality, the designer thinks about assessing learners' performance before and while developing an instructional strategy. As a matter of fact, a designer generally begins to construct assessment instruments[1] as soon as the instructional objectives have been identified. This is done to help ensure that the items match the objectives. In other words, the conditions and behavior specified in the objectives are considered in the writing of each assessment item. This is why the stage for writing test items appears where it does in the design model.

In this way we create what are called criterion-referenced assessment items. You can imagine how easy it is for someone to create an item immediately after writing the following objective: "Given a list of objects, some of which are transparent, the learner should be able to circle those objects that are transparent." All the designer must do at this point is fulfill the conditions of the objective; that is, list a number of objects for the learner, some of which are transparent, and through the directions (which are part of the assessment instrument) tell the learner to circle the transparent objects. There is a definite benefit to writing assessment items immediately after writing objectives. First, the intentions of the objectives are fresh on your mind. Secondly, if you cannot write an item for the objective, then you know that you probably need to revise the objective in some way so that students' performance on it can be measured. So, a good time to write test items is immediately after writing objectives. Of course, the success of developing good assessment instruments is heavily dependent on the quality of the objectives that you have written. If these do not really reflect the intentions of the instruction, then the assessment that is based upon them certainly will be inadequate.

When designing assessment items for a lesson one must do the following:

1. Identify the purpose of the assessment instrument and the type of model that will be followed in its development.
2. Determine what kinds of assessments are necessary and where they should occur in the instructional strategy.

3. Determine what forms the items should take (essay, multiple choice, checklist, etc.) to adequately assess the type of learning that is represented by the objective.
4. Write test items and directions that are clear to the learner, originally in the form of item specifications.
5. Determine how many items are needed to assess learners' performance on an objective and what constitutes an adequate performance.
6. Determine how to select among objectives or what proportion of objectives should appear on the assessment instrument by writing an instrument blueprint.

We will discuss each of these issues in the following sections. Good test-writing is a skill not quickly or easily learned. There are many texts on test writing, and most universities have entire courses on the subject. However, as you will see later in the chapter, there are specific approaches to developing assessment items in the context of instructional design that may differ considerably from traditional techniques for test design. We will overview some of the most critical information in this chapter.

*P*urposes and Models of Assessment of Learners' Achievement

In educational and training environments there typically are two rather diverse reasons for assessing learners' achievement: (1) to determine level of competence and (2) to compare or rank learners' abilities. The results of these assessments allow teachers, trainers, administrators, and learners to make two rather different kinds of decisions.

A performance assessment designed to determine whether a physical therapist can correctly adjust the height of crutches is an example of an assessment of competence. The scores from this assessment might enable the instructor to determine which learners are competent in this area and are ready for further study and which learners need more instruction on the topic. The information provided by this assessment might also be used by licensing or accrediting agencies to determine

<hr>

[1]We have intentionally used the terms *assessment, assessment instrument,* and *assessment item* rather than *testing, test,* and *test item* to avoid connotations and preconceptions that interfere with learning techniques suggested in this text. For example, many novice designers assume when the term *test* is used that we are referring to a pencil-and-paper assessment. As you will find, there are many formats for assessing learner achievement, only one of which is a written test format.

whether an individual has the skills and/or knowledge to be licensed or accredited as competent in the field. Instruments designed to assess competence or identify gaps in learning are termed **criterion-referenced** assessment instruments. (They are also called *objective-referenced* or *domain-referenced* instruments.) Although criterion-referenced assessments are effective for determining who is "competent" and where individuals' weaknesses are, they are not very effective in enabling decision-makers to compare or rank learners.

The Graduate Record Exam (GRE) is an example of an assessment designed to enable comparison or ranking of individuals. The GRE is designed to provide scores that assist admissions officers in selecting individuals for admission to graduate school. The goal of the test is to obtain a spread of scores that gives the admission officers a clear picture of ranking and maximizes the ability to compare students. Instruments of this type are termed **norm-referenced** tests. Although instruments designed with this purpose in mind are good at aiding selection decisions, they are much less helpful in determining whether an individual is competent in a particular skill or possesses particular knowledge. They are even less helpful in aiding an instructor (or learner) determine where the learning gaps are and where remediation is needed.

While an assessment instrument might be designed with both purposes in mind, ordinarily one purpose or the other is predominant. It is important that assessment designers have a clear purpose in mind for their tests because the methods in which instruments are designed for these two purposes are somewhat different. In most cases, an instrument that is designed to rank or compare learners is designed using a norm-referenced model, and tests developed to determine competence are designed using a criterion-referenced model. As a rule, instructional designers are involved in designing tests to assess competence and to determine areas needing remediation; consequently, instructional designers typically use criterion-referenced models and instrument development procedures.

The two models of assessment design differ in the manner in which they define the content that is to be assessed and in the manner in which they choose items to include on an instrument. Typically, norm-referenced test designers define

the scope of the material for the assessment instrument more broadly and with less precision than do criterion-referenced test designers. In contrast, when developing criterion-referenced instruments, designers use the precise objectives that they developed in the learning task description phase (as discussed in Chapter 4) to specifically guide their selection of skills and knowledge to be assessed. Therefore, the domain or scope of the type of items that are appropriate for assessment is carefully defined.

When determining which items will be included on an instrument, norm-referenced designers follow a procedure in which they administer a trial form of the exam to a sample of individuals who represent the target audience of the test. After the administration of the test, the designers look at the difficulty level of each item (the ratio of the number of people who answered the item correctly to the total number of individuals taking the exam). They then eliminate items that were extremely easy (answered correctly by most individuals) or extremely difficult (answered correctly by only a few individuals).

This procedure for selecting items in norm-referenced instruments helps obtain a spread or variation of scores, leading to what is often described as "normal distribution" or a *bell curve* of scores. This promotes the ability to discriminate between the performance of individuals and rank them. Once this form of the test has been developed, it is again administered to a large group of individuals who are representative of the population for whom the test is being developed. Using the scores from this administration, performance "norms" are obtained. That is, information is collected so that in later administrations, once a score is obtained, the teacher and learner can be provided with information as to how well the learner's score compares to others of his age or experience level. Often these scores are reported as percentiles; that is, what percent of scores an individual's score ranks above.

In contrast, the criterion-referenced test designer writes items that match the objective in terms of conditions presented and performance required. If the objective has a range of possible difficulty levels, the writer will write several items to sample across the difficulty levels. In looking at test scores on items after trials of the test, the instructional designer will certainly not routinely discard items that are answered correctly by the majority of learners, as this is a desirable outcome. It indicates instruction was effective. Rather, the designer will look at items that are missed by many individuals to determine if the item is well-written. Then she will examine the instruction to determine whether the coverage of that particular objective is adequate.

The criterion-referenced assessment designer is much less concerned with obtaining a wide spread of scores on an instrument than the norm-referenced designer. Quite often scores from criterion-referenced instruments do not represent a "normal distribution." They are often "skewed" by many individuals performing well: Instructional designers often argue that if instruction is effective, test results will not form a normal distribution on a well-designed test. So, Jim Evans, whose workshop experience was described earlier in this chapter, should not be satisfied with his test results simply because he obtained a normal distribution. His workshop goals were to develop a high level of competence for developing good visuals in *all* of the participants, not to compare or rank them. Therefore, he should actually be disturbed by his test results. (You might like to refer back to Bloom's Model of Mastery Learning in Chapter 1, in which the inappropriateness of "normal distribution" of scores on tests after instruction is discussed.)

*E*xercises A

1. Given below are descriptions of some assessment situations. Beside each situation, write whether a criterion-referenced model (C) or a norm-referenced model (N) is most appropriate for guiding assessment development.

    _____ a. Determine which students should be licensed as physical therapists.

    _____ b. Determine which applicants to admit to a graduate program with limited positions.

    _____ c. Determine whether a learner is ready to begin the next unit of study.

    _____ d. Determine which students should receive a scholarship.

    _____ e. Determine how one state's students compare to those in another state in reading ability.

    _____ f. Determine in which areas a learner needs remediation.

2. In your own words, describe the differences in development of a norm-referenced and a criterion-referenced assessment.

*T*ypes of Assessments

There are three types of tests that may be given during instruction: entry skills assessments, pre-assessments, and post-assessments.

Entry Skills Assessments

As we discussed in Chapter 4, there are often skills and knowledge that students must have to begin instruction on a particular topic. For instance, we would wish our learners to know how to add, subtract, multiply, and divide before they begin instruction in statistics. We can avoid a lot of grief by checking to make sure that learners have the prerequisite skills before they begin instruction on a current lesson. One should not assume that because students have had a course that included treatment of a particular topic that they ever learned, or have retained, the necessary skills and knowledge in that topic needed as prerequisites for a lesson. A good way to determine whether learners have these skills and knowledge is through an entry skills test. This test can be given prior to the instructional lesson, in combination with the pretest, or as a way of reviewing the prerequisite skills.

During the actual implementation of instruction, we may choose to omit an entry skills assessment if learners have just completed a valid and reliable post-assessment of the skills that would be included in the entry test. For example, if learners have just completed a prerequisite course to a course that is currently being designed, and the completed course has a valid and reliable assessment of the skills and knowledge that would be included in the entry assessment, you might omit the entry skills assessment for the latter course. However, we recommend that you retain the entry assessment in the formative evaluation phase of design, so as to confirm that you indeed have made a valid assumption regarding the skill level with which the learners will enter the course.

Pre-assessments

We often wish to know what learners already know about the topic that they are about to learn about through instruction. For example, the learners in your target audience may already know some of the enabling objectives, or some of them may already be able to achieve the terminal objective. A pretest can be given to determine what learners already know with regard to the objective(s) at hand. This pre-assessment may be given before a lesson begins, or it may be used as a way to gain students' attention and to inform them of the objective(s) of the lesson. Through a pre-assessment, the instructor can determine what the students need to learn. Then the instructor can help the learners focus on that portion of the instruction that has not been previously learned.

You may design pre-assessment so that the supervising instructor (or the computer program) can terminate the assessment if learners have evidenced that they cannot answer the items related to the new information to be learned. In this way, you may avoid possible frustration and negative feelings on the part of the learners. During formative evaluation, you can monitor learners' performance on the pre-assessment and the advent of negative emotions as learners begin to encounter items that they cannot answer.

Post-assessments

After learners have completed a lesson, they are ready for the "assess performance" event, which usually takes the form of a post-assessment. Ideally a post-assessment will assess whether the learner can achieve both the enabling objectives and the terminal objective of a lesson. Although tests that provide assessment of both enabling and terminal objectives can be time-consuming to write (and to take), they provide a great deal of useful information. If we were to test only for the terminal objective of a lesson, and the students were unable to perform well on those items, we would have no information as to where further instruction may be needed. If, however, we have tested the enabling objectives, we have some information as to where learning has "gone wrong." The teacher or instructional materials can then send the learners to appropriate remedial instruction. With the ex-

ception of items to test achievement of declarative knowledge objectives, the items that are included on the post-assessment should be different from those included on the pre-assessment and on practice items within the instruction.

Occasionally, to deal practically with the limitations of time in assessment development, the pre-assessment and the post-assessment may include only the most critical subordinate objectives, such as the objectives that reflect the major information-processing steps in the task, and the terminal objective.

Exercises B

1. Figure 5.1 shows the results of a prerequisite analysis. Indicate which objectives (identified by the letters A–Q) should appear on each of the following assessments.

   a. Entry skills assessment: _____

   b. Pre-assessment: _____

   c. Post-assessment: _____

2. In the situation just described, suppose "testing" time is severely limited for the post-assessment. Which objectives would you assess? Why? What risks do you run in using this type of assessment?

Characteristics of Good Assessment Instruments

"Good" criterion-referenced assessment instruments have several necessary qualities: validity, reliability, and practicality. We will discuss each of these characteristics below.

Validity

An assessment instrument is valid if it actually assesses or measures what it claims to assess or measure. For objective-based assessment instruments, an instrument is valid if: (1) its individual items are consistent with the objectives they claim to assess, (2) the items for each objective are representative of the range of items that are possible to develop for that objective, and (3) objec-

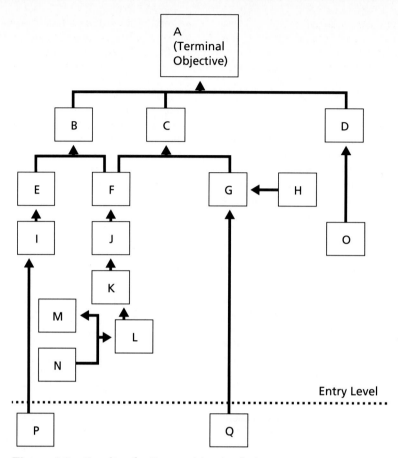

Figure 5.1: Results of a Prerequisite Analysis

tives upon which the instrument is based are adequately sampled.

An individual item is congruent with its objective if the conditions and performance specified in the objective are represented in the item. Consider the objective that Jim Evans gave for his workshop:

Given a description of the audience characteristics, purposes of the presentation, and source materials, the learner will be able to develop a transparency master that incorporates the principles of visual design and good lettering.

Now consider one of the items that he developed for the test that concluded the workshop:

Which of the following is not a characteristic of the design element surface?

a. texture

b. color

c. value

d. form

Although the item does possibly represent prerequisite knowledge that the learners might need to know to be able to perform the objective, it certainly does not match the conditions of the objective, "Given a description of the audience characteristics, purposes of the presentation, and source materials," nor does it match the performance specified "the learner will be able to develop a transparency master that incorporates the principles of visual design and good lettering.'' This is a typical error for designers to make. To achieve a more objective or easier-to-administer test, designers often create items that step back from the level of realism or directness that is specified in the objective. Designers such as Jim Evans develop items over more easily tested declarative knowledge or verbal information that may support the actual objective but certainly do not adequately assess it. A much more valid item would, of course, provide a scenario that describes an audience, the purpose of a presentation, and key resource information related to the topic. Then it would direct the learner to create a transparency master to convey the critical information.

Often a designer may find, when attempting to write a valid item for an objective, that it is impossible to create a way to assess the objective as written. This may be because the objective is too nebulous or because the designer has described a situation that is not practical to assess, such as performance of the targeted skill or knowledge on-the-job. We suggest that if you find you are unable to devise a way to assess an objective that you retain the original objective as a reference point and write a revised objective that reflects your closest intent that *can* be assessed. This could involve reducing the level of directness or realism, such as employing a simulation or pencil-and-paper test rather than an observation. Or, it might involve some disciplined clarification of your intentions.

The exercise of trying to write an assessment instrument can often help you determine the actual purpose of your instruction, which will certainly simplify the process of designing an instructional strategy. Revising objectives at this stage does not mean that you should reduce your intent to something that is easy to assess, such as reducing intellectual skills to declarative knowledge. This is a very common error that we see often in both training and public school environments. Reducing instruction to declarative knowledge levels simply to make writing objectives and test items easier makes a mockery of the process of instructional design and simply should not be done. You must be very creative to develop objectives and related test items that reflect as closely as possible your original intent.

There are procedures that will support the development of a valid instrument, such as writing item specifications and test blueprints, which we will discuss later in this chapter. A review by a subject matter expert and an instructional designer of these item specifications and blueprints during early formative evaluation can validate the parameters of the assessment instruments. These reviewers should be given copies of the objectives with their matched item specifications and the blueprint of the entire assessment instrument. They should also be asked to validate that (1) its individual items are consistent with the objectives they purport to assess, (2) the items for each objective are representative of the range of items that are possible to develop for that objective, and (3) objectives upon which the instrument is based are adequately sampled.

The characteristic of validity is critical to all assessments. If a test does not measure what it purports to measure, the test is worthless, or perhaps worse, misleading. Developing valid criterion-referenced instruments is based on procedures described in this chapter.

Reliability

An assessment instrument is reliable if it consistently measures what it claims to measure and if we have a high degree of confidence in the scores that it produces. We would like to be able to say with confidence that (within a modest amount of inevitable error) learners who achieve a high score on an assessment are competent, and learners who score poorly are not competent. We would like to believe that if we gave the same or a carefully matched assessment tomorrow or next week (without any intervening learning) that learners would achieve basically equivalent scores on both assessments. What instrument characteristics would interfere with our being able to draw these conclusions? What makes an instrument unreliable?

Anything that causes unpredictable error in an instrument makes it unreliable. There are a number of factors that can lead to this error. The lack of objectivity of an instrument can cause it to be unreliable. For example, an instrument that cannot be objectively graded can lead to errors in grading that make its measure unreliable. An instructor might grade an essay question quite differently today versus a day next week. The instrument would not yield a consistent score. ''Objective'' assessment formats, such as multiple-choice, true-false, and matching, are easier to evaluate objectively than "constructed" responses such as short answer, essay, simulation, or observed performance. Often, however, to assess an objective as realistically as possible we utilize the constructed response format. The use of checklists, model responses, and other criteria, such as looking for key words or phrases in an essay response, can help to ensure more objective evaluation.

One of the goals of a criterion-referenced assessment may be to differentiate between individuals who are competent or incompetent with regard to a particular objective or set of objectives. This is the goal of a licensing assessment such as those used to certify barbers, nurses, physical therapists, physicians, and pilots. A test that does not differentiate between a skilled and unskilled learner is not a reliable test. The assessment designer attempts to eliminate or reduce factors that would allow incompetent learners to appear competent or would cause competent learners to appear to be incompetent.

One of the primary means by which an incompetent learner may appear to be competent is found in the role that guessing can play in acquiring a correct answer. "Objective" test formats such as multiple-choice or matching are more vulnerable to the effects of guessing than constructed response items. Any time learners can select from possible answers, there is a chance that with no or incomplete knowledge, learners can guess and correctly answer some items. For this reason we typically recommend that you do not use true-false items in assessment: There is a fifty-fifty chance that learners can get a true-false item correct. It is also preferable that multiple-choice items have as many options, sometimes called *foils,* as possible. Each additional foil reduces the possibility of correctly answering by guessing.

Other factors that can contribute to the error in an instrument are the length of an instrument, the clarity of the items, the quality of the directions, or other problems in the administration of the assessment. With regard to test length, fewer items assessing an objective mean the greater the possibility that a learner's knowledge may be inaccurately reflected in the responses. An instrument that uses too few items to evaluate an objective may not achieve a reliable measure. For example, if we used only one item to assess whether a learner can balance a chemical equation, a simple mathematical error may interfere with a learner's getting that item correct. Or, a lucky guess may allow some learners to get the item correct even though they have not actually acquired the procedural rules to solve the problem. This is why we typically try to create several items to assess each objective. As we stated earlier, it can be difficult to write more than one item for a declarative knowledge objective; it is difficult to think of a number of ways to ask for the capitol of Texas. However, intellectual skills, cognitive strategies, motor skills, and attitude objectives generally can have multiple forms. We usually suggest that you use an odd number of items to assess an objective. The odd number simply allows you to make a decision about the achievement of an objective without "ties." This way, the learner can, for example, achieve two out of three or five out of seven of the items. Beyond this guideline, the number of items per each objective ultimately is affected by practicality and efficiency issues.

The reliability of an instrument is also affected by the clarity of the items and their directions. The instrument should be so designed that if a learner has actually acquired the skill associated with an objective there is nothing that will interfere with the learner's demonstrating this skill. Ambiguity in the statement of an item, incomplete directions, unfamiliar vocabulary, or unfamiliar context of items can cause a skilled learner to fail to demonstrate this skill. For example, learners who were skilled in locating the main idea of prose performed poorly when they were asked to "Circle the statement that gives the gist of the preceding paragraph." Subsequent questioning of the learners indicated that the fourth-grade learners were not clear on the meanings of both *gist* and *preceding.* Formative evaluation of items with representative members of a target audience can help eliminate some of these problems.

It is also possible that conditions surrounding the administration of the assessment can cause learners to perform at a less than optimal level. For example, unfamiliar assessment formats, such as administering a computer-delivered exam to learners who have never experienced this format, can lead to unreliable test results. Classroom conditions, such as excess heat or cold or other unpleasant physical conditions, can also sometimes lead to unreliability. In addition, unpleasant emotional conditions, such as excessive anxiety, can also lead to unreliable group performance. Prior planning for the administration of the assessment can usually eliminate these threats.

The reliability index of criterion-referenced assessments is generally obtained in a somewhat different manner than norm-referenced assessments. For example, for those assessments that require constructed responses (written or physically performed), it is often important that the grader establish some measure of reliability. Use of a checklist or rating form, as well as the practice of grading all of one question for the entire class set, can encourage a more consistent measure. If it is desirable that the grader report an index of reliability, the grader may choose to have several graders rate a sample of the performances or written tests based on the scale used. Then an index of "inter-rater reliability" can be obtained by correlating the scores that each of the graders assigned. (See Chapter 10 of Schrock & Coscarelli, 1989, for a more detailed description of this procedure.)

Test developers have traditionally used a measure of "internal consistency" such as the Kuder Richardson 20, Kuder Richardson 21, or Cronbach's *alpha* to report the reliability of written tests. Although such measures work well with tests built on a norm-referenced model, they can be very problematic for tests based on a criterion-referenced model. An index of internal consistency basically measures the consistency of responses from test respondents. It answers these questions: Do test respondents who make a high score tend to score high across all items? Do respondents who make a poor score tend to score poorly across all items? (For more information on determining the reliability of norm-referenced tests, refer to a traditional educational measurement text, such as Mehrens and Lehman [1991].) The problem with this approach to estimating reliability is that criterion-referenced tests tend to assess several objectives at one time, and it would be entirely feasible that a test respondent would perform well on items testing one objective but not well on items for another objective. Norm-referenced assessments relate not to specific objectives but to underlying abilities possessed by test takers, as those abilities might relate to achievement in some subject area. Thus, whereas the norm-referenced test should possess internal consistency, there is no reason that a criterion-referenced test must. In addition, the statistics in calculating KR 20, KR 21, or Cronbach's *alpha* depend on the high variance of scores that tests constructed with norm-referenced techniques obtain. As you recall, it is quite common to obtain many high scores with little variation on criterion-referenced assessments because items on which many students score correctly are not eliminated from the test, as they are in norm-referenced tests.

So, how is an index of reliability obtained for criterion-referenced tests? The most common procedure followed is to report the consistency of measurement across two administrations of a test (test-retest reliability). However, instead of correlating scores, the test-retest looks at the consistency of assignment to the master and non-master categories. Essentially, the test developer determines a criterion score for the test for which those who score above it are considered "masters" or competent in the content, and those who score below the criterion are considered non-masters. (We will discuss setting a mastery criterion later in this chapter.) The test (or parallel form of the test) is administered twice to a group of individuals, some of whom are considered already knowledgeable in the content, some of whom are not. The tests are administered within a few days of each other with the admonishment to the test-takers that they do not study the content in the interim. Then the consistency of assignments of the master/non-master groups is measured using correlation statistics. (For a more detailed review of these procedures see Chapter 11 of Schrock & Coscarelli, 1989.)

Practicality

Given the recommendations above to develop a valid and reliable test, you might conclude that the optimal assessment might be a many-itemed, constructed response or performance (observational) exam that is as close as possible to the real-life situation in which the learners will apply their knowledge, for all objectives, with a carefully developed set of criteria for evaluating the responses. This is occasionally possible. However, generally there is a trade-off between our desires to create a valid and reliable test and the realities of the assessment situation. Assessment resources are generally limited: We do not have many student hours for assessment, the instructor does not have unlimited grading time, we do not have many skilled evaluators available to help the instructor with evaluating performances, and the lag time between when assessment is administered and when scores must be reported is limited. For example, a terminal objective for a course in instructional design might be "Given a subject matter expert, materials resources, and a target population, the learner will be able to design, develop, produce, evaluate, and revise instructional materials to meet an instructional need." An ideal assessment for this objective would be the complete design of several courses for varying situations to ensure a valid and reliable measure of competence. However, it is unrealistic to expect that in the course of a semester learners could develop several complete designs, nor is it feasible that one instructor could evaluate them. Therefore, design courses often have learners complete designs for one situation for some degree of validity and use printed scenarios in written assessments in an attempt to obtain some degree of reliability.

Trade-offs in Assessment Design

As you can see, we must make carefully considered decisions as to which factors are most important for the particular assessment situation and then make trade-offs among the factors of validity, reliability, and practicality. One of the bases upon which these trade-offs may be made is the consequences of the wrong decisions that might be made with a less than ideal assessment.

In the instructional design class previously described, the assessment is not ideally reliable because it really has an insufficient number of "items" to allow the instructor to conclude that the learners will be able to design for a variety of situations. In an attempt to compensate for this lack of items the instructor might create printed scenarios in which the learners complete one part of the design process, or the instructor might develop situations in which the learners must evaluate and revise faulty, already-created portions of a design project. This reduces the validity of the assessment as it does not match the conditions of the

stated objective. Let us explore the implications of such a compromise.

It is possible that on the basis of the information provided from these assessments, given the compromises made among reliability, validity, and practicality, the instructor might mistakenly certify an instructional design student as competent who is actually unable to achieve the stated course objective. It is less likely that a learner who was unable to perform on these assessments would actually be able to perform the terminal objective as stated. The consequences of mistakenly certifying the student as competent would certainly be regrettable from the learner's standpoint, the learner's future employer's standpoint, and the certifying institution's perspective because the mistake could result in frustration on the student's part, loss of time and money on the employer's part, and loss of professional image on the institution's part. However, these consequences are not life threatening. In life-and-death situations, such as training learners in CPR, training parachute packers, or training employees in safety practices, we should be less willing to make compromises in validity and reliability to bow to issues of practicality. Resources should be made available to ensure the most reliable and valid instruments possible in such circumstances. In contrast, in cases of informal education, such as a community center course on embroidery, the consequences of incorrect assessment of competence may not have severe consequences for anyone, in which case more radical compromises might be made for the sake of practicality.

*E*xercises c

1. In the situation described at the beginning of this chapter involving Jim Evans's workshop, describe the ideal type of assessment.
2. Then, supposing that Jim's resources and time are limited, what might be a compromise form of assessment?
3. With this alternate assessment, what threats are made to validity and reliability?
4. Describe the possible consequences of these threats to validity and reliability.

*F*ormats for Assessment

There are three major formats of assessment that can be used in assessing learners' performance: observation, simulations, and pencil-and-paper tests.

On-the-Job Observation

Probably the best way to see if students have learned what we really want them to learn at the level we wanted them to learn it is to actually take them out into the real world and have them show us that they can perform what they have been instructed to do. For instance, we could take an electronics technician to a TV repair store, hand her a malfunctioning VCR, and tell her to locate the problem and repair it. Then we could confirm that the learner can actually find the problem and fix it and that she goes about it in a proper way. In this case our test instrument might be a checklist containing all the things the learner should do in order to adequately repair the VCR. Of course, to provide a *reliable* measure, we would probably want to see whether she could repair several malfunctioning VCRs with several problems before we were sure she could deal with the variety of problems we had taught her to repair. However, it is unlikely that we could find a sufficient number of VCRs with all the appropriate problems and in sufficient quantities to assess all learners. Even if we could find enough VCRs with the right problems, it is unlikely that many customers would like to have their VCRs repaired by novices.

Learners occasionally are assessed in on-the-job situations. In this case the teacher or evaluator usually uses a rating scale or a checklist as the assessment instrument. Rating scales and checklists can be used to assess the quality of the process as the learner performs a particular skill (or skills), or they can be used to evaluate the product or outcome of this performance. For example, if we were assessing learners' skill in making bread we could assess the learners' actions while making the bread: Do they wash their hands before beginning? Do they knead the bread properly and for the correct length of time? Or, we could evaluate the end product of the endeavor. Is the bread the proper consistency? Is it browned to the correct color? Or, we could choose to evaluate both the process and the product and combine these two assessments into one grade or score according to some predetermined formula.

Checklists generally list behaviors that should be observed or characteristics that should be observed in the product. You ascertain these behaviors or characteristics from an examination of the task analysis for the particular skills being assessed. These behaviors or characteristics are then judged dichotomously: present/absent, yes/no, appropriate/inappropriate, acceptable/unacceptable, correct/incorrect. Sometimes we need a more refined evaluation of a process or product than just whether it is correct or incorrect, so we use a rating scale that indicates degrees or levels of quality for a performance or quality. Figure 5.2 is an example of a checklist and a rating scale that could be expanded to be used to assess the quality of work performed by an intern instructional designer.

Simulations

Since it is often impractical or undesirable to assess a student's performance in real-life circumstances, we may wish to simulate real-life circumstances. We would not want learners to experience an actual house fire to assess whether they can apply principles they had learned about getting out of a house safely. However, we may use a simulation that creates an environment like real life in critical aspects in which learners must show that they can apply the principles of evacuating a burning house.

In addition to being excellent instructional strategies, simulations are excellent assessment forms, particularly for assessment of higher-order rule learning and attitude change. Simulations can be delivered with print, video, group interactions, computers, or interactive video. An example of a print-based simulation is the "in basket" assessment. For example, an assessment in an instructional management class might portray the scenario that an instructional designer has been hired to replace a project manager of a design project who left suddenly three months ago. The learner would be provided with all the memos and correspondence that had collected in the past three months (what would be in the manager's "in basket") and be asked to provide written responses to

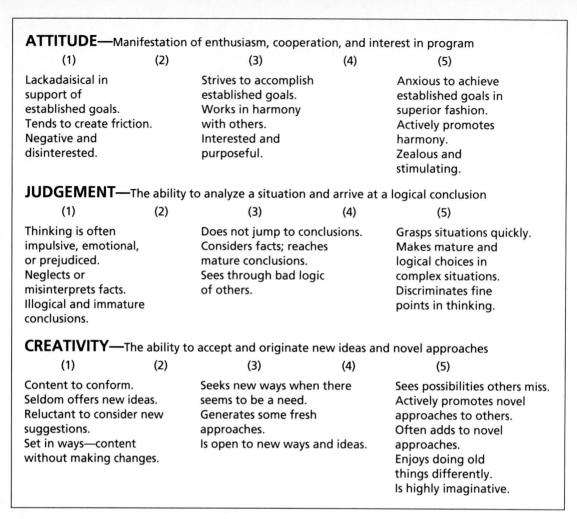

ATTITUDE—Manifestation of enthusiasm, cooperation, and interest in program

(1)	(2)	(3)	(4)	(5)
Lackadaisical in support of established goals. Tends to create friction. Negative and disinterested.		Strives to accomplish established goals. Works in harmony with others. Interested and purposeful.		Anxious to achieve established goals in superior fashion. Actively promotes harmony. Zealous and stimulating.

JUDGEMENT—The ability to analyze a situation and arrive at a logical conclusion

(1)	(2)	(3)	(4)	(5)
Thinking is often impulsive, emotional, or prejudiced. Neglects or misinterprets facts. Illogical and immature conclusions.		Does not jump to conclusions. Considers facts; reaches mature conclusions. Sees through bad logic of others.		Grasps situations quickly. Makes mature and logical choices in complex situations. Discriminates fine points in thinking.

CREATIVITY—The ability to accept and originate new ideas and novel approaches

(1)	(2)	(3)	(4)	(5)
Content to conform. Seldom offers new ideas. Reluctant to consider new suggestions. Set in ways—content without making changes.		Seeks new ways when there seems to be a need. Generates some fresh approaches. Is open to new ways and ideas.		Sees possibilities others miss. Actively promotes novel approaches to others. Often adds to novel approaches. Enjoys doing old things differently. Is highly imaginative.

Figure 5.2: Example Performance Rating Scale (portion) for use with Intern Instructional Designers

all the correspondence. This would be one way to assess whether the learner could apply all the principles that were to be learned during the course. Another example of a print-based simulation is a case study. Case studies are widely used for both instruction as well as assessment in such fields as management, law, and medicine.

Simulations may be administered to a group, as in a role-playing situation, though it may be difficult to assess individual performance within a group sim-

ulation. With the interfacing of microcomputers with videotape or videodisk, realistic simulated environments may be presented to individuals.

Checklists and rating scales may be utilized to determine that learners go through an appropriate process to solve the simulated problem. Some of this evaluation may be automated via a micro- or mainframe computer. Elaborate simulators used in pilot and astronaut training are probably the most sophisticated examples of this form of testing.

Pencil-and-Paper Tests

A third type of assessment form is the pencil-and-paper test. This is what we usually think of as a "test." Since such tests may now be computer-delivered, the term *pencil-and-paper test* may be misleading. There are numerous types of items that fall into this category: multiple-choice, true-false, matching, completion (fill-in-the-blank), short answer, and essay.

Generally all of the test item forms, with the exception of the essay exam, can have a finite and relatively small number of correct responses. A correct response to an essay question may vary considerably in terms of sequence, language, and specificity, not to mention correctness of style and grammar. This sometimes makes it hard to objectively evaluate essay items. Often designers develop checklists or rating scales to evaluate essay exams to help eliminate some of the subjectivity in the assessment of essay questions. However, with imagination and ingenuity, multiple-choice, matching, completion, and short answer items may be used to assess declarative knowledge, intellectual skills, attitudes (to some extent), cognitive strategies, and portions of motor skills.

*E*xercises D

1. Ann is developing a lesson to teach students how to properly use a photographic copy stand to make slides of graphics and other flat art. She plans to use a performance simulation in which the students will use the copy stand to make slides of art that they will be supplied. There are 220 students per year in the classes that will use this instruction. Has Ann made a good selection of the format of her assessment? Why or why not?
2. What other ways might Ann assess the skills included in this unit? What trade-offs will she have to make? Use the terms *reliability, validity,* and *practicality* in your response.
3. This exercise consists of a situation and a question.

    The situation: Willi has just completed writing the objectives for a lesson she is writing on behavior modification techniques that can be used by pet owners to encourage desirable be-

havior in their dogs. Her class will include 30 pet owners each six weeks. Sometimes she will teach the class, and sometimes it will be taught by other workers at the Humane Society. She has determined that her terminal objective is "Given the portrayal of a desirable or undesirable behavior by her dog, the pet owner will appropriately respond based upon the principles of behavior modification."

Willi has determined three different types of assessment forms:
a. An observational rating form to be used while observing the pet owner and her pet over a period of 10 minutes.
b. A videotape of several scenes, five in which the dog behaves in a desirable manner, five in which the dog performs an undesirable behavior. After each scene the videotape narrator asks, "What should the dog owner do now?" The participants must write their answers on a printed form.
c. A paper-and-pencil instrument in which the learners are given descriptions of situations in which dogs behave desirably or undesirably. The description explains the subsequent behavior of the dog owner. The learners are asked to rate the owner's behavior as "appropriate" or "inappropriate" and explain their answers.

The question: Evaluate the adequacy of the a, b, and c methods to assess the objective by comparing their relative validity, reliability, and practicality.

*F*orms of Test Items

You will recall that in Chapter 4 we introduced you to a way of categorizing learning into types of learning outcomes. We commented that the advantage to categorizing learning outcomes is that it promotes later phases of design: more detailed task analysis, including identification of prerequisites, specification of objectives, development of instructional strategies, and creation of assessment instruments. Indeed, forms of assessments will vary according to type of learning outcome, and regardless of the content, assessments for the same type of learning will take a similar form. Before we describe assessment for each of the types of learning we will present two types of assessment items that are common to all types of learning.

Across the different types of learning outcomes, assessment items can be designed in three different forms: recall, recognition, and constructed answer.

Recall Items

We generally use recall items to assess declarative knowledge objectives, or the declarative knowledge component of another learning outcome, such as the declarative knowledge routine that supports motor skills. Recall items ask learners to simply reproduce the knowledge that they have been presented in instruction, either in verbatim or paraphrased form. These items place a high demand on memory but less demand on higher reasoning processes. They generally take the form of written items, such as short answer, fill-in-the-blank, or completion items.

Recognition Items

Recognition items require the learner to recognize or identify the correct answer from a group of alternatives. This type of item may be used to assess declarative knowledge that has been memorized, such as the following item:

1. Which of the following is the first step in loading a camera?
   a. Set the film speed dial.
   b. Raise the rewind hatch.
   c. Open the back of the camera.
   d. Place the film cartridge in the left slot.

Or, recognition items may require the use of the higher cognitive skills involved in intellectual skills. They may require that learners apply the rules or concepts that they have acquired to recognize a correct answer:

2. Which of the following shutter speeds allows the shutter to remain open twice as long as a shutter speed of 15?
   a. 30   c. 60
   b. 4   d. 8

In the above example, answer d is correct. Even if the learner had memorized shutter speeds, the presentations of the shutter speeds as whole numbers rather than fractions, as well as the fact that 15 and 8 are not exact multiples, forces the learner to apply concept-level knowledge of shutter speeds, rather than respond from rote memory.

Although multiple-choice are the most commonly used type of recognition item, matching and true-false items also can be used as recognition items.

Constructed Answer Items

Constructed answer items require that learners actually produce or construct a response. These responses may be actions that can be observed in an on-the-job situation, actions or written responses during a simulation, or written responses in a pencil-and-paper assessment (or computer-based assessments). The difference between constructed answer items and recall items is that the constructed answer items require more than memorized responses: They require the higher reasoning of intellectual skills. These items differ from recognition items in that they place a higher demand on memory and cognitive strategies. They are also less cued and the options are less limited than in a recognition item. For example, the second example just given could be converted to a production item:

3. What shutter speed would allow the shutter to remain open twice as long as a shutter speed of 15?

In this item, the respondents not only must apply the rule that describes the relationship of shutter speeds to amount of light, they must also recall the shutter speeds that are available on a camera. As a recognition item, the possibilities were restricted to four and the options available were cued because they were listed. This support was not available when the question was converted to a constructed answer item. Generally, constructed answer items are more cognitively demanding than recognition items. They take more time to answer; therefore, the test designer can include fewer items per objective. However, constructed answer items are often more congruent with the real-life situation that may be described by the objectives and, therefore, they may be a more valid assessment.

Exercises E

Identify the following assessment items as constructed answer or recognition.

1. The situation: You are a middle school librarian working with a social studies teacher. The teacher is developing a unit on the life of the Native American in the years 1850–1900.
   The question: Based upon Dale's Cone of Experience, what would be a concrete medium/activity in learning about Native Americans? Why?
2. Match the instructional technologist to his contribution.

   _____ a. Teaching machines   1. Crowder
   _____ b. "Branching" instruction   2. Skinner
   _____ c. Programmed instruction   3. Pressey
                                               4. Dale

3. What does the number 500 on the shutter speed knob of a camera mean?
   a. The film speed of the film is 500.
   b. The shutter opens and shuts 500 times per minute.
   c. The shutter stays open for 500 seconds.
   d. The shutter stays open for 1/500 of a second.
4. Name a professional organization for educational technologists.

Assessment by Learning Outcome Types

In this section we will describe and give a number of examples of the types of items that can be used to assess each of the types of learning outcomes that you will design for.

Declarative Knowledge Objectives

Assessment of declarative knowledge objectives involves learners' ability to recall or recognize, either in verbatim or paraphrased form, information that has been presented to them. Items can also be constructed in which the learners must produce a response. Declarative knowledge items should not assess learners' ability to *apply* this knowledge, which would be use of the information as an intellectual skill; rather they should assess learners' ability to *remember* the information.

These items may take the form of recall items such as fill-in-the-blank or short answer. The information in the stem of the question may be in either verbatim form from its original instructional source (e.g., textbook, film, lecture) or it may be in a paraphrased form that is synonymous in meaning. The response may be accepted in only verbatim form, or a paraphrased response may be acceptable. When using verbatim forms the designer can only determine that the learner has memorized a response, whereas paraphrased forms may tap learners' *understanding* of the information. The following is an example of a recall, declarative knowledge question:

The component of the computer that is sometimes referred to as the "brains" of the computer is the _____ .

This item happens to be a verbatim item, using the exact language from the text. It could be carefully revised to take the form of a paraphrased question:

The brain is to a human as the _____ is to a computer.

Of course, the designer would wish to ensure that the learners were familiar with answering questions in an analogy format like that above, or he might threaten the reliability of the question.

Recognition items are also used to assess declarative knowledge objectives. These questions require the learner to recognize the correct answer. The stem and foils (options) may be verbatim from the instructional source or paraphrased. Below are examples of verbatim items:

1. *Write "T" for true and "F" for false.*
   _____ *RAM is called the "brains" of the computer.*
2. *Which of the following computer components is called the "brains" of the computer?*
   a. *CPU*   c. *RAM*
   b. *ROM*   d. *DOS*

3. *Match each term to its definition by writing the letter of the definition beside the term.*

   _____ *a. CPU*   *1. permanent memory*
   _____ *b. ROM*   *2. "brains" of computer*
   _____ *c. RAM*   *3. temporary memory*
   _____ *d. DOS*   *4. binary code*
                       5. language of communication between computer and disk drive

These items could be converted to paraphrased questions by carefully revising the language in the definitions to synonymous language:

a. Write "T" for true and "F" for false.
_____ RAM is to a computer as brain is to a human.

    Constructed answer items may also be written in the declarative knowledge domain. These items are almost always essay questions in a paraphrased form. They require the learner to select, recall, summarize, and synthesize information into a cogent form. Below is an example of a production form declarative knowledge item:

In your own words (100 words or less) summarize the similarities and differences between behavioral and cognitive theories of learning.

Discriminations

Most discrimination assessments are recognition items in which the directions ask the learners to "choose the one like this one." Below is an example of a recognition item for a discrimination.

An audiotaped message plays, "Listen to the target note that is played. It will be followed by four more notes. On your paper write 1, 2, 3, or 4 depending upon whether the first, second, third, or fourth note is the same tone as the first note."

It is possible with concrete objects that a learner might be sent out to "find one that looks like this." This type of item would be a constructed answer in which the learners have a number of real-world objects from which to choose. Here is an example:

"Go find a leaf that has this shape."

Discrimination outcomes are not typically evaluated with recall items.

Concepts

Concepts are evaluated on the basis of whether a learner can recognize or construct an example of the given concept. Assessment of concepts may be developed in three major forms. First, the assessment may involve two different kinds of recognition: (1) the learners explaining why a given, previously unencountered instance is or is not an example of a concept, or (2) the learners categorizing given instances as examples and nonexamples of a concept, with or without an explanation of the thinking processes behind the learners' categorization. The assessment may involve a constructed answer, with the learners (3) constructing their own examples of a concept, with or without explanation. Here are two examples of recognition items.

1. *Which of the following is opaque?*
   a. clear water
   b. a white net
   c. a dog in front of a TV set
   d. a frosted mug of soda
2. *Write "True" or "False."*
   _____ A mirror is translucent.

    Of course, to be a valid assessment of the learners' ability to apply this concept, rather than their ability to recall examples given in class, the options given in item *1* and the example given in item *2* should not be examples used during presentation of information or practice in the lesson.

    A constructed answer item would ask the learner to supply an instance of the concept that was not presented in class:

3. *Give an example of something that is transparent. (Do not use one of the examples that we used in class.)*

Concepts cannot be assessed with a recall item because the concept must be applied, rather than recalled, for us to say that the learner has acquired the concept. Related declarative knowledge, such as the definition of the concept, may be tested with a recall item, but this is not an assessment of the acquisition of the concept itself.

Occasionally, to obtain a more reliable assessment of concept learning we combine the recognition and constructed answer formats into an item that looks like the following:

4. *Is chocolate milk translucent?*_____
*Explain why or why not.*_____

Such an item requires the learners to recognize whether chocolate milk is an example of the concept "translucent." It also requires that the learners produce an adequate explanation of their choice. This type of item helps to eliminate the possibility that learners have guessed in answering the question.

Rules

To apply a rule or principle, learners must first determine which rule should operate in a particular situation. Then, they must apply the rule correctly. These two operations may be assessed separately or together in either recognition or constructed answer formats. For example, in applying the procedural rule relating to using negative exponents, we might ask the learner to determine which rule is appropriate by asking a recognition question:

a. *In solving the problem $1/2^{-2}$ = _____ what should you do first?*
   1. *multiply $1/2 \times 1/2$*
   2. *divide $1/2 \div 1/2$*
   3. *invert the fraction 1/2 to 2/1*
   4. *multiply the fraction times itself three times $1/2 \times 1/2 \times 1/2 \times 1/2$*

Application of a relational rule of pronoun usage could be assessed with the following recognition item:

b. *What grammar rule is violated in the following sentence?*
   The doghouse was built by Tim and myself.
   1. *subject-verb agreement*
   2. *pronoun reference*
   3. *reflexive pronoun*
   4. *no rule is violated*

The procedural rule involving negative exponents could also be assessed through a constructed answer by asking the following:

c. *In solving the problem $1/2^{-2}$ what should you do first?*

_____

And the relational rule of pronoun agreement could be assessed with a constructed answer item such as this:

d. *What grammar rule is violated in the following sentence?*
   The doghouse was built by Tim and myself.

_____

Note that these items are not declarative knowledge recall items because they demand that the learner determine which rule (from all those that the learner may have acquired) is to be used in this particular instance.

The above items do not actually assess whether the learner can actually apply the rule. The accurate application of a rule can also be assessed in both recognition and constructed answer forms. For example, recognition items would be the following:

e. *What is the answer to the problem*
   $1/2^{-2} =$ _____ *?*
   (1) 2
   (2) 4
   (3) 1/4
   (4) 16
f. *Which of the following sentences is grammatically correct?*
   (1) The doghouse was built by Tim and I.
   (2) The doghouse was built by Tim and me.
   (3) The doghouse was built by me and Tim.
   (4) The doghouse was built by Tim and myself.

One limitation of recognition problems of this sort is that due to the limited number of options, it is possible that learners could determine the answer either through guessing or elimination, while being unable to solve the problem in a production form. It is also sometimes difficult to develop plausible foils. We suggest in constructing recognition problems for assessing rule application that the designer determine the common errors that learners make in solving such problems and then create foils that represent each of these errors.

Of course, a constructed answer item involving the use of the rule would have the learners actually solve the problem using a rule.

g. $1/2^{-2} =$ _____

h. *You and Tim have built a doghouse. Complete the sentence below that tells this thought. (Do not use your name in the blank.)*
The doghouse was built by Tim and _____ *.*

You can combine recognition and constructed answer in items like the following:

i. *The directors of reading curriculum in the No Waste School District are favorably impressed by Schank and Minsky's work on "scripts and plans" and their impact on learning to read. The director develops a module about these models. He expects that the reading teachers will learn to use these models while teaching reading. When the director observes reading classes six months later, there is no evidence that the model is being incorporated into the reading instruction.*

   What principle of dissemination and diffusion have the directors violated? What might the directors have done differently?

Of course, as with assessing concepts and discriminations, the instances that are used in assessing rules should be examples that were not presented during the instruction, including practice items. If you used these old instances, you would be assessing recall of declarative knowledge, not the ability to apply the rule.

Rule use cannot be assessed with recall items because recall items test strictly recall of information, not its application. However, rule use has component declarative knowledge, such as the verbal statement of a rule or the list of steps in a procedural rule that can be tested in a recall format.

Problem Solving

Domain-specific problem solving involves the identification of the knowns and unknowns in a problem, the selection of relational rules to solve the problem, the application of procedural rules defining the order in which these relational rules should be applied, confirmation of the correct application of rules, and "fix up" if the rules have

not been correctly applied. Although the rules differ across domains, problem-solving tasks require these common steps. Each of these steps can be assessed separately as recognitions or constructed responses, or all the steps can be assessed together in a recognition or constructed response form.

Below are examples of a recognition type of item that could be used in assessment of skills in chemistry.

Below is a balanced equation.
$$2HCl + Ba(OH)_2 \rightarrow BaCl_2 + 2H_2O$$
It has been converted to a net ionic equation. Which of the conversions is correct?
   a. $2Cl^- + 2OH^- \rightarrow BaCl$
   b. $2H^+ + 2OH^- \rightarrow 2H_2O$
   c. $2H^+ + 2Cl^- + Ba^{2+} + 2OH^- \rightarrow$
      $Ba^{2+} + 2Cl^- + 2H_2O$
   d. $Ba^{2+} \rightarrow 2Cl^-$

This item is similar to the confirmation step in problem solving. The item also requires that the learners actually solve the problem, so it assesses whether they can correctly select and apply the rules. The item is somewhat less demanding than a constructed response problem that requires the solution of the problem; however, it may, in some cases, be a more practical format for assessment. Here is a recognition problem that assesses whether the learners can select from available rules those that are applicable to a particular problem:

Below is a balanced equation.
$$2HCl + Ba(OH)_2 \rightarrow BaCl_2 + 2H_2O$$
Which of the following rules for converting must you apply to convert the equation to a net ionic equation?
   a. *Rule of binary acids*
   b. *Rule of ternary acids*
   c. *Rule of polyprotic acids*
   d. *Rule of (writing) gases*

This chemistry problem is a problem-solving task rather than a rule-using task because the learner must choose from several rules and apply them in the correct order to solve the problem. However, it does not assess whether the learners can actually solve the problem. The first constructed response item *does* assess this skill.

Constructed response problems could resemble the following:

Below is a balanced equation.

$$2HCl + Ba(OH)_2 \rightarrow BaCl_2 + 2H_2O$$

Convert the above equation to a net ionic equation. Write your answer in the space below.

You could also combine the formats above in a number of ways to create an item that is both recognition and constructed response:

Below is a balanced equation.

$$2HCl + Ba(OH)_2 \rightarrow BaCl_2 + 2H_2O$$

It has been converted to a net ionic equation. Which of the conversions is correct?
- *a. $2Cl^- + 2OH^- \rightarrow BaCl$*
- *b. $2H^+ + 2OH^- \rightarrow 2H_2O$*
- *c. $2H^+ + 2Cl^- + Ba^{2+} + 2OH^- \rightarrow Ba^{2+} + 2Cl^- + 2H_2O$*
- *d. $Ba^{2+} \rightarrow 2Cl^-$*

List below the rules that you used to determine your answer.

Cognitive Strategy

Cognitive strategies are not often assessed, as they are rarely explicitly taught. However, should they be taught, their assessment can very closely resemble the assessment of problem-solving objectives. As you may recall from Chapter 4, application of a cognitive strategy requires the following steps: analysis of the requirements of the learning task, selection of an appropriate strategy, application of the selected strategy, monitoring and evaluation of the effectiveness of strategy use, and revision of strategy use as required. Each one of these steps or the total use of the strategy may be assessed. You might assess whether the learners can perform each of the individual steps by giving them a task and then prompting them to perform each step. For example, learners who have been taught a strategy for studying prose materials might be given the following problem:

The attached chapter from a geography text describes the topography, culture, economy, and politics of Peru, comparing it to Brazil, which you read about in the previous chapter. The test that you are preparing for will ask you general questions about major characteristics of Peru and how it compares to Brazil, as well as specific factual questions about the topography, culture, economy, and politics of Peru. Answer the following questions based upon the "structured notes" strategy that you have learned in the past weeks.
1. *What is the reading task?*
2. *Why is the structured notes strategy appropriate?*
3. *What overall text structure is used in the chapter? What are the clues to this structure?*
4. *What other text structures are used in the text?*
5. *Outline the chapter using structured notes. Which parts of this information should you review most carefully?*

Although this assessment evaluates whether the learner can perform each step of a strategy when prompted, it does not evaluate the learners' ability (1) to select from all the strategies that have been learned the one that is most appropriate, or (2) to perform the strategy when not prompted. You can develop such an assessment in either recognition or constructed answer formats. For example, learners who have been taught several cognitive strategies for dealing with prose may be given the following recognition item:

Jane was given the attached history chapter to study for a unit exam. The teacher has told Jane's class that they must remember the main ideas from the chapter and how these ideas relate together, but they do not need to recall all the dates and facts in the chapter. Here is a copy of Jane's notes and a videotape of Jane studying. Has she selected the appropriate study strategy? Is she applying it correctly? Circle the correct answer:
- *a. Jane has selected the appropriate strategy, but she is not applying it correctly.*
- *b. Jane has selected the appropriate strategy, and she is applying it correctly.*
- *c. Jane has not selected the appropriate strategy, but she is applying the strategy that she selected correctly.*
- *d. Jane has not selected the appropriate strategy, and she is applying the strategy that she selected incorrectly.*

You can see that the above item could be adjusted to become a combination of recognition and constructed response by asking the learners to explain their answers, or to suggest an alternate strategy if Jane's approach is not appropriate.

A constructed response item to assess the use of cognitive strategies might look like this:

Here is a chapter in a history book that you will be tested on later. The test will consist of items that require you to remember main ideas and how those ideas are related to each other. Here is an example of the type of item that might be asked: "How did the introduction of the automobile contribute to the changing morals of rural people in the 1920s?"

Select a strategy that is appropriate for studying and note-taking. Study the chapter using this strategy. When you have finished, write down a description of the strategy that you used and why you selected it, and predict how well you will perform on the exam. Turn in this description and a copy of your notes to your teacher.

In addition to the learners' written products, the instructor might use a checklist or a rating scale to observe the learners' study behaviors to confirm that they are applying the strategy appropriately. This observation might not be practical, however, if there are many students in the class or if several observers are not available.

Attitudes

In instructional design situations, it is less common for the designer to have affective objectives than cognitive objectives. One of the reasons for this is that it is more difficult to assess affective objectives than cognitive objectives. In assessing affective objectives we hope to determine learners' attitudes, values, preferences, or interests regarding objects, people, or ideas. Often in instructional arenas we hope to not only develop a skill in a particular area, such as mathematics, but also a more positive attitude or interest in that area than what a learner might have already developed. So we often evaluate (1) whether the learner has acquired a skill (the cognitive component of the attitude objective) and (2) whether the learner is now predisposed to use that skill (the affective component of the attitude objective). Occasionally, the focus of instruction is primarily to *change* an attitude rather than form a new attitude, such as attitudes toward individuals with AIDS. In these cases, there is a critical cognitive component, but

this cognitive knowledge is merely a vehicle by which to change attitudes. At any rate, we generally need to assess two things when assessing attitudes, values, or interest: (1) Can the learner perform the skill or demonstrate the knowledge desired? and (2) Is the learner predisposed to use this skill or knowledge? (With the second question, the designer tries to discern whether the learner will *choose* to use this skill or knowledge.)

There are three general types of instruments that can be used to assess affective objectives: direct self-report, indirect self-report, and observation. The first two approaches are similar to recognition items, and the latter resembles a constructed response item. Each of these types of instruments has advantages and disadvantages, which we will discuss and exemplify in the following paragraphs.

In assessment of attitudes we attempt to devise instruments that predict whether learners will behave in a desired manner (the manner dictated by the precepts of the attitude). One way to assess these predispositions is direct self-report; that is, to ask learners how they currently perform or how they would perform in the future. For example, if we had just completed a unit on protecting the environment and wished to assess learners' attitudes (as indicated by behavior) toward recycling, we might use the following questions in an instrument that is administered several weeks after instruction.

Directions: In the following questions circle the descriptor that best describes your current level of activity in recycling household products. There are no right or wrong answers, so answer as honestly as you can.

1. We recycle aluminum cans.
   Always   Often   Occasionally   Rarely   Never
2. We recycle glass products, such as bottles and jars.
   Always   Often   Occasionally   Rarely   Never
3. We recycle newspapers and other paper products.
   Always   Often   Occasionally   Rarely   Never
4. We recycle oil products, such as car engine oil.
   Always   Often   Occasionally   Rarely   Never

Or you might change the directions by asking learners to compare their level of activity prior to instruction with their current level, or you might administer one questionnaire prior to and one following instruction to determine changes. Or, immediately following instruction you might ask learners how they plan to behave in the next month.

The primary problem with direct self-reported attitude questionnaires is that people tend to respond in the manner that they believe will be seen as the most socially acceptable—in other words, in the manner they think they are supposed to respond. So such questionnaires give us a reading of how much learners think they are supposed to choose to perform in a certain way, but the questionnaire is susceptible to learners giving you what they think that you want. Therefore, we often choose to use a somewhat less direct measure than the straightforward questionnaire form described above. For example, we might devise a questionnaire that presents scenarios in which there is some competition for the main character's time or other resources, to determine the learners' level of commitment toward recycling. For example, the following items might be used to assess these predispositions toward recycling behaviors:

Directions: Read each of the following scenarios and decide the extent to which you agree or disagree with the behavior of the main character. This behavior is underlined in the scenario. Circle the descriptor that most nearly reflects your level of agreement or disagreement.

1. It is Tuesday morning and Greg is getting ready to go to school. Tuesday is the morning that the recycled newspapers and bottles must be placed in separate boxes on the curb for pickup. Greg's friend Skip arrives to walk to school with him, but Skip is in a hurry because he wants to talk to the science teacher before school. Greg decides that it won't hurt to not recycle this one week, so he throws all of the bottles and newspapers in the regular dumpster in the alley and leaves for school with Skip.

Strongly agree   Agree   Disagree   Strongly disagree

As it is sometimes difficult to discern why a learner chooses a particular position toward a behavior, you may obtain a more valid "reading" of the learners' attitude by asking the learners *why* they circled the responses that they did.

The indirect self-report is less susceptible to error from responding as is most socially acceptable than the direct self-report. However, the indirect self-report is still vulnerable to learners responding more in line with how they think they should respond, rather than how they would actually respond if they were in the situation themselves. Therefore, often it is desirable to actually observe learners' behaviors to see what they actually choose to do. For example, to assess learners' actual behavior regarding recycling, a teacher might set up a recycling center in the corner of the classroom and observe the frequency and duration of each learner's contribution to the recycling effort. A checklist instrument might be used, in which the teacher unobtrusively observes the recycling center for a specified amount of time each day over the period of a month. The checklist might look something like this:

Directions to observer: Beside each student's name for each occurrence in which the learner properly contributes to the recycling center, enter the date of the contribution.

Name	Paper	Plastic	Cans	Bottles
Sylvia Smith	2/14			
Bob Stone				
Lydia Perez				
Mildred Zuni				
Lloyd James				
Tom White				

Obviously, observational measures require a lot of time, effort, and persistence to obtain a reliable measure of an attitude for a group of learners. However, it is the most valid measure of how learners choose to perform. As assessment of attitudes is so difficult, we often try to use more than one measurement to obtain a clearer picture of the learner's actual attitude. For example, with the recycling example, we might wish to employ one self-report and one observational measure and combine the two measures in some way to get a final measure of learners' attitudes. In general these changes in attitude are not reflected in learners' grades, primarily because of the difficulty in validly measuring performance and difficulties in determining what is an acceptable level of performance. However, we commonly use aggregated group measures to assess the overall effectiveness of our instruction during formative or summative evaluation.

Psychomotor Skills

The *psycho* or cognitive portion of psychomotor tasks can be assessed in the manner we have just described. For example, many psychomotor tasks involve the learners' ability to apply a procedural rule or rules, such as the mental procedure of selecting the appropriate place to stand, the proper placement of the body, and the procedure for getting the racket back, connecting, and following through when performing a serve in tennis. There are also many declarative knowledge, concept, and rule objectives relating to following the rules and scoring in many sports that involve psychomotor skills. All of these can be assessed in a manner similar to the categories described in the previous sections.

However, the *motor* portion of these skills must be assessed in a somewhat different manner. Generally, these skills must be assessed by learners' demonstrating or producing the behavior (constructing a response). This type of assessment will be the most valid. Generally, learners are given a number of instances or trials to perform the behavior. This ensures a reliable measure. Checklists or rating scales are often used as the instrument to evaluate the learners' performance. For example, the following rating scale is based upon a portion of Rink's (1985) task analysis of the psychomotor skill of dribbling in basketball:

Directions to observer: Learner should be observed dribbling during the course of a regular game of basketball. Rate learners on the frequency of their performance of each of the desirable behaviors listed below.
1. *Effectiveness*
   * *Keeps the ball away from the defense.*
     Always   Often   Occasionally   Rarely   Never
   * *Uses the dribble to put the team in a better position.*
     Always   Often   Occasionally   Rarely   Never
2. *Efficiency*
   * *Uses pads of fingers and wrist action.*
     Always   Often   Occasionally   Rarely   Never
   * *Keeps ball close and slightly to the side of the dribbling hand when stationary.*
     Always   Often   Occasionally   Rarely   Never
   * *Keeps ball close and out in front when traveling with more speed.*
     Always   Often   Occasionally   Rarely   Never

* *Keeps knees flexed when stationary.*
  Always   Often   Occasionally   Rarely   Never

The previous rating scale was based upon the frequency of learners performing in a certain way. It might also have been based upon degrees of acceptability. For example, the anchors might be labeled *Excellent, Good, Fair, Poor,* etc., or simply *Acceptable* and *Unacceptable.* Your subject matter expert should be able to help you determine what features and anchors are most critical for the skill and the level of the learner. Other factors that might be evaluated in assessing motor skills are accuracy, time or duration, speed in completing the task, distance (such as in shot put throws), height or weight (e.g., in pole-vaulting and weight lifting, respectively).

You may choose to use recognition assessment items upon occasion, such as asking a learner to recognize whether a performer's body position is correct or incorrect. However, this assessment will not substitute for learners' actually demonstrating the movement themselves. It may evaluate prerequisite skills, such as a learner's ability to recognize correct or incorrect body motions.

*E*xercises F

Write a constructed response and a recognition item for each of the following objectives. Explain which (recognition or constructed response) is the most valid measurement of the objective and how the objective might need to be revised to reflect the measurement item.

1. The learner can locate a word in a dictionary.
2. The learner can determine the rate of speed for a train when given distance and time.
3. The learner can score a tennis match.
4. The learner can label the parts of a car engine.
5. The learner can touch-type on a keyboard.

*A*ssessment Item Specifications

Once you have a clear idea of the type of learning outcomes described by the objectives you will be assessing and the forms of items that are available to you for those objectives, you can begin to write items. All too often designers begin by simply writing items that reflect the objective. For one objective they may write items that will be included in the pre-assessment and post-assessment, and they may even construct items that can be used during practice in the lesson. It is difficult to adequately cover the range of difficulty and scope of content covered by an objective by haphazardly constructing items in this manner. The hapless designer ends up constructing very easy items for all of one assessment and makes all items difficult for a later form. Or, she might include only items that assess the ability to apply knowledge from only a small portion of the possible content to which the knowledge may apply.

For these reasons, it is most helpful to use a test design device suggested by Popham called *item specifications*. This concept has evolved from Hively's (1974) concept of test item shells for developing domain-referenced tests. In writing **item specifications,** the designer describes the characteristics of the items and the forms that responses will take. Although development of item specifications can be a bit tedious at first, designers report their use to be invaluable in on-the-job situations. On design projects in which time and resources are fairly adequate, these specifications are formally written, reviewed, and revised as part of early formative evaluation. This formal statement of item specifications is especially necessary when design and development are a team effort, perhaps with some members writing objectives and others writing the assessment items. It is not unusual on large contracts for the writing of assessment items to be subcontracted to another group. In such a case the item specifications must be precisely written because they serve as a clear statement of intention. During less ideal projects, designers may use item specifications as a mental tool in the development of assessment items.

Designers ideally develop assessment item specifications for each objective to be assessed on an instrument. According to Popham (1978), item specifications include the following components:

1. Objective
2. Description of test form
3. Sample item
4. Question characteristics
5. Response characteristics
6. Number of items and mastery criterion

Part *1,* the statement of the objective, will guide the rest of the development of the item specifications. The objectives should be composed of the components described in Chapter 4: conditions, performance, and perhaps a standard or criterion. If the criterion was not written into the objective, it should be added at this time in part *6* of the specifications. You may wish to elaborate on the objective if you feel the simple statement of the objective leaves some of the intention of the objective unclear.

Part *2,* the description of the test form, is a statement of the form that the assessment item will take. This statement may be as simple as "multiple-choice form" or as complex as "a computer-based simulation that presents graphic situations with a malfunctioning VCR, presents options for diagnostic procedures, provides output from these diagnostic procedures, and presents options to select from as solutions to the problem." The more clarity and detail that is provided in this step, the easier the following steps will be.

Part *3,* the sample item, should be representative of the type of item that assesses the ability to perform the behavior described in the objective under the conditions described in the conditions portion of the objective. The sample item should include the directions that will accompany all items of this type. The preparation of this sample item helps to clarify the intentions stated in the objective. It also may make later sections of the specifications more clear, as one example is often worth a hundred words.

Part *4,* the question characteristics, defines the qualities of the questions, pencil-and-paper assessments, scenarios in simulations, or situations that will be observed during on-the-job assessments. This section is the most critical in the entire assessment specification. In this section you specify the domain of content and range of difficulty of items to which the learner will respond. This section defines those features that must be included and those features that should not be included in the items. In all items there are factors that can be varied in the question as we generate items. It is the purpose of this section to identify those factors and the range of each factor's variation.

Let's look at an example of test item specifications from a topic that is fairly easy to define— mathematics. We will begin with the following rule-using objective:

When given a division problem with a two, three, four, or five digit dividend and a two-digit divisor, the learner can determine the quotient, including any remainder.

Given this objective, we have a number of options as to item form: matching, multiple-choice, short answer, and even true-false. In this case, we specify the test form as the following:

The test form will be short answer in which the learner will write in the value of the quotient.

Our sample item would have directions, and we have included three ways that the problem itself could be presented:

Directions: Write in the quotient of the following problems. Show your work on each problem.
1475 / 25 = _____

$25\sqrt{1475}$ = _____

1475 ÷ 25 = _____

A considerable amount is already pointed out in this objective and the sample item. We can determine that there are three factors that may vary in the presentation of the problem: the value of the dividend, the value of the divisor, and the format of the presentation of the item (i.e., which of the three possible forms shown in the sample item will be used). Not so obvious, but apparent to all who have written such items, is the relationship between the dividend and the divisor. Will the problems have a remainder, or will the dividend and divisor be selected so that their quotient will be an integer? Will the problems be so devised that the quotient can contain a zero?

Part 4, the question characteristics, will vary for this objective, depending upon the answers to the above questions. They read as follows:

1. Division problems will follow the form $y\sqrt{x}$, where x is the dividend and y is the divisor. Space will be provided above the problem for a one-, two-, or three-digit quotient. Space will be provided below the question for the partial solutions associated with long division.
2. The dividend may be a two-, three-, four-, or five-digit numeral. It may contain zeros in all of the place values, except the left-most place.

3. The divisor must be a two-digit number. It may contain a zero (i.e., be a multiple of ten), except it should not contain a zero in the tens' place.
4. The problems will be constructed so that they do not have remainders in their quotients. The problems should not result in zeros or fractions in the quotients.
5. Approximately 10 percent of the problems should have two-digit dividends, 40 percent three digits, 40 percent four digits, and 10 percent five digits.

Notice that the question characteristics give both the breadth and the limitations of the type of questions that are appropriate for this objective. Our question characteristics have also described, without specifying a fixed number of problems, the proportion of problems that should represent each type of possible problem that can be constructed using this specification. In this case, these proportions are based upon difficulty—simple (10%), medial (80%), and difficult (10%)—with the number of digits in the dividend being the determinant of difficulty. Also note that in this particular case it has been determined that items with remainders and zeros in the dividend are not appropriate.

The form of the description of part 5, response characteristics, differs depending upon whether the item is a recognition item, in which the learners select an answer, or a recall or production item, in which they enter their own constructed answers.

Recognition Item Response Characteristics

In describing responses to recognition items, the designer must outline the characteristics of the correct answer to be selected, which is relatively easy, and the incorrect answers, which is much more difficult. In describing the correct answers, it is often possible to actually list the entire pool of possible correct answers that could be assessed, such as on an instrument evaluating learners' ability to select a correct aperture size for a certain exposure. (There are a finite number of f-stops on common 35mm cameras.) On other occasions it may be fairly easy to describe the correct answer option. For example, in mathematics questions you can simply state that the correct answer, perhaps in a specific form, will serve as the correct answer option.

It is more difficult to describe the incorrect options to be used in a multiple-choice, true-false, or matching question. We suggest that you identify common misconceptions that learners may mistakenly acquire during learning and transform these misconceptions into the incorrect options to be selected. These plausible options not only create an assessment that can discriminate between skilled and unskilled performance, they also can provide data for remediation by indicating the kind of faulty learning the learner is utilizing. In many content areas, the common "bugs" have been identified in the literature of the field. In other areas, instructors with experience in teaching the content may be able to provide these common errors. If these sources are unavailable, the designer may choose to use a recall or constructed response format in the instrument or use this constructed format during early formative evaluation to obtain a number of responses. It is quite likely that among these responses will be some incorrect responses, and among these incorrect responses will be some clusters of incorrect responses that will be suitable for plausible foils (called *distractors*) in a selected response item. For our math example on division, if we used a selected format, rather than the open response that we have identified, our response characteristics could look like this:

1. Learners will be asked to circle the letter of the correct answer. Each item will include four options—the correct answer and three distractors.
2. The correct answer will be the quotient of the problem—a one-, two-, three-, or four-digit number with no remainder. The quotient should not contain a zero.
3. One distractor should represent misplacing the "place value" of the quotient (e.g., 280 instead of 28).
4. One distractor should represent a subtraction error in the partial products.
5. One distractor should represent a failure to correctly "bring down" values from the dividend while calculating partial problems during the solution.

Production Item Response Characteristics

The response characteristics for a recall or constructed answer have a different set of problems. It is fairly easy to specify the form that the answer should take. It may be difficult, however, to specify the characteristics of a correct response. The math example is fairly simple: There is only one correct answer. Most of us would agree on the answer. So the response specifications could be as follows:

1. Answers should be written in the area above the dividend. They should be mathematically correct as confirmed by a calculator and should include no remainder, including no R = 0.
2. Partial products and related subtraction should be shown and should be precisely calculated.

But suppose the question asked, "Give an example of an object that is translucent. Do not use an example from those given in the instruction." The number of possibilities for a correct answer is almost infinite, so what we must do in this case is define the characteristics of a correct response. We might use this type of definition of response characteristics:

1. Response must be a single, concrete object that has the following property: It must be an object that will allow light to pass through it but other objects must not be clearly visible through it.
2. Examples of correct responses are a frosted mug, a frosted light bulb, a pink umbrella, and sheer lingerie.
3. Correct response should not include an object that was described as translucent in the instruction, either information presentation or practice.
4. Correct spelling should not be considered a criterion for correctness.

Often, to determine the characteristics of a correct response we must construct a number of correct responses and attempt to analyze those features that make it a correct answer. This may also involve referring back to the instruction to review the critical characteristics of the skill that is being assessed, as we did when we referred back to the definition of the concept "translucent." In describing the response characteristics for problem-solving, psychomotor skills, and cognitive strategies, we may wish to develop a checklist that should be used to evaluate the learner's constructed response. A checklist will include a list of features that should be present in the response and, perhaps, features that should not be present.

The final segment of the item specifications, part *6*, describes the number of items that should be used to assess the objective and suggests a criterion for mastery. As you will recall from our discussion of objectives in Chapter 4, we believe the decision as to number of assessment items and the criterion or standard for mastery is a decision that is more logically made while devising test items than when writing the objectives. At this point in development of item specifications we have clearly described the form of the items that will be used to assess the objective, and we have a sense of the time and mental demands on both the learner and the grader. Therefore, we can make a more realistic estimate of how many items should be included for this particular objective and how many of these items should be correct for one to confidently certify the performance as ''competent'' or ''skilled'' or ''mastery.''

In systematically designed instruction, we are typically more concerned with whether a student can demonstrate a certain skill or knowledge than we are with whether the student performs better or worse than his peers. In such cases, we use what is called the **mastery approach** to learning and testing. In a mastery system of instruction, we identify for each objective the percentage of items learners must get correct for us to say they have achieved, or ''mastered,'' that objective. In determining the number of items that we will ask on a particular objective, we weigh the considerations that we discussed earlier concerning reliability and practicality. Then we determine what percentage of those items students must answer correctly for us to say that they have achieved the objective.

How do we determine this percentage? This decision is typically based upon the experience of the instructor, and is often, therefore, left for the instructor to determine. Designers, in consultation with instructors, may set this level of mastery. They should determine a figure, generally between 70 and 100 percent, depending upon the nature of the learning involved and the potential consequences of learners not learning to 100 percent mastery. Most of us would prefer that our dentists, surgeons, airline pilots, and parachute packers have learned their skills to 100 percent mastery. In this light, it is not so important that

children learn their multiplication facts to the same level of proficiency.

We may not only describe how many of the items the learner must get correct, we may also describe how many of each type or level of difficulty the learner must answer correctly. This is because it might be possible for a learner to reach a certain proficiency level over all items but still miss all of one particular type. For example, in the division example, we might describe the number and criterion section as follows:

1. Number of items may range from a minimum of 10 to a maximum of 30.
2. Mastery level is 70 percent. However, in addition, learners must get at least one correct out of the easy, medial, and difficult categories.

These descriptions are for an intellectual skill objective that involves application, so evaluation must assess the learner's ability to apply knowledge across several instances. Hence, more than one item is necessary. The percentages ascribed to the easy, medial, and difficult levels in the question specifications are 10 percent, 80 percent, and 10 percent. So a minimum of ten problems is necessary. Thirty problems is optimal as this would allow at least three items for each type of question. Production items for problem solving, psychomotor skills, and cognitive strategies may be of such length that only one item may be practically possible. Even if this is the case, the previous descriptions of questions and responses should be developed completely. For a question that requires a checklist for evaluation, the criterion of mastery may include what percentage of the criterial features must be included or what average rating must be included. The checklist may also include features that must be present or undesirable features that must be absent for the performance to be rated as ''mastery.''

Here is one more complete item specification for a map-reading skill learned by upper elementary level students.

Objective

Given a line drawing map that includes at least five landmarks and a scale, the learner can identify the landmark that is a certain direction and distance from a designated landmark.

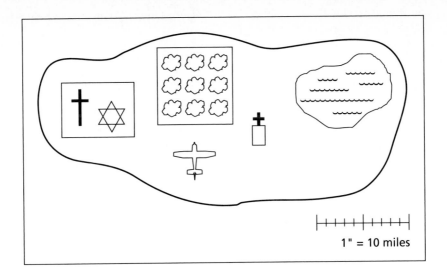

1" = 10 miles

Sample Item

Directions: Look at the map that comes with each question. Read the question carefully. Circle the name of the landmark that answers the question.

Which landmark is 5 miles northeast of the airport?

1. a park
2. a temple
3. a cemetery
4. a lake

Question Form

Multiple-choice with four foils.

Question Characteristics

1. Map should be a free form line drawing of approximately 4" × 3".
2. Five symbols should appear on each map: the designated symbol and four other symbols at various locations (see response characteristics for specific locations).
3. Question format will be "Which landmark is ___X___ miles ___Y___ of the ___Z___?"
4. X (distance) may be any value between 2 and 40 miles.
5. Y (direction) may be north, south, east, west, northeast, northwest, southeast, or southwest.

6. Z (designated landmark) may be symbols for any of the following:

temple	bridge
woods	cemetery
railroad station	airport
lake	factory
campground	school
hills	traffic cloverleaf
shopping center	park
mountains	

7. Scale should be included with one inch equal to an even number of miles up to ten (e.g., 1" = 8 miles). Increments for each mile should be marked on the scale.

Response Characteristics

1. Correct answer will be randomly assigned to any foil position: a, b, c, or d.
2. Distractors can be any of the names for the symbols included under Z in question characteristics.
3. One distractor will be the name of the symbol that is located in the correct direction from the designated symbol but an incorrect distance.
4. A second distractor will be the name of the symbol that is located a correct distance from the designated symbol but in an incorrect direction.
5. A third and fourth distractor may be (a) the name of a symbol randomly placed on the

map and (b) the name of a symbol not included on the map but easily confused with the correct symbol.

Number of Items and Mastery Criteria

1. Objective should have a minimum of eight items with one each from the eight possible directions. A maximum number of items is 24, with 3 items from each direction.
2. Mastery is 75 percent of the items correct.

Exercises G

Write test item specifications for the following objectives.

1. Given values of initial velocity, final velocity, and time, the learner will be able to calculate acceleration. (Hint: acceleration = change in velocity divided by time)
2. Given a list of the symbols for chemical elements and a list of names of the elements, the learner can match the symbol to the name. (Some of these elements and symbols are provided below.)

Aluminum	Al	Iodine	I
Barium	Ba	Iron	Fe
Boron	B	Lithium	Li
Bromine	Br	Mercury	Hg
Calcium	Ca	Nickel	Ni
Carbon	C	Nitrogen	N
Chlorine	Cl	Oxygen	O
Copper	Cu	Phosphorus	P
Fluorine	F	Platinum	Pt
Helium	He	Radium	Ra
Hydrogen	H	Silicon	Si
Sodium	Na	Sulfur	S
Uranium	U	Zinc	Zn

3. Given a list of scenarios, the learner can recognize those that represent the concept "ethnocentrism." (Definition of ethnocentrism: Tendency of a group's members to regard their own culture as superior and to regard other cultural groups as inferior.)

Assessment Instrument Blueprints

You have created item specifications that outline the characteristics of items to assess individual objectives, but usually an assessment instrument evaluates learners' performance on more than one objective. Therefore, the assessment designer must consider all the item specifications together and define the entire instrument. This plan is sometimes called an *instrument blueprint*. A blueprint includes the following components:

1. Objectives
2. Forms of items
3. Total number of items in instrument
4. Proportionality of items
5. Directions for administration
6. Scoring methods
7. Weighting of items
8. Passing or cutoff level

If you have completed item specifications for each of your objectives then you have parts 1 and 2 of the assessment blueprint completed. The next six components consider the item specifications together.

The first factor to be considered is the total number of items for the instrument. This may be to determine the number of written items, the number of simulation experiences, the number of on-the-job observations, or the total of combined items. You have already identified the number of items that you have determined to adequately assess each individual objective. At this point, when you have considered all the objectives that must be assessed with an individual instrument, you may decide that it is practically impossible either due to limited assessment time or grading time to assess each objective, even with a minimum number of items. In this case you must determine the optimal trade-off. If you must have information for each prerequisite objective in a unit or course—for instance, if you are conducting formative evaluation or your primary purpose in assessment is to determine where remediation must occur—then you may choose to break the instrument up into several assessment periods. If this is not feasible, you may decide to reduce the number of items for the more subordinate objectives and give ample number of items to the superordinate objectives, such as the terminal objective(s).

Often beginning instructional designers point out that it is unnecessary to assess subordinate objectives because if you have the task analysis correct and students perform well on the superordinate objectives, then we can assume that they can perform the subordinate objectives; and this is so. However, suppose students are unable to correctly complete items for the superordinate objectives. If you have not adequately assessed the lower objectives, you have no information as to where learning broke down. There is no simple solution to this problem. In each individual design project you must determine which is more important—efficiency of assessment or completeness of information. The purpose of your assessment can guide your decisions regarding this trade-off.

Proportionality of items, the percentage of items that come from each objective, is closely related to the total number of items. Assigning a greater proportion of items to specific objectives is one way to give attention to the more critical objectives in a unit or course. As you look at your task analysis related to a particular goal, you will note that there are certain key objectives within that analysis. These are often the terminal objectives and the next level of subordination within the task analysis. You will wish to assign a greater proportion of items to these objectives. You will also quite naturally develop more items for intellectual skills objectives than for declarative knowledge objectives, because valid measurement of concept and rule learning requires that the learner demonstrate proficiency in multiple instances.

Some test designers suggest that in situations in which you cannot include all the items you would desire you should randomly sample across the possible objectives and items. We do not recommend this practice because sampling across objectives implies that all objectives are of equal importance. As we have pointed out earlier, this is generally not true. If one must sample, we suggest that you sample from possible items within a single objective, rather than sampling from the objectives themselves.

As you wrote your item specifications, you determined the directions that are necessary for each type of item. You will also need to write directions for the entire instrument for the students and directions to administrators of the instrument. Directions to students may include the length and time limit of the instrument. Directions may also include cautions to notice particular instructions within the instrument and explain how responses should be reported (e.g., ''completely fill in the bubble with a no. 2 lead pencil''). Directions to administrators may provide information as to how to respond to students' questions, how to set up the assessment area, what materials are needed during the assessment, time length, or other pertinent information that may be necessary to ensure the reliability, validity, or practicality of the assessment.

You have already provided general information concerning the form responses should follow as you prepared your item specifications. At this point, however, you have fulfilled those specifications and have actual sample items for your objectives. This is the point at which you can create your scoring key. This key may be a simple template for items such as multiple-choice and true-false items, or it may need to be as complete and detailed as possible to alleviate errors in scoring other forms of items such as on-the-job observation, simulations, and essay items.

Since all objectives that are being assessed may not be of equal importance, you may give weight to those important objectives by including more items for those objectives. Another way to give weight to items for the more critical objectives is to value those individual items more in scoring than some other items. This is often done by making certain items ''worth'' more than others on the assessment. This is a legitimate practice, but if it is followed, it is important that the values for all items on the instrument are identified for the students.

You have already identified mastery levels for the items assessing individual objectives. At this point, you may wish to assign or suggest a ''passing'' or ''mastery'' criterion for the entire test. Instructional designers have been known to use the 80/80 criterion (i.e., in order to ''pass,'' learners must achieve at least 80 percent of the items on at least 80 percent of the objectives). While this standard may be appropriate in some contexts, it is often inappropriate. For example, using this criterion it might be possible to pass a learner who correctly answered none of the items that assessed the terminal objective(s). We suggest that in setting your criterion you use a general performance level, such as 80 percent, but that you include a minimum performance level on critical objectives such as the terminal objective. This statement might be as simple as "To pass, learners must also correctly answer (or perform) 80 percent of the items representing the terminal objective."

Many times designers must use the combined expertise and judgement of instructors and subject matter experts, as well as their own judgement in setting cutoff scores. However, in some situations it is possible to gather information over a period of time to validate and even suggest and change mastery cutoff scores. Consider, for example, courses designed for the military service for which information about student performance on tests given is available after the students leave the course for a prescribed number of years. Test designers with access to this sort of data from large numbers of students can follow the progress of students who made scores of 60 percent, 70 percent, 80 percent, and so on. They can obtain information such as superiors' evaluation of the performance of trained personnel on jobs related to the skills taught in the course. They can obtain other data, such as the trained personnel's own opinions about their preparedness to perform their jobs, accident rates, and other quality control data. Based upon this information, test designers can, over time, empirically ascertain a minimum criterion level that predicts an acceptable performance after leaving the course, and they may find it necessary to adjust the criterion level.

The careful planning that is required to create an assessment blueprint ensures that assessment designers consider the factors that may threaten the validity, reliability, or practicality of the instrument. Often you must make compromises among these factors, but in creating your blueprints you will have the opportunity to seriously consider these factors and make conscious, informed decisions.

Constructing Assessment Items

Numerous lists of guidelines for developing different types of test items have been published, so it is unnecessary for us to list all these guidelines again.

However, there are some problems that we often see in instrument design that we hope you will avoid. So, following are a few suggestions.

Across All Item Types

1. Make all language as simple as possible. The difficulty within an item should not arise from having to decipher complex or convoluted text.
2. Be careful not to "give away" the answer with language forms, such as use of singular or plural verbs or adjectives that give clues to the correct answer.

Multiple-Choice Items

1. State the stem in the form of a question or an incomplete sentence.
2. Include in the stem any words that might be repeated in the options.
3. Avoid the use of a negative in the item stem. If you must use a negative, emphasize it with underlining or boldface.
4. Make all options grammatically correct with the stem and in a similar form of speech (e.g., all verb phrases or all complete sentences).
5. Avoid, when possible, options that are subsets of each other or overlap in other ways.
6. Avoid words such as *all, always, none,* and *never* within options. Also avoid terms such as *most, generally,* and *some.* The former cue an incorrect answer; the latter cue a correct answer.
7. Make all options approximately the same length or otherwise screen out the tendency to make the correct response the longest one.
8. List options in a logical order (e.g., chronologically or in increasing or decreasing value).
9. Use the options *all of the above* and *none of the above* sparingly and only when they conceptually make sense as options.
10. To reduce the effects of guessing, include at least four options.

Fill-in-the-Blank Items

1. Use fill-in-the-blank items for only those objectives that have a unique and critical single-word answer.

2. Avoid including more than one blank per sentence.
3. Avoid the temptation to copy information verbatim from text. Paraphrase textual materials. Blanks should be key terms or important concepts.
4. Blanks should be positioned toward the end of a sentence.
5. Try not to give cues, such as *a* or *an,* in the body of the sentence.
6. Blanks should be long enough to accommodate answers and should be a standard length.

Matching Items

1. Statements or terms within a column should be as homogeneous as possible in terms of grammatical structure and conceptual content.
2. Lists of responses should be relatively short, such as less than ten responses.
3. Directions must precisely state how matches should be indicated.
4. To reduce guessing, the question should include items that will not be used. This should be noted in the directions.
5. Statements and terms within each column should be listed in a logical order (e.g., increasing or decreasing size).

Checklists

1. Directions for expected performance should be made explicit to learners.
2. Behaviors or characteristics that are to be observed should be of similar level of detail. Include only the most critical behavior(s).
3. Behaviors or characteristics that should not be observed should be listed in a separate section of the checklist and clearly identified with an emphasized negative (e.g., Cook did NOT attempt to put out grease fire with water.)
4. Behaviors and characteristics should be stated in such a way that they can be evaluated in a dichotomous manner (e.g., yes/no, present/not present, and performed/not performed).
5. Make it clear in your directions to the checklist whether and how the sequence of behaviors should be taken into account.
6. If the list of behaviors or characteristics becomes greater than ten statements, divide these into sub-divisions or categories.

Rating Scales

1. Use an odd number of anchors, from three to seven, on your scale line.
2. Statements of behaviors or characteristics should be stated in the positive.
3. If possible, label the lowest and highest anchor with descriptors (e.g., *very poor* and *excellent*).
4. For the highest anchor, describe the best you actually expect to see (not the best possibility in an ideal world), and for the lowest anchor, describe the worst you actually expect to see (not the worst scenario imaginable).
5. Behaviors or characteristics that are to be observed should be of a similar level of detail. Include only the most critical behaviors.
6. Make it clear in your directions to the checklist whether and how the sequence of behaviors should be taken into account.
7. If the list of behaviors or characteristics becomes greater than ten statements, divide these into sub-divisions or categories.

*E*xercises H

Below are several assessment items. Determine whether each follows the guidelines described in this section of the text. Rewrite items that do not follow the guidelines so that they do so.

1. *Inertia* is the _____ to _____ in an _____ _____ .

2. What is the correct aspect ratio for art for overhead transparencies?
   a. 5 : 7
   b. 2 : 3
   c. 4 : 5

3. Only about 20 percent of Japan is suitable for farming because
   a. much of the land is mountainous.
   b. of the poor soil in most of the country.
   c. most areas suffer from harsh climate.
   d. Many areas in Japan have very limited rainfall during the majority of the year.

4. Match each term in column A with the letter of the correct phrase in column B. (See the exercise on the next page.)

A	B
_____ 1. subsistence agriculture	a. a place in the desert where there are wells and springs
_____ 2. Bedouin	b. a blue-white metal
_____ 3. chromium	c. belief in one God
_____ 4. commodity	d. Muslim name for God
_____ 5. Allah	e. founder of Islam
_____ 6. Great Rift Valley	f. migrating desert herder
_____ 7. monotheism	g. evidence of the oldest human settlement
_____ 8. Muhammad	h. production of only enough crops to support one's family
_____ 9. oasis	i. valuable economic good, such as a product of agriculture or mining
_____ 10. Muslim	j. has one of the highest per capita incomes in the world
_____ 11. Iran	k. Ayatollah Khomeini was powerful political force in this country
_____ 12. Kuwait	

Summary

In this chapter, we looked at the assessment of student learning, or in common language, "testing." We began by noting that evaluation activities can be put toward two purposes: (1) assessing the learner's learning and (2) evaluating the quality of the instruction. This chapter deals with the first issue, and Chapter 16 addresses the second issue.

After contrasting norm-referenced and criterion-referenced assessment models, we found that the criterion-referenced approach generally fits the needs for assessments of products of systematic instructional design efforts.

Three types of assessments were discussed: entry skills (to see if learners are ready for the instruction), pre-assessments (to see what learners already know of the material to be taught), and post-assessments (to see what learners learned from instruction). Next, we looked at the characteristics of assessment instruments: validity, reliability, and practicality. We found that trade-offs must frequently be made among these qualities in designing assessments. Next we discussed the three major formats for assessments: observation, simulations, and pencil-and-paper tests. We looked at forms of assessment items: recall, recognition, and constructed answer. We also reviewed example recognition and constructed answer items for each type of learning outcome. This gives one a good idea of the options available for assessment items.

We described a procedure for constructing tests, beginning with development of assessment item specifications and assessment instrument blueprints. The item specifications are targeted to individual test items and have the purpose of ensuring that items are of an appropriate form and content for the objectives to which they relate. Item specifications help improve the quality of assessment items. We looked at how to develop instrument blueprints for the purpose of improving the quality of an entire test or other instrument. The blueprint builds upon item specifications and adds consideration of such things as proportional coverage of the content domain(s), number of items, weighting, and the minimum passing or cutoff level. Finally we presented a few item construction tips for different forms of assessment items. Figure 5.3 summarizes key points in this chapter.

Job Aid

1. Identify the purpose of your assessment instrument and the type of model that you will follow in its development.
2. List the kinds of assessments (entry-level assessments, pre-assessments, etc.) that are necessary and when they should occur in the instructional strategy.
3. Write the item specifications for each objective that you determined in your task analysis.
4. Write an instrument blueprint for each of the assessments identified in number 2 of the Extended Example.
5. Write complete instruments using item specifications and blueprints as a guide.

Purposes of Evaluation Are . . .

to assess learners' achievement of objectives, and to evaluate effectiveness of instruction.

Assessment Models

Norm-referenced—Developed to rank the order of learners.
Criterion-referenced—Developed to determine learners' competence on particular objectives.

Characteristics of Assessment Instruments

Validity—Does it measure what it purports to measure?
Does it sample the possible domain of items adequately?
Reliability—Is the measure objective and consistent?
Can one have confidence that scores represent learners' true abilities?

Assessment Item Specifications

Objective
Sample item
Question form
Question characteristics
Response characteristics
Number of items and mastery criteria

Figure 5.3: Summary Diagram for Chapter 5

Extended Example

Due to space limitations we cannot include all item specifications for the entire photography course. However, we have included sample item specifications and a unit test blueprint as examples of these products. You may wish to refer to the task analysis in the extended example at the end of Chapter 4.

1. *Identify the purpose of your assessment instrument and the type of model that you will follow in its development.* The purpose of the assessment will be to determine whether the learners are able to demonstrate the performances identified in the objectives, to establish competency level, and to determine what kinds of remediation are necessary. Learners will not be compared to each other or ranked. Therefore, a criterion-referenced model will be used.

2. *List the kinds of assessments (entry-skills assessments, pre-assessments, etc.) that are necessary and when they should occur in the instructional strategy.* Entry-skills assessment should occur during review of prior knowledge events in lessons in which entry level skill is prerequisite. Pre-assessment should occur prior to instruction on unit. Post-assessment should occur immediately following instruction on unit.

3. *Write the item specifications for each objective that you determined in your task analysis.* Due to space limitations we cannot include all item specifications for the entire photography course. However, we have included sample item specifications and a unit test blueprint as examples of these products.

Sample Item Specification

1. Terminal objective: Given a setting (shutter speed and f-stop) that will yield a correct exposure and a clear image, and a changing condition (lighting, motion, depth of field, or film speed), learner can determine (and explain) a correct setting, film speed, or other accommodations that will yield a correctly exposed, focused photo under the changed condition.

2. Item type: Multiple-choice

3. Sample item:
   Directions: Read the following situation. Determine what accommodations must be made to the change in the situation. Circle the answer that best compensates for the change. Then explain in your own words why you chose the answer that you did.
   You are vacationing on Malibu Beach on a slightly overcast afternoon. Your film data sheet suggests an exposure of f/8 at 1/125 of a second. Suddenly, you see Robert Redford jogging up the beach. You must have a clear picture of him to show your friends! Which of the following exposures would "freeze" Redford's action and give you a good exposure?
   a. f/5.6 at 1/125 sec.
   b. f/4 at 1/250 sec.
   c. f/4 at 1/500 sec.
   d. f/5.6 at 1/500 sec.

4. Question characteristics:
   Item form is the following:
   a. If the lighting situation is X, condition of the subject is Y, f-stop is Z, shutter speed is Q, film speed is O, and change is N, then what will be the correct f-stop and shutter speed?
   b. Lighting intensity (X) may be bright sunlight, cloudy but bright, heavy overcast, or open shade.
   c. Subject information (Y) will involve depth of field (within a shallow, moderate, or deep depth of field) and motion (static, moving less than 5 mph, 6–25 mph, or 26–75 mph).
   d. F-stop values (Z) may be 1.4, 2, 2.8, 4, 5.6, 8, 11, or 16.
   e. Shutter speeds (Q) may be 1, 1/2, 1/4, 1/8, 1/15, 1/30, 1/60, 1/125, 1/250, or 1/500.
   f. Film speed (O) may be 64, 100, 160, 200, 400, or 1000.
   g. Change (N) may be change in light intensity, desired depth of field, motion of subject, or film speed.

5. Response characteristics:
    a. There will be four foils (one correct and three distractors).
    b. Each foil will contain an f-stop value and a shutter speed value.
    c. Correct answer will be randomly assigned to a position.
    d. One distractor will change the f-stop value but leave the shutter speed the same as in the problem.
    e. One distractor will give the correct f-stop but undershoot or overshoot the correct shutter speed by one speed.
    f. One distractor will give the correct shutter speed but will undershoot or overshoot the correct f-stop by one stop.
6. Number of items and criterion for mastery: The minimum is three items with mastery of 2/3. The preferred method is seven items with mastery of 5/7.

4. *Write an instrument blueprint for each of the assessments identified in number 2.* Here is a blueprint for a photography unit on the relationship between shutter speed to exposure and focus. Following each objective is the number of items that should be used to assess that objective.

- **Objectives**—Due to time constraints, only the top three levels of the hierarchy will be assessed. Objective 3 is a performance skill that will be assessed via observation, along with performance skill objectives from other units. Objective 13 will be assessed because its knowledge is prerequisite to most of the other objectives, and if other superordinate objectives are missed, it will be important to know if learners were able to perform objective 13.

Terminal Objective

Given a description of the intensity of the light in a given situation, action, and the desired image of the subject, the learner will be able to produce an image that is correctly exposed and focused. (5)

Objective 1. Given a description of the light intensity conditions and a selection of four possible shutter speeds, the learner will be able to select the appropriate shutter speed so that the image would be correctly exposed. (3)

Objective 2. Given the action characteristics of the subject of a photo (still, slowly moving, etc.), the desired "effect" of the photo (e.g., subject clearly focused, background blurred), and a selection of four possible shutter speeds, the learner will be able to select the appropriate shutter speed so that the image will be focused as desired. (3)

Objective 4. Given descriptions of the light intensity conditions in four situations, the learner will be able to classify the situations as high, medium, or low intensity light. At least three of the four classifications must be correct. (4)

Objective 5. Given six descriptions of the action of the subject in a potential photo, the learner can correctly classify the actions as either fast, medium, slow, or still in at least four of the six situations. (6)

Objective 6. Given six shutters speeds, classify them as fast, medium, or slow. (6)

Objective 13. The learner will list all of the settings in a typical range of shutter speed settings from slowest to fastest. This list should include at least ten settings. None of the settings included should be incorrect or out of order. (1)

- **Forms of items**—Multiple-choice and matching
- **Total number of items in instrument**— 27
- **Proportionality of items**—The number of items that should be used to assess each objective is marked in parentheses beside each objective.
- **Directions for administration**—Students should not be allowed to use a list of shutter speeds, nor should they be allowed to refer to a camera. Part of the test, items related to objective 13, is to aid recall of this information.
- **Scoring methods**—A scoring key should be attached.
- **Weighting of items**—Each correct item in the terminal objective and objectives 1 and 2 should be scored with 2 points. Each item in

objectives 4–6 and 13 should be scored with 1 point.

- **Passing or cutoff level**—At least four of five items for the terminal objective must be correct, and the total score should be 28 or higher.

5. *Write complete instruments using item specifications and blueprints as a guide.* Entire test should be included here. We have omitted this due to space limitations.

Readings and References

Baker, E. L., & O'Neil, H. F. (1987). ''Assessing instructional outcomes.'' In R. M. Gagné (Ed.) *Instructional technology: Foundations.* Hillsdale, NJ: Lawrence Erlbaum.

Gronlund, N. E. (1985). *Measurement and evaluation in teaching* (5th ed.) New York: Macmillan.

Hively, W. (1974). *Domain referenced testing.* Englewood Cliffs, NJ: Educational Technology.

Mager, R. M. (1962). *Preparing instructional objectives.* Palo Alto, CA: Fearon.

Mehrens, W. A., & Lehman, I. J. (1991). *Measurement and evaluation in education and psychology* (4th ed.). Fort Worth: Holt, Rinehart, and Winston.

Morris, L. L., & Fitz-Gibbon, C. T. (1978). *How to measure achievement.* Beverly Hills, CA: Sage.

Morris, L. L., & Fitz-Gibbon, C. T. (1978). *How to measure attitudes.* Beverly Hills, CA: Sage.

Popham, W. J. (1978). *Criterion-referenced assessment.* Englewood Cliffs, NJ: Prentice-Hall.

Priestley, M. (1982). *Performance assessment in education and training.* Englewood Cliffs, NJ: Educational Technology.

Rink, J. E. (1985). *Teaching physical education for learning.* St. Louis: Times Mirror/Mosby.

Shrock, S. A., & Coscarelli, W. C. C. (1989). *Criterion-referenced test development.* Reading, MA: Addison-Wesley.

Instructional Strategy

six

Chapter Objectives

At the conclusion of this chapter you should be able to do the following:

- Describe the function of the instructional strategy stage in the instructional design process.

- Recognize and explain examples of the three categories of instructional strategies: organizational strategies, delivery strategies, and management strategies.

- List, describe, and identify examples of the expanded instructional events.

- Describe how a typical lesson proceeds from the standpoint of instructional events.

- Explain the differences between supplantive and generative organizational strategies and the advantages and disadvantages of each.

- Given a description of a strategy, identify it as more supplantive or more generative.

- Given a description of context, task, and learners, specify whether you would choose a more supplantive or more generative strategy, and justify your answer.

- Recognize examples of world-related, inquiry-related, concept-related, utilization-related, and learning-related macro-organizational strategies.

- Explain how a content could be organized according to the Elaboration Model.

Overview of Instructional Strategy Concerns in Instructional Design

Try to imagine this lesson. It is in the form of a printed booklet. The lesson begins with a graphic of a cartoon character puzzling over a sentence with nonparallel sentence construction:

To grow to the correct size, swallow the contents of the bottle marked "SMELL ME," dancing in a circle, and write your name in the air three times.

The next paragraph tells students that the lesson is on the parallel construction of sentences and paragraphs and that nonparallel structure is one of the most common problems that adult writers exhibit. This paragraph also states that nonparallel structure greatly confuses readers. Next, the lesson reviews the concepts of verb, participle, verb tense, infinitive, noun, adverb, adjective, clause, and phrase. The following page displays the rule that parallel construction requires that each element of information presented in a series should be in a parallel form of a clause or phrase. Then on subsequent pages, examples of the correct application of the rule are presented with textual information explaining why the rule is correctly applied. In addition, violations of the rule are shown with textual and graphic information explaining why the writing sample is incorrect and showing how to correct it. Then learners are presented with sentences and paragraphs and asked to tell whether they are parallel or nonparallel. When learners correctly identify nonparallel structure, they are asked to edit the sentence so that it is parallel. Feedback follows, which tells learners several correct methods of editing.

The above description outlines the instructional strategy of a lesson with a relational rule objective. You will notice that the lesson is carefully organized to support learners' cognitive processes of attention, encoding, and retrieval of information. This chapter will present you with information and practice on designing the organizational elements of an instructional strategy.

According to Reigeluth (1983) instructional strategies are composed of three different aspects: organizational strategy characteristics, delivery strategy characteristics, and management strategy characteristics. **Organizational strategy** characteristics refer to how instruction will be sequenced, what particular content will be presented, and how this content will be presented. **Delivery strategy** characteristics deal with what instructional medium will be used and how learners will be grouped. **Management strategy** characteristics include the scheduling and allocation of resources to implement the instruction that is organized and delivered as planned within the previous two strategy aspects. These strategies can be planned at the course or unit (macro) level or at the lesson (micro) level. By *lesson* we generally mean the amount of instruction that can typically be completed in one meeting (although *lessons* may also extend across two or three days, if little time is spent each day).

In this chapter we will discuss organizational strategy concerns that apply at both the lesson and course levels. In the following chapters we will focus on how to design an organizational strategy for each of the major types of learning outcomes: concepts, rules, problem-solving, cognitive strategies, verbal information, psychomotor skills, and attitudes. In Chapter 14, we will discuss delivery and management strategies.

We will begin this chapter by discussing organizational strategies at the lesson level because this level is addressed more often in instructional design literature, and then we will discuss course- and unit-level strategies.

*E*xercises A

Below are descriptions of designers' activities. Identify the activity as to which of the following the designer is preparing: organizational strategy (O), delivery strategy (D), or management strategy (M).

_____ a. Designer determines that practice questions will be completed in groups with five students in each group.

_____ b. Designer plans the clustering and sequence of the objectives for the lesson.

_____ c. Designer writes an instructor's guide that suggests the scheduling of the unit across six weeks.

_____ d. Designer determines that a lesson will be mediated with an instructor and print-based materials.

_____ e. Designer lists in the teacher's manual the materials, supplies, and equipment that will be required for the course.

_____ f. Designer decides that the lesson will follow an inquiry strategy.

_____ g. Designer determines what will occur during each of the events of instruction.

Lesson-Level Organizational Strategies

The predominant decisions that must be made at the lesson level are organizational strategy decisions: What content should be presented? How should this content be presented? What sequence should the instruction follow?

By way of introduction to these aspects of instructional strategy, we would like to outline in very general and simple terms what is believed by psychologists to happen cognitively when students learn. These mental activities may occur at either conscious or unconscious levels. You may remember this sequence of learning as it was portrayed in Chapter 1 in our discussion of information-processing theory.

First, students are immersed in a plethora of sensory inputs—sounds, sights, tactile stimuli, odors, and tastes. For learning to occur students must choose to attend to those stimuli in the learning environment that are related to the learning task (the instruction) and to ignore competing stimuli, such as the band practicing outside nearby. This process is called *selective perception*. Following perception, information is momentarily stored in short-term memory. Next, students "take in" the information in the instruction, using things they already know to help them understand the new information. During this process of relating what they already know to what is new, much of the new information is stored (encoded) into long-term memory, adding to or modifying what students already know. Either immediately or later, students retrieve from memory their new learning to answer questions, solve problems, or understand yet more new information.

The organizational strategy the designer selects should facilitate these mental operations. Instructional and cognitive psychologists have researched extensively what the characteristics of organizational instructional strategies should be. As we have mentioned previously, these characteristics may vary according to the type of objective (e.g., verbal information, concrete concepts, etc.). However, there are some general characteristics of an organizational strategy that seem to facilitate learning, whatever the objective. One of these characteristics is that the organization of a lesson should generally follow this pattern:

- Introduction
- Body
- Conclusion
- Assessment

Sometimes assessment is not included in an individual lesson but is delayed until a number of objectives across several lessons can be assessed at one time. However, the other three sections of a lesson are commonly included in most instructional theorists' lists of the episodes that comprise a lesson organization. What should be included in the introduction, body, assessment, and conclusion? R. Gagné (1972) has suggested that lessons include nine **"events of instruction"**:

1. Gaining attention
2. Informing the learner of the objective
3. Stimulating recall of prerequisite learning
4. Presenting stimulus materials
5. Providing learning guidance
6. Eliciting performance
7. Providing feedback
8. Assessing performance
9. Enhancing retention and transfer

Traditionally, instruction in training environments, such as military training, has included the following events:

1. Gain attention
2. Promote motivation
3. Give overview of lesson
4. Explain and demonstrate knowledge
5. Learner practice with supervision
6. Evaluation
7. Summary
8. Remotivation
9. Closure

We will combine these two groups to suggest a list of **expanded instructional events** that a lesson should include:

Introduction

1. Activate attention to lesson (gain attention to lesson)
2. Establish purpose (inform learner of instructional purpose)
3. Arouse interest and motivation (stimulate learner's attention)
4. Preview the lesson (provide overview)

Body

5. Recall relevant prior knowledge (stimulate recall of prior knowledge)
6. Process information and examples (present information and examples)
7. Focus attention (gain and focus attention)
8. Employ learning strategies (guide or suggest use of learning strategies)
9. Practice (elicit response)
10. Evaluate feedback (provide feedback)

Conclusion

11. Summarize and review (provide summary and review)
12. Transfer learning (enhance transfer)
13. Remotivate and close (provide remotivation and closure)

Assessment

14. Assess performance (conduct assessment)
15. Evaluate feedback and seek remediation (provide feedback and remediation)

(You may notice that in contrast to the instructional events presented by Gagné and the training lesson pattern, these expanded instructional events are stated in such a way that they reflect either what the learner does during the lesson or, as provided in parentheses, what the source of the instructional message may provide [such as a teacher or materials].) We have stated the events neutrally so they can accommodate strategies in which the predominant source of control of processing may be the learner, as well as those situations in which guidance of processing is supplied by the instruction. We have presented the instructional events in this fashion in contrast to earlier descriptions because we feel that it is very important that designers consider that these events may actually be provided by the learner; some instruction may either stimulate learners to generate instructional events themselves or assume that learners will generate the instructional events within themselves. On the other hand, the events may be provided entirely by the instruction, or they may be considered a shared responsibility between learner and instruction. The events describe instruction that is either structured or exploratory. We will return to this idea when we discuss supplantive and generative instructional strategies later in this chapter.

While these instructional events have been synthesized from a review of research, if you observe master teachers, you may see them including these events whether they have heard of them or not. Teachers probably follow this pattern because they have discovered that students who experience these events tend to learn better than students who do not. We will review the expanded instructional events in the following sections.

Introduction

The introduction prepares learners for the lesson, promoting their selective attention and bringing relevant memories to working memory, where the existing knowledge may aid in making new information understandable. In addition, the introduction establishes an expectancy for a particular learning goal, which aids the learners in employing strategies that will facilitate their learning. Although we typically imagine a presentation of some sort to be associated with the idea of an introduction, we want to ensure that you don't restrict your thinking to presentations or expository instruction. Regardless of the form of instruction, there will be a beginning for any given unit or lesson. Even when instruction is largely self-directed, the functions of the introduction and the events described within it are equally appropriate and needed.

Activate Attention. The purpose of this event is for learners to focus their attention on the learning task. As mentioned earlier, there are many stimuli in the learners' environment, so it is important that they are encouraged to attend to the part of the environment that is crucial to the learning task. We have all experienced this event when our teachers said, ''Please open your textbooks to page 43 and look at question number 1.'' Older learners may be able to supply this event for themselves, but even they may benefit from direction as to what portion of the learning task should be attended to at any one time. This is one event that can be delivered similarly across all learning outcomes. For example, learners' activation of attention for a rule learning task is much the same as their activation of attention for verbal information learning. Many older learners are able to supply this event for themselves, without much prompting by the instruction. This event is often combined with the other events in the introduction.

Media-based lessons may gain learners' attention in a number of ways: sounds, graphics (either static or animated), a change in the text on the screen, or verbal information that has high relevance to the learner or appears ''attractive'' because of its games, fantasy, or human interest aspects. For instance, a program might begin with a short segment of animated graphics to introduce a topic such as the relationship between wavelength and frequency. A major concern of designers is that they include enough stimulation in this event to draw students' attention to the learning task, but not so much stimulation that students' attention is directed only toward the attention-directing device and distracted from the learning task. In addition, designers should weigh the costs in production time and hardware requirements for highly complex presentations such as animated graphics for the attention-gaining function. Just because technology can do some very attractive things does not mean that it is always worth the cost to do so. Sometimes an alternative method that is less costly may be just as effective. Chapter 12 contains more information on gaining and maintaining attention.

Establish Purpose. As we mentioned in an earlier discussion, telling students what they are about to learn seems to facilitate learning. Knowing the learning goal can establish an expectancy in learners, arousing their interest and giving them a goal toward which to direct their cognitive energies. This event can be easily combined with the event of activating attention by stating the purpose of instruction in a way that attracts students' atten-

tion. Only rarely will designers express the objectives to the learners in the same forms that were used when designing instruction. Objectives that are stated in such formal terms may be too detailed, and they may actually interfere with students' learning. The designer may choose to state the objective in terms of a question or to demonstrate what the learner will be able to do after instruction. Or, the objective may be stated informally as, ''Today you will learn to. . . .''

In general, informing the learners of the purpose of the lesson allows them to ''sit in the driver's seat'' in the lesson. In informal, voluntary-attendance classes this may mean that the learner can choose whether to attend a particular meeting. In addition, having a clear idea of the purpose of the instruction allows learners to summon from long-term memory prior content and general world knowledge that may be appropriate to the task. It also allows them to recall learning strategies that they have found to be useful in learning similar kinds of objectives. Furthermore, knowing the purpose and goal of the lesson allows learners to monitor their own learning and to actively seek help or clarification when they sense that they are not achieving the objective. There may be occasions when you decide not to inform the learner of the objective because of the strategy you are planning. For example, if you plan to use a discovery or inquiry approach in which the learners induce a rule or concept, you may not choose to reveal the concept or rule in advance. Omitting a statement of the objective is acceptable in such circumstances, so long as you ensure at the conclusion of instruction that learners are indeed aware of what they have learned.

The specification of the objective may vary somewhat from learning type to learning type. For example, for verbal information objectives, the instruction can specify exactly what the learner must be able to list, summarize, or recall. For intellectual skills objectives, the instruction may simply describe kinds of problems learners will be able to solve, or it may demonstrate what learners will be able to do. A demonstration of the desired behavior may also be appropriate for a description of the objective of motor skills or attitude instruction.

It is not uncommon to design materials that are appropriate for multiple purposes. For example, many instructional databases may satisfy a variety of learner purposes. In such cases, the learner takes much of the responsibility in defining the instructional objectives and selecting content and sequence that are appropriate to meet these purposes.

Arouse Interest and Motivation.   We will discuss in much more detail how to create a motivating and interesting lesson in Chapter 12. In brief, it can be said that the critical aspect of this part of the introduction is that learners are informed of the importance and relevance of the lesson and/or encouraged to explore the personal relevance of the lesson. The information gained in the learner analysis will be very beneficial at this point in helping you determine why learning may be important to the learner. In courses for which attendance is voluntary, learners may have already made their own determinations as to why the course may be personally relevant, in which case the designer may only need to indicate how this particular lesson relates to the goal of the course. In cases in which learners' attendance is mandatory or a course is required, establishing the importance of the objective may be more of a challenge. In training environments for adults, indicating how attaining the lesson objectives may relate to job responsibilities may be sufficient. In other adult learning situations and in many public school environments, the actual application of learning to everyday life may lie in the distant future or even be unclear. In such cases, the designer may wish to stimulate curiosity in the objective through unusual anecdotes or graphics related to the objective. Or the designer may choose to present a challenging situation in which learning to achieve the objective will allow the learner to resolve the dilemma.

Preview the Lesson.   In this phase, the instruction itself may summarize the procedure or process that will be followed in the lesson, or the learners may choose or be encouraged to preview the lesson using whatever strategies they already possess. A very supportive lesson might provide an overview that includes a brief content outline as well as an overview of the instructional approach to be used. For example, an instructor might say the following:

In this lesson we will first review the portions of the Constitution that allocate powers to the federal government and the state government. Then we will

discuss how the contradictions in these two sections of the Constitution lead to an ambiguity that creates two camps of interpretation—loose versus strict constructivism. Finally, you will learn how to recognize positions that represent these two camps. You'll get to practice recognizing these two positions. Next week on our unit test you'll be tested on your ability to recognize examples of these two diverse interpretations of the Constitution.

As we stated earlier, being informed of the instructional purpose helps the learners feel expectant and begin to summon knowledge and strategies that will help them achieve the objective. In addition, previewing the process or procedure that will be followed in the lesson will also put the learners "in the driver's seat" by allowing them to anticipate the order and character of the instruction.

Body

Recall Relevant Prior Knowledge.   During this phase of instruction, learners are stimulated to retrieve knowledge from long-term memory that is necessary or helpful in learning the new objective. In the case of rule-learning objectives this event may be a review of concepts that comprise the rule to be learned. For verbal information objectives, this event may be an advance organizer that relates previously acquired, organized verbal information to new information that will be acquired in the lesson. In the case of motor skills, learners may be reminded of component motor skills they may have acquired that are similar to the skills to be learned. Learners may also be encouraged to recall cognitive strategies that can be employed to learn the new information.

This event may be in the form of a totally learner-controlled review of relevant knowledge in which the learner, being aware of the instructional purpose, searches memory for relevant knowledge. An experienced student beginning to read a text chapter accomplishes this event when, after reading enough of the chapter to get an idea of what it is about, he looks up from the text and thinks, "Now let's see, what do I already know about this?" Or the event may be accomplished through the instruction directly encouraging the learner to review particular prior knowledge. The instruction may encourage such a review through use of a comparative advance organizer, an analogy, an expository review, or a questioning of the learners. A comparative advance organizer (Ausubel, Novak, & Hanesian, 1968) provides a framework, or schema, for new learning by comparing a similar known entity to it. For example, Ausubel mentions that an organizer for a lesson in which Westerners are to learn about Buddhism might be a review of the features of Christianity and a feature-by-feature comparison of them to those of Buddhism. An analogy might compare a known concept (sometimes called the *vehicle*) to the concept to be learned (sometimes called the *topic*). For example, a lesson on the aperture of a camera often compares it to the iris of the human eye (relevant prior knowledge). The similarities (sometimes called the *grounds*) of the aperture and the eye might be discussed. It is also important that the ways in which the eye and the aperture are not similar (sometimes called the *limitations*) be carefully presented. An expository review might be a simple summary or restatement of relevant prior knowledge that learners have learned in previous lessons. Or, learners might be guided through questions to recall this information. An entry-level assessment followed by feedback is a rather structured method of reviewing this critical prior knowledge.

The recall of prior knowledge may also be intermixed with the next event, processing information and examples. For example, in lessons in which the learners are encouraged to carry much of the instructional burden, they might be asked to invent appropriate analogies or other comparisons as they are presented with new information. These comparisons are made between concepts that the learners already possess and new information. This mental activity is sometimes called *elaboration,* as the learner is required to elaborate on new information by searching for relevant personal experiences or memories that extend the new information by making it personally meaningful.

In addition to considering helpful and prerequisite prior knowledge, it is often useful to point out to the learners or encourage learners to consider for themselves prior knowledge that is not useful, is incompatible, or may interfere with learning of new information. The application of prior knowledge to situations in which it is not applicable is termed *negative transfer.* The application of English word order rules (particularly for nouns and their adjectives) when learning Spanish is an example of negative transfer.

Process Information and Examples.   During this event of instruction, learners encounter the material they will be learning. This information may be presented in an expository (didactic) form in which generalities such as concept definitions or statements of rules are presented prior to their examples. Or, the sequence may be more discovery (inquiry) in which the learners are presented with examples of the concepts or the applications of rules and are allowed to induce the generality. For example, if they are learning a new defined concept, like "transparent," they are often presented with the definition of the concept and examples and nonexamples of the concept. This is an **expository sequence.** Learners might, however, be presented with examples and be encouraged to induce the concept. This is a **discovery sequence.** If they are learning a rule or principle, the rule may be stated and followed by examples of the rule's application. This would be an example of expository sequence. Or, learners might be exposed to examples of the application of the rule and be encouraged to "discover" the principle or rule that is operating. Although inquiry instruction is somewhat less efficient than expository instruction, many educators feel that learners recall and are able to transfer learning more easily when it is acquired from a discovery-type approach.

Although there are many choices to be made in how this event is approached, some general patterns exist for certain types of learning. For example, motor skill instruction at this point may be comprised of a statement of the procedural rule either as a whole or in parts and a demonstration of the execution of the motor skill. Motor skill instruction seldom follows a discovery sequence. For problem-solving learning this event may be delivered by simply stating a problem to be solved; this would be a discovery sequence. Verbal information is simply stated at this point (either in the form of facts, lists, or organized information) in an expository form.

Designers have a great deal of flexibility in delivering the information and examples event, depending upon the chosen medium. Well-designed print-based materials utilizing graphics can be very effective. Audio information may be presented via audiotape, videodisc or videotape, or audio synthesizer. Audio presentation may vary from beeps to the human voice. The stimulus material may also be presented textually by a microcomputer in ways that cannot be delivered on a printed page. For instance, instead of presenting a complete block of text on the screen as it might appear on a page, the designer may plan to have only a portion of the instruction revealed at one time. Graphics may be presented as a whole or may be progressively revealed at appropriate points in the instruction. Interactive video capability (interfacing a microcomputer with a videodisc or videotape player) allows the designer to provide learners with realistic visuals. With microcomputer capabilities, it is possible to allow the learner to select the form of stimulus—auditory, textual, graphic, or video. Learners may also be allowed to select the rate of the presentation of the stimulus.

Focus Attention. Although the learner's attention was invoked at the beginning of instruction, it must be continuously refocused throughout the lesson. This event may be supplied by the learners as they highlight or underline critical parts of a textual passage, as they take selective notes, or as they mentally rehearse sections of the instruction. This event may also be supported by the instruction. For example, the instruction might ask "leading" questions to help students attend to the most critical features of the lesson. Pointing out distinctive attributes of a concept is also an example of focusing attention. (For example, "Notice that in a trapezoid only two sides are parallel.") During motor skills instruction, this event might be delivered by an instructor who reminds the learner of the procedural rule that controls the muscular actions. Textual information either in a print- or computer-based format may direct attention by using boxes, boldfacing, underlining, bulleting, or other attention-directing devices. Video segments may focus attention through such techniques as zooming-in on critical portions of a scene. Graphic overlays (such as arrows, boxes, and circles) and cues in the narration are also used to focus the learner's attention.

Employ Learning Strategies. Throughout the expanded events of instruction we have pointed out many ways in which the learners might "take charge" of the learning process. When learners do this, they are employing learning strategies they already possess. (In Chapter 11 we will discuss how these learning strategies may be taught.) The purpose of this event is to assist learners to use effective strategies, and that purpose is essentially accomplished by prompting learners to use appropriate learning strategies. Generally, during the body of the lesson, this means suggesting to learners how they might encode information so that it can be accurately retrieved. This might involve suggesting to learners that they create mental images of the content, that they take a particular kind of notes, or that they employ a certain kind of mnemonic strategy. Just as the optimal type of content treatment varies from learning outcome type to learning outcome type, so does the appropriate learning strategy. So we will suggest appropriate strategies in the following chapters on particular learning outcomes.

Although most media can prompt learners to use learning strategies, few have the capability of judging the appropriateness of their use. Print and video can suggest that learners employ a strategy, but they cannot assess whether a strategy has been used. Computer-based instruction, including interactive video, can determine if the learner is doing something (entering information); however, it is generally unable to judge the efficacy of the learners' actions. Although a human can make this judgement, it is improbable that the instructor can assess all learners' use of strategies across all events with large classes of learners. This difficulty leads many designers to design more "controlling" instruction than they would like (see the discussion of supplantive versus generative strategies later in this chapter). Designers do this to ensure that learners are getting all the assistance they need during instruction.

Practice. At this point in the lesson, the learners can be given the opportunity to actively interact with the material being learned and see if they are ready to proceed with the next part of the lesson. It is not the purpose of this event to evaluate the students for grading, but rather to (1) provide for learners' active participation in the learning process, and (2) assess how learning is progressing so that remediation may be provided if students are not learning. Inclusion of this event—more than all others—allows the learners to be active participants in learning rather than passive observers. Due to its fundamental importance this event should not be left out of any instructional sequence.

It is important that the learner have the opportunity to practice across the range of variability of the learning objective. You have defined this range in your assessment specifications, so you can use these specs to help you determine what practice should be made available to the learners. This means that they should have the opportunity to practice across the range of the content with which they should be skilled and that they should be able to practice across the range of difficulty of the objective. Although practice may be sequenced from simpler to more complex items, the need remains for the complete range of complexity to be practiced. It is not uncommon for designers to feel that since learners are just encountering the content they should not be required to practice at the level of complexity they will be tested on later. However, this decision is predicated on the assumption that learners will experience spontaneous learning over time. Although this is feasible, the active practicing of new learning (especially at more complex levels than learners have been exposed to) should not be left to chance. Novices in a content area may not have the experience to imagine how the content might be applied; consequently, provision of instruction with explicit practice items is very important.

The particulars of how practice is provided will vary considerably from learning type to learning type. For example, during concept learning, students may be given a variety of examples and nonexamples of the concept and be asked to identify those which are examples of the concept, or they may be asked to supply their own examples of the concept. For rule learning objectives, students may be asked to state the rule or principle they are learning and then demonstrate the application of that rule. Response may be elicited when students are learning problem solving by giving them a problem to solve and having them solve it or by having students state which rules seem appropriate for the solution of this particular problem. In learning verbal information, students may be asked to state, summarize, recognize, or list part or all of the information they are to learn. Students learning psychomotor skills may be asked to recall the procedural rule that controls the skill as well as to demonstrate the whole or part of the psychomotor skill.

When operating under the principles of behaviorism, designers created practice that was almost ''error-proof,'' anticipating that a benefit of totally successful practice would be more motivated learners. More recently, designers have tended to design practice so that it might evoke any misconceptions that learners might have developed about the new information. This direct addressing of common misconceptions actually seems to pique learners' interest even more than successful experience. So, as you design the practice event, you can consider the ways that learners might go wrong with the content—how learners might overgeneralize or undergeneralize a concept, or how learners might draw incorrect inferences from verbal information. Then you can design practice experiences that will allow them to confront these ''bugs'' in their learning.

Performance can be elicited in a number of well-known ways. Practice items, whether true/false, multiple choice, short answer, or essay, are probably the most widely used. Simulations, role playing, or even on-the-job performance opportunities are all methods of practicing learning. Learners should have several opportunities to practice the performance related to a specific objective to promote overlearning and automaticity of skilled performance. In addition, it is often very useful to include an extra set of practice problems for learners who may have difficulty during the first set of practice exercises. These learners may benefit from the feedback and need another opportunity to practice their skills.

Microcomputers are particularly good at providing the practice event because of their interactive capabilities. Computers can interact with all learners, asking them to respond and then checking the accuracy of the learners' responses. Software can be designed so that learners are required to respond in a particular way, eliminating the possibility of learners ''coasting'' on other learners' performance, as can happen in group-based discussions and practice. A limitation of computer-based software, however, is that it is not generally ''intelligent.'' That is, it cannot think or learn on its own. The computer's lack of intelligence has an impact on eliciting performance because the designer must be cautious in the types of questions or other response-eliciting situations the instruction poses. If learners are to be provided with accurate and meaningful feedback, the designer must ensure that the questions or situations posed will produce responses that can be judged by the microcomputer. Intelligent tutoring systems can be developed to deal (to some degree) with production responses, such as short written answers. However, these systems can be very expensive and time-consuming to develop, so they will not be easily available across all content areas for some time. For practice in which open-ended responses are required, a teacher or other human will generally be needed to assess the appropriateness of the learners' responses.

Evaluate Feedback. Feedback is so important that we couldn't even talk about the previous event without mentioning it. Often educators use the term *feedback* to refer to the positive reinforcements, such as ''good work,'' ''good for you,'' and other responses to learners' efforts that may not be necessarily contingent on the appropriateness of learners' responses but are constructed more to encourage, addressing the affective aspects of learning. Although this type of reinforcement can be very important, the type of feedback that we are referring to in this event is called **informative** or **informational feedback,** rather than motivational feedback. The purpose of informative feedback is to give learners the opportunity to consider information about the appropriateness of their responses during practice. Feedback is a critical event in instruction, and it is one that is too often slighted or overlooked. Several types of information can be provided through feedback:

1. Learners may simply be told if they are correct or incorrect. This type of feedback seems particularly appropriate for verbal information learning.

2. If learners are incorrect, they may be given the correct answer. This type of feedback is often used with verbal information and intellectual skills objectives.

3. Learners may be given information so they can determine if they are right or wrong and why

they are right or wrong. This type of feedback is particularly appropriate for intellectual skills learning.

4. Learners may be given information about the faulty solution strategies they are using, with hints for more appropriate strategies, without being explicitly told whether they are correct or incorrect.

5. Learners may be shown the consequences of their responses. This type of feedback can be used for problem solving or principle learning, particularly with instruction that is delivered via a simulation.

6. Particularly with psychomotor skills, learners may experience proprioceptive (internal sensory) feedback during or after demonstration of a skill. Learners may have to be taught to recognize these sensory cues. Videotape replays, which allow learners to see themselves, are a form of augmentation of sensory feedback.

7. Learners may be given cumulative information on their progress during practice. For example, they might be told what pattern of errors they are making or how close they are to reaching mastery or a pre-stated criterion of performance.

Feedback may be coupled with second tries with practice items so that if learners are incorrect they can use the feedback to correct the error on that very problem. For example, all the feedback types just mentioned (except 2—providing the correct answer) may be used in conjunction with several tries so that learners have the opportunity to apply the feedback to correct their own learning. In contrast to assessment, during practice and feedback one expects learning to continue through the practice and feedback events. In other words, practice and feedback are formative, not summative.

As you might surmise, the computer is especially good at providing individualized and immediate feedback to learners. Unlike most other instructional media—other than a human tutor—the feedback learners receive can be adjusted to the answers they gave. With other types of media, such as workbooks and conventional textbooks, you will probably be restricted to the "question and answer" method of feedback. Live humans are the best at communicating feedback because of the nature of production responses in which many answers may be equally correct. However, as we mentioned during our discussion of learning strategies, it is unlikely that an instructor can give tailored feedback to each learner in a class after each practice response. This limitation often leads designers to provide more information than some learners might require to ensure that enough feedback is given.

Conclusion

The conclusion events allow learners to review and elaborate recent learning so that it can be available for further application and use. As time is often short at the end of a lesson, designers have a tendency to abbreviate these events. However, these events are critical in that they support learners' attempts to synthesize and consolidate new learning.

Summarize and Review. The purpose of the summary is to ensure that the learners recall and synthesize the critical parts of the lesson into a memorable and applicable whole. New learning can be quite confusing, so it is helpful at the conclusion of the lesson to remind learners of what they have just learned. As with many of the other instructional events, lesson summaries may be constructed by the learner or provided by the instruction. It is important that summaries provided to learners not include any new information but rather restate the gist of the lesson itself. Often with transitory instruction, such as computer-, video-, or lecture-based instruction, learners can be provided (or encouraged to produce) a permanent and portable summary in the form of print-based notes.

The actual content of the summary will vary depending on the learning outcome. For example, a review of a procedural rule might be a restatement of the steps in completing the procedure or a demonstration of the procedure itself. A review of verbal information might include a restatement of a topical outline of main points or a clustered review of paired information, such as acronyms and the words they represent. A summary of concepts might include a restatement of the definition or the critical attributes of the concepts that have been learned. One particularly useful technique for aiding summarizing is called a *graphic organizer;* it visually and spatially shows the main points in a lesson and how those points are related to one another. You have encountered these graphic organizers at the conclusions of some of our chapters. Designers have found that providing learners with partially completed graphic organizers that the learners must complete is more effective than providing learners completed organizers or asking them to create the summary from scratch.

Review involves extended practice of the new learning. It can occur in the lesson itself, as an outside class assignment, or as the "review of prior knowledge" event in subsequent lessons. Review may also involve a cumulative practice over several lessons, which allows learners practice in distinguishing among newly learned facts, concepts, or rules. Learners also practice selecting the appropriate information, concepts, or rules from their new repertoire of knowledge to apply to specific situations. It is this ability to appropriately select and apply new learning that supports its integration and usefulness. In the case of verbal information, intellectual skills, motor skills, and perhaps cognitive strategies, spaced (over time) practice of the new learning can facilitate retention and recall. Of all the learning outcomes, verbal information learning and psychomotor skill learning seem to require the most review. Older and more capable learners may be able to construct their own review schedules and their own review items. Younger and less capable learners generally need more assistance in preparing and conducting reviews.

Transfer Learning. The process of transfer—the application of new knowledge and skills to a variety of real-life situations and future learning tasks—can be enhanced by giving learners opportunities to apply their learning to a variety of circumstances. Transfer is particularly critical for learning concepts, rules, problem-solving, cognitive strategies, psychomotor skills, and attitudes. The primary transfer task for learning verbal information is the ability to draw correct inferences from the information. Transfer of learning can be described in terms of a continuum from what is termed *near transfer* to what is termed *far transfer.*

Near transfer is the application of learning in a way similar to the manner in which it is applied during learning and to situations similar to those in which it was exemplified and practiced. Far transfer is the ability to apply learning in different ways and in situations that are very different from those in which the learning was acquired and practiced. For examples of near transfer and far transfer, let's consider an objective in our course on photography. One of the objectives in our course is "Given a correct exposure and information on aperture setting, shutter speed, and film speed, and given a description of a change in the situation, the learners can determine a change in aperture, shutter speed, and/or film speed that can compensate for the change." Examples of the changes that the learners encountered in learning were adjusting to the subject's change in motion, the light's intensity, and the desired depth of field. Questions that assess the learners' ability to solve problems similar to those practiced and defined in the objective are near transfer. A far transfer task, as envisioned by Bromage and Mayer (1986), is to describe a situation in which one or more of the components in a camera are malfunctioning and the learners must think of a way to compensate for this malfunction.

With regard to near transfer, the major goal of the transfer event is to enable learners to generalize their new learning to situations in which it is appropriate but not to overgeneralize the learning to situations in which it is not applicable. This ability requires that learners can recognize key features of a new situation that are similar to the critical features of similar situations that they have learned. For learners to be able to recognize the features in a situation that calls for the application of specific skills, they must have experienced many situations in which the noncritical features of the situation varied greatly and the critical features were present. In addition, learners must have been either explicitly instructed or been encouraged to explicitly elucidate the critical features of a task that call for application of a particular skill or body of knowledge. For example, learners will be more likely to appropriately transfer cognitive strategies to generalized situations if they are explicitly informed or are encouraged to explicitly express the characteristics of a learning task that might call for a particular strategy. Encouraging learners to create "rules of thumb" to determine whether partic-

ular new learning is appropriate can promote their ability to apply this new learning. Transfer activities may involve asking students to find examples or apply rules in real-life conditions they would anticipate encountering subsequent to instruction.

The factors that contribute to far transfer are somewhat less clearly defined by instructional research. However, Clark and Voogle (1985) suggest several activities that may influence far transfer. These include (1) encouraging learners to develop their own examples and applications, (2) analogies between new learning and prior knowledge, and (3) paraphrases of verbal information lessons. Other aspects of transfer are well described in Butterfield and Nelson (1989).

Remotivate and Close. As you will read in Chapter 12, learners' attitudes toward learning and new content will greatly influence how well the learning will be acquired initially and how well that learning will be retained. That is why we suggest that the lesson conclude as it began: with a statement, in terms that are relevant to the learners, of the importance of the learning. In particular, learners should be encouraged to explore how they may use this new learning immediately and what future applications they envision. Note how this event supports transfer by allowing learners to consider possible situations to which their new knowledge may, indeed, be transferred. It is not uncommon for learners to be uncertain of the applicability of newly acquired information, so the instructor should be prepared to supply much of this event for the learners. It may also be helpful to point out the learners' success with learning the content to promote their satisfaction with their own learning.

The function of closure is twofold: (1) to let the learners know that, in fact, the lesson is over and (2) to conclude the lesson on a positive note. Anyone who has ever written a piece, whether essay, research review, or novel, will remember the difficulties in writing a satisfying conclusion. However, it is important that learners are cued that the lesson is completed so they can consolidate their thoughts and relax their mental efforts. In a video this is often simply cued with a change in music and rolling the credits. In a textbook, it may be signaled with a listing of references. In teacher-lead instruction, closure statements may be as simple as "You've all been very attentive; we'll study a related concept tomorrow. Class is dismissed." You will note how ending the lesson positively may seamlessly merge with comments regarding students' successful learning in the remotivation phase. This merging might be accomplished by adding "I can tell that you are able to use concept *X* very well now" to the previous statement.

Assessment

Assess Performance. The purpose of this event is to assess whether learners have achieved the objective(s) of the instruction. Assessment information is critical to the designer, instructor, and the learners. Designers use the information to continuously revise instruction. Teachers use the information to guide their plans for remediation and scheduling. Learners use the information to evaluate the efficacy of their study strategies as well as to guide their search for remediation. This event differs from practice in two ways: (1) The decisions made as a result of the measures are more summative (conclusive) in nature, for they lead to grading, and (2) assessment instruments are developed more carefully than practice to obtain a reliable and valid measurement of learning. The way the attainment of an objective is assessed is closely related to the statement of the objective. This relationship will be discussed further in the following chapters. As is discussed in Chapter 5, pencil-and-paper tests are only one of many methods of assessing learners' ability to perform a required skill. Assessments may include on-the-job performance and simulations of various levels of realism and complexity.

The assess performance event may not occur during the lesson itself. As mentioned earlier in the chapter, it is a common practice to combine the assessment of several objectives into one assessment period, such as a unit test. It is important that if assessment is delayed then review is planned particularly carefully. Also, when many objectives are assessed together, instruments can become quite lengthy, and designers may be forced to make tough decisions between practicality and reliability or validity. Consequently, careful planning for the assessment event may result in the specification of more than one assessment period so that adequately reliable and valid measurements can be employed.

Four media capabilities that are especially helpful for supporting the assessment of performance are the ability to do the following: (a) randomly select items from a composed test pool, (b) present a variable number of items depending upon the learners' responses, (c) score tests easily to provide feedback to learners as quickly as possible, and (d) score and analyze the scores of a number of students.

The first capability allows the designer to assess a number of students without having exactly the same test for each student. This capability is especially important when students are proceeding at their own pace and the designer wishes to guarantee some degree of test security.

The second capability, the ability to present a variable number of items, allows the designer to create a test with a composition that can be changed during execution. Such tests are called *adaptive tests*. For instance, the designer could create a test that would continue to ask questions at a certain level until the learner gets a certain proportion correct or misses a predetermined number of questions.

The third capability, the ability to score tests and provide immediate feedback, is important to promote timely remediation for learners, as well as to respond to learners' desire to have immediate information on their performance.

The final capability, the ability to store and analyze data, allows the designer to establish a management system for the teacher/trainer and to collect and organize data with regard to the effectiveness of the instruction.

Among the varieties of media from which to choose, two seem best suited to supply these capabilities: first, teachers, in conjunction with print, and second, computers. Unfortunately, teachers cannot accomplish the task quickly when many learners require assessment during one time period, which makes a computer an ideal medium for many types of assessment. You will remember that one limitation of computer-based assessment is that it is generally unable to precisely evaluate production-type answers. Often, in such cases a computer may collect and compile learners' responses, but a teacher or other human is ultimately required to judge the adequacy of those responses. Other media, such as video, are used when learners must encounter realistic images in their assessment situation.

Evaluate Feedback and Seek Remediation. The feedback learners receive after assessment is often more cumulative—such as a percent correct or a number of objectives mastered—than the feedback received after practice. Although item-by-item feedback may be provided upon request, it is not generally designed into the strategy, as the feedback is planned to be more informative than corrective. This evaluation usually leads to a conclusion on the learners' (and often the instructor's) part, such as a grade or an overall judgement of the learners' mastery of the content.

The designer may plan for remediation activities for learners, such as additional practice sets or another presentation of the body of the instruction in an alternate form (e.g., with a more concrete explanation or a different media). Remediation may address specific objectives, or it may address the learning strategies that the learners apparently failed to employ. This remediation plan may be optional, with recommendations to the learner, or it may be program-controlled, requiring the learner's completion before proceeding to subsequent lessons.

Hints on Sequencing the Expanded Events of Instruction

A typical lesson generally follows this sequence of events:

1. Introduction
2. Body
3. Body
4. Body
5. Conclusion
6. Assessment

The repetition of *body* indicates that in lessons that have several objectives, the objectives may be grouped in such a way that after the lesson introduction, information pertaining to the first group of objectives is presented and that skill is practiced; then a second group of objectives is presented and practiced, and so on through the groupings of objectives. The exact number of objectives that should be grouped together for presentation and practice depends upon the relationships of the objectives, the instructional context, and the characteristics of the learners. After all groups of objectives have been taught, the lesson conclusion is

provided. Then the assessment of all objectives may be conducted. Sometimes assessment is not delivered during a single lesson but is delivered at the same time for several lesson objectives in the form of a unit test. This procedure seems to create efficient instruction.

Although the order from introduction to body to conclusion rarely varies, the order of particular items within these events may not follow their numbered order or may be seamlessly combined into fewer perceivable events. They may even be interspersed across lesson sections. For example, the event involving recollection of relevant prior knowledge may start in the introduction and then be addressed more specifically in the body of the lesson. These events should be used creatively and considered a guideline rather than required protocol.

As mentioned earlier in the chapter, the instructional events may be provided by the instruction, prompted by the instruction, or provided by the learner. There are advantages and disadvantages to having the lesson control the learners' processing or in expecting the learners to control their own processing. We will discuss these advantages and disadvantages in the next section on supplantive versus generative organizational strategies.

*E*xercises B

Provided below are descriptions of several of the expanded instructional events. Decide which event (or events) is being delivered in each description.

1. A frame states that this lesson is about the "lifeboat ethic," a concept in the study of world ecology. Another frame tells students that they will learn the definition of "lifeboat ethic" and learn to recognize examples of its use.

2. A lesson asks students to recall situations in which lifeboats are used. Instruction reminds students of a previous lesson's description of the relationship between (1) waste of natural resources and (2) a nation's dependence on other countries for raw materials.

3. The first frame of the lesson shows an animated graphic, a cartoon of a globe sinking into an ocean with people rowing away. Some people are swimming in the ocean, and some are

drowning. Boats are capsizing. Some people seem to be marooned on the sinking globe. A title, *Lifeboat Ethic*, is printed on the frame.

4. A frame points out that the "lifeboat ethic" has been used in this lesson to discuss exploitation of natural resources but that it can apply to national, international, and interpersonal relations in other areas. The lesson suggests that students review current periodicals to find examples of the "lifeboat ethic" in international monetary systems, military relations, and so on.

5. A frame presents a definition of "lifeboat ethic" and subsequent frames present examples in worldwide use of natural resources.

6. Scenarios are given and students are asked to classify them as examples or nonexamples of the concept "lifeboat ethic."

7. Information is given as to whether students' responses during event 6 were correct or incorrect. If they were incorrect, students are told what the correct answer is and why that answer is correct.

8. Examples and nonexamples of the "lifeboat ethic" are given, and students are asked to highlight portions of the scenarios that give clues as to whether the scenario is an example or nonexample. The student may check a later section to receive a more detailed explanation as to why the scenario is an example or nonexample of the "lifeboat ethic."

9. Students are presented with scenarios that are examples or nonexamples of the "lifeboat ethic," which they are to classify. No cues or explanations are given. After students have answered all questions, they are told which questions they missed, and this information is recorded on score sheets.

Supplantive and Generative Strategies of Instruction

Several years ago we attended a discussion between Robert Gagné, one of the pioneers of the field of instructional design, and Claire Weinstein,

a well-known researcher and writer in the area of learning strategies. The focus of the discussion was whether strategies should be "built into" the learner or into the materials. The issue that they addressed is critical to the field of instructional design because it asks, "Which should be the locus of control of information processing, the instruction or the learners?" Although most of us would immediately respond that it is most desirable that the learners themselves initiate and control their own processing, upon careful consideration one will notice that *any* instruction is constructed to guide learners' processing to some extent. For example, we do not throw jumbled words at learners for them to decipher; we organize them into sentences and paragraphs. We do not leave students to imagine what a new component of equipment looks like; we provide an illustration. We do not inundate novice learners with unstructured databases from which to interpret procedures; we present procedural steps in a carefully selected sequence. So the question for designers is not which is preferable, learner processing or lesson control of processing, but where on the continuum of locus of processing control instruction should fall.

The availability of potentially exploratory learning environments, such as hypermedia and some intelligent tutoring systems, has created situations in which implementation of many of the key instructional variables can be placed in the hands of learners. High technology is said to empower learners from a tool-using standpoint so that the learner learns through magnification of her own intellect, not through outside manipulation of material to be learned. So the question of locus of processing control has become even more pressing because we have the capability to mediate instruction in which the learner has much of the initiative (i.e., control) in the learning process. This option has stimulated some instructional designers to consider highly generative instructional strategies, which were not seriously utilized by many instructional designers in the past. **Generative strategies** (Wittrock, 1974) are those approaches in which learners encounter the content in such a way that they are encouraged or allowed to construct their own idiosyncratic meanings from the instruction by generating their own educational goals, organization, elaborations, sequencing and emphasis of content, monitoring of understanding, and transfer to other contexts. In other words, learners "control" the preponderance of information processing during learning by providing much of the events of instruction themselves. Wittrock's model of generative learning emphasizes the critical role of an active learner in the learning process. He subscribes to the "constructivist" view of learning, the position that meaning is not transferred to the learner during instruction, but that the learner must actively construct meaning for learning to occur. It is called the *generative* model of learning because Wittrock emphasizes the importance of the learner generating associations between new information and prior learning, a process that is enhanced by the learner carrying the major responsibility for the events of instruction.

The outgrowth of Wittrock's model has been studies that contrasted supplying learners with "provided instructional devices" (i.e., instructional "control" processing), such as summaries, headings, underlining of key ideas, and pictures, which indicate the relationships among ideas for the learner, with asking the learners to generate these devices for themselves (e.g., asking the learners to generate summaries, headings, underlining, pictures). Generally, studies of this sort have found that learners perform better on comprehension and recall tests if they have generated associations for themselves rather than having the associations supplied. Often, this effect is explained in terms of depth of processing (Craik & Lockhart, 1972). The more the learner is required to relate information to his own cognitive structure, the greater the depth of processing, which results in better learning. In addition to supporting better learning, such strategies have been purported to be highly motivating by placing learners in an autonomous situation in which they may pursue their own specific interests regarding the content. Generative instructional strategies also allow learners to engage, practice, and refine their learning strategies. However, this approach places a high cognitive demand on learners' working memory by requiring them to acquire new learning while taking the responsibility for structuring that learning situation. This could possibly lead to cognitive overload and emotional frustration. Due to the large amount of processing by the learner, generative learning may require a large amount of time. Its success may also be highly dependent

upon the learner's prior knowledge of the content and the breadth of learning strategies the learner possesses. Because of the very nature of the strategy, learning outcomes from such an approach can be idiosyncratic and interpretations of content can be highly personal.

Traditionally, instructional designers have elected to use relatively supplantive (sometimes labeled *mathemagenic*[1]) strategies within their instruction. This instruction, as compared to generative instruction, tends to supplant (Salomon, 1979) more of the information processing for the learner by supplying all or part of the educational goal, organization, elaboration, sequencing and emphasis of content, monitoring of understanding, and suggestions for transfer to other contexts. In other words, **supplantive strategies** explicitly and overtly provide much of the events of instruction, actively gaining learners' attention, informing learners of the objective, explicitly providing a preview of the lesson, and so on. Supplantive instruction tends to conserve learners' cognitive capacity for acquiring skills and knowledge related to the learning task by limiting the amount of responsibility they must carry for structuring the learning situation. It may lead to more focused and predictable learning outcomes. It may be more efficient than generative learning strategies: More material may be learned in a shorter period of time. Learners with a limited level of prior knowledge and a limited repertoire of learning strategies might be expected to be more successful with this approach. However, as the strategy engages fewer of the learners' mental processes, it can lead to less depth of processing, and consequently less complete learning. It may lead to less personally meaningful learning. It may appear too contrived and sterile to the learner and be less challenging and consequently less motivating to some learners. Over time it may "short-circuit" learners' critical information-processing skills to the point where learners are dependent rather than independent learners.

Although the comparable advantages of these two diverse forms of environment have not yet been thoroughly empirically investigated, several

---

[1] *Mathemagenic* refers to processes or events that stimulate learning. The term, coined by Ernest Rothkopf in 1970, is composed of two Greek roots: *mathe* (learning) and *genic* (giving birth to).

bodies of theory and research suggest that neither approach is universally superior, but that there are many factors that may influence the efficacy of one instructional approach over the other. Among the related research areas are the following: research on generative versus mathemagenic teaching methods (Jonassen, 1985; Osborne & Wittrock, 1985; Wittrock, 1974), learner control in computer-based instruction (Hannafin, 1984; Steinberg, 1977; Tennyson, 1984), discovery versus expository learning (Herman, 1969; Ray, 1961), and cognitive capacity and allocation of mental resources (Burton, Niles, & Lalik, 1986; Britton, Westbrook, & Holdredge, 1978; Craik & Lockhart, 1972; Duncan, 1980; Watkins, 1983).

This research and theory suggests that indeed the decision as to whether to design instruction with more generative or more supplantive strategies is not a simple one. As illustrated in Figure 6.1, the decision is like a balancing act. Generative strategies require greater mental effort and consequently lead to greater depth of processing that results in better learning. However, cognitive capacity in the form of working memory is limited, so if learners are required to carry too much of the instructional burden, they may be overloaded and unable to learn. So, when designing organizational strategies, the designer must balance these two competing demands: (1) the need to require sufficient mental effort to lead toward learning and (2) the need to support the learners' processing

sufficiently in a way that does not overload their working memory.

Factors within the learners, the learning context, and the learning task itself may suggest to which side of the balance the strategies should be tipped in any particular case. For example, if time is limited, one might expect that a more supplantive strategy might be more effective, as generative strategies can be expected to be more time-consuming. If learners' prior knowledge on a particular content level is high (for instance, if they are about to learn a problem-solving task and have already learned the related rules required in the problem-solving task), a more generative strategy may be more effective. If learners are generally lower aptitude then they are more likely to have limited learning strategies, so a more supplantive strategy may be designed. If you were designing instruction for a training environment in which the primary goal is that the learners are able to perform certain skills, and less that the learners become more facile learners, then you might conclude that a more supplantive strategy might be more effective. However, if you were designing for a public school environment in which one of the primary goals of instruction is the acquisition of learning strategies, then generative strategies should be included when possible to allow learners the opportunity to practice these strategies. There are additional situations that might also help the designer determine which side of the balance is more

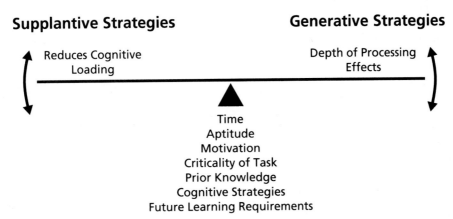

Supplantive Strategies   **Generative Strategies**

Reduces Cognitive Loading   Depth of Processing Effects

Time
Aptitude
Motivation
Criticality of Task
Prior Knowledge
Cognitive Strategies
Future Learning Requirements

Figure 6.1: The Balance of Generative and Supplantive Strategies

appropriate to the situation, such as the motivation level of the learners, the philosophy of the institution, and the facility of the teachers/instructors with particular strategies.

We have taken care to describe the expanded events of instruction neutrally with regard to generative and supplantive strategy options. Using the events as we have labeled them, instruction can be designed so that the learners take more responsibility for their processing or so that the instruction itself guides the learners' processing. In the following chapters we will continue to present these options so that you will be prepared to design on either end of the continuum or somewhere in the middle. But before we move on to describing the events of instruction for all the learning outcome types, we will briefly discuss organizational strategies that are appropriate at the macro level. We will discuss how to organize units or entire courses.

*E*xercises c

1. Given below are descriptions of events that occurred during a lesson. Identify whether the strategy leans more on the side of a generative strategy (G) or more on the side of a supplantive strategy (S).

    _____ a. Students underline key points in a print-based lesson.

    _____ b. Students create their own mythical countries that exemplified the concept "fascism."

    _____ c. Students watch a video-based summary of factors leading to the Civil War.

    _____ d. Students select from a number of instances those that represent the concept "loose constructionism."

    _____ e. Students run a number of example computer programs using subroutines and determine which procedural rules must be used to make programs that don't "crash."

2. Following are descriptions of two instructional strategies to teach the same relational rule—the relationship of pitch to length, tightness, and thickness of a plucked

string. The strategies are labeled *A* and *B*. One of the strategies is more generative; one is more supplantive. Write the type of strategy in the blanks below, and explain your answers.

   • Strategy A _____
     (Generative or Supplantive?)
   • Strategy B _____
     (Generative or Supplantive?)

Strategy A

Materials:
Violin, other stringed instruments, tom-tom and other drums, whistle with sliding stopper, piano, xylophone, elastic string, and rubber bands
Procedures:
Teacher statement: We've been talking in this science unit about the "bounce of sound." You will remember that sound is caused by the vibration of the molecules in an object. For instance, when I strike this bell, I set the molecules in the bell vibrating. This causes sound. Yesterday we discussed what causes the pitch of a vibrating object to be low or high. The pitch of the sound an object makes when struck or plucked depends upon how fast the molecules in the object vibrate. Remember when we talk about high and low pitch (demonstrates) we're not talking about loud and soft (demonstrates). A high pitch can be loud (demonstrates) or soft (demonstrates).

Today we'll talk about why when some objects are struck their molecules vibrate more rapidly and they have a higher pitch, and when some objects are struck their molecules vibrate more slowly and they have a lower pitch. The pitch of the sound an object makes when struck or plucked depends upon the length, tightness, or thickness of the object. (Writes the words *thickness, length,* and *tightness* on chalkboard.)

Demonstration #1: Teacher demonstrates with running explanation that the thickness of the strings on a violin affects the pitch of the strings. Teacher presents the rule that the thicker the string, the lower the pitch.

Practice #1: Students make predictions about the pitch of various thicknesses of string and then try out and make note of their pitches.

Demonstration #2: Teacher demonstrates with running explanation that tightening and loosening a string on the violin affects the pitch of the string.

Teacher presents the rule that the tighter the string, the higher the pitch.

Practice #2: Students make predictions about the pitch of various degrees of tightness of a string and then try out their predictions, noting the pitches and the accuracy of their predictions.

Demonstration #3: Teacher demonstrates with running commentary that pressing on the string effectively shortens the length of the string and affects the pitch produced. Teacher presents the rule that the shorter the string, the higher the pitch.

Practice #3: Students make predictions about the pitch with various lengths of string and then try out their predictions, noting the pitches and the accuracy of their predictions.

Demonstrations #4–10: Teacher demonstrates the rules on a variety of musical instruments and has the students predict the effects of changes in length, thickness, and tightness upon the pitch of the instruments. Students try out other instruments on their own. The lesson continues until the rules are obviously learned and the students' predictions are consistently true.

Strategy B

Materials:
Ukuleles, xylophones, sliding whistles, rubber bands, chimes, drums, and strings
Procedures:
Teacher's statement: I saw many of you at the symphony orchestra's concert yesterday. Which songs were your favorites? Which instruments did you like the best? Have you ever wondered what it is about an instrument that enables it to make higher and lower pitches? Today we have a number of instruments with which you may experiment to try to find out what makes the pitch of instruments go from low to high. Why don't you start with a ukulele? Try to figure out what makes a ukelele string make a higher or lower tone.
Stimulating questions:
   a. Yes, I can feel that "buzzy" feeling when you strike the chime. What causes that? What happens with the shorter chime?
   b. Yes, striking harder on the xylophone makes the sound louder. Is that the same as higher? How can you make the pitch higher?
   c. How can you find out if thicker strings make lower tones?

   d. Carlos, what do you think of Sheila's idea that the pitch of the whistle has to do with how far the slide is pushed in?
   e. Zenia, how can you check out your guess about what makes one chime's pitch high and another's low?
   f. Kenneth, the pitch of your voice is very low but Sue's voice is high. Why do you think that is so? Where can you go to find out?
3. Discuss as completely as you can the comparative advantages and disadvantages of generative and supplantive strategies. Use examples from Question 2 to provide a context for your answer.
4. Suppose you were planning the organizational strategy to teach hiring practices that are in accordance with new federal laws to a group of 50 mid-level managers. The managers have only a three-hour class period available for the training. The learners are quite skilled but impatient with anything other than "the facts." The manager who will be delivering the instruction is very knowledgeable in the content but less skilled in modes of delivery other than lecture/discussion.

   The question: Should you use a more supplantive or more generative strategy for this lesson? Explain your answer.

Macro-Organization Strategies

The expanded instructional events provide an excellent organizational structure for designing a lesson that may range from one to a few class meetings. However, the events are not an adequate macro-organizational pattern for organizing an entire course or unit (although you may see some valuable suggestions for introducing or closing a course within those events).

The scope, organization, and sequence of content at the macro level is most often considered under the rubric of curriculum design. (As a rule curriculum designers are more concerned about what to teach as opposed to how to teach. See Dick (1986–87) and Foshay & Foshay (1981) for further distinctions between these two fields.) After reviewing numerous curricula over all content areas and across a variety of age groups, Posner (Posner & Strike, 1976; Posner & Rudnitsky, 1978) classified curriculum organization patterns into five major categories: world-related structure, inquiry-related structure, utilization-related structure, learning-related structure, and concept-related structure. We will discuss each of these briefly. Then we will describe a particular concept-related model, the Elaboration Model, in detail.

World-Related Structure

A world-related structure clusters and sequences content according to the way things in the world seem to be organized—by time, by space, and by physical characteristics. An example of organizing by time or chronology would be teaching music history with units organized by historical periods and sequenced from earliest music through Renaissance, Baroque, Classical, Romantic, and Contemporary periods up to the present day. An example of organizing by spatial relationships, grouping and sequencing according to how things occur spatially in the world, would be teaching world geography by grouping units according to continent, and teaching geography of all countries in one continent at a time. When content is organized by physical characteristics, content that is similar in its physical attributes is clustered together. Generally, then, the entities with the least complex physical attributes are taught first. For example, a biology class might be organized by beginning with the least complex units, cell and sub-cell levels, then moving into more complex organisms. Or a course in chemistry might be organized around the clustering of elements into their groups, such as inert gases, metals, nonmetals, and so on.

Inquiry-Related Structure

An inquiry-related sequence and organization teaches ideas together because they represent similar phases of inquiry. Following this scheme, a designer would sequence and organize instruction by the steps of inquiry that the scientists in that field pursue. For example, a course in educational research would be organized and sequenced according to the steps that an educational researcher would follow in studying a question: formulation of a question, review of the literature, statement of

hypotheses, design of a study, data collection, data analysis, and drawing conclusions. The SMSG mathematics curriculum revision of the 1960s—called at the time *new math*—represented an attempt to improve mathematics learning by restructuring the curriculum along the lines of "how mathematicians think."

Utilization-Related Structure

A utilization-related organization groups ideas together according to how skills will be used in the future, either personally, socially, or vocationally. Following this orientation, groups of concepts, facts, procedures, or theories are grouped together and taught in priority sequence so that the first to be taught are those topics that will be used first, the next topics taught are the next used, and so forth. For example, this text is sequenced in the order that a professional designer follows in designing instruction, starting with analysis, continuing with strategy development, and concluding with evaluation of developed instruction. Using another form of utilization-based sequence, we teach the most frequently used knowledge first. For example, teaching the commonly used statistical tests, such as correlation and t-tests, could precede teaching more specialized and less frequently used tests such as path analysis.

Learning-Related Structure

Learning-related structures organize information in such a way that new learning builds on relevant prior knowledge. One way to organize using a learning-related structure is a prerequisite-based structure. If a designer conducted an information-processing analysis of the tasks related to all of the goals for an entire course, the outcome of that analysis would indicate the prerequisite relationships of all the information and skills in that course. An investigation of this analysis would reveal that there are some fundamental concepts, skills, or knowledge that are foundational for the entire course. Using a strictly prerequisite-based organization, these would be the skills taught first. For example, in a computer programming course, the ability to use the hardware and ability to apply principles of the disk operating system are prerequisite to any later hands-on experiences in programming.

A second perusal of the task analysis would reveal a second tier of concepts, rules, or information that are prerequisite to later, more complex skills. There may be several groupings of these ideas within the second tier of analysis. The information and skills in this tier would be taught next. For example, in the computer programming course, the next ideas to be taught might be the concepts relating to program structure, such as the program body and subroutines and related commands. These concepts would be introduced next in a prerequisite-structured course. The pattern of "moving up" the hierarchy of the task analysis should be followed until learners are taught to achieve the most complex skills in the course. For example, in the programming course, the next level of prerequisites would involve teaching the most fundamental commands for accepting keyboard inputs, displaying information, judging inputs, manipulating data, and controlling flow of the program. Then, more esoteric commands for each of the programming needs could be learned. Finally, learners would be prepared to solve complex programming problems by putting together the commands that they have learned.

You may have noticed that one element of the micro-organization of lessons is the building on prerequisites. Going through the body of the expanded events repeatedly is often driven by the need to teach prerequisites before teaching more complex skills in a lesson. The prerequisite-based structure is the most commonly utilized macro-organizational strategy in the field of instructional design. A disadvantage of prerequisite-based structure is that learners have a tendency to lose the "big picture" as they acquire skill with individual prerequisites. They may lose sight of how the prerequisites relate to each other and to the goal of the course. For this reason, prerequisite-based organization may be less motivating than other forms of structure.

A less formal approach to prerequisite-based instruction is predicated on teaching the familiar before the unfamiliar. For example, in religion class, the aspects of the more commonly prevailing religion might be studied before moving on to the more unfamiliar. Or, in a world geography class, the study of the geography of one's own country might precede the study of more distant locales.

Concept-Related Structure

Concept-related structures use the structure of the discipline to organize the content. The most superordinate, all-inclusive concepts or principles are taught first, and then the more specific cases of the concepts or applications of the principles are taught later. One of the advantages of this structure, in contrast to the prerequisite-based structure, is that the resulting learning may be integrated, with relationships of ideas clear. Many of the science programs developed during the curriculum reform movement in the 1960s in the United States, such as BSCS biology, were developed based upon the concept-related macro-structure. An example of such an organization in a general science class would be teaching about the properties of matter before teaching about atoms, and teaching about atoms before teaching about electricity. Reigeluth's Elaboration Model, which is described next, is a particular example of a concept-related macro-structure.

*E*laboration Model

Concept-related structures have many advantages; in particular, they instruct in a sequence that supports the manner in which many cognitive theorists suggest that information is stored in the brain, with more specific information being subsumed under superordinate concepts. However, their disadvantage—and the reason why most instructional designers structure courses according to prerequisites—is that they fail to consider levels of learning outcomes (discriminations, concepts, rules, problem-solving) and how these levels are prerequisite to each other. This failure to consider prerequisites leads to learners' either encountering levels of information that they lack a background for or their only encountering the information at the verbal information and concept levels, never at the higher levels of learning, such as rule-using or problem-solving. Reigeluth devised an organizational pattern to take advantage of positive aspects of both the concept-related and prerequisite-based macro-strategies and to diminish the disadvantages of each with his Elaboration Theory (Reigeluth, 1979; 1983).

Reigeluth focused on organizing an entire course according to one of three major types of outcomes: concepts, principles, and procedures. He suggested that a particular content may be taught by setting out to achieve any of the three outcomes. (For example, statistics may be taught by emphasizing the concepts in statistics, the principles of statistics, or the procedures for calculating statistics.) He stated that it is one of the first actions of the designer to determine which of the three content structures—conceptual, theoretical (principle-based), or procedural—should be emphasized in a particular unit or course.

Reigeluth then suggested that the designer identify the most overarching, fundamental concepts, principles, or procedures (depending upon which structure is selected). These overarching generalizations should be taught first at the application level in what Reigeluth called an *epitome*. For example, when Wedman and Smith (1989) developed a theoretically-based unit on the principles of camera operation, they taught the relationships among aperture size, shutter speed, and film type at their most basic level (e.g., if film type is constant, to keep exposure equal if aperture is made larger, shutter speed must be faster) without reference to numerical values of shutter speed, aperture size, or film speed. Learners were required to apply the relationships they had learned to solve problems. For example, they were asked what they might do if the lighting changed and the shutter speed had to remain constant. Any of several answers could be correct and indicate that the learners had acquired the general principles relating shutter speed, film speed, and aperture size.

After the epitome is taught and practiced at the application level, then more detailed instruction, an "elaboration" of the content, is presented. For example, in the first level of elaboration in the photography unit, learners received instruction on the details of f-stops, shutter speeds, and film speeds. Then, content was taught in a more detailed level of elaboration, and so on. In the photography unit, this meant that learners were taught about how motion interacts with shutter speed and how depth of field relates to aperture size. This continuing elaboration of general ideas is similar to Bruner's concept of the "spiral curriculum" (1960), Ausubel's concept of "progressive differentiation" (1968), and Norman's concept of "web learning" (1973). Within each level of elaboration, information is taught according to prerequi-

sites. Instruction at each level of elaboration is tied to the other levels with synthesizing and summarizing statements that integrate the levels of elaboration. Reigeluth likens this form of instruction to the "zooming in" of the camera to pick up details in a visual field and then the "zooming out" to give the viewer a perspective of the whole picture.

Reigeluth has predicted that when used with large bodies of content, such as units or courses, elaborated instruction will result in more integrated and motivated learning. However, studies of short segments of instruction (one to several lessons) have failed to substantiate these predictions (Beukhof, 1986; Wedman & Smith, 1989). Nevertheless, the model has such intuitive appeal that designers continue to use it to organize large segments of instruction. We recommend it as a structure for designing units and courses. For more information on the particulars of design we recommend that you read Reigeluth's own description of the model (Reigeluth, 1983) and his example of the model's application (Reigeluth, 1987).

*E*xercises D

1. Given below are descriptions of course structures. Write beside each the type of macrostructure employed: world-related (WR), inquiry-related (IR), utilization-related (UR), learning-related (LR), or concept-related (CR).

    _____ a. Teach anthropology from the earliest appearance of humankind on the earth to present day.

    _____ b. Teach the concept of "velocity" before teaching the concept "acceleration," a change in velocity.

    _____ c. Teach biology in the sequence that a researcher follows in the scientific method: Examine data, construct hypotheses, select likely hypothesis, test hypothesis, examine data, and accept hypothesis or consider alternate hypotheses.

    _____ d. Teach math by teaching the most commonly used operations first, followed by the next most commonly used operations.

_____ e. Teach phonics skills before teaching students how to read sentences.

2. Explain how you might teach an instructional design or a computer programming class following the Elaboration Model.

Writing Organizational Strategy Plans

As you can see in the Job Aid below, organizational strategy plans include (1) a description of where a lesson falls within a unit or course, (2) a description of the plan for the macro-organization of the unit or course into which a lesson falls, (3) a grouping of the objectives for a particular lesson, and (4) a plan for the lesson that follows the expanded instructional events. The plan for the expanded instructional events may cycle through the body of the lesson several times, so we suggest that you make multiple copies of the Job Aid section that relates to the body of the lesson. You will make one of these plans for each grouping of the objectives. These objectives might be at several levels of outcomes. For example, you might have one grouping that teaches the concepts in the lesson, one grouping that teaches the related rules, and one grouping for the problem-solving objective that uses the rules.

Job Aid

I. Course and Lesson Organization Plan

    A. Diagram of How This Lesson Fits Within Course or Unit
    B. Macro-Organization of Course or Unit

II. Lesson Organization Strategy Plans

    A. Sequencing and Grouping of Lesson Objectives
    B. Introduction Strategy
        1. Activate **Attention** to Lesson
        2. Establish Instructional **Purpose**
        3. Arouse **Interest and Motivation**
        4. **Preview** Lesson

Objectives for Grouping (Must Be Repeated for Each Cluster)

    C. Body
        5. Recall Relevant **Prior Knowledge**
        6. Process **Information and Examples**
        7. Focus **Attention**
        8. Employ **Learning Strategies**

Objectives for Grouping (Must Be Repeated for Each Cluster)

        9. **Practice**
      10. Evaluate **Feedback**

Conclusion

      11. **Summarize** and Review
      12. **Transfer** Learning
      13. **Remotivate and Close**

Assessment

      14. **Assess** Performance
      15. Evaluate **Feedback** and Seek **Remediation**

Summary

During the *develop the instructional strategy* stage, we take the information that we acquire during the analysis stage and use it to help us make decisions about the instructional strategy. At the lesson level, the designer uses the expanded instructional events as the framework of the lesson. At the conclusion of this stage, the designer has developed a strategy for the lesson. The lessons themselves are not produced yet. In other words, they are not in their mediated, or final, form. Figure 6.2 summarizes key points in this chapter.

Components of Instructional Strategies

Organizational Strategies

- Macro-Strategies— scope and sequence structures
- Micro-Strategies— expanded instructional events

Delivery Strategies

- Media selection
- Grouping strategies

Management Strategies

- Scheduling
- Acquisition of resources

Expanded Instructional Events

Introduction

- Activate attention
- Establish instructional purpose
- Arouse interest and motivation
- Preview lesson

Body

- Recall prior knowledge
- Focus attention
- Employ learning strategies
- Practice
- Evaluate feedback

Conclusion

- Summarize and review
- Transfer knowledge
- Remotivate and close

Assessment

- Assess performance
- Evaluate feedback and remediate

Figure 6.2: Summary Diagrams for Chapter 6

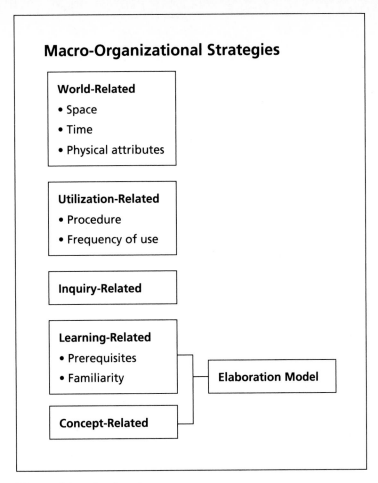

Figure 6.2: *Continued*

Extended Example

1. *Course and Lesson Organization Plan.* Following are diagrams of how a lesson on depth of field fits within a course or unit. We decided to use the Elaboration Model as the macro-strategy for our photography course. Figure 6.3 shows the structure of the epitome for a unit on coordinating shutter speed, aperture, and film speed.

The first level of elaboration, as shown in Figure 6.4, introduces more detail regarding

shutter speed, aperture, and film speed. Specifically, it addresses the relationships among settings and their effects.

The final level of elaboration, as seen in Figure 6.5, relates aperture and shutter speed to the composition features of depth of field and subject action.

2. *Lesson Organization Strategy Plans.* See examples at conclusion of Chapters 7–13.

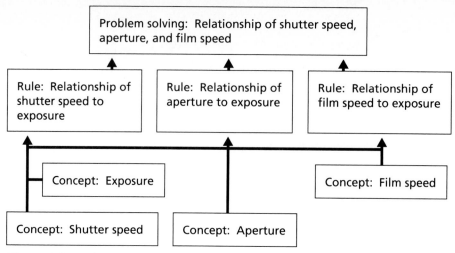

Figure 6.3: Epitome Diagram

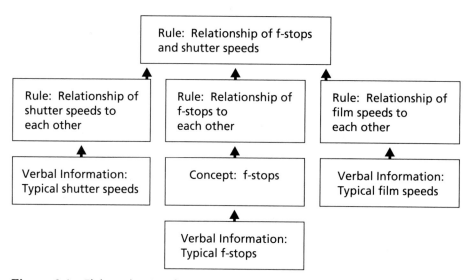

Figure 6.4: Elaboration Level 1

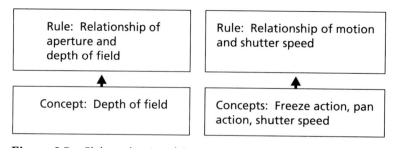

Figure 6.5: Elaboration Level 2

Readings and References

Ausubel, D. P., Novak, J. D., & Hanesian, H. (1968). *Educational psychology: A cognitive view* (2nd ed.). New York: Holt, Rinehart, & Winston.

Beukhof, G. (1986). *Designing instructional texts: Interaction between text and learner.* Paper presented at the meeting of the American Educational Research Association, San Francisco.

Britton, B. K., Westbrook, R. D., & Holdredge, T. S. (1978). Reading and cognitive capacity usage: Effects of text difficulty. *Journal of Experimental Psychology, Human Learning, and Memory, 4* (6), 582–591.

Bromage, B. K., & Mayer, R. E. (1986). Quantitative and qualitative effects of repetition on learning from technical text. *Journal of Educational Psychology, 78* (4) 271–278.

Bruner, J. S. (1960). *The process of education.* New York: Vintage Books.

Bruner, J. S. (1966). *Toward a theory of instruction.* Cambridge, MA: Harvard University Press.

Burton, J. K., Niles, J. A., & Lalik, R. M. (1986). Cognitive capacity engagement during and following intersperse mathemagenic questions. *Journal of Educational Psychology, 78*(2), 147–152.

Butterfield, E. C., & Nelson, G. D. (1989). Theory and practice of teaching for transfer. *Educational Technology Research and Development, 37*(3), 5–38.

Clark, R. E., & Voogel, A. (1985). Transfer of training principles for instructional design. *Educational Communication and Technology Journal, 33* (2), 113–123.

Craik, F. I., & Lockhart, R. S. (1972). Levels of processing: A framework for memory research. *Journal of Verbal Learning and Verbal Behavior, 11,* 671–684.

Dick, W. (1986–87). Instructional design and the curriculum development process. *Educational Leadership, 44* (4), 54–56.

Duncan, J. (1980). The demonstration of capacity limitation. *Cognitive Psychology, 12,* 75–96.

Foshay, W. R., & Foshay, A. W. (1981). A father and son exchange letters. *Educational Leadership, 38,* 621–625.

Gagné, R. M. (1972). *The conditions of learning.* (2nd ed.). New York: Holt, Rinehart, & Winston.

Hannafin, M. J. (1984). Guidelines for using locus of instructional control in the design of computer-assisted instruction. *Journal of Instructional Development, 7*(3), 9–14.

Herman, G. (1969). Learning by discovery: A critical review of studies. *Journal of Experimental Education, 38,* 58–72.

Jonassen, D. H. (1985). Generative learning vs. mathemagenic control of text processing. In D. H. Jonassen (Ed.), *Technology of Text II,* Englewood Cliffs, NJ: Educational Technology Publications.

Norman, D. A. (1973). Memory, knowledge, and answering of questions. In R. L. Soso (Ed.), *Contemporary issues in cognitive psychology: The Loyola symposium.* Washington, D.C.: Winston.

Osborne, R., & Wittrock, M. (1985). The generative learning model and its implications for science education. *Studies in Science Education, 12,* 59–87.

Peck, S. (1988). Informal presentation at the University of Texas, Austin, Texas.

Posner, G. J., & Rudnitsky, A. N. (1978). *Course design: A guide to curriculum development for teachers.* New York: Longman.

Posner, G. J., & Strike, K. A. (1976). A categorization scheme for principles of sequencing content. *Review of Educational Research, 46*(4), 665–690.

Ray, W. E. (1961). Pupil discovery vs. direct instruction. *Journal of Experimental Education, 29*(3), 271–280.

Reigeluth, C. M. (1979). In search of a better way to organize instruction: The elaboration theory. *Journal of Instructional Development, 6,* 40–46.

Reigeluth, C. M. (1983). The elaboration theory of instruction. In C. M. Reigeluth (Ed.), *Instructional design theories and models.* Hillsdale, NJ: Lawrence Erlbaum Associates.

Reigeluth, C. M. (1987). Lesson blueprints based on the elaboration theory of instruction. In C. M. Reigeluth (Ed.), *Instructional theories in action.* Hillsdale, NJ: Lawrence Erlbaum Associates.

Rothkopf, E. Z. (1970). The concept of mathemagenic activities. *Review of Educational Research, 40,* 325–336.

Royer, J. M. (1979). Theories of the transfer of learning. *Educational Psychologist, 14,* 53–69.

Salomon, G. (1979). *Interaction of media, cognition, and learning.* San Francisco: Jossey-Bass.

Steinberg, E. (1977). Review of student control in computer-assisted instruction. *Journal of Computer-Based Instruction, 3,* 84–90.

Tennyson, R. (1984). Application of artificial intelligence methods to computer-based instructional design: The Minnesota adaptive instructional system. *Journal of Instructional Development, 7,* 17–22.

Watkins, D. (1983). Depth of processing and the quality of learning outcomes. *Instructional Science, 12,* 49–58.

Wedman, J. F., & Smith, P. L. (1989). An examination of two approaches to organizing instruction. *International Journal of Instructional Media, 16*(4), 293–303.

Whitener, E. M. (1989). A meta-analytic review of the effect on learning of the interaction between prior achievement and instructional support. *Review of Educational Research, 59*(1), 65–86.

Winn, W. (1989, March). Rethinking cognitive approaches to instructional design. A paper presented at the annual meeting of the American Educational Research Association, San Francisco.

Wittrock, M. C. (1974). Learning as a generative process. *Educational Psychologist, 11,* 87–95.

Strategies for Declarative Knowledge Lessons

seven

Chapter Objectives

At the conclusion of this chapter you should be able to do the following:

- Recognize three forms of declarative knowledge.

- Identify and describe three critical features involved in learning declarative knowledge.

- Given a declarative knowledge objective, design strategy plans for that objective.

Review of Declarative Knowledge Learning

Declarative knowledge involves "knowing that" something is the case. It is often what we mean when we say we want learners to "understand" a content. You may recall from Chapter 4 that the term *verbal information* is also frequently used to refer to the same sort of learning as declarative knowledge. Words that we use to describe declarative knowledge performance are *explain, describe, summarize,* and *list.*

Although declarative knowledge learning is often disparaged as mere rote memorization, uninteresting, and unimportant, it is the substance of much of our thinking. Declarative knowledge is a critical part of what we learn throughout life. Although the acquisition of declarative knowledge is often equated with "rote learning," rarely is it or should it be acquired via such a strategy. To the contrary, declarative knowledge is generally acquired within meaningful structures.

When people say that a person is "educated," often what they mean is that the person possesses a large amount of declarative knowledge. During the Persian Gulf War in 1991, surveys indicated that many students were unable to locate countries in the Middle East. Many citizens were astounded by this deficit. The task of locating and labeling the countries in the Middle East is a declarative knowledge learning task. The recent outcry over the lack of "cultural literacy" among school students often refers to learners' lack of declarative knowledge.

Declarative knowledge is also strongly tied with other types of learning. Much of concept learning is the *understanding* of ideas and how they relate to each other. Declarative knowledge of a list of steps is necessary to complete procedures and psychomotor skills. Declarative knowledge is necessary to understand problems in order to solve them.

Although declarative knowledge is a major type of learning, there are some important distinctions that can be made within this category of learning. Gagné and Briggs (1979) identified three sub-types, each of which involves slightly different cognitive processes: labels and names, facts and lists, and organized discourse.

The learning of labels and names involves pairing of information. This type of learning re-quires that learners mentally make a connecting link between two elements. This link may be propositional or image-based. The more labels that we need to remember, the more similar the information among the pairs, or the less meaningful the connection between the two ideas, the more difficult the learning.

The learning of labels and names is sometimes referred to as *paired associate learning* and is somewhat distinct from the other two forms of declarative knowledge. Examples of learning labels and names are foreign language vocabulary learning, learning the names of the state capitols, learning the valences of the chemical elements, and learning to label the parts of a camera. In each case, a pair is linked together, as in "hat" to "sombrero" or "Illinois" to "Springfield" or "oxygen" to "minus 2" or a particular image to "shutter release lever." It is worth noting that learning labels does not necessarily require learning the meaning of the two linked ideas but rather learning that one thing links to the other. In learning that *sombrero* is the Spanish word for *hat,* we aren't necessarily learning what a hat is — that is a concept learning task. When learners do not already possess concepts, it makes the learning of labels much more difficult because they lack meaning.

The learning of facts and lists is fundamentally propositional in nature. A fact is usually a statement that describes a relationship between or among concepts, such as "Ann Richardson was the governor of Texas in 1991." A list is a group of elements that must be remembered together. The order of elements in a list may or may not be important. To be remembered, facts and lists must be made meaningful by integrating them with prior knowledge. The isolated, non-meaningful memorization of facts is rarely a worthwhile learning objective.

Facts and lists may, however, be learned as individual facts, seemingly apart from other information (e.g., "The discount store closes at 7:00 P.M. on Fridays") and as networks of interconnected information, such as the local football team's wins and losses. The discount store's closing time is a meaningful thing (for those who shop there), even though it is an isolated fact. The more isolated a fact is, the more difficult it is to learn; consequently, if we ever manage to remember when the discount store closes on Fridays, it is generally because that is important information to us. Once we have some knowledge, it becomes increasingly easy to add to it. As the network or knowledge base becomes larger and more complex, it also becomes easier to add yet more. This seeming impossibility (the larger and more complex, the easier it is to add to it) is a result of the way in which we learn declarative knowledge—linking, elaborating, and organizing. Having a large knowledge base makes it easier to acquire more knowledge.

The learning of organized discourse is also propositional in nature. But whereas facts and lists are discrete, the phenomenon of ''discourse'' itself involves the comprehension of a thread of meaning that runs through an extensive body of information, such as a passage of prose. The archetype for discourse learning is learning through reading a text (typically expository text). For the activity to result in learning, the discourse, which is itself an integrated body of knowledge, must be tied with existing knowledge.

Novice designers often confuse learning connected discourse and learning concepts. As a matter of fact, it is in the midst of conceptual learning that we divide declarative knowledge from intellectual skills. According to Gagné's scheme, which we employ here, much of what is commonly referred to as *concept learning* is described as *connected discourse learning*. For example, ''perestroika'' is a concept that can be understood in the declarative knowledge sense; the term literally means ''a fast-moving sleigh.'' With such declarative knowledge a learner can interpret a conversation or text that uses this word. In addition, having declarative knowledge allows the learner to do the following: (1) explain the meaning and etiology of *perestroika* in its recent use referring to political reforms in Russia, (2) describe the history of the term, and even (3) make inferences, such as making associations between the conceptual knowledge and prior knowledge. The propositional network associated with the concept ''perestroika'' may be rich and highly differentiated. The strategies to teach this sort of conceptual knowledge are the same as those used to teach connected discourse. But the sort of concept learning that we have categorized under intellectual skills (along with rules and problem solving) is a different kind of learning. It involves pattern recognition productions (i.e., if the presented instance has certain features, then it is an example of perestroika). Concept learning as an intellectual skill is a classifying rule.

Neither type of ''concept''—declarative knowledge or classifying rule—is a superior kind of learning. Each type of learning meets certain requirements as a basis for future learning or application to life circumstances. The only reason that we make a differentiation between them is that the instructional strategies required for learning are quite different. If you are interested in reading more about these two ways of looking at ''concept'' we suggest you read Tessmer, Wilson, and Driscoll (1990).

A final point that should be clarified regarding the relationship between declarative knowledge and intellectual skills is the sequence in which they should be learned. We tend to fall somewhere between Anderson (1985) and R. Gagné (1985) regarding the prerequisite relationship of declarative knowledge and intellectual skill (procedural) knowledge. Gagné believes that although declarative knowledge can be useful as prior knowledge for acquiring intellectual skills, it is not essential. Anderson models all procedural learning (i.e., intellectual skills) as being initially represented as declarative knowledge. Through practice, this declarative knowledge is formed into productions (if-then rules). It appears that Anderson believes procedural knowledge must pass through a declarative knowledge stage. We conjecture that in many cases declarative knowledge is essential to learning intellectual skills because the declarative knowledge helps make the intellectual skill meaningful.

As we discuss instructional strategies for declarative knowledge, we will provide separate prescriptions depending on which of these three subtypes (labels and names, facts and lists, and organized discourse) is involved.

Cognitive Processes of Learning Declarative Knowledge

Before we discuss the processes involved in learning declarative knowledge, it is important to describe how theorists suggest that declarative knowledge is stored. Since most, if not all, of our knowledge is interrelated in some fashion, the primary form of representation of our declarative knowledge is theorized to be in **propositional networks** (Anderson, 1976). A proposition is somewhat similar to a sentence. For example, the sentence ''Pat gave a large bone to Sarah, a smooth collie'' contains three propositions:

1. Pat gave a bone to Sarah.
2. The bone was large.
3. Sarah is a smooth collie.

The difference between sentences and propositions is that (1) sentences may contain more than one proposition (as the sentence above), and (2) propositions *are* the ideas, and sentences are what we commonly use to express the ideas. Propositions may also be expressed as diagrams or illustrations, mathematic expressions, musical notation, and other forms of languaging.[1] A network of propositions is the collection of many propositions linked together in some fashion. The links that are formed in a propositional network are idiosyncratic to a large extent and are almost as important to the ''knowledge'' as is the content of the propositions themselves.

Another theoretic construct that has been used to describe knowledge structures is schema theory (Minsky, 1975; Rummelhart & Ortony, 1977). Schemata (plural of *schema*) are clusters of related ideas. For example, most of us probably have a ''restaurant schema,'' which includes not only the sequence of events that generally occur in a restaurant but also the objects and people you would expect to see there. Schemata are said to have slots, or categories, that can be filled with particular information. For example, the ''dessert slot'' may be occupied by ''Baked Alaska'' one evening at a particular restaurant and by ''Hot Fudge Sundae with Nuts'' at another time and place. In either case, propositional networks or schemata, the significance of the relatedness of knowledge in memory is the same: In order to learn declarative knowledge, it must be linked to existing knowledge.

The learning of all declarative knowledge has certain requirements. E. Gagné (1985) summarizes the process of learning new declarative knowledge in four steps: (1) new knowledge is presented via some medium and apprehended by the learner, (2) the material presented is translated by the learner into propositions, (3) related propositions in the learner's memory are activated, and (4) elaborations are generated by the learner as new connections stimulate the making of inferences. These steps underscore the active nature of declarative knowledge learning. The current view about how this learning takes place sharply contrasts with the view of the learner as a passive receiver absorbing material like a sponge. Rather, learners perform certain critical cognitive activities when they are engaged in learning declarative knowledge. These activities are linking, organizing, and elaborating.

Linking with Existing Knowledge

To be easily learned, recalled, and used, new declarative knowledge must be tied to the learner's existing (i.e., prior) knowledge. As a matter of fact, to be stored in long-term memory, incoming information must be meaningful. What makes new information meaningful? When we have some prior knowledge that links to it, incoming information can be meaningful. In cases in which there is little prior knowledge to link to, learners will have to employ artificial (rather than intrinsically meaningful) links. These links tend to focus on surface similarities, such as similar sounds, shapes, sensory impressions, or motor procedures. So, when a learner is working in an unfamiliar area, early learning may lean heavily on sound associations, similarity in physical features such as letter sequences, or other non-meaningful sources of connection. When even these ''trick'' links cannot be made, one has to resort to sheer rote repetition to get the information to be stored into long-term memory.

A result of linking is construction of meaning. In fact, the heart of the process of learning declarative knowledge is this creation of meaning. In other words, the way we acquire new, meaningful knowledge is by making sense out of new information. In this process, we are constructing meaning and, thereby, are acquiring new declarative knowledge. This takes more time than is frequently

---

[1] Although not in common use, *languaging* is a term from the linguistics field and refers to the engagement of language behavior. The term is used in visual literacy discussions and is a useful one when pointing to language events that involve symbol systems that are not immediately or commonly recognized as ''language.''

allowed in instruction. It takes the learner 10 seconds to encode one new bit of information according to Simon (1974). The rate of information presentation in rate-controlled media (such as television and film) is frequently too fast for learners to process new information and therefore remember it. Later in this chapter we will see instructional strategies that make use of linking to assist in learning declarative knowledge.

Organizing

Organizing new information is another cognitive activity that facilitates the learning of declarative knowledge. As we receive new information, we actively organize it by clumping sets together, separating sets from one another, subordinating, and making relationships among sets. Such organization may simplify the cognitive load of handling and remembering masses of data, as seen in the common subdivision of telephone numbers. Which sequence of numbers is easier to learn?

15557568902 or 1 (555) 756 8902

Organization may add meaning by placing new unfamiliar material into some existing "slot." Slots can assist recall by providing a beginning point for recall of the rest of the schema, or a slot may aid recall by limiting the spread of activation of memory to a smaller and more germane area (only the schema and related schemata).

Although organization is something learners do internally, instruction may either provide organization for the learner or help learners to engage in organization themselves. Later in this chapter we will discuss instructional strategies that either provide organization (such as advance organizers) or assist the learner to organize information (such as concept mapping).

Elaborating

Another activity that is important for declarative knowledge learning is elaboration of information. When we receive new information, such as in reading or listening, we tend to add to that information, partly so that it makes sense to us and partly so that the information will be more retrievable. We elaborate by filling in gaps, making inferences, imagining examples, and so forth. The activity of elaboration is more inevitable in learning—and thus more important to instruction—than was generally acknowledged until recent years. Previously, elaboration was frequently thought of as being analogous to decoration: a nice addition but not necessary. Closer attention to learners' cognitive processes during declarative knowledge learning has led us to realize that elaboration is a basic process by which links are made within information being received as well as for connecting new information to existing knowledge and structures. Computer studies attempting to develop artificial intelligence have provided us with an appreciation for how much of our natural language in speech and writing requires inferences to make sense. The ambiguities of natural language provide an excellent illustration of the need to transcend the words being used. Schank (1984, p. 93) cites the difficulty of getting a computer to correctly interpret the meaning of the verb *gave* in these sentences:

1. John gave Mary a book.
2. John gave Mary a hard time.
3. John gave Mary a night on the town.
4. John gave up.
5. John gave no reason for his actions.
6. John gave a party.
7. John gave his life for freedom.

If we instruct the computer to infer that *Mary now possesses a book* when it encounters the word *gave* in the first sentence, we can see how the computer (which is less able to actively generate elaborations than humans) would interpret the remaining sentences in the list: *Mary now possesses a hard time, Mary now possesses a night on the town, John possesses up,* and so forth. Unlike computers, people who are listening or reading with comprehension actively make leaps of inference as a part of the sense-making process of declarative knowledge learning.

Although humans are well equipped to engage in elaboration, it does not mean that they always do so when needed. The unmotivated learner, the learner who is not skilled in employing needed learning strategies, the learner with little prior knowledge, or the learner who is fatigued may not engage in the mental activity needed to learn declarative knowledge being presented, even though the material may be presented clearly and accurately. Hence, instructional strategies need to encourage learners to perform the elaborations required to learn the material.

The three functions—linking, organizing, and elaborating—will provide the foundation of the information-processing aspect of instructional strategies that we will describe later in the chapter.

Conditions Supporting Declarative Knowledge Learning

The number and variety of possible appropriate strategies for declarative knowledge instruction sometimes present a chaotic picture. There seem to be more specific techniques for assisting the learning of declarative knowledge than for any other type of learning. West, Farmer, and Wolf (1991), for example, present a total of 35 specific cognitive strategies, all of which are applicable to declarative knowledge learning. Their eight major categories represent a good set of instructional strategy tools: organization strategies, classification frames, concept mapping, advance organizers, metaphoric techniques, rehearsal strategies, mnemonics, and imagery. These and instructional techniques suggested by other sources can be categorized into three major types of strategies: linking, organization, and elaboration. We will use these three types of strategies to organize our description of instructional techniques, providing a view of strategy design for declarative knowledge instruction that is both theory-based and functional.

Many events of instruction in lessons for declarative knowledge may be either supplied by instruction or generated by learners. Of the many micro-strategies that we present, only one—advance organizers—seems inappropriate for learners to generate for themselves. The vast majority of the strategies can, therefore, be implemented as either supplantive instruction or generative. The decision as to where the strategy is expected to originate should be based on factors such as time available, learner aptitudes, and prior knowledge. The engagement in the appropriate cognitive activity is the critical feature: whether that activity is something controlled and delivered by instruction or whether that activity is something that instruction facilitates the learner doing is a matter of choice for the designer. If consideration of the factors of time,

learner aptitude, and prior knowledge fails to provide a direction, logistical considerations and the need for variety may influence the decision.

In the following application of the expanded instructional events to the design of instruction for declarative knowledge instruction, we will use two lessons as examples. The first, from a high school chemistry course, involves learning the names and symbols for 103 chemical elements, and the second, from a college music history course, is learning the names, composers, and stylistic periods of musical passages from the Baroque, Classical, and Romantic periods.

Example A: The Elements. Labels learning task.
Setting: High school chemistry class. College prep.
Audience: Teenagers, age 16 to 18. Class enrollment of 28.
Task: Given the symbol for a chemical element, the learner can supply the name of the element, or given the name of the element, the learner can supply the symbol.

There are 103 named elements on the periodic table. Here is a sample:

Aluminum	Al	Iodine	I
Barium	Ba	Iron	Fe
Boron	B	Lithium	Li
Bromine	Br	Mercury	Hg

For this instruction we have selected a computer-assisted instruction module as the delivery system.

Example B: European Music from 1600 through 1900. Organized discourse learning tasks within that course.
Setting: College elective music history course.
Audience: Adults, undergraduate college students. Class enrollment of 28.
Tasks:

1. Given a musical passage, the student will be able to recognize it and identify it by title, composer, and stylistic period.

2. The student will also be able to describe the major events and identifying characteristics of music from the Baroque, Classical, and Romantic periods.

For this instruction, we have selected instructor delivery, with audiovisual media (primarily compact disks and an overhead projector) and independent student work involving listening and use of printed materials.

Introducing Declarative Knowledge Lessons

Deploy Attention

Arouse Interest and Motivation

A variety of techniques is appropriate for attention, interest, and motivation in declarative knowledge lessons. Since the learning of declarative knowledge may be a more onerous task than some other types of learning, it is particularly helpful to plan a strategy to increase curiosity and interest through such techniques as using novel, conflictual, and paradoxical events or providing an abrupt change in stimulus. Throughout the lesson, the use of anecdotes and other devices that interject personal and emotional elements can increase interest, as well as make information relevant by relating instructional goals to learners' life goals, job requirements, and opportunities for advancement. Finally, an important part of motivation, particularly for older learners, can be provided by making it clear how this learning relates to other learning tasks.

In our chemical elements example, attention might be established in the introduction through animated graphics with sound in the computer-assisted instruction, similar to the way computer games often begin. Here, animation showing atoms of various structures could spin and interact, and then become the title screen. The program would include material related to subsequent instructional events, as well as describe the necessity of knowing the names and symbols for the elements so that the next work with forming compounds will be easier and more meaningful. (For example, if we learn that salt is *NaCl,* it will be more meaningful if we already know that *Na* is the symbol for sodium and *Cl* is the symbol for chlorine.) An additional appeal for college prep students might be the statement "You can improve your score on the SAT exam by knowing the symbols for the elements."

In our music history class, we can initially attract attention to the subject by playing a short passage of particularly compelling music (e.g., the "Presto" movement of Bach's *Italian Concerto,* BWV 971), and then change the stimulus by turning the music off. This would immediately shift attention to the instruction. A conflictual/paradoxical event could be supplied by juxtaposing classical composers with the pandering gossip of a supermarket tabloid. The instructor could use humorous headlines to gain students' attention, such as the following: "J.S. Bach won't stop using counterpoint in front of his children," and "Is Amadeus perverting the allegro tempo to please his wife?" and "Beethoven shocks Vienna with the Third!"

Establish Instructional Purpose

There are excellent approaches to establishing the purpose of lessons that are useful for all sorts of learning, not just declarative knowledge, such as relating instructional goals to personal life goals or job requirements and encouraging learners to make the instructional goal personally relevant. In addition, there are some considerations for establishing purpose that are particular to this type of learning. Due to the potential for declarative knowledge learning goals to appear more dull than higher-order learning tasks, an effort to present the goal in an interesting, dynamic format may be worthwhile. It is also worthwhile to tie the purpose of the lesson with learning strategies that are effective in learning this particular kind of task.

For example, in learning the names and symbols for the chemical elements, if students had previously learned to use a mnemonic technique to help them learn the names of state capitals, a good practice would be to remind students of the similarity of the two types of learning, the strategy used for the previous task, and how it could be used to help learn the new material.

Also, the specific requirements for successful attainment of the learning goal should be pointed out. The learners' expectancy for success can be increased, thereby increasing the likelihood of success. This could be accomplished in our chemical elements instruction with a statement such as "You will be able to write the name of the element for any symbol that I show you, and if I give you the name first, you will be able to write the symbol for it."

It will assist learning if instruction will let learners know in what form they must remember the material (recognize or recall, recite verbatim or

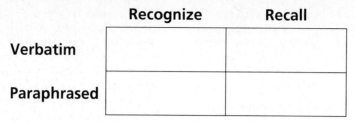

	Recognize	Recall
Verbatim		
Paraphrased		

Figure 7.1: Four Forms of Declarative Memory

paraphrase). Figure 7.1 illustrates the four possible combinations of form of memory. Knowing in advance the nature of the performance that is expected will assist learners to activate the appropriate cognitive strategies for the acquisition of the required learning. Consequently, in our chemical elements module, the instruction will explicitly say, "You will be able to write the name of the element," rather than being vague about what the learners will be expected to do.

In our music history course, we will be explicit about the learning that is expected, saying (and providing equivalent information on a printed handout): "You will learn to recognize musical passages and identify their composers and stylistic periods. On an exam, after I play a passage of music, you will write in a blank the name of the composer of that passage and from what musical period that music came. Also you will be able to describe the major events and identifying characteristics of music from three periods in an essay exam." Notice that the wording here is quite similar to that of the objective but with changes made that direct the statement *to* the learner, rather than talking *about* the learner. Here, we say, "You will learn to . . ." as opposed to "The learner will be able to. . . ."

Previewing the Lesson

Previewing the lesson should include an overview of both what will happen and the nature of the material to be learned. In previewing what will happen in a lesson in which information will be repeated, it is important to ensure that learners know that the information *will* be repeated and reviewed. Learners should know they don't have to grasp it all at once. Knowing what will happen in

the lessson gives learners a chance to prepare to use cognitive strategies, even if they are routine.

The overview of the material to be learned in a lesson can be included in an advance organizer. Although advance organizers can serve as an excellent means to provide a preview of material to be learned, they have important roles in other instructional events as well. A key point to be covered in the overview of material is the way that information in the lesson will be organized. Knowledge of the organization of the material, especially in learning organized discourse, can well be provided through an expository advance organizer and can clarify the relationships among ideas. Two primary types of advance organizers are (1) expository organizers and (2) comparative organizers.

Expository organizers provide and clarify the hierarchical relationships among ideas. They are best for laying the groundwork for broad areas of new, unfamiliar material for which there is no relevant knowledge that the new knowledge can be compared to.

Comparative organizers make orienting comparisons between current knowledge and material to be learned. They are best for learning for which there are similar bodies of knowledge that can be compared to new knowledge on several major points.

The following example of an advance organizer for our music history course serves as both a preview for the course as well as providing a link between previously learned general history—what was happening in Europe at the time the music under study was being written—and the musical periods under study.

The instructor might begin the class by saying, "Think back to your courses on world history.

What were some major figures and events in Europe during the 17th, 18th, and 19th centuries? Let's see, what was happening in the 1600s?'' Quickly get a few student contributions, relating those to a time-line transparency for the 17th century (a graphic organizer). Point out a few memorable events if needed and allow some time for students to look at the chart. ''And what was going on in the 1700s?'' Similarly conduct recitation and review the time-line transparency for the 18th century. ''And in the 1800s?'' Do similar recitation and review. ''In this class, we are going to study what was happening in the world of music in Europe during this period. We will get to know what is now called the Baroque period, and you'll get to know the style of music from that period.'' Play a very short selection from Bach's *Brandenberg* Concerto no. 2. ''We will learn about the music of what is now called the Classical period, its composers, and the musical forms that developed. You'll learn what that style is like and how it is different from Baroque music.'' Play a very short selection from Mozart's Symphony no. 36. ''And finally we will learn about the Romantic movement and how it came to be.'' Play a selection from Beethoven's Third Symphony. ''We'll also examine what made the Romantic period unique and what contributions it made to our world today.'' Play a selection from Saint-Saëns' Third Symphony. The above advance organizer has elements of both an expository and a comparative organizer. This advance organizer might be most appropriate at the very first of the first class, coming before the more detailed information on the objective, described in the previous section.

An idea related to the advance organizer is the epitome, a concept which is part of Reigeluth's Elaboration Model (described in more detail in Chapter 6). An epitome, like an advance organizer, is an initial learning experience covering the whole of a body of material to follow, but unlike the advance organizer, the epitome presents the key ideas and has the learners use this knowledge (paraphrasing, making inferences) before moving on to more details. For example, in music, briefly describing each period and how it relates to other periods would be an epitome. Later in the course, the instruction would provide more details for each period.

Body

Stimulating Recall of Relevant Prior Knowledge

Two powerful techniques for the stimulation (and linking) of prior knowledge to new declarative knowledge are the use of advance organizers and the use of metaphoric devices. A fundamental characteristic of advance organizers is that they bridge old and new knowledge; thus, they are extremely useful in stimulating recall of relevant prior learning. As noted earlier, advance organizers frequently apply to more than one event of instruction. Hence, we have seen their applicability in both previewing the lessons and in stimulating recall of relevant prior learning.

Metaphoric devices can provide a link between the known and the unknown as well as provide intellectual stimulation and interest through the figural use of concrete images. Metaphoric devices often include the use of metaphors, in which a known vehicle is used to convey a new topic through setting up an identity, such as ''the white blood cells (new topic) are soldiers (vehicle).'' Metaphoric devices can also use analogies, in which the vehicle is used to convey the topic through a relationship between pairs, such as ''white blood cells attack infections just as soldiers attack their enemy.'' Although there are dangers in using metaphoric devices (such as the learner generalizing too much or taking the comparison literally rather than figurally as intended), metaphoric devices can be powerful learning tools, whether used in verbal or visual form (Smith & Ragan, 1990; West, Farmer, & Wolf, 1991). An example of a metaphoric device for our music history course would be to compare the sonata form to the commonly used essay form of an introduction, a body, and a conclusion.

A final means of stimulating recall of prior learning in declarative knowledge instruction is to perform a straightforward review of prerequisite concepts. It is easy to come to the conclusion that concepts are always learned after declarative knowledge. (Bloom's taxonomy mistakenly suggests this relationship.) The meaningfulness of declarative knowledge is buttressed by links to previously learned concepts and other declarative knowledge. Without such links, the learner is forced to engage in rote learning if the material is to be learned at all—hardly an efficient or salutary approach in any event.

For our chemistry class instruction, we will stimulate recall of prerequisites by reviewing the previously learned concepts that are embodied within the periodic table (e.g., the concept of a chemical element and learning from a prior lesson on the organization and structure of the periodic table, including the concepts of atomic weight and atomic number).

Process Information

Many specific techniques are available for the processing of information in learning declarative knowledge. Some techniques are appropriate only for one or two of the three sub-types of declarative knowledge. We will look at each sub-type separately.

Some mediation of processing can be provided by instruction, and some should be required of the learner. For example, the use of images is a powerful tool in processing information for learning labels and names, as we describe below. This use of images can be supplied by the instruction, providing learners with images to associate with the content. Or, the images can be supplied by the learner, as mental images perhaps, with the role of instruction to stimulate the learner to think of appropriate images.

A number of specific techniques are available for assisting the information processing of declarative knowledge learning. One set of techniques assists learners to make associations that aid learning. We will call these **associational techniques.** They include the use of mnemonics, images, and analogies. Another set of techniques helps the learner organize information to be learned. These **organizational techniques** include clustering and chunking by categories, use of graphic organizers, generation of expository and narrative structures, and the use of advance organizers. A third set of techniques involves making elaborations on the material being learned. These **elaborative techniques** include elaboration into sentences and devising rules.

Certain of the techniques outlined above will apply to one or more of the forms of declarative knowledge and not to others. The techniques will be brought up and discussed as they apply in each category.

Labels and Names. An organizational technique that is useful in learning labels and names is that of clustering and chunking into categories. It is so commonplace to organize information along some structural pattern that we may forget that this is a particular instructional strategy element and a cognitive strategy for learners to employ. The periodic table of the elements is clustered in various ways including columns of elements clustered into categories (metals, nonmetals, noble gases) and the table is frequently color-coded in categories for solids, liquids, gasses, and synthetic elements. Clustering and chunking may be employed by learners, for example, by choosing to work on particular subsets of the periodic table, either by columns or by rows or by some other grouping principle.

An elaboration technique for learning labels and names is the elaboration of the material into sentences. An example of elaboration of a label would be an explanation of how *Hg* became the symbol for mercury. Elaboration of labels into sentences may lead to their being learned as concepts rather than remaining declarative knowledge, depending on a variety of factors, such as the practice available on examples and nonexamples. Note that the instructional event being implemented at this point is ''processing information.'' While elaboration may constitute excellent practice, it can also be used to initially engage the learner with the material. The music history course could make use of elaboration into sentences by having learners write a sentence for each term as it is being explained.

Facts and Lists. A primary associational technique for processing information in the learning of facts and lists is the use of images. Many techniques are available that employ images to assist in the memorization of facts and lists. Use of images, either instruction-supplied or learner-generated, includes far too many specific possibilities for us to be able to describe it thoroughly here. Texts in audiovisual media (Heinich, Molenda, & Russell, 1989; Locatis & Atkinson, 1984) do an excellent job of presenting and discussing the use of visuals in instruction. A few examples of visual techniques include (1) making mental images of sentences and prose passages, (2) the method of loci in which the locations of objects in an imagined space such as a room are associated with points to be remembered and (3) the use of illustrations such as pictures, graphs, and maps, either learner-generated or instruction-supplied.

Organizational techniques for processing information in learning facts and lists include the use of expository structures and narrative structures. Expository and narrative structures are more commonly used in connected discourse learning; however, it is possible that lists might be learned by organizing them in such a way that they reflect a common structure. Certainly a chronological structure is commonly employed in recalling lists. We describe expository and narrative structures in more detail in the following sections on connected discourse.

Another organizational technique for processing information in learning facts and lists is recognizing patterns. Frequently, patterns exist among facts that are to be learned. These patterns may not be apparent to learners, and, if pointed out by instruction, can be of assistance in the learning of them. For example, the patterns inherent in the columns and rows of the periodic table can be pointed out to learners, making it easier for learners to remember the elements.

Another useful organizational strategy for processing information in learning lists is clustering and chunking. Chunking is the technique that is commonly used to group telephone numbers and social security numbers into smaller subsets that are easier to remember.

Another organizational strategy is elaboration. Adding meaningful information around lists and facts can make them more memorable. For example, information as to why the elements are clustered into the row and column organization that is used in the periodic table may help the learner recall the list of elements.

Organized Discourse. Just as we have done with the other two forms of declarative knowledge, we will discuss the processing of information for organized discourse in terms of three types of strategies: associative, organizational, and elaboration. A great deal of the instructional intent of reading organized discourse, such as the material that you are now reading, is reflected in the term *comprehension*. We find *comprehension* used frequently to describe the outcome of processing organized discourse in conventional print such as books and

journals and in speech such as lectures. We do not find the term *comprehension* used often in other contexts, such as learning from simulations, computer-assisted instruction (CAI) and video. Comprehension of organized discourse involves apprehending the thread of ideas in prose language and following the flow, much as a surfer rides the crest of a wave. Strategies for information processing for this kind of learning may be supplied in the instruction and thus constitute suggestions for writing prose, or they may be generated by learners and thus constitute suggestions for cognitive strategies.

Associative strategies for processing information for organized discourse include the use of imagery and the use of metaphoric devices. Imagery has been described previously in the context of learning facts and lists. In the context of organized discourse, considerations change somewhat even though much of what was noted earlier remains applicable. As a supplantive technique, imagery in organized discourse includes the use of verbal descriptions of images, which sometimes can invoke more vivid mental imagery than is possible to achieve on film or video. In part, the power of the printed word to invoke images is illustrated by the fact that given a good novel and a good motion picture rendition of the novel, the mental images created by reading the book are almost always more vivid and memorable than those that are depicted on film or which remain in the memory after seeing the film. In our high-tech world of film, video, and multimedia, skillfully crafted words remain an exceptionally powerful technique for creating images. Figure 7.2 presents a paragraph from a fiction work, used here to serve as an illustration and reminder of the power of the printed word to invoke images.

In addition to the imagery that words may convey, supplantive uses of images for processing attention in organized discourse include uses of illustrations in text. Images can be explicative and represent information, in addition to their uses in attentional and retentional roles (Duchastel, 1978). Guidelines for selecting and using illustrations in text are provided in Chapter 15. Further information on using illustrations in text can be found in the references for that chapter (especially Willows & Houghton, 1987; Houghton & Willows, 1987; Jonassen, 1982; and Jonassen, 1985).

The tail of the white horse swished back and forth as he trotted briskly down empty avenues and boulevards. He moved like a dancer, which is not surprising: a horse is a beautiful animal, but it is perhaps most remarkable because it moves as if it always hears music. With a certainty that perplexed him, the white horse moved south toward the Battery, which was visible down a long narrow street as a whitened field that was crossed by the long shadows of tall trees. By the Battery itself, the harbor took color with the new light, rocking in layers of green, silver, and blue. At the end of this polar rainbow, on the horizon, was a mass of white—the foil into which the entire city had been set—that was beginning to turn gold with the rising sun. The pale gold agitated in ascending waves of heat and refraction until it seemed to be a place of a thousand cities, or the border of heaven. The horse stopped to stare, his eyes filled with golden light. Steam issued from his nostrils as he stood in contemplation of the impossible and alluring distance. He stayed in the street as if he were a statue, while the gold strengthened and boiled before him in a bed of blue. It seemed to be a perfect place, and he determined to go there.

Figure 7.2: A Passage Illustrating Image-Invoking Prose

Source: *Winter's Tale,* by Mark Helprin, pp. 5–6. Copyright 1983 (held by the author).

Metaphoric devices are also applicable as associative strategies to the processing of information in organized discourse. Metaphor use in organized discourse is similar to imagery use, which we discussed previously: Both are powerful language tools for the subtle, impactive, or memorable conveying of a message. Often metaphors, analogies, and similes are employed in text that evokes images, such as the sample passage used earlier in Figure 7.2. Although they can be highly useful, metaphoric devices are not without their dangers. Zeitoun (1984) presents critical factors in the use of analogies in instruction, including the need for learners to be familiar with the vehicle of the analogy, the need for learners to be capable of analogical reasoning, the need for the learner to be able to identify the limitations of the analogy, and the need to visualize verbally presented analogies. (For additional information on instructional design considerations for using analogies, particularly visual analogies, see Smith & Ragan, 1990.)

Organizational strategies for the processing of information in organized discourse learning include use of expository structures and graphic organizers. **Expository structures** that are often suggested are description, chronology, comparison-contrast, cause-effect, problem-solution, and problem-solution-effects. In addition, certain contents have common structures that they follow. For example, science content may follow a structure describing a system. Within this structure are common "slots" of function, parts, "how it works," or problems/prevention and solution (Armbruster & Anderson, 1985). Such structures can be supplied by instruction, or the structure may be imposed by the learner as a learning strategy. Selecting the appropriate structure is a constant concern of textbook authors, teachers, and instructional designers. **Narrative structures** can similarly be employed in either a supplantive or generative strategy, placing the information being studied into the structure of a story's events.

Research has suggested that text that is organized using one of these structures is more easily learned (Armbruster & Anderson, 1985; Meyer, 1985; Smith & Tompkins, 1988). In our music history course example, the three historical periods Baroque, Classical, and Romantic provide a chronological structure. Further structure may be employed with regard to composers—comparison-contrast is one good alternative. The musical forms, such as minuet and trio, scherzo, rondo, theme and variations, and sonata allegro, lend themselves to a description structure or comparison-contrast structure.

	Dates	Composers	Forms	Innovations
Baroque				
Classical				
Romantic				

Figure 7.3: Frame Organizer for Music History

Expository structures have potential relevance in generative instruction as well as their supplantive implications. One research study by Smith and Friend (1986) is an example of generative use of an organizational strategy. Students improved their comprehension of text material by applying a procedure that they were taught to use, that of determining and coding the text structure of material being studied. Sometimes gifted students discover such strategies on their own; certainly it is unusual for young children to consciously perform structural analyses of material they are reading, yet there is reason to believe that such a skill can be taught to practically anyone.

Graphic organizers can be of great assistance in the information processing of organized discourse learning. Graphic organizers of all sorts may be used for learning facts and lists, but perhaps their most powerful use is in the organization of discourse. Holley and Dansereau (1984) describe the use of such graphics as ''spatial learning strategies'' and include among these strategies networking, concept structuring, schematizing, and mapping. All strategies are similar in that they require learners to identify and represent ideas presented in instruction and spatially indicate the relationships among these ideas. West, Farmer, and Wolf (1991) call such organizers *frames*. The periodic table is arranged in just such a frame. The composers and periods could be cast into a frame for our music history course (see Figure 7.3).

Another technique involving use of a graphic organizer is concept mapping. **Concept mapping,** like outlining, is a graphic means of depicting relationships among ideas. Like outlines, concept maps may be part of a presentation, or they may be generated by learners. In concept mapping, a wide variety and flexibility exists in arranging elements and depicting their relationships. West, Farmer, and Wolf (1991) describe three types of concept maps: spider, hierarchy, and chain, illustrated in Figure 7.4. A supplantive application of concept mapping is employed in the summary diagrams in this text.

In organized discourse the function of graphic organizers such as frames, networks, and concept maps can be to assist in the tuning of cognitive structures and, at times, in assisting restructuring. Graphic organizers provide a visible, distanced[2] pattern on which to build a schema. Graphic organizers may be provided by instruction or generated by learners themselves. An example of learner-supplied graphic organizers is found in the study performed by Smith and Friend (1986). Learning-disabled elementary school students were taught to generate and use visual imagery of text structures to improve comprehension of the text material. A comparison of the recollections of students who used the imagery technique and other students who did not use the technique suggested that the imagery technique assisted comprehension and recall of the material studied. Instruction of learners in creation and use of learner-supplied images—both in

---

[2] The term *distanced* may be unfamiliar to many readers. It refers to one of two forms of language: evanescent and distanced. Evanescent language, like the spoken word and sign language, exists in the moment only and is not available for inspection, manipulation, and so forth. On the other hand, distanced language, like the written word and graphics, is available for inspection and manipulation.

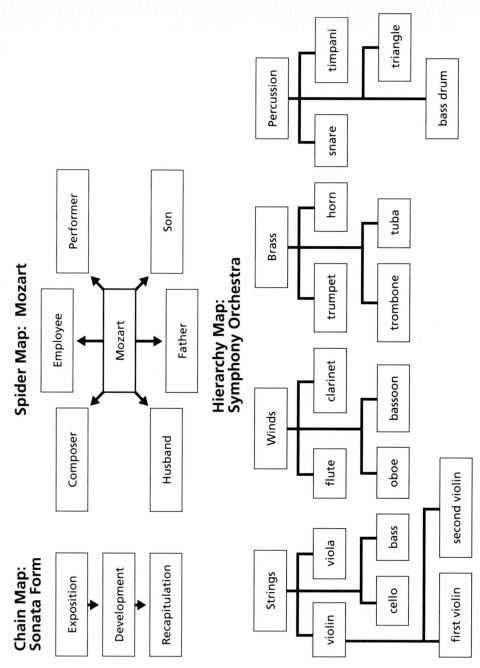

Figure 7.4: Three Forms of the Concept Map

creation of concrete visuals such as drawings, photos, and videos, as well as creation of mental images—is a central concern of the Visual Literacy movement (see Heinich, Molenda, & Russell, 1989, pages 70–76).

Focus Attention

The primary need for attention-focusing in learning labels and names is for focusing on distinctive features. In the learning of facts, attention needs to be focused on key elements. In organized discourse, the learner's attention toward organization of the material is of the most importance. Two particular attention techniques are (1) the procedure of underlining, listing, and reflecting, and (2) the use of questions.

A widely useful technique for focusing attention in declarative knowledge learning is underlining, listing, and reflecting. A good example can be seen in our chemistry lesson by asking the learner to underline each element name using a computer mouse or other pointing device. The learner could list the elements by name and symbol on paper. Reflection could be stimulated by asking the learner to read through the list of elements, pausing at each element and, with eyes closed, silently saying the name of the element and its symbol before moving on to the next.

A great deal has been written about the use of questions in teaching and in instruction (e.g., Gall, 1970; Rothkopf & Bisbicos, 1967; Wager & Wager, 1985). In addition to other mathemagenic functions that they can serve, questions are a powerful tool for establishing and maintaining attention. Their attention function, in large measure, is accomplished through stimulating information processing on the part of the learner. Questions also have an effect on incidental learning. Questions tend to focus the learner's attention on material related to the question, reducing the amount of learning in areas not related to the question (Bull, 1973). When learning goals require a substantial amount of exploratory learning of text material, the attention-focusing capability of questions may be more powerful than desired.

Attentional uses of questions can be served by pre- and post-questions as well as by embedded questions. Pre- and post-questions are perhaps first thought of in their assessment role. However, questions about the content to which the student is expected to respond will have the effect of drawing the student's attention to that content, regardless of other uses to which the student's response may be put. Embedded questions can also serve to hold attention to the material under study. **Embedded questions** are questions within the body of the instruction—ranging all the way from probing, exploratory questions to simple questions of fact. There is no doubt as to the attentional effect of questions. Schramm (1964) concluded, after an extensive review of the research literature on teaching machines and programmed instruction, that the primary effect on learning from frequent, active learner response in programmed instruction was substantial in amount, and it was attributed primarily to the effects of attention on the processing of information under study.

In our chemical elements module, embedded questions will form a great deal of the material provided in the computer-assisted instruction. These questions will at the same time serve a practice function.

In our music history course, embedded questions will be employed by the instructor during the classroom lessons. In addition, embedded questions will be provided in the printed materials supplied for individual student use.

Employ Learning Strategies

Learning strategies that are appropriate for declarative knowledge include the use of mnemonics, elaboration strategies, imagery, analogy, organization, chunking, linking, graphic organizers, and rehearsal. All of these strategies, except mnemonics and rehearsal, were previously discussed as information-processing strategies that could either be supplied by instruction or generated and controlled by the learner. When the learner generates and controls a strategy such as elaboration or imagery to assist in learning desired material, that strategy is being used as a learning strategy. In addition to providing critical training in learning strategies, instruction should guide the learner in the choice of appropriate learning strategies for particular learning tasks. For example, if students were working on the memorization of the names of all the elements in the periodic table, instruction should point them in the right direction, toward use of learning strategies that would be of most assistance in promoting the desired learning. In this case, since the learning task is fact/list, one of the mnemonic techniques, such as single-use coding, pegwords, or method of loci, would be helpful.

Mnemonic techniques of various sorts are particularly potent associational techniques in processing information for learning of facts and lists. Although quite potent, they should be used as a last resort, only when meaningful associations cannot be made. A popular mnemonic device, termed *single-use coding* by West, Farmer, and Wolf (1991), involves the use of letters in words or the first letters in sentences to help learn a list. Common examples in music include using the letters in the word *face* to remember the notes on the spaces on a treble clef, and using the first letter of each word in the sentence "Every good boy does fine" to remember the notes on the lines (E, G, B, D, and F). These are examples of mnemonics that instruction could supply. Alternatively, students may be taught to devise their own instead of using a supplied mnemonic. Single-use coding is involved in the use of rhymes, stories, or jingles, such as the song that begins "Thirty days hath September. . . ." It is also used in any rhyme, story or jingle that a learner might invent. An example of single-use coding for our periodic table instruction would be learning that the symbol for sodium is *Na,* associating table salt with sodium and recalling that too much sodium in the diet is not healthy, and then inventing the slogan, "Just say nay to sodium!"

A complex but powerful mnemonic technique is the use of pegwords, in which a list of things is arbitrarily associated with a sequence of numbers beginning with one, such as "one is for sun; two is for shoe; three is my knee," and so forth. For the list of words to be remembered, the first word is juxtaposed with the sun, the second with shoe, and so forth. If our list to learn were hydrogen, helium, and lithium, we could first imagine the sun with a big *H* on it, then the shoe being lifted by helium balloons, and finally my knee with lithographic printing all over it (suitable only for those with *lithography* in their vocabulary).

Similar to the pegword technique is the time-honored method of loci. The method of loci was a significant part of a memory system used by the Sophists of ancient Greece, a sect known for their amazing ability to memorize large bodies of information. To commit a list of words or topics to memory, one imagines a familiar location, such as a room, including its items, such as furniture. One way to do this is to visualize your own living room. Using a systematic sweep pattern, the living room is scanned in the mind's eye, say, in a clockwise direction, beginning with the northeast corner. As each item of furniture or decoration "appears," an association is made between that item and the next topic or word on the list. Given practice in using the method of loci, learners can commit very large amounts of material to memory in a short amount of time (West, Farmer, & Wolf, 1991).

Another mnemonic, the keyword technique (Atkinson, 1975; Pressley, Levin, & Delaney, 1982), involves a particular kind of operation to assist in the association of a pair of elements, such as a label or a name. In essence the technique involves creating a memorable image that will stimulate recall of the pair in question. For example, if we wanted to apply the keyword technique to assist us in remembering that the symbol for potassium is *K,* we would need to create images evoking keywords that either sound like or remind us of potassium and the letter *K*. Keywords can be put together to form a combined image. So, we will select *potato* for potassium and for *K* we will select *kangaroo*. The image of a kangaroo playing with a potato (or a potato carved in the shape of a kangaroo) is easy to remember. Studies indicate that although bizarre images have been commonly recommended, either bizarre or commonplace images can be effective. The factors that govern the memorability are interaction of the elements in the image, vividness, uniqueness, and the time spent forming the image (Higbee, 1979).

While the linking process used in keyword mnemonics may sound complex, it is easy to perform and results in a surprisingly good memory aid with only a modest amount of mental effort. Either the instruction may supply keywords and their images for learners to use, or learners may be assisted in generating these themselves (Higbee, 1979). In general, an advantage of learners generating keyword images themselves is that the learner-generated associations may be better remembered. An advantage of instruction-supplied associations is that their use requires less instructional time.

Although fascinating in themselves and highly recommended by many sources, each of which draws from many research studies (e.g., Higbee,

1979; Joyce & Weil, 1986; and West, Farmer, & Wolf, 1991), we would emphasize that mnemonic techniques should be used only when equally effective approaches that use meaningful associations have failed. The use of constructed, arbitrary, and artificial meanings, which is required by mnemonics, leaves the learner with a "memorized" learning that is not as lasting or useful as that which is built upon meaningful links.

Rehearsal may be the first and only learning strategy that many learners may be able to come up with on their own. Too many school children and trainees spend countless unnecessary hours engaging in the repeated practice that rote memorization requires. But when rehearsal is placed within the context of use along with other appropriate strategies it can be quite valuable and appropriate. True rehearsal is not accomplished through meaningless repetition. The concept "rehearsal," as developed in cognitive psychology tradition, involves thinking. A minimalist version of rehearsal would be to think aloud. Many of the previously described techniques involve rehearsal, and they engage it in more powerful and interesting ways than the minimalist version. (However, thinking aloud is often exactly what a person needs to do to learn a subtle bit or a complex body of declarative knowledge.) Instruction needs to assist the learner in making appropriate use of rehearsal as a learning strategy. We will have more to say about rehearsal later under the next instructional event, practice.

Practice

The strategies discussed to this point require very little rehearsal or practice for mastery of material. Providing for adequate practice is a necessary part of instructional design. One consideration in designing practice is determining whether the learning task requires recall or whether it only requires recognition. Practice requirements for recognition— all other things being equal (such as learning strategies employed)—are much less than for recall. Another consideration in determining the amount of practice needed is, if recall is required, whether the recall should be verbatim or if it may be paraphrased. Again, assuming we use the same learning strategies, a verbatim performance will require more practice than a paraphrased one.

Another factor in practice, particularly for the learning of labels, facts, and lists, is the importance of spaced practice. Massed practice, as is seen in all-night cram sessions for final exams, will generally not be as efficient as the same amount of time spent in practice spaced over a period of time.

Practice is generally associated with reaching automaticity in the performance of a skill. However, automaticity is also involved in declarative knowledge. Some declarative knowledge performances require more automaticity than others. For example, remembering a list requires less automaticity than reciting a poem. The material under study needs to be practiced until the learner reaches the desired level of automaticity. In determining the degree of automaticity for declarative knowledge, the designer needs to imagine the context in which the knowledge will be applied. For example, a high level of automaticity will be needed for recalling chemical symbols or elements because this knowledge needs to be available more or less instantly in applying rules and in problem solving.

Practice for labels should involve presenting one of the two elements in the association, such as presenting H and then requiring the learner to provide the other element—hydrogen. Practice for labels is almost always verbatim recall. Practice for labels could be verbatim recognition. However, usually the desired end result is that the learner can supply, rather than recognize, the elements, so practice should be at this level. But when learners are practicing supplying labels, if one element is likely to be consistently supplied in use, then that element should always be supplied in practice. For example, when learners learn to label a map with names, usually the map is given and the name must be supplied. The knowledge should be practiced this way. However, in some cases either element is equally likely to be supplied, so practice should be distributed so that each element is supplied and each is recalled.

Practice for facts and lists is generally verbatim recall. With a fact, usually a question is asked that supplies one of the concepts as a cue to elicit recall of the other concept (e.g., "Who is the governor of Texas?" or "In what year did J. S. Bach die?"). A question that asks for recall of a list usually supplies a keyword to cue the list (e.g., "Name the inert gases"). If sequence within the list is important, then the question should remind the learner of its importance (e.g., "Name the planets in the sun's orbit, starting with the planet nearest the sun and moving outward'').

Practice for connected discourse is most often in the form of paraphrased recall. Learners are asked to explain, summarize, and describe in their own words content that has been provided in the discourse. Occasionally, learners may be asked to recognize paraphrased statements that best represent the content. They may be asked to determine if a single statement accurately reflects the content. Practice of connected discourse learning usually requires the learners to evidence ''understanding.''

Practice requirements for our periodic table instruction should involve ''overlearning'' to reach the required level of automaticity. This means that learners will encounter the material frequently over an extended period of time. The activities involved in the events of instruction, such as processing information, focusing attention, and employing learning strategies, all provide for practice. However, due to the automaticity needed in this learning task, instruction will need to provide for repeated practice over time; this should be individually determined and administered. The use of computer-assisted instruction is particularly suited to satisfying this need. Although ''drill and practice'' uses of computers are abhorred in some circles, needed practice of the sort required here may be more interestingly and efficiently provided by this medium than other alternatives.

Feedback

For labels, facts, and lists, the requirements of feedback are relatively straightforward. Feedback for labels and facts should evaluate whether information is complete and associations are correct. Lists may have two elements, completeness and sequence, which must be evaluated. If answers reflect an incorrect combination of associations, the feedback might point out the error.

For organized discourse, provision of feedback generally requires that instruction either have an ''intelligent'' evaluator or provide model responses. An ''intelligent'' evaluator generally is a knowledgeable human; however, some computer-based intelligent tutoring systems (ITS) may incorporate sufficient natural language processing and ''intelligence'' to assess a constructed answer. A model response should be constructed with attention to organization and the essential features of a model answer. The marking of essay examinations provides a commonplace example of organized discourse feedback (assuming exams are returned to the student). As all good teachers know, to do a good job of evaluating and providing feedback to students on their essay performances the instructor must know what a good answer to the question is. This good answer could be either written or in the teacher's head, although we would recommend the written version, with levels of quality illustrated (see Chapter 5). The same sort of good answer or model response is needed to provide feedback on practice.

Conclusion

Summarize and Review

The summary and review process is critical to declarative knowledge learning. As cognitive structures are being tuned and adjusted by new knowledge, summaries are needed as practice and to assist consolidation. Summaries serve somewhat different needs in organized discourse as compared to the other forms of declarative knowledge. A summary of organized discourse, particularly with lengthy and complex material, serves to clarify and ensure the schema-tuning needed to assimilate the material. For the other forms of declarative knowledge the summary and review function will be more related to needs for practice and repetition. So, in learning labels/names and facts/lists, a summary and review can provide an opportunity to work with the material using a different strategy from that which was used in information process-practice-feedback phases. For example, if the designer had chosen to employ a mnemonic strategy for learning a list of technical terms in an electronics course, a summary/review could be conducted using a graphic organizer.

Learners may be more involved in the generation of summary/review activities than has been the case in traditional instruction. The traditional pattern, certainly for didactic, supplantive instruction, has been for the instruction to supply a summary. We are so accustomed to this approach that it might be difficult to imagine summaries being accomplished any way other than by the instructor or other medium. However, student-processed summaries are a powerful learning tool, particularly for organized discourse. Hidi (1985) devised and studied a technique for training learners in generating summaries of text material. The training proceeds from teaching learners to paraphrase paragraphs in relatively simple material through the summarizing of long, complex bodies of material. The researchers found that although the training required of learners to become proficient at summarizing can be extensive and difficult, student-generated summaries were better than instruction-supplied summaries for retention of material studied.

A final concern with regard to summaries is the need for them to be employed more than once, over time. Sometimes the impression is left that summarizing is a single event. There is a need, particularly in complex and difficult material, for interim summaries. Interim summaries provide opportunity for consolidation before the material in working memory is replaced by subsequent material. Interim summaries also provide excellent transition vehicles from one sub-topic to the next.

A summary of our elements module could be provided by a review of the categories into which elements are grouped. The summary could indicate how the categories are related and could provide a review of the elements and the label for each element.

For our music history course, we might have each student create a musical summary (through editing audio materials onto tape). The summary should be accompanied by a short written verbal explanation.

Transfer

The most critical part of transfer in declarative knowledge learning is that information is available for retrieval to be combined with new information. In other words, to apply a fact or make use of a list, it must be easily brought to mind so that it can be used. Everyone has experienced being stuck, unable to go on in a conversation or project because the word, phrase, or number needed is on the "tip of the tongue" but not available. Procedures—motor skills and procedural rules—have a declarative knowledge component requiring that learners remember a list of steps. Rules often require declarative knowledge recall, such as a formula or a constant such as the value of pi. Understanding and ability to perform can be stymied by mere lack of ability to remember a simple fact. The governing factor in retrieval of labels, facts, and lists is the strength of the relationships between elements in an association. The more relationships between elements that are established the more easy the retrieval is. Therefore, to enhance transfer, the knowledge should be elaborated in as many different situations as is feasible. Once declarative knowledge is used, it becomes more easily retrieved for further use. The key to connected discourse recall is organization. The organization or structure of a lecture or text provides retrieval cues, much as retrieving a folder in a file allows us to retrieve the information in the file.

Transfer often involves making inferences—bridges between knowledge that have not been made for the learner. Inferences usually involve invoking prior knowledge combined with new information. In building expertise in a body of knowledge, such as a scholar or expert in a specialty does, one can have the experience of "discovering" links and patterns between and among sets of information that were learned as separate, distinct entities. College students experience the joy of seeing relationships within their knowledge that seem to deepen and personalize knowledge, making it truly "their own." Opportunities for this sort of transfer to occur are increased when instruction encourages learners to make inferences from the material learned to other possible areas.

In our chemistry instruction, we want learners to be able to apply their knowledge of chemical names and symbols in reading chemical formulas. Practice within instruction or that provided during assessment of recently learned symbols in the context of chemical formulas can assist transfer.

Opportunities for transfer of the learning from our music history course will be available throughout the students' lives and will be actualized depending on whether the student chooses to do so. Certainly the structure provided by the course can assist recall of the ideas in the course and can provide the learner with building blocks for a richly developed knowledge and appreciation of music.

Remotivate and Close

In remotivation and closure of declarative knowledge instruction it is important to re-emphasize the utility of the knowledge that has been learned.

It is also important to encourage the learners to mentally manipulate the information on their own. For facts, labels, and lists, this mental manipulation may be rehearsal. For organized discourse, it may be elaboration with more information or seeking out redundancies, contradictions, or inferences.

Assessment

The final two events in the expanded instructional events, Assess Performance and Evaluate Feedback/Seek Remediation, are described in Chapter 5. Also see the discussion of feedback from practice previously discussed in this chapter.

Summary

In this chapter, we have taken a close look at designing instruction for the learning of declarative knowledge. In a review of declarative knowledge, we saw that declarative knowledge, also called verbal information, is viewed as being represented in memory as propositional networks, or schemata, linking nodes of information by relationship. We discussed three kinds of declarative knowledge: labels/names, facts/lists, and organized discourse. We also discussed three activities that are common to all declarative knowledge learning: linking, organizing, and elaborating. Using the expanded instructional events as a framework, we looked at particular instructional techniques for declarative knowledge instruction. Within the discussion of the instructional events, illustrations from two example applications were provided, one for a module on the periodic table (a facts/list task) and a second involving music history (an organized discourse task). The following table recasts the remainder of the chapter's content into a summary frame.

Conditions of Learning by Event for Declarative Knowledge Learning

Introduction	Deploy attention. Arouse interest and motivation.	• Use of novel, conflictual, and paradoxical events, the interjection of personal/emotional elements, and making clear how the present learning relates to other learning tasks
	Establish instructional purpose.	• Relate instructional goals to personal life goals or job requirements; make instructional goals personally relevant; present the goal in an interesting, dynamic format; remind learners of relevant learning strategies; point out requirements for successful attainment of the objective; and let learners know the form in which they need to remember the material.
	Preview lesson.	• Advance organizer or epitome can be useful form of preview; outlines or maps are also helpful.
Body	Recall prior knowledge.	• Advance organizers, use of metaphoric devices, and reviews of prerequisite concepts

	Process information.	• Labels/names
		    Organization: clustering and chunking
		    Elaboration: elaboration into sentences

Body (continued)		• Facts/lists
		  Association: use of images
		  Organization: expository and narrative
		  structures, recognizing patterns, clustering and
		  chunking, and elaboration
		• Organized discourse:
		  Association: imagery, metaphoric devices
		  Organization: analysis of expository and
		  narrative structures, use of graphic organizers
		  such as frames and concept maps
		  Elaboration: Elaboration Model

	Focus attention.	• Underlining, listing, and reflecting; pre-, post-, and embedded questions

	Employ learning strategies.	• Previously noted strategies (all but advance
		  organizer)
		• Mnemonic techniques such as single-use coding,
		  pegwords, the method of loci, keywords, and the
		  use of rhymes, stories, or jingles
		• Rehearsal

	Practice.	• The role of practice; consider differential needs
		  for practice for recall versus recognition learning
		  tasks and for verbatim versus paraphrased recall;
		  consider needs for spaced practice; and the role of
		  automaticity in declarative knowledge

	Evaluate feedback.	• Consider feedback needed for labels, facts, and
		  lists (evaluate correctness of associations of
		  elements) as contrasted with the feedback needed
		  for organized discourse (''understanding'').

Conclusion	Summarize and review.	• Tuning cognitive structures, learner-generated summaries, interim summaries

	Transfer knowledge.	• Increase the number of possible connections in
		  the learner's mental map, the role of application
		  in a variety of settings, learners making
		  inferences

	Remotivate and close.	• Show how learning can help the student.
Assessment	Assess performance.	• Refer to Chapter 5.
	Feedback and remediation.	• Refer to Chapter 5.

Job Aid

Use the Job Aid from Chapter 8 to plan concept lessons or lessons that combine declarative knowledge and other outcomes.

Extended Example

Learning Task: List the common f-stop numbers.

Review of Learning Task

Learning the common f-stop numbers is a facts/list task. This module is to follow instruction on f-stops as concepts and rules. In other words, learners will already know what f-stops are and have some knowledge of how to use them. Possession of these intellectual skills, however, does not assure that the learners possess the declarative knowledge of what the common f-stop numbers are. Such knowledge is seen as useful in actual photography work, in which the easy recall of numbers is used to solve problems. In other words, knowledge of the f-stop numbers helps keep the photographer from getting confused when working on exposure.

Synopsis of Instructional Approach

For learning the f-stop numbers, the method of loci combined with rhyming will be used, and it will be delivered using a CAI module. Rhyming objects will be assigned to the numbers one through ten, to associate with the ten f-stop values to be learned. The method of loci will help encode and stimulate recall of the sequence. The computer will assist the learner in the process of devising and assigning mnemonics and provide practice as well as evaluation.

On following pages, the lesson will be described in terms of the expanded instructional events.

Introduction

1. Deploy attention to lesson.
2. Establish instructional purpose.
3. Arouse interest and motivation.
4. Preview lesson.

The title frame and introductory frames of the CAI lesson will achieve the functions of the introduction. In short paragraphs the student is told what the lesson will be about and what specific learning will be expected: "When you complete this module, you will know the common f-stop numbers used on 35mm camera aperture controls. In the posttest, you will be asked, 'What are the common f-stop numbers?' You will be able to list all ten of them, in the correct sequence." For motivational purposes, the utility of this knowledge will need to be conveyed, since the task is intrinsically relatively uninteresting, and the utility of memorizing f-stop numbers is not likely to be already realized by learners as a product of their prior learning. Finally, the learner will be told, again in a short paragraph, how the lesson will proceed. The lesson will involve a keyword (or pegword), technique and practice, and a posttest. A short paragraph will describe the pegword method:

Your learning of the f-stop numbers will be made easier through the use of a memorizing aid called the pegword method. Using a rhyme and counting one through ten, you will make up words that will rhyme and help you associate the f-stop numbers in their correct sequence.

Body

5. Recall relevant prior knowledge.

The concept of aperture and certain rules regarding aperture are relevant prior knowledge. A pretest will be used to both screen for prior knowledge and review. Feedback from the pretest offers review in another form, consolidating it. For learners who complete the pretest successfully, the review will state the following:

Excellent. You knew that the aperture is the lens opening, controlling how much light gets onto the film. You also remembered that f-stop numbers are the denominators of fractions that represent the ratio between the size of the lens opening and the focal length of the lens. You knew that because f-stops are the bottom numbers of fractions, then the larger the number, the smaller the aperture (1/16 is smaller than 1/2; f/16 is smaller than f/2). Let's now go on and learn the common f-stop numbers.

6. Process information and examples.
7. Focus attention.
8. Employ learning strategies.

The instruction will first present the list of f-stop numbers and ask the learner to read them aloud, one by one: 1.4, 2, 2.8, 4, 5.6, 8, 11, 16, 22, and 32. The instruction will then proceed to help the learner memorize the numbers. First, the learners will be stimulated to imagine a room with which they are familiar and told that they will mentally place objects around the room and use those objects as a memory aid. The learner will be guided in the formation of images for 1.4, 2, 2.8, and so forth. While learner-generated objects could be used, we chose to provide them:

- The door is 1.4.
- A shoe is f-stop 2.
- A big old plate is 2.8.
- A mess on the floor is f-stop 4.
- A bunch of sticks is 5.6.
- A wooden crate is our f-stop 8.
- A painting of heaven is 11.
- A sofa of green is f-stop 16.
- A chair of blue is 22.
- A big old gnu is 32.

The instruction will tell the learner, "Now imagine 1.4 painted on your front door. Now say, 'The door is 1.4.' Close your eyes and visualize the front door with 1.4 on it." Subsequently, after practice, feedback, and review events, the next number is associated in a similar fashion. F-stop 2 would be represented by the shoe of a camera salesperson stuck in the doorway. The associations proceed, placing each object in the room in a clockwise sequence around the room.

One additional information-processing strategy is provided by explaining why there is not an immediately obvious consistent progression in the numbers (the fact that they are the denominators of fractions). The instruction will show that a pattern does exist in the numbers: Alternate numbers are doubles (1.4 times two is 2.8; 2 times two is 4; 2.8 times two is 5.6; and so forth). If the learner remembers the first two numbers (1.4 and 2), the entire list can be reconstructed (the only exception being 5.6 times two being rounded to 11).

9. Practice.
10. Evaluate feedback.

The instruction provides the opportunity for practice of each number before moving to the next number. The learner is asked to complete the rhyme:

The door is _____ .
A shoe is _____ .

Conclusion

11. Summarize and review.

After each new number is presented, a review beginning with 1.4 is provided to assist consolidation, including a review at the end of the entire set of ten numbers. The f-stop numbers will be related to the size of the lens aperture.

12. Transfer learning.

After the learner has completed the mnemonic section with associated practice, opportunity is given to remember the set of numbers under different stimulus conditions. The learner is presented with an illustration of a camera without any numbers on the aperture ring. The student is to fill in the f-stop numbers on the aperture ring. In this exercise, the student will be given help if stuck, but if help is given, the instruction will return to providing practice instead of moving on.

13. Remotivate and close.

Remotivation will follow the assessment phase. For remotivation, the module will briefly illustrate the utility of knowing f-stop numbers: "When the aperture is set to f/16 you know immediately that there are two smaller f-stops available, or if you need two f-stops larger than the current opening, you know that you need f/8. As you work with the camera, the f-stop markings on the aperture ring will become more familiar. With practice, you will be much more 'at home' with your camera.''

Assessment

14. Assess performance.
15. Evaluate feedback and seek remediation.

A posttest will be given within the CAI module to provide for assessment. For the posttest, the student will be asked to type the f-stop numbers in sequence. After all numbers have been entered, the computer will compare them with the correct responses and present the learner with results. If all were correct, the learner is given hearty congratulations and the lesson is concluded. If any were missed, the program returns to practice.

Readings and References

Anderson, J. R. (1976). *Language, memory and thought.* Hillsdale, NJ: Lawrence Erlbaum Associates.

Anderson, J. R. (1985). *Cognitive psychology and its implications* (3rd ed). New York: W. H. Freeman.

Armbruster, B. B., & Anderson, T. H. (1985). Frames: Structures for informative text. In D. H. Jonassen (Ed.), *The technology of text, Vol. 2.* Englewood Cliffs, NJ: Educational Technology Publications.

Atkinson, R. C. (1975). Mnemotechnics in second-language learning. *American Psychologist, 30,* 821–828.

Ausubel, D. P. (1968). *Educational psychology: A cognitive view.* New York: Holt, Rinehart, & Winston.

Bull, S. G. (1973). The role of questions in maintaining attention to textual material. *Review of Educational Research, 43,* 61, 83–87.

Duchastel, P. (1978). Illustrating instructional texts. *Educational Technology, 1978, 18*(11), 36–39.

Gagné, E. D. (1985). *The cognitive psychology of school learning.* Boston: Little, Brown, & Co.

Gagné, R. M. (1985). *The conditions of learning* (4th ed.). New York: Holt, Rinehart, & Winston.

Gagné, R. M., & Briggs, L. J. (1979). *Principles of instructional design.* (2nd ed.) New York: Holt, Rinehart, & Winston.

Gall, M. D. (1970). The use of questions in teaching. *Review of Educational Research, 40* (5) 707–721.

Heinich, R., Molenda, M., & Russell, J. D. (1989). *Instructional media and the new technologies of instruction.* New York: Macmillan.

Hidi, S. (1985). *Variables that affect how children summarize school texts and the amount they learn during this activity.* A paper presented at the annual meeting of the American Educational Research Association, Chicago.

Higbee, K. L. (1979). Recent research on visual mnemonics: Historical roots and educational fruits. *Review of Educational Research, 49* (4) 611–629.

Holley, C. D., & Dansereau, D. F. (Eds.) (1984). *Spatial learning strategies: Techniques, applications, and related issues.* Orlando, FL: Academic Press.

Joyce, B. & Weil, M. (1986). *Models of teaching,* (3rd ed.) Englewood Cliffs, NJ: Prentice-Hall.

Locatis, C. N. & Atkinson, F. D. (1984) *Media and technology for education and training.* Columbus: Merrill.

Meyer, B. J. F. (1985). Signaling the structure of text. In D. H. Jonassen (Ed.), *The technology of text, Vol. 2.* Englewood Cliffs, NJ: Educational Technology Publications.

Minsky, M. A. (1975). A framework for representing knowledge. In P. H. Winston (Ed.), *The psychology of computer vision,* pp. 211–280. New York: McGraw-Hill.

Posner, G. J., & Strike, K. A. (1976). A categorization scheme for principles of sequencing content. *Review of Educational Research, 46,* 665–690.

Pressley, M., Levin, J. R., & Delaney, H. D. (1982). The mnemonic keyword method. *Review of Educational Research, 52* (1), 61–91.

Reigeluth, C. M. (1979). In search of a better way to organize instruction: The elaboration theory. *Journal of Instructional Development, 2,* (3) 8–15.

Reigeluth, C. M. & Stein, F. S. (1983). The elaboration theory of instruction. In C. M. Reigeluth (Ed.), *Instructional-design theories and models: An overview of their current status.* Hillsdale, NJ: Erlbaum.

Rothkopf, E. Z. & Bisbicos, E. E. (1967). Selective facilitative effects of interspersed questions on learning from written materials. *Journal of Educational Psychology, 58,* 56–61.

Rummelhart, D. E. & Ortony, A. (1977). The representation of knowledge in memory. In R. C. Anderson, R. J. Spiro, and W. E. Montague (Eds.), *Schooling and the acquisition of knowledge,* pp. 37–53. Hillsdale, N.J.: Lawrence Erlbaum Associates.

Schank, R. C. (1984). *The cognitive computer: On language, learning, and artificial intelligence.* Reading, MA: Addison-Wesley.

Schramm, W. (1964). *The research on programmed instruction: An annotated bibliography.* Washington: U.S. Dept. of Health, Education and Welfare, Office of Education. Publication number OE 34034.

Simon, H. A. (1974). How big is a chunk? *Science, 183,* 482–488.

Smith, P. L. & Friend, M. (1986). Training learning disabled adolescents in a strategy for using text structure to aid recall of instructional prose. *Learning Disabilities Research, 2* (1), 38–44.

Smith, P. L., & Ragan, T. J., (1990). Designing visual analogies for instruction. *Journal of Visual Language, 10*(2), 60–83.

Smith, P. L., & Tompkins, G. E. (1988). Structured notetaking: A new strategy for content readers. *Journal of Reading, 32* (1), 46–53.

Sternberg, R. J. (1987). The psychology of verbal comprehension. In Glaser, R. (Ed.) *Advances in instructional psychology,* vol. 3, pp. 97–152. Hillsdale, NJ: Erlbaum.

Tessmer, M., Wilson, B., & Driscoll, M. (1990). A new model of concept teaching and learning. *Educational Technology Research and Development, 38*(1), 45–53.

Wager, W. & Wager, S. (1985). Presenting questions, processing responses, and providing feedback in CAI. *Journal of Instructional Development, 8* (4), 2–8.

West, C. K., Farmer, J. A., & Wolf, P. M. (1991). *Instructional design: Implications from cognitive science.* Englewood Cliffs, NJ: Prentice Hall.

Zeitoun, H. H. (1984). Teaching scientific analogies: A proposed model. *Research in Science and Technological Education, 2,* 107–125.

Strategies for Concept Lessons

eight

Chapter Objectives

At the conclusion of this chapter you should be able to do the following:

- Given descriptions of several learning tasks, identify those that are concept learning tasks.

- Given examples of an instructional strategy plan, identify those that are inquiry and those that are expository.

- Given a concept, describe the criterial attributes of that concept.

- Given sets of concepts, identify those that are coordinate concepts.

- Given a concept, develop a concept map of that concept, indicating its relationship to superordinate and subordinate concepts.

- Given a concept, determine the "best example" and a poor initial example for that concept, and justify your choices.

- Given a concept, develop a matched example and nonexample and explain your choice.

- Given a concept, explain the processes of generalization and discrimination as they apply to that concept.

- Given a concept, explain the processes of overgeneralization and undergeneralization as they apply to that concept.

- Given a concept objective, design a strategy plan for a concept lesson.

Review of Concept Learning

In Chapter 4 we identified concept learning as one of the intellectual skills. Learning that is classified as an intellectual skill involves the ability to apply knowledge across a variety of instances or circumstances. Intellectual skills are most often confused with verbal information learning. Intellectual skills differ from verbal information learning in that verbal information involves a memorization of an association between two or more entities; for example, the association of a dog's appearance with its name. Intellectual skills involve the ability to apply knowledge across a variety of previously unencountered instances—in the case of a concept, the ability to respond "dog" to an infinite variety of usually four-legged, furry, sometimes barking mammals. One definition of concept that we find particularly useful is the following:

A concept is a set of specific objects, symbols, or events which are grouped together on the basis of shared characteristics and which can be referenced by a particular name or symbol. (Merrill & Tennyson, 1977, p. 3)

Examples of concepts are listed below:

computer	impressionism
house	Cold War
adverb	igneous
theory *Y*	hunter-gatherer
haiku	norm
profit	pulley
cartoon	scapegoat
forehand serve	bull market
triangle	beard
prime number	tax-sheltered annuity
blue	solid
reptile	cumulus cloud

You will remember from your reading of Chapter 4 and from examining the list of concepts above that there are two distinctly different kinds of concepts: concrete and abstract (sometimes called *defined concepts*). **Concrete concepts** are known by their physical characteristics, which may be discerned by any of the senses—sight, smell, taste, touch, or hearing. In the preceding list, *computer, house, cartoon, forehand serve, triangle, blue, reptile, igneous, pulley, beard, solid,* and *cumulus cloud* are most known by their physically perceivable characteristics, so they are concrete concepts. Ideas like "profit," "haiku," "norm," "bull market," and "tax-sheltered annuity" are not perceivable by their appearance; indeed, some of them, like "bull market," have no appearance. They are **abstract concepts.** Members of this category are known only as they fit a particular definition.

Some of the above examples might fall into either category, concrete or abstract, depending upon the level of sophistication of the learners. For example, for a primary school child a computer is a concrete, physically perceivable object. However, a college student knows that some television sets, dishwashers, and cash registers may also be considered to be "computers," because they have the built-in capability of digital processing of information. The college student knows the concept "computer" by the definition that includes a function, rather than solely by its physical appearance. The same concrete-to-abstract continuum might be applied to the concepts "cartoon," "triangle," "blue," and perhaps others.

As you can see, the distinction between abstract and concrete concepts can become quite muddy; therefore, we will not ask you to classify examples as concrete or abstract. However, in the actual design of instruction, when you know the level of sophistication of your learners, you will wish to consider whether you are teaching a particular concept at the concrete or the abstract level because the way you address the design of the two types of concepts is somewhat different.

At this point it is helpful to review what concept learning is *not*. Concept learning is frequently confused with verbal information. Two misunderstandings are particularly common. One is confusing the learning of a concept with learning of the definition of that concept. For example, if a child were to memorize the definition of a triangle as "a three-sided plane figure" but was unable to find the triangles in a set of figures, then the child would only have learned "triangle" at the verbal information level. Another misunderstanding has to do with the labeling of things versus identification of membership in a class of things. A child who points to our dog and says "Gracie" has acquired verbal information. If she points to our dog and says "golden retriever," she has acquired a concept. Verbal information learning enables a person to identify a particular member of the concept category, such as saying, "That is Mt. Kilimanjaro." Concept learning allows a person to identify something when given a picture not previously seen such as saying, "That is an extinct volcano."

Concept learning is also not the application of a rule that contains that concept. For example, learning the concept "the commutative property of addition" would involve recognizing its application. Consider this example:

In which of the following problems is the commutative property applied?

$$2 + 3 = 3 + 2$$
$$2 + 3 = 4 + 1$$
$$(1 + 1) + (2 + 1) = 1 + (1 + 2) + 1$$

The actual application of the commutative property as a rule would require the solution of a particular math problem using the property, such as:

$$2 + 3 = \underline{} + 2$$

A learner who has acquired a concept is able to use that concept to classify previously unencountered instances as members of that concept class or not. We say "previously unencountered instances" because if we assess learners' acquisition of concepts with examples they have encountered as examples in initial instruction or in practice, they may simply have memorized the association rather than actually being able to apply the concept.

Learners who have acquired concepts are also able to supply their own examples of the concepts and apply the concepts appropriately in day-to-day encounters. For example, learners have acquired the concept "bourgeois" if they use it appropriately in speech or writing and understand its meaning when they hear it used. Concepts have both a declarative knowledge aspect and a procedural (intellectual skill) knowledge, pattern recognition aspect (Tessmer, Wilson, & Driscoll, 1990). In this chapter we will discuss the procedural knowledge aspect of concepts.

Cognitive Processes and Structures in Concept Learning

We say that learners have acquired a concept when they have learned to recognize a "pattern" in their surroundings and consistently respond to that pattern no matter what nonessential features may appear along with that pattern. Learning a concept requires two cognitive processes—generalization and discrimination. When learners are first exposed to a member of a concept they must learn to **generalize** beyond the single instance of that concept to others that fall into the same category. For example, a young child who sees a picture of cows in a pasture may point to one of the animals and ask, "What's that?" The instructor will respond, "A cow." It is very likely that if the child has not yet learned the concept "cow," then he will point to another of the cows in the picture and ask, "What's that?" The faithful instructor (or parent) will respond again, "A cow," Eventually, the child will point to another animal in the pasture and ask, "Cow?" and receive all the feedback and encouragement he needs. The child has generalized the concept of "cow" beyond the single first instance encountered to other examples of the concept.

However, as people are learning concepts they have a tendency to **overgeneralize.** For example, the child who has learned that a large, four-legged animal is a cow may have a tendency to respond "cow" to a picture of a horse, zebra, moose, and many other large, four-legged animals. Gradually, the child learns to **discriminate** between examples of the concept and nonexamples that may share some features with the concept but do not share the critical attributes that make one instance a member of the class. For example, cows' general body shapes, as well as the shapes of their heads, hooves, and tails, make them distinct from other large, four-legged mammals. The instructor helps the child make these discriminations by saying, "No, that's not a cow. Look at how thin and long the head is. That's not the head of a cow. Look again at the cow's head. It's short and wide."

Please note that it may be possible that in learning concepts, learners first make discriminations that certain entities are similar to each other and that other entities are distinctly different from the group, and then make generalizations. We do know that learners must be able to distinguish differences among entities before they are able to move on to form a concept around one or the other of them. For example, learners must be able to distinguish that a figure that is a circle is different from a figure that is a square before they can acquire the concept "square." It may be slightly more efficient to encourage learners to generalize before they are encouraged to consciously discriminate the distinctive features of a concept. You will see later that we suggest two slightly different sequences of instruction—one that encourages generalization first and one that encourages discrimination first.

Another necessary generalization of a concept is learners' ability to transfer the concept to settings other than the setting in which they first encountered it. We know that the child has really acquired the concept "cow" when she identifies cows in settings other than the picture in which she first started learning "cow" (for instance, when she points to the billboard advertising a milk company whose logo is a cow and says, "cow," or when she points to a real cow and identifies it as a "cow").

Concept learning can go wrong in two ways. First, learners can continue to overgeneralize, as with the child who continues to say "cow" in response to four-legged animals other than cows. Or, learners can **undergeneralize,** as with a child who thinks only black and white animals with cow features are "cows." In each case, particular instructional strategies can prevent or remediate overgeneralization and undergeneralization of the concept.

You will note how critical learning the class label or concept name is to acquiring the concept. While it is theoretically possible that a learner could respond to a class of things without knowing the class's name, the learner must have some label that he is using to mentally represent that class. To have efficient communication, learners must be able to respond to examples of the concept with its name.

Cognitive psychologists theorize that concepts are mentally stored in the form of productions, an if-then representation. For example, the concept "rhombus" might be stored in the following form:

IF the figure is a polygon,
   and the figure is a parallelogram,
   and the figure's sides are equilateral,
   and the figure's angles are oblique,
THEN the figure is a rhombus.

These productions result from the generalization and discrimination processes. You will notice how closely this production mirrors our information-processing analysis of the task of learning the concept "rhombus" in Chapter 4. It is quite possible that these productions are not on the conscious level but rather are automatic for learners who are proficient in the application of a particular concept. We often find this automaticity to be the case when conducting an information-processing analysis of a concept learning task. Sometimes quite lengthy and probing questioning is required to ascertain the qualities that an expert uses when assigning entities to categories.

*E*ssential Conditions of Learning Concepts

The essential conditions in a concept lesson are the features that promote generalization and discrimination and reduce over- and undergeneralization. Although the most critical features of a concept lesson lie in the events within the body, we will describe important features within each of the four main components of the lesson. You will notice that we do not list each of the expanded events in the order in which we first introduced them. This variation further underscores the notion that the order of these instructional events may vary with the learning task, learners, and context.

Two General Strategies of Concept Instruction

Concept instruction may follow one of two general strategies: a predominantly generative strategy or a more supplantive one. One type of generative strategy is termed an **inquiry approach.** It is contrasted to a more typically supplantive strategy called an **expository approach.** Neither approach is particularly better than the other, but one may be more appropriate than the other depending upon the context, the learners, and the learning task.

An inquiry strategy is often referred to as an *exploratory strategy* or a *discovery approach.* An inquiry strategy presents examples and nonexamples of the concept and prompts the learners to "discover" the concept underlying the instances. Joyce and Weil's (1986) concept attainment model is an example of an inquiry approach to teaching concepts. In this strategy learners are presented with a group of matched examples and nonexamples in verbal, auditory, or visual form. The examples are labeled with the word *yes*, and the nonexamples are labeled with the word *no*. The learners are invited to join in a guessing game to discover the secret (the concept) as to why some instances are labeled *yes* and others *no*. Learners are encouraged to develop a tentative hypothesis as to the concept underlying the categorization. Then, they are presented with more examples and nonexamples labeled with *yes* and *no*. The learner is prompted to confirm her hypothesis by determining if it would predict the categorization of the new instances. Next, learners are invited to state their hypotheses regarding the concept. Some hypotheses may be fallacious, some may be unrelated to the targeted concept (these should be accepted but not further investigated at this time), and other hypotheses will be correct. These hypotheses should be formalized into a statement of the concept. Finally, learners are encouraged to think of their own examples of the concept and receive feedback regarding the accuracy of their examples. (The example lesson on the concept "art deco" that appears later in this chapter is an example of a slightly different inquiry approach.)

An expository approach presents the concept, its label, and its critical attributes earlier in the lesson sequence than in the inquiry approach. Expository instruction does present many examples and nonexamples; however, these instances follow a discussion of a best example and how it embodies the characteristics of the concept. In an expository approach, learners are encouraged to develop their own examples; however, it is after the attributes of the concept have been carefully explained. The sequence that we use in the following discussion of the expanded instructional events employs a more expository sequence. The extended example that teaches the concept "depth of field" at the end of the chapter uses an expository approach.

Introduction

Deploy Attention
Arouse Interest and Motivation

In text-based concept lessons, attention is often aroused in as simple a manner as using boldface type or otherwise highlighting a new term. That term is then further explored in the remainder of the lessons. Inquiry strategies are often highly attention provoking, interest arousing, and motivating. An unusual picture or humorous story relating to the concept may also stimulate interest and attention. Information about the origin or history of the concept to be learned may also promote these two events. The instruction may even present the first matched set of examples and nonexamples of the concept to focus learners' attention on the characteristics of the task, pique their curiosity, and begin to inform them of the objective, all in one step. A matched set of examples and nonexamples is provided by a clear example of the concept and an instance that is similar in some features but is not an example of the concept. For many older learners and adults, information is also provided about how knowledge of this concept will relate to future tasks or problems.

Establish Instructional Purpose

Instructional purpose may be selected by the individual learner ("I'm going to learn the difference between Level 1, Level 2, and Level 3 interactive video"). Or it may be provided by the instruction ("Today we're going to learn to distinguish among the legislative, executive, and judicial branches of a government"). A statement of the objective is more typical in an expository form of instruction. A lesson that is structured in an inquiry organization may not inform the learners of the specific purpose of the lesson at the beginning of the lesson, as this revelation would short-circuit the inquiry process; however, it is critical that within the summary and closure events it is confirmed that learners clearly understood the purpose of the lesson.

Preview Lesson

The preview of an expository lesson may, if desired, not only provide an overview of the content to be learned but also provide an indication of how the lesson will proceed, such as explaining to learners that they will see examples and nonexamples of the concept under study until they are able to demonstrate that they are able to distinguish examples of these concepts. An inquiry preview may set up the "problem" of the inquiry task, letting learners know that they will be discerning the categories of instances and determining the characteristics by which the instances were placed in these categories, such as a teacher saying, "You will decide what boxes we will make up, and you'll also decide what goes in each box."

Body

Recall Prior Knowledge

The most critical prior knowledge in learning a concept is the knowledge of concepts that comprise the criterial attributes or characteristics of the concept. For example, to learn the concept "rhombus," learners must already possess the concepts "figure," "polygon," "parallelogram," "side," "equilateral," "angles," and "oblique." It is quite likely that before learners reach this point in instruction, they have already acquired these concepts. If not, these prerequisite learnings must be taught before (or concurrently with) instruction on the concept "rhombus." Teaching the concepts concurrently has some advantages in efficiency, but it may sacrifice some clarity as the concepts are not coordinate and are, therefore, more difficult to teach at the same time.

If the prerequisite concepts have been learned previously, a brief review of these concepts is very useful. This review may take the form of (1) informal questioning of the learners to ensure that they remember the concepts, (2) a formal pretest with feedback, (3) a formal review of each of the prerequisite concepts, or (4) an integrated review of each prerequisite concept as it becomes important in discussing the concept's critical attributes in the processing of information and examples event.

For concepts that have less esoteric prerequisites (those with criterial prerequisites that come from general world knowledge), the designer may choose to remind the learners of this general world knowledge through the use of an advance organizer. Ausubel, Novak, and Hanesian (1968) suggested the advance organizer as a way to tie prior knowledge with new learning. One particular kind of advance organizer, the comparative organizer, seems most appropriate for teaching concepts. Borrowing from Ausubel's example, suppose you were wishing to teach the concept "Buddhism." One way to bring relevant concepts to working memory is to review the critical characteristics of the dominant religion of the learners in the target audience. These attributes provide a basis of comparison for the new religion being introduced, and

the attributes of the new concept can be made more meaningful by being compared to the familiar. In other words, a comparative organizer reviews a coordinate concept that the learners have acquired previously to allow learners to make clear comparisons between the two concepts.

Process Information and Examples

The most critical feature to ensure these processes is the nature of examples and nonexamples that learners encounter in the initial processing of information relating to a targeted concept and in the practice of that concept. When possible, the first example (sometimes called the *best example* or *prototype*) of the concept should be carefully selected. This example should clearly embody all of the necessary attributes (sometimes called *criterial attributes*) of the concept with few distracting or irrelevant attributes, and it should be familiar to the learners. For example, if the concept to be learned is the concept "transparent," then the first example should concisely represent the concept. A glass window pane is a good best example because (1) it is unequivocally transparent, (2) there are few situations in which a glass window pane would not be transparent, (3) window panes generally vary little in their characteristics, and (4) window panes are familiar objects.

A poor example would be a light bulb because clear glass light bulbs are transparent, but some bulbs are frosted and therefore translucent. Another poor example would be the front surface of a mirror. Although it is transparent, this is difficult to visualize as transparent. Later in the lesson, these difficult examples should be used to help the learners refine their generalization and discrimination, but they are not sufficiently obvious to use as first examples.

Focus Attention

The instruction should point out, either by the definition or a description of the criterial attributes of the concept, why the example represents the concept. Pointing out the criterial attributes is called **attribute isolation.** For some learners, such as those who possess lower aptitude, those who possess few learning strategies, younger students, or extremely anxious learners, providing visual cues to the attributes as they are isolated may be helpful. These visual cues for concrete concepts could be simplified illustrations to highlight the attributes in the instance that make it an example or a nonexample. For abstract concepts, highlighting may also be used within the definition or within the verbal instance to focus the learners' attention on the criterial attributes of the concept and the relevant features of the instance.

Once the learners understand why the example is an example of the concept, they should encounter a matched nonexample of the concept. The nonexample should be matched with the best example on all the nonrelevant attributes so that the characteristics that are criterial will be distinctive. For example, a wall, which is clearly not transparent, shares many of the nonrelevant attributes with a window (e.g., it is flat and vertical), and it would be a good matched nonexample. Again, a discussion of why the nonexample is not an example of the concept is essential. Occasionally, it may be useful to teach two related and easily confused concepts, such as stalactite and stalagmite, together. When concepts are grouped together in instruction, they are called **coordinate concepts.** When you teach coordinate concepts, the examples of one concept can serve as nonexamples for a coordinate concept. Examples of coordinate concepts are convex and concave lenses, loose and strict constructionism, systolic and diastolic pressures, deciduous and coniferous trees, and synonyms and antonyms.

This step should be followed by the processing of additional examples and matched nonexamples that become more and more difficult, such as the clear light bulb example, the front surface of a mirror, or the glass in front of a television screen. Increasing the complexity of the examples encourages the learners to make finer and finer discriminations of the critical and nonrelevant attributes of the concept. In addition, the examples and nonexamples should be as widely dispersed across settings as possible to encourage learners to generalize and transfer the concept to as many appropriate settings as possible. For a more generative strategy, this step may be supplied by the learners themselves, if the medium of instruction allows for accurate feedback to the learners as to whether their examples and nonexamples are appropriate. For example, teacher-led instruction can allow for confirmation of the accuracy of learners' examples. Print-based instruction cannot be so accurate. Unless the number of possible examples is fairly limited, computer-based instruction is limited in giving specific feedback to learners.

Practice

Exposure to examples and nonexamples should be followed with practice across the range of difficulty of the concept from something very simple to discriminate to a most difficult instance. Although the practice may be built from simple practice to more difficult discriminations, it is useful if the settings from which the examples and nonexamples are drawn are as random as possible. This practice should include learners distinguishing between previously unencountered examples and nonexamples of the concept, including the learners isolating the key attributes of the examples and nonexamples. Learners should occasionally be asked to explain their answers. The examples and nonexamples used should be carefully selected to elicit any misconceptions the learners might have. These examples and nonexamples should provide opportunities for learners to overgeneralize and undergeneralize the concept. In addition learners should practice producing their own examples (if feedback is possible).

Evaluate Feedback

Feedback provided to the learners should include an explanation of why an instance is classified as an example or nonexample. This explanation may include criterial attribute isolation, which for abstract concepts may refer to the definition. If learners have *overgeneralized* the concept, they should be provided with clear information as to why the nonexamples they said were examples are not actually examples of that concept. They should be informed of what criterial attributes they are overlooking. If learners have *undergeneralized* the concept, they should be encouraged to determine which features of examples they chose are not actually criterial attributes of the concept. These learners have narrowed the concept inappropriately in some way and need to recognize that they have done so.

Feedback for production answers—answers in which learners provide their own examples of the concept—may be direct when a human is evaluating the practice answers. For other delivery systems, such as computers, feedback for production answers can be accomplished by providing guiding questions keyed to the criterial attributes of the concept. These questions allow learners to evaluate the adequacy of their own answers: "Is the example that you gave of a transparent object an object through which an image can be clearly seen? If so, it is a transparent object.''

Employ Learning Strategies

Some strategies that a learner may employ in acquiring concepts have already been mentioned — elaborating by inventing one's own examples, and isolating attributes and highlighting these attributes in some way. These strategies may be ''built into the instruction'' (within the body, conclusion, or remediation events), provided by the learner, prompted by the instruction, or a combination of all three. Other strategies that may be provided in learning concepts are the development of concept ''trees'' or ''maps,'' analogies, mnemonics, and the use of imagery. **Concept trees** are hierarchical, graphic representations of a targeted concept that show that concept's relationship to superordinate and subordinate concepts. Figure 8.1 shows an example of a concept map developed by Driscoll and Tessmer (1985) to show the relationship of five easily confused coordinate concepts: positive reinforcement, the Premack principle, negative reinforcement, punishment, and extinction. You can see that they included not only the labels for these concepts but also verbal descriptions of their criterial attributes and an example of each. To engage the learning strategy, learners might construct the entire map or complete a partially developed map.

Analogies also help learners understand and remember concepts, particularly concepts for which learners possess little related prior knowledge. Analogies may be presented by the instruction, or the learners may be prompted to develop their own verbal or visual analogies. The development of analogies may be useful for both abstract and concrete concepts; however, analogies may be most helpful in making abstract concepts more concrete. An example of an analogy that can be used in learning a concept is the analogy between the iris of an eye and the aperture of a camera. The point(s) of similarity between the new concept and the familiar concept should be related to the criterial attributes of the concept. For example, the similarity between the eye's iris and a camera's aperture is that they both allow light to pass through to a receiving medium (the film or the retina) and that they control the amount of light passing through by expanding or contracting the opening. It is important that learners are encouraged to consider where

the analogy breaks down so they do not develop misconceptions about the concept. For instance, one of the differences between the iris and an aperture is in the nature of the receiving medium. Film becomes overexposed if too much light falls upon it: It has a finite limit of the length of time that it should be exposed to light. While the retina can receive too much light, such as when viewing the sun in an eclipse, this overexposure has to do with the intensity rather than the duration of the light falling on the retina.

Mnemonics are more often used to remember verbal information than in concept learning. However, there are verbal information components to learning a concept. One of these components is the association of the concept label to the concept. Particularly when coordinate concepts are learned, learners may have difficulty in relating the correct label to the correct concept. When these associations cannot be easily made meaningful, use of mnemonics may be helpful. Many of us learned proper associations of the terms *stalactite* and *stalagmite* by remembering that stalactites ''hold *tight* to the cave's ceiling'' and stalagmites ''reach for the cave's ceiling with all their *might*.'' Mnemonics may also be used to aid learners in remembering the multiple, critical attributes of a concept. These mnemonics may be provided by the instruction or created by the learners.

Imagery is another useful strategy to use in learning certain concepts. Although creating mental images may be easier with concrete concept objectives, some learners may find that developing a visual that concretely represents an abstract concept is very helpful. For example, you can see in Figure 8.2 how one of our students chose to represent the concept ''rule'' (one of Gagné's types of learning outcomes). Such images may be manipulated mentally or committed to paper for future reference. Instruction may provide such images, or learners may be encouraged to produce their own images.

Conclusion

Summarize and Review

At this point in the lesson, it is very helpful to provide an opportunity for a restatement of the definition or criterial attributes of the concept associated with a clear restatement of the concept

Principles of Behavior Management

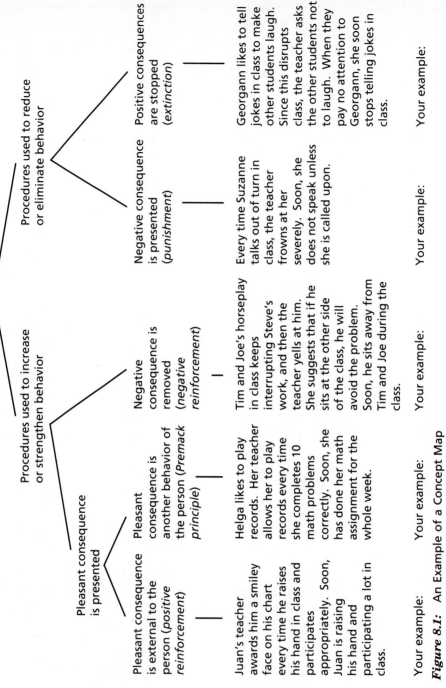

Procedures used to increase or strengthen behavior

Pleasant consequence is presented

Procedures used to reduce or eliminate behavior

Pleasant consequence is external to the person (*positive reinforcement*)

Juan's teacher awards him a smiley face on his chart every time he raises his hand in class and participates appropriately. Soon, Juan is raising his hand and participating a lot in class.

Your example:

Pleasant consequence is another behavior of the person (*Premack principle*)

Helga likes to play records. Her teacher allows her to play records every time she completes 10 math problems correctly. Soon, she has done her math assignment for the whole week.

Your example:

Negative consequence is removed (*negative reinforcement*)

Tim and Joe's horseplay in class keeps interrupting Steve's work, and then the teacher yells at him. She suggests that if he sits at the other side of the class, he will avoid the problem. Soon, he sits away from Tim and Joe during the class.

Your example:

Negative consequence is presented (*punishment*)

Every time Suzanne talks out of turn in class, the teacher frowns at her severely. Soon, she does not speak unless she is called upon.

Your example:

Positive consequences are stopped (*extinction*)

Georgann likes to tell jokes in class to make other students laugh. Since this disrupts class, the teacher asks the other students not to laugh. When they pay no attention to Georgann, she soon stops telling jokes in class.

Your example:

Figure 8.1: An Example of a Concept Map

Source: Driscoll & Tessmer (1985).

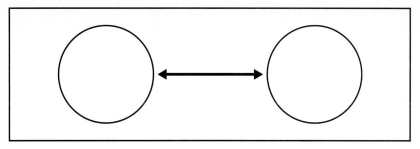

Figure 8.2: Visual Representation of the Concept "Rule"
Source: Smith & Smith (1991).

name. It is not uncommon for learners to forget the name of the concept they have just spent so much time learning, so emphasizing this association is important. It is also useful, if possible, to paraphrase this statement of the definition rather than present the original statement verbatim. This way, learners are encouraged to attend to the meaning rather than the exact terms used in the definition. This might be the point where learners are encouraged to develop or complete a concept map of the concept(s) just learned.

Transfer Knowledge

Learners should be encouraged to locate examples of the concept they have learned in everyday context, perhaps bringing them up for class discussion and confirmation of their categorization. In addition, learners should be encouraged to use the concept label appropriately in conversation as much as possible. It is also useful to encourage learners to begin to make inferences from the concept. For example, if learners have just learned the coordinate concepts "deciduous" and "coniferous," then they might be asked, "If Mr. Rogers hates to rake leaves in the fall, what kind of trees should he plant in his yard?"

Remotivate and Close

To experience this event in conjunction with the transfer event, learners may be encouraged to predict how the newly acquired concept may be applicable in daily life and how it might be useful in future job responsibilities or learning tasks. Since learning concepts is usually a preamble to learning rules and problem solving, the instruction may preview how this new learning will be useful and what learning task will be addressed in the next class meeting.

Assessment

Assess Performance

You will remember that assessment of concepts may involve learners doing the following: (1) explaining why a given, previously unencountered instance is or is not an example of a concept, (2) categorizing given instances as examples and nonexamples of a concept, with or without an explanation of the thinking processes behind the learners' categorization, and/or (3) producing their own examples of a concept, with or without explanation. As with practice, learners should be assessed across the range of difficulty of the concept. Recognition items should be constructed so that learners who have not acquired the concept have an opportunity to overgeneralize or undergeneralize the concept.

In addition, learners may also be assessed on their ability to use the concept to draw inferences, consider the implications of the concept, and use the concept in writing or oral conversation. These transfer items should be separated from the "nearer" transfer items (the performance related to the stated objective), so that learners are not surprised by their appearance.

Evaluate Feedback and Seek Remediation

Feedback should be given to the learners in terms of whether they appear to have mastered the objective. Their mastery should include not only the ability to identify examples and nonexamples but also the ability to use the concept correctly by developing their own examples. In addition, if transfer items are included, learners' ability to transfer the concept should be reported separately from their ability to meet the objective as stated.

Remediation should consider learners' ability to identify examples and nonexamples, their ability to explain their categorization, and whether they are over- or undergeneralizing the concept. Overgeneralization may be remediated by presenting learners with matched examples and nonexamples and isolating the attributes that make the examples viable and the nonexamples not viable. Undergeneralization may be remediated by presenting the learners with an extremely broad range of examples of the concept, with attribute isolation emphasizing that despite the variability of the examples, all of them fall into the concept category.

Exercises

1. Which of the following are concept learning tasks? Justify your answer.

    _____ a. State the definition of *refraction*.
    _____ b. Listen to the following music intervals. Which are fifths?
    _____ c. Explain the kinetic theory of matter.
    _____ d. Circle the pronouns in the sentence.
    _____ e. Read the following sentences. Write the correct form of the verb in the blank in the sentence.
    _____ f. Solve this quadratic equation.
    _____ g. Give an example of a minority.
    _____ h. What is a vegetable?

2. Refer to the examples of generative and supplantive strategies in the Exercises on pages 154–155 of Chapter 6 (numbers 1 and 2). Which of the examples follows an inquiry approach? Which follows a more expository approach? Explain your answer.

3. Which of the following would be considered criterial attributes of the concept "yuppie"? Which are irrelevant attributes of the concept? Explain your categorization.

a. Well-dressed
b. Conservative
c. Brown-haired
d. Drives a Swedish car
e. Short in stature
f. Obsessed with money
g. Good-natured
h. Under 40 years of age
i. Is teased by siblings

4. Which of the following groups of concepts could be considered coordinate concepts? Explain your answer.

    _____ a. Inquiry and expository strategies
    _____ b. Reptile and snake
    _____ c. perennial and annual flowers
    _____ d. dependent and independent clauses
    _____ e. lever and seesaw
    _____ f. solid, liquid, and gas

5. Construct a concept map representing the relationship of the coordinate concepts "deciduous" and "coniferous" to each other and to superordinate and subordinate concepts.

6. What would be a good best example for the concept "mammal"? Why? What would be a poor best example for the concept "mammal"? Why?

7. Give a matched example and nonexample for the concept "verb." Why do you consider the two instances to be matched?

8. Using the concept "stringed instrument," and the best example "violin," explain what would occur as the learner passed through the phases of generalization and discrimination in learning the concept.

9. Explain what a learner might do if he overgeneralized the concept "bicycle." What might he do or say if he undergeneralized the concept "bicycle"?

Preview of the Example Lesson

Analysis of the Task, Context, and Learners

In the next section an example concept lesson will be presented, a lesson on recognizing examples of the concept "art deco." (This is in addition to our Extended Example on photography.) To preview the lesson, we will briefly describe the instructional task, the context, and the learners.

Task Analysis. The lesson objective is the following:

Given a series of color photographs of architectural elements, some of which are examples of art deco and some of which are representative of other art periods, the learner will be able to identify those that are examples of art deco.

This is a concrete concept objective. One can point to an instance of art deco: It is known by its physical attributes.

The production for art deco identification looks something like this:

IF the object or its decoration includes forms that are rectilinear
    and symmetrical
    and streamlined
    and have smooth lines
THEN the object is art deco.

Art deco is a more ambiguous concept than some of the previous concepts that we have discussed in that it has some additional common characteristics that are not present in all forms. Specifically, art deco has the following common characteristics (although not all of these features are required in a form for us to categorize the form as "art deco"):

1. Materials:
   - Precious stones or metals—obsidian, crystal, onyx, ivory, silver, jade
   - Human-made materials—chrome, plastics

2. Motifs:
   - Animals—especially sleek and fleet animals such as deer, antelopes, and gazelles
   - Nude female figures
   - Stylized lightning, leaves, sunbeams, rainbows
   - Geometric patterns

3. Colors: orange, black, silver
4. Form: While the form must include all of the criterial attributes (rectilinear, symmetrical, streamlined, and smooth lines), additional features that aid in the finer distinctions between art deco and other modern forms are the materials, motifs, and colors included in the forms. It will be important that these additional attributes are included in a discussion of criterial attributes.

Context. This objective is for a lesson in a unit on twentieth century art and design for high school students in an art class. The unit itself is organized in a chronological sequence. The class meets in a classroom that has both typical desks and a lab area. Traditional equipment is available, including a video playback unit, a slide projector, and bulletin board areas.

Learners. Students in this class are high school juniors and seniors who have already taken one year of art in high school. The year focused on production techniques of drawing, painting, and sculpting. The second year includes these production techniques in a more elaborated fashion. In addition, this course also attempts to help learners put their work into a context of the history of art. The learners are all quite skilled in production techniques, although there is a range in these skills. Both art classes are electives, so the students are voluntarily enrolled in the class. There are equal numbers of females and males in the class. Many (although not all) of the students anticipate post-high school training in some facet of art. Traditionally, students in this class tolerate the art design and history aspects of the course so they can move on to the related production aspects. The lesson previous to this one was on the concept "art nouveau" (a period of design that spanned the period from approximately 1890 to 1910), an immediate predecessor to art deco. Students in this class learned to identify examples of art nouveau by its major criterial attributes (curvilinear, asymmetrical designs that often included flower- or plant-like motifs as well as flowing female figures). The students saw examples of art deco in their lesson on art nouveau as nonexamples of art nouveau. (Please note that these two concepts, art nouveau and art deco, could be taught together as coordinate concepts. To simplify the presentation of the example lesson, we will teach only the art deco concept, but it should be clear to you how the two concepts might be easily taught together.)

*E*xample Concept Lesson— Art Deco

The lesson will follow an inquiry approach; therefore, you will see how some of the expanded events are resequenced to accommodate this strategy. Although the actual form of mediation may not be finalized until after the strategy design, it is not uncommon for the designer to begin to imagine the appropriate medium to deliver the events. We have selected five media of instruction: video, realia, photographs and line drawings, slides, and a human teacher.

Introduction

Deploy Attention

Arouse Interest and Motivation

As students enter the class a videotape will be playing. The videotape includes clips of scenes from films and cartoons of the 1920s that utilize art deco forms, either in the drawings, as with the cartoons, or in the sets, as in the films. The soundtrack is popular music of the period. The videotape is approximately 15 minutes long. The tape continues to play as learners prepare for class. Students are directed to notice the style of the sets and the cartoons.

Establish Instructional Purpose

Preview Lesson

The teacher informs students that today they will study the design style that followed art nouveau and learn to recognize examples of design from that period. They are given their first task, which is to discover the key features of this period.

Body

Process Information and Examples

Students are placed into groups of four to six around lab tables. Each group is handed a packet of 10 line drawings on cards and given directions to group the cards according to design styles. They are told that one particular style, the style to be studied today, has the most examples. The packet contains 10 line drawings, 5 of which are unambiguous, "best examples" of art deco, and 2 of which are examples of art nouveau. The remaining 3 are clearly non-examples of art deco, including 2 modern designs and one design from the period that followed art deco called "arts and crafts." These line drawings are of objects that are matched according to function. For example, the two line drawings in Figure 8.3 are included in the packet; one is an art deco teapot, and the other is an art nouveau pitcher. Other objects included vary from jewelry to architectural elements to household decorations.

Students are directed to group the drawings according to style. They are told that there is one predominant style and that the rest of the design periods will vary. When they have the drawings grouped, they are asked to determine the distinguishing features of the design style in the predominant group. When all groups have finished this sorting task, the teacher asks one group to tell how

Figure 8.3: Art Nouveau Pitcher and Art Deco Teapot

they sorted the drawings. If they failed to sort them according to style but rather by function, they are asked to quickly re-sort them by styles. If they have sorted by style, they are asked to describe the features in the drawings that caused them to sort as they did. (The criterial attributes of the concept relate to the lines of the design, so eliminating all irrelevant attributes beyond the lines, such as color, texture, etc., should ensure a predictable sorting by these attributes.) If learners have included drawings from other periods in the art deco pile, they are asked to reconsider according to the attributes they have identified as critical attributes. If they have included attributes that are not criterial, they should be encouraged to notice that not all of the drawings in their pile include this attribute.

Eventually, when the piles are sorted with all art deco examples in one pile, the teacher can ask if any learners know the name of the style represented in the largest pile. If none know it, the teacher can state that the design style is called *art deco*. The teacher can note on the board the criterial attributes of the concept (rectilinear, symmetrical, streamlined forms, with smooth lines). For review purposes the teacher may also ask the learners if they recognize any familiar styles in the remaining line drawings, which should stimulate a quick review of the features of art nouveau.

Recall Relevant Prior Knowledge

The criterial attribute terms written on the board are concepts that the learners have already acquired, but *rectilinear* may be unfamiliar. If any terms are unfamiliar, they should be reviewed with examples and nonexamples.

Process Information and Examples (continued)

Focus Attention

The teacher will project (via two projectors to facilitate simultaneous comparison) color photos that relate to each matched pair in the line drawings. The students are asked to point out the critical attributes of art deco in each photo, noting how the attributes are not present in the nonexample. To facilitate this attributes isolation, the line drawing of the image is superimposed over the photo for the

first two or three pairs of images. This superimposition will allow students to easily focus on the critical attributes.

Ten more examples of art deco are projected. These examples may vary considerably in function, setting, and in tightness and length of rectangular lines. Within these examples, common motifs, materials, and colors are represented across several examples. Students are then asked to comment on common motifs, colors, and materials. The teacher points out that though these common features are not required to be considered art deco, they are found very commonly in examples.

Now the teacher may set the art deco period in chronological perspective by showing on a timeline how the period followed the art nouveau period. The period may also be set in conceptual perspective by students or by the teacher pointing out that the clean, sleek lines of the art deco movement may have been a reaction to the intricacies and fussiness of the art nouveau period. The teacher may also inquire if learners see the influence of any other art movements on art deco. If no students notice, the teacher can point out the effects of cubism in the rectilinear forms.

To set the art deco movement into historical context, the teacher may also point out that this movement was at the height of the Industrial Revolution and that the art deco movement was an attempt to rectify a failure of the art nouveau movement. One of the goals of art nouveau designers was to create a style that was appropriate for mass production. However, the intricacies of the nouveau style did not facilitate mass production. The elongated, simple lines of the deco style were appropriate for mass production. (The teacher may elaborate the context of the period more; however, this contextual information should be focused on how the period influenced the particular criterial attributes of art deco. Providing too much background information should be avoided to eliminate the possibility of it interfering with the targeted objective, which is recognizing examples of art deco.)

Employ Learning Strategies

As students are second-year art students, which may mean that they have become highly visual learners, they may have difficulty with recalling

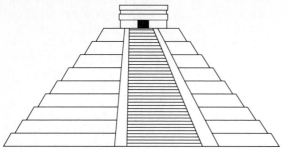
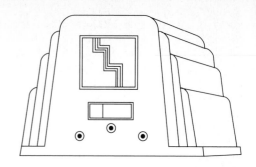

Figure 8.4: Aztec Temple and "Aztec" Radio

the verbal label of the concept with the visual attributes (especially since they will be learning many such labels in an art and design history unit). They are encouraged to develop their own mnemonic to tie the label to the criterial attributes. If they are unable to do so, the teacher may supply a mnemonic. One such mnemonic might be a rhyme, formed by the tie between the influences of Aztec art and art deco. To emphasize this relationship, learners can be shown the visual of an Aztec pyramid and the stepped shape of an art deco radio (sometimes known as an *Aztec radio,* as shown in Figure 8.4). This was inspired by Hillier's (1968) text on art deco.

Practice and Feedback

Practice 1. Students are asked to write the numbers from 1 to 15 on a sheet of paper. They are then presented with 15 slides of images, 10 of which are previously unencountered examples of art deco, ranging in function, colors, motifs, materials, and difficulty of identification. Five are nonexamples, all modern styles including at least 2 examples of art nouveau. Each slide is numbered. Some of the nonexamples should include art deco motifs, materials, or colors. Students are asked to write "yes" beside the number of the slide if it is an example of art deco and "no" if it is not. They are asked to be prepared to justify their answers.

Feedback 1. Students are asked to reveal their decisions and explain their answers. Explanations should include how the criterial attributes are represented. In addition, students may discuss the other common features that may be included in art deco style. If students overgeneralize these common features, the teacher points out that the common features in and of themselves do not constitute the criterial attributes. If students undergeneralize, they should be encouraged to notice the range of the examples that are indeed art deco, and the teacher should try to discover and remediate the misconceptions of irrelevant attributes that students are mistakenly considering to be criterial.

Practice 2. The teacher asks students to think of any examples of art deco that they may have seen. Examples may include local examples, the carpet at Radio City Music Hall, skyscrapers such as the Chrysler Building in New York City, and so forth.

Feedback 2. If the teacher is unfamiliar with the examples, the students are encouraged to sketch their examples. In each case, the example is compared to the criterial attributes of art deco.

Conclusion

Summarize and Review

Remotivate and Close

Transfer Knowledge

The videotape that was used at the beginning of the lesson is replayed and students are asked to point out examples of the art deco style. (The tape can be paused. The students are asked to explain their answers by stating how the criterial attributes that distinguish art deco from other design styles are represented in the tape.)

In closing the lesson, students are reminded that they now can identify the art deco style and the art nouveau style and distinguish the difference between them. Students are encouraged to find examples, either realia or photos, of the two styles and bring them into the classroom to an interest area, which is separated into deco and nouveau areas. They are also assigned to design via drawings one of the following in art deco style: bookends, a stained glass window, or a book cover. (Examples of none of these items were shown in the examples in the body of the lesson, so students must actually apply the concept in their production.) The students are reminded that 60 percent of the grade on this design project will be based on how nearly the design embodies the criterial attributes of the style. Forty percent of the grade will be derived from the quality of the rendering of the drawing.

Assessment

Assess Performance

Evaluate Feedback and Seek Remediation

Assessment will be delayed until the end of the unit. Part of the assessment of this objective will be the assessment of the adequacy of the design project that was just discussed. The teacher uses a checklist that details the criterial attributes of art deco, as well as criteria for production derived from course goals, to evaluate the project. Feedback will take the form of written comments regarding the match between the attributes and the design, as well as the adequacy of the rendering. (The teacher may also wish to consider the adequacy of any examples that learners bring to the interest area as part of the assessment.)

The second aspect of the assessment will be a more conventional exam in which students are shown slides of all the styles learned during the unit. The learners will identify each style on paper. At least 10 examples from the art deco style should be allowed so that the teacher has a reliable measure of the learners' performance on this objective. In addition, careful attention should be given in selecting these examples so that they cover the range of nonrelevant and common attributes. On at least some of the items learners should be asked to justify their answers.

Learners are provided with not only a summary score from the entire assessment but also a score on mastery in identifying each of the specific design styles. Patterns of overgeneralization and undergeneralization are identified and remediated as students are shown the slides as a group and are asked to identify the styles. As with the feedback following practice, isolating the criterial attributes in the examples and pointing out their absence in the nonexamples can encourage remediation of any misconceptions the learners may have developed.

Summary

The following table highlights the chapter's key points in a summary frame.

Conditions of Learning by Event for Concept Learning

Introduction	Deploy attention.	• Highlight concept label, use unusual picture or humorous story regarding concept, provide interesting information on origin or history of concept, and present first matched example and nonexample. Use inquiry approach.
	Arouse interest and motivation.	
	Establish instructional purpose.	• State explicitly in expository lesson. Delay statement in inquiry lesson.
	Preview lesson.	• Overview process of inquiry approach. Point out importance of examples and nonexamples and practice in lesson.

Body	Recall prior knowledge.	• Review concepts constituting critical attributes of concept. Use techniques such as informal questioning, formal pretest, advance organizer, or analogy.
	Process information.	• Expose to best example and/or definition. Emphasize criterial attributes. Consider matched examples and nonexamples. Present concept in range of settings with diversity of nonrelevant attributes.
	Focus attention.	• Isolate critical attributes in examples with highlighting such as boldface type, color, or a simplified drawing.
	Employ learning strategies.	• Generate concept maps, analogies, mnemonics, or images.
	Practice.	• Identify examples from previously unencountered instances, which range in difficulty and settings. • Explain categorizations. Generate examples.
	Evaluate feedback.	• Feedback contains attribute isolation.
Conclusion	Summarize and review.	• Restate criterial attributes. • Repeat or paraphrase key information.
	Transfer knowledge.	• Apply outside classroom. • Provide further examples.
	Remotivate and close.	• Show how learning can help student.
Assessment	Assess performance.	• Test ability to isolate criterial attributes in examples and to point out their absence in nonexamples. • Test including range of common and nonrelevant attributes.
	Feedback and remediation.	• Provide score or other performance summary. • Identify problems of over- and under-generalization.

Job Aid

Use the Job Aid from Chapter 5 to plan concept lessons or lessons that combine concepts and other outcomes.

Extended Example

Objectives: Given a photograph of a scene with lines marking distances within the scene, the learner will be able to identify the area within the scene that represents the depth of field.

Given three photographs, one with shallow depth of field, one with deep depth of field, and one with moderate depth of field, the learner will be able to label them as *shallow, deep,* and *moderate*.

This lesson will be mediated in a print-based, self-instructional text.

Introduction

Deploy Attention

Arouse Interest and Motivation

Show two shots of the same scene. The scene should include objects at uniformly spaced intervals from the foreground to the background of the scene. One has an extremely shallow depth of field; one has an infinite depth of field, as in Figure 8.5 below. Ask learners to determine how the photos differ. Feedback points out that the amount of the scene that is in focus from front to back differs in the two photos. Explain that this area of focus is called the ''depth of field.'' Discuss the differences in the composition of the two photos and their effects on the viewer. Point out that one of the

advantages of a manual exposure camera, such as a 35mm reflex camera, is the ability to control the depth of field in a photo. Give an example of a situation in which you wish to send a picture of your new cat to your mother. However, the cat is napping amongst the clutter that you have accumulated in the living room. What other alternatives do you have besides cleaning the living room? One option is to focus narrowly on the cat and make the background blurry.

Establish Instructional Purpose

Preview Lesson

Text states that the purpose of the lesson is to teach learners to recognize depth of field in a photo and to identify whether a photo has shallow, moderate, or deep depth of field. Explain that this lesson will teach learners to recognize depth of field and that the following lesson will teach learners how to manipulate it.

Body

Recall Relevant Prior Knowledge

Point out that the cameras most learners used while growing up were designed to have a fixed depth of

Figure 8.5: Shallow and Deep Depth of Field
The left photo has shallow depth of field. The right photo has deep depth of field.

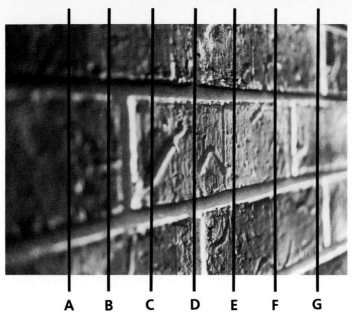

A   B   C   D   E   F   G

Figure 8.6: Determining Depth of Field

field, which made all area from foreground to background in focus. This is because people use these cameras for many situations, including taking photos of landscapes, that require all the area to be in focus. However, this fixed depth of field can be a problem—remember the picture of your cat in the cluttered living room.

Show a photo with deep depth of field that includes identifiable objects in the foreground and background. Review the concepts "foreground" and "background."

Show a photo totally out of focus and one with deep depth of field. Review the concept of "focus."

Show a photo that has a clear point of best focus, such as a photo of a person, along with an illustration of a camera lens distance scale, indicating that the lens has been set to focus at a particular distance. Review the concept of "focal point."

Process Information and Examples

Focus Attention

Employ Learning Strategies

Define *depth of field:* the area from foreground through to background, on either side of the focal point (the distance on which you actually focused), that is in sharp focus.

Present an example photo with moderate depth of field. There should be superimposed lines over the photo from foreground to background, as in Figure 8.6. The lines are labeled with letters. Ask students to determine the depth of field in the photo. Give feedback on the exact depth of field of this photo.

Emphasize that the area to be considered in depth of field is from foreground to background, not from side to side. Also emphasize that depth of field extends both toward the foreground and toward the background from the focal point. Explain that the areas of focus within the depth of field are not equal in front and behind the focal point. One-third of the depth of field is in front of the focal point, and two-thirds is behind the focal point. Refer learners to an illustration similar to Figure 8.7.

Practice

Feedback

Present three more examples of various scenes. The latter two scenes do not have uniformly spaced objects. Lines are superimposed as in Figure 8.6. Ask learners to identify the depth of field in each. Provide feedback with explanation as to why each answer is correct.

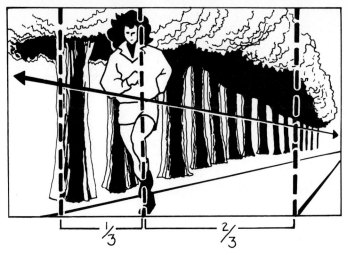

Figure 8.7: The Focal Point and Depth of Field
One-third of the area that is in focus is in front of the center of
interest, and two-thirds is behind it.

Present Information and Examples

Focus Attention

Employ Learning Strategies

Provide three matched images of the same scene. One has deep depth of field, one has moderate depth of field, and one has shallow depth of field. Label each photo according to depth of field. Explain that deep, moderate, and shallow depth of field are comparative terms and can only be considered relatively. When people see a single image and say that it has a shallow depth of field, they are comparing the depth of field of that photo to the depth of field of photos that they usually see. However, deep depth of field usually means that all of the areas of the photo are in focus. Deep depth of field contains the maximum amount of information. It is more like seeing the actual object because the viewer can determine what to attend to. Shallow depth of field means very little of the photo besides the focal point, usually the subject, is in focus. Use of shallow depth of field emphasizes one object as opposed to others in the scene. It merely suggests what surroundings are. Moderate depth of field places an image in its immediate surroundings, but the foreground and the background of the scene are blurry.

Recall Relevant Prior Knowledge

Ask if a near-sighted person's perspective of a scene is similar to moderate depth of field. Point out that moderate depth of field is not like a near-sighted view of a scene because for a near-sighted person, depending upon the severity of the vision problem, the foreground is in focus but the background is out of focus. With moderate depth of field, the immediate foreground is out of focus, the area one-third in front of the focal point is in focus, the area two-thirds behind the focal point is in focus, and the remainder of the background is out of focus. With near-sightedness, the out-of-focus part is always at the near distance, regardless of what the person is trying to focus on. With depth of field, the out-of-focus part depends on where the lens focus point has been set.

Practice

Feedback

Provide three sets of three photos for each student. The sets of photos should vary in settings and subjects. Ask students to identify which photo in each set has shallow, moderate, and deep depth of field. Provide feedback that specifies the relative depth of field of each photo in the set, and explain the categorization by specific reference to the amount of the scene that is in focus.

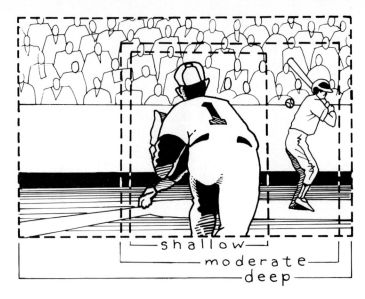

Figure 8.8: Shallow, Moderate, and Deep Depth of Field
This diagram shows the areas of focus for shallow, moderate, and deep depth of field.

Conclusion

Summarize and Review

Restate the definition of *depth of field*. Use a diagram similar to Figure 8.8 to summarize depth of field.

Transfer Knowledge

Suggest that learners examine collections of photos in books and note the depth of field in each. Provide some suggestions of books to examine. Ask learners to hypothesize why the photographers selected the depth of field that they used. Ask them to consider how the depth of field affects the composition and the aesthetic aspects of the image.

Ask students to consider how different types of lenses, such as telephoto or wide angle, influence the depth of field of a scene. (This will involve relatively complex transfer, unless students learn a great deal about lens focal length characteristics in other lessons.)

Remotivate and Close

Remind students that they have learned an element of composition of a photo that can greatly influence the message that it conveys as well as its aesthetic qualities. Point out that in the next lesson they will learn how to control depth of field.

Assessment

Assess Performance

On a cumulative exam, provide at least one item (if possible, three items) similar to Figure 8.6 and have learners identify the area of the photo that is its depth of field. Provide at least one item that contains a set of three photos in which the learners must identify which has shallow, moderate, and deep depth of field.

Evaluate Feedback and Seek Remediation

Provide information as to whether learners are able to identify depth of field as shallow, moderate, or deep. Human assistance may be required to point out distinctive features within the test photos. Remediation may involve the use of art photo books, in which learners practice (with a knowledgeable peer or teacher) identifying depth of field.

Readings and References

Ali, A. M. (1981). The use of positive and negative examples during instruction. *Journal of Instructional Development, 5*(1), 2–7.

Ausubel, D. P., Novak, J. D., & Hanesian, H. (1968). *Educational psychology: A cognitive view* (2nd ed.). New York: Holt, Rinehart, & Winston.

Driscoll, M. P., & Tessmer, M. (1985, April). *Application of the concept free and rational set generator for coordinate concept learning.* A paper presented at the annual meeting of the American Educational Research Association, Chicago.

Gagné, R. M. (1985). *The conditions of learning* (4th ed.). New York: Holt, Rinehart & Winston.

Hillier, B. (1968). *Art deco.* New York: Schocken Books.

Joyce, B., & Weil, M. (1986). Attaining concepts. In B. Joyce and M. Weil (Eds.), *Models of teaching* (3rd ed). Englewood Cliffs, NJ: Prentice-Hall.

Klausmeier, H. J. (1980). *Learning and teaching concepts.* New York: Academic Press.

Merrill, M. D., & Tennyson, R. D. (1977). *Teaching concepts: An instructional design guide.* Englewood Cliffs, NJ: Educational Technology Publications.

Newby, T. J., & Stepich, D. A. (1987). Learning abstract concepts: The use of analogies as a mediational strategy. *Journal of Instructional Development, 10*(2), 20–26.

Smith, M. A., & Smith, P. L. (1991). The effects of concretely versus abstractly illustrated instruction on learning abstract concepts. In Michael Simonson (Ed.), *Thirteenth Annual Proceedings of Selected Research Paper Presentations at the 1991 Annual Convention of the Association for Educational Communications and Technology* (pp. 804–815). Ames, IA: Iowa State University.

Tennyson, R. D., & Cocchiarella, M. J. (1986). An empirically-based instructional design theory for teaching concepts. *Review of Educational Research, 56*(1), 40–71.

Tessmer, M., & Driscoll, M. P. (1985, April). The effects of design methods for teaching coordinate concepts via concept trees and testing concept learning via rational set generators. A paper presented to the annual meeting of the American Educational Research Association, Chicago.

Tessmer, M., Wilson, B., & Driscoll, M. P. (1990). A new model of concept teaching and learning. *Educational Technology Research and Development, 38*(1), 45–53.

Wilcox, W. C., Merrill, M. D., & Black, H. B. (1981). Effects of teaching conceptual hierarchy on concept classification performance. *Journal of Instructional Development, 5*(1), 8–13.

Wilson, B. G. (1987). What is a concept? Concept teaching and cognitive psychology. *Performance and Instruction, 25*(10), 16–18.

Wilson, B. G., & Tessmer, M. (1990). Adult's perception of concept learning outcomes: An initial study and discussion. In M. Simonson and D. Frey (Eds), Eleventh Annual Proceedings of Selected Research Paper Presentations of the 1990 Annual Convention of the Association for Educational Communications and Technology. Ames, IA: Iowa State University.

Strategies for
Rule Lessons

nine

Chapter Objectives

At the conclusion of this chapter you should be able to do the following:

- Given a description of a task, determine whether it is a rule and whether it is relational or procedural.

- Given a relational rule or principle, identify its component concepts.

- Given a procedural rule, determine whether it is simple or complex.

- Given a rule/principle objective, design a strategy plan for the rule lesson.

Review of Rule Learning

As you may recall from our discussion of rule learning in Chapter 4, rules may be of two types: relational rules and procedural rules. Relational rules prescribe the relationship(s) among two or more concepts. These relationships are often described in the form of an if-then or cause-effect relationship. Boyle's law is an example of a relational rule: When temperature of a gas remains constant, if pressure increases, then volume decreases (and vice versa). Other terms that have been used for relational rules are *propositions, principles, laws, axioms, theorems,* and *postulates.* Equations from mathematics and science are abbreviated forms of relational rules because they state the relationships among concepts. We find examples of relational rules in every subject matter, including mathematics, science, the social sciences, language learning, as well as in the arts, such as music. Here are some examples of relational rules:

1. From mechanics: Power = Work/Time (e.g., if a certain amount of power is expended in a certain amount of time, if you halve the time and keep work constant you will double the power).
2. From sociology: If a society undergoes industrialization, then the population will grow rapidly at first and then level off as a result of successive reductions in death rates and birth rates.
3. From statistics: If the mean, median, and mode of a distribution are the same, then the distribution is normally distributed.
4. From optics: The greater the curvature of a convex lens, the shorter the focal length is.
5. From mathematics: The associative property in addition can be represented as follows: $(a + b) + c = a + (b + c)$.
6. From economics: The principle of diminishing marginal utility is as follows: The more units of a certain economic product a person acquires, the less eager that person is to buy still more (of that product).

You can see how a rule describes the relationship among the concepts in the rule. These concepts are often in the form of variables—factors that can have many values. The application of a rule enables learners to predict what will happen if one of the variables is changed. Rules also allow the learner to explain what has happened. For example, why did sales of yo-yos decline during the late 1950s? (The principle of diminishing marginal utility can help you explain this situation.) Finally, knowing a rule allows you to control the effects of variables upon each other. For example, using the rule from optics describing the relationship between lens curvature and focal length, consider John, who needs new glasses. What lens curvature does he need—more or less than his current lenses—if his problem is that he cannot focus as closely as he needs to in order to read?

Procedural rules are a generalizable series of steps initiated in response to a particular class of circumstances to reach a specified goal. Procedures are often strictly defined—all steps are included with no ambiguity in each step. Another term for such a strictly defined procedure is *algorithm.* Many procedural rules are algorithms. For example, mathematics operations are procedural rules that are algorithmic. The procedure for subtracting by "borrowing" is an algorithm: The steps in the procedure are fairly invariant. Procedural rules may be simple, with only one set of steps that the learner goes through linearly, or they may be complex, with many decision points. (Each decision point could lead to a different path, or branch, through the algorithm.) Decision points are points in a procedure at which the learner must determine which of two (or sometimes more) situations exist. (Making decisions at these points requires a kind of concept recognition. An example would be "Is the battery charging?") Based upon this determination, one branch or another of the procedure will be followed.

Some procedures may be somewhat less clearly prescribed. In such cases, there may be incomplete knowledge of the steps involved, unreliable consequences of the application of the procedure, or a mass of steps with much ambiguity at decision points. Dealing with situations in these areas may require the application of "rules of thumb" or heuristic knowledge. Two examples are techniques for reducing cholesterol level and protocols for treating certain illnesses. In such cases, we recommend teaching the procedures in these areas as problem-solving tasks rather than as procedural rules.

Some examples of procedural rules are the executive subroutines for psychomotor skills, such as throwing a javelin or performing the broad jump. Many tasks in mathematics that we term "problem-solving" are really applications of procedural rules. Some of these tasks are dividing fractions, finding the average of a series of numbers, determining the area of a polygon, constructing a pentagon within a circle, and solving a quadratic equation. Many training goals and objectives are procedural rules, such as those tasks for operating a piece of equipment, readjusting the timing of an engine, or doing an if-then analysis on a spreadsheet.

It is not uncommon for a learner to learn a procedure to complete some task (such as solving for an unknown in an equation) and, as a product of applying the procedure, learn the relational rule that underlies the procedure. Or, the reverse sequence may occur: learning the relational rule first and then the procedure. For example, learners learn the relational rule that states how the amount of current flow in an electrical current is related to volts of electricity put into the circuit and the resistance of the current ($I = V/R$). However, when learning to solve many such problems quickly, learners will discover or be taught a procedure for solving such problems: First, determine what values are known, and then determine which form of the equation will solve for the unknown. With this approach learners can acquire an efficient means to deal with solving for an unknown (by applying a procedure), but at the same time they truly "understand" what is occurring when the procedure is employed through learning the relational rule. We recommend tying the two rules together, teaching procedures so that learners have efficient means of dealing with a given circumstance; but the instruction should also explain the procedure in the context of the underlying relational rule so the information is more meaningful and, therefore, more memorable and transferrable.

The acquisition of a rule, either relational or procedural, should not be confused with the ability to state the rule. The ability to state a rule is declarative learning knowledge. The acquisition of a rule involves the ability to *apply* that rule to a variety of previously unencountered situations. The ability to verbally state the relationship among concepts or to state the steps in a procedure may be helpful in learning to apply a rule; however, stating the rule is not sufficient evidence that the rule has been learned. A rule must be applied to show that it has been learned.

The mental operations involved in applying rules are called *productions* (Anderson, 1985). As you may recall, productions are hypothesized mental operations that generally take the form of if-then representations. Productions are implicit in all of the intellectual skills. We will see examples of productions in the following section on cognitive processes of learning relational rules.

Exercises

Write *RR* in the blank if the outcome is an example of relational rule learning. Write *PR* if it is an example of a procedural rule. Write *X* if it is not a rule. Explain your answer.

_____ 1. Demonstrating the technique for "jump starting" a car
_____ 2. Determining the amount of energy released from a nuclear reaction with the equation $E = mc^2$
_____ 3. Stating the law of supply and demand
_____ 4. Recognizing examples of deviant behavior
_____ 5. Determining what to do when a traffic light is red
_____ 6. Deciding whether to use *a* or *an* before a noun
_____ 7. Showing how to make bread
_____ 8. Soldering two wires together
_____ 9. Determining the length of a hypotenuse of a triangle given the length of the two sides
_____ 10. Conjugating a regular verb in Spanish

Cognitive Processes of Learning Relational Rules

The cognitive processes required to learn how to apply a rule are slightly different for the two types of rules. Therefore, we will discuss the processes separately. The processes underlying knowing a relational rule can be identified in the productions associated with them:

IF the situation described involves key concept *A*
and IF the situation described involves key concept *B*
THEN rule *Q* applies in this case (concept recognition).

The relational rule explains the relationship of these two concepts:

IF concept *A* changes in direction *R* with magnitude of *Z*
THEN concept *B* will change in direction *M* with a magnitude of *N*.

Prior knowledge of the concepts represented in the relational rule (in the above production identified as concepts *A* and *B*) is prerequisite to learning a relational rule. One of the main cognitive tasks in learning a rule is learning to recognize the situation in which these two or more concepts are related in a way such that the rule applies. This recognition requires the generalization of the rule to more contexts beyond those instances first encountered. It also requires discrimination in which the learner learns to recognize occasions in which the rule does not apply. The learner must also be able to state the relationship of these concepts (a verbal information component of the task). Next, the learner must determine which concept or concepts have changed and the magnitude and direction of the change. Finally, the learner must determine what effect these changes will have on the other concept(s).

An example of this cognitive operation is the task of learning Ohm's law, which most of us learned in general science. It is prerequisite to learning many advanced rules and concepts in electronics. Ohm's law states that voltage is directly related to both current and resistance.

1. Determine what variables are involved in the situation.
2. Determine which rule applies. (If the situation relates current, voltage, and resistance, then Ohm's law applies.)
3. Determine which variables' values are known.
4. Determine which variables' values are unknown.
5. Determine the direction and magnitude of the known variables.

6. Using the rule (Ohm's law), determine the effects of the known variables on the unknown variables by determining the value of the unknowns.
7. Determine if the value makes sense.

The final step in the task analysis is critical for learners to complete to evidence fundamental understanding of the relationships underlying the task. For example, voltage is directly related to both current and resistance: One symbolic relationship of these variables is $V = I \times R$. Suppose a learner had a situation in which the current was 2 amps and resistance was 60 ohms. If she calculated an answer of 10 volts, it would clearly not make sense. The importance of understanding the principle underlying this relationship is one reason we suggest that relational rules should be learned as relational rules rather than as procedures (although you can see how easily we could convert the information-processing analysis into a procedure to follow for solving problems involving Ohm's law).

*C*onditions Supporting Rule Learning — Relational Rules

The design for relational rule lessons is quite similar to the design of concept lessons. Just as with designing concept lessons, when designing a strategy for relational rules, the designer can choose between an inquiry or an expository approach. An inquiry strategy for teaching relational rules involves presenting learners with examples and nonexamples of the rule application and encouraging the learners to discover the rule (i.e., the relationships among the concepts in the situation). Both Taba (1967) and Suchman (1964) suggest how inquiry methods may be used in teaching rules. We will briefly describe Suchman's Model of Inquiry Teaching. Suchman suggests the following instructional process:

1. Present the learners with a puzzling situation that shows the relationship among the variables. Such a situation may be a demonstration or description.

2. Allow learners to ask the teacher (or an "intelligent" computer) questions about the situation

that can be answered in the form of "yes" or "no." Students' questions should eventually move through questions verifying the nature of the situation, to gathering more data about the situation, to isolating the relevant variables in the situation, to forming hypotheses about the situation, to testing their hypotheses to confirm cause-effect relationships.

3. At the conclusion of the experience, learners should be able to state a formal principle or rule about the relationships of the concepts involved.

4. Learners should also be encouraged to discuss the inquiry process itself, including those approaches that were fruitful and those that were not. (This practice will encourage the development of cognitive strategies, discussed in Chapter 11.)

Although an inquiry approach may be extremely useful for teaching rules, especially for extremely abstract rules or in situations where learners are particularly skilled in prior knowledge or cognitive strategies, such a strategy can be more time consuming and potentially confusing to unskilled learners than an expository approach. Occasions may arise in which the optimal sequence of instruction is more expository: the rule is stated, demonstrated and learners have an opportunity to practice the rule's application.

We will describe each of these approaches in more detail as we describe the expanded events of instruction for relational rule lessons.

Introduction

Deploy Attention

Learners' attention should be directed toward investigating the relationships among key concepts in the principle or rule. This may be done by highlighting the concepts verbally or visually. An inquiry strategy can gain learners' attention quite quickly by presenting an anomalous situation involving the key concepts and their relationships. For both inquiry and expository strategies, attention may be piqued through demonstrations or scenarios of the application of the rule.

Establish Instructional Purpose

In an inquiry strategy, the purpose may be originally defined as a puzzle to solve. Before the lesson is concluded, it is important that the purpose of the lesson be explicitly stated in terms of the acquisition of the rule. For more expository lessons, the purpose may be stated explicitly by verbally stating the rule that relates two or more particular concepts together, such as "Today, you will learn how to determine the change in volume of a gas when given a specified change in pressure." Or, the instructor may ask a question regarding the nature of the relationship among concepts and point out that the purpose of the lesson is to determine this relationship.

Arouse Interest and Motivation

An inquiry approach itself may sufficiently stimulate interest. We would suggest moving directly into the puzzling situation to promote such interest. Puzzling situations may also be posed in an expository lesson. In addition, learners may be shown previous experiences that have involved the rule or principle. Motivation may also be encouraged by stating how the use of the rule may be utilized in explaining, controlling, or predicting everyday situations. Older learners and learners with high aptitude may also be motivated by a discussion of how the rule will be later combined with other rules to solve problems.

Preview Lesson

For instruction using an inquiry strategy, this event will involve giving directions to the solution of the puzzle as well as an overview of how the entire lesson will progress. In a more expository lesson, the preview may involve an outline of how the lesson will allow the learners to solve a puzzle or resolve a scenario that has been presented.

Body

Recall Relevant Prior Knowledge

The most critical prior knowledge to acquisition of a relational rule is acquisition of the concepts underlying the rule. Learners should have more than a verbal information knowledge of the concepts (i.e., they should be able to apply the concept, not just state its definition or characteristics). For example, the rule that gas expands when heated has three concepts—"gas," "heated," and "expands."

It is not uncommon for the concepts that are incorporated in a rule to be taught in the same lesson as the rule itself. In such a case, learners should experience instruction on the concepts, including practice and feedback, until they are skilled with the concepts, before instruction on the rule begins.

Rule analogies may be used in tying prior knowledge to new learning. For example, consider teaching the use of the "GOTO" command as opposed to the "GOSUB" command in BASIC programming. (This involves if-then relational rules.) An analogy to flipping pages in a book may be used to distinguish the differing needs of a programming situation. (For example, if you plan to return to the page, you put your finger in that page. That's a GOSUB. If you don't plan to return, then you flip the pages completely over. That's a GOTO command.)

Process Information and Examples

At this point in the instruction, the learners may be presented with a statement of the rule or principle and presented with subsequent examples of the rule's application, or the learners may be presented with examples of the rule's application and asked to induce the rule. If the rule is stated first, it is usually stated in an if-then form, although other ways of stating this generality are also acceptable. Examples of statements of a rule include the following:

- If a stamp has complete perforations, then it is more valuable than if it has incomplete perforations.
- If a musical phrase contains a crescendo, then begin the phrase singing at the volume indicated and gradually increase the volume to the level indicated by the music (or by the director).
- If a plant's leaves are drooping and its soil is dry to the touch, then water it.
- If a fire breaks out on the kitchen stove and the material that is burning is grease, then don't spray it with water, but do cut off the oxygen to the fire.
- When incorporating material written by others in your own writing, clearly designate those ideas that are directly borrowed from others.

- To get wax out of your ears, use drops to break down the wax, and then use a gentle spray of water to wash out the wax.

In expository instruction, these principles will be stated in a form that is appropriate for the audience in terms of vocabulary and sentence complexity. It may be helpful to display a statement of the rule on a poster, bulletin board, transparency, or chalkboard for learners to refer to during the initial portion of the lesson. Later, you will wish to remove the statement of the principle so that learners will rely on their own memory of the rule.

It is often useful to explain the *why's* of a principle or rule to make it meaningful and therefore, more memorable. For example, in our principle stated above regarding a grease fire, an explanation as to why one should not spray water on it is necessary. The explanation should be at a level that is understandable to the audience, based upon their prior knowledge. It should help them to remember and apply the rule. Often, this explanation uses knowledge of relational rules that the learners have already acquired.

Inquiry strategies will, of course, not state the rule immediately but will lead the learners to develop a statement of the principle that is operating, after they have observed the action of the concepts in examples of the application of the principle.

Once learners have been exposed to the statement of the rule in expository strategies, or initially in inquiry strategies, they should experience applications of the rule. These applications can be directly experienced or demonstrated. For example, the principle that the tighter a string is pulled, the higher its pitch when plucked could be demonstrated by the instructor or directly experienced by learners who are given string or rubber bands. Often, instruction may include demonstration first and then direct experience. Generally, learners find direct experiences of application of rules more engaging and interesting. However, the context, characteristics of the learners, and characteristics of the instructional task may dictate whether direct experience is possible. For example, the principle that if molecules are heated, they move more rapidly cannot be directly observed. It may only be simulated (for example, through video animation).

Applications may show how the rule can be used to predict effects (e.g., Will the pitch be higher or lower than the previous pitch?), to explain outcomes (Why was the pitch lower than the previous pitch?), or to control the outcomes of a situation (How can I make the pitch lower?). As with concept learning, it may be helpful to first present learners with a best example of the rule. This example should clearly demonstrate the application of the rule, with few extraneous (noncritical) aspects in the situation. It is very helpful if this example has some features such as humor, analogy, novelty, or personal relevance to make it more memorable.

The outcomes of a rule or principle application may be discrete, as in the correct conjugation of a verb; it may be continuous, as in the result from applying Ohm's law to calculate the amount of current in a circuit when given the voltage and resistance; or it may be general, as when predicting the effects of industrialization on population growth. Learners should encounter sufficient examples of the application to have a clear idea of the character of the answers that can be acquired when applying the rule.

Unlike learning concepts, matched nonexamples may not be critical to learning rules. For example, it may not be possible to think of a reasonable nonexample to the principle relating the tightness of a string and its relative pitch when plucked. On the other hand, it is important to use contrasting examples and nonexamples when teaching learners about how to select from the nominative and subjective forms of pronouns in a sentence ("Tim brought the present to Gracie and *I*" versus "Tim brought the present to Gracie and *me*.")

When a rule guides a clear choice among several alternatives, then matched examples and nonexamples should be included early in the presentation of application of the rule. If, however, the application of the rule yields multiple outcomes, such as varying pitches in the rule example above, or multiple values of volume of a gas when pressure on that gas changes (Boyle's law), then often there is not a reasonable match in terms of results of application. However, once the learners have begun to learn to apply the principle, it may be useful to point out to them common errors or misconceptions regarding the relationship of the concepts in the rule. For example, with the principle relating string tautness and pitch, a common misconception is that plucking the string harder will change its pitch. (The learners are confusing pitch with volume: To change the volume of the sound coming from a plucked string, pluck it softer or harder.) With regard to Boyle's law, a common misconception is that pressure and volume of a gas is directly (rather than inversely) related. These misconceptions may be directly addressed or evoked and corrected during practice.

As learners experience the application of a rule, it is important that they be encouraged to identify which features of the situation surrounding the rule application suggested that a particular rule should be employed. For example, in the situation of changing the pitch of a plucked string, the learners should be able to identify that the critical features in the situation are the following:

- There is a string.
- The string will be plucked.
- We wish to change the pitch of the sound resulting from the plucked string.

So the learners can be aware of the breadth of the domain to which the rule is applicable, they should also be encouraged to identify noncritical aspects of the rule application. For example, in the situation just mentioned, the rule is equally applicable if the strings are different colors, attached to instruments or unattached, or of different materials and thicknesses (although this does introduce another rule as well) from those with which the learners practiced.

Focus Attention

Learners may require assistance in determining which concepts are being related by the rule and how the concepts are related. These features may be highlighted in the rule statement by inflection, if the rule is stated orally, or by typography, if the rule is in written form. In addition, as learners are exposed to applications of the rule, they should be encouraged to focus on these key features in each application. Learners also should be encouraged to note the direction and magnitude of changes in one variable (concept) when another variable has been changed.

Employ Learning Strategies

To support retention of the rule statement, learners may be asked to develop their own mnemonic, or if they are unable to do so, they may be presented with a mnemonic to aid them in recalling a rule. For example, many of us were taught the mnemonic "*i* before *e* except after *c*" to help us remember a spelling rule. Learners may also be taught techniques to support application of the rule. When given the sentence "Tom gave the horn to Molly and me/I," removing the noun *Molly* from the sentence will allow the learner to determine the appropriate form of the pronoun. Learners might also be encouraged to illustrate or diagram the relationships of concepts as presented in the rule.

Practice

When practicing rules learners should practice at four levels. First, they should practice stating the rule. Although research results are somewhat mixed regarding the necessity of actually being able to state a rule to apply it, it is very useful for learners to have practice in stating the principle or rule. Learners may also be encouraged to state the principle in their own words, with the instructor providing feedback as to whether their statements accurately reflect the intention of the principle. Instructors can often gain useful information as to any misconceptions that the learners may have developed by observing their paraphrased statements of the rule.

Second, they should practice recognizing situations in which the rule is applicable. For example, after studying Boyle's law, learners might be given practice items in which pressure and volume of liquids are changed, temperature and pressure of gases are changed, and pressure and volume of gases are changed. Students could be asked to identify those situations in which Boyle's law is applicable. If students have previously learned related rules that might be easily confused with the application of the current rule, this practice may include questions that require the learners to distinguish among them.

Third, they should practice applying the rule. Students should have the opportunity to actually practice applying the rule to predict, explain, or control the effects of one concept on another. This practice should be across the range of difficulty and applicability of the rule so that learners are exposed to the range of situations in which the rule is applicable. The situations should vary as much as possible on noncritical aspects. Some of the practice items should require learners to explain their answers. Depending upon the availability of a medium that can provide feedback to production questions—a human or an "intelligent" computer system—some items may ask students to provide their own examples of the application of the rule.

And finally, learners should practice determining whether a rule has been correctly applied. It is important that learners do not practice at this level until they are skilled at applying the rule because they should not be confused by incorrect applications of a rule before they are skilled in its correct application. However, it is important that they be able to scan a solution to a practice item in which the rule has been applied and determine if the solution is reasonable and appropriate. They must have this skill to "check" their own solutions; therefore, it can be helpful for them to be presented with carefully constructed incorrect solutions and be asked if the answers are reasonable. The incorrect solutions could represent common misconceptions or errors that learners make when applying a particular rule. After learners have identified whether the rule has been properly applied, they should be asked to explain their decisions. This explanation is important in this situation because with a dichotomous answer (yes/no), learners have a strong possibility of guessing the answer correctly without actually being able to apply the rule. Requiring an explanation ensures that to be able to answer the question correctly the learners must truly be able to apply the rule.

Evaluate Feedback

Feedback varies for each type of practice question. For items that practice stating the rule, feedback should provide information as to whether learners' statements contain the key concepts of the rule and relate these concepts appropriately. Feedback might also include identification of any extraneous or incorrect information included in the statement of the rule. With some media, such as print or computer-based instruction, feedback might be limited to a model answer, with a highlighting of critical features of the statement. Such feedback might also include identification of common errors and factors that should not be included in the answer.

Items that practice recognizing situations in which the rule is applicable should be followed with feedback that identifies (1) whether the rule under consideration is applicable and (2) what features of the situation make the rule applicable or not applicable.

For items in which learners actually practiced applying the rule, feedback should provide the outcome of the application of the rule. This may be a single answer, as in the case of the determination of which pronoun form is appropriate to a situation; or it may describe the direction and magnitude of the change in one concept (variable) when there is a change in another variable. It is also helpful to provide explanatory feedback in the form of a step-by-step solution of the item, a highlighting of critical features in the item that influence the application of the rule, or a graphic illustrating how the solution can be drawn by applying the rule to the information given.

Feedback for items in which the learners determined whether a rule has been correctly applied should include a clear indication of the correct answer. Additionally, for situations in which the rule has not been correctly applied, the feedback should specifically point out the error in the application and how the rule should have been applied.

Conclusion

The conclusion of a rule learning lesson should allow the opportunity for learners to consolidate their learning into a form that can be readily applied in a variety of circumstances and that can be transferred to higher-order learning tasks.

Summarize and Review

A summary and review of a rule learning task should include a restatement of the rule in a form that is paraphrased from the original statement in the lesson. The review may present this rule in a graphic format, such as an illustration or diagram that graphically presents that relationship of the concepts that are associated in the rule. The instruction may also refer back to any best example that was presented earlier in the instruction, with a clear review of why this example epitomizes the application of the rule.

Transfer Knowledge

The most common transfer of a rule is its application in concert with other rules in problem-solving situations. It can be quite helpful to support this transfer by stating in the conclusion of the lesson how this rule may be applied later in combination with other rules. Students should also be encouraged to locate situations in their daily lives in which the rule's application is demonstrated. An area of the classroom, such as a bulletin board, may be set up to document these observations.

Remotivate and Close

Remotivation in the lesson may be supported by learners identifying the relevance of the rule's application in their later instruction or in their daily lives.

Assess Performance

Assess Performance

As suggested in Chapter 5, performance assessment for a rule may include the following types of items:

1. Stating the rule.
2. Recognizing situations in which the rule is applicable.
3. Applying the rule.
4. Determining whether a rule has been correctly applied.

Of course, the items represented by item 3 most nearly assess the intention of the objectives of most rule learning lessons. Items 1, 2, and 4 represent skills that support the application of the rule. Therefore, the majority of the items should involve application of the rule to predict, explain, or control the influence of one variable on another. In assessments in which it is practical, you may wish to also assess 1, 2, and 4 because these items may provide information as to learners' ability in skills that support the application of the rule. The items should assess across the range of applicability and difficulty levels of the rule. Several related and/or easily confused rules may profitably be assessed at the same time to ensure that the learners know how to differentiate among applications. However, the designer must be careful not to develop items that require the selection and multiple application of several rules, as this is problem-solving learning.

Evaluate Feedback and Seek Remediation

Feedback for assessment should generally be in the form of cumulative information, such as whether the learner has acquired the ability to apply the rule or not. Correct answer feedback may also be helpful after assessment.

Remediation should address misconceptions the learners have evidenced in their responses. For instance, learners may indicate that they have overgeneralized the rule. Remediation can highlight and review the features of the situations that call for the application of the rule. Remediation of overgeneralization should also involve more practice in identifying situations that require application of the rule.

Remediation may also be necessary for undergeneralization. Learners who evidenced this problem can be helped with practice across the full range of the applicability of the rule.

Preview of an Example Lesson — Relational Rules

Task Analysis. This lesson focuses on the grammar rule that guides the selection of *who, which,* or *that* in a sentence such as "The Mozart Mass in C, _____(who/which/that) is sometimes called the *Coronation Mass,* was written in 1779." The objective and productions associated with this rule are listed below.

Objective: Given a sentence with a blank in it, the learner will determine whether the pronoun *who, which,* or *that* is appropriate for filling in the blank.

Productions:

IF the noun referent is a person
THEN use the pronoun *who.*
IF the noun referent is an animal, object, or idea,
and IF the pronoun begins a nonrestrictive clause,
THEN use the pronoun *which.*
IF the noun referent is an animal, object, or idea,
and IF the pronoun begins a restrictive clause,
THEN use the pronoun *that.*

Learners. The learners for this lesson are undergraduate college students in a technical writing class. This class is an elective course for programs from diverse subject matter areas such as science, sociology, nursing, and English. All learners in the class have passed an exam that assesses high school graduate-level skills in punctuation, grammar usage, and composition.

Context. The technical writing course follows a PSI (Personalized System of Instruction, see Chapter 14) instructional management system in which students receive individualized instruction for some components of the course and group-delivered instruction for other segments. The current lesson will be designed for a segment of individualized instruction on pronoun usage. For the purposes of this example, we will predetermine the medium to be computer-based instruction (although, ideally we would delay making a media selection decision until after we had determined how the expanded instructional events might be implemented).

Example Lesson for Relational Rules

Introduction

Although an inquiry approach could be used for this lesson, we will use an expository approach to exemplify a lesson of a more expository nature than that presented in Chapter 8 on concepts.

Deploy Attention

The supermarket _____ has the freshest produce will be our supplier.
    Who?   Which?   That?

Establish Instructional Purpose

Arouse Interest and Motivation

The ability to select the appropriate pronoun to use in a descriptive pronoun phrase, particularly to select between the pronouns *which* and *that,* is a distinctive skill of technical writers.

Many writers are unaware that the words *which* and *that* are not interchangeable.

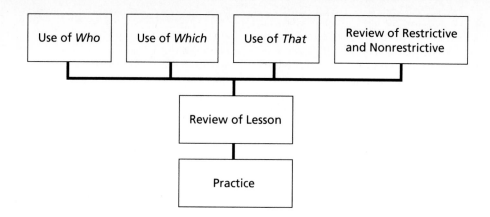

In this lesson you will learn to determine which relative pronoun to use in sentences in which you must choose among *who, which,* and *that.*

Preview Lesson

You have some options as to the order of the lesson. The figure above shows how the lesson is arranged. Click on the point in the lesson where you would like to begin.

Body

Recall Relevant Prior Knowledge

Relative Pronouns:
As you recall from the previous lesson, relative pronouns are the pronouns *who* (or *whom*), *which,* and *that.* A relative pronoun is a pronoun that does two things:

- It takes the place of a noun.
- It connects a dependent clause and a main clause.

Process Information and Examples

Focus Attention

The Use of Who

You use the pronoun *who* when you are writing a phrase to describe a person.
    For example, here are some correct uses of *who:*

- The driver **who** drove persistently in the left lane was a menace on the road.
- Bob Fields, **who** designs cardboard houses, lives in Rockport, Maine.
- The carousel operator **who** went to sleep at the controls gave the children a long ride.

    It is incorrect to use the pronoun *who* to begin a phrase that describes an animal, an event, or an idea.
    The collie who lives in the corner house sat in the shade of the oak tree.
    The truck who was going 80 mph was stopped by the highway patrol.
    The parade who turned the corner onto 6th Street was drenched by a sudden shower.

Employ Learning Strategies

Notice that *who* is used incorrectly in the sentences at the top of page 223.

Practice

Directions: Click on the blank of each sentence in which the word *who* could fill the blank.

    1. The meteorologist _____ had been up for 26 hours stumbled over his words in the emergency broadcast.

The collie who lives in the corner house sat in the shade of the oak tree.

The truck who was going 80 mph was stopped by the highway patrol.

The parade who turned the corner onto Sixth Street was drenched by a sudden shower.

2. Make sure that you put the cat ____ is on the special diet in the front cage.

3. Chuckles the Clown, ____ entertained children on TV for years, has retired to Pago Pago.

4. The boy ____ dropped the ball is standing up.

5. The town of Rolla, ____ is in the rolling hills of Missouri, is near Fort Leonard Wood.

Evaluate Feedback

✔ 1. The meteorologist <u>who</u> had been up for 26 hours stumbled over his words in the emergency broadcast.

✗ 2. Make sure that you put the cat <u>who</u> is on the special diet in the front cage.

✔ 3. Chuckles the Clown, <u>who</u> entertained children on TV for years, has retired to Pago Pago.

✔ 4. The boy <u>who</u> dropped the ball is standing up.

✔ 5. The town of Rolla, <u>which</u> is in the rolling hills of Missouri, is near Fort Leonard Wood.

Review Relevant Prior Knowledge

To understand the correct use of *which* and *that* you must be able to determine whether a phrase or clause that modifies that noun is restrictive or nonrestrictive.

A **nonrestrictive** phrase or clause is a phrase or clause that has the following characteristics:

- It modifies a noun.
- It does not limit (i.e., restrict) the meaning of the noun.
- Thus, it can be removed from the sentence without changing the essential meaning of the sentence.
- It is often separated from the remainder of the sentence by commas.

Here are some examples of nonrestrictive phrases and clauses:

- The paper, **which was due yesterday,** was to be 10–12 pages long.
- The agent, **who lives in Anaheim,** arranged contracts for two authors.
- The car, **which had flame decals on the sides,** was stuck in the car wash.

Notice how the meaning of the sentences would not be substantially changed if the nonrestrictive phrases were omitted.

Restrictive phrases and clauses have the following characteristics:

- They restrict or limit the meaning of the noun they modify.
- Thus, they cannot be removed without substantially changing the meaning of the sentence.

Here are some examples of **restrictive** phrases and clauses:

- All students **who fail to turn in the final project** will receive F's.
- The classes **that had fewer than five students** were cancelled.
- Cats **that have not been immunized** are at risk of catching distemper.

Notice how the meaning of the sentences would be substantially changed if the restrictive phrases were omitted.

Process Information

Focus Attention

The Use of Which

Use the relative pronoun *which* to begin phrases or clauses that have the following characteristics:

- They describe animals, ideas, or events (any noun other than a person).
- They are nonrestrictive phrases or clauses.

Here are a few examples:

- The paper, **which was due yesterday,** was to be 10–12 pages long.
- The car, **which had flame decals on the sides,** was stuck in the car wash.
- The computer, **which was purchased with department funds,** required additional memory to run the software.

The Use of That

Use the relative pronoun *that* to begin phrases or clauses that have the following characteristics:

- They describe animals, ideas, or events (any noun other than a person).
- They are restrictive phrases or clauses.

Here are a few examples:

- The classes **that had fewer than five students** were cancelled.
- Cats **that have not been immunized** are at risk of catching distemper.
- The TV program **that began at four o'clock** was not over until nine o'clock.

Employ Learning Strategies

A comparison of *which* and *that* follows:

- Organizations **that** follow the plan can expect to experience improved employee relations.
- Organizations, **which** often are built from a "mom and pop business," can apply for information regarding the new tax laws.
- This instrument, **which** is called a 3-bar roller, can be used to straighten twisted pipeline.
- The instrument **that** the burglar used to pry open the window was left in the bathroom.

Practice

Directions: Type in the correct pronoun: *which* or *that*.

1. The bear, _____ entered the room through the window, knocked the cannisters off the kitchen shelves.
2. The book _____ was listed as a required text was not available in the bookstore.
3. The computer, _____ Dad purchased for the family, was surrounded by 15 children from the neighborhood.
4. The law, _____ had been long forgotten by many, prohibited teachers from dating.
5. I have been writing books _____ are modern versions of Greek tragedies.

Feedback

1. The bear, <u>which</u> entered the room through the window, knocked the cannisters off the kitchen shelves.

2. The book <u>that</u> was listed as a required text was not available in the bookstore.

3. The computer, <u>which</u> Dad purchased for the family, was surrounded by 15 children from the neighborhood.

4. The law, <u>which</u> had been long forgotten by many, prohibited teachers from dating.

5. I have been writing books <u>that</u> are modern versions of Greek tragedies.

Conclusion

Summarize and Review

In review, here are three rules for *who, that,* and *which:*

- Use *who* in phrases or clauses that describe people.
- Use *that* in phrases or clauses that are restrictive (i.e., the meaning of the sentence would be substantially changed without the phrase or clause).
- Use *which* in phrases or clauses that are nonrestrictive (i.e., the meaning of the sentence would not be substantially changed without the phrase or clause).

Transfer Knowledge

Some punctuation has been intentionally omitted from these sentences. Fill in each sentence with *who, that,* or *which.* Then, punctuate the sentence correctly.

1. The cat _____ broke its leg is unable to move far from its bed.

2. The minister _____ wore a robe entered the sanctuary from the side door.

3. The soda _____ was in a red can was tucked into the door of the refrigerator.

4. The photograph _____ was printed on glossy paper created a glare when it was filmed.

5. Sally _____ was the first on the scene of the accident administered first aid.

6. The disk _____ was stuck in the disk drive was warped from the heat.

Feedback

1. The cat <u>that</u> broke its leg is unable to move far from <u>its</u> bed.

2. The minister <u>who</u> wore a robe entered the sanctuary from the side door.

3. The soda, <u>which</u> was in a red can, was tucked into the door of the refrigerator.

4. The photograph <u>that</u> was printed on glossy paper created a glare when it was filmed.

5. Sally, <u>who</u> was the first on the scene of the accident, administered first aid.

6. The disk <u>that</u> was stuck in the disk drive was warped from the heat.

Remotivate and Close

Here is an assignment:
Look for examples of the use of *who, which,* and *that* in newspapers, magazines, and textbooks. Can you find instances in which they are used incorrectly?

Practice using these relative pronouns correctly in your own writing. Soon, using them correctly will seem automatic to you.

Assess Performance

Assessment would resemble the practice exercises by requiring the learner to demonstrate application of the rule. In addition, student writing products could be evaluated for correct usage.

Evaluate Feedback and Seek Remediation

Feedback would provide the learner with information as to whether the use of each pronoun had been adequately learned.

Cognitive Processes Supporting Learning Procedural Rules

Just as with relational rules, procedural rules require that productions be learned. Below is a generic format for productions:

> IF the situation contains certain distinguishing features *X, Y, Z* (usually understood as concepts)
> THEN follow procedure *P.*

An information-processing analysis for procedural rules is somewhat different from that for relational rules:

1. Recognize a situation in which the procedural rule is applicable.
2. Recall the procedural rule.
3. Apply the steps in the procedure.
4. If required, make decisions at the decision points.
5. If required, choose correct branch(es).
6. Complete steps in required branch(es).
7. Ascertain that the procedure has been applied appropriately.

An example of such a procedure might be the procedural rule of applying CPR.

1. Determine if the person is unconscious. (There is an entire sub-procedure to determine this.)
2. Open an airway. (This is another sub-procedure.)
3. Determine if the person is breathing (another sub-procedure). If there is no breathing, go to Step 4; if the victim is breathing, go to Step 5.
4. Give four breaths (another sub-procedure).
5. Determine if there is a pulse (another sub-procedure).
6. If there is no pulse, provide CPR (another sub-procedure).

In addition to recognizing an initial situation that calls for the use of a procedural rule, many procedural rules have decision points within them that also require classification of situations and branching into alternate paths depending upon the decisions. Step 3 above is an example of a decision point.

Procedural rules (1) determine if a situation requires that the learner learn to do a particular procedure for cognitive tasks (i.e., concept recog-

nition); (2) recall the steps in the procedure (i.e., verbal information); (3) complete the steps in the procedure; and (4) analyze the completed procedure and confirm/disconfirm that the procedure has been correctly applied. In addition, if the procedure is complex, procedural rules require that the learner make decisions within the procedure.

Steps in a procedure may be "decision" steps or "operation" steps. Decision steps are those like Step 3 above that require the learner to (1) determine whether a certain set of circumstances exists and (2) follow alternate pathways depending upon the decision. Procedures that do not have decision steps are termed *linear* or *serial*. Procedures that do have decision steps are termed *branching* or *parallel*.

Procedures may be classified as simple or complex, depending upon the type and number of steps to be completed. It is important for the designer to classify procedures as simple or complex because they are taught somewhat differently. A linear procedure may be considered simple if it only has a few (five to seven) steps (Schmid & Gerlach, 1990). The age, sophistication, and prior knowledge of the audience, as well as the difficulty of each step, should help you determine whether to use five or seven as your cutoff point for simple procedures.

Simple procedures with no decisions may be taught and practiced as a unit. The procedure for calculating an average is a simple procedure:

1. Add the values together.
2. Determine the number of values.
3. Divide the sum of the values by the number of values.

A branching procedure is considered to be a complex procedure. The CPR example above is a complex procedure. We will discuss how instruction might be varied depending upon the complexity of the procedure in the following paragraphs on the expanded instructional events.

Conditions Supporting Rule Learning—Procedural Rules

General Design Decisions

Writing the Procedure. Before a procedure is taught, the designer must clarify the procedure and list the steps and decisions of the procedure in an unambiguous form. Some guidelines for verbally describing the procedure follow:

- Steps should be described in clear, unambiguous sentences.
- Steps should result from a careful cognitive task analysis.
- Each operation step should represent a single, elementary action.
- When possible, each decision should be dichotomous, resulting in the selection of one of two possible paths. If the decision must result in more than two options, the branches resulting from a decision should not exceed five.
- Decision steps should be stated in the form of a question.
- Operation steps should be stated as imperative sentences (beginning with a verb).

Figure 9.1 presents an example of a procedure description for selecting film of an appropriate speed.

Simple vs. Complex Procedures. Simple procedures may be taught in a straightforward manner in which a step is presented and demonstrated and then practiced. In some cases it may be useful to present and practice the procedure in a reverse order, beginning with the last step first. Then the learners will learn and practice the next to the last step, and so on (Gilbert, 1978). This gives the learners the satisfaction of completing the procedure over and over.

Complex procedures must be simplified for their initial instruction. Then later the procedure can be elaborated into its more complex form. Some methods for simplifying (adapted from Wilson, 1985) are to teach the following items first:

- The simplest or most common path
- The major branches
- A simplified initial case

(One could also provide output of difficult or time-consuming steps, and/or chunk related steps together.)

One popular way to simplify a complex procedure is to choose the simplest or most common path through the procedure and teach that first. The procedure is taught with its decision steps; however, there is only one route through the procedure,

so it is initially linear. In such a case the learners need not learn all the branches and steps in the first stages of learning. What they do learn can be built upon in subsequent elaborations of the procedure. An example of this approach would be to give instruction on the most common repair on a piece of malfunctioning equipment first and then move on to more difficult repairs.

Providing instruction and practice on separate major branches is also a common simplifying procedure. It is quite common in complex procedures to have a first decision point that sends the learner through two or more separate and distinct paths. One approach to teaching a procedure of this kind is to teach one branch from beginning to end before moving to other branches. (You will see an example of this approach in our sample lesson in this chapter on scientific notation.)

A third method of simplifying a complex procedure is by simplifying the original instructional case. Much as we select best examples that embody critical characteristics when we are teaching concepts, we can begin instruction on a procedure with a simple case. The instruction may limit the sheer volume of the original case so that the entire procedure can be demonstrated in a short period of time. This is the approach we use when we have students apply the instructional design procedure to a single objective lesson. It is also the method math teachers use in explaining the procedure of "borrowing" in subtraction.

When the completion of individual steps in a procedure is extremely time-consuming, tedious, or otherwise complex, it may be helpful in initial presentation and practice to provide learners with the output of individual steps. In such a case, the learners can complete the entire procedure as a whole, without becoming frustrated or distracted with the details of completing any single step. For example, when we teach students to use a page-processing software program, we initially provide them with a text file and a graphics file. This is so that they initially do not have to go through the extended process of creating these files, but they still have the experience of completing the page processing related to the software. Another example is instruction on completing a tax form. An initial pass through the instructional events might provide the learners with some of the calculated values so that completion of calculations is needed only on the most critical and meaningful parts of the form.

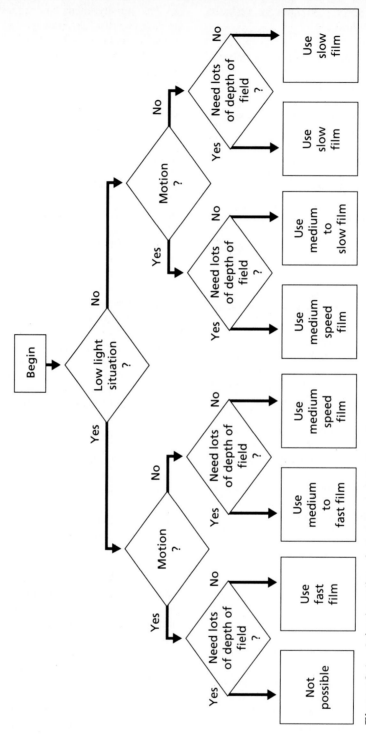

Figure 9.1: Selecting Film of an Appropriate Speed

If a particular procedure is made complex by the sheer number of steps or many steps in addition to decision steps, one way to simplify the instruction originally is to chunk the steps into stages or phases. Then the learners can learn to complete and practice those steps together as a whole, rather than being overwhelmed by the entire task. Ultimately the individual steps in a stage may be mentally "compiled" (Anderson, 1985) so that they represent one cohesive unit. Thus, they are easily dealt with in the entire procedure. We could use this approach with students in a car mechanics class learning to tune-up a car. First, we provide instruction on tuning-up the ignition system. Learners can practice this procedure before moving on to learn how to adjust the valves. Finally, they can learn to tune-up the carburetion system. Eventually, learners can be given instruction and practice on completing all three phases of a tune-up.

Expository or Discovery Strategy. A didactic, expository approach, rather than a discovery approach, seems to be generally best for teaching procedural rules. As procedures are efficient means for the repeated solution of situations that might otherwise be solved by the application of a relational rule or through problem solving, it makes sense to teach the procedure as efficiently as possible. The best strategy appears to be a straightforward presentation of the procedure with demonstrations of the applications of the procedure, rather than having learners struggle with discovering the procedure for themselves. However, Landa (1983) suggests that in some cases it may be useful to support learners' discovery of their own procedures, which may be somewhat idiosyncratic. We believe that such a discovery approach may be appropriate if one of the primary goals of the instructional system is for learners to acquire skills in generating procedures. However, we believe that such an instructional task would more appropriately be considered a problem-solving task than a procedural rule task.

Introduction

Deploy Attention

Attention to the instructional task may be gained by asking a question that presents a situation requiring the application of the procedure, or through demonstrating the actual application of the procedure itself. Attention may also be encouraged by pointing out the efficiency of the procedure over trial and error techniques.

Establish Instructional Purpose

Learners may be informed of the purpose of the lesson both in terms of which procedure is to be learned and its range of applicability. In addition, it is important that learners are aware of the efficiency of learning a procedure instead of continuing to respond to each situation with a trial and error approach. In many cases the procedure may be demonstrated to clarify the purpose of the lesson (and to preview the lesson).

Arouse Interest and Motivation

Learning procedures can be intrinsically motivating because they allow learners to complete tasks more efficiently and more reliably than they did using trial and error approaches before instruction. Since the learning of procedures can appear to be rote and meaningless to the learner, it is important that the purpose of learning a procedure (in terms of its efficiency and reliability) be emphasized. This efficiency might actually be demonstrated to the learners. If learners have experienced the situations as trial and error tasks, they may have already begun to formulate their own procedures to deal with these tasks more efficiently. Learners should be encouraged to compare any procedures they have developed to the procedure being taught on the basis of efficiency and effectiveness.

Preview Lesson

The procedure should be previewed during this phase of the lesson. If the procedure is fairly simple, with approximately seven steps or fewer (even fewer steps for younger learners) and has no or few decision points, then the procedure may be previewed by demonstrating the complete procedure. If the procedure is complex, with many steps and decision points with related branches, then the overview may be a summary of the procedure with several steps grouped together, such as our previous description of the complex CPR procedure. Such an overview may be made concrete with a verbal or visual outline of the steps.

It is important that it be made clear to the learners that the demonstration is to give them an overview and that they are not expected to learn the entire procedure via this one demonstration. Learners can become very anxious if it is not made abundantly clear that they will be explicitly taught the individual steps of the procedure.

Body

Sequencing and clustering of the steps of the procedure are important decisions at this stage in the strategy plan. For very simple procedures, the entire procedure may be taught first in its entirety and then practiced. However, most procedures will require that the procedure be simplified in some way and be taught and practiced in segments. Teaching the procedure in stages will require that the events in the body of the lesson be repeated for each stage of the procedure.

Recall Relevant Prior Knowledge

Prior knowledge that can support the acquisition of a procedure may be concepts that are known and that must be used in recognition of a situation, such as the concept "pulse" in the CPR procedure. Concept knowledge may also be involved in completing a step of the procedure, such as recognition of certain tools in the procedural repair of equipment. These concepts should be reviewed.

As we stated earlier in the chapter, learners may have been taught a relational rule (such as the relationship of distance, time, and rate) and later be taught a procedure to efficiently and reliably solve problems involving these variables. It is helpful to review the relational rule underlying the procedure to make the procedure meaningful.

Often, learners have previously learned less complex procedural rules that will be combined with other procedures to form a new and complex procedure. For example, learners may have already learned to take a pulse in another context before taking a course on CPR. This procedure should be reviewed at the appropriate time in the sequence of learning to administer CPR.

Process Information and Examples

As we stated earlier, to learn a procedural rule learners must learn to recognize situations that require a particular procedure, complete the steps in the procedure, recall the steps in the procedure, and determine if the procedure has been properly applied. In addition, if the procedure is complex, the learner must learn to make decisions within the procedure by classifying situations and choosing branches of the procedure depending upon the decisions that are made. Although we are suggesting that the instructional sequence occur in the following order, we recognize that other sequences may also be appropriate.

1. *Learning to determine if the procedure is required.* To make the procedure meaningful, the first information that should be processed is the context or situation(s) in which the procedure is applicable. This is a prerequisite "pattern recognition" or concept learning that should be learned and practiced first in the lesson. A strategy for teaching concepts will be appropriate for this phase: Learners should see examples of the variety of situations in which the procedure is applicable and the characteristics of the situations that make them appropriate for the application of the procedure. Situations that have similar nonessential features should be contrasted so that learners can clearly identify the attributes of the situations that are critical to the use of the procedure. For example, part of learning the procedure for changing the oil in a car is knowing how to recognize that the car is low on oil. The presentation of these matched examples and nonexamples should be followed with practice and feedback.

2. *Learning to complete the steps in the procedure.* This phase of presenting and processing information differs depending upon whether the procedure is a simple procedure or a complex procedure. Simple procedures may be learned in a single pass through the process information event and practiced as a whole, or each individual step may be learned and then practiced. Complex procedures may be taught in an elaborated instruction (see the discussion of Reigeluth's Elaboration Model in Chapter 6) in which learners move through the events multiple times with increasingly complete experiences. For example, if the designer uses a most common path simplification of the procedure, then each iteration of the events might present instruction on steps that are in less and less common paths.

Each step of the procedure may be presented as a live demonstration, a video, or in some cases, audio representation, computer frames, or illustrated textual materials. Generally, each individual step should be considered and demonstrated separately. The importance of this principle becomes apparent when we consider examples of print-based instruction such as that developed to teach the assembly of equipment. Designers often are tempted to save space and cost by combining steps when teaching and illustrating them. This almost always leads to learners' confusion in distinguishing what actions should precede others. Although presentation and processing of individual steps can be tedious and costly, such thoroughness is generally beneficial.

You will recall that in our discussion of concepts and relational rules we suggested using matched nonexamples. There has been some controversy among designers as to the utility of presenting nonexamples when teaching procedures. Based upon the scanty research that is currently available, we suggest that it *is* useful to show learners common errors in completing individual steps. This presentation should occur only after the correct application of a step has been clearly demonstrated with several examples. This will avoid possible confusion about the correct procedure. The statement of the error should be couched in a general form rather than in terms of the specific error in a particular example. For example, the study on which this suggestion is based (Marcone & Reigeluth, 1988) taught the procedure for constructing a musical interval on a scale. The researchers used the following warning: "BE CAREFUL: You should begin counting on the note given and NOT the line or space above it. THIS IS THE MOST OFTEN MADE MISTAKE!!!" The study found that it was more beneficial to state the warning and show the error exemplified on a staff than to show the error without the warning.

After each step is demonstrated, the learners should have the opportunity to practice that step until they are proficient. Then the next step should be presented and practiced along with the previous step. (We will discuss this practice in the next section.)

3. *Learning to list the steps in the procedure.* After learners have gone through the iterations of step demonstration and practice, they must learn to combine the steps into an articulated whole that flows from one step to the next. This integration is partly a result of practicing the steps together as a whole. It is also a result of learners acquiring a mental representation of the sequence and nature of the steps. For simple procedures, a recollection of the order of the steps and what each step entails may be easy; simply practicing the procedure with spaced review on the order and nature of the steps will generally be sufficient for learning what the steps are.

Complex procedures will be more difficult to remember because of the number of steps and the branching possibilities. It is important for a designer to determine whether the learner must actually remember the order and nature of the steps. Memorizing the steps may not be necessary for the following types of procedures: (1) those that are exceedingly complex with multiple decision points, (2) those that are rarely executed, (3) those that will always be completed in one particular location, (4) those that do not have to be completed speedily, and (5) those that are very similar and easily confused with related procedures. Such procedures may be supported with a printed list of steps and decisions (a job aid), often in the form of a checklist or flowchart. For example, the procedures for troubleshooting malfunctioning equipment are often exceedingly lengthy and involve many branches. It is very common to support these procedures with flowcharts that the repair persons carry with them. If job aids are to be used in the application setting, then learners should have them available to them during all the events of instruction (including assessment) and be taught to use them effectively. Instructing learners to use job aids effectively involves modeling of the use of the job aid and feedback to the learners.

The following types of procedures must be recalled without the help of a job aid: (1) procedures that must be completed in crisis situations, (2) those that may be required in many and unexpected locations, and (3) those that must be completed often and routinely. Occasionally, especially with complex procedures, initial instruction may include a job aid to support the learners' first practice attempts. If this support is provided, however, the instruction should include transition instruction that teaches learners how to develop a mental representation of the information on the job aid. Learners should practice without the job aid until they are proficient. The instruction should also include spaced practice without access to the job aid.

Another strategy that may enhance the retention of these steps is a discussion of the meaningfulness of the particular sequence of the steps as they appear; i.e., why the steps are ordered as they are. If the information regarding the order and nature of the steps can be made personally meaningful to the learners, they may remember the steps more easily.

4. *Learning to check the appropriateness of a completed procedure.* Part of learning a procedure is learning to determine whether it has been correctly applied. This skill depends upon the learner being able to mentally review the procedure (after it has been applied) and confirm that each step and decision was completed appropriately. The previously described instruction in concert with practice in reviewing procedures completed by others will support this learning. In addition, learners should receive instruction on how to judge the adequacy of the output of a procedure. For example, learners could have practice in being given the input and then estimating the output of a mathematical procedure. This would give them a feel for the range of acceptable outputs of the calculation. Other types of procedures may have specific cues to signal a correct application of a procedure, such as auditory cues of a correctly tuned car or the appearance of a correctly baked soufflé. Most of us were taught to check the result of subtraction by adding the difference (answer) to the bottom number (subtrahend). This skill is an example of instruction on monitoring the successful completion of a procedure. Direct instruction on judging the adequacy of the output of a procedure should be included in the instructional events so that learners may become good monitors of their own performance.

Focus Attention

1. *Learning to determine if the procedure is required.* As with other pattern recognition (i.e.,

concept) learning tasks, it is important that the criterial features of the situation that requires the application of the procedure be highlighted and contrasted to noncritical features within the situation. These features can be emphasized by pointing out the critical features in a comparison of examples and nonexamples of situations that require the procedure.

2. *Learning to complete the steps in the procedure.* As the students learn to complete each step in the procedure, it is important that their attention be focused on the key cues that indicate when a particular step should be initiated and when it has been completed correctly. These cues may be visual, auditory, tactile, or olfactory. In addition, they should be presented (or encouraged to develop) keyword summarizers of each step. These keywords should generally be verbs that signal the learners' performance during each step. These keywords should be emphasized during instruction and review.

3. *Learning to list the steps in the procedure.* The important features that should be emphasized during this part of instruction are sequence and keyword performances. If a job aid is used and its continued use is anticipated, then sequence and keyword verbs should be highlighted.

4. *Learning to check the appropriateness of a completed procedure.* As in learning to complete individual steps, learners' attention should be focused upon the cues within the situation that signal the successful completion of the procedure. Examples of these cues would be the correct threading of paper through a printer, the cessation of blood leaving a wound, and having all blanks filled in on a form.

Employ Learning Strategies

If the criterial features of a situation that would elicit the procedure are difficult to recall, such as the particular symptoms of a medical emergency, it may be useful to provide the learners with a mnemonic device to aid them in recalling these characteristics. Or, learners may be encouraged to develop their own mnemonics.

As the exact order of the steps may be difficult for a learner to remember over time, particularly if the procedure is not used often, the instruction may provide or encourage the learners to invent a mnemonic to remember the steps. For instance, CPR training often includes the mnemonic ABC to remind the learners to first establish an airway (A), then to commence breathing (B), and then to begin cardiac massage (C). Learners might also be encouraged to develop visual mnemonics or other visual images that represent the sequence of steps in the procedure.

Instead of providing learners with a job aid, it may be useful to encourage them to develop their own job aids. Such activity will help them to consolidate their own learning and may make the learning more memorable. If they have not had previous experience in developing job aids, time should be set aside to provide guidance and instruction in the purpose and possible formats of a job aid. In addition, instructors should provide feedback on the usefulness and efficiency of the job aids that the learners have developed.

The monitoring of output of a procedure is a learning strategy that applies beyond the characteristics of this type of learning. As with other learning, it is important that learners acquire the habit of estimating the results of their actions. Then they can compare the actual end results of their actions with their estimates. If the conclusion is far off the estimate, one can either revise the estimate or reapply the procedure. This monitoring of progress may also be employed at the conclusion of some individual steps. For example, when learning to fill in blanks on an income tax form, learners may learn to monitor whether each of the values "makes sense" in the context of the procedure.

Practice

Although the ultimate goal of learning a procedure is the ability to perform all four of the components of completing a procedure, it is usually helpful to practice each of these components before moving on to the next component.

1. *Learning to determine if the procedure is required.* This skill, which is prerequisite to performing the entire procedure, may be practiced by presenting situations in which the procedure might be useful. Learners should then decide whether or not the procedure should be applied. It is also critical at this point to have learners

justify their answers to ensure that they have truly identified the situation by its critical attributes. Learners' practice should begin with situations that clearly require the procedure. Then they can move on to situations that are less clear due to extraneous details. If learners have previously learned other procedures that are easily confused with the new procedure, they should be presented with some of these situations in order to have practice in distinguishing between these potentially confusing situations.

2. *Learning to complete the steps in the procedure.* In general, each individual step of the procedure should be practiced immediately after it is presented. This practice may be practicing a decision step by determining which of two or more conditions exists, or it could be practicing an operation step by completing a performance step in the procedure. Landa (1983) suggests that the first step be demonstrated and practiced, then the next step be demonstrated and practiced, and then steps one and two be practiced together. Next, step three is demonstrated and practiced. Then it is practiced with steps one and two. Landa proposes that this "snowballing" effect of practicing new steps with previously learned steps will enhance learners' learning the entire procedure as a whole. As you will read in Chapter 13, Gilbert suggests a similar approach to practicing procedures. He, however, suggests that for some procedures it may be helpful to learn and practice the steps in a reverse order. In such an approach, the last step would be learned and practiced, then, the next-to-last step would be learned and practiced, and then the two steps would be practiced together. For some procedures and some learners this "backward chaining" may be very effective and motivating, especially for tasks in which completing the last step is highly satisfying.

After having the practice of completing the individual steps, learners should have practice in completing the entire procedure a number of times. With a complex procedure this practice might, after initial instruction, involve only simplified cases. However, after instruction with more complex cases, the practice should occur with situations across a wide range of possible situations. These should include some situations that require the simplest or most common path, some that require a more complex and extensive path, and some that do not require the procedure at all.

For procedures that are to be performed without a job aid, practice should either not include a job aid or have the job aid removed during practice toward the end of the practice event. For procedures in which the job aid will be employed during the projected actual application of the procedure, practice should include use of the job aid. In addition, some practice items may ask learners to note the portion of the job aid that is relevant to a certain portion of the procedure to ensure that the learners are able to use the job aid as a guide and reference.

3. *Learning to list the steps in the procedure.* After learners have practiced executing the procedure, it is critical that they practice recalling the sequence and nature of the steps in the procedure. If learners are learning to complete a procedure that is supported by a job aid, of course, this type of practice will not be necessary. However, if they will be required to remember the steps of the procedure in the correct order, then they must be provided with ample opportunity to actually recite this order. In addition, they should be able to recall critical keywords that summarize the performance in each step. It will also be useful at some point in practice to require learners to expand upon these keywords to ensure that they do indeed denote the entire step of the procedure to the learner.

This type of recall is a verbal information learning task and will profit from suggestions for practice presented in Chapter 6. Of these suggestions, the suggestion for spaced review and practice is particularly important in learning procedures.

4. *Learning to check the appropriateness of a completed procedure.* Practice should also include an opportunity for learners to view the process and/or product of a procedure and determine whether the procedure was correctly performed. This practice should include their overt reviewing of their own performance, as well as the opportunity to review the performance of others. Reviewing others' performances or products allows the learners to note errors that they may not have made yet in their executions of the procedure but might commit later in their performance. As a part of this practice learners may be encouraged to identify the source of the error and suggest approaches for rectifying the problem.

Evaluate Feedback

1. *Learning to determine if the procedure is required.* Of course, the first feedback that should be provided is confirmatory feedback as to whether the learner has appropriately identified the situations that require the application of the procedure. In addition, some explanatory feedback should be available to the learner as to why a particular situation does or does not require the application of the procedure. Such feedback should include a discussion of the critical attributes of the situation and a mapping of these attributes on to the situation, indicating where the attributes do or do not match.

2. *Learning to complete the steps in the procedure.* Learners should be provided with feedback as to the accuracy of their completion of each step of the procedure. During initial learning phases when each step is first learned, this feedback may be more detailed than in later practice of the entire procedure. Feedback on decision steps will include information as to whether the learner correctly assessed the nature of the situation and made the correct decision, leading to choosing the correct path in the procedure.

Feedback on completion of operation steps should include not only dichotomous information as to whether the step was correctly completed but also qualitative information as to (1) whether the inputs into the operation were appropriately selected, (2) whether the outputs of the operation reached any prescribed criterion, and (3) whether the step was completed with acceptable precision and efficiency.

Procedures with operation steps that have a significant observable motor component may be videotaped so that learners observe their own behavior while reviewing any written or spoken feedback. In addition, learners can be taught to judge the adequacy of the completion of individual steps in the procedure, just as they can be taught to judge the adequacy of the completion of the entire procedure. For some procedures that have a motor component, learners can also learn to recognize the kinesthetic feedback when an operation step is completed appropriately.

3. *Learning to list the steps in the procedure.* For procedures that must be completed without a job aid, feedback on whether all the steps of the procedure were remembered in the correct order is also useful. In initial practice this feedback may be in response to a verbal information exercise, such as "List the steps of *X* procedure in the correct order." Later, when the entire procedure is practiced, feedback as to whether all steps were completed and whether they were executed in the correct order may be included in the feedback. Additional feedback might include such hints as to what characteristics of an antecedent step cued the step that followed.

4. *Learning to check the appropriateness of a completed procedure.* Feedback for this type of practice should include correct answer feedback as to whether the given procedure has been correctly completed. The learners can then compare this judgement to their own assessments of whether a demonstrated procedure has been executed properly. This general feedback might be followed with a detailed explanation of why a particular decision was made.

Conclusion

The conclusion should give learners an opportunity to compile their representation of the procedure across all the variations of the procedure that they may have experienced during the instruction.

Summarize and Review

Transfer Knowledge

The summary of a procedural rule lesson often begins with a review of the types of problems, goals, or situations to which the procedure applies. This review will also support the transfer of this learning. The instruction or the learners may supply these situations; however, it will be helpful if the situations are classified into categories if they

tend to be of several types. For instance, some situations require a simple form of the procedure, while other situations require a more complex form.

A summary may also include a reiteration of the relationship between the procedure and a relational rule (or rules) from which it is derived. This review will add meaningfulness, which might not have been as apparent at the beginning of the lesson when this relationship was first described. Any increase in meaningfulness should enhance retention of the procedure.

Next, the form, nature, and variations of the procedure should be summarized and reviewed. This summary can be supplied by the learners, perhaps by their creation of a graphic organizer. Or, the summary can be provided by the instruction. For example, the instruction might present the sequence of steps for a simplest case and then add overlays to outline the procedures for increasingly complex cases. The presentation of these procedural steps might also be presented in clusters to aid learners' compilation of the steps into larger units. This compilation will enhance retention and automaticity, particularly within clusters.

The instruction should also review any particularly difficult or confusing steps within the procedure and the features that indicate a correctly completed procedure.

As there is a considerable verbal information component in learning a procedure, spaced review, and practice of the procedure, including the variations of the procedure should be planned into subsequent lessons. This spaced practice may encourage greater efficiency or precision in execution of the procedure. This spaced practice might be combined with instruction that encourages transfer of the procedure to other learning tasks. The procedure, or parts of the procedure, may be incorporated in other tasks, such as the Heimlich maneuver being incorporated into a CPR procedure. Or cognitive strategies acquired while learning a procedure, such as self-monitoring techniques, may be incorporated into a procedure. In addition, a simpler procedure may be elaborated on in later lessons.

Remotivate and Close

Part of the remotivation may occur in the previous event as learners are reminded of the breadth of utility of the new procedure. In addition, here at the conclusion of the lesson, the learners should again be reminded of the usefulness of the procedure over other ways of solving problems: the efficiency and the reliability of the outcome if the procedure is correctly applied. The closing statement of the lesson should include a name for the procedure to ensure that the learners can recall the procedure by its label.

Assess Performance

The ultimate assessment for a procedure is the learner's ability to correctly apply the procedure across as diverse a range of difficulty and situations as the designer has prescribed. If possible, the designer will develop several items across this range in order to obtain a reliable and valid assessment of the learner's skill. It is often desirable to assess component (prerequisite) skills—the identification of situations that call for the procedure, the listing of steps in correct sequence, and the evaluation of a completed procedure as to its correctness. If these component skills can be assessed, their results can provide information if remediation is required. Occasionally, it is possible to gather information as to learners' skills in these components by observing learners' demonstration of the procedure—by having them "show their work"—or by reviewing their final product to determine their correct use of the process.

Evaluate Feedback and Seek Remediation

Feedback can inform learners as to their skill in completing the procedure at its various levels of complexity and common errors they have made when applying the procedure. When learners' performance is poor, it can also inform them of what specific component skills have not been mastered.

Preview of Example Lesson — Procedural Rule

Task Analysis

The procedural rule for this lesson is to convert numbers from standard notation to scientific nota-

tion. For purposes of brevity we will limit the objective to positive numbers. The objective for the lesson is the following: "Given a number greater than one in standard notation, the learner can convert the number to scientific notation."

The production for this task is:

> IF a number is in standard notation
>   And IF the number is greater than ten thousand
>   Or IF it is necessary to report the number compactly
> THEN convert to scientific notation by using the following procedure. (See Figure 9.2 for a flowchart of this procedure.)

Learners and Content

The learners for this example lesson are eighth-grade students in general science classes. The required general science class includes a survey of earth science, physics, biology, and chemistry. This lesson occurs early in the year-long course.

In the learners' mathematics classes in both sixth and seventh grades, students have learned the meaning and use of exponents. They have also learned the concepts of place value and base ten numbers.

This lesson will be mediated in print because it is a simple, straightforward procedure. Feedback for this particular objective can be presented even for constructed response items. You will notice that, as in previous lessons, we have resequenced the expanded instructional events as needed for this particular lesson and these particular learners.

Example Lesson — Procedural Rules

Introduction

Deploy Attention

Establish Purpose

Arouse Interest and Motivation

The lesson will begin by presenting scenarios in which scientists and students must present very large numbers used in science, such as the distance

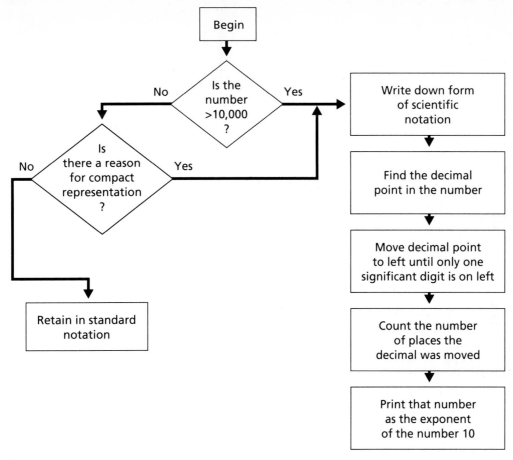

Figure 9.2: Conversion to Scientific Notation

between planets, the number of bytes of information the human brain can store, or the mass of the earth. These scenarios should be portrayed as humorously as possible. Other scenarios should depict situations in which large numbers must be presented compactly. Instruction should state that the purpose of this lesson is for students to learn to represent large numbers in a more compact form. This compact form is called *scientific notation*. Instruction points out that learners will learn to follow a procedure for converting numbers to scientific notation. Students could find the answer without using the procedure, but they will reach the answer more reliably and efficiently with this procedure.

Preview the Lesson

The overview should indicate that the instruction will answer the following questions:

- What is scientific notation? What is standard notation?
- When should I use scientific notation?
- How do I convert a number from standard to scientific notation?

(Notice we do not review the steps of the process here because some concepts must first be learned for the process to make any sense.)

Body

Process Information

Employ Learning Strategies

Focus Attention

Review Prior Knowledge

The instruction lists several large numbers in standard notation and labels them as such. It then defines *standard notation*. The lesson points out that *standard* usually means "common" and that *notation* comes from the word *note*. Then the lesson lists a series of numbers and labels them as *standard notation*.

Next, the lesson presents these same numbers in scientific notation. It juxtaposes the same values in scientific and standard notation. It highlights the form of scientific notation:

$$\underline{\quad ? \quad} \times 10^{?}$$

The lesson asks the learners to notice that the value in the blank is a number between 1 and 10. It may contain fractional parts in the form of a decimal. Then the lesson emphasizes that the value of the exponent tells how many times the 10 would be multiplied by itself. The lesson also states that in standard notation the base must always be 10.

Practice

Several numbers are presented, including numbers in standard notation, scientific notation, and numbers (not 10) with exponents. The learners are asked to label the numbers as *scientific notation, standard notation,* or *other*.

Evaluate Feedback

Provide numbers with correct labels. Explain why numbers with exponents in which the base number is not 10 are not scientific notation.

Recall Prior Knowledge

Take one of the examples from earlier and show how the number in scientific notation actually represents the number. Review place value to show how this notation actually works.

Process Information

Discuss the two types of numbers for which scientific notation is preferable: (1) numbers larger than 10,000 and (2) numbers smaller than 10,000 that must be presented compactly. (Point out that later in their studies they will be introduced to additional reasons.) Review several situations in which scientific notation would be appropriate, and contrast these with somewhat similar situations in which scientific notation would be unnecessary. Emphasize that scientific notation can be used with any numbers but that it is generally unnecessary to make the conversion except in the situations just mentioned.

Practice

Present a variety of situations in which scientific notation is and is not necessary. (Be creative, and make the practice fun by presenting humorous number problems.) Ask students to label the situations and explain their decisions.

Evaluate Feedback

Give the learners feedback by presenting each number in both forms and then discussing which is the preferred form. Each decision should be briefly explained.

Preview the Lesson

Preview the process for converting to scientific notation. Emphasize the keywords for each step. Remind students that each step will be explained and practiced later.

1. Write the shell for scientific notation.
2. Find the decimal point in the number in standard notation.
3. Move the decimal point to the left until only one number is to the left of the decimal. Write this number in the first blank.
4. Count the number of places the decimal was moved to the left. Write this number as the exponent of the 10.
5. Check the number mentally by converting it back to standard notation.

The lesson should be in a parallel, two-column format to demonstrate the conversion of a number beside each step.

Process Information

The first step should be labeled with the heading 1 — *Write the shell*. Review the term *shell* from their computer literacy classes. Show the form of the shell:

$$\underline{\hspace{2cm}} \times 10$$

Explain that two values must be added to complete the scientific notation. Review the nature of these two numbers.

Practice

Have students write the form of the shell, circle the two places where the number will be added, and explain the nature of the numbers that should appear in these two places.

Evaluate Feedback

Provide a shell with locations for two additional values circled and an explanation of these two values.

Process Information

Focus Attention

Begin this section with the heading 2—*Find the decimal*. Present several numbers, some of which contain decimals and some of which have "understood" decimals. Highlight the location of the decimals.

Practice

Evaluate Feedback

Present several numbers, some of which contain decimals and some of which have "understood" decimals. Ask students to locate the decimal. Then present these numbers with decimals highlighted.

Summarize and Review

List the first two steps of the procedure. Use a sample problem and take learners through the first two steps.

1. Write the shell for scientific notation.
2. Find the decimal point in the number in standard notation.

Practice

Give several numbers in standard notation that are appropriate for standard notation. Ask students to complete the first two steps in converting to scientific notation.

Evaluate Feedback

Each step should be shown and labeled explicitly for each number

Process Information

Focus Attention

The third step should be presented with the heading *3—Move the decimal*. The object of this step should be emphasized—to get only one number to the left of the decimal. Several examples should be demonstrated with the first two steps completed and the third step demonstrated. The number written in the first blank of the shell should be highlighted. The lesson should emphasize that this number must be between 1 and 10 (but will never *be* 10). The lesson also emphasizes that the movement is to the left, not the right.

Practice

Evaluate Feedback

Several numbers suitable for scientific notation are presented. The learners are given the first two steps completed for each number and are asked to complete the third step by entering the value of the number in the first blank of the shell. Feedback is provided by showing the third step for each practice number.

Practice

Several numbers suitable for scientific notation are presented. The learner is asked to complete the first three steps of the procedure for converting to scientific notation.

Feedback

The first three steps of the procedure should be presented for each of the practice numbers.

Process Information

Focus Attention

This step should be labeled *4—Count the moves*. An example should be shown with the first three steps completed. The fourth step should be visually demonstrated. The procedure of moving the decimal should be emphasized with a dotted line stopping at each place the decimal is moved. An arrow should point to the location where the decimal will now appear. The arrow should indicate that the movement was to the left. The number of moves should be indicated with a number below the dotted line. The connection between the number of moves and the exponent should be visually emphasized. The shell should be completed with the exponent of the 10 completed. Several examples should be shown. Following these, the text should explain that this step is just a procedural way of determining the place value of the significant digit that is given in the first blank. It should also be emphasized that the count stands for the moves, not the places the decimal is moved.

Practice

Evaluate Feedback

Several numbers that are appropriate for scientific notation should be presented with the first three steps completed. The learners should be directed to complete the fourth step by entering the exponent for the 10. Feedback should provide the completed shell.

Present more numbers that are appropriate for scientific notation. Learners should be asked to complete the first four steps of the procedure. Feedback should be presented in the form of a completed shell for each number.

Process Information

Focus Attention

Employ Learning Strategies

The fifth step, 5—*Confirm answer,* should be introduced as a critical step in all procedures. Learners should be presented with some examples of numbers in standard and scientific notation, some of which have been converted correctly and some of which have the correct form but an error in conversion. Some of these numbers should contain zeros in both the initial and in medial positions. The instruction should suggest three approaches for checking the answer: (1) checking the format of the number, (2) reapplying the procedure, or (3) converting the number back to standard notation. The procedure for converting a number from scientific to standard notation should be demonstrated with appropriate graphic devices that emphasize the procedure.

Practice

The learners should be presented with several numbers written in scientific notation with their standard notations. Some of these should be incorrectly computed, with moves incorrectly counted, more than one number as a significant digit, and other common errors. Learners should be asked to mark each conversion as correct or incorrect. Beside those that they mark as incorrect, they should be asked to explain their answers.

Feedback

Feedback should include the number in its given standard notation and scientific notation, with the statement *correct* or *incorrect*. Each incorrect answer should be explained with a statement of which approach would be most likely to locate a problem: (1) checking the format of the number, (2) reapplying the procedure, or (3) converting the number back to standard notation.

Practice

Feedback

Several numbers should be presented in an application context, some of which are appropriate for conversion and some of which are not. Students should be directed to determine which numbers should be converted and then convert them. Feedback should indicate the numbers that should be written in scientific notation in that form. A brief explanation as to why some numbers were not converted should be included.

Practice

Feedback

Learners should be asked to list the five steps in converting a number to scientific notation. Feedback should provide a list of these steps.

Conclusion

Summarize and Review

Employ Learning Strategies

The five steps for conversion to scientific notation should be presented with the keywords emphasized. Learners should be encouraged to shut their eyes and visualize these steps either in words or in representative pictures. The situations that require scientific notation should be reviewed. The process should be demonstrated with one last number.

Transfer Learning

Learners should be informed of a number of situations in which they will be asked to use scientific notation in future units. They should be asked to locate numbers in texts and other publications in which scientific notation is used or should have been used. They could be given a number that is negative (but with an absolute value of 1 or more) and asked to convert to scientific notation and provided with feedback. They might also be given a number that is less than 1 (and appropriate for scientific notation) and asked to guess how it might be converted. Feedback should be provided.

Remotivate and Close

Learners should be given an exciting, interesting, or humorous scenario in which they must convert a number to scientific notation. They should be encouraged to explain why this is a useful skill to have.

Assessment

Assess Performance

If this lesson is to be assessed independently from other objectives, then several separate items may be included to assess if learners can do the following: (1) identify situations in which scientific notation should be used, (2) apply the procedure to convert a number from scientific notation to standard notation, (3) list the steps for the procedure, and (4) determine whether the procedure has been correctly applied. If assessment time is limited, only components (2) and (4), or perhaps just (4), may be assessed.

Evaluate Feedback and Seek Remediation

Feedback should be provided in a generalized form. Information can be provided as to whether the learners have difficulty in identifying situations appropriate for scientific notation, applying the procedure, listing the steps, or monitoring an answer. Even if separate items of each type were not administered individually, the grader may be able to view the learners' responses and draw some inferences about the source of the problems. In addition, the grader may be able to identify for the learners any common or consistent errors they are making.

Job Aid

For designing relational and procedural rule lessons, use the Job Aid in Chapter 6.

Summary

The following tables summarize key points from the chapter.

Conditions of Learning by Event for Relational Rule Learning

Introduction	Deploy attention.	• Curiosity-evoking situation/problem
	Establish instructional purpose.	• Understand/apply principle, relationship between concepts
	Arouse interest and motivation.	• Curiosity-evoking situation
	Preview lesson.	• Inquiry = directions; expository = outline
Body	Recall prior knowledge.	• Review component concepts.
	Process information.	• Present/induct relationship; state in principle form; demonstrate application.
	Focus attention.	• Direction and size in change of one variable when other variables change
	Employ learning strategies.	• Mnemonic rule statement, diagram of relationship
	Practice.	• Predict, explain, and control changes in concept(s) based on change of another; recognize situations where rule applies; and determine whether rule was correctly applied.
	Evaluate feedback.	• Information on whether rule is applicable, outcome of application

Conditions of Learning by Event for Procedural Rule Learning

Introduction	Deploy attention.	• Ask questions, demonstrate procedure, and describe efficiency.
	Establish instructional purpose.	• Describe procedure to be learned and the range of applicability.
	Arouse interest and motivation.	• Emphasize efficiency and reliability of procedure.
	Preview lesson.	• Preview procedure in chunks.
Body	Recall prior knowledge.	• Review component concepts, sub-procedures, or related principles.
	Process information.	• Simplify complex procedures, situations that require procedure steps in procedure, order of steps, how to evaluate the correct application. • May elaborate over several iterations.

Visual	*Audio*
Title slide: The smaller the aperture, the greater the depth of field.	Yes, the principle is the smaller the aperture, the greater the depth of field. Or conversely, the larger the aperture, the more shallow the depth of field.
Two images contrasted side by side with f-stops labeled at bottom.	Here is another example. Notice how the depth of field compresses as the aperture is made larger.
Two more images contrasted side by side with f-stops labeled at bottom.	Here is another example. Notice how the depth of field becomes deeper as the aperture is made smaller.
Image of large and smaller aperture and light rays being focused upon plane of film.	The physics of why this relationship occurs is fairly complicated.
Image of kid reading book by flashlight in a darkened room. Book is held closely, kid is frowning.	But if you need a trick for remembering the relationship between aperture and depth of field, remember how, as a young child, you were told not to read in the dark.
Image of a dilated eye.	Remember when you are in the dark your eye adjusts to the low light by opening its aperture (the iris). Why is it hard to read in low light? Your eye's depth of field has been reduced due to the large aperture, so your eye muscles must strain to keep the image in focus.
Image of kid reading in brightly lit room with book set comfortably in front of him, followed by slide of an image of eye with small iris.	Under bright light, when the eye's aperture is ''stopped down'' to a small opening, you have lots of depth of field and can focus on close objects more easily.

Practice

Feedback

Title shot: Practice	Now let's see if you can remember and use this relationship.
Slide of two apertures, one f/5.6, one f/11.	Which of these two aperture settings will have the shallower depth of field?
Slide of two images, one labeled 5.6 with a shallower depth of field and one labeled f/11 with deeper depth of field.	Yes, the shot with the larger aperture (smaller f-stop) has the shallower depth of field.
Slide of two apertures, one f/16 and one f/5.6.	Which of these two aperture settings will have the deeper depth of field?

Visual	*Audio*
Slide of two images, one labeled f/16 with deeper depth of field and one labeled f/5.6 with shallower depth of field.	Yes, the shot with the smaller aperture (larger f-stop) has the deeper depth of field.
Slide of two apertures, f/2.8 and f/5.6.	Which of these two aperture settings will have the deeper depth of field?
Slide of two images, one labeled f/2.8 with shallower depth of field and one labeled f/5.6 with deeper depth of field.	Yes, the shot with the smaller aperture (larger f-stop) has the deeper depth of field.

Conclusion

Summarize and Review

Transfer Knowledge

Remotivate and Close

Title slide:	The smaller the aperture, the deeper the depth of field.
Review:	The larger the aperture, the shallower the depth of field.
	To review, repeat these principles aloud: The smaller the aperture, the deeper the depth of field. The larger the aperture, the shallower the depth of field.
Slide of earlier problem with dog in cluttered living room.	Now you may have some suggestions for solving Pat's problem. Her current aperture setting is f/11 with a shutter speed of 1/125. What can she do to have only her dog in focus?
Slide of dog with remainder of living room blurred.	You are correct if you suggested that the f-stop be made smaller, like f/5.6 so that only the dog is in focus. This smaller f-stop gives you a larger aperture (opening).
Slide close-up of aperture with f-stops.	In a later lesson you will learn to estimate the area that will be in a depth of field when given a subject and an f-stop.
Slide close-up of shutter speed control.	You may have suspected that a change in the aperture will require a change in the shutter speed. That is correct. In a later lesson we will discuss this problem as well. For now, it is sufficient that you remember the principle relating the size of aperture to depth of field.

Assessment

Assess performance

Feedback and remediation

Very likely this objective will be assessed along with other related objectives or as a component of a problem-solving objective. The assessment should allow the instructor to determine if the learners have acquired the principle, especially if they recall the relationship correctly.

Readings and References

Anderson, J. R. (1985). *Cognitive psychology* (2nd ed). New York: Freeman.

Gagné, R. M. (1985). *The conditions of learning* (4th ed). New York: Holt, Rinehart and Winston.

Gilbert, T. (1978). *Human competence: Engineering worthy performance.* New York: McGraw-Hill.

Joyce, B., & Weil, M. (1986). Teaching inductively: Collecting, organizing, and manipulating data. In B. Joyce and M. Weil (Eds.), *Models of teaching* (3rd ed). Englewood Cliffs, NJ: Prentice-Hall, pp. 40–53.

Joyce, B., & Weil, M. (1986). Inquiry training. In B. Joyce and M. Weil (Eds.), *Models of Teaching* (3rd ed). Englewood Cliffs, NJ: Prentice-Hall, pp. 55–69.

Landa, L. N. (1974). *Algorithmization in learning and instruction.* Englewood Cliffs, NJ: Educational Technology Publications.

Landa, L. N. (1983). The algo-heuristic theory of instruction. In C. M. Reigeluth (Ed.), *Instructional design theories and models.* Hillsdale, NJ: Lawrence Erlbaum, pp. 163–211.

Marcone, S., & Reigeluth, C. M. (1988). Teaching common errors in applying a procedure. *Educational Communications and Technology Journal, 36*(1), 23–32.

Mitchell, M. C. (1980). The practicality of algorithms in instructional development. *Journal of Instructional Development, 4*(4), 10–16.

Reigeluth, C. M. (1987). *Instructional theories in action.* Hillsdale, NJ: Lawrence Erlbaum.

Scandura, J. M. (1983). Instructional strategies based on the structural learning theory. In C. M. Reigeluth (Ed.), *Instructional design theories and models.* Hillsdale, NJ: Lawrence Erlbaum, pp. 213–246.

Schmid, R. F., & Gerlach, V. S. (1990). Instructional design rules for algorithmic subject matter. *Performance Improvement Quarterly, 3*(2), 2–15.

Suchman, J. (1964). Studies in inquiry training. In R. Ripple and V. Bookcastle (Eds.), *Piaget reconsidered.* Ithaca, NY: Cornell University.

Taba, H. (1967). *Teacher's handbook for elementary social studies.* Reading, MA: Addison-Wesley.

Tennyson, R. D., & Tennyson, C. L. (1975). Rule acquisition design strategy variables: Degree of instance divergence, sequence, and instance analysis. *Journal of Educational Psychology, 67*(6), 852–859.

Wilson, B. G. (1985). Techniques for teaching procedures. *Journal of Instructional Development, 8*(12), 2–5.

Strategies for
Problem-Solving Lessons

ten

Chapter Objective

At the conclusion of this chapter you should be able to do the following:

- Given a problem-solving objective, design strategy plans for that objective.

*R*eview of Problem-Solving Learning

The term *expert* is used to describe someone who can apply knowledge to solve problems in a particular field of endeavor. We define *problem solving* as a specialized skill within a domain of knowledge rather than a generalized skill that applies across a variety of content areas. **Problem solving** is the ability to combine previously learned rules (both relational and procedural), declarative knowledge, and cognitive strategies within a domain of content to solve previously unencountered problems. This activity yields new learning as learners are more able to respond to problems of a similar class in the future. This type of problem solving is often described as "domain-specific" or "semantically rich" problem solving because it emphasizes learning to utilize rules in a specific content area. The sort of problem solving that this chapter addresses encompasses a great deal of what is meant by the term *expertise*.

For some time educational psychologists have attempted to describe problem solving and identify aspects that might be transferrable to various domains of endeavor (Dewey, 1933; Polya, 1945; Newell & Simon, 1972). A number of curricula of instructional materials (e.g., the Productive Thinking Program, Covington, Crutchfield, Davies, & Olton, 1974 and the *Cognitive Research Trust*, or "CoRT," de Bono, 1973) have been developed to teach generic problem-solving skills. We will describe some of these in our discussion of cognitive strategies in Chapter 11. Cognitive strategies are the outcome in Gagné's category system, which is similar to generic problem-solving. However, it has become more and more clear that the single key ingredient to skill in problem solving in any domain is knowledge within that domain, particularly knowledge of relational and procedural rules (R. Gagné, 1985). So, attention is concentrated on how experts in particular fields are able to solve problems and on identifying appropriate instructional strategies for domain-specific problem solving, rather than trying to identify and teach generic problem-solving skills.

Problem solving differs from rule learning because problem solving requires the selection and combination of multiple rules in order to solve a problem, rather than a single rule. Problem solving as we describe it is often not what is termed *mathematical* problem solving. Mathematical problem solving can be application of single rules or procedures, rather than selection and application of multiple rules. For a learning goal to be termed *problem solving* according to our criteria, it must involve the almost simultaneous consideration of all the rules and procedures within a domain, the careful selection of the rules that are applicable, and the sequencing of the application of the rules so a problem has been solved.

This category of learning is congruent with the term *heuristic* problem solving; in other words, problem solving for which no clear procedural rule exists. Application of a procedural rule is sometimes termed *algorithmic* problem solving, but we have chosen to include the algorithmic problem solving in the rule learning category because its instruction is quite different from heuristic problem solving. One thing that may make the distinction between procedural rule learning and problem solving difficult is the following: A learning task may be taught first as a problem-solving objective, and then later, learners may form their own solution algorithm or they may be taught one so that they may employ a procedure to accomplish work rather than use the more taxing problem-solving process. How the learning is initially approached (with or without algorithm) helps us decide what type of learning it is and, therefore, what the instructional strategy should be.

Another form of problem solving is not addressed in this chapter. Solving a problem as a result of random activity or trial and error is possible. As ludicrous as it may seem on the surface, under certain circumstances this is a desirable activity. However, problem solving that results from uninformed trial and error does not result in the kind of learning that can be applied in the future. Thus, this kind of problem solving is not useful in learning about effective ways to solve problems either in a subject domain or in a general sense.

Examples of Problem Solving

Goals that require the application of multiple rules and that are generally taught as problem-solving outcomes include learning to do the following tasks:

- Construct geometry proofs (selection and application of appropriate laws and theorems in the correct sequence).
- Read music.
- Write computer programs.
- Design a house or, more simply, select and position the windows in a house.
- Plan and conduct an experiment.
- Make a medical diagnosis.
- Troubleshoot malfunctioning equipment when no algorithm is provided.
- Practice law.
- Respond to an emergency call as a police officer.

Problem-solving tasks can be complex or simple. One of the things that makes problem solving simpler is when fewer rules must be considered (e.g., designing a house versus designing the windows for a house). Another feature that relates to complexity in problem solving is the clarity of the problem. Some problems are much "fuzzier" than others. In order to understand what makes a problem unclear we need to define some common terms related to problem solving.

A *problem,* according to Duncker (1945), is present when one has a goal but does not know immediately how this goal can be reached. The goal cannot be reached without a "search process" (Gilhooly & Green, 1989). To solve problems learners must search through their long-term memory for relevant rules, knowledge, and strategies that might apply to this problem. In so doing, they begin to clarify the "problem space." The problem space (Anderson, 1985) includes the goal state (i.e., the desired end state of the situation: what conditions would be like if the problem were solved), the given state (the current situation, including its restrictions and obstacles), and the intermediate states that must be overcome to move from the given state to the goal state. The clearer the given state and the goal state are, the less "fuzzy" the problem is. A clear given (or initial) state has all the relevant information explicitly provided, requiring that less information be inferred or researched. A clear goal precisely states the criteria for determining if the problem has been solved. Although not universally true, it appears that problems in much of the mathematics and science that are taught (as opposed to advanced theoretical

studies) tend to be more clear than problems in the social sciences. Problems are often described as "ill-defined" or "well-defined." In addition, "ill-defined" problems may not possess a specific order in which rules should be applied to solve the problem.

Cognitive Requirements of Problem-Solving Learning

In order to solve problems in a domain, learners must possess and apply three kinds of knowledge: rules, declarative knowledge, and cognitive strategies (R. Gagné, 1980, 1985; de Jong & Ferguson-Hessler, 1986). The ability to apply rules seems to be the most critical component to problem solving; however, it is clear that without declarative knowledge and cognitive strategies, the learner may not be able to adequately identify or search the problem space. (For a more complete review of how domain knowledge and cognitive strategies interact, see Alexander and Judy [1988]). We will describe these three components of problem solving in more detail.

Ability To Recall and Apply Relevant Rules

In order to select from and apply multiple rules, learners must know those rules. They must be able to identify situations in which the rules can appropriately be applied; they must be able to apply the rules; and they must be able to confirm that the rules have been correctly applied. It is not wise to assume that learners can discover the rules while they are learning to problem solve. Too often we find educational situations in which this assumption is made. For example, many teachers have used simulations for learners to practice problem solving in a domain without giving learners prior experience with the rules that must be considered and sequentially applied to solve the problem presented in the simulation. In such a case, rules should have already been learned and practiced. It is possible to teach rules in the same lesson as problem solving. However, the problems must be carefully limited so that the number of rules that must be considered are few. For example, in one lesson a learner might first learn to apply the rules singly and then to select and apply the rules in concert. It is generally preferable that a learner can apply these rules automatically prior to trying to apply them in a problem-solving situation.

As you will recall from Chapter 9, rules are theorized to be stored in memory as productions. These productions have an if-then structure. For example, in the photography content in our Extended Example, there are rules relating to (1) how to adjust exposure with shutter speed and aperture, (2) how to select film types and speeds in particular conditions, (3) how to obtain particular effects through composition, and (4) how to adjust field of view and size of image through lenses. To solve photography problems, these rules must be considered almost simultaneously because they are so interrelated. Those rules that are pertinent to the particular problem conditions must be selected from among all the interrelated rules. Then these rules must be applied in the correct order. Once the photograph is produced, it must be evaluated to see if it solves the identified "problem."

Ability To Recall Declarative Knowledge

Declarative knowledge helps the learner understand the problem and limit the problem space (i.e., goal state, starting state, possible solution paths) of the problem. This declarative knowledge may organize the rule productions into meaningful relationships, both hierarchically (as some rules may be superordinate to other rules), and conceptually (as some rules may have similar conditions or similar actions). The more this knowledge is related by "deep structure" (i.e., with meaningful and conceptual links) rather than by similarities on "surface features" (e.g., similarities in actual wording, similarities in contexts in which learning occurred), the more the knowledge will support facile problem solving. Additional declarative knowledge in terms of the actual propositional statement of the rule or in terms of organized information regarding how the rule was discovered or has been applied may also be stored in long-term memory. Also stored in long-term memory may be ties between the rules and prior experiences and world knowledge that make the rules meaningful. Other related information in the form of facts or labels, as well as concepts stored in declarative forms rather than as productions may also support problem solving. Declarative knowl-edge is generally considered to be stored as schemata with conceptual nodes and relationship links.

In the photography example, information about film speeds, aperture sizes, shutter speeds, lens types, types and possible locations of lighting, as well as many experiences, both vicarious and personal, form an interrelated network of declarative knowledge for the photographer. The actual organization of this information may differ. (We have informally asked skilled photographers to represent how they organize this knowledge, and indeed it does seem to differ. Regardless of these differences, experts do have their knowledge highly structured.)

Ability To Recall and Apply Cognitive Strategies

Problem solving requires cognitive strategies in addition to the content knowledge represented as rules and declarative knowledge. In addition to specific cognitive strategies, problem solving also requires metacognitive awareness and monitoring, which we will address more fully in Chapter 11. Cognitive strategies can facilitate the learner's (1) understanding and representing the problem; (2) decomposing the problem into subgoals; (3) searching, selecting, and combining relevant knowledge; (4) sequencing application of knowledge; and (5) monitoring the relative success of solutions. Learners use a number of strategies in solving problems. Some of these strategies are generic (applicable across multiple content areas), and some are more specifically applicable to solving problems within a particular domain. Generic strategies are considered to be less potent and less efficient than strategies specific to a content domain (Anderson, 1985). Examples of generic problem-solving strategies are Dewey's (1933) five-stage reflective thinking pattern (recognize problem, formulate hypotheses, design the inquiry, test hypotheses, and draw conclusions) or Polya's (1945) four stages of problem solving: understand the problem, devise a plan, carry out the plan, and look back.

Four generic strategies that have been identified as search and decomposition strategies are means-ends, difference reduction, working-backwards, and analogy. A learner employing the means-ends strategy mentally jumps back and forth between the desired end and the current state, identifying intermediate states and the rules to convert each state to the next intermediate state. We prepare dinner using this strategy. Our goal is to have a hot meal. The difference between the initial state and the final state is hot, prepared food. How do we get hot, prepared food? Well, we must go to the store and buy it. How do we get to the store? We travel in a car. What do we have to do to use the car? Fill it with gas. How do we fill it with gas? Go to the gas station. And so on.

The difference reduction strategy attempts to select rules to enact upon the current state to get it to look more and more like the desired state. You may have seen this strategy used by a sculptor who carves away clay and adds material to make the image resemble the desired figure. The process is repeated many times. This may not be the most efficient problem-solving strategy for this task, but it is a very common and effective one.

A learner employing the working-backwards strategy starts with the desired end state and then selects and applies the rules that will back up to the intermediate state just before the desired state. Then the learner moves to the next-to-next-to-last step, and so on until the intermediate state is reached. You've probably employed this strategy in solving mazes.

When using an analogy strategy, the learner finds a similar but simpler situation or problem in a very different context for which a solution is apparent and then applies that same solution to the problem at hand. For example, students could use an analogy strategy to solve Duncker's (1945) problem:

Suppose you are a doctor faced with a patient who has a malignant tumor in his stomach. It is impossible to operate on the patient, but unless the tumor is destroyed the patient will die. There is a kind of ray that can be used to destroy the tumor. If the rays reach the tumor all at once at a sufficiently high intensity, the tumor will be destroyed. Unfortunately, at this intensity the healthy tissue that the rays pass through on the way to the tumor will also be destroyed. At lower intensities the rays are harmless to healthy tissue, but they will not affect the tumor either. What type of procedure might be used to destroy the tumor with the ray, and at the same time avoid destroying the healthy tissue? (pp. 307–308)

In Gick and Holyoak's (1980) study, they gave some students a hint in the form of an analogy: An army is attempting to take over a fortress that is surrounded by mined roads, which detonate only when large forces travel on them. The solution is dividing the forces and having them all converge upon the fortress from different directions. Ninety-two percent of the students who were given this hint were able to solve the tumor problem. Only ten percent of the students who were not given the hint were able to solve the problem.

Specific cognitive strategies developed for a particular domain tend to be more potent and efficient than generic strategies. One example of a specific strategy is Schoenfeld's (1979) problem-solving heuristics for solving problems in mathematics: (1) draw a diagram; (2) if there is an integer parameter, look for an inductive argument; (3) consider arguing by contradiction or contrapositive; (4) consider a similar problem with fewer variables; and (5) try to establish subgoals (cited in Mayer, 1985, p. 38).

Problem-Solving Task Analysis

What *is* the generic task analysis for problem solving? Now that you know a bit more regarding problem solving, we have elaborated our task analysis from Chapter 4 with some more precise terminology and additional steps. Although a single approach is not clearly identified in the research or theoretical literature, it seems that it is common in problem-solving conditions that the following stages often occur. They may not occur in the same sequence as described as follows:

1. Clarify the given state, including any obstacles or constraints.
2. Clarify the goal state, including criteria for knowing when the goal is reached.
3. Search for relevant prior knowledge and declarative, rule, or cognitive strategies that will aid in solution.
4. Decompose the problem into subproblems with subgoals.
5. Determine a sequence for attacking subproblems.
6. Consider possible solution paths to each subproblem using related prior knowledge.
7. Select a solution path and apply production knowledge (rules) in the appropriate order.
8. Evaluate to determine if the goal is achieved. If not, revise by returning to Step 1 above.

In a specific content area, this schema may be employed with specific content knowledge filling in the "slots." We do not suggest that instruction teach this strategy in a content-free context. The eight steps provided can be used in analyzing specific problem-solving tasks within content domains, helping the designer to find and structure the primary sub-tasks.

Mental Representation of Problem-Solving Knowledge

How does the knowledge used in problem solving become organized in long-term memory? It is clear that in some way the declarative knowledge and procedural knowledge must become interwoven. Perhaps these forms of knowledge are stored in problem schemata. There may be superordinate productions in the if-then form with the *if* representing the salient conditions for a particular class of problems (along with all the related declarative knowledge and rules related to this condition) and the *then* representing the cognitive strategies and rules to support the solution of the problem.

Johnson-Laird (1983) hypothesized a cognitive structure that seems to be appropriate for describing the mental representation of the three kinds of knowledge listed above. He conjectures that knowledge is stored in a "mental model" of the information related to a domain. This mental model is an interweaving of declarative knowledge propositions and rule-based productions. The mental model is subject to restructuring with experience, additional learning, and the type of problem presented.

The actual structure of problem-solving knowledge remains unclear at the moment. The processes of problem solving have been studied with much more detail. One of the ways that psychologists have studied problem-solving processes is to compare how experts in a field solve a problem to how novices solve it.

Differences Between Expert and Novice Problem Solvers

Psychologists have spent much of the past 30 years trying to describe the processes of expert and novice problem solvers. Psychologists have studied problems in the domains of chess (Chase & Simon, 1973; de Groot, 1965), physics (Chi, Glaser, & Rees, 1982; Larkin, 1989), mathematics (Schoen-

feld & Herrmann, 1982), political science (Voss, Greene, Post, & Penner, 1983), and medical diagnosis (Norman, 1985) to name but a few. These studies and others (de Jong & Ferguson-Hessler, 1986; Frederiksen, 1984; Larkin, 1980; Mayer, 1983; Simon, 1980; Simon & Chase, 1973) have marked the following differences between novice and expert problem solvers, indicating that experts have the following:

1. A "perception-like" recognition of problem types (i.e., pattern recognition)
2. More domain-specific knowledge
3. Better organized and integrated domain-specific knowledge
4. The ability to represent problems and their similarities to other problems by abstract, "deep structure" (semantically), rather than by surface features (e.g., similarities in unimportant physical or spatial properties)
5. Compiled knowledge, so application of rules is more automatic
6. Related rules chunked together in memory
7. The ability to recognize when a problem is solved and solved appropriately
8. A tendency to use a working-forward strategy rather than a working-backwards strategy
9. The ability to develop solution hypotheses quickly but delay acting upon them
10. More schema-driven than search-driven solution strategies

Although we have quite a refined description of the differences between novices and experts, we have few research-based principles regarding how to facilitate the transformation from novice to expert. In the remainder of the chapter we will describe some principles of instruction for problem solving. Some have been tested with research. Others seem logical given what we do know with regard to the cognitive processes of problem solving. Hopefully, future research will provide empirical validation of our recommendations.

*M*acrostrategies for Problem-Solving Instruction

Unfortunately, educators and trainers often employ one of two equally ineffective strategies for teaching problem solving. The first is to teach the relevant rules (sometimes only in their declarative form, without any instruction in their actual application) for problem solving and assume that learners can select and combine these rules for problem solving without any instruction, including practice, in problem solving in the domain. The second, more common strategy is to provide opportunities for problem solving without any instruction on the rules that must be applied in order to solve problems; this makes the assumption that the learners can induce the rules from the context. Each of the approaches might be effective with very bright learners who have a great deal of prior knowledge to draw upon, good cognitive strategies, and successful experience in filling in the gaps left by faulty instruction. However, both of these teaching approaches should be avoided. With such incomplete instruction, slower learners will not learn to problem solve, and the most able learners may have to struggle and worry more than is profitable.

This stance does not mean that we necessarily recommend didactic, expository instructional strategies for teaching problem solving. It simply means that we feel that the prerequisites for problem solving should be taught and that problem solving itself is new learning that should also be taught using appropriate instructional strategies. (Both the Extended Example and the sample lesson on computer programming within this chapter employ a combination of supplantive and generative instructional strategies.) A highly generative strategy may be selected, or a more supplantive one may be more appropriate, depending on many factors that the designer should consider.

A second concern, in addition to instructional strategy type, is the sequencing of the related rule learning with regard to problem-solving learning. It is possible to provide instruction on prerequisite rules first and then just teach how to integrate the knowledge, rules, and cognitive strategies to solve problems using the rules. The Extended Example at the end of this chapter will use this approach. Or, the instruction on rules and problem solving can be interwoven, providing instruction on a certain subset of rules, along with instruction on how these rules can be used to solve a certain subset of problems within the content domain. The example on computer programming that follows later in this chapter follows this approach.

There are advantages and disadvantages to each approach, and the superiority of one approach over the other has not been established by research.

There are a number of exciting macrostrategies for teaching problem solving. Most of them are amenable to a "guided discovery" approach. That is, the learners must discover how the rules and knowledge can be combined to solve problems, but the instruction hints and occasionally directly teaches the appropriate rules, knowledge, or strategies to use along the way. The hints and direct teaching can gradually be dropped out during practice, so that learners are required to do more and more of the information processing for themselves. This guided discovery approach with diminishing amounts of guidance should be motivational and effective in promoting transfer of problem-solving skills. Thus, with the amount of prior knowledge of content that learners usually possess before they begin a problem-solving lesson when guided discovery of prerequisite knowledge has been employed, designers can usually use a more generative strategy for problem-solving instruction itself.

Elaboration Model

One of the best macrostrategies for teaching problem solving involves the presentation of carefully sequenced problem sets. The first set of problems should be the most fundamental of those to be learned. Students may learn these rules far in advance of the problem-solving instruction or just prior to the problem-solving instruction. If the instruction of the rules occurs just prior to instruction on combining the rules in problem solving, the designer should definitely ensure that sufficient examples and practice have been incorporated so that the application of each independent rule is fairly automatic. After learners have received instruction on selecting and combining the rules to solve a class of problems, then instruction may move on to learning additional rules and combining these rules with the old ones to solve a larger class of problems. You may recognize this approach as an adaptation of the Elaboration Model (Reigeluth & Stein, 1983). We will use this approach later in this chapter in our description of a computer programming course.

Socratic Dialogue

Another macrostrategy, which may or may not involve the Elaboration Model, is **Socratic dialogue.** Our prototype example of this approach is the instructional strategy that Professor Kingsfield used in the movie/TV series *The Paper Chase.* You may remember that in trying to teach his students to apply contract law, Professor Kingsfield described a problem and then required students to use laws in order to unsnare the legal problem. His pointed questioning guided the learners in both the selection of the appropriate laws (rules) and how they applied them to the particular problem.

Socratic dialogue is a powerful technique for teaching problem solving. It is very demanding for the teacher, requiring exceptional skills in attention to learners, the ability to infer the learners' line of reasoning, and a clear conception of the ultimate goal of the instruction. It is easy for a less-skilled teacher to be distracted by unimportant details or to be unable to construct a question (rather than a lecture) to guide the learners' reasoning. Another negative aspect of Socratic dialogue is that the questioning can involve only one student at a time. Other learners may vicariously experience the interactions, but the line of questioning may not really address their own misconceptions or faulty lines of reasoning. Computer-based programs (often described as intelligent tutoring systems) that engage learners in Socratic dialogue have been developed in a number of domains. Although experimental and limited at the moment (primarily due to computers' inability to understand natural language), this technology ultimately has the potential for giving all learners in a class the opportunity to experience this instructional interaction intimately. Collins and Stevens (1983) suggest several types of interactions that the teacher may originate (or the teacher may guide the learners to generate) in Socratic dialogue: positive or negative examples of rules, counterexamples of rules, hypothetical cases, hypotheses, tests of a hypothesis, predictions and alternate predictions, entrapping of students, tracing consequences to contradiction, and questioning authority (p. 260).

Simulations

A simulation can also be used effectively as a macrostrategy for problem-solving instruction. A **simulation** is an activity that attempts to mimic the most essential features of a reality but allows learners to make decisions within this reality without actually suffering the consequences of their decisions. Simulations generally portray a problem situation and then require the learner to interact with the problem. With every action of the learner, there is a response within the simulation. Simulations are often computer-based so that the quality of the feedback to the learners' response can be lifelike and immediate. An example of a computer-based simulation to teach problem-solving skills was the "Fruit Fly Simulation" that was originally delivered on the PLATO system (Hyatt, Eades, Tenczar, & Denault, 1968). It was devised to give learners the opportunity to apply multiple rules of genetics for predicting and controlling inheritance of factors for the fruit fly. The learners could see the effects of their manipulations of parents on the offspring for several generations within a few minutes rather than waiting to see the actual effects of a live genetics experiment.

Simulations can occur with written material, such as an in-basket simulation in which a learner must deal with all the mail that has built up in an in-basket within an environment. Simulations can also be group-based, as with simulations in which the learners must role-play within a prescribed environment. Tennyson (1988) listed the advantages of simulations noting that simulations can do the following:

1. Portray a meaningful context.
2. Be quite complex.
3. Expose learners to alternative solutions.
4. Require problem solving in situations in which there is no single correct answer.
5. Allow learners to see the consequences of their solutions.
6. Require learners to predict the effects of their actions.

Another advantage of simulations is that they can be constructed so that in initial phases the problem and goal state are simplified. This way, it is within the capabilities of the learners early in the instruction to solve the problem. Then, the problem and related solution can be made more and more complex (like real life) to require the learner to employ more selection and processing strategies. Simulations, particularly those that are computer-based, may be run a number of times by learners so that they have multiple practice opportunities.

Unfortunately, good simulations can be quite difficult and time consuming to create. In designing a simulation, the designer must carefully plan the description of the environment, the actors within the environment, and the rules that govern (1) when and how the actors may act, (2) how these actions will affect the environment, and (3) how the environment will react to the actors' actions. All the elements in the design must mirror reality. The cause-and-effect rules governing the actors and the environment should be those rules that the learners are learning to manipulate in problem solving. Rowe (1984) has described guidelines that designers must consider in designing simulations. These guidelines are categorized into guidelines which deal with (1) variables (those factors that are influenced by the rules) and their parameters, (2) questions to the user, (3) display of simulation results, (4) simulation behavior in general, and (5) overall organization of the simulation. These rules give some impression of the complexity of designing good simulations. Other sources that provide guidance for developing simulations are Greenblat and Duke (1981), Adkinson (1977), Maidment and Bronstein (1973), Shirts (1975), and Walcott and Walcott (1976).

Once a simulation is developed, it is imperative that designers carefully outline the suggested use of the simulation within instruction. For example, it is extremely critical that prior to encountering simulations learners acquire the rules that must be combined in the simulation. Even with multiple passes through a simulation, learners cannot be expected to induce the rules that have been interacting within a simulation. As noted earlier, although the most able or gifted learners may be able to perform the mental leaps necessary to induce unknown rules from working with multiple problems, such an approach is inefficient for even the best students and will not work for the vast majority of students in any event. Also, the debriefing following the simulation is critical. It is quite possible for learners to have been successful within a simulation and still not have acquired the ability to apply the rules in concert to other cases. Their behavior within the simulation may have been

trial-and-error or based on faulty, albeit successful, reasoning. During the debriefing, learners should be required to explain their understanding of the given state, the goal state, their selection of rules to solve the problem, and how their actions moved the situation from the given state to the goal state. Joyce and Weil (1986) and Kozma, Belle, and Williams (1978) present suggestions for the actions of a teacher during a simulation. As designers develop their simulations and related teacher/trainer guides, the activities of teachers or other media that introduce and conclude the instruction should be carefully considered and explained because introduction and conclusion are very critical to the effectiveness of the simulation.

Case Studies and Case Problems

Case studies can be similar to simulations in that they present a realistic situation and require the learners to respond as if they were the person who must solve a problem. Case studies also require learners to select and manipulate multiple rules and principles in order to solve problems. Hudspeth and Knirk (1989) describe case materials as follows:

[Case materials are] problem oriented descriptions of a believable event which provide sufficient detail to allow the reader to analyze the problem/solution process. A complete case describes an entire situation and includes background information, the actions and reactions of persons involved, the solution, and the possible consequences of the actions taken. Case materials should have enough background information and detail so that they are readable and believable. (p. 31)

An example of a case study might be developed to teach the problem-solving skills in an instructional design class, such as application of the rules involved in selecting instructional media. A single case study or multiple case studies might be written that provide a full description of the instructional environment (including time and resources available for the development project), the potential learners, and the instructional task. Given this information, learners in the class could examine the givens, identify the goal state, select the principles that would be appropriate for determining optimal media, apply the principles to determine optimal media, and evaluate the quality of their solutions.

Case studies are particularly useful in learning to problem solve in situations in which there is more than one correct solution to the problem. As with simulations, case studies can be written in sets with increasing levels of detail, complexity, and irrelevant information so that learners can manipulate more and more rules and employ more cognitive strategies as they proceed through instruction. Case studies may be completed individually or in cooperative learning groups. Another advantage of case studies is that they aid transfer to real-life situations. They are also a highly motivating strategy.

Case studies are more difficult to develop than might be immediately apparent. If the designer begins with a problem and attempts to invent a situation for its context, the designer will find that ''fleshing out'' the situation so that it appears realistic and has sufficient irrelevant detail can be tedious. The result can appear very contrived. If, in contrast, the designer models the case study on a real-life problem, the designer will find that real problem situations can be too complex to use, at least in initial problem-solving instruction. We find it to be most effective to begin with a known case and simplify it by eliminating some of the problems or omitting some of the extraneous detail. We occasionally combine characteristics of two known situations to make one clear problem case. Although not much is written on developing good case materials, you will find some excellent suggestions in Hudspeth and Knirk (1989) and a set of publications by Harvard Business School Case Services (no date).

Expert Systems

Expert systems are computer-based programs that when given data are able to solve problems within a limited domain of expertise. Expert systems were originally developed to substitute for expertise within esoteric domains of expertise in which the number of humans who possess the expertise are limited. For example, two expert systems were developed—one related to the repair of steam-driven train engines and one related to the cleaning of chemical tanks—when it became clear that the

experts in these two areas were nearing retirement and no one had been specifically trained to solve problems in these two areas. So, as they are developed, expert systems are designed to preclude the need for problem-solving instruction within a domain. At present the development of expert systems is extremely time-consuming, even with the assistance of shells (Grabinger, Wilson, & Jonassen, 1990). Of course, the broader the domain of problem solving and the more complex the potential problems, the more difficult the development will be.

Expert systems are composed of two components, a knowledge database and an inference engine. The knowledge base is composed of domain-specific declarative knowledge and rules. The inference engine is composed of generic and domain-specific strategies that determine how the knowledge base should be combined. When an individual uses an expert system to solve a problem, the expert system asks the individual for information about the given and the goal state. If this information is adequate, the system can provide the user with a solution. If the information is inadequate, the rules are incomplete, or the domain is ''fuzzy,'' the system can provide the user with information as to how probable its solutions are.

If they are available or feasible to develop, expert systems can be used in problem-solving instruction. Simply using an expert system to help solve problems probably will not teach the learner to solve problems independently. Or, if a learner could induce the rules and cognitive strategies, it would be a very inefficient instructional strategy. Although we cannot find this hypothesis confirmed through empirical research, it seems analogous to the situation of learners using calculators to complete math problems. We would not expect that the learners would learn math facts by using a calculator. However, there are at least three ways in which expert systems could be used to learn problem solving in a domain: sequenced problem sets, intelligent tutoring systems, and building an expert system.

Use of sequenced problem sets is one way in which expert systems can be used to assist instruction in problem solving. Some expert systems when queried will display the rules that were used to solve a problem and the sequence in which the rules were employed. Some systems also show the declarative knowledge within the system and the information provided by the user that was used to solve the problem. Problem-solving instruction that uses an existing expert system should ensure that learners already can apply the rules individually. Then it should provide learners with carefully selected and sequenced problem sets to give to the expert system. Learners should be taught how to access, read, and interpret the system's explanation of its reasoning. Learners should have the system solve problems in the first problem set (the simplest class of problems in the domain). They should study and explain the reasoning of the system. Learners should solve similar problems on their own and then give the problems to the system for feedback. Finally, they should solve problems in the set independently and evaluate the adequacy of their solutions. Then, they can move on to the next problem set and follow the same pattern. For more information on expert systems, we suggest you read McFarland and Parker (1990) and Lippert (1988).

Intelligent tutoring systems (ITS) are computer-based instructional systems that include not only a knowledge base and an inference engine but also a teacher model and a student model. The teacher model (sometimes called the *pedagogical component, tutor,* or *coach*) contains knowledge and rules regarding instruction. The student model contains a model of the rules and knowledge that the learner has acquired. As the learner learns more, the student model is updated to reflect the learners' new knowledge. ITS programs are designed to be self-contained and sufficient in teaching learners a particular content. ITS programs are very complex, expensive, and time-consuming to develop and, at present, are mostly used for research rather than implemented as instruction in schools and training facilities. Some ITS programs have been developed to teach problem solving, such as programs designed to teach programming, physics, or medical diagnosis. Others teach declarative knowledge or concepts. Considering the cost and complexity of ITS development, developers will probably reserve them for research and for the most critical and difficult to learn skills; these would be skills for which learners may have very diverse prior knowledge and for which it is difficult to predict how learners' prior knowledge will interact with the new content. For more informa-

tion on ITS systems, we suggest you read Polson and Richardson (1988).

A third strategy for using expert systems to teach problem solving is to have the learners develop an expert system that can solve problems in the specific content domain that they are learning. Expert system shells are available that allow nonprogrammers to develop a simple expert system. Using these shells varies in difficulty, and their power also varies (Grabinger, Wilson, & Jonassen, 1990). However, educators have reported their successful use with both high school and college-age students (Starfield, Butala, England, & Smith, 1983; Trollip & Lippert, 1988; Wideman & Owston, 1988). Such an endeavor would require intense teacher training and considerable time and resources. Students would need to be skilled in application of individual rules before developing the system. For more information on developing an expert system, we suggest you read Grabinger, Wilson, and Jonassen (1990).

Other Macrostrategies

A number of other suitable macrostrategies may be most appropriate for problem solving in particular domains of content. For example, Suchman's Inquiry Training and the Biological Sciences Curriculum Inquiry Model (Joyce & Weil, 1986; Schwab, 1965) are most appropriate to problem solving in the sciences. They outline methods for teaching science through experimentation. The Jurisprudential Inquiry approach (Joyce & Weil, 1986; Oliver & Shaver, 1966) and the Social Science Inquiry approach (Joyce & Weil, 1986; Massialas & Cox, 1966) were developed especially for problem solving in the social sciences. The Jurisprudential model would be appropriate for problem solving with human-made rules, such as laws, which may have values and attitudes attached to them.

*I*nstructional Events for a Problem-Solving Lesson

Often when novice instructional designers begin to design the instructional strategies for a problem-solving objective, they imagine that there is really nothing to "teach," as all the rules have been learned prior to the problem-solving lesson. They suggest that the only thing remaining is for learners to practice combining the rules. Indeed, practice is a critical part of a problem-solving lesson; however, there are additional instructional events that can support the acquisition of problem-solving skill.

Remember that the prerequisites (rules and their associated concepts, declarative knowledge, and cognitive strategies) for problem solving can be taught in lessons prior to problem-solving lessons. Or, instruction on rules, concepts, declarative knowledge, and strategies can be taught in sets interspersed with instruction on how to combine this knowledge for problem-solving.

Introducing Problem-Solving Lessons

Deploy Attention

Presenting an interesting and challenging problem that the learners will learn to solve can gain attention and begin to identify the purpose of the instruction. If novel stimuli such as graphics or video are used to present the problem, learners are likely to be more interested.

Establish Instructional Purpose

The instructor may describe the class of problems that the students will learn to solve. If a challenging problem has been presented to promote motivation and attention, the instructor may explain how this problem is representative of the class of problems to be learned. If the strategy being employed is inductive or if the instructor feels that overtly stating this information at this point may reduce the learners' interest in the problem, this event may be omitted and the learners can be asked to demonstrate their induction of the characteristics of this class of problems during the conclusion.

Promote Interest and Motivation

Suggesting how problem solving in this domain may assist learners in everyday problems can promote interest. Problem solving, if completed successfully, can be motivating in itself. The instruction should be constructed to provide successful practice as quickly as possible. If a relatively short simulation is to be used within the instruction, learners might view a portion of the simulation.

Preview Lesson

The instruction should inform the learners that they will be going through a succession of problems with increasing complexity. The instruction may preview the primary strategies that will be employed and the learners' responsibilities within the strategies.

Body

The events described within this section will be cycled through several times in a problem-solving lesson.

Reviewing Relevant Prior Knowledge

If declarative knowledge, concepts, rules, or strategies appropriate to the task have been previously learned and applied, then the knowledge can be overtly reviewed by doing the following:

- Review declarative knowledge related to the area; this should cause learners to bring to working memory the information needed to understand the nature of the problem.
- Review general problem-solving strategies, directly suggesting an appropriate structure for attacking the problem and suggesting any modifications that are particularly appropriate to this domain.
- Review the type and source of rules (and their associated concepts) related to this problem, ensuring that learners have access to rules and examples of their application.

Or, if the instruction on this knowledge was recent and learners evidenced a high level of skill with it, the recall of this knowledge could be interspersed in places that are immediately appropriate. This knowledge could be reviewed less directly, with the instructor modeling problem solving or using guiding questions as learners practice solving problems.

If learners have acquired the prerequisite knowledge over a period of time or if it is likely that they have knowledge structured in a manner that will not facilitate problem solving, the learners could be encouraged to restructure their knowledge so that it is appropriate to solve the new class of problems. One way to do this will be illustrated in the Extended Example by using a spatial strategy, a networking technique, to show the relationships of concepts or rules, with the instruction imposing a new structure on previously learned concepts or rules. The learners would then fill in the network with additional concepts, knowledge, and rules. Diagrams or visuals could be added to this spatial representation to make it more concrete. This reorganization of knowledge should be in a form that emphasizes the underlying generalities of the concepts and rules, rather than their surface similarities (such as the use of similar terms in two rules). This rearrangement may show hierarchical relationships among concepts and/or rules. Or, it may be organized functionally, as illustrated in the Extended Example.

If learners have solved problems that have similarities to the current class of problems, then this similarity should be explicitly mentioned and the differences between these classes of problems should be clearly identified.

Strategies that intersperse acquisition of rules and concepts with problem solving should review the knowledge relevant to them at the point where the instruction occurs.

Processing Information

The instruction, whether computer-based or human, must determine whether a more supplantive or a more generative approach should be used to support the events of processing information, focusing attention, and employing learning strategies. If the learners have well-organized and extensive content knowledge, good cognitive strategies, high aptitude, high motivation, and a sufficient amount of time, then a more generative strategy would be appropriate. If learners' prior knowledge is limited and not organized well, cognitive strategies are limited, aptitude is not high, motivation is low, time is short, and a high level of skill is required by all learners, then a more supplantive strategy would be appropriate.

The most generative strategy that we recommend is presenting sets of increasingly complex problems for the learners to solve, with the guiding questions of the instruction used to evoke the processing, attention focusing, and strategies described in these events. A slightly more supplantive approach would be to present a problem and have the instructor (whether computer or human)

model the solution to the problem by thinking aloud. The model should utilize the processing, attention focusing, and strategy techniques that seem appropriate. Using this level of support, the students would next be provided with a problem in which they would do some of the processing and the instructor would also provide some. Finally, the learners would solve this type of problem with only the support of guiding questions. This sequence would be repeated with increasingly complex problems.

The most supplantive strategy that we recommend is for the instructor to present an example problem, talking through the solution with a full explanation of each step of the solution to the problem. Practice might be broken into smaller chunks, such as merely clarifying and verbalizing the given state of the problem. After this deliberate and careful presentation and explanation of a solution (and practice with individual steps along the way), the learners would be provided practice with complete problems and guided through a solution with the instructor's explicit instructions or guiding questions.

Regardless of which approach is taken, the following main aspects of presentation of information and processing must occur.

1. *Presentation of the problem.* Problem presentation should usually employ a simplified version first. The problem may be simplified in a number of ways: limiting the number of rules that must be accessed, providing external representations of these rules as cues, providing the solutions to parts of the problem, limiting the extraneous information presented in the problem, or clarifying the given state or goal state. The simplified problem should be prototypical of problems of its class, with clear delineation of attributes that make the situation typical and a minimum of distracting information. Problems may be presented in case studies, simulations, or in written or graphic formats.

2. *Problem space.* Learners must learn to recognize the problem space (although we would not use the term *problem space* because it would confuse more than clarify in instructional use). The instructor should encourage the learners (perhaps by modeling) to do the following:

- Review the task instructions for relevant information by verbalizing and elaborating on the characteristics of the goal state. This is done by inspecting the solved problem and systematically scanning the task instructions for situational cues and other relevant information regarding the given state.
- Construct a network of relationships of the variables in the given state with those in the goal state, either mentally or with a diagram.
- Analyze the relationship of the given and the goal states for a pattern that is recognizable as identifying a given set of problems.
- Identify what is not known, what learners can make inferences about, and what topics about which learners must seek more information.
- Decompose the problem into intermediate states (subgoals) between the given state and the goal state. This usually involves recognizing where particular rules can operate on the givens to transform them to the point where another rule can be employed.

3. *Appropriate rules.* Learners must also receive direct instruction or guidance on how to select appropriate rules to move from each intermediate state to the next state.

Focusing Attention

The instruction can use guiding questions or direct statements to focus learners' attention on key aspects of the problem state or the given state, relevant rules, or problem-solving strategies.

Learners may also need assistance in focusing their attention during the pattern-recognition task of identifying the critical features of the given state and the goal state.

Employing Learning Strategies

Both general and specific strategies may be suggested. If learners are being successful and their strategies are not faulty or inefficient, they should be encouraged to continue to use them. If their strategies are ineffective (or may prove to be with more complex problems) or inefficient, then the instructor may promote the acquisition of new strategies. Learning strategies may be taught through direct instruction, modeling, or guiding questions. The initial strategies taught may not be the strategies that experts would use, as their

knowledge is consolidated and organized differently from novices. However, the strategies that are taught should be effective given the state of their representations of knowledge and rules. The instruction may supply learning strategy assistance by providing any of the following:

- Alternate ways of representing the problem—graphic, analogy, etc.
- Ways of limiting the number of alternative approaches
- Hints at the general form of the solution or sub-solutions
- Search strategies for retrieving relevant information
- Monitoring techniques for appraising the appropriateness of the solution
- Mental imagery tactics for recognizing problem types or solution types
- Methods for providing external storage to deal with memory limitations, such as creating job aids or graphics
- Generic strategies such as hypothesis and test, working forward, working backward, and means-ends
- Specific strategies for representing problems or retrieving solutions for the particular domain

Practice

Chase and Chi (1980) suggest that thousands of hours of practice may be needed to transform a novice into an expert problem solver. After learners have experienced the solution of example problems, then they should have the opportunity to solve problems of similar difficulty. Instructional guidance, such as hints, guiding questions, presentation of a database of rules, and suggestions for strategies, should be gradually phased out. Sufficient practice should be provided so that (1) knowledge can be reorganized and elaborated in a manner that supports problem solving, (2) pattern-recognition skills become automatic even with complex problems, (3) identification of subgoals and related rules becomes automatic, and (4) selection and application of strategies is automatic.

Initial practice may involve performance of only one stage of problem solving, such as (1) identifying the goal state, (2) identifying important information in the problem, (3) identifying relationships among variables, (4) constructing a representation of variables in given and goal states, (5) identifying pertinent rules that should be applied, and (6) confirming the appropriateness of a solution. Each phase should be followed by feedback, rather than having the learner apply the entire process. Later, following initial practice and feedback, learners should practice solving the entire problem before receiving feedback.

Practice should start with problems that have easily recognizable, distinctive features in given and goal states, with little extraneous detail. Gradually more ill-structured problems should be introduced.

Feedback

Initial feedback may be in the form of hints or guiding questions if the learner's solution has gone awry. Feedback may also be specific in terms of information used or misused.

Feedback should include information regarding not only the appropriateness of the learners' solutions but also the efficiency of the solution process. As learners make the transition from novice to expert, they will include more automaticity in their problem solving. Therefore, as learners become more and more expert their approaches to problems, their solutions should be more and more streamlined. Feedback on the efficiency or speed of problem solving is necessary to the extent that genuine expertise is often expected as part of the learning goal.

Feedback information, especially early in the instructional process, may also include whether the learner has correctly identified the problem, correctly defined the goal state, appropriately decomposed the problem, considered the relevant alternatives, selected a viable approach, and reached the goal state.

One way to provide feedback regarding effectiveness and efficiency is to present a model of the solution process. Or, if the solution process produces artifacts of the stages of the solution (such as intermediate written solutions), the learners may be given a written or visual model answer to the solution. This model may include a description of how the solution led from the given state to the goal state and how the solution represents the goal state.

Conclusion

Summary and Review

The summary and review, whether provided by the learners or the instruction, should include the following:

- A review of the characteristics of problems that make them members of the class of problems that can be solved in a similar manner
- A summary of effective strategies for this domain of problems
- Suggestions of methods for organizing the problem schema for storage and later retrieval

Transfer

Transfer of problem-solving skill, particularly transfer of strategies, does not occur spontaneously. For transfer to occur, learners need explicit hints that point to the utility of this learning to similar and dissimilar problems from this lesson. They also need reminders in subsequent instruction, of which knowledge, rules, or strategies may be useful.

The guided discovery approach that we have recommended (with three levels of processing support) will tend to encourage transfer of specific and, to some degree, general problem-solving skills. In addition, learners should be encouraged to identify similar kinds of problems in real-life situations or within more complex problems.

Learners can also be encouraged to develop their own problem descriptions that fall into this same class of problems and construct their own solutions. Or, learners may be encouraged to give the problems to fellow students.

During subsequent instruction, transfer can be explicitly supported by hinting that strategies used in this lesson can be applied to the new one. Learners can be reminded of knowledge representations that they constructed in this lesson, and then those representations can be elaborated upon during new instruction.

Remotivation and Conclusion

Learners may be sufficiently remotivated and the lesson successfully concluded by reminding learners of the amount and utility of the skills that they have acquired in the lesson.

Assessment

The assessment of problem-solving skills should require learners to solve problems of the class that the instruction has targeted. The problems should be from contexts similar to those that were used as examples and practice in the lesson. Task instructions should also be similar to those provided in instruction. However, the problems themselves should be novel and previously unencountered. Simulations and case problems may be used during assessment.

A key difficulty in evaluating problem-solving skills is that often the time required to solve a single problem may be extensive. It is, consequently, difficult to provide a sufficient number of items during an assessment period to feel confident in the reliability of the measure. In such cases designers of assessment instruments may wish to include some partial problems, such as problems in which the learners must evaluate the appropriateness of a provided solution, in addition to the one or two complete problems that the learners must complete.

Example Problem-Solving Lesson—BASIC Programming Course

Audience: The class consists of undergraduate and graduate students, most of whom are education majors. Learners are heterogeneous regarding experience with computers and programming. Some have prior knowledge of programming; however, many report that they have forgotten what they learned in previous programming courses. Few have used any programming skills in the previous year. Usually, about two-thirds of the class has used a computer for applications, such as word processing. A few students are fearful of using the computer. Every semester there are some students who describe themselves as "not very analytical" and are uncomfortable with analytical approaches to problems. Two-thirds of the class are educational technology students who are seeking an advanced degree.

Setting: The class meets weekly for 2 1/2 hours for 15 weeks in a classroom with 12 Apple II e's. (Apple II's are used because they are available, they have BASIC in ROM, and their DOS is relatively simple to learn.) Usually the class has 15–24 students, which requires some or all learners to share a computer. The classroom has a display system for demonstrations that allows the instructor to show the output of his computer to the entire class.

Learning Task: The goals of the course are that learners can do the following: (1) interpret and "debug" BASIC code; (2) given an instructional problem (up through difficulty levels involving the use of random access files), code a program that will solve the problem; (3) implement fundamental principles of instructional design in the development of an instructional program; (4) use programming and CAI development terminology appropriately; and (5) appreciate the tediousness and time-consuming nature of programming and given a desired characteristic of an instructional program, estimate the feasibility, difficulty, and amount of time that it would take to code that part of the program.

The objective for the problem-solving lesson that will be described in the following example lesson is as follows: Given a problem that can be solved by the use of the BASIC commands INPUT, PRINT, IF . . . THEN, HOME, GO TO, FOR . . . NEXT, and END, the learners can write, enter, and debug a program to solve the problem.

Description of Problem-Solving Lesson

Before we describe the lesson, we will briefly describe the entire course because each lesson is a problem-solving lesson that leads to the skills represented by the course goals. The macrostrategy for the lesson is the Elaboration Model. The course begins with a lesson in which the students learn to apply the most basic programming commands and fundamental syntax rules. Each subsequent lesson merely elaborates a single instructional program—a program designed to teach the concepts "transparent," "translucent," and "opaque." Each lesson in the course adds some additional instructionally sound elaboration to the CAI lesson and teaches the commands and syntax needed to program the new part of the concept lesson. For the most part, each BASIC lesson follows the same structure as the lesson described here, except that the lessons become more and more generative, with the learners supplying more and more of the processing as they build up knowledge, rules, and strategies. Each chapter of the textbook (Ragan & Smith, 1989) that accompanies each lesson is divided into four major sections: (1) design of the CAI lesson (instructional design with its consequent programming structure); (2) programming of the CAI lesson (a line-by-line description of the function of the code), (3) summary, and (4) exercises.

The first lesson in the semester provides needed background in procedures for operating the computer and caring for disks. It also introduces the concept of ''computer program'' and gives two examples (DOS and BASIC). The first lesson ends with an overview of the entire semester and a viewing of sample final projects from the previous semesters.

The following paragraphs will describe the second class in the semester.

Introduction

Deploy Attention

Establish Purpose

Promote Interest and Motivation

Preview Lesson

Review Relevant Prior Knowledge

The instructor does the following:

- Tells students that today they will learn the seven most fundamental BASIC commands and how to put them together in programs to solve problems
- Tells students that once these commands are learned, they will know over 50 percent of the commands used in most programs
- Explains that the lesson will involve analyzing a program to see what it does, entering it into the computer, learning what each individual command does, and doing some exercises that require them to write some programs of their own
- Compares the instructional strategy that he will use to meaningful approaches to learning to read and write. (Children are taught a few words by

sight so they can read sentences very quickly.) This technique is similar in that the learners will learn a few commands with which they can make useful programs after today's lesson.

Body

Review Relevant Prior Knowledge

The instructor asks learners to explain what a computer program is (reviewing relevant concepts). The instructor also reminds them of experiences with programmable toys they may have operated and discusses how specific a program must be to get desired results (reviewing analogous strategies).

Process Information (relational rules—commands)

Practice

Employ Learning Strategies

Focus Attention

Materials consist of an orienting, beginning computer program entitled ''Sampler,'' which is supplied on computer disk to students along with a printed listing and explanation of the program. The program itself is trivial, yet it provides a beginning point for what a program is, beginning commands, and putting commands together.

The learners run the previously described program on a provided disk several times, using the strategy suggested by the instructor. The first time they view the program, they notice what the program does in general. During the second run of the program, the students are to note the different things (operations) that the program does. The third time they view the program, they note the sequence of events within the program. Learners run the program additional times, answer the displayed questions in different ways, and attend to how the program responds to different answers.

Feedback

The instructor runs the program and asks the students to explain generally what the program does, the major operations of the program, the sequence of the operations, and how the program execution varies with different inputs.

The instructor also points out operations that learners miss, such as the clearing of the screen, and categorizes the functions (display, keyboard input, conditional, looping, and program flow).

Review Relevant Prior Knowledge (concepts RAM and ROM)

Process Information (relational rules—syntax)

Focus Attention

The instructor does the following:

- Reminds the students of how explicit they had to be in programming programmable toys in terms of sequence, correctly spelling commands, and including all desired operations
- Explains that they must employ the same care in giving commands for the Apple computer to execute
- Reviews computer memory—RAM and ROM
- Displays the program code and explains that this is the code that is in RAM when the program is run
- Asks learners to note program line numbers and asks why these are included in program
- Explains "rules of thumb" regarding numbering program lines and why these rules are appropriate
- Asks learners to note the spacing of words and the use of uppercase letters in the program code
- Explains rule about spaces when typing in code

Process Information (relational rules— commands and syntax, concept, string variable)

Review Relevant Prior Knowledge (variable)

Practice

Focus Attention

The instructor does the following:

- Asks the learners to note how each line of code is constructed and runs each line of code to show the students what each line does
- Reviews what each command does and how each command works within the program
- Gives hypothetical questions requiring the use of only one command and asks learners to provide the code

- Asks students to explain what a variable is, asks them to find a variable in the program, and asks the function of the variable
- Introduces the concept "string variable," explains its function, gives examples and nonexamples of the use of variables, and asks the learners to give examples and nonexamples of the use of variables
- Explains the syntax of string variable names, gives examples and nonexamples, and asks students to give examples and nonexamples

Process Information (procedural rules)

Review Relevant Prior Knowledge (concept, DOS commands)

Practice

Focus Attention

The instructor demonstrates the following:

- The function of the NEW command and explains its criticality, warning students about what can happen when it is not used
- How to type in lines of code, how to correct typing errors, and how to insert lines of codes
- How to save the program to disk, reminding students that this is a DOS function and why it is so classified

The students type in the sample program (two per computer for cooperative learning and moral support).

The instructor answers questions and reminds students of syntax rules.

Process Information (problem solving)

Practice

Focus Attention

Employ Learning Strategies

The students run the program and attempt to debug it.

The instructor helps with debugging, asking guiding questions that stimulate the students to recall command use, syntax rules, and procedural rules for operating the computer. The instructor also suggests debugging strategies.

Practice

The students complete exercises that require them to employ the commands, procedural rules, and syntax rules to new problems. The students run and debug their programs.

Feedback

Focus Attention

Employ Strategies

The instructor does the following:

- Asks guiding questions that help learners recall rules
- Suggests strategies for planning the solutions to the problems
- Praises students who solve problems and encourages those who have difficulty
- Answers questions

The computer provides feedback as to whether problems are solved correctly.

Conclusion

Summary and Review

Remotivation and Conclusion

The instructor reviews the following:

- Commands and their functions
- Rules of syntax and why they are important
- The concept "string variable"
- The means for beginning a new program, saving a program, and running a program from disk

The instructor also reminds the students of how much they have learned in just one day and previews the next week when additional functions will be learned.

The students read the text, which restates the rules learned during class.

Transfer

For homework, the students write problems that require the functions learned in this lesson, and they write a paper solution. Next week they will try their solutions in the computer and try to stump other students with their problems.

Assessment

The instructor provides ungraded review of excercises provided in the chapter as an ongoing assessment. A mid-term examination and final project are used in post-assessment.

*E*xercise

Using the expanded instructional events as a framework, describe the design of a lesson to provide instruction for the following situation. Make sure you describe any preceding instruction.[1]

Setting. This is a high school biology class (college prep).

Audience. The class enrollment is 28 students, ages 16 to 18.

Task. Given the phenotype and genotype of a parent generation, the learner can determine the phenotype and genotype of the offspring and explain the answer using rule statements.

Sample Problem. Suppose a woman who has normal vision but is a carrier of color blindness marries a color-blind man. What is the probability of having a color-blind son or daughter? Show the possible phenotypes and genotypes for all possible offspring. Explain how you determined your answer.

This should be approximately a 1-hour lesson. Using the events of instruction, outline the sequence and content of the lesson.

Related Rules

1. If an organism's genotype has one dominant and one recessive gene, the organism's phenotype will show the dominant trait.
2. If an organism's genotype has two dominant genes, then the organism's phenotype will show the dominant trait.

---

[1]You may have difficulty with this exercise from a subject matter standpoint. Finding subject matter that is appropriate for exercises such as these in the problem-solving area and that is familiar to all potential users of the text has proved to be impossible. You may wish to review the subject using a high school science text or discuss the topic with a subject matter expert.

3. If an organism's genotype has two recessive genes, then the organism's phenotype will show the recessive trait.
4. If a member of a human generation is a male, then it has both an X (from the mother) and Y (from the father) chromosome.
5. If a member of a human generation is a female, then it has both an X (from the mother) and an X (from the father) chromosome.
6. If a human is color-blind, (s)he carries that gene on an X chromosome.
7. If a male is color-blind, he carries the recessive color-blind gene on the X chromosome.
8. If a female is color-blind, she carries recessive color-blind genes on both X chromosomes.
9. Previous events do not affect the probability of later occurrences of the same event.
10. The probability of independent events occurring together is equal to the product of the probabilities of these events occurring separately.
11. Procedure for making a Punnett square

Summary

Our definition of *problem solving* is the ability of a learner to combine rules and principles from a content domain to solve novel problems in that domain. This definition refers to "domain-specific" problem solving. Although many psychologists have struggled to identify generic problem-solving skills that can transfer to multiple domains, we agree with those who suggest that even these generic strategies should be taught as part of domain-specific problem-solving.

Experts are those who are able to combine their knowledge to solve problems within a particular domain. There appear to be numerous differences between the way experts and novices solve problems. One of the most striking differences between novices and experts is the amount of domain-specific knowledge that they possess. Learners are unable to solve problems unless they have content knowledge in the form of declarative knowledge, rules, and associated concepts. Learners also must acquire cognitive strategies that enable them to manipulate this knowledge.

Although research has clarified to some degree how people solve problems, many questions remain as to the qualities of instruction required to teach people to solve problems. Five macrostrategies appear to be useful: the Elaboration Model, Socratic dialogue, simulations, expert systems, and case studies. A summary of our suggestions for how the expanded instructional events might be delivered for problem-solving follows.

Conditions of Learning by Event for Problem-Solving

Introduction	Deploy attention. Arouse interest and motivation.	• Present a challenging and interesting problem that is represented in a novel manner.
	Establish instructional purpose.	• State the class of problem that learners will learn to solve. • Delay statement in inquiry lesson.
	Preview lesson.	• Point out that problems will become increasingly complex throughout lesson.
Body	Recall prior knowledge.	• Explicitly review relevant prior knowledge: rules, declarative knowledge, and strategies. • Suggest ways that learners can reorganize knowledge in a more conducive form. • Attend to similarities and differences with other problem-solving learning.

Body (cont.)	Process information.	• Encounter simplified, prototypical versions of the problem first. • Verbalize task requirements. • Provide model think-alouds. • Decompose the problem into subgoals.
	Focus attention.	• Isolate critical attributes in the given state and goal state.
	Employ learning strategies.	• Generate networks and analogies. • Monitor success of solutions. • Ask guiding questions and provide hints. • Represent problem in alternate forms. • Use print or other media as a form of external storage.
	Practice.	• Practice identifying and clarifying given and goal states. • Practice decomposing the problem. • Practice evaluating adequacy of a provided solution. • Practice with well-defined problems first.
	Evaluate feedback.	• Model the solution process or provide models of solution. • Give hints or ask questions. • Provide information on efficiency and effectiveness of solution.
Conclusion	Summarize and review.	• Restate criterial attributes of the problem class. • Summarize effective strategies. • Suggest ways of organizing knowledge for storage and retrieval.
	Transfer knowledge.	• Find similar problems outside the classroom. • Explicitly state when strategies may transfer to other problem types.
	Remotivate and close.	• Review the importance and breadth of what has been learned.
Assessment	Assess performance.	• Test ability to solve similar but novel problems, both well-defined and poorly defined. • Test ability to isolate criterial attributes of the goal and given states. • Test ability to evaluate others' solutions. • Test ability to justify solutions.
	Feedback and remediation.	• Identify whether problems are in pattern recognition, decomposition, explaining solution, etc.

Job Aid

1. How will prerequisite rules and concepts be taught—prior to the problem-solving lesson or interspersed with problem solving?

2. What macrostrategies will be used?
3. Fill in the expanded instructional events provided in Chapter 6.

Extended Example

After learners have completed instruction and can apply rules, concepts, and declarative knowledge regarding composition, exposure, focus, films, selection of shutter speed, selection of aperture size, and the relationship between shutter speed and aperture size, they are ready to solve complex, real-life problems.

Objective. Given information as to current (1) shutter speed, (2) f-stop, (3) desired composition, and (4) film speed and a changing condition that interferes with composition, exposure, or focus, the learner will determine what changes must be made to obtain good composition, exposure, and focus.

General Strategy. We could have easily developed the course around the Elaboration Model. Indeed, Wedman & Smith (1989) have developed such a photography unit. However, to present an alternative macrostrategy to the example strategy on programming instruction that we presented in this chapter, we will assume that the lesson has been sequenced in a hierarchical manner. The prerequisite rules and declarative knowledge for this course have been learned and practiced in previous lessons in the semester in the following order.

The instructional strategy in some ways may appear piecemeal; however, it might legitimately be selected if there were a wide variance in the knowledge and skills of the target audience so that the prerequisite declarative knowledge, rules, and concepts had to be presented in separate modules for individualized study. Within these models they will have completed one simple problem-solving task, combining rules regarding the relationship of aperture size to exposure and the relationship of shutter speed to exposure. Learners should have acquired prerequisite knowledge relating to the following content:

1. Camera parts and functions
2. Light and how film works
3. Obtaining a proper exposure
   - Underexposure
   - Overexposure
   - Correct exposure
   - Aperture
   - F-stops
   - Shutter
   - Shutter speeds
   - Relationship of f-stop and shutter speed
   - Lighting—natural, flash, photofloods
   - Light meters
4. Film
   - Film types
   - ASA, film speeds
   - Film data sheet
5. Focus
   - Blur—good and bad
   - Good/poor focus
   - Lenses
   - Field of view
   - Depth of field
6. Composition
   - Subject and field of view (framing, leading lines)
   - Rule of thirds
   - Depth of field
   - Motion
   - Angle of view
   - Perspective
   - Balance
   - Lighting

This part of the instruction will include the following media: instructor, videotapes, transparencies, and print handouts. The lesson will extend over several class meetings.

Introduction

Deploy Attention

Establish Purpose

Promote Motivation and Interest

Preview Lesson

The learners view a videotape that shows a photographer in a situation in which from her position on the sidelines she must take photos of the new hotshot, a freshman basketball player whose specialty is the "slam dunk." She is in a low-light situation, and the use of flash is forbidden during play. The video describes the film type in the camera (ASA 200, 36 exposure, only 6 frames already shot), the aperture (f/2.8), and the shutter speed setting (1/30) that gives an adequate exposure, as indicated by her light meter. The camera is a standard single-reflex camera with a regular 50 mm lens, f-stops from 1.4 to 22, and shutter speeds from 1/500 to 1 second. The video stops after the givens and the goal state are presented, and the narrator asks, "What problems will the photographer encounter in shooting the pictures? How might she solve these problems?"

The instructor does the following:

- Asks the learners to consider the problem as stated and asks how many feel that they could identify problems and suggest a solution. (Those that feel competent are asked to write down their solutions for now.)
- Explains that the learners have acquired a great amount of knowledge and principles regarding photography in the current semester, but that many students at this point feel somewhat unclear about how to combine their knowledge to solve problems like this one
- Suggests that photography truly is a content in which all of these factors must be considered simultaneously in order to solve common problems. Therefore, a lesson that promotes the combining of this knowledge is necessary. As with other types of problems, many problems in photography have more than one solution; often these solutions have trade-offs in terms of characteristics of the final product.
- Points out that this lesson will prepare learners to combine their learning in order to solve many problems

Body

Review Relevant Prior Knowledge

Employ Learning Strategies

The learners' organization of their current knowledge may very much resemble the outline of prerequisites identified above, with ideas considered linearly, related only by the categories presented. In order to facilitate their problem solving the instruction will suggest an alternative organization, which should promote more effective problem solving.

The instructor presents a transparency of the following graphic presented in Figure 10.1. The instructor does the following:

- Explains what each represents and gives an example of each
- Suggests that organizing what learners know concerning the subject, the desired photo, the camera, and the related equipment is very useful for problem solving in photography
- Distributes a handout that is the beginning of a network (semantic map) of the concepts above. On a second page are listed a number of concepts and principles, such as motion, contrast, perspective, depth of field, aperture, lens focal length, film speed, and so on.
- Explains that the learners will design a semantic map that relates all these concepts together
- Presents instruction on networking
- Asks students to complete the network on photography
- Shows several examples and has students explain how they related the concepts and rules

Process Information

Focus Attention

Employ Learning Strategies

The learners view the remainder of the video with the basketball game photography problem. The video does the following:

- Models with a think-aloud coordinated with video sequences. It demonstrates the analysis of the characteristics of the scene: content within scene, subjects within scene, amount of motion present in scene, amount of contrast,

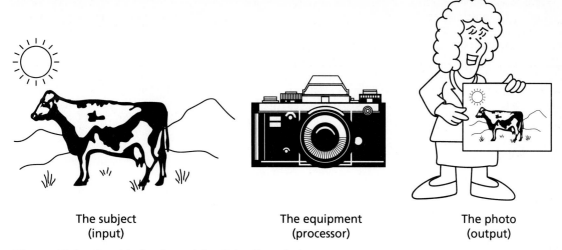

The subject	The equipment	The photo
(input)	(processor)	(output)

Figure 10.1: Graphic for Organizing Prior Knowledge

and light levels (intensity, direction of light, and whether flash or photofloods are possible).

- Models visualizing and thinking aloud regarding the completed photo in terms of the desired (1) placement of the subject, (2) the field of view, (3) depth of field, (4) action of the subject and how this motion should be portrayed, (5) message or emotion desired, (6) perspective, and (7) sharpness of images. The video actually demonstrates these factors being manipulated. The final frame shows the photographer saying, "That's it!"

- Models with think-aloud the photographer's manipulation of the camera to reach the desired state. The steps are (1) considering the low light situation; (2) realizing that the shutter is not quick enough to freeze the action; (3) considering speeding up shutter to 1/250; (4) realizing that to maintain adequate exposure, the aperture must be bigger; (5) determining that this aperture must be f/1.4; (6) estimating the effect of a large aperture on depth of field and determining that it is unacceptable; (7) pursuing options of getting more light on the subject; (8) considering using "faster" film; and (9) selecting a pan-with-action shot using a slower shutter speed than would freeze action. (The last scene of the video shows the photographer with the final photo.)

The instructor does the following:

- Points out how the photographer clarified and considered the situation (the given state), clarified and visualized the final product (the goal state), and considered and evaluated the alternative operations to move the given to the goal state
- Asks if learners can suggest other solutions
- Asks the learners to evaluate the solutions that were proposed

Practice

Feedback

The learners practice with separate well-defined problems in which they must clarify the critical features of the given state or the goal state.

The instructor asks guiding questions and gives hints to help learners clarify these states.

The learners practice completely solving well-defined problems and practice explaining their solutions and evaluating the soundness of others' solutions.

The instructor confirms the viability of the learners' solutions and discusses the effectiveness and efficiency of their solution strategies.

The learners practice answering poorly-defined problems in which (1) much extraneous information is present, (2) information is missing, (3) inferences must be made about the given or goal state, or (4) no solution is perfect and trade-offs in quality must be considered. They also practice explaining their solutions and evaluating the soundness of others' solutions.

The instructor confirms the viability of the learners' solutions and discusses the effectiveness and efficiency of their solution strategies.

Conclusion

Summarize and Review

Transfer

The instructor does the following:

- Displays the transparency, which shows the main concepts of scene, camera, and product
- Asks learners to supply concepts underlying each superordinate concept
- Asks learners to suggest rules that tie concepts together
- Assigns learners six photography assignments, which will require problem-solving, camera,

and film. Four of the problems are situations in which relatively unlimited time for problem solving is available. Two of the problems will require learners to problem solve quickly. The learners must actually go out and shoot the photos and bring the developed prints to class the next week (near transfer).

- Identifies the structure of the organization as "given state," "goal state," and "operators"
- Suggests that this is a typical problem-solving pattern
- Gives examples of problem solving that follow the same pattern
- Asks learners to find other similar problem forms

Assessment

In order to have sufficient variability of context and difficulty level and sufficient items for obtaining a reliable measure, we suggest a pencil-and-paper assessment that portrays problems similar to that given in the introduction. Some problems should be well-defined, and others should be poorly defined. Learners should be required to explain why they chose the solution that they did.

Readings and References

Adkinson, F. D. (1977). Designing simulation gaming activities: A systems approach. *Educational Technology, 17*(2), 38–43.

Alexander, P. A., & Judy J. E. (1988). The interaction of domain-specific and strategic knowledge in academic performance. *Review of Educational Research, 58*(4), 375–404.

Anderson, J. R. (1985). *Cognitive psychology and its implications* (2nd ed.). New York: Freeman.

Chase, W. G., & Chi, M. T. H. (1980). Cognitive skill: Implications for spatial skill in large-scale environments. In J. Harvey (Ed.), *Cognition, social behavior, and the environment*. Potomac, MD: Erlbaum.

Chase, W. G., & Simon, H. A. (1973). Perception in chess. *Cognitive Psychology, 4,* 55–81.

Chi, M. T. H., Glaser, R., & Rees, E. (1982). Expertise in problem solving. In R. Sternberg (Ed.), *Advances in the psychology of human intelligence* (pp. 161–183). Hillsdale, NJ: Erlbaum.

Collins, A., & Stevens, A. L. (1983). A cognitive theory of inquiry teaching. In C. Reigeluth (Ed.), *Instructional-Design Theories and Models*. Hillsdale, NJ: Erlbaum.

Covington, M. C., Crutchfield, R. S., Davies, L. B., & Olton, R. M. (1974). *The productive thinking program: A course in learning to think*. Columbus, OH: Merrill.

de Bono, E. (1973). *CoRT thinking materials*. London: Direct Education Services.

de Groot, A. E. (1965). *Thought and choice in chess*. The Hague: Mouton.

de Jong, T., & Ferguson-Hessler, M. G. M. (1986). Cognitive structures of good and poor novice problem solvers in physics. *Journal of Educational Psychology, 78*(4), 279–288.

Derry, S. J., Hawkes, L. W., & Tsai, C. (1987). A theory for remediation problem-solving skills of older children and adults. *Educational Psychologist, 22*(1), 55–87.

Dewey, J. (1933). *How we think*. Boston: Heath.

Duffield, J. A. (1991). Designing computer software for problem-solving instruction. *Educational Technology Research and Development, 39*(1), 17–29.

Duncker, K. (1945). On problem solving. *Psychological Monographs, 58* (Whole No. 270).

Foshay, W. R. (1991). What we know (and what we don't know) about training of cognitive strategies for technical problem-solving. In G. J. Anglin (Ed.), *Instructional technology: Past, present, & future, 344–353*. Englewood, CO: Libraries Unlimited.

Frederiksen, N. (1984). Implications of cognitive theory for instruction in problem solving. *Review of Educational Research, 54*(3), 363–407.

Gagné, E. D. (1985). *The cognitive psychology of school learning*. Boston: Little, Brown, & Co.

Gagné, R. M. (1980). Learnable aspects of problem solving. *Educational Psychologist, 15* 84–92.

Gagné, R. M. (1985). *The conditions of learning* (4th ed.). New York: Holt, Rinehart, and Winston.

Gick, M. L. (1986). Problem-solving strategies. *Educational Psychologist, 21*(1 & 2), 99–120.

Gick, M. L., & Holyoak, K. J. (1980). Analogical problem solving. *Cognitive Psychology, 12,* 306–355.

Gilhooly, K. J., & Green, A. J. R. (1989). Learning problem-solving skills. In A. M. Colley & J. K. Beech (Eds.), *Acquisition and performance of cognitive skills*. New York: Wiley and Sons.

Glaser, R. (1989). Expertise and learning: How do we think about instructional processes now that we have discovered knowledge structures. In D. Klahr and K. Kotovsky (Eds.), *Complex information processing*. Hillsdale, N.J.: Erlbaum.

Gorrell, J. (April, 1990). *Effects of cognitive monitoring and implicit rule presentation on problem solving*. A paper presented at the annual meeting of the American Educational Research Association, Boston.

Grabinger, R. S., Wilson, B., & Jonassen, D. H. (1990). *Building expert systems in training and education*. New York: Praeger.

Greenblat, C. S., & Duke, R. D. (1981). *Principles and practices of gaming/simulation*. Beverly Hill, CA: Sage Publications.

Greeno, J. G. (1978). A study of problem solving. In R. Glaser (Ed.), *Advances in instructional psychology, Vol.1*. Hillsdale, NJ: Erlbaum.

Greeno, J. G. (1989). Situations, mental models, and generative knowledge. In D. Klahr and K. Kotovsky (Eds.), *Complex information processing*. Hillsdale, NJ: Erlbaum.

HBS Case Services (Harvard Business School, Boston, MA 02163): Culliton, J. W. (n.d.). *Handbook on case writing*. Lawrence, P. R. (n.d.). *Preparation of case material*. Culliton, J. W. (n.d.). *Case method*. Sanford, M. J. (n.d.). *Case development and teaching notes*. McNair, M. P. (n.d.). *McNair on cases*. Towl, A. R. (n.d.). *Case-course development: The case method of learning administration*.

Heller, J. I., & Hungate, H. N. (April, 1984). *Theory-based instruction in description of mechanics problems*. A paper presented at the annual meeting of the American Educational Research Association, New Orleans.

Hudspeth, D. & Knirk, F. G. (1989). Case study materials: Strategies for design and use. *Performance Improvement Quarterly, 2*(4), 30–41.

Hyatt, G., Eades, D., Tenczar, P. J., & Denault, J. M. (1968). *Drosophila genetics*. Urbana, IL: University of Illinois Computer-Based Education Research Laboratory.

Ingram, A. L. (1988). Instructional design for heuristic-based problem-solving. *Educational Communications and Technology Journal, 36*(4), 211–230.

Johnson-Laird, P. (1983). *Mental models*. Cambridge, MA: Harvard University Press.

Joyce, B. & Weil, M. (1986). *Models of teaching* (3rd ed.). Englewood Cliffs, NJ: Prentice-Hall.

Kotovsky, K., & Fallside, D. (1989). Representation and transfer in problem solving. In D. Klahr and K. Kotovsky (Eds.), *Complex information processing*. Hillsdale, NJ: Erlbaum.

Kozma, R. B., Belle, L. W., & Williams, G. W. (1978). *Instructional techniques in higher education*. Englewood Cliffs, NJ: Educational Technology Publications.

Larkin, J. H. (1980). Teaching problem solving in physics: The psychological laboratory and the practical classroom. In. D. T. Tuma & F. Reif (Eds.), *Problem solving and education: Issues in teaching and research*. Hillsdale, NJ: Erlbaum.

Larkin, J. H. (1989). Display-based problem solving. In D. Klahr & K. Kotovsky (Eds.), *Complex information processing*. Hillsdale, NJ: Erlbaum.

Lippert, R. C. (1988). Expert systems: Tutor, tools, and tutees. *Journal of Computer-based Instruction, 16*(1), 11–19.

Maidment, R., & Bronstein, R. H. (1973). *Simulation games: Design and implementation*. Columbus, OH: Merrill.

Massialas, B., & Cox, B. (1966). *Inquiry in social studies*. New York: McGraw-Hill.

Mayer, R. E. (1983). Can you repeat that? Qualitative effects of repetition and advance organizers on learning from science prose. *Journal of Educational Psychology, 75,* 40–49.

Mayer, R. E. (1985). The elusive search for teachable aspects of problem solving. In J. A. Glover and R. R. Ronning (Eds.), *A history of educational psychology*. New York: Plenum.

Mayer, R. E. (1989). Models for understanding. *Review of Educational Research, 59*(1), 43–64.

McFarland, T. D., & Parker, R. (1990). *Expert systems in education and training*. Englewood Cliffs, NJ: Educational Technology Publications.

Newell, A., & Simon, H. A. (1972). *Human problem solving*. Englewood Cliffs, NJ: Prentice-Hall.

Norman, G. R. (1985). The role of knowledge in teaching and assessment of problem-solving. *Journal of Instructional Development, 8*(1), 7–11.

Oliver, D., & Shaver, J. P. (1966). *Teaching public issues in the high school*. Boston: Houghton-Mifflin.

Perkins, D. N. (April, 1988). *Understanding and expertise: The double helix of mastery*. A paper presented at the annual meeting of the American Educational Research Association, New Orleans.

Polson, M. C., & Richardson, J. J. (1988). *Foundations of intelligent tutoring systems*. Hillsdale, NJ: Erlbaum.

Polson, P. G., & Jeffries, R. (1985). Instruction in general problem-solving skills: An analysis of four approaches. In J. W. Segal, S. F. Chipman, & R. Glaser (Eds.), *Thinking and learning skills, vol. 1*. Hillsdale, NJ: Erlbaum.

Polya, G. (1945). *How to solve it*. Princeton, NJ: Princeton University Press.

Ragan, T. J. & Smith, P. L. (1989). *Programming instructional software*. Englewood Cliffs, NJ: Educational Technology Publications.

Reigeluth, C. M. & Stein, F. S. (1983). The elaboration theory of instruction. In C. M. Reigeluth (Ed.), *Instructional-design theories and models: An overview of their current status*. Hillsdale, NJ: Erlbaum.

Rowe, N. C. (1984). Some rules for good simulations. In D. F. Walker and R. D. Hess (Eds.), *Instructional software: Principles and perspectives for design and use*. Belmont, CA: Wadsworth.

Schoenfeld, A. H. (1979). Can heuristics be taught? In J. Lochhead & J. Clement (Eds.), *Cognitive process instruction* (pp. 315–338). Philadelphia: Franklin Institute Press.

Schoenfeld, A. H., & Herrmann, D. J. (1982). Problem perception and knowledge structure in expert and novice mathematical problem solvers. *Journal of Experimental Psychology: Learning, Memory, and Cognition, 8,* 484–494.

Schwab, J. J. (1965). *Biological sciences curriculum study, biology teachers' handbook*. New York: Wiley and Sons.

Shirts, R. G. (1975). Ten "mistakes" commonly made by persons designing educational simulations and games. *SAGSET Journal, 5,* 147–150.

Simon, H. A. (1980). Problem solving and education. In D. T. Tuma & R. Reif (Eds.), *Problem solving and education: Issues in teaching and research*. Hillsdale, NJ: Erlbaum.

Simon, H. A., & Chase, W. G. (1973). Skill in chess. *American Scientist, 61,* 394–403.

Starfield, A. M., Butala, K. L., England, M. M., & Smith, K. A. (1983). Mastering engineering concepts by building an expert system. *Engineering Education, 74,* 104–107.

Suchman, J. R. (1962). *The elementary school training program in scientific inquiry*. Report to the U.S. Office of Education, Project Title VII. Urbana: University of Illinois.

Tennyson, R. D. (April, 1988). *Problem-oriented simulations to develop and improve higher-order thinking strategies.* A paper presented at the annual meeting of the American Educational Research Association, New Orleans.

Trollip, S. R. & Lippert, R. C. (1988). Constructing knowledge bases: A process for instruction. In M. H. Chignell, P. A. Hancock, & Lowenthal, A. (Eds.), *Intelligent interfaces: Theory, research, and design.* Amsterdam, The Netherlands: North Holland Press.

Voss, J. F., Greene, T. R., Post, T. A., & Penner, P. C. (1983). Problem solving skill in the social sciences. In G. H. Bower (Ed.), *The psychology of learning and motivation: Advances in research and theory* (Vol. 17, pp. 165–213). New York: Academic Press.

Walcott, C., & Walcott, A. (1976). *Simple simulations: A guide to the design and use of simulations/games in teaching political science.* Washington, D.C.: American Political Science Association.

Wedman, J. F., & Smith, P. L. (1989). An examination of two approaches to organizing instruction. *International Journal of Instructional Media,* 16, (4), pp. 652–660.

Wideman, H. H., & Owston, R. D. (1988). Student development of an expert system: A case study. *Journal of Computer-Based Instruction, 15*(3), 88–94.

Strategies for Cognitive Strategy Lessons

eleven

Chapter Objective

At the conclusion of this chapter you should be able to do the following:

- Given a cognitive strategy objective, design strategy plans for a cognitive strategy lesson.

Review of Cognitive Strategy Learning

As we discussed in Chapter 4, cognitive strategies are those techniques that learners use to control and monitor their own cognitive processes. R. Gagné (1985) has identified two primary kinds of cognitive strategies: strategies for learning and strategies for thinking. Cognitive strategies for learning are mental tactics for attending to, organizing, elaborating, manipulating, and retrieving knowledge. Cognitive strategies for thinking are mental tactics that lead to discovery, invention, or creativity.

Cognitive strategies that support learning are sometimes called *learning strategies*. These learning strategies are the same skills that we have suggested in our expanded instructional events, which instructional designers explicitly plan to prompt or encourage. The cognitive strategies that we call *thinking strategies* are of a different sort than previously discussed in this book. We described these thinking strategies as "generic problem-solving skills" in Chapter 10. These general problem-solving skills are a form of thinking strategy that is different from the domain-specific problem solving discussed in Chapter 10. In this chapter we discuss the nature of both learning strategies and thinking strategies, and we discuss how both learning and thinking strategies may be taught so that they are within a learner's repertoire and available for use. We will give more attention to learning strategies within this chapter, primarily because they have been more clearly described and their related instructional strategies have proven to be more successful than more general thinking strategies. The chapter will include integration into the expanded instructional events and a sample lesson for learning strategies only.

Learning Strategies

Cognitive strategies may control the processing of information that does not lead to learning (as *learning* was defined in Chapter 1), such as a strategy for recalling a phone number long enough to dial it. However, much cognitive strategy instruction is instruction to support acquisition of learning strategies. Learning strategies are those tactics employed by learners to facilitate the acquisition of knowledge and skills. When learning strategies are employed, the learners guide their own processing, rather than having the processing guided or supplied by the instruction (Derry & Murphy, 1986; Weinstein, 1982; Gagné & Driscoll, 1988; Davidson, 1988). We have suggested that processing strategies can be "built into" the instruction or "built into" the learners. In other words, portions of cognitive processing can be supplanted by the instruction or generated by the learners. Learning situations in which the learner takes the major responsibility for processing is termed *self-regulated learning* (Zimmerman & Schunk, 1989).

The instructional designer must consider a number of factors in determining how much cognitive processing can be supplied by the learner. One of these factors is whether learners possess appropriate strategies. Learning strategies are not often directly taught (Norman, 1980): They are more often discovered by good students. Unfortunately, they are seldom discovered by poorer students (Brown, 1978; Torgesen, 1979). Therefore, it appears that for many learners direct instruction on cognitive strategies may be beneficial. To date, several studies have indicated that training in cognitive strategy use can be effective (Brown, Campione, & Day, 1981; Weinstein & Mayer, 1986; Dansereau, 1985).

Although strategies are by nature cognitively based processes, they are often categorized as cognitive or affective. **Cognitive domain strategies** are used to support information processing: selecting information to attend to, promoting encoding and storage of information, and enhancing retrieval. Weinstein and Mayer (1985) categorized cognitive strategies as organizing strategies, elaborating strategies, rehearsing strategies, and comprehension monitoring strategies. *Organizing* strategies are used to structure information in memory and to store new information in memory within an appropriate structure (e.g., within an appropriate schema). Examples of organizing strategies are techniques such as grouping similar information together, developing graphic organizers, or outlining content. *Elaborating* strategies are used to establish associations between new information and previously acquired knowledge. Tactics such as mental imagery, analogies, the keyword method, paraphrasing, generating personal examples, and generative note taking are examples of elaborating strategies. *Rehearsing* strategies assist in the encoding and retrieval of information that is not easily structured or elaborated. An example of such strategies would be a learner actively reciting or naming items. *Comprehension monitoring* strategies assist the learner in determining whether they are understanding or learning. An example of a monitoring strategy would be self-questioning. **Affective domain strategies,** sometimes called *support strategies,* are those self-motivational skills that influence an individual's active engagement in a learning task and maintain a psychological attitude conducive to learning (Dansereau, 1978; McCombs, 1984). Examples of such strategies would be time management, stress reduction techniques, and positive self-talk (McCombs, 1984; Weinstein & Underwood, 1985). These strategies are sometimes referred to as *metacognition* or *executive skills*.

Instruction in cognitive strategies, especially if it is appropriately "situated" within a continuing discussion of cognition, can enhance the development of metacognition (Brown, Campione, & Day, 1981; Flavell & Wellman, 1977). Metacognition involves students' awareness of their own cognitive processes, their ability to control these processes by selecting among cognitive strategies, and their ability to monitor, evaluate, and revise their strategy use (Brown, 1978; Flavell, 1977; Weinstein & Mayer, 1986).

Learning strategy instruction has been increasingly advocated, particularly for learners in public schools. However, even in training environments, such as the military, increasing attention has been given to developing skills in "learning how to learn" (Derry & Murphy, 1985; McCombs, 1981–82). Following our treatment of thinking strategies, this chapter will consider the most effective instructional strategies for the teaching of learning strategies and promoting their transfer.

Divergent Thinking Strategies

The category of cognitive strategies that we label *thinking strategies* includes techniques and strategies intended to help learners solve problems or generate new ideas, regardless of the domain of application. As noted above, this "creative problem solving" or "general problem solving" is quite a different matter from "domain-specific problem solving" discussed in earlier chapters. Whereas domain-specific problem solving involves application of rules from within a subject area to problems within that domain, creative problem solving involves techniques or skills that may be applied to a variety of situations requiring invention. A commonly used framework for creative problem solving is what has been labeled "divergent-production" (Polson & Jeffries, 1985). Approaches to improving thinking skills that employ this paradigm focus on divergent thinking and the generation of many possible hypotheses. These approaches usually employ the general problem-solving heuristics developed by Polya (1957).

A variety of thinking strategies have been proposed and studied. Stein (1974, 1975) describes various individual procedures: techniques used to exert influence from a personality standpoint, including role playing, hypnosis, and psychotherapy; techniques used to assist hypothesis formation, such as Osborne's "brainstorming," Zwicky's "morphological analysis," and Crawford's "attribute listing"; techniques of forced relationships; Taylor's nine-step "PakSA" technique; General Electric's Input-Output technique; and miscellaneous techniques such as "use of the ridiculous," "modification," and "fresh eye." Group procedures for stimulating creativity include brainstorming; Parnes' Creative Problem-Solving; Gordon's Synectics; and Crutchfield, Covington, and associates' "Productive Thinking Program." The four primary divergent-production problem-solving strategies identified by Polson and Jeffries (1985) are Crutchfield, Covington, and associates' "Productive Thinking Program"; deBono's "CoRT Thinking Lessons"; Rubenstein's "Patterns of Problem Solving"; and Wickelgren's "How to Solve Problems." Techniques from the information-processing perspective, also as identified by Polson and Jeffries, include work by a variety of researchers on search strategies such as the "generate and test" strategy and "means-ends analysis." They also include techniques involving both understanding and search, such as "planning by abstraction," "decomposition," and various techniques for acquisition of problem-solving skills through enhancing one's awareness of self as a problem solver.

One serious limitation of much of the work in thinking strategies (particularly work from the divergent-production perspective) is a lack of sufficient attention to the need for knowledge in the area or topic in which the learner is to become creative or to which general problem-solving skills will be applied. Successful inventors, musical composers, architects, artists, and good problem solvers in business and industry all tend to be *very* knowledgeable in the area in which they are working. Domain-independent thinking strategies tend to grossly underemphasize the need for expertise in the domain to which the strategies are to be applied. Stein (1974, 1975) notes some elements of divergent thinking for which no technique appears to exist in the creative problem-solving literature: inspiration, intuition, and selecting the "good possibility." In describing the lack of direct investigation on inspiration, Stein notes "it might be said that to achieve a state of inspiration an individual would have to prepare himself intensively in his field and devote himself sincerely to the work he has undertaken" (p. 202). Similar statements can be made of how individuals come to possess the talent for making shrewd guesses, proposing good hypotheses, and selecting the best possibilities from among a variety of hypotheses. It is interesting to note that Newell (1980), in discussing the importance of search strategies in problem solving, classifies the two "general" search strategies previously noted (generate and test; means-ends analysis) as "weak methods." Newell noted that their weakness derives from their generality—trading the power of a domain-specific search for the generality of an approach that can be used across many tasks. This may be a good characterization of thinking strategy instruction and its role in instructional design. Approaches to assisting learners' creative problem-solving skills that claim great power and at the same time neglect the importance of knowledge in the area of application should be viewed with extreme caution.

An Example of a Thinking Strategy Instruction Model

The Synectics approach developed by Gordon (1961) was selected by Joyce and Weil (1986) as a model for teaching creativity and is an instructional strategy for promoting divergent thinking strategies. The Synectics approach emphasizes the use of metaphoric thinking, primarily through generation of analogies. Joyce and Weil present one strategy derived from Synectics that involves six phases, directed toward helping learners generate new ideas (i.e., new ways of looking at a familiar concept). The first step is description of the present condition; that is, clarifying the task at hand. This phase is generally initiated and directed by a teacher, with student involvement. The second phase is generation of direct analogies. In this phase, students are stimulated to (1) generate analogies that relate to the problem, (2) select one analogy, and (3) explore that one analogy further. In the third phase, students generate personal analogies. Students are assisted in translating the direct analogy into a personalized form—students "become" the analogy selected in the first phase. In phase four, students engage in what is described as "compressed conflict." Compressed conflict involves generating two-word descriptions of an object that contradict; that is, oxymorons. Examples include *dark brightness* and *prideful modesty*. Joyce and Weil (1986) cite two from Gordon: *life-saving destroyer* and *nourishing flame*. Compressed conflicts used in this process are to be taken from analogies generated in phases three and four. Students are directed to select one compressed conflict from the set created. Phase five involves development of another direct analogy, but this time it must come from the compressed conflict selected in phase four. Phase six involves reexamination of the original task in light of the last analogy developed or helpful products from any of the previous phases.

The Synectics model can add richness and variety to students' thinking about a topic. Used by a skillful teacher, it can stimulate new ideas about a familiar topic, increasing the quality of thinking and helping cut through stereotypes and clichés.

Cognitive Requirements of Cognitive Strategy Learning

An information-processing analysis of the procedure that is involved in applying a cognitive strategy clarifies the requirements of the learning task. This analysis was developed from an extensive review of literature and identifies the overarching cognitive processes involved in applying a cognitive strategy:

1. Analyze the requirements of the learning task.
2. Analyze one's ability to complete the task, including the predictable demands on and limitations of memory.
3. Select an appropriate strategy.
4. Apply the selected strategy.
5. Evaluate the effectiveness of the strategy used.
6. Revise as required.

This overarching process, which is mentally employed by the learner, strongly resembles the information-processing analysis of traditional problem solving. Selection, application, and evaluation of a cognitive strategy is indeed very similar to problem solving. However, cognitive strategies tend to be applicable across a variety of domains of content, rather than domain-specific. Step four in this process is the application of a procedural rule, which will vary depending upon the specific cognitive strategy. The learner's analysis of the task and her own ability to cope with the task, the selection of an appropriate strategy, the evaluation of the success of the strategy use, and the revision of the process depending upon this evaluation are all metacognitive skills that must be learned along with the ability to apply a particular cognitive strategy.

General Approaches to Teaching Cognitive Strategies

Pressley, Snyder, and Cargilia-Bull (1987) reviewed the learning strategies literature and categorized six alternative approaches to strategy instruction. We have added a seventh approach (self-instructional training):

1. *Discovery and guided discovery.* Typically the discovery approach is the way most students learn cognitive strategies, as formal instruction in strategies is not common. The guided discovery approach involves a more direct instructional technique, in which the instructor, through questioning, leads the learner to discover a particular strategy.

2. *Observation.* Observation of a model demonstrating the use of a cognitive strategy is a technique suggested by social learning theory (Bandura, 1977). According to Pressley et al., the delivery system for an observation strategy might involve cooperative application of cognitive strategies with paired learners, expert demonstration by a teacher, or symbolic modeling by a fictional character, which is presented visually or textually.

3. *Guided participation.* Guided participation depends heavily upon a teacher who guides students through the use of a strategic procedure in day-to-day school tasks. As tasks are encountered, the learners and teacher together determine the characteristics of a learning task, identify strategies to facilitate the learning task, and determine effective ways to employ the strategy. This type of activity normally does not involve direct instruction regarding the strategy.

4. *Strategy instruction in books and courses.* This category describes "prepackaged" instruction on strategies (some of which were noted earlier in our discussion of thinking strategies), such as de Bono's (1983) CoRT thinking skills program, Feuerstein's Instrumental Enrichment Programme (Feuerstein, Rand, Hoffman, & Miller, 1980), Higbee's (1977) text on cognitive skills, and Covington's (1985) Productive Thinking Program. Pressley et al. suggest that one disadvantage of this approach is that it may lack practice in applying the strategies to the types of materials that the learners encounter in their school tasks and may, consequently, fail to promote transfer to the very contexts in which the strategies must be applied.

5. *Direct explanation, largely teacher directed.* This type of instruction teaches learners not only the procedure of the strategy but also provides them with information on when and where the strategy should be applied. Direct instruction includes "concrete examples, modeling, and practice" (Pressley et al., p. 97).

6. *Dyadic instruction.* Dyadic instruction involves a one-to-one interaction between the learner and a knowledgeable adult. The adult

demonstrates strategy application, making thought processes as obvious as possible to the learner, perhaps through think-aloud procedures. The technique also involves the learner reciprocating by demonstrating the strategy to the adult, and the adult providing advice and supervision of this strategy application.

7. *Self-instructional training.* Although not described by Pressley et al., Meichenbaum's (1977) self-instructional training clearly is an approach to teaching cognitive strategies. The approach includes (in addition to self-instruction) active interactions with a teacher who may also model strategy use and provide feedback to the learners. A critical part of the approach (and the characteristic that makes it a "self-instructional" approach) is the encouragement of learners to engage in private speech, perhaps initially overtly, and later covertly.

While Pressley et al. detail advantages of these instructional techniques, they suggest that direct explanation may be the most successful and the most applicable in classroom situations. This position is supported by many, including Weinstein (1978), who found that students who received explicit training in strategy use outperformed students who were informed that a use of a particular strategy would be helpful.

Analysis of these seven instructional strategies reveals that they vary in their relationship to instruction on content-related objectives (Rigney, 1980). Certain strategies may be characterized as "embedded," in which instruction on the technique in question is part of (or embedded within) instruction on content-related objectives. For example, strategy 3, *Guided participation,* would always be employed within the context of a lesson on some particular topic. Other strategies may be characterized as "detached," in that instruction on the learning strategy stands alone—it is the topic at hand. An example of a detached technique is 4, *Strategy instruction in books and courses.*

Each approach (embedded or detached) has general advantages and disadvantages. Embedded training can be superior to detached training in transfer to real-life tasks. On the other hand, the embedded training may suffer from insufficient attention to the learning strategy caused by pursuing it at the same time as content objectives. Detached training may provide more time and emphasis on learning the strategy itself but may not be as readily transferred to real application. The way we are approaching cognitive strategies in this chapter is as "detached" strategies. However, the same techniques that we are teaching can be used in an "embedded" approach. The Extended Example at the end of Chapter 10 included an application of embedded cognitive strategies, in which instruction on a "networking" strategy—which will help learners make use of previously learned concepts and rules—is provided within the problem-solving lesson.

In the final analysis, instruction that is designed to involve both embedded and detached approaches may be ideal (Derry & Murphy, 1986). Initial learning may best be acquired through a direct approach. As learners acquire the fundamentals of a learning strategy, their application can be encouraged and prompted in content instruction. Over a period of time, prompting of applications can be faded to the point where learners determine to use the strategy when needed. Such an approach is completely consistent with instruction in cognitive strategies as suggested by this chapter. Using strategies in lessons directed at achievement of other objectives, as suggested by the expanded instructional events throughout this text, is consistent with the idea of embedded strategy learning.

Davidson and Smith (1990) found in the recommendations of many scholars seven specific events that are recommended for instruction in a cognitive strategy (Deshler, Alley, Warner, & Schumaker, 1981; E. Gagné, 1985; Meichenbaum, 1977; Pressley, Snyder, & Cargilia-Bull, 1987; Weinstein, 1981). Those events are the following:

- Specific identification of the utility of the strategy—when and where to use it
- Overview of the specific steps in the strategy
- Demonstration or modeling of the strategy
- Examples and nonexamples of application of the strategy
- Practice using the strategy across a wide variety of appropriate situations with graduated difficulty of situations requiring the strategy
- Corrective feedback
- Explicit encouragement to transfer the strategy to appropriate contexts

These seven critical attributes of successful instruction in cognitive strategies highlight the more detailed treatment of instructional events that follows.

Events of Instruction for Teaching Cognitive Strategies

We describe this instruction as primarily mediated by a teacher because we believe that there is an interplay and complex feedback mechanism that may be best supplied through the rapid and complex analysis and processing that is available through a live teacher. It is quite possible, however, that many of the instructor demonstrations might be videotaped in order to obtain a practiced and replicable model. As of this writing, research is under way involving development of a multimedia, self-contained, detached learning strategies lesson to examine what portion of strategies training may be available to the individual and to small groups.

Introduction

Deploying Attention

Establish Instructional Purpose

Arouse Interest and Motivation

One way to begin instruction on a specific strategy is to give learners a task that requires use of the particular strategy and then ask them to complete it. In doing so, the learners demonstrate their prior knowledge of the requirements of the task and particular strategies that they currently have available, enabling the teacher/trainer to (1) diagnose the learners' level of knowledge and skill and (2) build upon that knowledge and skill. A discussion of the utility and efficiency of the strategies that the learners used can lead into a statement of the purpose of the current lesson — to learn a particular strategy that can be applied effectively to a certain category of tasks. The active involvement of the learners at this point and the attention to relevancy of the task should activate the learners' attention to the lesson. If there is a clear mismatch between learners' current approach and the requirements of the task,

learners may choose to change their tactics and learn to employ the new strategy.

We also suggest that to arouse motivation the specific strategy being learned should be discussed within the context of metacognition and executive processes. This discussion can include the importance, effectiveness, and efficiency of active, purposeful learning. Pressley, Borkowski, and Schneider (1987) suggest that the introductory message include the points (1) that good strategy users know that there are many strategies that can be used and that all are useful in attaining specific goals and (2) that they are aware that good performance is tied with effort. In particular, with regard to effort, learners should know (and perhaps believe) the following: ''(1) personal effort often increases the likelihood of success; (2) although effort per se is important, effort channeled into strategic activity is better than working hard; (3) specific strategies are not tied to one task but can be matched to new situations; and (4) if strategic actions and plans are to be successful, they should be shielded from competing behaviors, distractions, and emotions'' (pp. 1, 25–28).

Preview Lesson

The steps in the cognitive strategy can now be overviewed and a model can demonstrate the use of the strategy for a straightforward situation appropriate for the strategy. The model might be the teacher/trainer, a knowledgeable student, or a fictitious student presented in a video. The model can follow a think-aloud procedure that explicitly points out the critical features of the strategy, including what about the learning task cued the use of this particular strategy. This presentation allows the learners to gain a perspective as to what is meant by the strategy, explicitly what the steps to the strategy procedure are, and how the various steps fit together.

Body

Review Relevant Prior Knowledge

If other strategies have been explicitly taught or if other strategies that include similar steps are already in the learners' repertoire, then these strategies may be contrasted with the new strategy.

Later, such a comparison may also be made on the utility of the strategy as compared to other strategies.

Process Information and Examples

Focus Attention

The next information to be presented to the learners is when and where the strategy can be appropriately applied. First, the instructor can provide an explicit description of the learning tasks to which this strategy is applicable. Then, the teacher/trainer can present the learners with situations that are appropriate for the strategy, asking them to point out what characteristics of the situation suggest the strategy. To promote transfer, these examples should vary on as many noncriterial attributes as possible, including content, task type, time length of task, and context of task. Next, the instructor can give the learners examples in which the strategy is inappropriate. These nonexamples should be as "matched" on noncriterial attributes (such as content) as possible. (You may notice that recognizing the context appropriate to a particular cognitive strategy is a concept performance, sometimes termed *pattern recognition task*. The instructional strategy for learning to determine when a particular cognitive strategy should be used is similar to the instructional strategy for teaching concepts as identified in Chapter 8.)

The learners may be asked to point out why certain situations are inappropriate for the application of the strategy, with the instructor confirming and correcting their comments. The learners can be asked to supply example situations in which the strategy is appropriate and situations in which it is inappropriate. The instructor, in collaboration with the other learners, may provide feedback and correction as to the appropriateness of the examples that are presented.

Employ Learning Strategies

This new strategy may be contrasted with other strategies that have been taught or already exist in the learners' repertoire. Other strategies that may have similar application may be compared as to their efficiency or effectiveness. They may also be contrasted on the purpose of the instructional task or other aspects that may make the new strategy superior to other strategies.

Practice

Evaluate Feedback

Learners can now be provided with example situations in which they specify whether the new strategy is appropriate or not. They should be encouraged to substantiate their answers based upon the requirements of the learning task and the utility of the strategy. If learners have learned related strategies or have other strategies in their repertoire, they should be encouraged to explain why this strategy may be superior to others as they identify a strategy as appropriate to the situation. As with other pattern recognition practice, some of the instances should be very easy and obvious, while others should involve fine discriminations in order to determine that the learners are neither undergeneralizing nor overgeneralizing the utility of the strategy. Feedback may be presented that not only informs the learners of the correctness of their responses but also provides information as to why a particular response is correct or incorrect. The learners might also be provided with a video of an age-appropriate student applying the strategy in a particular context. The learners might be asked to appraise whether the student is appropriately applying the strategy and be asked to explain their answers.

Process Information

Focus Attention

The sequence of instruction that is followed next depends upon the complexity of the cognitive strategy being taught. If the strategy is complex, involves many steps, or involves many decision points with alternate steps that depend upon the decision, then a part-whole technique for presentation and practice will be appropriate. If the strategy steps are few, with few decision points, then the strategy may be presented and practiced in its whole from the outset.

The instructor (or another model) can again demonstrate a part of a complex strategy or the entire simple strategy. In this demonstration, the instructor can use a think-aloud procedure that emphasizes the cognitive processes required of the strategy. In addition, the instructor should demonstrate the steps in the metacognition relating to this strategy: He should think-aloud the analysis of the requirements of the task, the selection of this strategy as appropriate to the task, the application of the strategy, the evaluation of the strategy in terms of its effectiveness, and any ''fix-up'' techniques involved in revising the strategy use.

Employ Learning Strategies

The instructor may find a self-questioning pattern appropriate to represent this metacognitive processing, particularly monitoring success of the strategy (e.g., ''What is it that I'm supposed to do with this task? Have I fulfilled the requirements of the learning task?'').

Practice

Evaluate Feedback

The learners now should be given the opportunity to practice applying the strategy (or the part of the strategy). This practice may be supported with a checklist or flowchart that reminds the learner of the steps to follow. This practice may involve reciprocal teaching in which learners are paired. One learner can demonstrate the strategy with its accompanying metacognition in a think-aloud mode, while the second learner plays the role of a coach-evaluator, using a checklist as a guide. Then the roles can be reversed.

The materials for the learning task in this second practice should be reduced to simple, straightforward, and short applications of the strategy to which the strategy is clearly applicable. After the learners have each had an opportunity to practice, the instructor may provide group feedback (through demonstration), learner demonstration, or attention to specific aspects of the strategy with which the learners displayed difficulties. This feedback may involve reviewing any artifacts of the strategy (such as notes) as good and poor models of the outcomes of strategy application. The learners can be encouraged to contribute their observations acquired during the dyad practice to this feedback.

Process Information

Focus Attention

Employ Learning Strategies

If the strategy is complex and was broken up into a part-whole presentation, the next event would be to present the next part of the strategy following steps previously described through each of the individual parts, and then through the entire strategy.

Following this complete part-whole presentation or instruction on the entire simple strategy, the next presentation of information should be an instructor's (or other model's) think-aloud demonstration of the strategy with more complex and naturalistic tasks and materials. There should also be a presentation with tasks and materials that do not require the strategy at all.

With these demonstrations the entire metacognitive sequence, from assessing the task to evaluating the success of the strategy use and ''fix-up'' techniques, should be followed.

Practice

Evaluate Feedback

Here, perhaps in dyads again, the learners should be provided the opportunity to practice the strategy on more naturalistic, complex materials across a variety of contents and tasks. The practice should also include some tasks to which the newly acquired strategy is not applicable in order for the learners to practice this decision point in the metacognitive process. This practice may extend across several days, or even weeks, depending upon the scope of the application of the strategy, the time each application takes, the amount of interchange among dyads, and the complexity of the feedback. After each application, there should be opportunity for feedback and discussion of the strategy.

Conclusion

Summarize and Review

Transfer Knowledge

This event is perhaps the most critical to the development of the executive control and metacognition processes. This event can extend over many months or even years. As learners acquire other learning strategies and the contexts in which they should be used, the learners should be encouraged to consider whether previously learned strategies are viable alternatives to the newly learned strategy, or whether the new strategy is useful in learning situations that are unique.

In addition, the newly learned strategy may be moved from a detached strategy to an embedded strategy by the instructor's prompting or the use of the checklist or flowchart detailing the strategy. All instructors that interact with the learners, whether they explicitly teach the strategy or not, should be skilled in the strategies being taught and aware of the schedule upon which the strategies are taught so that they can explicitly and consciously prompt the learners to employ the strategies appropriately. The instruction should explicitly review how the learners may monitor and evaluate the effectiveness of the strategy use. It should suggest modifications of the strategy that may be appropriate when the strategy does not seem to be effective. Gradually, the instructor and external prompts should be "faded" so that the learners are depending upon their own cognitive processes to evoke and employ the strategy. When there is evidence that the learners are not using the appropriate strategies, the strategy should again be "detached" and reviewed. This event should be done carefully and conscientiously, even to the point of being organized into a curricular scope and sequence. This event is critical to the success of strategy and metacognitive development.

Assess Performance

Feedback

Remediation

The ideal assessment of the learners' ability to apply the strategy would be individual assessments of the learners' think-aloud protocols by the instructor or other skilled strategy users. However, realistically, the use of the strategy may require assessment at a less direct level of evaluation, such as evaluation of the concrete artifacts of the strategy use or learners' evaluation and suggestions for a videotape of a learner applying the strategy. This assessment should be ongoing and may be included in the teaching of subsequent strategies (by including the strategy and tasks to which it is appropriate as the nonexamples for the new strategies). Feedback might include the following: (1) whether the strategy was applied to appropriate learning tasks, (2) whether the strategy was applied correctly, and (3) whether appropriate monitoring of strategy use and adaptation to problems was used.

*E*xample Cognitive Strategy Lesson

The following example of strategy instruction was developed to teach a note-taking technique that involves the use of graphic organizers representing typical text structures found in expository prose (e.g., chronology, cause-effect, problem-solution). The instruction is intended for high school students, and it is to be used in content area classes such as English or social studies. Although it is especially beneficial for low-ability students, we have found that average and above-average students also feel that this note-taking strategy facilitates comprehension and retention of content area reading materials. Prior to this instruction, the students have already learned to recognize the major types of text structure and their graphic representations; students are now learning the strategy that employs these structures. The instructional procedure involves the following steps.

Introduction

Deploy Attention

Establish Instructional Purpose

Arouse Interest and Motivation

The instructor assigns a naturalistic reading assignment. Students are asked to read and study the assigned section as they normally would. After students have completed the assignment, the teacher leads a discussion of the techniques that they employed and the relative success or lack of success of the strategies. The objective of the lesson—learning a note-taking strategy—is presented.

The teacher and students discuss the purposes for taking notes. Students are encouraged to discuss note-taking techniques and problems that they have in taking notes. The teacher points out that many students have difficulties taking notes, such as trouble in deciding what to include or trouble in organizing notes. Students are told that they will be learning a strategy that may help them when taking notes.

The teacher points out to the learners that students frequently think that merely trying hard will lead to success. She emphasizes that effort does promote success, but that success in learning also requires the use of appropriate strategies.

Body

Review Relevant Prior Knowledge

The teacher reviews the content structures and their graphical representations that students learned to recognize in prior lessons. The structures include time-order, comparison-contrast, problem-solution, problem-solution-results, cause-effect, description, and definition-example.

Process Information and Examples

Focus Attention

Employ Learning Strategies

The teacher points out that the strategy of read-think-aloud is appropriate for expository reading assignments. (The teacher should review the concept "expository" with examples as required.) He also points out that this strategy is most appropriate when the learning task is to "understand" main ideas and interrelationships of ideas, rather than to recall isolated facts. The teacher then discusses the utility of this strategy for taking notes over written passages and well-organized and overviewed lectures. Students are also told that this strategy can be used for recopying less-structured lecture notes. In addition, the fact that this strategy requires time is emphasized. The teacher compares this strategy to the known strategy of note taking—outlining—and discusses the types of assignments and purposes for which the new strategy and the outlining strategy are each appropriate.

The learners view a video in which a model (a student who is approximately their age) demonstrates the use of the entire note-taking strategy, thinking aloud all the cognitive steps in the strategy, including determining that this particular strategy is appropriate to the task. The steps in the strategy are listed and displayed for later reference:

1. Determine that the task requires fitting ideas together and understanding the whole, rather than the recall of isolated facts.
2. Determine that the passage is expository.
3. Skim the passage to determine its overarching structure.
4. Represent this structure in a graphic on the notes page and fill in the main ideas for this structure.
5. Read the passage carefully, determining the underlying structures, representing these structures graphically, and filling in key words to explain these ideas.
6. Check comprehension of how ideas in the passage relate to one another.
7. If comprehension is spotty, scan back through the passage to find key connecting ideas, and then repair notes.

Practice

Evaluate Feedback

The teacher provides learners with example passages in which students must determine whether the strategy is appropriate to use. They should substantiate their answers by stating whether recall and understanding of main ideas or individual details are required. Feedback is provided regarding the correctness of students' responses; if errors occur, an explanation of appropriateness is provided.

Process Information and Examples

Focus Attention

Employ Strategies

The learners view a videotape of a student using an explicitly structured passage from a content area textbook, approximately five to ten paragraphs in length. The student models the note-taking strategy using a read-think-aloud procedure (Flower & Hayes, 1981). The student states a purpose for reading the passage, scans the passage, and comments upon the overarching structure when it becomes evident. Then the student in the videotape uses the structure to predict subsequent content and rectify misconceptions within predictions as she encounters new information. The student continuously scans back and forward to check on ideas that support the structure. After reading in this manner, the student in the videotape creates a structure-based graphic organizer, filling in main ideas and detail information, fleshing out the graphic summary by referring back to the text, and adding pictorial cues to represent main idea or important detail information. When filling in the organizer, where possible, the student paraphrases rather than using verbatim wording from the text.

Practice

Evaluate Feedback

The learners are provided with one explicitly structured and one implicitly structured three-to-five paragraph expository passage. They are then asked to break up into pairs and practice the note-taking strategy using the read-think-aloud procedure, starting with the explicitly cued passage. One student in each pair should read the passage aloud and take notes, describing his mental processes orally. The other student should provide feedback and encouragement. Then students should switch roles and work with the implicitly cued passage.

Process Information

Focus Attention

Employ Learning Strategies

The instructor should introduce a chapter-long segment of expository material that has explicitly cued, clear combinations of structures. It may be necessary to revise existing materials to have such a clear-cut example for this learning experience. The instructor can model the note-taking strategy using the read-think-aloud technique. The instructor should underline or create marginal notes to highlight the structure. This process should generate a graphic organizer that embodies the combinations of structures included in the chapter. The instructor can point out that there is no single correct form of organizer but that the organizer that is developed should present the top-level structure as well as the other structures used in the passage.

Practice

Evaluate Feedback

The students should be provided with chapter-length, explicitly cued and clearly structured expository material that they have not encountered previously. In pairs, they should use the note-taking strategy to generate a graphic organizer. The instructor should collect and review structured notes that the learners produced. The instructor can choose two or three sets of notes to discuss and evaluate in a subsequent lesson. In the discussion, the instructor provides feedback on the selection of structures, layout on page, selection of main ideas, and details included on the organizer. Next, the

learners should complete a similar activity independently.

Conclusion

Summarize and Review

The learners should review the steps involved in applying the strategy. The emphasis should be on understanding the strategy rather than memorizing verbatim the steps in the strategy. Learners should explain how each step leads naturally into the next. The learners should also review the occasions for which the strategy is appropriate and how to monitor the effectiveness of the strategy.

Transfer Learning

One way to promote transfer is for the instructor (or another model) to demonstrate the read-think-aloud procedure using the note-taking strategy with implicitly structured and poorly organized materials. The learners should be presented with alternative structures that might be used in creating graphic organizers, and they should discuss how selection of alternate structures yields emphasis on different points. Then the learners can practice the note-taking strategy with implicitly organized and poorly organized chapter-length materials.

Another way to promote retention is to discuss how the level of detail of the content in the notes and the amount of elaboration within notes may vary depending upon the purpose for reading. The instruction can present two sets of structured notes created over a chapter that students read earlier. One set should include a high level of detail and be more verbatim from the text, reflecting the type of notes suitable when students are preparing for an exam composed of multiple-choice and short-answer types of questions. The second set should show an emphasis on main ideas and the integration of information with prior knowledge (such as a comparison-contrast structure, comparing new information in the text to information obtained in other sources). The second set of notes would be more appropriate for preparation for class discussions and essay-type exams.

Remotivate and Close

The lesson should conclude with a restatement of why the strategy is important and an emphasis upon the significance of both effort and selecting the appropriate strategies in learning.

Assess Performance

The teacher should prepare a test situation in which the students are to use the read-think-aloud procedure. Chapter-length expository material would most appropriately evaluate their ability to transfer the strategy to natural settings. This time students are asked to complete the task using the strategy on an individual basis. The notes can be collected and reviewed for accuracy. The assessment may also include observation as to how students are performing. If appropriate, this strategy could be tested using videotaped or audiotaped sessions.

Impediments to Strategy Use

As noted earlier, throughout the chapters on instructional strategies we have included in our expanded instructional events learning strategies that would be appropriate for learners to employ while engaged in a lesson for a particular kind of learning outcome. Within a lesson learners may be prompted with a greater or lesser degree of directness to employ these strategies. Evidence from research suggests that many learners do not employ cognitive strategies spontaneously. There are factors that inhibit the use of strategies. We will describe these factors and how they may influence strategy use.

1. *Low skill in strategy use.* As we have stated throughout this chapter, instruction on cognitive strategies must be provided, most learners do not "discover" the most effective strategies, and most do not induce metacognitive information regarding the application of the strategy. For example, one of the greatest problems in strategy application is transfer. Learners tend to have difficulty in recognizing similarities between a current situation and situations in which strategy was learned. Consequently, when confronted with a new learning task, they may have an appropriate strategy in their repertoire but not recognize its usefulness. We have suggested direct instruction and practice in identifying critical characteristics of a learning task that suggest a particular learning strategy. If attention is given

to this aspect of strategy training, transfer should be enhanced.

2. *Low motivation.* Although strategy use can become automatic, it generally requires the learner's conscious, willful effort. Employment of strategies is a very private matter. It often presents no observable evidence of activity. Therefore, strategy use may not be subject to social reinforcement by teachers or fellow students. Internal motivation to achieve the learning task must consequently be high in order for learners to engage in what they may perceive as "extra" effort of applying strategies. In order to encourage such motivation, designers should consider employing tactics that encourage attention, relevancy, confidence, and satisfaction.

3. *Learners' feelings of self-efficacy are low, and attributions of success are external.* For learners to use cognitive strategies, they must believe that the additional effort they expend in using the strategy will pay off. This factor is closely related to motivation, but it is of sufficient importance and distinction for us to mention it separately. If learners tend to perceive themselves as poor learners and/or if they ascribe extreme success or failure in learning to factors external to themselves (external locus of control), then they may tend to believe that the effort required for cognitive strategy use is pointless. Learners who employ strategies tend to be more successful and, consequently, tend to acquire greater self-esteem. They also tend to become more internal regarding their learning attributions. Learners who are impeded by feelings of low self-efficacy or external attributions may need more prompting to employ strategies. They may also benefit from more explicit and overt reward systems. They should be encouraged to note the causative relationship between their employment of strategies and their success with a learning task. A classroom situation that encourages learners to externalize their cognitions and that provides social reinforcement for cognitions that employ appropriate strategies should promote strategy use by learners with feelings of low self-efficacy or external attributions.

4. *Learners' lack of awareness of their own memory and processing characteristics.* Learners

must be sufficiently aware of their own cognitive capabilities to determine when strategy use will be needed. They must be able to reflect on their own cognitions and predict when a learning task or learning context will require the additional support of a strategy. They must be able to monitor their own learning and determine when strategic behavior must be employed. This type of metacognitive knowledge takes time, both in terms of purposeful instructional attention to it (such as with a teacher modeling prediction and monitoring) and in terms of the years of experience and practice required to become learners who are aware of their own metacognition.

5. *Lack of knowledge of task characteristics.* In order for learners to assess the match between (1) their memory and processing characteristics and (2) the learning task, they must be aware of the learning task, and they must be able to assess the cognitive demands of the learning task. We alluded to this factor when we discussed informing learners as to the purpose of instruction within a lesson. If learners are uninformed as to what they are to learn and to what degree or depth they must learn, they will have difficulty in ascertaining whether strategies must be engaged and which strategies are appropriate. In addition to having a knowledge of instructional goals, learners must be able to analyze a goal in terms of its cognitive demands. In our chapters on each of the types of learning outcomes, we have tried to outline for you what appears to be the required cognitions, and we have related them to the characteristics of the instructional strategy. In a similar, although perhaps simplified fashion, as part of describing the learning task the instruction may suggest the type and depth of cognitive activity that is required for successful acquisition of the learning goal.

6. *Devoting/allocating insufficient time.* The dual-level processing that is required in order to employ strategies and process new content may take more time than more superficial processing of content. (Of course this time-on-task variable is often a confounding factor in studies on the efficacy of cognitive strategies.) Learners must be provided with enough time to engage strategies and reflect on their cognitions. The newer the strategy is for learners, the more time that must be allocated to a lesson in which they will be encouraged to use it. This demand for time often leads designers, particularly in training situations, toward supplanting more of the processing in order to proceed through the instruction more rapidly. Of course, as we discussed in Chapter 6, this supplantation can lead to more superficial processing and ultimately, less learning.

7. *Insufficient content knowledge.* In order to make sense out of the learning task and thereby determine the cognitive demands of the task and the consequent appropriate strategies, the learners must have some prior content knowledge. In addition, the more foreign the content is, the more cognitive capacity that must be allocated to comprehending the instruction; this also means that there will be less available capacity for employing the strategy. Therefore, in initial contacts with new content, if the designer expects for the learners to engage cognitive strategies, then much additional time and support must be set aside for the instruction. Or, the designer might plan more supplantive instruction as learners are encountering initial concepts and principles and more generative instruction later on, capitalizing on cognitive strategies that have been learned.

When analyzing the task, the learners, and the context during the process of designing the instructional strategy, the designer should carefully examine whether any of these inhibiting factors is present. If these factors are present, the designer may devise a method to ameliorate them or may determine to facilitate the use of the strategies with more direct prompting or supplant the particular processing with more complete and direct instruction.

Summary

The following table highlights the chapter's key points in a summary frame.

Conditions of Learning by Event for Cognitive Strategy Learning

Introduction	Deploy attention. Arouse interest and motivation. Establish instructional purpose.	• Experience task that requires the strategy. • Discuss role of strategic thinking in learning.
	Preview lesson.	• Demonstrate entire strategy model.
Body	Recall prior knowledge.	• Recall previously learned strategies or tasks that seem similar.
	Process information.	• Experience situations for which application of the strategy is appropriate and inappropriate. • Model demonstrates strategy with think-aloud procedure.
	Focus attention.	• Critical attributes of tasks to which strategy is appropriate. • Cues that indicate successful application of strategy.
	Employ learning strategies.	• Thinking aloud about cognition and monitoring effects of the strategy.
	Practice.	• Identify contexts/tasks to which strategy is appropriate and explain why. • Apply strategy to increasingly difficult tasks. • Reciprocal practice.
	Evaluate feedback.	• Peer evaluation. • Group feedback—model appropriate application and examine artifacts of strategy use.
Conclusion	Summarize and review.	• Summarize steps and review tasks to which the strategy is appropriate.
	Transfer knowledge.	• Move from detached to embedded with prompts, and then withdraw prompts. • Compare strategy to others learned later.
	Remotivate and close.	• Importance of effort coupled with strategy use.
Assessment	Assess performance.	• Directly observe. • Examine artifacts of strategy use.
	Feedback and remediation.	• Was appropriate strategy selected? • Was strategy applied correctly? • Was success of strategy monitored, and were ''fix up'' strategies employed?

Extended Example

This strategy was proposed to be taught as an embedded strategy within the Extended Example in the problem-solving chapter. This lesson suggested that an effective strategy for facilitating learners' reconceptualization of photography principles was the use of a conceptual "networking" strategy (Dansereau, Collins, McDonald, Holley, Garland, Diekhoff, & Evans, 1979). Although they suggest the strategy for initial encounters with a text-based material, we suggest its use here as a method for reorganizing a large body of knowledge that has been learned in smaller units.

Objective: While or after studying a body of conceptual knowledge, learners can visually indicate the relationships of concepts within the body of knowledge by presenting them in a "network."

Introduction

Deploy Attention

Establish Purpose

Promote Motivation and Interest

The teacher points out to students that they have been learning concepts and principles in units rather than considering them as they work together. The teacher also presents the following list of concepts and asks students to suggest how they would go about relating the concepts together.

Light level	Object shapes
Aperture	Film
Focus	Angle of view
Light angle	Textures
F-stops	Lenses
Depth of field	Perspective
Contrast	
Shutter	
Composition	
Atmosphere	
Shutter speeds	
Subject	
Movement	
Light meters	
Field of view	

The teacher then does the following:

- Asks learners how they feel when confronted with such a task.
- Asks learners to describe some of the approaches that they would use and then asks students to comment on the efficacy of the strategies.
- Considers students' suggestions and comments on those strategies that would be productive.
- Comments that many students have a tendency to relate the ideas linearly in outlines.
- Points out the limitations of linear representations: They can take a lot of effort, which may not be the best use of time.

Preview Lesson

In the lesson preview, the teacher demonstrates the networking technique. She decides to use a content area other than photography for this demonstration. She tells the students that she had recently attended a seminar in computer applications in education. At the seminar, a lot of content was presented in a linear way without any overarching organization. She points out that she wants to find a way to link these ideas about computer use together to help make them meaningful and help her see relationships among main ideas that were presented linearly. So, she decided to use a "networking" strategy with this material. She uses a think-aloud technique to demonstrate the thought processes necessary to use this strategy. She thinks aloud that the three main areas of computer applications in education are the following: (1) using the computer as a productivity tool, (2) using the computer to teach something, and (3) programming.

Using the blackboard as her notepaper, the teacher then demonstrates how she uses these three organizing ideas to organize hierarchically many concepts presented in the seminar. She refers to her notes from the seminar and relates ideas within each category together via links. She marks these relational lines with letters to indicate the type of relationships among ideas. Then she shows relationships among concepts between categories, such as using word processing (a productivity tool) as a method for teaching writing skills. She conjectures about some relationships among ideas and puts question marks beside these lines to indicate a need to seek further information.

The teacher points out that this strategy can be used to relate the concepts in the photography course and other learning tasks.

Body

Review Relevant Prior Knowledge

The teacher relates the strategy to other strategies that students have used, such as outlining or using text structures. She encourages the learners to point out the similarities and differences in the strategies in terms of applicability, efficiency, and actual procedure.

Process Information

The teacher gives an example of a situation for which the new strategy is appropriate and a situation in which the strategy would not be appropriate, such as needing to recall detail information. The teacher then asks the students to provide their own examples and nonexamples and helps the students determine which examples are appropriate for the strategy and which are not.

Focus Attention

The teacher asks the students to explain why they selected situations as examples or nonexamples and helps them focus on the critical characteristics of a situation that make this strategy useful (e.g., many concepts learned over time, the need to relate main ideas rather than details, and so on).

Employ Learning Strategies

The students are encouraged to recognize the need to identify the task characteristics, their limitations and strengths as students, and the benefits of the strategy when determining which strategy is appropriate. They are encouraged to evaluate their own characteristics (both cognitive and affective) in dealing with large volumes of information. The teacher suggests ways of determining what the goal of a learning task is and whether it fits with this strategy.

Practice

The teacher presents the learners with descriptions of situations that identify the task and learner char-

acteristics, and learners are asked to identify whether the networking strategy would be effective and to justify their answers.

Evaluate Feedback

Students give their answers and justifications. The teacher confirms those conclusions that are correct and provides descriptions of the critical characteristics of the situation that call for the networking strategy.

Body

Review Relevant Prior Knowledge

The teacher uses the example of the taxonomy of living things as they are organized in a biology class to show how ideas can be related together. She points out that the relationships presented in this taxonomy can be described by using the phrase *type of* (e.g., a mammal is a *type of* vertebrate).

Process Information

The teacher presents the information that the three major types of relationships among ideas are hierarchies, chains, and clusters. Then she shows examples of each kind of relationship. Then she subdivides each major type into sub-types (Dansereau et al., 1984):

- Hierarchy: Part of (P), Type of (T), Example of (Ex)
- Chain: Leads to (L)
- Cluster: Characteristic (C), Evidence (E), Analogy (A)

She gives examples of each relationship, draws a line between the two concepts, and uses the identifying letter to label the line.

Employ Learning Strategies

The learners create their own examples of each kind of relationship and point out the critical features of each example that make it that type of relationship. The learners create their own job aid to help them to remember the relationships.

Practice

The teacher gives the learners pairs of concepts and asks them to relate them with the appropriate labeled relationship.

Evaluate Feedback

The learners consider the correct answers and ask for clarification of any labels that they don't understand.

Process Information

The teacher demonstrates using the strategy to relate a list of concepts from a study of adult human development. She demonstrates on a transparency how she physically represents and relates the ideas with words, lines, and letter labels. She thinks aloud the task requirements and her thought processes as she relates the concepts. She refers to notes when it is appropriate. She mulls over what type of relationships ideas have. She restates the concepts so that they can grammatically and semantically relate to other ideas.

Employ Learning Strategies

Learners are encouraged to ask for explanations as to why the teacher chose to represent ideas in a certain way. The teacher points out to students that there are many ways to represent the relationships of concepts. She tells them that there is no one "correct" representation.

Practice

Learners are divided into pairs and given the assignment to relate the concepts presented at the first of the class (see list of concepts on page 291) using the networking strategy. The purpose of the task is to see the relationships among and between the major photography units that they have studied. They are given markers, note cards with the concepts listed on them, and blank note cards. They are also given cards with the three organizing illustrations in Figure 11.1 to use as principle organizing concepts. The students are encouraged to modify the concept statements to make them relate semantically and grammatically. They are reminded to use their written job aids in completing the task. They are reminded that there is no one "correct" answer.

Evaluate Feedback

The teacher collects the completed networks. She identifies appropriately completed networks and duplicates them to show students during the next class. She identifies common errors and prepares examples of these errors to show during the feedback session.

Conclusion

Summarize and Review

The teacher shows a videotape of an age-appropriate student modeling the complete strategy, including deciding whether the strategy is appropriate.

Transfer Knowledge

The teacher points out that this strategy can also be used as a note-taking strategy to organize information as it is first encountered. She encourages students to think of other ways that the strategy might be used, such as planning the organization of a writing project or analyzing a paper that they have written to determine which relationships of ideas are not clear.

Students are encouraged to apply the strategy, and the strategy is reviewed at intervals in later classes.

Remotivate and Close

Students are encouraged to point out the utility of the strategy. The teacher emphasizes that effort alone cannot lead to successful learning but that effort must be accompanied by judicious choices and the application of strategies. The teacher points out that the more often the strategy is used, the easier and less time-consuming the strategy use becomes.

Assess Performance

After students have had an opportunity to practice the strategy for several months, they are given an exercise that requires them to relate ideas from the previously studied unit using the networking strategy. The written networks are collected.

Evaluate Feedback and Remediation

The teacher examines the networks and evaluates the networks in two ways: (1) Is the content accurately reflected? and (2) Has the strategy been appropriately applied? An error related to the first question will indicate a need for remediation in the content. An error related to the second question will indicate a need to remediate use of the strategy.

Light level	Aperture	Focus
Light angle	F-stops	Depth of field
Contrast	Shutter	Composition
Atmosphere	Shutter speeds	Subject
Movement	Light meters	Field of view
Object shapes	Film	Angle of view
Textures	Lenses	Perspective

The subject	The camera	The photo

Figure 11.1: Three Organizing Illustrations

Readings and References

Bandura, A. (1977). *Social learning theory.* Englewood Cliffs, NJ: Prentice-Hall.

Battig, W. F. (1979). Are the important ''individual differences'' between or within individuals? *Journal of Research in Personality, 13,* 546–558.

Brown, A. L. (1978). Knowing when, where, and how to remember: A problem of metacognition. In R. Glaser (Ed.), *Advances in instructional psychology (Volume 1).* Hillsdale, NJ: Lawrence Erlbaum Associates, Inc.

Brown, A. L., Campione, J. C., & Day, J. D. (1981). Learning to learn: On training students to learn from text. *Educational Researcher, 10,* 12–14.

Brown, A. L., & Smiley, S. S. (1978). The development of strategies for studying texts. *Child Development, 49,* 1076–1088.

Covington, M. C., Crutchfield, R. S., Davies, L. B., and Olton, R. M. (1974). *The productive thinking program: A course in learning to think.* Columbus, OH: Merrill.

Dansereau, D. (1978). The development of a learning strategy curriculum. In H. F. O'Neil (Ed.), *Learning strategies.* New York: Academic Press.

Dansereau, D. (1985). Learning strategy research. In J. W. Segal, S. F. Chipman, and R. Glaser (Eds.), *Thinking and learning skills (Volume 1)*. Hillsdale, NJ: Lawrence Erlbaum Associates, Inc.

Dansereau, D. F., Collins, K. W., McDonald, B. A., Holley, C. D., Garland, J., Diekhoff, G., & Evans, S. H. (1979). Development and evaluation of a learning strategy training program. *Journal of Educational Psychology, 71* (1), 64–73.

Dansereau, D. F., McDonald, B. A., Collins, K. W., Garland, J., Holley, C. D., Diekhoff, G. M., & Evans, S. H. (1979). Evaluation of a learning strategy system. In H. F. O'Neil and C. D. Spielberger (Eds), *Cognitive and affective learning strategies* (pp. 3–45). New York: Academic Press.

Davidson, G. V. (1988, January). *Training children to use learning strategies to improve their ability to attain concepts.* Paper presented to the Association for Educational and Communications Technology, New Orleans.

Davidson, G. V. & Smith, P. L. (1990). Instructional design considerations for learning strategies instruction. *International Journal of Instructional Media, 17*(3), 227–243.

de Bono, E. (1983). *CoRT thinking: Notes.* Oxford: Pergamon Press.

Derry, S. J. & Murphy, D. A. (1986). Systems that train learning ability. *Review of Educational Research, 56,* 1–39.

Deshler, D. D., Alley, G. R., Warner, M. M., & Schumaker, J. B. (1981). Instructional practices for promoting skill acquisition and generalization in severely learning disabled adolescents. *Learning Disabilities Quarterly, 4,* 415–421.

Deshler, D. D., Warner, M. M., Schumaker, J. S., & Alley, G. R. (1983). Learning strategies intervention model: Key components and current status. In J. McKinney & L. Feagans (Eds.), *Current topics in learning disabilities.* New York: Ablex Publishing Corporation.

Feuerstein, R., Rand, Y., Hoffman, M., & Miller, R. (1980). *Instrumental enrichment.* Baltimore: University Park Press.

Flavell, J. H. (1977). *Cognitive development.* Englewood Cliffs, NJ: Prentice-Hall.

Flavell, J. H. & Wellman, H. M. (1977). Metamemory. In R. V. Kail & J. W. Hagen (Eds.), *Perspectives on the development of memory and cognition.* Hillsdale, NJ: Lawrence Erlbaum Associates, Inc.

Flower, L., & Hayes, J. R. (1981). A cognitive process theory of writing. *College Composition and Communication, 32,* 365–387.

Gagné, E. (1985) *Cognitive psychology and school learning.* Boston: Little, Brown & Company.

Gagné, R. M., (1985). *The conditions of learning* (4th ed.). New York: Holt, Rinehart, and Winston.

Gagné, R. M. & Driscoll, M. A. (1988). *The essentials of learning for instruction.* New York: Holt, Rinehart, and Winston.

Garner, R. (1990). When children and adults do not use learning strategies: Toward a theory of settings. *Review of Educational Research, 60* (4), 517–530.

Garner, R., & Alexander, P. A. (1989). Metacognition: Answered and unanswered questions. *Educational Psychologist, 24*(2), 143–158.

Gordon, W. J. (1961). *Synectics: The development of creative capacity.* New York: Harper & Row.

Higbee, K. L. (1977). *Your memory: How it works and how to improve it.* Englewood Cliffs, NJ: Prentice-Hall.

Holley, C. D., & Dansereau, D. F. (1984). Networking: The technique and empirical evidence. In C. D. Holley and D. F. Dansereau (Eds), *Spatial learning strategies: Techniques, applications, and related issues* (pp. 81–108). Orlando, FL: Academic Press.

Jonassen, D. H. (1985). Learning strategies: A new educational technology. *Programmed Learning and Educational Technology Journal, 22*(1), 25–34.

Joyce, B., & Weil, M. (1986). *Models of teaching* (3rd ed.). Englewood Cliffs, NJ: Prentice-Hall.

Levin, J. R. (1986). Four cognitive principles of learning-strategy instruction. *Educational Psychologist, 21*(1,2), 3–18.

Mayer, R. E. (1980). Elaboration techniques that increase the meaningfulness of technical text: An experimental test of the learning strategy hypotheses. *Journal of Educational Psychology, 72,* 770–784.

McCombs, B. L. (1981–82). Transitioning learning strategies research into practice: Focus on the student in technical training. *Journal of Instructional Development, 5*(2), 10–21.

McCombs, B. L. (1984). Processes and skills underlying continuing intrinsic motivation to learn: Toward a definition of motivational skills training interventions. *Educational Psychologist, 19*, 199–218.

McCombs, B. L., & Marzano, R. J. (1990). Putting the self in self-regulated learning: The self as agent in integrating will and skill. *Educational Psychologist, 25*(1), 51–70.

Meichenbaum, D. M. (1977). *Cognitive behavior modification*. New York: Plenum.

Newell, A. (1980). One final word. In D. T. Tuma & F. Reif (Eds.), *Problem solving and education*. Hillsdale, NJ: Erlbaum.

Newby, T. J., & Stepich, D. A. (1990). Teaching cognitive strategies. *Performance and Instruction, 29*(1), 44–45.

Newell, A., & Simon, H. A. (1975). *Human problem solving*. Englewood Cliffs, NJ: Prentice-Hall.

Norman, D. A. (1980). Cognitive engineering and education. In D. T. Tuma & F. Reif (Eds.), *Problem solving and education*. Hillsdale, NJ: Lawrence Erlbaum Associates, Inc.

Polson, P. G., & Jeffries, R. (1985). Instruction in general problem-solving skills: An analysis of four approaches. In J. W. Segal, S. F. Chipman, & R. Glaser, (Eds.), *Thinking and learning skills, vol. 1: Relating instruction to research*. Hillsdale, NJ: Erlbaum.

Polya, G. (1957). *How to solve it* (2nd ed.). Garden City, NJ: Doubleday Archer.

Pressley, M., Snyder, B. L., & Cargilia-Bull, T. (1987). In S. M. Cormier & J. D. Hagman (Eds.), *Transfer of learning*. San Diego: Academic Press.

Pressley, M., Borowski, J. G., & Schneider, W. (1987). Cognitive strategies: Good strategy users coordinate metacognition and knowledge. In R. Vasta & G. Whitehurst (Eds.), *Annals of child development (volume 4)*. Greenwich, CT: JAI Press.

Rigney, L. B. (1978). Learning strategies: A theoretical perspective. In H. F. O'Neil (Ed.), *Learning strategies*. New York: Academic Press.

Rigney, L. B. (1980). Cognitive learning strategies and dualities in information processing. In R. E. Snow, P. Federico, & W. E. Montague (Eds.), *Aptitude, learning and instruction (volume 1)*. Hillsdale, NJ: Lawrence Erlbaum Associates, Inc.

Rohwer, W. D. (1980). An elaborative conception of learner differences. In R. E. Snow, P. A. Federico, & W. E. Montague (Eds.), *Aptitude, learning and instruction (volume 2)*. Hillsdale, NJ: Lawrence Erlbaum Associates, Inc.

Ross, S. M., & Rakow, E. A. (1982). Adaptive instructional strategies for teaching rules in mathematics. *Educational and Communication Technology Journal, 30*, 67–74.

Salomon, G., & Perkins, D. N. (1989). Rocky roads to transfer: Rethinking mechanisms of a neglected phenomenon. *Educational Psychologist, 24*(2), 113–142.

Schmitt, M. C., & Newby, T. J. (1986). Metacognition: Relevance to instructional design. *Journal of Instructional Development, 9*(2), 29–33.

Schunk, D. H. (1990). Goal setting and self-efficacy during self-regulated learning. *Educational Psychologist, 25*(1), 71–86.

Siegler, R. S. & Jenkins, E. (1989). *How children discover new strategies*. Hillsdale, NJ: Lawrence Erlbaum.

Singer, R. N., & Gerson, R. F. (1979). Learning strategies, cognitive processes, and motor learning. In H. F. O'Neil & C. D. Spielberger (Eds.), *Cognitive and affective learning strategies*. New York: Academic Press.

Smith, P. L., & Friend, M. (1987). Training LD students in a strategy for using test structure to aid recall. *Learning Disabilities, 2*, 338–344.

Stein, M. I. (1974). *Stimulating creativity, volume 1: Individual procedures*. New York: Academic Press.

Stein, M. I. (1975). *Stimulating creativity, volume 2: Group procedures*. New York: Academic Press.

Sternberg, R. J. (1986). Intelligence, wisdom, and creativity: Three is better than one. *Educational Psychologist, 21*(3), 175–190.

Taylor, I. A., & Getzels, J. W. (1975). *Perspectives in creativity*. Chicago: Aldine Publishing Co.

Tennyson, R. D. (1981). Use of adaptive information for advisement in learning concepts and rules using computer-assisted instruction. *American Educational Research Journal, 73,* 326–334.

Thomas, J. W., & Rohwer, W. D., Jr. (1986). Academic studying: The role of learning strategies. *Educational Psychologist, 21*(1,2), 19–42.

Torgesen, J. K. (1979). Factors related to poor performance on memory tasks in reading disabled children. *Learning Disability Quarterly, 2,* 17–23.

Torrance, E. P. (1979). *The search for satori & creativity.* Buffalo, NY: Creative Education Foundation.

Weinstein, C. E. (1978). Elaboration skills as a learning strategy. In H. F. O'Neil (Ed.), *Learning strategies.* New York: Academic Press.

Weinstein, C. E. (1981). Learning strategies: The metacurriculum. *Journal of Developmental and Remedial Education, 5,* 6–10.

Weinstein, C. E. (1982). Training students to use elaboration learning strategies. *Contemporary Educational Psychology, 7,* 301–311.

Weinstein, C. E. & Mayer, R. E. (1986). The teaching of learning strategies. In M. C. Wittrock (Ed.), *Handbook of research on teaching* (3rd ed.). New York: Macmillan.

Weinstein, C. E. & Underwood, V. L. (1985). Learning strategies: The how of learning. In J. Segal, S. Chipman, & R. Glaser (Eds.), *Learning and thinking skills (volume 1).* Hillsdale, NJ: Lawrence Erlbaum Associates, Inc.

Winn, W. (1983, April). *Learning strategies and adaptive instruction.* Paper presented at the meeting of the American Educational Research Association, Montreal.

Winn, W. (1986, February). *Emerging trends in educational technology research.* Paper presented at the meeting of the Association of Educational and Communications Technology, Las Vegas.

Zimmerman, B. J. (1990). Self-regulated learning and academic achievement: An overview. *Educational Psychologist, 25*(1), 2–18.

Zimmerman, B. J., & Schunk, D. H. (Eds.). (1989). *Self-regulated learning and academic achievement: Theory, research, and practice.* New York: Springer-Verlag.

Strategies for Attitude Change, Motivation, and Interest

twelve

Chapter Objectives

At the conclusion of this chapter you should be able to do the following:

- Translate broad goals that involve affective learnings into specific affective objectives that can be used in designing instruction for their achievement.

- Given an affective goal, devise a hierarchy of affective objectives related to it.

- Given an attitude objective, design a strategy plan for that objective.

- Relate three instructional conditions (role model, role playing, and reinforcement) to the learning components to which they lead.

- Describe techniques to promote interest and motivation in lessons for all learning outcome types.

- Given an instructional activity or instructor's statement, categorize that activity/statement as to motivational strategy type, attention, relevance, confidence, or satisfaction.

Introduction

In Chapters 7 through 11, we discussed instructional strategies for achieving learning objectives in the cognitive domain, and in Chapter 13 we will address instructional strategies for objectives in the psychomotor domain. This chapter is concerned with the affective domain. The affective domain has been relatively neglected over the years in educational practice. We hope to redress the balance by devoting this chapter to (1) instructional strategies for objectives in the affective domain and (2) the affective component of lessons in the cognitive and motor domains.

In the first half of this chapter, we will treat designing instructional strategies for objectives within the affective domain, particularly objectives that have to do with attitude formation or change. In the second half of this chapter, we will look at a body of theory and some specific techniques for enhancing the motivational qualities of the instruction for all domains.

Instruction for Attitude Objectives

Although attitude objectives are not as frequently stated in explicit form as cognitive or even psychomotor objectives, there are times when we want to form or change an attitude. In public education, such objectives are seen in drug education, sex education, health education, and in the implementation of many of the schools' socially derived goals such as cooperating to achieve common goals, democratic values and processes, and so forth. In the exercise at the end of this section, we present public school goals that are attitudinal in nature and illustrative of just how pervasive attitude objectives are in school work, even when they may not be explicitly stated. (Several of these goals are very similar to much of corporate America's training needs and goals.)

In addition to school learning, higher education and training environments have more of their goals involving attitudes than might be anticipated. In something as seemingly cut-and-dried as an engine mechanics unit in an aircraft mechanics course, building appropriate attitudes and dispositions toward work and tasks may be the most difficult and important part of the training design

problem. Likewise, in another training environment—managerial training—attitude objectives form a large portion of the actual intent of training. Many educators and trainers frequently assume, in both education and training settings, that the affective domain is somehow "off limits"—that it cannot be dealt with through instruction. This is not the case. As we will see in this chapter, there are viable instructional strategies to promote attitude formation and change. If you find it difficult to identify affective objectives in the setting with which you are most concerned, look toward the more general goals or mission statements of the organization or agency. A school's broadest goals will, upon close examination, often be almost entirely affective. In translation to specific objectives, due to such factors as tradition and lack of imagination, most designers fail to do justice to needs for development in the affective domain. We hope that this chapter will help you to translate broad goals that involve affective learnings into specific affective objectives that can be used in designing instruction for their achievement.

Exercises A

From the set of goal statements in Figure 12.1, identify those that represent or involve attitude formation or change. The source of these goals is a 1938 statement of educational goals for U.S. public schools from the National Education Association (Educational Policies Commission, 1938). Although these statements appear to us now to be goal statements, their original form was as "objectives."

Instruction for Attitude Change or Formation

In the following pages, we will look at instructional design that has attitude change or formation as its goal. We will discuss how attitudes are learned and the components of attitude learning. Then we will present a framework for attitude learning involving use of a taxonomy of objectives in the affective domain. Next we will look at three

Label	Objective Statement	Label	Objective Statement

The Objectives of Self-realization

_____ The inquiring mind:

_____ Speech:

_____ Reading:

_____ Writing:

_____ Number:

_____ Sight and hearing:

_____ Health knowledge:

_____ Health habits:

_____ Public health:

_____ Recreation:

_____ Intellectual interests:

_____ Esthetic Interests:

_____ Character:

The educated person . . .
has an appetite for learning.

speaks the mother tongue clearly.

reads the mother tongue efficiently.

writes the mother tongue effectively.

solves his problems of counting and calculating.

is skilled in listening and observing.

understands the basic facts concerning health and disease.

protects his own health and that of his dependents.

works to improve the health of the community.

is a participant and spectator in many sports and other pastimes.

has mental resources for the use of leisure.

appreciates beauty.

gives responsible direction to his own life.

The Objectives of Human Relationships

_____ Respect for Humanity:

_____ Friendships:

_____ Cooperation:

_____ Courtesy:

_____ Appreciation of Home:

_____ Conservation of Home:

_____ Homemaking:

_____ Democracy in Home:

The educated person . . .
puts human relationships first.

enjoys a rich, sincere, and varied social life.

can work and play with others.

observes the amenities of social behavior.

appreciates the family as a social institution.

conserves family ideals.

is skilled in homemaking.

maintains democratic family relationships.

The Objectives of Economic Efficiency

_____ Work:

_____ Occupational Information:

_____ Occupational Choice:

_____ Occupational Efficiency:

_____ Occupational Adjustment:

_____ Occupational Appreciation:

_____ Personal Economics:

_____ Consumer Judgment:

_____ Efficiency in Buying:

_____ Consumer Protection:

The educated producer . . .
knows the satisfaction of good workmanship.

understands the requirements and opportunities for various jobs.

has selected his occupation.

succeeds in his chosen profession.

maintains and improves his efficiency.

appreciates the social value of his work.

plans the economics of his own life.

develops standards for guiding his expenditures.

is an informed and skillful buyer.

takes appropriate measures to safeguard his interests.

The Objectives of Civic Responsibility

_____ Social Justice:

_____ Social Activity:

_____ Social Understanding:

_____ Critical Judgement:

_____ Tolerance:

_____ Conservation:

_____ Social Applications of Science:

_____ World Citizenship:

_____ Law Observance:

_____ Economic Literacy:

_____ Political Citizenship:

_____ Devotion to Democracy:

The educated citizen . . .
is sensitive to the disparities in human circumstance.

acts to correct unsatisfactory conditions.

seeks to understand social structures and social processes.

has defenses against propaganda.

respects honest differences of opinion.

has a regard for the nation's resources.

measures scientific advance by its contribution to general welfare.

is a cooperating member of the world community.

respects the law.

is economically literate.

accepts his civic duties.

acts upon an unswerving loyalty to democratic ideas.

**Figure 12.1:** A Set of Educational Goals

Source: Educational Policies Commission (1938), p. 41.

instructional conditions for learning attitudes, and finally we will apply the expanded instructional events to attitude learning as a structure for design of attitude instruction.

Review of Attitude Learning

The basic idea of attitudes is captured in the idea of choosing to do something. When a person has an attitude toward something, the most salient influence that this attitude has on the individual's behavior is on choices that she makes. No matter if the topic is practicing ''safe'' sex, or practicing conservation, or settling arguments nonviolently, or voting, whether we have made an influence on our students' attitudes will be evidenced by what our students *choose to do* with regard to them. Since much of what we actually wish to achieve as a product of instruction is seen in our learners' behavior in matters of what they choose to do (after school or training is completed), one can see that attitude learning is fundamental.

There have been many psychological theories that have dealt with attitude change and formation over the years. Martin and Briggs (1986, pp. 118–138) summarize five of them in their discussion of selected theories of attitude change that have instructional implications:

1. *The Yale Communication and Attitude Change Program.* This is a reinforcement-based approach that stresses, in addition to the use of reinforcement, the necessity to address the cognitive elements of beliefs and opinions.

2. *Festinger's Cognitive Dissonance Theory.* This theory stresses the importance of the cognitive element of dissonance—a tension created by inconsistencies in an individual's beliefs—and the need to reduce that dissonance.

3. *Cognitive Balancing.* This resembles Cognitive Dissonance theory, a theory that involves balancing and accommodation, but here, both affective and cognitive components are employed.

4. *Social Judgement Theory.* This theory describes how attitudes change through a judgment process involving internally held subjective refer-

ence scales of acceptability that people use to judge their own positions or values in contrast to competing values offered by persuasive communications.

5. *Social Learning Theory.* This approach describes attitude change through learning from (a) direct experience (as a consequence of one's own behavior); (b) vicarious experience (through observation of a model), or experience through reading or hearing about; or (c) through emotional associations.

In Fleming and Levie's (1978) text, *Instructional Message Design,* the authors' treatment of attitude instruction is based on a communications perspective. The authors present 69 research-based principles for attitude change through persuasion, organized along the basis of source, message, channel, and receiver variables. Their compilation and discussion of these principles provides a communications and message-design perspective. In Figure 12.2, a summary listing of 22 principles related to message structure in persuasive communications, (adapted from Fleming and Levie) is presented. The structure and delivery of effective persuasive communications is a large topic, beyond the scope of this book. The principles listed in Figure 12.2 may be used as a reminder of persuasion techniques that you have previously learned, or it may stimulate you to further study. In the final analysis, the design of successful attitude instruction can be facilitated by use of persuasive techniques, but their use is not always necessary.

Components of Attitude Learning

Attitudes, even though they are generally ''affective'' in nature, have three components that we can derive from the previous review of attitude learning: cognitive, behavioral, and affective. If, for example, we wanted students to learn the attitude of ''safe driving,'' the students would have more to do than just acquire an affective disposition toward driving safely.

1. The *cognitive component* consists of ''knowing how.'' Before the student can practice any attitudes about safe driving, the student must know how to drive. Although it is reasonable

Sequencing Variables

1. When a communicator wishes to reveal some ''con'' arguments, they should be presented after the ''pro'' arguments if the receiver is not familiar with the ''con'' arguments. When the receiver is familiar with the ''con'' arguments, present and refute them before presenting the ''pro'' arguments.
2. When the receiver has relatively little interest in the issue but may be favorable to your viewpoint, present your conclusion first and use an anticlimactic order in presenting your arguments. When the receiver is involved in the issue and is initially opposed to your viewpoint, present your arguments in a climactic order and then present your conclusion.
3. Present information that leads to pleasant contingencies first.
4. Present need-arousing information prior to need-satisfying information.
5. The adverse effects of a low credibility source can be lessened if the source is identified after, rather than before, the message.
6. Repetition helps.

Appeals to Emotions or Reason

7. Fear appeals can be effectively used to change attitudes and behavior.
8. The effectiveness of fear appeals is related to the receiver's final level of anxiety, a moderate anxiety level being more effective than either very high or very low levels of anxiety.
9. The level of threat in fear appeals should be moderated when the message is complex and places demand upon comprehension.
10. Fear appeals should include specific and effective recommendations for preventive action.
11. The effects of humor on persuasion are generally unpredictable.

Attitude Change via Behavioral Change

12. If a person can be induced to perform an important act that is counter to the person's own private attitude, attitude change may result.
13. When a person is induced to perform an attitudinally discrepant act because of promise of reward or punishment, attitude change will occur only to the degree that the person feels the magnitude of the reward was insufficient to justify the attitudinally discrepant behavior.
14. People value things they have worked hard to achieve, even when the things turn out to have little manifest value.
15. Role playing can have powerful persuasive impact.
16. Active participation produces more attitude change than passive reception of information.
17. Attitudes can be changed when the receiver becomes involved with a human model.

Figure 12.2: Some Message Structure Principles for Attitude Change Through Persuasion

Miscellaneous Flamboyant Techniques	18.	Persuasion may be more effective if the receiver overhears the message rather than receives it directly, particularly when the conclusion is agreeable to the receiver.
	19.	Persuading a person to comply with a small request increases the likelihood that the person will later comply with a more important request in the same area.
	20.	Reducing covert counter-argumentation by presenting distracting stimuli along with the message may enhance persuasion when the message is easy to comprehend.
	21.	In general, it is probable that persuasion will be enhanced if the receiver is in a "positive frame of mind" or is engaging in an enjoyable activity.
	22.	Confronting people with inconsistencies in their own attitude-value system may lead to self-dissatisfaction that produces changes in attitudes and long-term behavior.

Figure 12.2: *Continued*
Source: Fleming & Levie (1978), pp. 221–242.

to think of the cognitive component as a prerequisite learning, it is a prerequisite that will always be present in all examples of attitude learning; therefore it is something we can think of as being part of the attitude itself.

2. The *behavioral component* of attitude learning is seen in the need to apply the attitude—to engage in behavior. Thus, to actually internalize the attitude of safe driving, it will be necessary for the students to do it—to drive safely and receive feedback about it.

3. The *affective component* is the "knowing why," the urge or desire to drive safely. The most fundamental condition for achievement of the affective component is provision of a role model. A role model is a respected person who demonstrates the desired behavior. Thus, in the case of learning to drive safely, a person the student respects must demonstrate (or "model") safe driving.

The Cognitive Component in Attitude Change and Formation

It is important to remember the existence of the cognitive component in attitude learning. Many failures and difficulties in attitude learning are mistakenly attributed solely to the affective component; often, a deficit in the cognitive component needs to be remedied first. For example, when a student displays poor study habits, it is commonplace to place the blame on the student's lack of desire to study. But often, the student does not know how to study. An attitude includes both knowing how to do something and choosing to do it.

We will see a little later how the three components of attitude learning can be provided in a single lesson, although much attitude instruction is interwoven within other lessons for longer spans of time than individual lessons.

Attitudes are but one of many types of affective objectives that can be objects of instruction. There have been many attempts to describe and categorize types of learning outcomes in the affective domain (Krathwohl, Bloom, & Masia, 1964; Gephart & Ingle, 1976; Brandhorst, 1978; Nunnally, 1967; and Martin & Briggs, 1986). For our purposes, the most suitable categorization scheme is the taxonomy developed by Krathwohl and associates. We will describe the Krathwohl taxonomy to help you see a wider range of types of objectives other than attitudes. The Krathwohl taxonomy also lends increased precision to our descriptions of affective learning outcomes, including attitudes, since commonly used affect-related terms such as *attitudes, values, appreciations,* and

1.0 Receiving (or "attending")	1.1 Awareness
	1.2 Willingness to receive
	1.3 Controlled or selected attention
2.0 Responding	2.1 Acquiescence in responding
	2.2 Willingness to respond
	2.3 Satisfaction in response
3.0 Valuing	3.1 Acceptance of a value
	3.2 Preference for a value
	3.3 Commitment
4.0 Organization	4.1 Conceptualization of a value
	4.2 Organization of a value system
5.0 Characterization by a Value Complex	5.1 Generalized set
	5.2 Characterization

Figure 12.3: Summary of the Taxonomy of Educational Objectives in the Affective Domain
Source: Krathwohl, Bloom, & Masia (1964).

interests are broader and less precise than the terms set forth and described by the taxonomy.

The Krathwohl taxonomy has five major categories, with subcategories within each major category. Figure 12.3 presents a summary of the taxonomy. To illustrate the meanings of each of its categories, let's select a topic area and see how that topic might be reflected in activities and learning outcomes throughout the taxonomy. For our example, let's use "appreciation of classical music." Although some of what the taxonomy addresses is far beyond the idea of "appreciation," this is a commonly understood way to start. We will begin our example with this scenario: You have taken on a mission to convert your friend George, who hates classical music, into a person who has, at the very least, a positive attitude about classical music.

1. *Attending.* At the beginning, we have a problem with even getting George to listen to classical music. In the attending category, we begin with the small, but real, achievement of just getting George to be *aware* of the music (1.1 in Figure 12.3), to be *willing* to actually listen to it (1.2), and to even be able to *focus* in on parts of it—to pay close attention to the music (1.3).

The attending level is where we always begin, in any instructional situation, and if we were completely thorough in our learning task descriptions, we would include it as a prerequisite or part of all of our instruction. (We will discuss this further in the second part of this chapter when we discuss attention and motivation.) Although attending is an implicit part of all instruction, rarely would we expect to see attending as the the actual objective of instruction. When our objective is in the affective domain, attending will be a prerequisite—part of an affective learning hierarchy.

2. *Responding.* It's one thing for George to be willing to listen to the classical music, and it's another for him to actually take satisfaction in it. We can observe the difference—even though it is difficult to detect sometimes—between George's mere attention to and his responding to the music. George may perhaps move from *acquiescence* (2.1) to *willingness* to respond (2.2) to taking *satisfaction* in response to the music (2.3). When he achieves this level of affective learning with regard to classical music, we may observe subtle evidences of his response, perhaps with facial expression and bodily movements.

The responding level is right at the center of what is generally meant by *appreciation* in common language. As you can see, *responding* is a more precise description, one that we may use in a performance objective. In our mission to convert George, this may be as far as we had intended to go when we started, but as we will see, this goal may be extended into how deeply and pervasively George internalizes (or "appreciates") classical music.

3. *Valuing.* If George finds himself enjoying classical music in one or more instances, we are likely to find that he achieves the next level in the hierarchy, valuing. Like the other categories treated so far, valuing has subcategories that we may find George experiencing. He may begin with *acceptance* of the value of classical music (3.1). For example, when asked, "Do you think classical music is any good?" he may change his response from "No" to "Yes, I guess some of it is." Then he may experience *preference* (3.2) in which, for example, he goes to the record store and finds that he goes to the classical section first. Finally, he may experience *commitment* (3.3) in which, for example, he chooses to spend time or money on his classical music interest, such as buying season tickets to the symphony orchestra concerts, taking time off from other activities to go to a concert, or helping the orchestra in its annual fund-raising drive.

Many school and training affective objectives will be in the valuing category. We want the learners to not just respond positively to our topic but to internalize an interest in the topic so that it becomes something that they value. The final two categories in the Krathwohl taxonomy take the idea of valuing and deepen or extend it.

4. *Organization.* George's mind is full of conflicting and contradictory value structures and systems. He doesn't have all of his values organized into a consistent, carefully constructed system. You can see that just having achieved the valuing level described above does not automatically mean that George will make the mental effort of *conceptualizing* (4.1) his valuing of classical music. For example, he might become a "true believer" in classical music and shun good jazz in a snobbish fashion, as is often the case

with those who have acquired commitment to a value but have not yet conceptualized it. Having conceptualized his valuing of classical music, George can take one step deeper and begin to form an *organized value system* (4.2). At this point, George goes beyond his newfound eclecticism and links with other values outside classical music itself. Now George is reading literature of a higher quality than he formerly did, he has joined an ethics and philosophy discussion group, and he has begun to study computer programming for aesthetic reasons. His views on politics have even changed.

Organization goes beyond what we typically attempt to do in school or training situations, although our most general goals often reflect this level of achievement. The goals of graduate study, for example, seem to involve this level of functioning, especially with respect to the field of study itself. It is important that the student (1) know things, (2) have skills in the field, and (3) acquire particular affective learnings tied to particular skills and knowledge. And, for the health of the field itself, it is important that the student have the organized system of beliefs, commitments, and preferences that one associates with a person in that particular field.

5. *Characterization.* It would be hard to imagine George going any further with this classical music business than he already has, but the characterization level gives us an opportunity to take him even further. At the characterization level, we see not an individual who merely possesses certain organized sets of values, but rather someone whom we would look to as a source of those values—a model. Over time, given the behaviors and affective states that we saw George experiencing at the organization level, we may see George take on what is known as a *generalized set* (5.1). The clichés such as the tweed sport coat with elbow patches, the dignified gray beard, and a pipe communicate at a superficial level what is meant by a generalized set—all the things associated with being a connoisseur of classical music. More technically, *generalized set* refers to a predisposition or consistent response to a wide variety of situations. Thus, rather than just being completely obsessed by his "classical music jag," we hope that George now possesses

an orientation that is made up of organized sets or clusters of related values. The final level that George could aspire to is itself called *characterization,* (5.2). At this level, we would look to George to find a reflection of interest in classical music. In fact, the last we heard of George, he was teaching a music appreciation class with great success.

The characterization level is the level we hope our teachers and professors have achieved with regard to the subjects and fields they are teaching. People functioning at this level are our actual, genuine role models. Perhaps this need is one that underlies the need for classroom teachers who have undergone extensive teacher education as well as excellent subject matter preparations. Certainly we hope for professionals — physicians, lawyers, teachers, and others — to possess the depth reflected by the characterization level. Rather than blindly wishing for professionals to randomly reach this level of functioning, we can draw upon the Krathwohl taxonomy and other concepts to design instruction that will intentionally educate for this goal.

*E*xercises B

For the following goal statements from the 1938 Educational Policies Commission report, develop a learning hierarchy related to each goal. Use the Krathwohl taxonomy as a guiding framework.

1. The educated person has an appetite for learning.
2. The educated person protects her own health and that of her dependents.
3. The educated person observes the amenities of social behavior.
4. The educated citizen acts to correct unsatisfactory (social) conditions.

*I*nstructional Conditions for Attitude Objectives

From our review of attitude learning, we have derived three key instructional conditions for its attainment. Although many variations are possible,

we would offer these three conditions as primary and critical: (1) demonstration of the desired behavior by a respected role model; (2) practice of the desired behavior, often through role playing; and (3) reinforcement of the desired behavior. Other conditions include persuasive communications, dissonance establishment and reduction, and use of group discussions (see Martin and Briggs, 1986, pp. 137–140 for more information on these latter conditions).

As we elaborate on the three primary conditions for instruction, the three components for learning an attitude should be recalled: the cognitive component (knowing how), the affective component (knowing why), and the behavioral component (opportunity to practice). As we describe the three instructional conditions for forming or changing attitudes, you can see how these learning components relate to the design of instruction.

1. *Demonstration of the desired behavior by a respected role model.* We have already seen how important a role model is in our discussion of the Krathwohl taxonomy. Gagné (1985) underscores the utility of modeling as an instructional technique by noting, "One of the most dependable methods of establishing attitudes is by means of a set of learning conditions that includes human modeling" (p. 241). Conditions that Martin and Briggs (1986) present as essential with regard to the use of role models include the importance of the learner's "comprehend(ing) and see(ing) the model demonstrating the behavior *and* being reinforced" (p. 139). Gagné (1985, p. 238) presents a four-step procedure for the use of human models in attitude learning:

   a. Establish the appeal and credibility of the model.
   b. Stimulate the learner's recall of relevant knowledge and concepts.
   c. Demonstration or communication of desired action by the model.
   d. Demonstration or communication of reinforcement of the model as a result of the action taken.

2. *Practice of the desired behavior (role playing).* As pointed out earlier in the discussion of

attitude learning, learner activity with regard to the attitude in question is a powerful tool in attitude formation and change. The technique of role playing offers the opportunity for learner activity within an instructional environment, as well as constituting another means by which modeling can be employed. In the case of role playing, the actor (the learner or another person) "plays out" the role rather than using an actual role model. According to Gagné (1985), in addition to particular role-playing methods that may be employed, such as case studies and simulations, conventional group discussion is also a legitimate means for practice of a desired behavior. In a discussion, as each student contributes from the point of view of the attitude at hand, that student serves as a role model for the attitude. The discussion leader has the opportunity to provide reinforcement for the discussant/role model, and as the discussion progresses, the attitude may be expressed with more and more precision.

3. *Provide reinforcement for the desired behavior.* Behavioral techniques have remained a substantial part of instruction for attitude learning. Even in role model use (and role playing), reinforcement is an integral part of the process. In these circumstances, the reinforcement, as well as the role model per se, is thought to function in a surrogate or vicarious fashion for the learner. Research from the social learning standpoint has pointed out that reinforcement is such a potentially powerful tool in these situations that even observing a model being reinforced can be a condition for attitude formation or change (Martin and Briggs, 1986, p. 178). However, the most powerful reinforcers will be those that apply directly to the learner as a product of the learner's own behavior. That behavior may be a demonstration of the desired behavior in an actual situation, in role playing, with discussions, or in other contrived situations.

Reinforcement is a slippery concept, and defining what reinforcers actually *are* turns out to be somewhat circular. No particular type or category of event may be guaranteed to be a reinforcer. A reinforcer is technically defined as a stimulus that increases the probability of the preceding behavior reoccuring. In day-to-day use,

reinforcers are generally thought to be rewards, but not all rewards are reinforcing. In the case of reinforcement for taking an action of choice, the most powerful reinforcers seem to be those which we can call "natural consequences." The thanks from someone you have helped, the safe passage through a dangerous situation, and seeing the benefit gained from help you supplied are all much more direct and powerful reinforcers than praise or reward from a teacher. In fact, in many situations, praise and reward can be worse than no attempt to reinforce at all. A teacher's role in providing reinforcement can be seen as assuring that learners are put in contact with and apprehend the feedback resulting from their actions.

*E*xercises c

For each of the three instructional conditions for attitude learning previously discussed, describe what learning components (cognitive, behavioral, affective) are being provided.

*E*xample Attitude Lesson

The preceding paragraphs have outlined some fundamentals of attitude learning and considerations for instructional design. Now we will expand on these basics and put together an example lesson that employs both the fundamentals discussed to this point as well as the expanded instructional events as a strategy development framework for an entire lesson.

For our example attitude lesson, we will use the following objective: Given an interpersonal conflict situation, the student will choose to respond in a nonviolent manner, resolving the conflict if possible. (This objective arose out of a personal experience one of the authors had as a classroom teacher in an elementary school in which there was a definite and clear need for the students to achieve this particular learning objective.) We would classify the objective in the Krathwohl taxonomy as a valuing objective, either at the level of preference for a value (3.2) or at the commitment level (3.3).

Introduction

Attention

Establish Instructional Purpose

Arouse Interest and Motivation

Preview Lesson

Our instruction in "nonviolent solutions" might begin with the teacher showing a videotape that depicts a common classroom conflict situation, perhaps a conflict between two elementary students over a pencil: "You've got my pencil!" "No I don't!" "Oh yes you do!" As the argument becomes truly heated, the teacher stops the video and asks, "What would you do?"

The introduction to this lesson, although it does not follow a strict set of steps, seems to be an appropriate one and fulfills the functions of gaining attention, arousing interest, and in a vague, perhaps dramatic way, establishing a direction.

One important characteristic of the videotape is that at least one of the characters on the tape be a person who functions as a role model for the students. If the tape is locally produced, the person might be an older student whom students in this class would probably respect. If the tape is commercially produced, it will help if the character is portrayed by an actor who is particularly popular with students in the class.

Body

Recall Relevant Prior Knowledge

Process Information and Examples

When the teacher stops the tape, a class discussion may focus on answering the question "What would you do in this situation?" The teacher will need to have in mind (or on a lesson plan used as notes) anticipated responses from the students, some of which might include "I would hit him and get my pencil back" and "I would get the teacher to settle it" and "I would see if we could figure out whose pencil it was and where the other pencil went." For each case, the teacher needs to be able to discuss what the results of this type of response are likely to be. For example, if the suggestion is to hit the other student and take the pencil back, what is likely to happen if that is the action taken? If we call in the teacher, what is

likely to happen? If we negotiate or talk it out, what is likely to happen?

In attitude change, if a persuasive communication is used and discussion is also to be employed, the persuasive communication should be employed before discussion, in order to minimize public commitment to the old attitude and lessen the resistance to change (Hoban & Van Ormer, 1950). This principle would suggest that before the discussion begins, the entire videotape should be shown because the role model demonstrates the desired choice.

Focus Attention

Employ Learning Strategies

We can consider two different approaches, both potentially effective, for continuing the lesson. The teacher could employ a persuasive communication technique to describe the consequences of the desired nonviolent approach, if the students have not already done so in their discussion. The other alternative would be to have the videotape continue, depicting the hero (role model) settling the difference in a nonviolent fashion. It is important that the dramatization end with the role model receiving reinforcement for having chosen the action taken. Depiction of acceptance and admiration by peers is an appropriate reinforcer for all age groups.

Practice

Evaluate Feedback

The group discussion could be considered as practice and feedback; it certainly is for the cognitive component of the objective. However, additional practice and feedback is completely feasible in this example and should be used. Role playing by students in a variety of contrived (but believable) situations could be an excellent part of the instruction. (This is not a discussion of an individual lesson because we anticipate this work to go on for a period of time.) One of the goals of the role playing would be to help students gain a repertoire of nonviolent responses to a variety of situations, experiencing the learning in all three components: cognitive (knowing some ways to respond to conflict situations other than violently); affective (knowing why—gaining the disposition to choose to respond nonviolently); and behavioral (practice in responding nonviolently with feedback experienced for that behavior).

Conclusion

Summary

Transfer Knowledge

Remotivate and Close

It is appropriate to end each session or lesson with a conclusion that includes the events of (1) summary, (2) transfer knowledge, and (3) remotivate and close. The specifics of each conclusion would vary with what has been done during the particular session. A clear restatement of the desired behavior by a respected model would be a good summary. This restatement will leave learners with no doubt regarding the purpose of the instruction. (We *do* believe that the purposes of affective instruction should be explicitly stated at some point to lessen the impression of manipulation.)

Assessment

Assess Performance

Evaluate Feedback and Seek Remediation

The primary and fundamental assessment would be in observation of the students' future behavior in conflict situations. Even so, other forms of assessment are appropriate—their gain in reliability offsets the losses in validity from the ideal (of actually observing what each student does in all future conflict situations). Role playing, again, would appear to be an excellent means of assessment. The role-playing situation may not adequately bring out the affective component of the objective. (This is because students may make different choices when they are out of the teacher's sight.) However, observations of role-playing situations can do a good job of providing for assessment of the cognitive and behavioral components of the objective.

*P*romoting Interest and Motivation in Learning

The other side of the coin in the affective domain is its role in instruction for objectives in the other domains—cognitive and psychomotor. Here, our concern is finding and using those aspects of our student's affective functioning that are necessary and helpful in the learning process, regardless of what is being learned. Although all aspects of af-

fect are possible candidates for our attention in this regard, the area of *interests and motivation* is the most critically important.

Interests and motivation are desired learner characteristics. We all know who the ''disinterested'' and ''unmotivated'' students are. Yet even the most unmotivated students have motivation (except in cases of clinical depression). They may be motivated to work on their cars after school, they may be motivated to get dates, they may be motivated to make some money, or they may be motivated to do any of a myriad of activities and interests that have nothing to do with their schooling. When we talk about wanting our students to be motivated, we mean, of course, that they be motivated toward the instruction they are receiving. We want the students to choose to attend to instruction and choose to apply effort in learning it.

In order for learning to take place, the learner must *attend* to the material. In Chapter 1, we saw the fundamental requirement of attending reflected in the third criterion for high quality instruction: appeal (in addition to the criteria of effectiveness and efficiency). The phenomenon of attending is one we have all experienced, and readers of this text can recognize the phenomenon subjectively in its absence. (Many students in schools and training agencies, however, cannot). We have all looked up from reading an assignment and said to ourselves, ''Oops, I've been reading for the past page or two but my mind was on something else. Let me see, where did I leave off?'' These unfortunate incidents illustrate that it is possible to go through the motions of studying or being in class without attending. And as we also know from our own experience, if you aren't attending, you're not learning.

In recent years we have become increasingly cognizant of the need for appeal in instruction, and we have become correspondingly interested in the topic of motivation in instructional design. We will devote the remainder of this chapter to a discussion of principles of instructional design that can improve the motivational qualities of all of the instruction you design.

*K*eller's ARCS Model

In the late 1970s John Keller began work on motivation in instruction, which was an outgrowth of his interest in effort and its variability. He was frustrated that so much of the interest in psychology—especially research and theory that accounted for learner differences in achievement—was concentrated on differences in learner ability. To account for performance differences, Keller felt that it was necessary to understand and model the influence of effort and the contributors to effort. He determined that among the various constructs that might be applied to the problem of variation in effort, that of motivation was the most appropriate and useful (Keller, 1983).

By the mid-1980s, Keller had developed the ARCS Model, a model for influencing learners' motivation to learn and for solving problems with learning motivation. ARCS is an acronym containing four major conditions for motivation: Attention, Relevance, Confidence, and Satisfaction. The four categories constitute, as a set, the conditions that Keller's research led him to presume are needed to "produce instruction that is interesting, meaningful, and appropriately challenging" (Keller, 1983, p. 395). Each of the four major categories contains specific motivational strategy prescriptions for its attainment. In addition to the four motivation strategy categories, the ARCS Model also includes recommendations for what he calls "motivational design"; in other words, how motivational concerns may be included in the instructional design process. We will describe each of the four motivation strategy categories and the motivation design process model, and we will look at how the ARCS Model may be applied by using suggestions from it within our expanded instructional events.

Four Motivation Strategy Categories

The following discussion of the four categories of motivating strategies borrows heavily from Keller's description of them (1987, pp. 4–5).

Attention Strategies. You may have noticed some of the following strategies in our introduction to many of the lessons included in Chapters 7–13, particularly in the Deploy Attention and Arouse Interest and Motivation events. These strategies represent means to draw student attention to the material being learned and frequently involve very specific techniques of content presentation or treatment. Keller describes six kinds of attention strategies: (1) incongruity and conflict, (2) concreteness, (3) variability, (4) humor, (5) inquiry, and (6) participation. The first attention strategy is that of providing *incongruity and conflict,* such as introducing a fact that appears to contradict the student's experience or playing the devil's advocate in discussing an issue or current event of interest to the students. The second attention strategy is *concreteness,* in which visual presentations or concrete verbal presentations, such as anecdotes and biographies, attract the student's interest. In the third attention strategy, *variability,* the student's attention is caught or maintained by changes such as tone of voice, movements, instructional format, medium of instruction, layout and design of print material, and changes in interaction patterns such as changing from student-instructor interaction to student-student interaction. Examples of the use of *humor,* the fourth attention strategy, include such techniques as using puns during redundant or necessarily repeated information presentation, making humorous analogies, and telling jokes in introductions and conclusions. The fifth attention strategy, *inquiry,* includes frequent engagement in problem-solving activities and providing opportunities for learners to select topics, projects, and assignments that can capitalize on their interests. (See the description of inquiry and expository strategies in Chapter 6.) The sixth attention strategy is *participation,* which may involve such activities as games, role playing, or simulations that involve active participation of the learners. Participation strategies are described in the Practice events discussions in all of the strategy chapters, Chapters 7–13.

From the various attention strategies, we see that not only is there a variety of strategies to select from—both those provided as well as others you may be stimulated to devise given the example techniques—but also there is a need to consider attention needs throughout the entire instruction. It is relatively easy to get attention for a moment. What is needed, and much more difficult, is to direct that attention to the learning needs at hand and to maintain the attention at an optimal level, having students becoming neither bored nor overstimulated. Novices in the field of instructional technology are occasionally so intrigued by what media can do to gain learners' attention that they overuse attention-gaining techniques so that learners' attention is directed more toward the device than to the content. The same effect can result from the gratuitous use of humor. Attention strategies should direct the learners' attention to the task.

Relevance Strategies. As a group, relevance strategies are intended to assist students in attaching value to the learning task and in deepening the internalization of that value. These strategies influence how the learning task is portrayed to the student, rather than impacting directly on the content itself. Keller describes relevance strategies with the terms *experience, present worth, future usefulness, need matching, modeling,* and *choice*.

The first strategy suggested to assist in relevance, *experience,* suggests that instruction should tell learners how new learning will use their existing skills, that analogies be used to relate current learning to prior experience, and that instruction be related to learner interests.

The second relevance strategy, called *present worth,* suggests that instruction explicitly state the current value of instruction, as opposed to stressing its value in the future. Imagining the current value of some learning task may be very difficult. It is sometimes productive to engage the students themselves in establishing immediate purpose.

Future usefulness, the third relevance strategy, suggests explicitly tying instructional goals to the learner's future activities and having learners participate in activities in which they relate the instruction to their own future goals. As you might predict, this strategy is often more useful with older students than younger students.

The fourth relevance strategy is called *need matching,* which may be accomplished by capitalizing on the dynamics of achievement and risk taking, power, and affiliation. This involves activities that give students the opportunity to have achievements under conditions of moderate risk, activities that provide opportunities for students to exercise responsibility, authority, and influence, and activities that provide opportunities for cooperative interaction utilize matching strategies.

The fifth relevance strategy is *modeling*. Some example activities that use this strategy include the use of alumni as guest lecturers, allowing studentswho finish self-paced work first to serve as deputy tutors, and modeling through teacher enthusiasm.

The sixth strategy that can enhance relevance is *choice,* which may be implemented by allowing students to employ different methods to pursue their work or allowing students a choice in how they organize their work.

Relevance strategies, as a group, represent various ways to help students see why what they are learning should be important to them. In our expanded instructional events, the examples that we have frequently employed in our discussions of two instructional strategies—Arouse Interest and Motivation, and Remotivate and Close—have been applications of the relevance strategies of Keller's *experience, present worth,* and *future usefulness.* The strategies of *need matching, modeling,* and *choice* illustrate how different organizational strategies of instruction may influence motivation; the strategies produce motivational effects of *how* something is taught rather than producing effects of *what* is taught.

Confidence Strategies. The five confidence strategies are described as (1) learning requirements, (2) difficulty, (3) expectations, (4) attributions, and (5) self-confidence. These strategies tend to focus on various aspects of learner performance in the learning process.

The first confidence strategy, *learning requirements,* emphasizes that students should clearly know what is being taught. Example techniques provided include the incorporation of learning goals into the instructional materials, providing self-evaluation tools and skills, and providing explanation of the criteria used in evaluation.

The second strategy for improving confidence is *difficulty.* Keller suggests that the difficulty of learning materials should be sequenced in order of increasing difficulty, providing a continual but reasonable challenge. Instruction that builds on prior knowledge and instructs on prerequisites incorporates this principle.

Expectations strategies are suggestions for helping students acquire realistic and positive outlooks toward working with the material, through such techniques as letting students know the likelihood of success given different amounts of effort, teaching students to plan their work productively, and helping students set realistic goals for progress and achievement. Many of these skills are taught under the umbrella term *meta-*

cognition. (See a discussion of this concept in Chapter 11.)

The fourth confidence strategy is *attributions,* and it involves helping students to attribute their successes to the effort they employ. In other words, to encourage learners to have a more internal locus of control with regard to learning tasks. (See our discussion of internal/external locus of control in Chapter 3.) Some techniques that teachers/instructors can use to promote internal locus of control are (1) ensuring that students know that their successes were the product of their effort rather than luck or other external factors (when that is the case) and (2) encouraging students to "verbalize appropriate attributions for both successes and failures" (Keller, 1987, p. 5).

Self-confidence is the fifth confidence strategy, and it includes a variety of example techniques to help students build self-confidence, including allowing students to experience increasing independence as they work at learning a skill; providing practice of skills under realistic conditions following initial learning under more sheltered, low-risk conditions; and helping students avoid the mental traps of perfectionism rather than taking too much satisfaction in their accomplishments.

Confidence strategies are particularly helpful in preventing "blocks" that keep learners from beginning to engage in practice and other necessary learning activities, such as maintaining student persistence in efforts associated with the learning task. People with different levels of confidence approach application exercises, practice, assignments, and tests very differently, and the confidence strategies represent powerful means of fostering the development of confidence and "form the impression that some level of success is possible if effort is exerted." (Keller, 1987, p. 5) The very careful and systematic design of instruction that promotes high levels of performance across ability levels tends to encourage learners' self-confidence by leading to many successful learning experiences.

Satisfaction Strategies. There are five satisfaction strategies: (1) natural consequences, (2) unexpected rewards, (3) positive outcomes, (4) avoidance of negative influences, and (5) scheduling. They, in general, affect motivation through management of the consequences of student activity and learning.

The first satisfaction strategy is *natural consequences,* in which positive consequences of learning that are intrinsic to the accomplishment are maximized, such as letting students use their skills in realistic settings as soon as possible and allowing students who have mastered a task to help students who have not yet finished.

The second strategy to enhance satisfaction, *unexpected rewards,* offsets boring tasks with extrinsic rewards that the learner can anticipate ahead of time; it also enhances tasks that are intrinsically interesting by providing unexpected, noncontingent rewards. Maintaining effort during the performance of boring tasks can be made easier by the expectation of reward. With a task that is interesting, knowledge that an external reward is coming will not be particularly motivating. But an unexpected reward can surprise and delight a person who is working on a pleasant task without distracting him from that task.

The third satisfaction strategy, *positive outcomes,* is illustrated by instruction-supplied actions such as verbal praise, personal attention, helpful feedback, and motivating feedback (praise) immediately following task performance.

The fourth satisfaction strategy, *negative influences,* illustrates the need to avoid the negative. This involves avoiding (1) the use of threats, (2) the use of surveillance practices (as opposed to positive attention), and (3) external performance evaluation when student self-evaluation is possible.

Scheduling, the fifth satisfaction strategy, refers to the scheduling of reinforcements, such as scheduling frequent reinforcement when learners are new at learning a task and intermittent reinforcement as they become more experienced. The overall schedule of reinforcement should vary, in terms of both interval and quantity. For example, in the early phases of an employee safety training program, particular attention should be paid to providing frequent benefits and recognition to employees who participate in the program. As the program proceeds, rewards should not become routine or predictable but be awarded with some element of surprise. The most powerful reinforcement schedule (as anyone who has observed people playing slot machines knows) is a variable schedule, or random reinforcement pattern.

In general, the satisfaction strategies operationalize Thorndike's Law of Effect which holds that if a stimulus is followed by a response that is followed by a satisfier, than the stimulus-response connection will be strengthened. A variety of techniques for providing extrinsic reward and intrinsic satisfactions have been presented. When a task is intrinsically satisfying, extrinsic reward techniques can actually be demotivating, so care must be employed in the use of these techniques. When properly selected and used, these techniques can be very powerful.

The Motivational Design Process Model

Keller's ARCS Model also contains, in addition to the four categories of motivational strategies, a process model for assisting designers in incorporating motivation strategies into instruction. Figure 12.4 presents this model alongside our own Instructional Design Process Model so that you can see how the two models coincide. The model is comprised of four phases: Define, Design, Develop, and Evaluate. The simplicity of structure and choice of commonly employed phases makes its recommendations easy to fit within whatever overall design model the designer is using.

The ARCS Define phase dovetails well with the Analysis phase of our model, particularly at the steps of Learning Environment and Learners. Motivation problems can run the gamut from the need to increase the relevance of instruction for students who are generally cooperative and interested to the need to establish attention and expectancies of success for an essentially indifferent or even hostile population of learners. In the Define phase, we determine if the motivational problem is one that is amenable to solution through the tools offered by the ARCS model, and if so, we proceed in analysis of audience and objectives.

In the first step, Classify Problem, we determine if the motivational problem at hand is within the range of problems that the ARCS model can reasonably be expected to address. The example of the sort of motivational problem to which the ARCS model was not intended to be applied are problems involving individual learners' personality or emotional disorders. Keller notes that the ARCS model is not a behavior change model, suggesting that its use is not a substitute for counseling or psychotherapy. The activities of the Learning Environment step of our model coincide well with the requirements of this step.

In the second step, Analyze Audience Motivation, we look at the motivation of the particular students or the target audience being taught. The

---

Analysis
    Learning Environment
    Learners
    Learning Task

Instructional Strategy
    Determine Organizational Strategy
    Determine Delivery Strategy
    Determine Management Strategy

    Write and Produce Instruction

Evaluation
    Write Assessment Instruments
    Conduct Formative Evaluation

    Revise Instruction

Define (motivation issues)
    Classify (motivational) Problem
    Analyze Audience Motivation
    Prepare Motivational Objectives

Design (of motivation)
    Generate Potential Strategies

    Select (motivational) Strategies

Develop (motivation elements)
    Prepare Motivational Elements
    Integrate with Instruction

Evaluate
    Developmental Tryout
    (of motivational elements)

    Assess Motivational Outcomes

Figure 12.4: The Motivational Design Model in Context of the Instructional Design Process Model

designer should attempt to find out what the general level of motivation is for learners upon entry and what particular audience interests and needs may exist that can be built on to assist the extrinsic appeal of the instruction. The four categories of motivation strategies—attention, relevance, confidence, and satisfaction—may be used as a framework for this analysis. The analysis can take place as a natural part of the Learners step of our design model.

In the third step, Prepare Motivational Objectives, we use knowledge gained from the first two steps of the Motivational Design model (along with other knowledge from the Analysis phase of our model), to develop specific objectives for motivation. Motivation objectives are like instructional objectives in that they deal with outcomes in the learner and need to be expressed in performance terms. An example motivation objective would be ''By the end of the introduction to the lesson, each student will be able to describe two tangible benefits of learning to solder electrical circuit components.'' Two other examples are ''Within the practice phase of instruction, each student will persist in attempting exercises of increasing difficulty to the point of completion of all prescribed exercises'' and ''When beginning the final project for the course, each student will express confidence in being able to successfully complete the final project given sufficient effort.'' The preparation of these motivational objectives can take place during the Learning Task step of our design model, perhaps at the end of it so that the learning task objectives are known and stated before the development of motivational objectives.

During the ARCS Design phase, we determine the particular motivational strategies that will be employed. Two steps complete this phase. These steps fit well with other activities in our own model's Instructional Strategy phase.

The first step is Generate Potential Strategies, in which motivation strategy options are brainstormed to develop an extensive set of possibilities from which to choose. This step can be done during the Instructional Strategy phase of our model (specifically, in the Determine Organizational Strategy step).

The second step is Select (motivational) Strategies, in which the list of options is screened against the criteria of time required, fit with instructional objectives, cost to develop in terms of time and money, fit with learner characteristics, and compatibility with other aspects of instructional design and delivery. A good sequence within our model would be to perform these tasks during the Determine Management Strategy step, just prior to Write and Produce Instruction.

During the ARCS Develop phase, the plans and materials for the motivation are created. If instructional materials have already been created, this phase would require some adjustment and adaptation of the instructional materials, but it seems more ideal if plans and materials for motivation are developed alongside and integrated with instructional materials. So, the two steps in this phase, Prepare Motivational Elements and Integrate with Instruction, should be performed during our Write and Produce Instruction step.

The ARCS Evaluate phase includes two steps that fit well within our Evaluation phase. First, the Developmental Tryout of motivational materials and procedures should be conducted during our steps Conduct Formative Evaluation and Revision Instruction because the process is the same for motivational materials as it is for the rest of the instruction. The step Assess Motivational Outcomes would be a product of the conclusion of our Conduct Formative Evaluation step, in which field trials establish or ''validate'' the revised instruction.

Promoting Interest and Motivation

Introduction

To assist deploying attention to the lesson, Keller's attention strategies of *incongruity* and *humor* contain excellent ways to begin a lesson in a motivating way, potentially stimulating curiosity and drawing attention to the material. These strategies are good examples of attention ''grabbers'' that may at the same time clearly relate to the topic at hand.

In establishing instructional purpose, the confidence strategies of *learning requirements* and *expectations* may be used to contribute to learner confidence while establishing the learning objective. These strategies suggest that if instruction contains clearly stated and appealing goals with clear criteria for evaluation, the learner's confidence in learning may be enhanced.

For arousing interest and motivation, the relevance strategies of *experience, present worth,* and *future usefulness* will be most germane at this point in the instruction. These are strategies that assist the learner in seeing why the knowledge or skill being studied will be helpful.

Within the preview of the lesson, as before, the confidence strategies of *learning requirements* and *expectations* may also be used here to assist the motivational qualities of the lesson preview as the instructional purpose is elaborated.

Body

Information Presentation. To enhance motivation during the events of recalling relevant prior knowledge, processing information and examples, focusing attention, and employing learning strategies, motivational strategies of attention and relevance will be the most helpful. For example, attention strategies of *concreteness* and *variability* illustrate techniques to enhance the interest qualities of presentations, and *inquiry* and *participation* are attention strategies that involve non-expository forms of instructional delivery that are intrinsically interesting. The relevance strategies of *need matching, modeling,* and *choice* likewise address how material may be brought into contact with learners in ways that compel interest and involvement.

Practice and Feedback. To enhance motivation during practice and feedback, there are many different motivational strategies that may be employed. Key ones to consider are the following: within the relevance category, *need matching* to capitalize on needs for achievement, power, and affiliation; within the confidence category, the techniques of *difficulty* management to provide continual but reasonable challenge, *attribution* techniques such as those that assist students to credit effort rather than luck for success, and *self-confidence* techniques that use independence and risk management; and all of the strategies within the satisfaction category—*natural consequences* of accomplishment, *unexpected rewards* from task completion, provision of *positive out-*comes for work and task accomplishment, avoiding *negative influences* such as threats, and *scheduling* of reinforcement.

Learning Strategies. Learners can be taught to employ many of the strategies themselves to control and promote their own motivation and interest. Indeed, in the spirit of our promoting generative strategies when possible, we believe that the gradual handing over of these strategies to learners is a very important instructional goal.

Conclusion

A similar pattern of use of motivational strategies is appropriate for use in the conclusion as well as the introduction. Attention strategies, confidence strategies, and relevance strategies will be useful in the conclusion in the same way that they were in the introduction. However, there will be a shift in tense—from future tense emphasis ("Why should I learn this?") to a past tense emphasis ("Now that I know it, how can I use it?").

Assessment

One technique within the *need matching* strategy has particular relevance to assessment: to provide opportunities to achieve excellence under conditions of moderate risk. Two techniques from the satisfaction category may also be applicable to assessment activities. First, the technique of avoiding external performance evaluations by helping the students to evaluate their own work is a motivational technique that should be considered in balance with needs for assessment information, which may or may not be possible to acquire without external evaluation. And second, *natural consequences* techniques may be used at the end of assessment. These techniques capitalize on learners' completion of assessment. If learners have achieved mastery, they may be allowed to put their new knowledge to real use as soon as possible or to help others learn the skill.

*E*xercises D

Following are lesson features that incorporate motivational strategies. Determine the strategy category or categories—attention (A), relevance (R), confidence (C), or satisfaction (S)—that the lesson exemplifies.

_____ 1. A computer screen shows animated images of planes flying toward each other at the same altitude. Before they collide, the planes take separate routes with different altitudes, one higher than the other.

_____ 2. The lesson begins with the professor's personal story regarding an embarrassing situation resulting from her lack of knowledge of the content that will be taught in the lesson.

_____ 3. When the teacher returns a good paper to a student, he says, "Good work. I can see that you worked hard on this paper!"

_____ 4. The lesson uses a mastery plan, and students are able to retake alternate versions of the final exam until they reach an established criterion.

_____ 5. At the beginning of a lesson on "drafting" in competition bicycle riding, students view a video demonstration of the skill. Then, the instructor replays the tape and points out the critical features of good technique.

_____ 6. In a computer program, when a learner has correctly answered ten questions on multiplication facts, she is allowed to play a computer game for three minutes.

_____ 7. A parent, after teaching a child to set a place setting, goes into the other room while the child sets the other places, rather than "hanging over the child's shoulder."

_____ 8. The instruction in a physics course relates Bernoulli's principle to students' experiences at a swim park.

Summary

In this chapter we have considered instructional design from the standpoint of the affective domain. In addition to looking at how to design instruction that supports the learning of attitude objectives, we have also discussed another affective topic—motivation. Specifically, we addressed the importance of motivation in instructional design and strategies for improving the motivational qualities of instruction.

In looking at design of instruction for attitude objectives, we began by discussing attitude learning from a variety of theoretical standpoints, involving both learning theory and a communication perspective. Following a discussion of the components of attitude learning, we broadened our scope somewhat and looked at a variety of kinds of objectives in the affective domain using the Krathwohl taxonomy. Then we presented instructional conditions for attitude learning and a sample attitude change lesson that illustrated use of the expanded instructional events in designing attitude instruction.

In the second part of the chapter we looked at how to promote motivation through instructional design. We described Keller's ARCS Model as an excellent guide for designing for motivation. We looked at the four major components of the model and the categories under which specific motivation strategies are classified: attention strategies, relevance strategies, confidence strategies, and satisfaction strategies. We discussed the Motivation Design Process Model, which is also part of the ARCS Model, and saw how it fit within our more general instructional design model. Finally, we looked at how motivation strategies can be used within the framework of the expanded instructional events. Figure 12.5 summarizes key points in this chapter.

Instruction for Attitude Learning

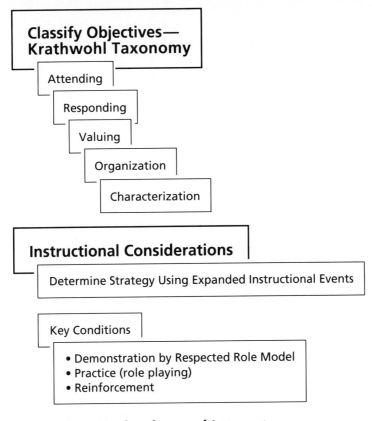

Classify Objectives—Krathwohl Taxonomy

Attending

Responding

Valuing

Organization

Characterization

Instructional Considerations

Determine Strategy Using Expanded Instructional Events

Key Conditions

- Demonstration by Respected Role Model
- Practice (role playing)
- Reinforcement

Promoting Motivation and Interest

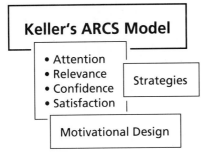

Keller's ARCS Model

- Attention
- Relevance
- Confidence
- Satisfaction

Strategies

Motivational Design

Figure 12.5: Summary Diagram for Chapter 12

Job Aid

I. Designing Instruction for Attitude (Affective) Objectives

State the terminal objective and classify it by a Krathwohl taxonomy category.

_____

_____

Krathwohl Taxonomy
1. Attending
2. Responding
3. Valuing
4. Organization
5. Characterization

State enabling objectives, using the Krathwohl taxonomy as an aid in suggesting the appropriate "next steps" in learning.

_____

_____

_____

_____

_____

Describe how each of the three key instructional conditions will be met.

_____

_____

_____

_____

1. Demonstration by a respected role model
2. Practice
3. Reinforcement of desired behavior

Describe the expanded instructional events (use the Job Aid from Chapter 6).

_____

_____

_____

_____

_____

II. Designing for Motivation in Instruction
A. Process Framework for Motivational Design (use as a worksheet)

ANALYSIS
Learning Environment
Learners
Learning Task

DEFINE (motivation issues)
Classify (motivational) Problem
Analyze Audience Motivation
Prepare Motivational Objectives

INSTRUCTIONAL STRATEGY
Determine Organizational Strategy
Determine Delivery Strategy
Determine Management Strategy

DESIGN (of motivation)
Generate Potential Strategies

Select (motivational) Strategies

Write and Produce Instruction

DEVELOP (motivaton elements)
Prepare Motivational Elements
Integrate with Instruction

EVALUATION
Write Assessment Instruments
Conduct Formative Evaluation
Revise Instruction

EVALUATE
Developmental Tryout
  (of motivational elements)
Assess Motivational Outcomes

B. Using the expanded instructional events descriptions for your instruction, consider how strategies for each of the four Motivation Strategy categories might be used in this lesson.

Attention Strategies

_____

_____

Relevance Strategies

_____

_____

Confidence Strategies

_____

_____

Satisfaction Strategies

_____

_____

Extended Example

This Extended Example will be a lesson on "appreciating black and white photography." Since, for primarily technical and aesthetic reasons, many of the photographs that students will be making will be black and white (B&W) rather than color photographs, we felt that the students' valuing of black and white prints would assist them in the other aspects of the course. In addition, the appreciation (or valuing) of B&W prints is a cultivated taste for some students.

Learning Task

Using the Krathwohl taxonomy, we established a terminal objective of "conceptualization of a value" (4.1). Although this is a somewhat higher level objective than "appreciation" would dictate, looking at our goal from the standpoint of how it might translate to various levels in the taxonomy caused us to choose this objective. Such translation processes are a benefit of the taxonomy that you should anticipate encountering in the future. (Throughout this section, the elements in parantheses indicate references to levels in the Krathwohl taxonomy in Figure 12.3. This provides additional information on the learning intent of each objective.) Our performance objective for this module of our course is the following:

Each student should choose to ascertain technical information (exposure, contrast, materials used, scene conditions, etc.) of B&W photographs encountered informally, as well as choose to study and analyze the print from an aesthetic and thematic standpoint, relating the technical and artistic qualities of the print in a verbal statement (such as that which might be spoken to a companion while looking at prints in a photographic exhibition). (4.1)

We described the objectives that support and lead up to the terminal objective for this module. The following two objectives appeared at the valuing level of the taxonomy:

Each student will frequently choose to create B&W images over color images in a variety of photomaking opportunities. (3.2)

Each student will typically choose to view the B&W version of old motion picture films over the colorized version, especially for films that have excellent cinematography. (3.2)

These objectives are illustrative of our desire for students to appreciate or value good B&W photography. These two objectives, although both at the same level in the Krathwohl taxonomy, vary widely with regard to ambition for student achievement. However, both are well within what we actually intend as outcomes for graduates of our course.

An objective at the responding level of the taxonomy follows:

Each student will experience pleasure in viewing B&W images. (2.3)

Finally, it seems that the instruction should have its first prerequisite objective at the attending level of the taxonomy, awareness (1.1). This objective relates to the need for students to learn to become aware of certain key elements in B&W images: contrast, exposure, and the aesthetic qualities of the images. The students' ability to evaluate photographs is not at issue, although it may at first glance appear to be so. Here, at the early stage in learning, we are concerned with the students being aware of certain things:

Given B&W pictures of varying quality based on differences in contrast, exposure, and aesthetic qualities, the learner will be able to select those which possess qualities of interest in any of the dimensions embodied in the images. (1.1)

The three components of affective learning are all clearly present in our terminal objective and prerequisite objectives. The cognitive component (knowing what) is seen clearly in the knowledge that will be needed that relates to particular aspects of B&W photography, including salient qualities, such as contrast and exposure, as well as qualities related to the theme and content of the image. The behavioral component (knowing how) can be seen in those activities that the objectives suggest: viewing photographs, making selections, making photographs, and choosing to view certain types of photos.

The effective component (knowing why) is most clearly seen in the students responding to images, discussing them, and internalizing values regarding B&W photographs. The cognitive component contains concept, rule, and problem-solving objectives. (Since we have described and amply illustrated how instruction for objectives in these categories may be designed, we will not perform that analysis or design here.)

Instructional Strategy

Although sequencing and selection of media is made after the design of instructional events, we will describe media for this lesson to help you conceptualize it. The totality of instruction for this module will take place over an extended period of time, but a few introductory lessons that form the core of the instruction will be offered as a short unit. The form of instruction will be a combination of teacher-led instruction with slide-tape (or slide-lecture), sound filmstrip, small group or individual work with study prints, and later, as the objectives of this lesson are pursued along with other objectives in the course, taking photographs and analyzing field work. The use of expensive teacher-led instruction is justified for this instruction due to the requirements that the affective learning goals impose. The teacher will serve as a guide for class discussions and as a role model in some instances.

*I*nstructional Events

We will devote our analysis of instructional events to the first lesson in the unit. This is a lesson to achieve the first objective: awareness of the unique aesthetic qualities of B&W photographs.

Introduction

Deploy Attention

To direct attention to the qualities of B&W photography and to establish a mental/affective set for the lesson (and, it is hoped, the remainder of the module), a biographical narrative will be presented about a pivotal figure in photography, Alfred Stieglitz. The narrative was developed to capitalize on identification as a motivational strategy, and it would be delivered with slides of photographs by Stieglitz and his

contemporaries. These B&W images are of such high quality, from both visual and thematic standpoints, that it is anticipated that they will catch the viewers by surprise. The narrative itself could be presented by a tape in a slide-tape format, but for our class we will use live teacher presentation to increase the attentional value of the presentation.

Alfred Stieglitz

Born in Hoboken, New Jersey, in 1864, Alfred Stieglitz became interested in the new and exciting process called "photography" as a teenager in the 1870s and later as a college student in engineering. His interest in photography became a passion and then an obsession. After five years of frustrating work running a small printing and engraving business in New York following college, he gave up the business and turned all of his energies to photography. He became a photographer with an extraordinary interest in the artistic potential of the medium. In 1897 he took over the editorship of the New York Camera Club's newsletter, *Camera Notes,* and he soon turned the newsletter into a platform for photography as a fine art through his selection of images and editorial content. In 1901 he began a movement called the Photo-Secession, a movement of photographers who had seceded from the mainstream of photography by insisting that good photography consider more than good technique—that it be considered an art form.

During the first decade of the 1900s, Stieglitz's focus became broader to include the championing of contemporary art, whether in the form of photography, painting, or sculpture. He introduced the work of the great European artists Rodin, Matisse, Picasso, Braque, and Cezanne to the United States through his galleries.

In 1915, Stieglitz met the major American artist Georgia O'Keeffe, who was at that time an art teacher in Texas. O'Keeffe had sent some drawings to a friend of hers in New York with instructions that the drawings were not to be shown to anyone. The friend ignored O'Keeffe's instructions and showed the drawings to Stieglitz, who was immediately impressed and began to exhibit them in his gallery. O'Keeffe came to New York and demanded angrily that her pictures be removed from the exhibit. Somehow Stieglitz not only convinced her to leave her pictures but also began a friendship that would last for the rest of their lives. They were married in 1924, and although they lived apart most of the time (she in New Mexico and he in New York), they maintained a warm, intimate, and mutually inspirational relationship. Stieglitz's last series of prints, widely acclaimed as his finest work, was a pictorial biography of his life with Georgia, focusing on his wife's face, hands, legs, and torso. This series of photographs has been described as "images that express the sublime nature of all human relationships" (Mason, 1970, p. 24).

Establish Instructional Purpose

Rather than merely restate the actual objective for this lesson or recast it as "a lesson on appreciation of B&W photography," the instructor should explain the actual idea of the lesson and unit. The learners should be informed that for technical and aesthetic reasons, many of the photographs they will be making in the course as well as in their future professional lives will be B&W rather than color. Creative control of photographic variables is easier with B&W. It is also easier to analyze in the finished product when using B&W. Their appreciation of B&W prints will assist them in the other aspects of the course. Also, the reasons for working with B&W photography, such as its importance in creating reasonably priced, realistic images for instructional texts, should be made clear so that students are not confused about the purposes to which their learning will be put.

Arouse Interest and Motivation

This unit underscores and celebrates B&W photography; part of its purpose is motivational for the rest of the course. For the lesson itself, it is important that students understand why they need to learn to be aware of the aesthetic qualities of B&W photographs. Some reasons were provided in establishment of purpose, but in addition, students may not realize the extent to which high quality B&W photography is important in instruction. B&W photographs will be the preferred form of illustration in many projects that are mediated by print, and the ability to make high quality B&W photographs is in part dependent on an appreciation of the medium's potential.

Preview Lesson

An outline of the schedule, required activities, and evaluation expectations will be presented.

Body

Recall Relevant Prior Knowledge

This lesson will build quite specifically upon previously learned concepts of exposure and contrast. *Objective 1:* Have an awareness of the unique aesthetic qualities of B&W photographs.

Process Information and Examples

A short illustrated lecture will point out B&W photographs in which the combination of (1) exposure and contrast elements with (2) compositional and thematic elements can create uniquely memorable or moving images in ways that color photos cannot. The lecture will employ poster photographs by Ansel Adams and W. Eugene Smith. The luminous quality of Adams' work and the chiaroscuro quality[1] of Smith's work will be pointed out, and techniques relating to exposure, contrast, composition, and lighting in B&W photography will be explained.

Focus Attention

The sound filmstrip "The Personal Journey of W. Eugene Smith" from the series *Images of Man* (1972) will be shown. Some of the images seen earlier as study prints are contained in the kit that includes the filmstrip. In this sound filmstrip Smith narrates photo essays he created as a *Life* magazine photographer during and after World War II.

Practice

Just before presenting the filmstrip, a one-page set of response questions will be distributed. Questions will focus on the aesthetic qualities of the photographs in the filmstrip. These questions will not be directed at memorization or even complete comprehension of all the ideas and visual techniques discussed in the filmstrip; they are directed at helping the student become aware of the qualities of the photographs. Additional practice for the cognitive component of this objective will be provided by an assignment to (1) search out three examples of B&W photogra

---

[1] The term, which literally means "light-dark," refers to style associated with paintings by the "Old Masters," such as Rembrandt, in which light portions of the image seem to glow in contrast with dark areas of the image.

phy that illustrate aesthetic qualities and (2) write one paragraph for each photo that describes its aesthetic qualities.

Following are condensed treatments of instructional events for the Body of the lesson for the remaining objectives in the unit.

Objective 2: Find pleasure in viewing B&W photographic images.

The instruction described previously should lead to achievement of the second objective because of the extremely compelling and dramatic images presented in the examples selected for viewing. The use of high quality filmstrips and prints, coupled with the provision of good viewing conditions, should also give the learners pleasure in viewing these materials.

Objectives 3 and 4: Choose to view B&W versions of films over colorized versions and choose to make B&W photos over color.

For this objective, a screening of a classic B&W film with excellent cinematography will be provided in a subsequent class meeting, followed by a screening of part of a colorized version. Discussion will be directed to differences between the images and why the B&W version of the film is better. Screening this film through videotape may be employed for practical reasons, although the images loose a great deal of their quality from the video transfer process. This fact will be pointed out. Later on in the course, excellent B&W student work can be pointed out and related to the qualities studied in these lessons.

Objective 5: Choose to ascertain technical information about B&W photos and choose to study these images from an aesthetic and technical standpoint.

Modeling of this behavior by the instructor in the presentations and activities described above will be the primary instructional condition; this will be in the context of the presentations and activities themselves providing instruction for the prerequisite objectives.

Employ Learning Strategies

Elaboration techniques in which the students draw examples from their own experiences will be quite helpful in supporting these objectives. If students do not spontaneously elaborate on the content, the instructor will assist the student by asking leading questions (Socratic method).

Practice

Evaluate Feedback

Viewing of the filmstrip will be followed by group discussion. The topic will be "The potential of high quality photography in instruction." This practice is closely related to the remotivation function, a situation not uncommon during lessons that contain affective learning objectives.

Conclusion

Summarize and Review

Transfer Knowledge

Remotivate and Close

Each lesson will conclude with a brief summary of what the main points were of that day's lesson and suggestions for how that learning will be applied in future lessons. Each lesson will conclude with the statement "Today's lesson is finished." For the whole photography class or unit, an entire class period may be devoted to conclusion events at the unit level. The lesson would itself be a summary, transfer experience, remotivation, and closure for the unit. Student presentation of final projects will serve other purposes in the class but will definitely serve well as a conclusion device.

Assessment

Assess Performance

Assessment will be in two parts: One part will be of the cognitive component of the objectives, and the other will assess the affective portion of it. The cognitive component will be assessed through an evaluated exercise in which students are provided with five examples of B&W photography that illustrate aesthetic qualities. Students will be asked to write a paragraph for each photo describing the qualities that the photo exemplifies. The affective component will be assessed later in the course. It will be based upon the selections that the students make when choosing from among color and B&W films for application projects.

(Note: An additional exercise for this chapter would be to find and list or describe the applications of the ARCS Model Motivation Strategies that are contained within this Extended Example.)

Readings and References

Bohlin, R. M. (1987). Motivation in instructional design: Comparison of an American and a Soviet model. *Journal of Instructional Development, 10*(2), 11–14.

Brandhorst, A. R. (1978). *Reconceptualizing the affective domain.* Williamsburg, VA: ERIC Document Reproduction Service No. ED 153 891.

Educational Policies Commission. (1938). *The purposes of education in American democracy.* Washington, D.C.: National Education Association.

Fleming, M., & Levie, W. H. (1978). *Instructional message design: Principles from the behavioral sciences.* Englewood Cliffs, NJ: Educational Technology Publications.

Gagné, R. M. (1985). *The conditions of learning* (4th ed.). New York: Holt, Rinehart & Winston.

Gephart, W. J., & Ingle, R. B. (1976). *Evaluation and the affective domain.* Proceedings of the National Symposium for Professors of Educational Research (NSPER). Phoenix: ERIC Document Reproduction Service No. ED 157 911.

Hoban, C. F., & Van Ormer, E. B. (1950). *Instructional film research, 1918–1950.* Pennsylvania State University Instructional Film Research Program. Port Washington, NY: U.S. Naval Training Device Center, Office of Naval Research, Tech. Report No. SDC 269-7-19.

Images of Man. (1972). (Filmstrip Kit). New York: Scholastic, Inc.

Keller, J. M. (1983). Motivational design of instruction. In C. M. Reigeluth (Ed.), *Instructional-design theories and models.* Hillsdale, NJ: Lawrence Erlbaum, Publisher.

Keller, J. M. (1987). Development and use of the ARCS model of motivational design. *Journal of Instructional Development, 10*(3), 2–11.

Kiesler, C. A., Collins, B. E., & Miller, N. (1969). *Attitude change: A critical analysis of theoretical approaches.* New York: Wiley.

Krathwohl, D. R., Bloom, B. S., & Masia, B. B. (1964). *Taxonomy of educational objectives: The classification of educational goals. Handbook II: Affective domain.* New York: Longman.

Martin, B. L., & Briggs, L. J. (1986). *The affective and cognitive domains: Integration for instruction and research.* Englewood Cliffs, NJ: Educational Technology Publications.

Mason, R. G. (Ed.). (1970). *The Print.* New York: Time-Life Books.

National Special Media Institutes. (1972). *The affective domain: A resource book for media specialists (Contributions of behavioral science to instructional technology, Handbook 1).* Washington, D.C.: Gryphon House.

Newby, T. J., & Stepich, D. A. (1990). Teaching attitudes. *Performance & Instruction, 29* (3), 48–49.

Nunnally, J. C. (1967). *Psychometric theory.* New York: McGraw-Hill.

Rossett, A. (1981). Relevance revisited systematically. *Journal of Instructional Development, 4*(4), 9–13.

Zimbardo, P. G., & Leippe, M. R. (1991). *The psychology of attitude change and social influence.* Philadelphia: Temple University Press.

Designing for Psychomotor Skill Lessons

thirteen

Chapter Objectives

At the conclusion of this chapter you should be able to do the following:

- Given a psychomotor objective, design a strategy for that lesson.

- Given a description of a situation, determine whether spaced or massed practice is needed.

- Given a description of a situation, determine whether part or whole practice is needed.

Introduction

In this chapter we will look at guidelines for designing instruction for psychomotor learning. It is important to consider psychomotor learning as a separate skill area because this domain of learning is commonly misunderstood in practice. On the one hand, learning tasks that are in this domain are frequently ignored or treated as if they were cognitive tasks (such as ignoring the motor skill aspect of learning to drive a car). On the other hand, we frequently see learning tasks that are not actually psychomotor tasks treated as if they were (such as writing an essay or doing long division with pencil and paper). Another reason why motor learning is important for us to study is its relative neglect in the instructional design literature. Although we are by no means starting from scratch with regard to this domain of learning, relatively little emphasis has been given to the specifics of instructional design for motor learning. However, a great deal of research in this area has been done in the physical education field. We can draw upon and use this research in the instructional design process.

In this chapter, we will look at what psychomotor learning is and how to accurately identify learning tasks in this domain. We will also look at instructional concerns and specific instructional strategies that are effective for psychomotor learning tasks. We will also look at the critical instructional events of performance and feedback for this type of learning task. In the conclusion of this chapter we will return to our continuing examples of the photography unit. Here we will look at a motor skill that is part of our unit, and we will show how this skill could be taught using the guidelines we have presented in the chapter.

Review of Psychomotor Learning

In Chapter 4, we introduced the type of learning called *motor skills* and used Gagné's (1985) characterization of them as "coordinated muscular movements that are typified by smoothness and precise timing." Let us begin our review of psychomotor learning by looking first at what is meant by the idea of skills, and then we will look more specifically at psychomotor skills as learning tasks.

The concept of "skill," in the broad sense, may be defined as a "completion of a task with ease and precision" (Robb, 1972, p. 39). Generally, when we think of skills, we have psychomotor capabilities in mind. Psychomotor tasks involve skills that are of a physical nature. We are using the term *psychomotor* rather than *motor* to emphasize the fact that there is a cognitive part to all motor skills. This cognitive component to a skill may be thought of as a schema that underlies the skill. Once we become actually skilled in a psychomotor capability, the cognitive or "thinking" part of the skill becomes automatic and we are no longer conscious of that part of the skill. Yet in learning a psychomotor skill, the cognitive part of the skill is an important part of the learning task.

Designers frequently have difficulty in accurately classifying psychomotor tasks, mistaking the physical manifestations of intellectual skills for the physical part of psychomotor skills. Learning to write an essay, for example, is not a psychomotor objective, even though physical movement may be observed as the student writes. The critical, distinguishing feature of the objective is the *new* learning that is involved. In learning to write an essay, the new learnings are not of a physical nature. The handwriting or typing involved in writing the essay is a psychomotor task—an important but distant prerequisite learning.

For learners to demonstrate that they possess an intellectual skill, they generally must use some muscular movement. Intellectual skills generally require muscle movement to demonstrate. For example, if you are asked to demonstrate your skill in long division, you must move your hand to write or your mouth to speak the answer. You may even engage in movements while you are solving the long division problem. In fact, good instruction of the concepts and rules involved in long division can involve manipulating objects and doing a lot of physical activity. But what is being learned—the new learning involved in learning long division—is a mental, not a physical skill. When the learner is working on a long division exercise or test item with paper and pencil, the manipulations of the pencil, although necessary, are not what we are interested in. At some earlier point in time, we were interested in the learner's manipulation of the pencil as a learning task. At that time, when the youngster was learning to write with a pencil, we *were* concerned with a psychomotor learning task.

Skills that are of a psychomotor nature have their own particular characteristics. In general, a learning task can be said to be a psychomotor task if it requires learning to perform coordinated muscular movements. Examples of psychomotor learning tasks include learning to dribble a basketball, form letters and words with a pencil, parallel park a car, and click a mouse button on a computer. Psychomotor tasks are skills that involve learning new muscular movement.

Researchers have developed various categories of psychomotor skills (Oxendine, 1984; Magil, 1985; Singer, 1980). One means of categorizing psychomotor skills relates to the distinctiveness of the beginning and ending points of skills: discrete versus continuous skills. **Discrete skills** have either a single step or a few steps and have distinct, task-determined beginnings and endings, such as using a key to unlock a door, clicking the mouse button on a computer, or hammering a nail. **Continuous skills** are those for which the beginning and ending points are more subtle and performer-determined, such as dribbling a basketball, swimming, and steering a car to stay within the traffic lane. A subcategory of discrete skills is called *serial skills,* in which a series of subskills are assembled to form a major skill. Forming letters to write words, parallel parking a car, and playing a violin are examples of serial skills. A particularly interesting and frequently encountered task that has characteristics of both continuous and serial skills is the tracking task, such as aiming at a moving target. The stimulus of a tracking task may be continuous—such as a steadily moving target—but research has revealed that acquisition of the target (aiming at it) frequently involves a complex series of decisions and actions rather than one continuous fluid motion as we subjectively experience it (Travers, 1977). Since it takes approximately one-quarter of a second to initiate movement in a direction, only two or three adjustments can be made in a second. Expert performance in tracking tasks demanding particularly fast response requires anticipation.

Another means of categorizing psychomotor skills involves determining how the skill relates to the environment: closed versus open skills. **Closed skills** are performed without active influence from the environment. **Open skills** are those in which the environment causes the performer to make continuous adjustments. Thus, bowling and golf involve closed skills, whereas playing basketball and hockey involve open skills. If all of basketball were comprised of doing slam-dunk demonstrations, without other players to contend with, then basketball would be a closed skill sport. Since those pesky opponents and the player's interactions with them do have a way of making the exact situation of making any shot unpredictable, we find that basketball involves open skills—skills performed in interaction with changing and dynamic external situations.

A third means of categorizing psychomotor skills involves classifying person and object motion (Fitts & Posner 1967; Merrill, 1972). The person may perform the skill either at rest or in motion, and the object may either be at rest or in motion. The two conditions of the person and the two conditions of the object are cast in a matrix in Figure 13.1. The four cells of the matrix represent four types of motor skills. Each of these types has different learning and performance concerns. Type I skills, in which both the performer and the object are at rest, such as clicking the mouse button on a computer or using a key to open a lock, will be concerned primarily with consistency of response, with little need for quickness of adjustment. Type II skills, in which a stable performer is working with a moving object, such as aiming at a moving target from a stationary platform, is an example of a partially dynamic task. Type III tasks, in which a moving performer is working with a stable object, such as making a slam-dunk shot in basketball, are also partially dynamic tasks. Practice requirements for Type II and Type III tasks will be greater than for Type I tasks due to the need to be prepared for varieties of situations that can be encountered. General recommendations also include the use of standard, ''most probable'' situations for initial practice until some competence is developed, such as might be seen in batting practice with a pitching machine. This should occur before encountering the more complex and demanding situations, such as batting to a big-league pitcher (Singer, 1980). Type IV skills, in which both the performer and the object are in motion, such as a spirited volley in badminton or catching a ball while running, involve the most complex dynamic

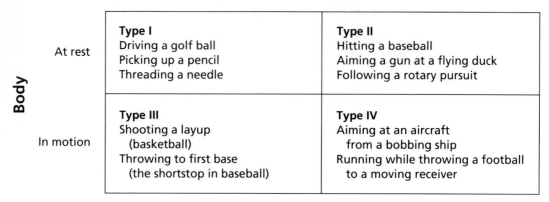

Environmental Object

	At rest	In motion
Body At rest	**Type I** Driving a golf ball Picking up a pencil Threading a needle	**Type II** Hitting a baseball Aiming a gun at a flying duck Following a rotary pursuit
Body In motion	**Type III** Shooting a layup (basketball) Throwing to first base (the shortstop in baseball)	**Type IV** Aiming at an aircraft from a bobbing ship Running while throwing a football to a moving receiver

Figure 13.1: Psychomotor Tasks Classified by Movement of Performer and Object
Source: Adapted from Merrill, M. D. (1972). Reprinted with permission.

interaction. Learning these skills is generally a long process, involving prior practice at levels II and III.

Clearly, each of the three different approaches to categorizing psychomotor skills sheds a somewhat different light on the nature of psychomotor skill learning and upon individual learning tasks as well. One task may be viewed under each of the three approaches because each way of looking at the task provides new insights into the learning requirements for that task.

As we mentioned previously, in addition to learning to control a muscular movement, psychomotor learning tasks have a cognitive component to them. This cognitive component is the *psycho-* part of the *psycho-motor* combination. If you will recall from Chapter 4, psychomotor skills usually contain within them a procedural rule that organizes the kind and sequence of actions performed. So, we see psychomotor learning as a process involving the acquisition of two basic components — muscular movements and a procedural rule.

*E*xercises A

Classify the following skills using each of the three categorization schemes. In the three blanks, label each skill as discrete (D), continuous (C), or serial

(S); and as open (O) or closed (C); and as type I, II, III, or IV.

_____ _____ _____ 1. touch-typing on a keyboard
_____ _____ _____ 2. ice-skating
_____ _____ _____ 3. returning a serve in tennis
_____ _____ _____ 4. shooting a clay pigeon
_____ _____ _____ 5. writing the letter *g* in cursive script
_____ _____ _____ 6. playing kettle drums in an orchestra
_____ _____ _____ 7. grabbing the brass ring on a carousel ride

Critical Elements of Psychomotor Skills

The two components of a psychomotor skill, as characterized in the research literature on human skilled behavior, can provide a foundation for prescribing the instructional strategy for this type of learning. There are two primary characteristics that distinguish skilled behavior from other activities. First, the act employs *executive subroutines* to control decisions and supply subordinate skills in a hierarchical organization or plan (Miller, Galanter, & Pribram, 1960, p. 16; see Robb, 1972, p. 43). Second, the act employs *temporal patterning* of skills to integrate the sequence of performance over time in which the skilled performer employs pacing and anticipation to enable the act to be performed with ease and smoothness (Robb, 1972, pp. 44–49).

Competing lines of theory in the specialty of motor learning include the "closed loop" theory (Adams, 1971) and a schema theory (Schmidt, 1982). Both theories attempt to describe the cognitive component of skills, often called *motor programs*, the role of internal feedback, and knowledge of results or *KR* ("information about the correctness of response from an external source such as . . . a teacher or coach." [Magil, 1985, p. 68]). We will have more to say about schema, particularly with relationship to automaticity, later in this chapter.

Much of what we do in providing instruction for psychomotor skills involves (1) a demonstration and explanation that leads to the verbal information and procedural rule learning that form the basis for the executive subroutines and (2) practice with feedback that leads to temporal patterning. Instructional strategies for learning procedural rules are described in depth in Chapter 9, and more about the cognitive component of psychomotor learning will be provided later on in this chapter. The other critical factor, that of practice, will be discussed here.

An aspect of psychomotor learning that has received a great deal of attention in the research literature is practice. Two issues with regard to practice deserve some attention here: distribution of practice (massed versus spaced) and chunking of skill elements (whole versus part).

Massed versus Spaced Practice. In massed practice the learner engages in one or a few intensive, extended periods of practice with little or no rest in between. The alternate form of practice, called *spaced practice,* is the form in which many relatively short practice sessions are distributed over time. The primary factors that interact with practice distribution are learner characteristics (such as age, skill level, and prior experience) and the type of skill to be learned (whether the skill is simple or complex, has few or many elements, is fatiguing, or demands close attention to detail). Harrison and Blakemore (1989) describe typical conditions under which spaced practice would be advisable:

Younger students and students with low ability levels fatigue easily and have shorter attention or concentration spans, and lower interest levels. Distributed practice sessions in which several skills are practiced during a class period are usually preferred for these students. . . . Strenuous activities often must be scheduled for shorter periods of time due to the effects of fatigue. (p. 95)

Figure 13.2 summarizes factors to take into account in making decisions on practice distribution.

	Shorter and More Frequent	**Longer and Less Frequent**
If the task	Is simple, repetitive, or boring Demands intense concentration Is fatiguing Demands close attention to detail	Is complex Has many elements Requires warm-up Is a new one for the performer
If the learner	Is young or immature (unable to sustain activity) Has short attention span Has poor concentration skills Fatigues easily	Is older or more mature Is able to concentrate for long periods of time Has good ability to focus attention Tires less easily

Figure 13.2: Factors in Practice Distribution
Source: Rothstein, A., Catelli, L., Dodds, P., & Manahan, J. (1981). p. 40.

Whole versus Part Practice. Another issue regarding practice that has received a great deal of research is the question of how best to "chunk" the parts of a skill. A skill may be practiced as a whole, such as practicing a tennis serve, or it may be practiced in parts, such as practicing first the toss of a tennis serve, then separately practicing the swing and the follow-through. In part practice, each separate part of a skill is mastered before assembling the parts into a whole. Notice that the concern here is with the chunking of practice; demonstrations and explanations of a skill may be chunked into separate parts even when whole practice is employed.

As with massed and spaced practice decisions, the primary factors that influence decisions about whole versus part practice are found within the learner and the learning task. The number, complexity, and interrelatedness of the subroutines in a skill can vary from relatively independent and isolated, such as tying a knot, to relatively integrated and simultaneous, such as riding a bicycle. Likewise, learner differences in attention span, memory span, and skill level will make a difference as to how much part practice will be necessary. Figure 13.3 summarizes primary factors that interact in decisions on whole versus part practice.

Even for cases in which part practice is necessary due to learning task and learner factors there is a drawback to it. The problem with part practice (even when it is required) is that learners may experience difficulty in putting the parts together. One technique that has been developed to overcome this problem is called the **progressive part method,** in which learners practice the first step, or part 1 of a skill, and then, in practicing part 2, practice it together with part 1. Then part 3 is practiced along with parts 1 and 2, and so forth.

A further refinement in progressive part practice can be seen in a technique called **backwards chaining,** in which the learner is exposed to and practices each step from last to first, in a progressive part fashion but in reverse order. For example, if we were to teach a young child how to tie her shoes, we would first show the whole operation as an overview. Then, we would quickly tie a shoe up to the last step in the process and direct the child's attention to that last step: "Now watch me pull the

	Emphasize Wholes	Emphasize Parts
If the task	Has highly dependent (integrated) parts Is simple Is not meaningful in parts Is made up of simultaneously performed parts	Has highly individual parts Is very complex Is made up of individual skills If limited work on parts or different segments is necessary
If the learner	Is able to remember long sequences Has a long attention span Is highly skilled	Has a limited memory span Is not able to concentrate for a long period of time Is having difficulty with a particular part Cannot succeed with the whole method

Figure 13.3: Factors in Chunking a Skill for Practice
Source: Rothstein, A., Catelli, L., Dodds, P., & Manahan, J. (1981). p. 38.

loop through the hole." After two or three repeats of this demonstration, the child is given the shoe with the knot all tied except for this last step, which the child gets to perform. The next thing that is demonstrated and practiced is the next-to-last step. Then the third-to-last step is demonstrated and practiced (along with the next-to-last and last steps), and so forth. The last thing that is shown and practiced is the first step. Backwards chaining compensates for the forgetting problem between explanations and demonstrations when there are many steps in a skill, each one of which requires practice.

Feedback Issues. In performing a motor task, the individual experiences feedback from internal sources called *proprioceptive feedback* and other sensory feedback such as vision. The nervous system, which sends commands to muscles to move, also sends signals back to the brain from the muscles and organs such as the skin. We experience a mild form of proprioceptive feedback loss with anesthetics for dental work. Sometimes we find we have chewed our tongue or cheek badly, something which proprioceptive feedback would have prevented had the nerves in the mouth not been temporarily deadened. An expert performer of a skill is heavily dependent upon the feedback that engagement in the task provides—visual, auditory, and proprioceptive sensations that performance of the task (and the situation) generates.

A great deal of the expertise in psychomotor functions lies in the skill of "reading" feedback generated by performance of a task. When a person is learning a new psychomotor skill, often it is not clear what to look for. The sensation of having properly performed the skill is not present because the person can't properly perform the skill yet. External (or instructionally provided) feedback may supplement the learner's built-in feedback. (The learner may think, "My swing was three inches too high.") Or, instruction may provide guidance to the learner on what to look for or be sensitive to. (The teacher/coach may say, "Feel it on the balls of your feet when you receive the serve.")

Two forms of feedback can be provided in psychomotor learning: feedback about the product (or "quality of response outcome") and feedback about the process or causes of the response out-

come (Magil, 1985). During early stages of learning, feedback about process may be most helpful to learning, and during later learning, feedback on outcome alone may be sufficient. Instruction-supplied feedback may not always be needed or even helpful. Early learning of simple motor tasks has been found to be improved by providing feedback on less than every response (Ho & Shea, 1978; Newell, 1974). Precision of instruction-supplied feedback can effect learning. It is possible to provide too precise a feedback to be useful, such as describing a distance in millimeters when centimeters would be more meaningful (Rogers, 1974). The precision offered by quantitative feedback has been found in some cases to be superior to qualitative feedback, such as "you're holding the ball two inches too high" versus "you're holding the ball too high" (Smoll, 1972).

*E*xercises B

For the following scenarios, label the practice distribution as massed (M) or spaced (S). Also label the practice chunking as whole practice (W), part practice (P), progressive part practice (PP), or backward chaining (BC).

_____ _____ 1. John and Theresa, both 7 years old, are each going to assemble a model airplane. Neither of them has ever built a model airplane. The kit has balsa wood pieces that must be fit together and glued. To complete the model, one must apply wet tissue paper to the wooden framework. Both children have the desire to build the plane, but the task will be a challenge because of their age. (Consider the task of building the whole kit as well as the sub-task of papering. Think of the children's learning, not just the successful completion of the kit.)

_____ _____ 2. Jean and Ray, both 10 years old, have joined a beginners soccer team. They will be learning all aspects of the game of soccer over the 4-month season.

_____ _____ 3. Juan and Bryan are graduate students in piano; each wants to improve his playing technique to the concert level. They are learning to control the cross from left to right hand in loudness changes, with each hand playing a rhythmic pattern. They are both practicing George Gershwin's "Rhapsody in Blue," a long piece that is extremely difficult to play. Juan has excellent technique, but his hands are not very strong. Bryan has very strong hands but is less coordinated than Juan.

_____ _____ 4. Barbara and Mark, both in their late 20s, are new employees at a chemical manufacturing plant. Their jobs involve moving large amounts of material from one part of the plant to another. Although aided by equipment, their jobs involve a great deal of strenuous work; they also must learn to operate hoisting and rolling equipment.

*T*ask Analysis of a Psychomotor Skill

Task analysis for psychomotor skills is described in detail in Chapter 4. We have noted that the learning of a psychomotor skill includes a cognitive component. Let's take a look at an example skill description, one that includes consideration of the cognitive component of the skill as subroutines in the skill.

The task of beginning bowling can be divided into three subroutines. These are (1) the approach, (2) moving the ball, and (3) the release of the ball. Further examination of each subroutine reveals that the approach consists of steps that get progressively longer and faster and end with a slide. Since this is not the way a person normally walks, the subroutine of walking will have to be modified. Conscious effort and practice will be needed to overcome his habitual walking pattern.

The second subroutine involved in the task of bowling is moving a ball through space. Although the performer is accustomed to swinging his arm, he is not familiar with moving a ball that weighs between 12 and 16 pounds.

The third subroutine involves the release of the ball. A smooth release is characterized by a roll of the ball rather than a drop or throw. Thus the beginner must learn to bend his left knee (assuming he is right-handed) and release the ball smoothly on the lane, not on the approach area. The ball should land on the lane like an airplane landing on a runway. (Robb, 1972, p. 143)

Some authorities break down the learning of a psychomotor skill into three phases: (1) cognitive phase, (2) associative phase, and (3) autonomous phase (Fitts & Posner, 1967; see Singer, 1982, p. 87). We can analyze the bowling example from this three-phase standpoint to better understand the role of the cognitive component in psychomotor learning.

During the beginning or cognitive phase of learning a psychomotor skill, learners begin to acquire the verbal information and procedural rule components of the psychomotor skill. They learn what they are to do and in what sequence. Note that the learners learn *what* is to be learned; they do not at this time learn *how* to do it in the physical sense. Explanations and demonstrations are part of what is required to achieve the cognitive learning requirements for psychomotor skills. In addition, learners may need repetition and rehearsal in order to remember the steps of the skill. Depending on the requirements of the skill at hand, repetition along with practice during the second and third phases might be sufficient, or the cognitive component may require its own repetition and application as one grouping of objectives in a lesson design. (You may wish to refer to Chapter 9 to review the design of instruction for learning procedural rules because many of that chapter's recommendations are pertinent to learning a procedural rule that is a part of a psychomotor skill.)

During the second (or associative) phase of learning a psychomotor skill, learners begin to learn how to physically perform the skill. In bowling, learners will at some point engage in their first few practice rounds. Actual performance is required during this phase of learning, in which the learner associates the cognitive knowledge of the skill with the muscular movements required to perform it. At this stage the procedural rule is deepened and made meaningful by the actual physical activity that accompanies each step in the procedure, but a smooth, highly skilled performance is not likely.

During the autonomous phase, practice and feedback allow the learner to progress from the jerky or fumbling efforts of the novice to the smooth, controlled, apparently effortless actions that characterize the expert performance of a psychomotor skill. The student bowler becomes more proficient at the skill, reaching what is called *automaticity*. As automaticity is attained the cognitive component becomes less and less at the conscious level, with each physical movement cueing the next physical movement. Automaticity may be parallel to schematization (the idea of "schema" was introduced in Chapter 7 and noted earlier in this chapter). When thinking about and studying the phenomenon of a skill becoming autonomous and no longer a matter of separate steps for a learner, a good explanation for what goes on may be found in thinking about schema. The same networking and unifying process that underlie schematization of knowledge and rules would appear to be a good explanation for the cognitive component of psychomotor skill learning in moving from novice to expert.[1]

A General Procedure for Teaching Psychomotor Skills

Singer (1982, pp. 109–110) provides a three-phase approach to the teaching of psychomotor skills that dovetails with the three phases of learning described above. The three phases for instruction which Singer describes are (1) prior to practice, (2) during practice, and (3) after practice. Let's elaborate these three phases to form a general procedure for teaching psychomotor skills, using our expanded instructional events as a framework.

---

[1]This linking of schema with automaticity is not the same idea as that held by Schmidt (1982) described earlier in this chapter. Yet there appears to be no contradiction between our discussion and Schmidt's "Schema Theory of Motor Learning." We are indebted to Rita Richey for this concept.

Instruction prior to practice needs to prepare the learners for learning the skill and to engage in the initial learning of the skill itself. To begin, learners need to know what is being learned, they need to know why they must learn it, and they need to know how they are going to go about learning this skill. In addition, it is during this stage of instruction that explanations and demonstrations are provided, supplying the conditions for achieving the cognitive phase of learning the skill.

If we apply our expanded instructional events, we can see that events that occur prior to practice include events from both our Introduction and Body phases. From the Introduction phase we see the following events: deploy attention to the lesson, establish instructional purpose, arouse interest and motivation, and obtain a preview of the lesson. Events during the Body of the lesson (but still prior to practice) include the recall of relevant prior learning, processing information and examples associated with an explanation and/or demonstration (at this stage of instruction, verbal and visual, not tactile), focusing attention to the demonstration/ explanation, and employing learning strategies.

Using our bowling example, let's examine the instruction.

Deploy Attention to the Lesson

The student's attention may be directed to bowling by merely being in the bowling alley, yet many distracting sights and sounds make it likely that the instruction will need to actively and explicitly direct the student's attention to the learning task frequently within the instruction. As an aid to continued attention, it will help if the learner can be made aware of how it will benefit her if she were to learn the skill that is going to be taught. Much of the value in the following two events is toward this very point: to help the learner continue to pay attention to and invest effort in the lesson as it proceeds.

Establish Instructional Purpose

Establishing the purpose can be done in many ways, but somehow the learner must be apprised of what is to be learned now. For this lesson, we might say, "Today, we are going to begin to learn to bowl," and the instructor might even at this point demonstrate what will be learned. The direction will be further refined when we actually preview the lesson.

Arouse Interest and Motivation

The learner should determine why he should learn the material at hand. Placing the material into a larger scheme (particularly when the learnings for the current lesson have a prerequisite function for subsequent lessons) can be sufficient for learners who are generally motivated in the course or program. For learners who are not such "self-starters," direct and personalized relating of how the material can help them may be required, including appeals to personal-social needs of the learners. For high school learners in our bowling lesson, some relationship of being skilled in bowling to being popular with peers might somehow be devised. Appeals to health and fitness might not be sufficient for high school students but might well hit home with a middle-aged population.

Preview of the Lesson

The preview should include both an overview of *what* will be learned as well as a preview of *how* the lesson will proceed. For example, a bowling lesson might be overviewed in terms of content by saying the following:

In today's introductory lesson in bowling, we will learn three main steps. First, we will learn the approach, in which we will see that we walk toward the line with steps of increasing length and increasing speed. Second, we will learn how to move the ball during the approach. Third, we will learn the release, in which we will learn to roll the ball out of the hand rather than drop or throw it.

Notice that a preview of exactly what is to be learned is presented. Next, we would preview how the lesson will proceed by saying something like the following:

The way we'll proceed is this. First, I will show you each of the steps and point out things to focus on. Each of you will have a chance to see what is involved in each of the steps—how to do it right. Then you'll have a chance to practice. I will be watching you and helping you. I'll offer correction if I see you're not doing something right. Then, after we've had a chance to practice the skill, I'll have each of you roll the ball a few times without help. At this point I'll be watching you to see how well you can do it. Ok, let's begin.

Recall Relevant Prior Knowledge

The skills of bowling build upon previously learned skills. The approach in bowling, for example, is a special form of walking. Immediately prior to the demonstration of the approach, it might be helpful to remind learners that what you are doing as you perform the approach is simply walking. During the practice phase, as well, learners can be assisted in their first tries at the approach by being advised to walk. The instruction might include verbal tips such as the following:

Walk to the line now. Just pretend you're on a stroll in the park. This time, though, just imagine that you're walking up to something with longer and longer and faster steps as you near your goal. That's it.

Process Information and Examples

In our psychomotor skill lesson, this event is accomplished by the explanation/demonstration of the skill itself. Still prior to practice, the instruction presents the skill itself. In some lessons, an explanation should precede a demonstration, and in others, the explanation and demonstration should occur simultaneously. The decision will depend upon the specifics of the skill being learned and is a fairly self-evident one. The instructional medium used for information and examples does not always have to be a live teacher; a videotape will frequently be a superior medium for delivering this event. Advantages of video include its ability to show close-up details, employ techniques such as slow motion, and provide the opportunity for individualized instruction. Regardless of the delivery medium employed, the explanation/demonstration should be clearly and explicitly organized in terms of the steps (or subroutines) of the skill, perhaps even providing verbal cues, such as *pause, left, right, left and back, release, slide,* and *follow through.* In our bowling lesson, we will demonstrate and explain simultaneously, repeating demonstrations that focus on each of the three bowling steps. In addition to live demonstration, a videotape will be used that shows the bowler from different angles (from the side, back, and front) and presents close-ups of the release itself in slow motion as well as normal speed.

Focus Attention

The learner's need to attend to instruction will be present throughout the lesson, but lapses of attention during presentation of information and examples are a frequent contributor to unsuccessful instruction. The learners' attention will be enhanced by the quality of the introduction as well as by characteristics of the explanation/demonstration itself. Also, during and after the practice phases of the lesson, the learner activity that is intrinsic to psychomotor skill lessons is potentially a built-in attention aid. But learner attention should not be taken for granted, even in psychomotor skill lessons.

Attention takes on particular importance in many psychomotor skill lessons, which involve skills that we can call *critical skills*. Critical skills are those that involve potentially life-threatening situations, such as piloting aircraft, performing surgery, and packing parachutes. Just because instruction involves potentially life-threatening situations does not necessarily mean that learners will be paying sufficient attention during all phases of instruction. The importance and relevance of the activities at hand should always be clear to the learner. Specific techniques for maintaining attention should be considered and employed as needed. Often with psychomotor skill instruction, attention-directing can be included as a part of carefully performing demonstrations. The instructor might say, "Notice that I . . . " or "See how he . . . " and so forth.

Employ Learning Strategies

Learners can be assisted in their acquisition of new skills by employing learning strategies. The instruction in the new skill may include assistance or suggestions that can lead the learner to employ learning strategies that she may not otherwise devise. In our bowling lesson, the instructor might suggest a visualization strategy by saying the following:

Before you step up to the lane, briefly close your eyes and try to visualize yourself executing the steps in bowling, smoothly and skillfully.

Another example of a possible learning strategy for our bowling lesson could be the use of a mnemonic or oral rehearsal of what the learner should be doing. One such mnemonic that has been used in tennis instruction, for the steps in returning a tennis serve, is SBSSF: "*S*ide to the net, racket *B*ack, *S*tep and *S*wing through the ball, and *F*ollow through." Analogies can also be used to support the recall of the steps in the procedural rule supporting the motor skill. For instance, many of us learned to tie a bow knot through an analogous story about a rabbit going around a tree, in a hole, and so forth.

During practice, instruction primarily needs to support appropriate practice. Here is where decisions about the distribution (part/whole) and scheduling (massed/spaced) of practice are made, as well as sequencing. Practice is a fundamental aspect of learning and perfecting psychomotor skills. Complex skills such as musical performance and athletics are refined over long periods of time involving repeated practice.

From the standpoint of our expanded instructional events, we can see that *all* of the events may legitimately take place in the "during practice" phase, but that the predominant events are practice and feedback.

Practice

Practice will involve the actual grasping of the bowling ball, walking to the line while beginning the arm swing, and so forth. During practice, guidance may be provided by a coach talking the learner through his first attempts or by providing hints and suggestions on holding the ball, placement of the feet, and so forth. Provision of learning guidance may also be seen in ensuring that the learner participates in repeated practice, appropriately scheduled and chunked. Much of the traditional role of a good athletic coach may be seen as an excellent example of the provision of learning guidance.

It is during this event that we have the opportunity to specifically apply what we know about practice distribution, scheduling, and sequencing. In the case of our bowling example, spaced practice will be required due to fatigue and task complexity factors. Many athletic skills are of this nature because the concept of "mastery" does not apply, and practice can lead to improvement over a period of years. In learning a skill such as bowling, practice will be required until the learner reaches automaticity.

Feedback

Feedback is obtained not only externally by the comments and suggestions provided by a coach or videotape replay but also internally by the learner's own built-in proprioceptive feedback mechanisms and senses of hearing and vision. The internal feedback that we receive from kinesthetic "feel" and from sensory systems is fundamental to learning psychomotor skills. For this reason, feedback is considered to be a "during practice" event rather than an "after practice" event. Learners may have to be taught to recognize proprioceptive feedback. For example, a coach might throw the ball at the "sweet spot" of the learner's tennis racket many times before the learner begins to recognize the "feel" of hitting the ball properly.

After practice we are primarily concerned with evaluation and conclusion of the lesson. We will reverse our usual instructional events sequence in this example. As noted in the introduction to the expanded instructional events in Chapter 6, the sequence provided is nominal, not strictly prescriptive. In the current example, our bowling lesson will include an assessment of the learners' skills within the lesson itself, followed by the conclusion phase of the lesson.

Assess Performance

A summative assessment of performance, or posttest, of psychomotor skills is frequently performed as a separate step from practice, in addition to observation of practice, to form the basis for assessment of competence in a skill. In either case, the assessment itself and communication of its results are conducted after practice. An informal assessment might be appropriate, in which the instructor watches the learners bowl a few frames, carefully observing their performance. An additional refinement could be the use of a rating scale to improve the reliability and consistency of the observations as well as provide a comprehensive yet convenient way to help appraise the learner of the assessment. Using an informal observation as a basis for assessment in our bowling example, the instructor could tell a learner that he is doing well on the approach but that the release needs some improvement. Another learner might be told that she is doing everything properly and should continue practicing.

Summarize and Review

The summary should recap the main points of the lesson. In our bowling example, the summary might go something like this:

Today we had our first lesson in bowling. You all learned to throw the ball correctly, which as you recall involves three things: first, the approach, where we learned to walk to the line with steps of increasing length and speed; second, we learned how to move the ball as we approach; and third, we learned the proper way to release the ball.

In the summary, it is important to emphasize the material that has already been covered. If new material cannot be resisted, it should not be allowed to interfere with the consolidating and clarifying function of the summary.

Transfer of Knowledge

Transfer is primarily accomplished by additional practice with accompanying learning guidance and feedback. Our bowling instructor might prescribe practice twice weekly for the next six weeks, with observation and feedback twice within the practice period. This is to reinforce what was initially learned during the first session. A further example of transfer could be to bowl in different alleys.

Remotivate and Close

The very last of our bowling lesson can consist of the instructor briefly reminding learners, now that they know the skill, how they can apply it in the future. The closure of the lesson will let the students know that the lesson is over.

So, now you have another alternative to going to the movies or watching TV. When you do go bowling with friends or on a date, you won't need to feel embarrassed at not being able to bowl—even if you're not an expert yet. Just remember how you did it. Go through the steps in your mind, and then let your body's memory do what it remembers. OK, see you Thursday.

Evaluate Feedback and Seek Remediation

Here, the learner processes what she knows about how well she can perform the skill and takes appropriate action. For example, one learner will need further instruction on the release of the ball. Another learner who is performing quite well will not need to concentrate on making any particular corrections, only to deepen and perfect the skills she has developed. An instructional system, such as a computer-managed instruction system, might take on some of the job of processing evaluation results and prescribing remediation.

Summary

In this chapter, we began with a review of psychomotor learning. We looked at what kind of learning characterizes psychomotor learning tasks—skills involving physical activity. We learned to look for the distinguishing feature of "what new learning is involved" to assist in accurately discriminating psychomotor tasks from other types of learning tasks.

In our review of psychomotor learning, we also looked at psychomotor learning from the "skilled performance" viewpoint. In addition, we reviewed issues in psychomotor learning regarding practice: massed versus spaced practice and whole versus part practice, including two techniques for improving part practice—progressive part practice and backward chaining.

Next we reviewed the task analysis of a psychomotor skill (using the example of bowling), in which we saw that the major steps of the skill, or major subroutines, form the basis of the skill. Also, we looked at the phases of learning of a psychomotor skill: the cognitive phase, the associative phase, and the autonomous phase.

We presented a three-phase approach to the teaching of psychomotor skills, in which we looked at the instructional events that should take place (1) prior to practice, (2) during practice, and (3) after practice. Finally, we used the expanded events of instruction to examine strategy decisions by using the bowling example. Figure 13.4 summarizes key points in this chapter.

Job Aid

Prior to Practice

1. Deploy attention. _____

2. Establish instructional purpose. _____

3. Arouse interest and motivation. _____

4. Preview of the lesson. _____

5. Recall relevant prior knowledge. _____

6. Process information and examples. _____

7. Focus attention. _____

8. Employ learning strategies. _____

During Practice

9. Practice
   Determine practice distribution (massed/spaced). _____

Components of Psychomotor Skills

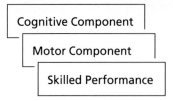

Cognitive Component

Motor Component

Skilled Performance

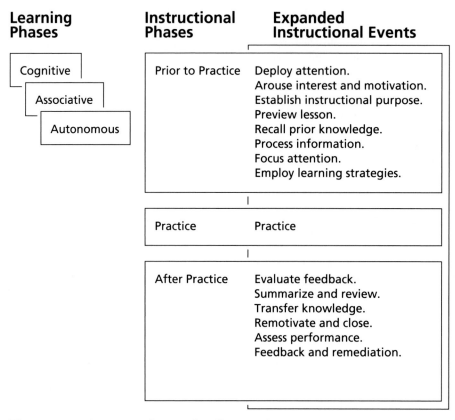

Learning Phases	Instructional Phases	Expanded Instructional Events
Cognitive	Prior to Practice	Deploy attention. Arouse interest and motivation. Establish instructional purpose. Preview lesson. Recall prior knowledge. Process information. Focus attention. Employ learning strategies.
Associative	Practice	Practice
Autonomous	After Practice	Evaluate feedback. Summarize and review. Transfer knowledge. Remotivate and close. Assess performance. Feedback and remediation.

Figure 13.4: Summary Diagram for Chapter 13

Practice schedule:_____

Determine chunking of practice (whole, part, progressive part). _____

10. Feedback _____

After Practice

11. Assess performance. _____

12. Summarize and review. _____

13. Transfer of knowledge. _____

14. Evaluate feedback and seek remediation. _____

Extended Example

Although photography involves physical activity, we find that learning outcomes that are of a psychomotor nature are few and far between. Although physically manifested, the setting of a lens aperture or shutter speed involves little if any actual psychomotor learning. In either case, knowing *how to determine* the correct lens aperture or shutter speed is what needs to be taught. Once we know that the shutter speed needs to be 1/125, the rotation of the shutter speed dial requires little if any instruction. Loading film into a 35mm camera is another possible example, depending on how difficult to load the camera you are using is. With some cameras, a particularly skilled manipulation of the film is necessary to get the film to thread properly into the camera parts. Other examples of psychomotor learning tasks in photography include releasing the shutter, loading film onto a stainless steel reel in a daylight developing tank, and panning on a moving object. We will use the last task in this example.

Task analysis reveals that panning on a moving object involves (1) visually following a moving object to gauge the speed of the pan that will be needed and (2) rotating the trunk of the body at a rate that will allow the camera to swing around so that the moving object remains within the view-finder through the majority of the arc of the pan. The skill also includes the ability to release the shutter at some time during the actual pan, not before it begins or after it is over. The skill is comprised of both a procedural rule and skill acquisition (motor learning). The procedural rule may be reflected as a sequence of steps:

1. Determine that a pan is needed.
2. Follow (track) the moving object.
3. Rotate trunk to swing camera at the matching rate.
4. Release shutter.

Deploy Attention

Establish Instructional Purpose

Arouse Interest and Motivation

We will begin our lesson with an introduction in which attention is directed to the topic. The student is assisted in this by the instruction showing bad, then good, pictures of moving objects. The instruction points out that the good pictures were taken by a photographer who knew how to pan. Motivation and interest in the topic will be deepened by making specific links between the students' success and their ability to perform this skill.

Preview Lesson

Still in the introduction to the lesson, we will overview the lesson by describing first the major parts of the skill (the tracking and estimating, the actual body trunk rotation, and the shutter release during the pan). Next, in the overview, we will describe how the lesson will proceed, indicating that the instructor will first explain and demonstrate each of the steps. Then, each student will practice them first with a video camcorder and next with an instant-developing camera. The overview further notes that after practice the students will each take one more picture with the instant-developing camera for a "test" of their ability to perform the skill. Notice that the overview covers both what will be taught and how it will be taught.

Recall Relevant Prior Knowledge

We begin the body of the lesson by demonstrating and explaining the skill of taking a pan shot. The instructor will build on previous learning by recounting experiences of watching tennis matches, auto races, or other situations in which a spectator follows a moving object. The instructor will also call attention to the shutter release.

Process Information and Examples

Two students will toss a basketball back and forth to provide a moving object to pan. The instructor will use a camcorder to demonstrate, providing a television monitor so that students may see what the instructor sees in the viewfinder.

A combined demonstration/explanation is selected in this case rather than a separate explanation followed by demonstration because the steps of the skill are few and, given the preview of them during the overview, a combined demonstration/explanation will not be confusing. Releasing the shutter will not be part of this initial demonstration.

Focus Attention

Employ Learning Strategies

Practice

Following the initial demonstration/explanation, a student performance phase will begin in which students will be directed and managed in taking turns using the camcorder to take a pan shot of the moving basketball. The camcorder was selected for the first round of practice because it is easier than using a camera. Timed release of a shutter is not needed, and viewing the video monitor provides continuous feedback at a time when the learner can adjust and compensate.

Evaluate Feedback

To provide additional feedback, the instructor will carefully supervise the performance and offer both encouragement as well as corrections as needed. The instructor might say the following: "You'll need to lead a little. You're behind the ball all the time," or "Don't wait until the time you want to take the picture; begin panning just as soon as the ball comes into range, maybe even a little before. You have to anticipate it." Another comment would be "Yes, that's good, you're keeping it right in the middle of the screen."

Recall Relevant Prior Knowledge

Process Information and Examples

Focus Attention

Employ Learning Strategies

A second demonstration/explanation phase will be conducted in which the instructor will use an instant-developing camera to demonstrate the complete skill—this time including the timing of the shutter release. The instructor will say, "Notice when I squeeze the shutter now." A different object might be employed, rather than the basketball, such as a moving car or running person. The speed of the object to track, as well as its distance and angle from the camera, should be tried out in advance by the designer to ensure that a challenging yet feasible photographic subject is provided.

Practice

Following the second demonstration, a second supervised performance phase will begin. Each student should have more than one opportunity to try the skill, along with instructor supervision and feedback. Again, as with the feedback following the first practice, the feedback will be informative and corrective.

Assessing the Performance

The instructor will make a clear transition from the supervised performance phase to an evaluation phase in the lesson. Students will be clearly informed of what will happen during this phase, including the condition that now they are to perform the skill independently, without help from the instructor or other students so that their proficiency can be observed. The instructor then conducts the evaluation phase of the lesson, observing the students' performance.

Evaluate Feedback and Seek Remediation

The evaluation phase concludes with a report to each student on her proficiency so that after the lesson the student can know how she did and can engage in further work with the material as needed.

Summarize and Review

The conclusion of the lesson includes a summary, which may involve a final demonstration of the skill by the instructor, and a short presentation on situations in which the skill can be used. The instructor will also discuss situations in which using the skill would not be appropriate.

Remotivate and Close

The instructor completes the lesson and establishes closure by stating that the lesson is concluded.

Transfer Knowledge

Additional practice of the skill in real-life situations, such as a shooting assignment, will be needed to sufficiently address the need for transfer.

Readings and References

Adams, J. A. (1971). A closed-loop theory of motor learning. *Journal of Motor Behavior, 3,* 111–150.

Briggs, L. J. (Ed.). (1977). *Instructional design.* Englewood Cliffs, NJ: Educational Technology Publications.

Fitts, P. M., & Posner, M. I. (1967). *Human performance.* Belmont, CA: Brooks/Cole.

Gagné, R. M. (1985). *The Conditions of learning* (4th ed.). New York: Holt, Rinehart & Winston.

Harrison, J. M., & Blakemore, C. L. (1989). *Instructional strategies for secondary school physical education* (2nd ed.). Dubuque, IA: Brown.

Ho L., & Shea, J. B. (1978). Levels of processing and the coding of position cues in motor short-term memory. *Journal of Motor Behavior, 10,* 113–121.

Jonassen, D. H., & Hannum, W. H. (1986). Analysis of task analysis procedures. *Journal of Instructional Development, 9,* 2–12.

Magil, R. A. (1985). *Motor learning concepts & applications,* (2nd ed.). Dubuque, IA: Brown.

Merrill, M. D. (1972). Taxonomies, classifications, and theory. In R. N. Singer (Ed.), *The psychomotor domain: Movement and behavior.* Philadelphia: Lee & Febiger.

Miller, G. A., Galanter, E., & Pribram, K. (1960). *Plans and the structure of behavior.* New York: Henry Holt.

Newel, K. M. (1974). Knowledge of results and motor learning. *Journal of Motor Behavior, 1,* 235–244.

Oxendine, J. B. (1984). *Psychology of motor learning.* Englewood Cliffs, NJ: Prentice-Hall.

Rink, J. E. (1985). *Teaching physical education for learning.* St. Louis: Times Mirror/Mosby.

Robb, M. D. (1972). *The dynamics of motor-skill acquisition.* Englewood Cliffs, NJ: Prentice-Hall.

Rogers, C. A. (1974). Feedback precision and post-feedback interval duration. *Journal of Experimental Psychology, 102,* 604–608.

Rothstein, A., Catelli, L., Dodds, P., & Manahan, J. (1981) *Basic stuff series I: Motor learning.* Reston, VA: American Alliance for Health, Physical Education, Recreation, and Dance.

Schmidt, R. A. (1982). *Motor control and learning: A behavioral emphasis.* Champaign, IL: Human Kinetics.

Singer, R. N. (1980). *Motor learning and human performance.* New York: Macmillan.

Singer, R. N. (1982). *The learning of motor skills*. New York: Macmillan.

Singer, R. N., & Dick, W. (1974). *Teaching physical education: A systems approach*. Boston: Houghton Mifflin.

Smoll, F. L. (1972). Effects of precision of information feedback upon acquisition of a motor skill. *Research Quarterly, 43,* 489–493.

Stepich, D. A., & Newby, T. J. (1990). Teaching psychomotor skills. *Performance & Instruction, 29*(4), 47–48.

Travers, R. M. W. (1977). *Essentials of learning* (4th ed.). New York: Macmillan.

Designing Delivery and Management Strategies

fourteen

Chapter Objectives

At the conclusion of this chapter you should be able to do the following:

- Describe and recognize the critical attributes of the instructional media of print, computers, video, interactive video, and teachers.

- Given the characteristics of the learners, the learning task, and the learning context, select the appropriate medium/media and provide a rationale that justifies the choice in terms of those factors and the attributes of the media selected.

- Given the characteristics of the learners, the learning task, and the learning context, select the appropriate grouping strategy.

- Describe two management strategies that were devised to manage instruction that contains individualized instruction.

*D*elivery Strategies

Delivery strategy decisions involve determining an appropriate medium (or media) of instruction and determining grouping strategies. These selections may be the same through all the events, or they may vary from event to event. For example, introduction events might be presented via videotape to a large group; events in the body of the instruction through computer-based instruction in an individualized format; and conclusion events with teacher and print in large groups.

Media Selection

The most common delivery strategy decision made at the lesson level concerns the instructional medium or media (print, teachers, computers, etc.) that will be used to deliver the instruction that was planned during the "determine organizational strategies" phase. When possible, instructional designers need to enter this portion of the lesson design process without an *a priori* decision as to the medium that will be used to deliver instruction. By **medium**, we mean the physical means by which the instructional message is communicated, such as television, print materials, teacher, or computer. Designers prefer to examine the demands of the instructional situation first and then decide which medium or combination of media will best meet the needs of the situation.

Generally, the media selection decision is made after the instructional analysis and at the time that the instructional strategy is being developed. This approach to media selection is particularly critical to those designers who have the capability or budgets to produce elaborate instructional materials, such as computer software or video productions. Too often these technologies become "solutions looking for a problem." High technologies are still scarce resources in educational and training settings. It is imperative that they be used well and only when they are the best choice of instructional medium.

Characteristics of Media. For several decades researchers have attempted to establish that certain media are superior to other media for delivery of instruction. Generally, these studies have operated in the absence of a theory base. Not surprisingly,

these media comparison studies have failed to establish the overall superiority of one medium over all others. In other words, neither computers nor television nor texts nor use of a live teacher is a generally superior way to conduct instruction. Clark and Salomon (1986) conclude the following: "Past research on media has shown quite clearly that no medium enhances learning more than any other medium regardless of learning task, learner traits, symbolic elements, curriculum content, or setting" (p. 474).

Despite the lack of a general superiority of one medium over others, we need to continue to pay attention to the characteristics of media that make them more appropriate for certain requirements of instruction. Instructional technologists have investigated how specific capabilities of a medium may support specific cognitive processes that are required for targeted learning tasks. For example, Salomon, who bridges some of the gaps between communication theory and learning theory, has developed a "media attribute" theory, which holds that "(1) both the media and the human mind employ symbols to represent, store, and manipulate information; and (2) that some of the symbol systems employed in cognition are acquired from the symbol systems employed by media" (Clark & Salomon, 1986, p. 468). Salomon contends that the closer the symbol systems of a particular medium are to the mental representations and skills required to complete a specific instructional task, the easier the learning will be. His classic example is the use of "zooming in and out" utilizing video technology, and how it supports some learners' ability to identify salient cues in a display. He calls this support *supplantation*. Salomon warns that while such supplantation can be very beneficial for learners who are unable to complete the cognitive processing required for a particular task, care should be used in including such supplantation in lessons in which learners already possess the mental skills required for the task. This is because it can actually depress the performance of skilled learners.

Another aspect of media that Salomon describes as critical in learning is learners' perception of the difficulty of a particular medium and how this perception relates to the amount of mental effort invested in learning. Salomon also addresses how these relate to the amount and quality of learning. Is there a difference between how students approach working with a book versus the anticipation of viewing a televised lesson? Salomon's research (1979, 1981, 1983) has indicated the media that learners perceive as ''most difficult'' are the media that learners invest the most mental effort upon.[1] Salomon's research and that of others (e.g., Britton, Westbrook, & Holdredge, 1978) has also indicated that the amount of mental effort applied is related (both correlationally and causatively) to the amount of learning. In other words, learners tend to learn more when they work harder at it, and, all other things being equal, students will tend to work harder with some media than with others.

A third characteristic of media that has been represented in theory and research is the identification of media as delivering single or dual channel information. For some years, theoreticians (Travers, 1967) have investigated single channel versus dual channel media, such as those that convey both visual and auditory messages, questioning whether there is any superiority to multimodal presentations. Contrary to earlier thinking, researchers in the 1950s found evidence for the superiority of single-channel presentations (Broadbent, 1957, 1958). More recent research led to conclusions that whether single or dual channel presentations are most successful depends on the learning task. Some have based their reasoning upon dual-encoding theories. These theories (Kosslyn, 1981; Kosslyn & Pomerantz, 1977; Paivio, 1977) have posited that visuals are encoded in different ways from verbal information, which is hypothesized to be stored in semantic (meaningful) propositions. Dual-encoding theories would suggest that if information is visual/spatial, then it should be represented with visuals to make it more easily stored in a similar form in memory. Other theorists (Pylyshyn, 1973, 1981) have concluded that there is a deep level of semantic encoding in memory that is similar for both visual and verbal information.

---

[1]This relationship has not always been replicated in research. For example, Cennamo, Savenye, & Smith (1990) found that undergraduate education majors perceived media that required more mental effort to be ''easier'' than media that required less mental effort, and that the students performed more poorly as a result of instruction delivered with the medium perceived to be more ''difficult.''

If one medium is no better than another, why do we not always choose the cheapest, most available medium, such as books, for all instruction? Some media are more capable than others of efficiently delivering the conditions that facilitate learning for particular kinds of outcomes and particular learners. We call these capabilities of a medium its **attributes.** So when we come to the point in design where we must select a medium, we consider a number of factors:

(1) The learning task along with the instructional conditions that facilitate the learning of that task
(2) The characteristics of the learners
(3) The learning context and other practical matters that influence the appropriateness of the medium
(4) The attributes of the potential media (what each potential medium can and cannot do with regard to the prior three factors)

During our discussion of the events of instruction we talked about the instructional conditions that facilitate achievement of each category of learning outcome. The conditions that different categories of learning require help the designer determine the attributes that are needed in the medium that will deliver these events. Media selection based on this factor is a matter of narrowing down our media options to include only those that will supply the necessary conditions for the efficient achievement of the category of learning at hand. Reiser and Gagné (1983) based their media selection flowchart on decisions based on attributes of media and their relationships to learning task types. See Figure 14.1 for a portion of the Reiser and Gagné flowchart.

For instance, the instructional event of presenting the stimulus for a motor skill may involve a demonstration of that skill. If a demonstration is required, this condition dictates that the medium should have the capability of showing motion. It may even require control over the rate of presentation of that motion (e.g., slow motion or time lapse). There are several media that have the attribute of motion: film, video, and a teacher.

Here is another example: Intellectual skill learning demands a medium that can present multiple examples of the skills, require the learner to

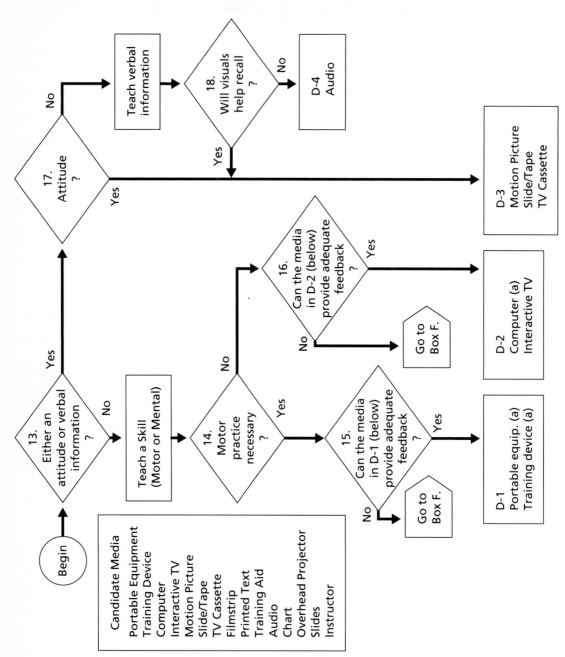

Figure 14.1: A Portion of a Media Selection Flowchart

Source: Reiser & Gagné (1983).

respond to questions about these examples, and give the learner feedback about the accuracy of responses. Several media have the capability of delivering these conditions—programmed texts, filmstrips, live teachers, and computers.

These media are not by any means necessary to learn intellectual skills. For instance, many generations have been educated without the use of computer-driven interactive video systems. However, one of these alternatives will be the medium of choice in instances where its attributes are needed. In other words, many intellectual skills are readily learned by all learners in the target population through books, handouts, or conventional media. Conventional media should be used when they will work as well as more elaborate technologies. However, some intellectual skills are just plain hard to learn when taught conventionally. With these "tough nut" intellectual skills that exist within every grade level and every specialty, it may be necessary to employ more elaborate technology to solve the instructional problem.

Characteristics of the learners dictate some fairly obvious matches with media attributes. For example, knowledge about learners' ability to read, hear, see, decode visual symbols, and understand abstract symbols will help the designer determine which media present symbols in a form that the learners can understand. Learners' familiarity with the operation of certain media hardware (such as computers) or with particular media conventions (such as time lapse photography in film and video) may provide direction as to which media are inappropriate for certain learners. Learners' attitudes toward certain media may influence whether those media are appropriate or desirable for instruction.

There are a number of practical and contextual conditions that will help the designer to determine the appropriateness of media. The availability of sufficient equipment is probably the foremost of these considerations. Other contextual factors that influence the selection of media are the classroom organization and facilities, scheduling, and funding. For example, instructional environments that are organized for self-paced, individualized instruction (e.g., "open entry" vocational education programs) are ideal environments for the efficient delivery of such instruction through computer-based instruction, programmed texts, or video delivered lessons.

You can see how the information about the learners, the learning environment, and the learning tasks that we acquire during the analysis phase of design can help us to make the decision as to which medium of instruction is the appropriate one for the task at hand.

Characteristics of Various Media

Since the attributes of various media are one of the critical determinants of media selection, we will briefly summarize the characteristics of six commonly used instructional media: microcomputers, print, video, interactive video, slides and filmstrips, and people.

Microcomputers. Microcomputers may be more like people than any other machine when it comes to instruction. A computer can adjust to the needs of the learners, analyze learners' problems, and give differential feedback. This is *not* to say that computers and people are the same but that the very flexibility of a computer makes it difficult to pin down what computers can and cannot do. Of course, the computer's capability depends upon what it was programmed to do; that is, its software. Some of the capabilities of microcomputers are as follows:

1. The microcomputer can hold a great deal of information in its memory, manipulate this information rapidly, and never make a mistake in this manipulation of data.
2. The microcomputer can deliver dynamic graphics, and the character of these graphics can be changed by input from the learner.
3. The microcomputer can foster a high level of interactivity. It can ask for student response and can respond to the student's response in a relatively individualized manner.
4. The microcomputer can adapt its presentation to the learner, adjusting the content of the instruction to the needs of the learner. It is a good medium to use when individualized instruction is desired.

5. The microcomputer can maintain a high level of control over what the learner is allowed to attend to at one time, or it can put this control in the hands of the learner.

6. The microcomputer can adjust the type of feedback that it gives to the type of response that the learner makes.

7. The microcomputer can retain and analyze records of the progress of the learner and use this information to adapt future instruction sequences to the needs of the learner.

8. The microcomputer can control other media, such as videotape/disk players, slide projectors, etc., and use these media and devices in an interactive way.

9. The microcomputer allows exact duplication of instruction at remote sites.

10. The microcomputer alone cannot efficiently present photo-realistic, motion graphics.

11. The microcomputer alone cannot efficiently present lengthy segments of high quality audio, particularly voice.

Print. Second only to humans, print is the most widely used instructional medium. The medium of print includes both text and graphic elements on paper, typically bound or stapled together in a book, booklet, or handout. Among the characteristics of the print medium are the following:

1. Print is relatively inexpensive to produce and duplicate. (Within the "relatively inexpensive" quality, the range of cost for production and duplication can be quite wide. One extreme can be seen when demands of visual quality, color, and graphic sophistication are kept low, as in a "ditto" handout prepared by a teacher or aide. Another extreme can be seen in the level of production quality exhibited in the typical "coffee table book," printed on glossy heavy paper, filled with high quality, full-color illustrations and photographs, and perhaps lavishly bound. Most instructional uses of the print medium fall somewhere between these two extremes.)

2. Print supports individual student use.

3. Print does not require equipment for use and is eminently portable.

4. In addition to being portable, print is a permanent record of instruction, the access of which requires no equipment.

5. The book format, as supported by page numbers and conventions such as the table of contents and index, is excellent for providing easy random access by individual users. (Both books and certain uses of computers have their own unique strengths in facilitating a learner's individual accessing of information.)

6. Print can be developed to provide a fair degree of interactivity.

7. Print is sensitive to learners' literacy skills.

Video. As a medium of instruction, video has very different attributes from print and computers. Although "video" can be taken to mean the reception of programs on a television set, it more often implies the use of a VCR. (Video may also be stored on videodisk.)

1. This is an audiovisual medium. Although video can depict text, the medium's primary strength lies in its ability to display images, in motion and color, along with sound.

2. Video can appear to compress time (i.e., time lapse) or expand time (i.e., slow motion) to support learners' attention.

3. Video can "zoom in" for enlarged close-ups or "zoom out" for a telephoto view.

4. Active, individualized learner interaction is difficult to support with video, unless it is used with a computer. (This can be very expensive for individual student use).

5. Presentation occurs via a prearranged sequence, which is difficult and awkward to modify by individual learners. (See the following discussion of interactive video.)

Interactive Video. Interactive video (IV), the combining of videotape or videodisc with computers, has many of the attributes of computers and video. However, interactive video (particularly when a videodisc supplies the video component of the medium) combines the positive instructional attributes of each component while obviating the negative attributes of each. For example, one of the limitations of video is its inability to promote interaction. Interactivity is computer-based instruction's forte. The attributes of interactive video are as follows:

1. IV can hold a great deal of information in its memory at one time, manipulate this

information rapidly, and never make a mistake in this manipulation of data.

2. IV can deliver dynamic graphics, and the character of these graphics can be changed by input from the learner.

3. IV can foster a high level of interactivity. It can ask for student response and can respond to the student response in a relatively individualized manner.

4. IV can adapt its presentation to the learner, adjusting the content of the instruction to the needs of the learner. It is a good medium to use when individualized instruction is desired.

5. IV can maintain a high level of control over what the learner is allowed to attend to at one time, or it can put this control in the hands of the learner.

6. IV can adjust the type of feedback that it gives to the type of response that the learner makes.

7. IV can retain and analyze records of the progress of the learner and use this information to adapt future instruction sequences to the needs of the learner.

8. IV can control other media, such as videotape-/disc players, slide projectors, etc., and use these media and devices in an interactive way.

9. Interactive video is an audiovisual medium. Although it can depict text, the medium's primary strength lies in its ability to display images, in motion and color, along with sound.

10. IV can appear to compress time (i.e., time lapse) or expand time (i.e., slow motion) in order to support learners' attention.

11. IV can "zoom in" for enlarged close-ups or "zoom out" for a telephoto view.

12. Random access to video segments can be provided.

13. There is limited local production.

14. The expense of individual student instructional stations can be significant.

Slides and Filmstrips. Although slides and filmstrips are not currently considered to be very exciting media, they are more readily available than some of the more exotic options. Their primary attributes include the following:

1. They provide color images that are realistic, intense, bright, and still.

2. The pace can be easily controlled by learners.

3. These media can use superimposed attention-directing devices.

4. These media can show close-up, enlarged details of an image.

People. It may seem a bit unusual to think of a person as a medium of instruction, but as long as we are talking about the attributes of different media, it is only natural to include the most popular one of all: the human being. When you use people as instructional media, you call them *teachers*. Teachers, just like other media, have their strengths and weaknesses. Although the individuality of people makes us all unique and different from one another, we all share certain characteristics. Human beings have various instructional media attributes in common with all other teachers. In addition to using people as teachers, people are used in instruction in other ways. For instance, students interact with each other, and people are often brought in as resources or examples. Humans have the following attributes:

1. Teachers are highly interactive (depending on the mood or wishes of the person).

2. Humans are extremely expensive to use.

3. Teachers are highly adaptable and flexible (depending on the skills and attitude of the person).

4. Humans are unreliable for doing the same thing over and over in exactly the same way, such as repeating the same lesson on Albania in the nineteenth century twenty-five times for twenty-five individual students.

5. Teachers possess and reflect empathy. Humans are the only medium that has this ability, and for certain learning tasks and situations it is an invaluable one.

(For a further discussion of people as instructional media, see Ragan [1982].)

In conclusion to this section, there are a number of models and techniques that have been suggested to aid designers in making media selection decisions. Reiser and Gagné's (1983) text on media selection is a good example. You may find such texts instructive in examining media selection issues in more detail. However, these techniques ultimately "boil down to" considering the interplay of features of the learning task, the characteristics of the learners, and the practical constraints and resources of the learning context.

An Example of Media Selection Decisions

Here is a description of a relatively common instructional situation. Read the following scenario and determine which medium (or media) is the most appropriate for the situation. (Hint: If it has been a while since you read Chapter 11 on attitude instruction, you might wish to review that chapter quickly before determining your answer.)

Dan Franklin, a social studies curriculum specialist, has noticed that many students in the middle school grades seem to lack the skills to settle disputes in nonviolent ways. He is designing a unit that will demonstrate such procedures and will have strong attitudinal messages to encourage their use. His strategy includes some practice, which will involve role playing. Dan's office has production equipment to produce slides, transparencies, videotapes, print-based materials, and computer-based instruction. Each school includes a media center that has all the equipment to present this software, plus a computer lab with 30 computers.

Stop for a minute and consider what your medium/media selection might be and the rationale for your decision.

You may recognize this task situation as similar to an objective in Chapter 11. There are several key attributes about the situation that suggest the need for particular media:

1. The instructional task is attitude learning; therefore, use of role models, role playing, and reinforcement of desired behavior will be needed. Role models may be supplied by live humans or realistic visuals such as those in video. Role playing generally requires a human to manage and encourage its use. Reinforcement requires the presence of a live human. A human teacher and peers will also be helpful in providing reinforcement for desired behavior.

2. The learners are middle-school teens. In the case of this particular learning task, it is important to consider who their role models are. Usu-

ally these models are not those people who serve as authority figures in their lives. Role models are more often found in members of their peer group or a slightly older group, as well as national figures in film, music, and sports. For this reason, it may be critical to secure an audio or video recording of role modeling.

3. The context is a rather well-endowed public school environment. Production of some materials appears reasonable. However, due to the cost factor, interactive video, which still remains a possible consideration in our selection, seems beyond the resources of our production unit.

Given all the features of the situation described above, a reasonable media selection seems to be video with a human teacher. The video can be used to introduce the instruction and to provide information. It can also be used to provide practice situations. Human teachers are needed for management and to provide reinforcement.

In the next section of this chapter, we will take a look at instructional grouping decisions, the second half of delivery strategies.

Exercises A

1. Provide at least one additional instructional attribute for the medium of print, one for the medium of video, and one for human beings as instructional media. (If you are familiar with computers, provide an additional attribute for computers.)

2. Describe other media that might be used in instruction and provide a short list of attributes for each.

3. Given below are descriptions of media attributes for print (P), computers (C), video (V), and teachers (T). Write the letter for the medium (or media) beside each of its attributes.

_____ a. Feedback tailored to the response of the learner

_____ b. Highly portable medium

_____ c. Presents information in only one sequence

_____ d. Highly adaptable and flexible

_____ e. Inexpensive to produce and duplicate

_____ f. Retains and analyzes student data

_____ g. Facilitates random access to information

_____ h. Can display motion easily

_____ i. Unreliable and unrepeatable

_____ j. Dynamic and interactive graphics

_____ k. Can reflect empathy

_____ l. Difficult to support interactive learning

_____ m. Random access of video images

_____ n. Realistic, still images

4. Given below are three brief descriptions of the information gathered during the analysis phase of instruction. Decide which medium would be the best medium of instruction. Give reasons for your selection.

Jean Herbert always dreads the time when she will introduce long division to her fourth-grade class. Some of the students catch on very fast. Many need to have the procedure shown and explained many times. Some students have not acquired the prerequisite math skills to actually begin learning about complex division. Ms. Herbert has available to her four micro-computers, a video playback machine, a nice office copier, and a part-time teaching assistant.

Bill Frankenberger is the training supervisor for a large department store chain. He is presently involved in preparing lessons for sales-people to help them deal with complaining clients. He hopes that not only will salespeople learn a process to use in speaking with clients but will also choose to use this process when they, too, feel angry. Frankenberger has a large training budget and can afford to develop custom-made instructional materials.

Maribelle Sanders is a training specialist for an international company, Big Boards, which produces building materials. New recommendations from the World Health Association in conjunction with other international agencies have a strong and immediate impact on the safety precautions for Big Boards employees. These recommendations pertain to the usage of certain chemicals that are employed in the manufacturing process. The training will include new techniques for handling chemicals and using new safety equipment. This training must be complete. It must be capable of documenting that employees have received the training and have passed the instruction, and it must be delivered within the next six months. Big Boards has excellent training centers with all equipment at numerous international sites. They also have computers on-site at all locations, some of which are dedicated to training.

Grouping Strategies

Introduction to Grouping Strategies

A frequently made assumption is that the work of instructional designers will always result in instruction that is to be delivered individually. Although this can be the case, it is not always so. An important question to answer in delivery is "What grouping(s) of students shall I use?" As we shall see, these decisions are not cut-and-dried; there is a great deal of latitude with regard to groupings and, although there are some guidelines, the selection of a grouping may be determined on a highly subjective basis. We feel that it will be useful for you to know the grouping options available and to know reasons that might be involved in selecting one option over another. Also, we will present a description of factors to be considered when making grouping decisions.

Because of the interaction among organizational strategies, media decisions, and grouping strategies, these decisions are often made concurrently (rather than linearly as our instructional design process model might imply).

Types of Groupings

Gagné, Briggs, and Wager (1988) present four basic grouping patterns that reflect variations in practice and differentiate primary interaction pattern alternatives provided by different groupings: two-person groups (tutoring); small groups (interactive); small or large groups (recitation); and large groups and very large groups (lecture). To this we would like to add a fifth: individualized (adaptive) instruction, which is a grouping option even though the "grouping" selected is one person. We will briefly discuss the primary characteristics of these grouping patterns.

Individualized Instruction. In individualized instruction, the learner works alone with materials. A primary characteristic of individualized instruction is that instruction may be adapted to the needs and traits of the learner. One of the common adaptations of individualized instruction is pace. In individualized instruction, learners proceed independently at different rates, pursuing their learning without the necessity of a human tutor. Materials-based individualized instruction allows many students to proceed individually in what is frequently a cost-effective fashion. Relatively recent refinements of individualized instruction that have been made possible by computer technology are learner control and adaptive instruction. (The characteristic attributes of computers that support these provisions are noted earlier in this chapter.) In learner-controlled instruction, individualization is provided for (1) when and what the student may study and (2) how instruction will proceed. *Learner control* refers to giving students control over instructional strategy elements of the lesson. *Adaptive instruction* refers to instructional delivery systems that change the form and content of instruction as a result of analysis of student learning progress. For example, an adaptive lesson might shift instructional strategies, perhaps from a generative to a more supplantive strategy, if the learner were having difficulty learning.

Group Learning. *Direct Teacher Input System* (lecturing), *Teacher Modification System* (lecturing with feedback), *One-Way System* (reflective lecturing), and *Two-Way System* (guided discovery) are all labels for technical descriptions of traditional lecture techniques provided by Romiszowski (1981). The lecture, in one form or another, delivered to either a medium-sized or large group is one of the most widely used forms of instructional delivery in both schools and training agencies. Yet lectures, particularly for large groups, are in some ways a very "individual" learning experience. Although learners may not proceed at their own pace during lectures—as they can in independent learning environments—one rarely finds a lecturer who allows, much less stimulates, interaction among audience members during the presentation. In other words, "individual learning" can imply "learning that does not involve interacting with other students," a condition that the lecture method generally supplies.

Group dynamics is a long-standing area of study in the communication field. More recently, in a training and performance development context, groups have been studied by Mink, Mink, and Owen (1987). Educators are increasingly capitalizing on the phenomena of group development and maturation, techniques enhancing group productivity in ideation and problem solving, and techniques of feedback use.

Reasons for Selecting Different Groupings

Learning Task Considerations. What is the relationship between the nature of the learning task and optimal groupings? Many of the relationships suggested by educators seem to possess several exceptions to the rule, but they are suggestive of ways to begin thinking about grouping decisions. Some beginning points include the use of cooperative learning for learning rules, the time honored group problem-solving approach suggested by Dewey (1924), and the use of individualized delivery for tasks in which there is reason to expect a wide variation in learning rate.

Romiszowski (1981) suggests that facts may often be efficiently learned through individual learning. This method may also be helpful for concept and procedure learning. Principles, particularly social principles and principles "discovered" through inquiry, are centrally appropriate to group learning. Concepts and procedures may also be learned in groups. Romiszowski argues that there is little need for a group if one is learning factual material, but for learning of principles he says that the opportunity to apply them in "analytical conversations" can be a helpful contribution that results from working in a group (p. 328).

The selection of grouping may also interact with media selection decisions, which are based on learning task factors. For example, inquiry and frequent interactions are possible in individualized, computer-based instruction, particularly via simulations and Socratic dialogue. Another example of the grouping-media bond is in situations that require human interchange, such as attitude objectives. In these cases, group instruction is preferable because it is efficient and involves human interaction.

Subject matter can sometimes bring with it "natural" groupings. For example, instruction in computer-related learning, such as programming and productivity software use, is typically conducted in pairs or triads—a "cooperative learning" environment. The intellectually demanding nature that so often characterizes these learning tasks, along with the externalization of thinking in interacting with the computer, have combined to make cooperative learning a tradition in this relatively young field of study.

Gerlach and Ely (1980) rest the primary decision making for groupings on questions teachers would ask related to the learning tasks at hand:

1. Which objectives can be reached by the learners on their own?
2. Which objectives can be achieved through interaction among learners themselves?
3. Which objectives can be achieved through your formal presentation and through interaction between you and the learner? (p. 16)

The assumption Gerlach and Ely make is that all objectives that *can* be reached through individualized instruction *should* be delivered via individualized instruction. This is an assumption that various considerations, such as media options available and other organizational factors, may contradict.

Learner Characteristics. In addition to the learning task, learner factors may sometimes enter into grouping decisions. Perhaps the single most important learner difference that impacts on grouping decisions is *locus of control*. (You may wish to refer to the discussion of this personality variable in Chapter 3.) As we have said, learners with a more internal locus of control generally attribute their successes and failures to factors within themselves. Learners with a more external locus of control tend to attribute their success or failure to factors outside themselves.

In one study (Daniels & Stevens, 1976) two methods of instruction—one an individualized instruction approach and the other a group-based approach—were employed with students who were classified as either "internal" or "external" in their locus of control. Whereas students with an internal locus of control did best under the conditions of individualized instruction, students with external locus of control had difficulty with the individualized instruction and performed well with group-based instruction.

Another learner factor that might influence grouping decisions is the degree of variation in the prior knowledge and ability levels of the learners. When a wide variation in learners' knowledge and/or ability exists, then large group instruction is generally not optimal. In such a case, the teacher tends to direct instruction to the lower middle of the class, boring the brighter students and losing the less skilled students. Two somewhat different grouping choices are available in such cases. One choice is to use individualized instruction that can be designed to adapt to different needs of learners. Individualized grouping is the most efficient and effective grouping option available for a highly variable audience. However, often the resources for development of individualized instruction are unavailable, and often the willingness to make basic organizational changes necessary for individualization is not present. Also, the tendency toward learner isolation evidenced in individualized instruction is sometimes perceived as being undesirable. In such cases, the second choice, cooperative learning groups, may be constructed. Membership in a cooperative group is based on knowledge and skill level and, hopefully, compatibility. Such a group will have some skilled and some less skilled learners. The group will be given a learning task assignment that they must complete together with their combined skills.

Learners' perceptions, experiences, skills, and preferences may also be considered in determining grouping. For example, learners are often not skilled or experienced in working in small groups. If small groups are clearly indicated as a desirable grouping, then students must receive some training in working effectively in groups. For the sake of motivation and interest, students' preferences for grouping should be considered whenever possible. However, preferences should not be the first factor considered for two specific reasons. First, students who are inexperienced with a particular grouping may not prefer a grouping strategy simply because they are unfamiliar with it. The lack of familiarity should not be an impediment to the use of the strategy. Second, ample research has indicated that learner preferences are often not highly predictive of a strategy's effectiveness.

Context Factors. Facilities, equipment, and production capabilities available in the learning setting can have a major impact on what groupings are employed. In many cases, using analysis of both the learning task and learners will yield no prescription for groupings; the task could be achieved individually or in group work. In such a case, context variables may become the deciding factors in grouping decisions. These variables involve the availability of learning spaces, instructional hardware/software, and media production resources. For example, if a school has an individual learning laboratory equipped with computers, some objectives that could employ group instruction to provide sufficient interaction could be taught better using computer-supported simulations. In another example, an institution might not have available lecture halls or halls equipped properly to support the required visual presentations. In such a case, small group presentation of such visuals may be required. The actual physical characteristics of a facility may preclude a certain grouping. For example, a large classroom with desks bolted to the floor may not permit small group work. When learning outcomes are equally supported by more than one grouping alternative in terms of efficiency, effectiveness, and appeal—and if facilities are available for more than one grouping alternative—choices can legitimately be made on the basis of economic and instructor factors. For example, costs may tip the decision to large group instruction for certain objectives, but if no one is available or willing to prepare and deliver the lectures, other groupings (and delivery) must be considered.

Teacher preferences and skill with certain grouping strategies often influence the ultimate decision. Factors within the context, such as teacher training resources, aides, and management devices, may broaden these preferences.

Media Selection Factors. As mentioned previously in this chapter, media selection and grouping choices are often made in relationship to each other. For example, a selection of a computer-based strategy often implies an individualized strategy (although cooperative groups can be used effectively with computer-based instruction). Grouping strategies can also influence media selection decisions. For example, a decision based upon economic factors to use large group instruction will determine what media are candidates. (For instance, although they are occasionally used for group-based instruction, computer-based and interactive video instruction are not commonly

group-based media and would not often be selected to deliver instruction to large groups).

Organizational Strategy. Organizational strategy decisions and grouping decisions are also highly interrelated. One difference among organizational strategies that can have a bearing on grouping decisions is the expository versus inquiry choice. If an organizational strategy is expository, there is generally no reason to select anything but an individualized approach; however, if the strategy is an inquiry-related one, the need for exploration, discussion, and application will frequently be present for cooperative learning in small groups. Yet, this distinction is not inflexible. Some highly effective inquiry-based computer lessons have been designed.

A particularly insightful treatment of the interaction among grouping decisions and other major instructional variables is provided by Gerlach and Ely (1980). They have considered the interactions of grouping decisions with time, space, media, and delivery strategy. Their model for instructional design, which addresses these interrelationships, is presented in Figure 14.2. As with media selection decisions, grouping decisions cannot be made on the basis of knowing which is the "best" grouping and always using it. The "best" grouping strategy depends on many factors and will therefore vary from event to event and lesson to lesson.

*E*xercises B

Provided below are two descriptions of learning situations. For each, select a grouping strategy or strategies and justify your answer.

1. Jack Roberts teaches a government class into which many special education students are placed. Consequently, the students are very heterogeneous regarding ability and prior knowledge. The class is about to study the concepts of "loose" and "strict" constructionism—whether legislative rights unenumerated in the Constitution are reserved to the federal government or the state government. Mr. Roberts plans to use an expository method for many of the events, but he plans to have students engage in transfer activities in which they look for examples of loose and strict constructionism in historical documents.

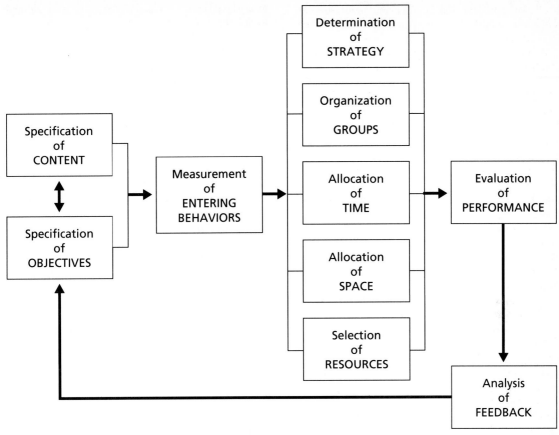

Figure 14.2: The Gerlach/Ely Model for Systematic Planning of Instruction
Source: Gerlach & Ely (1980).

2. Harriet Mills is designing instruction for nursing students regarding their attitudes toward caring for cancer patients. The class is relatively homogeneous with regard to background knowledge and ability. The students have utilized many media and grouping techniques throughout their instruction.

*I*nstructional Management Strategies

Instructional management strategies are those strategies that guide the orchestration of organizational and delivery strategies. These are the strategies that guide the scheduling of instructional events and the mechanisms for delivering these events. Management also coordinates the articulation among various delivery systems. With the amount of assessment and scheduling information inherent in many instructional systems, management strategies must also devise means of organizing and reducing this information into interpretable units and getting this information to the proper people in a timely fashion. Management strategies also involve techniques for getting the instructional resources to the learners who need them.

At the micro level, these management decisions can be dealt with by the teacher/trainer/facilitator. The teacher's guide is developed by the designer to give critical information about the instruction to inform management decisions. It also provides concrete instructional management suggestions that pertain to particular segments of instruction.

At the macro level, systems of instructional management often need to be devised. During the 1960s, as individualized instruction began to be considered a viable option for instruction in public schools, it became apparent that some explicit management systems were needed to manage such instruction. When almost every student in the classroom is at a different point in the curriculum, as is possible with individualized instruction, management strategies are critical if chaos is to be avoided. The remainder of this chapter will discuss some of the management strategies that were developed to specifically deal with individualized instruction.

PLAN. The Program of Learning in Accordance with Needs (PLAN) was developed in the 1960s jointly by the American Institute for Research (AIR) and Westinghouse Learning Corporation. An early example of computer-managed instruction (CMI), PLAN employed a mainframe computer to provide test scoring, diagnosis, prescription, and reporting to aid teachers in keeping track of students within a curriculum and to help them deal with the bewildering amount of data generated in an individualized system. Teachers in PLAN schools received daily computer printouts that detailed the progress of each student. Teaching Learning Units were prescribed by the computer, which were cooperatively developed by teachers and students into a program of studies.

AIS. The Advanced Instructional System developed by McDonnell Douglas Corporation in the 1970s is another example of individualization assisted by computer management. The functions of the AIS are similar to those provided by PLAN, except that the AIS contains its own instructional materials authoring system and is currently available commercially as computer software.

IPI. Robert Glaser of the University of Pittsburgh developed the Individually Prescribed Instruction system under his Research for Better Schools program. Key features of the IPI approach include detailed diagnosis of students' prior learning, careful placement of students into curriculum entry points, and the use of pretests, posttests, and "curriculum-

embedded tests." Under IPI, each pupil's work is guided by a written prescription and frequent communications between student and teacher. The student works independently using prescribed materials, frequently using semi-programmed instruction materials, workbooks, cassette tapes, and objects and occasionally doing small group work. The teacher's primary roles become those of decision-maker, tutor, and evaluator, with extensive use of teacher aides for scoring and tabulation.

LAPs. The idea of individualizing through Learning Activity Packets (LAPs) has no particular source that we can find. The concept of the LAP is a simple one: The materials that are needed for instruction are either included or specified in a print-based packet. First, material is presented that orients students to a learning task (providing for the Introduction events in our expanded instructional events). Then, learners are either provided with learning materials or referred to something such as a text, video, or filmstrip that will deliver the Body and Conclusion events. Third, learners are provided with problems and feedback to those problems, usually in the form of print-based instruction. Finally, learners are directed to assessment instruments, which are often distributed and monitored by a teacher or aide. The idea of providing instruction either internally or by specification gives the LAP concept a practical flexibility, which contributes to its widespread adoption.

Audio-Tutorial Instruction. The audio-tutorial instructional approach was developed in the early 1960s by S. N. Postlethwait, a professor of botany at Purdue University. The approach evolved in an experimental offering of Postlethwait's introductory botany class. At first, the professor provided tape-recorded lectures so that students could listen to them in the audiovisual center. With use, it became apparent that it would be a good idea for students to bring their texts so that they could refer to specific illustrations discussed on the tape. The final evolution of the concept occurred when it was realized that the tape recordings could be listened to in the laboratory so that the actual plants under discussion could be handled and inspected. Experiments could be performed by the student in the lab, as directed by the tape recording. Heinich, Molenda, and Russell note (1989), "Consciously or unconsciously, Dr. Postlethwait had moved his instructional technique from one focusing on abstract learning experiences (lectures) toward a multimedia system emphasizing concrete experiences—an integrated lecture-laboratory approach'' (p. 318).

PSI. A college teaching-based innovation developed by F. S. Keller in the 1960s, the personalized system of instruction (PSI) has seen wide adoption in colleges and universities and has an excellent record of success (Kulik, Kulik, & Smith, 1976). A key concept in PSI is mastery-based individualized instruction, as facilitated by *proctors*—assistant in-

structors or advanced students who volunteer their help. Proctors provide individualized help, test administration, scoring, and immediate feedback and personalized assistance to the student. The instructor for the course only occasionally conducts large group sessions, which are generally motivational in purpose. PSI is a good example of the judicious combining of grouping and other instructional factors into a general delivery strategy of real merit. Keller's PSI is not the only possible intelligent combination of delivery strategy elements; others of your own devising may be just as good.

Summary

Without systematic instructional design, ''modern technology'' has little impact on instruction. As we have seen, different media are not generally superior to one another, even the most modern and currently fashionable products of high technology. Yet some media are better than others under certain conditions. When we match the attributes of various media to the needs of the learning task, the characteristics of learners, and learning context considerations, we find that in fact some media *are* better than others for particular situations.

Decisions about grouping are also influenced by characteristics of the instructional tasks, learners, and instructional context. In addition, organizational strategy decisions and media selection decisions may strongly influence grouping decisions.

The outcome of organizational and delivery strategy decisions may involve the complex interrelationship of media and groupings. Management strategies are needed to orchestrate the instructional events that are supplied by various combinations of media and groupings. Figure 14.3 summarizes key points in this chapter.

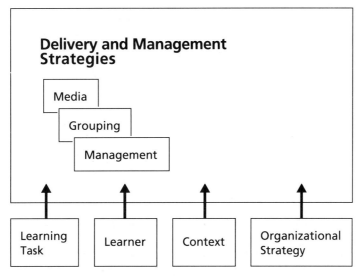

Figure 14.3: Summary Diagram for Chapter 14

Job Aid

Lesson Delivery Strategy Plans

1. Media Selection and Rationale

   a. Attributes required by context, task, and/or learners _____

   _____

   b. Ideal medium/media _____

   _____

   c. Medium/media of choice (by event) _____

   _____

   d. Rationale for medium/media selection _____

   _____

2. Grouping Strategies

   a. Grouping plans by events _____

   _____

   b. Rationale for grouping strategies _____

   _____

Extended Example

The Extended Example for this chapter might consist of a summary of the delivery strategies selected in previous instructional strategy chapters (Chapters 7–13). Three examples follow.

> Chapter 8: Concept Learning
> Topic: Depth of field
> Medium: Print-based text
>
> Chapter 12: Attitude Learning

Topic: Valuing B&W images (prints)
Medium: Teacher-led instruction using slide/tape, sound filmstrip, and study prints

Chapter 13: Psychomotor Learning
Topic: Panning a moving object
Medium: Teacher-led instruction using video camcorder and an instant-developing camera

Readings and References

Britton, B. K., Westbrook, R. D., & Holdredge, T. S. (1978). Reading and cognitive capacity usage: Effects of text difficulty. *Journal of Experimental Psychology: Human Learning and Memory, 4,* 582–591.

Broadbent, D. E. (1957). Immediate memory and simultaneous stimuli. *Quarterly Journal of Experimental Psychology, 9,* 1–11.

Broadbent, D. E. (1958). *Perception and communication.* New York: Pergamon Press.

Carroll, J. A. (1963). A model of school learning. *Teacher's College Record, 64,* 723–733.

Cennamo, K. S., Savenye, W. C., & Smith, P. L. (1990). Can interactive video overcome the ''couch potato syndrome''? In M. R. Simonson & C. Hargrave (Eds.), *Proceedings of selected research presentations at the 1990 Convention of the Association for Educational Communications and Technology.*

Clark, R. E., & Salomon, G. (1986). Media in teaching. In M. C. Wittrock (Ed.), *Handbook of research on teaching* (3rd ed.). New York: Macmillan.

Daniels, R. L., & Stevens, J. P. (1976). The interaction between the internal-external locus of control and two methods of college instruction. *American Educational Research Journal, 13*(2), 103–113.

Dewey, J. (1924). *Democracy and education.* New York: Macmillan.

Fleming, M., & Levie, W. H. (1978). *Instructional message design.* Englewood Cliffs, NJ: Educational Technology Publications.

Gagné, R. M., Briggs, L. J., & Wager, W. W. (1988). *Principles of instructional design* (3rd ed.). New York: Holt, Rinehart & Winston.

Gerlach, V. S. & Ely, D. P. (1980). *Teaching and media: A systematic approach* (2nd ed.). Englewood Cliffs, NJ: Prentice-Hall.

Heinich, R., Molenda, M., & Russell, J. D. (1989). *Instructional media and the new technologies of instruction* (3rd ed.). New York: Macmillan.

Johnson, D. W. & Johnson, R. T. (1975). *Learning together and alone: Cooperation, competition, and individualization.* Englewood Cliffs, NJ: Prentice-Hall.

Kosslyn, S. M. (1981). The medium and the message in mental imagery: A theory. *Psychological Review, 88,* 46–66.

Kosslyn, S. M., & Pomerantz, J. R. (1977). Imagery, propositions and the form of internal representations. *Cognitive Psychology, 9,* 52–76.

Kulik, J. A., Kulik, C. L., & Smith, B. B. (1976). Research on the personalized system of instruction. *Programmed Learning and Educational Technology, 13*(1), 23–30.

Lefcourt, H. M. (1976). *Locus of control: Current trends in theory and research.* Hillsdale, NJ: Lawrence Erlbaum.

Mink, O. G., Mink, B. P., & Owen, K. Q. (1987). *Groups at work.* Englewood Cliffs, NJ: Educational Technology Publications.

Paivio, A. U. (1977). Images, propositions and knowledge. In J. M. Nicholas (Ed.), *Images, perceptions and knowledge.* Dordrecht, The Netherlands: Reidel.

Pylyshyn, Z. W. (1973). What the mind's eye tells the mind's brain: A critique of mental imagery. *Psychological Bulletin, 80,* 1–24.

Pylyshyn, Z. W. (1981). The imagery debate: Analogue media versus tacit knowledge. *Psychological Review, 88,* 16–45.

Ragan, T. J. (1982). The oldest medium. *Educational Technology, 22* (5), 28–29.

Reiser, R. A. (1980). Interaction between locus of control and three pacing procedures in a personalized system of instruction course. *Educational Communications and Technology Journal, 28* (3), 194–202.

Reiser, R. A., & Gagné, R. M. (1982). Characteristics of media selection models. *Review of Educational Research, 52* (4), 499–512.

Reiser, R. A., & Gagné, R. M. (1983). *Selecting media for instruction.* Englewood Cliffs, NJ: Educational Technology Publications.

Romiszowski, A. J. (1981). *Designing instructional systems.* London: Kogan Page.

Salomon, G. (1979). *Interaction of media, cognition, and learning.* San Francisco: Jossey-Bass.

Salomon, G. (1981). *Communication and education: Social and psychological interactions.* Beverly Hills, CA: Sage Publications.

Salomon, G. (1983). The differential investment of mental effort in learning from different sources. *Educational Psychologist, 18,* 42–50.

Salomon, G. (1984). Television is ''easy'' and print is ''tough'': The differential investment of mental effort in learning as a function of perceptions and attributions. *Journal of Educational Psychology, 76* (4), 647–658.

Taylor, R. P. (Ed.). (1980). *The computer in the school: Tutor, tool, tutee.* New York: Teacher's College Press.

Travers, R. M. W. (Principal Investigator). (1967). *Research and theory related to audiovisual information transmission* (Revised ed.). Washington, D.C.: U.S. Department of Health, Education, and Welfare, Contract No. 3-20-003.

Trump, J. L. (1959). *Images of the future: A new approach to the secondary school*. Urbana, IL: Commission on the Experimental Study of the Utilization of Staff in the Secondary School, National Association of Secondary School Principals.

Walker, D. F., & Hess, R. D. (Eds.). (1984). *Instructional software: Principles and perspectives for design and use*. Belmont, CA: Wadsworth.

Production of Instruction

fifteen

Chapter Objectives

At the conclusion of this chapter you should be able to do the following:

- Describe the procedures involved in producing print-based instruction.

- Describe the role of flowcharts, pseudo-code outlines, and screen planning sheets in the production of computer-based instruction.

- Discuss the strengths and weaknesses of general purpose programming languages, authoring languages, and authoring systems in the production of computer-based instruction.

- Describe the role of a storyboard script in video production.

- Compare and contrast single-camera video production with studio production.

- Describe the procedures involved in producing teacher-based instruction.

*I*ntroduction

Production of the instructional materials themselves is the last step in the instructional strategy phase. After determining the organizational strategies (the expanded instructional events), delivery strategies (selection of media), and management strategies, then the design work that must precede actual production is completed. How do we translate the decisions and specifications made in previous steps into instructional materials and trainer guides? This chapter will answer that question.

There are entire texts on the production of media, as well as entire texts on producing materials for any one medium. This chapter will not attempt to replace these valuable resources; rather, it will assist you in making the link between the design work performed up to this point and the finished product. We will do this by taking a look at how some of the most frequently used forms of instruction are produced. In some projects, the designer performs the production work. Frequently this is the case with teacher-based instruction. In other projects, particularly those involving print, video, or computer-based instruction, the designer will work with a production specialist, programmer, or production team. Some knowledge of the production process is necessary on the designer's part in order to design more effectively prior to production and in order to communicate well with a production specialist. This chapter will give you sufficient background to communicate with producers. It will also give you some idea of where to begin as well as where to look for answers, (such as production texts), when you are producing your own media.

In this chapter, we will discuss the fundamentals of producing print-, computer-, video-, and teacher-based instruction. The instruction provided by these four media comprises the vast majority of current instruction being delivered today.

*P*roduction of Print-Based Instruction

Print is the most commonly used medium for delivery of instruction, exceeding even teacher-based instruction as the primary means of instructional delivery. The reasons for the widespread use of print include its relative low cost to produce, low cost to duplicate, modest demands in terms of production equipment required, widespread availability of production knowledge, ease of distribution, and various instructional media attributes including high image quality, portability, and ease of use.

Once the instructional strategy has been designed, the stages involved in actual production of print are as follows:

1. Draft text and thumbnail illustrations.
2. Select/design a layout grid and text specifications.
3. Create a dummy.
4. Create camera-ready copy (text and illustrations).
5. Duplicate/print the text.

Drafting Text and Illustrations

Ideally, the writing of text material is part of the production process, and the writing begins with a draft of the text and creation of thumbnail illustrations. The advantage of integrating writing with production is that content and form can work together. We recommend "a process approach," in which material evolves and improves through a process of generation, critical reading, and revision.

Text drafts should begin with outlines, and the designer will have these outlines as a product of previous steps in the design process. The designer will have an outline of the material to be written in the form of the expanded instructional events. From the outlines the designer or writer writes the prose of the text.

One of the first decisions that should be made is a determination of which expository text structure should be used to structure the information in the "present information" event of instruction. Common text structures that are often suggested are description, chronology, comparison-contrast, cause-effect, problem-solution, and problem-solution-effects. Research has suggested that text that is arranged in one of these common structures is more easily comprehended and remembered (Armbruster & Anderson, 1985; Meyer, 1985; Smith & Tompkins, 1988). These text structures can be selected based upon the type of learning outcome, as shown in Figure 15.1.

Outcome	Structure
Concept	Description
Coordinate concept	Comparison/contrast
Procedural rule	Chronology
Relational rule	Cause-effect
Problem-solving	Problem-solution, Problem-solution-effects
Cognitive strategy	Chronology or Problem-solution

Figure 15.1: Text Structures for Common Types of Learning

Text writers have also suggested that particular structures are used more commonly in certain content areas; for example, Armbruster and Anderson (1985) have suggested that science and technology texts often use a "systems" frame of reference that contains information on functions of systems, parts and functions in a system, how the system works, and problems and solutions within the system.

Assuming that the writer is beginning with material developed through use of a systematic design process as described in this book, primary concerns in text drafts will be writing quality and style. A good writing style for instructional text is very much a learned skill—one that requires a basic understanding of the language being used. For English writers, the reading of and frequent reference to a manual such as Strunk and White's *The Elements of Style* (1979) can be invaluable. A brief list of guidelines for writing instructional text is provided in Figure 15.2.

Illustrations that are included in instructional text can take the form of pictures (line drawings or photographs), diagrams, charts, tables, or graphs. Illustrations may be used to clarify, organize, summarize, or support recall of information. Illustrations can also influence attitudes or feelings about the content or about learning in general. Illustrations should be selected and crafted just as carefully as text. They should be carefully integrated with the text, and where appropriate, learning strategies should be suggested as to how the illustrations may be used by the learner.

Illustrations should begin as rough drafts, called *thumbnails*, which is a shortened form of "thumbnail sketch." A **thumbnail** is an early version of a visual, not the finished rendering. Thumbnails can be sketches, photocopies, photos, computer screen-dumps, or any form of an illustration that you intend to develop into finished form at a later time. Thumbnails are a beginning point for finished artwork in many cases. Also, the thumbnail is needed for planning in our next steps—selecting a grid and creating a dummy. Figure 15.3 presents a few basic guidelines for using illustrations in instruction.

Selecting/Designing a Grid

Before text and illustrations are rendered into final copy, we begin to determine the form that these elements will take on the page. The first step in this determination is the selecting or designing of a grid. A **grid** is a fundamental compositional tool for determining what will go where on a printed page. Although you may have already made extensive use of print that you developed for handouts, memoranda, letters, and so forth, you may not have had experience working with an instructional grid.

The idea of an instructional grid is an extension of a commonly used concept in print design, the "text grid." In multi-page documents, the placement of elements on a page needs a structure, and that structure is what the grid provides. At the most fundamental level, the grid controls margins. An example can be found in practically any published print material. Examine the structure of the text on this page. You should begin to see elements

1. Keep sentences short, simple, and concrete.
2. Avoid the frequent use of long introductory clauses.
3. Make pronoun references direct and clear. For example, in the following passage, the reader may not know to what *it* refers: "The 9mm wrench can be used to disconnect the framis. It can then be set aside." Does *it* refer to the wrench or to the framis?
4. Use the active voice rather than the passive voice.
5. Include the word *you* to aim messages directly at the students. For example, rather than say "One should consult the customer at this point," it is often better to say "You should consult the customer at this point."
6. Use personal names and personal pronouns when possible.
7. When introducing a new term, use an attention-getting technique (such as underlining, boldface type, or italics), and then explain what the term means. Here's an example: "The **hypotenuse** is the side of a right triangle that is opposite the right angle."
8. Use a different attention-getting technique for words you want to emphasize. For example, "Turn the skeezix nut *counterclockwise* in order to tighten it."
9. Use headings to break up the text into sections and to chunk related text.
10. Use transition words when appropriate. Examples include *then, now, next, first, second,* and *finally.*
11. After you have completed the first draft, use a commonly used formula for assessing readability level, such as the Fry Readability Graph. Simplify vocabulary and shorten sentences if the level is too high. Ninth- or tenth-grade reading level is appropriate for many instructional materials.
12. Make sure that the instruction is free from gender bias. Avoid sentences that reinforce stereotypical gender roles, and refrain from using sexist or gender-exclusive language.

Figure 15.2: Some Guidelines for Writing Instructional Text

1. Illustrations should employ an appropriate level of detail.
2. Familiar objects should be included in illustrations to enhance comprehensibility.
3. Illustrations of procedures should include as many frames or individual pictures as there are main steps in the procedure.
4. Use separate illustrations to show before/after, right/wrong, etc.
5. Use lines to indicate relationships between groups or sequenced illustrations.
6. In a series of illustrations, maintain a consistent point of view for the sake of continuity.
7. Put illustrations as close as possible to the text to which they refer, even if it requires repetition of the graphic on several pages.
8. Illustrations should be explicitly related to text using both captions and references within text.
9. Illustrations should be clearly labeled: Label key elements using arrows or lines connecting the label to the element being described.
10. Use focus devices (such as color, exploded drawings, and arrows) where needed to get the reader's attention and to clarify complex material.

Figure 15.3: Some Guidelines for Illustrations
Source: Adapted from Jones, Friedman, Tinzman, & Cox (1984).

that are specified and controlled by the grid. Margins are the most obvious element. In addition to the margins, there will be a certain number of columns on the page. One to three columns is common in textbooks; more are generally seen in newspapers and magazines. The form and placement of headings and other organizational devices, use and placement of page numbers, and page headers (such as book title, chapter title, and section title) are all determined by the grid. Some commonly used grids are illustrated in Figure 15.4.

Text specifications are further details regarding the form of the text, including font, leading, justification, and rules to follow for page breaks.

1. Fonts are the different type styles. Type is measured in units called *points*. Here are some examples of fonts and point sizes: Century Schoolbook, 12 point; Helvetica, 9 point; and *Zapf Chancery, 10 point*. Font selection influences legibility, and it provides subtle yet real influences on the impression that the text conveys. Different fonts do have different looks to them, and the font can definitely influence a reader's perception of text. For instructional texts, one should select a conservative and fairly common font, with an emphasis on clarity and legibility.

2. Leading refers to the amount of space between lines. With a typewriter, we have the choice between single- and double-spaced lines. With both traditional printing and desktop publishing the space between lines can be varied drastically. When deciding the amount of leading for a text, one should consider legibility and the length of the final printed text.

3. Justification has to do with where lines begin and end on the page. Text can be aligned on the left side only (leaving ragged right margins), centered (making both the right and left margins ragged), or justified (making both the left and right margins straight). Computers offer easy, instant selection of alignment, making it possible for the user to obtain justified margins even when this might not be the best choice. Generally ragged right margins are preferable.

4. Page breaks are a more important issue in instructional text design than in other text design

applications, such as paperback novels. In instructional text, it is often important for clarity's sake not to separate a text unit, such as a paragraph, into two separate pages.

There are two basic ways to reproduce a text: conventional (photo-mechanical) and by computer (electronic publishing). Whether you employ one or the other means to create text does not alter the steps that are taken in the print production process (we still start with a draft, make a grid, create a dummy, and so forth); however, the means by which the steps are carried out differs depending on the approach to text creation. Here, at the step of selecting and designing a grid, we take different paths.

Designing a grid for conventional print production is typically performed on a drafting table; a master page is created with pen on paper. This master page will specify, with grid lines, the location of margins, placement of columns, headers, page numbers, and so forth. This master page will be duplicated so that for both the dummy and camera-ready copy, text and illustrations may be pasted up in locations on the page specified by the grid.

Designing a grid for electronic publishing is typically accomplished with the help of computer software that is especially created for this purpose. This software is called *desktop publishing* software and is exemplified by PageMaker from Aldus Corp., Ventura Publisher from Xerox Corp., Frame Maker from Frame Technology Corp., and Interleaf Publisher from Interleaf, Inc. The details of how one goes about designing a grid when using desktop publishing software depend on the software being used, but the development of a grid, in one form or another, is fundamental to using the software. Rather than making lines on paper to denote margins and columns, the computer software enables you to make such decisions on the computer screen. The software also allows you to quickly and easily make changes and see the results of your changes. This ability to revise and immediately see what you would get as a result of the revision is perhaps the single most helpful contribution that desktop publishing software provides. The grid that desktop publishing software provides will accommodate both text and graphics, and the software facilitates the placement and manipulation of illustrations in the text.

Figure 15.4: Some Frequently Used Instructional Text Layout Grids

Creation of a Dummy

A dummy is a layout draft. Your text copy (now at a stage beyond first draft but still subject to revision) and your thumbnail illustrations are placed on pages in the form that you developed with your grid and specifications. A conventional dummy is made by pasting blocks of text and illustrations into place on master pages. Although rubber cement or wax adhesive makes it possible to change the placement of items, these changes are much easier when you use a computer. When using a computer, a dummy will result when you satisfactorily complete the placement of your text and illustrations in the computer file. The idea of making the dummy is to place the material where it will go using the grid. In making the dummy, there are typically several changes involving the placement of text and graphic elements as pages are developed. Making major changes in paste-up copy can be troublesome, but it is better to make changes on a dummy because changes to camera-ready copy are much more difficult and costly.

The completed dummy allows for review and revision. The idea of moving around text and graphic elements while making the dummy is an example of review and revision at the micro level. But review and revision is also performed at a higher level; this is the process of formative evaluation. (We discussed formative evaluation in Chapter 1.) You know that formative evaluation is the procedure by which instructional materials are reviewed, tried out, and revised. This process ensures that the instructional materials that are produced will be correct and effective. The dummy, being material with both the content and form of the finished product, can be reproduced and used for expert review, one-to-one trials, small group trials, and field trials with revision at the end of each step as indicated by feedback from the trial.

One special type of formative evaluation used with printed materials is the evaluation of readability. Readability refers to the level of text-processing skill needed by the reader to be able to comprehend the text material at hand. Common techniques used to assess readability are the Fry (1977) Readability Graph and the Gunning (1952) "Fog" count. (Further information on these techniques can be found in Hartley, 1985 and Rye, 1982.) Use of these readability indexes involves analyzing samples of text to determine how difficult they are to read. "Difficulty" is usually defined by (1) the complexity of sentences (usually measured by the average number of words per sentence in a sample) and (2) familiarity of words (usually measured by average number of syllables in a word). The Cloze technique (Taylor, 1953) is unusual in that its use involves trial reading by a sample of readers from the target population, rather than providing a technique for a person other than the reader to employ in analysis. Most readability techniques yield a grade-level estimate of the difficulty of the text. Readability indexes are easy to use and can provide useful information on the processing demands that a particular instructional text is likely to make on a reader. However, due in part to their simplistic basis (e.g., sentence length and word length), their ease of use, and the uncomplicated feedback that they provide, readability indexes have come under criticism for their overuse and the quality of information that they provide. We agree that use of readability indexes should not take the place of formative evaluation as we describe it in this text, but we still recommend use of readability checking as a part of the evaluation of text-based instruction.

A major difference in production between the use of conventional techniques and use of the computer is seen with regard to what it means to make and use a dummy. With conventional techniques, the paste-up dummy is relatively inexpensive to produce compared to the cost of making camera-ready copy through photo-mechanical processes. Thus, testing and revising a dummy will save a lot of time and money compared to using the final product for formative evaluation and revising that final, printed copy each time changes are needed. In the case of a computer-generated dummy, the physical quality of the dummy may be little or no different from the final product. The dummy of desktop publishing material is merely the version of the project with which you begin field testing; the final product is the last version of it, and often it is not printed in a more sophisticated form.

Creation of Camera-Ready Copy

After the dummy has been developed and formative evaluation has been accomplished, the camera-ready copy is produced. When using conventional techniques, finished art will replace thumbnail sketches for illustrations and type will be set for the text (although set type may be used for dummies as well). The text and illustrations will be pasted up and photographed with a large-format camera. The negative will be used to make reproduction plates. The creation of camera-ready copy when using desktop publishing techniques is to print out a final version. (Sometimes a higher quality printer is used to make the final print out of computer files.)

Duplication/Printing

Camera-ready copy is duplicated by some means appropriate to the number of copies that will be needed. Very short duplication runs may be handled by office copying equipment if color requirements can be met. Longer duplication runs and those that require color are generally handled with offset duplicators, presses, or xerographic duplicators. If the appropriate duplication process has been selected, significant economies of scale may be realized when large numbers of copies are made, so that the cost per unit of print-based instruction can be much lower than the cost of making few copies. A 50-page instructional module that costs $2.00 per copy when 10 copies are made may cost $1.00 per copy when 200 are made and may cost less than 50 cents per copy when 1,000 or more are made.

Production of Computer-Based Instruction

Design and development of computer-based instruction (CBI) is a major enterprise for instructional technologists. The prevalence of CBI (particularly in business and industry) combined with the large amount of effort that is required to develop high quality CBI, creates the need for many instructional designers with CBI design skills. Your knowledge of instructional design and a basic understanding of the development and production process used for CBI will give you a good orientation to this specialty.

The CBI developer must translate the specifications for instruction (expanded instructional events, delivery strategies, and management strategies) into instructional materials. Although the actual steps taken in production may vary, we will break the CBI development process into five steps: (1) development of functional flowcharts, (2) creation of screen designs, (3) creation of pseudo-code, (4) creation of code, and (5) test/revision of code.

Development of Functional Flowcharts

A flowchart describes events and decisions in a program in an algorithmic form; all of the events are present and there is no ambiguity as to what happens in each event. Although flowcharts have lost popularity with programmers due to changes in programming languages, flowcharts are still quite useful in the CBI development process. Functional flowcharts can be used to depict the structure, sequence, and decisions in a CBI program before programming begins. Flowcharts employ certain symbols for certain kinds of computer activity. The most fundamental and commonly used are the rectangle for information (such as a frame or screen) and the diamond for decisions. Figure 15.5 shows a flowchart for a CBI lesson.

Flowcharts may be written at different levels of detail. A good practice is to start with a more general representation, followed by additional flowcharts at increasing levels of detail. A total of three levels is generally sufficient to move from the most general representation to the most detailed. The flowchart depicted in Figure 15.5 is a somewhat detailed representation.

Creation of Screen Designs

Once the functional flow of a CBI lesson has been established, it is appropriate to determine what individual screen displays will look like. Screen content will be dictated by both content and functional concerns. For example, if learner control provisions are to be used in the lesson, certain information will need to appear on screens that otherwise would not be needed, such as "Press ctrl-H for Hint, ctrl-Q for Quiz, ctrl-E for Example." Paying attention to screen design makes it possible to not only ensure that functional elements are provided on-screen as needed, but also to lay out the screens in a consistent, functional, and pleasing manner. So, for example, as we design the screen for a lesson that will contain the learner control func-

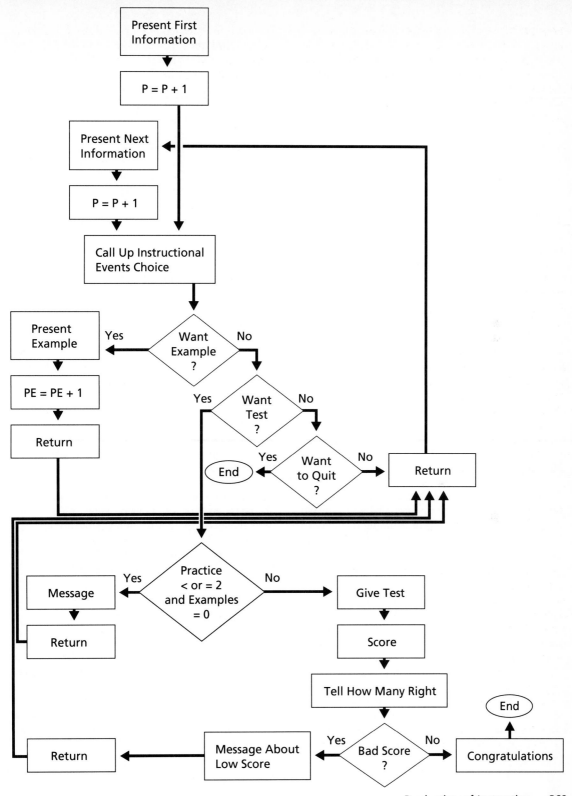

Figure 15.5: An Example Flowchart

tions previously noted, we should ensure that they appear on the screen in a consistent and appropriate location. Hannafin and Peck use the term *frame protocol* to refer to the "consistent designation of various zones of a frame for specific uses" (1988, p. 175). In fact, if all functions including information, response provisions, and wayfinding have a consistent look and layout, the utility and appeal of the CBI module can be improved.

Screen Planning Sheets are a useful tool for determining what each screen display will contain and how the screen should look. Screen planning sheets are typically developed at the same time as the detail-level of flowchart work. Figure 15.6 shows example screen planning sheets used in a project on geography.

Creation of Pseudo-Code

Before writing actual program code, many programmers find it helpful to outline the program, writing in the same general form of the language that will ultimately be used but leaving off the details of correct syntax and form that the actual computer code will use. An example of a pseudo-code outline for the same instruction presented in the previous flowchart example is presented in Figure 15.7.

Creation of Code

Three primary alternatives are available for use in developing the computer software that will support CBI: (1) general purpose programming languages, (2) specialized authoring languages, and (3) CAI/CBI authoring systems. With use of any of these approaches, computer-readable code is generated. When languages are used, the author is somewhat closer to the code than when authoring systems are used, in which case the actual code is not obvious or, in many cases, available for the author's inspection. But code is generated, nonetheless.

1. General purpose programming languages such as BASIC, Pascal, and C are the most flexible tools available, but they have the drawback of taking the most time to learn to use and being the most time-consuming to use. Pascal and C are usually used by people whose training and

specialty is in programming, and these are the languages typically used to develop the software on the commercial market. BASIC has lost popularity in recent years, but it can provide an introduction to the kind of environment that is experienced when working with a general purpose programming language.

2. Special purpose authoring languages and shells, such as Pilot, Super Pilot, Course Writer, and VP Expert, offer a balance between the difficulty of learning and using general purpose languages and the restrictions imposed by authoring systems. Authoring languages, in theory at least, are easier to learn to use than general purpose languages because their command set is restricted to a particular sort of application. They can also provide more flexibility than an authoring system, although this advantage is quickly being eroded by improvements in authoring systems.

3. Authoring systems, such as Course of Action, Phoenix, and HyperCard, are the easiest to learn and the least time-consuming to use of the development options. When using an authoring system the author makes selections from alternatives presented rather than writing lines of commands. Due to increases in computer power (speed and memory), authoring systems have become much more flexible than they were in the past. Whereas early authoring systems restricted the user to a single or narrow range of instructional strategy options, now the better authoring systems provide a flexible environment. HyperCard is not a CBI authoring system per se, but it has become one of the more popular authoring environments for CBI developers due to its combination of flexibility and development speed.

Testing and Revision of Code

In addition to the formative evaluation techniques described elsewhere in this text, CBI development entails its own special form of review and revision: debugging. Computer software does not always work or "run" as anticipated due to a variety of causes, such as coding errors, logical errors, and system flaws. The task of debugging is to find and fix these errors.

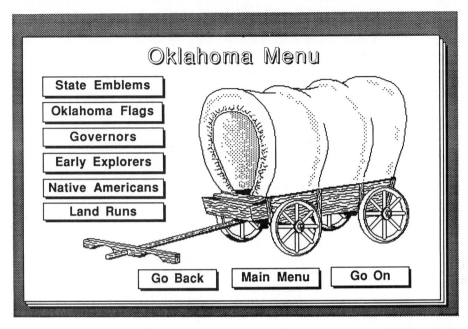

Screen 3: Oklahoma Menu

Screen 4: Emblems, bird

Figure 15.6: Example Screen Planning Sheet

```
Main instruction–present information
Accumulate "practice" variable (P)
Call up instructional events selection subroutine
 ▶Present options at bottom of screen
   Input learner choice
      CTRL E gets examples subroutine
       ▶Present examples
         Accumulate "examples" variable (PE)
       ▪Return
      CTRL T gets test subroutine
       ▶Evaluate P and PE
          If not enough practice
             Present "not enough practice" message
          ▪Return
          Otherwise–Give test
          Call up scoring and feedback subroutine
           ▶Score
            Tell score
            Evaluate
               If score low
                  Present low score message
               ▪Return
            Present congratulations
            End
   ESC ends
 ▶Return
```

Figure 15.7: Example Pseudo-Code Outline

Many software errors turn up only under a specific circumstance (for example, only when a particular key is pressed while a certain part of the program is being executed). The power and sophistication of current computers and authoring environments allow for the creation of software that is so complex that some errors are quite difficult to find. Furthermore, real-world users have a tendency to do the most unexpected and bizarre things while interacting with their computers. Therefore, computer software is normally subjected to review and testing by programmers/developers (frequently called *alpha testing*). It is also sent out to users who are expected to use the software in real settings and who will report any problems back to the software company (frequently called *beta testing*). Even after release, software may exhibit problems that must be repaired, sometimes more than once, resulting in the familiar ''version 4.1'' or ''version 5.8'' of a software item.

The review and revision process commonly employed in the development of computer software is similar but not identical to the formative evaluation processes commonly used in instructional design. Alpha testing is quite similar to expert review in formative evaluation. One difference between formative evaluation of instructional materials and beta testing is that in the case of formative evaluation of instructional materials, the person using the software is a novice in the subject matter being taught and may or may not be a novice at computer use; with beta testing, users are generally experts. When developing CAI materials, we would suggest that the first phase of formative evaluation, expert review, be expanded to include the empirical, user-based testing that is inherent in beta testing. The further testing and revision of the software (which subsequent phases of formative evaluation involves) are quite appropriate and still needed after beta testing.

Production of Instructional Video

Video is one of the most widely used instructional formats (Geber, 1989), due in large measure to the common availability of VCRs and to the instructional medium attributes of television. In this section we will discuss the three phases of video production (preproduction, production, and postproduction), the most commonly used video planning tool (the storyboard script), and the primary production techniques in common use.

Preproduction

The bulk of preproduction work needed for instructional video occurs in the analysis and instructional strategy planning found within the instructional design process. One particular preproduction technique that is unique to video (and related media such as film), is the use of storyboard scripts. Although not all video producers choose to use this form of preproduction planning, we recommend it to those who do not already have a better way to accomplish its functions.

The function of a storyboard script is related to the structure of video itself: Conventional video consists of a linear sequence of visuals with an accompanying linear sequence of audio. In other words, one shot follows another on the screen, with the sound that accompanies it. Determining what those shots will be and organizing them into a sequence that presents the instructional message is the job of the storyboard script.

Storyboards are sets of visuals, such as thumbnail sketches, on 3″ × 5″ cards, pinned to a bulletin board to allow arrangement and rearrangement. One card can be used for each shot in the finished product. Each card on the storyboard contains a sketch of what the shot will depict. Storyboard cards may also contain written information, such as shot number, a verbalized description of action within the shot, and technical information about the shot. In a storyboard script, the visual planning of a storyboard is combined with the audio planning provided by a script. Generally the visuals are on the left column and the script is placed on the right. An example storyboard script is provided in Figure 15.8.

Although most college graduate students are generally accustomed to the need for verbal continuity and know how to achieve it in prose, visual continuity and the means to achieve it are known by a smaller audience of specialists—people who work with film, television, and other visual media. Visual and audio continuity, along with interest factors, are special concerns of video preproduction planning. In the next section, we will discuss the widely used visual continuity technique of visual paragraphing.

Video Production

The wide variety of video production approaches may be summarized into two general forms: studio production and single-camera with editing. Any one project may involve both forms of production or, in some cases, one or the other production approach is selected. Whatever the form of production selected, the goal is a product that has the qualities we associate with "good" video. These qualities, beyond the most obvious ones relating to picture sharpness, stability, and clear audio, include a critical aspect called *visual paragraphing*.

Virtually all television material that is professionally produced possesses the quality of visual paragraphing. Visual paragraphing is achieved when the visual message is conveyed by a sequence of shots rather than one continuous shot; the change in point of view offered by the different shots corresponds to transitions in ideas. A single, continuous shot tends to be boring. Camera angle changes are needed for interest's sake, and the idea of visual paragraphing emphasizes the importance of making visual changes to reinforce and clarify the content while maintaining both visual and semantic continuity. The two primary techniques of video production described below may be thought of as alternative routes to achieve visual paragraphing. A given production might use one or the other or a combination of these two production approaches.

1. *Studio production.* The most basic and fundamental television studio houses two or more video cameras, one or more video recorders, equipment to enable switching and mixing the signal from the cameras into a recorder, audio devices such as microphones and an audio mixer, an intercom to allow communication between director and camera and videotape operators,

Video   Audio

Alternative
Method of
Fitting
Auxillary
Crutches

shot 1

Title slide

Notes: Smiling person
walking on crutches /w
title superimposed

shot 2

Mobile Society–People have a
need to continue with
activities despite injuries.
If properly fitted, auxillary
crutches will allow a person to
interact with the community
while the injury is healing.

Notes: Outside shot of
patient walking w/ crutches

shot 3

Axilla to heel + 4"

Two traditional methods
for measurement exit.

One measurement is the
axilla to heel plus four inches.

Notice that the patient must be reclining.

Notes: Therapist measuring
with patient reclining

shot 4

The other involves the patient
standing in parallel bars while
the therapist measures and
adjusts the crutches.

Notes: Patient standing in
parallel bars. Therapist squatting
to measure & adjust crutches

Figure 15.8: An Example Storyboard Script

lighting equipment, and sets/backgrounds. Using a storyboard script, the director in a studio production can direct a currently unused camera to be ready for the next shot. Then, when the action that the camera is to capture begins and the video switcher has connected that camera's output to the recorder, the camera previously in use is now free to film the next shot. This "leap-frog" from one camera to another, as guided by the director, who in turn is guided by a storyboard script, is the archetype for studio production of video.

Studio production offers the advantages of controlled lighting, a controlled acoustical environment, support staff, and, most importantly, high speed of production. Its drawbacks include the expense of the studio, equipment, and personnel, and the lower audience interest level that often results from material being taped in a studio environment rather than a natural environment.

2. *Single camera with editing*. As portable videotaping and editing equipment have become increasingly sophisticated, working on location with a single camera and then editing the results to achieve continuity has become more common. The different camera angles are achieved by stopping the action and the recording, moving the single camera to a new location, and beginning recording again. Because action must stop and wait for the next shot to be ready, single camera recording is generally more time-consuming than studio recording. After the shooting is complete, the videotape segments are edited into the finished product. Depending on the production design, the audio portion may be recorded and "dubbed" onto the videotape after the video shooting is complete. Editing consists of copying the video segments in the sequence desired, as well as editing the sound portions that accompany the video.

Single camera production offers the advantages of lower cost for capital equipment as well as the interest and variety offered by outdoor as well as indoor settings. A primary drawback of single camera production is that it is takes longer to produce a given amount of material than an equivalent studio production. Also, recording outside of the controlled environment of a studio frequently causes difficulties in getting good, clear audio. Producing a satisfactory sound portion of a videotape shot outside a studio is frequently the most difficult part of the production. "Voice over" production designs, in which we do not see the narrator speaking, are often an excellent way to achieve high quality audio while at the same time filming outside of a studio.

Postproduction

A large amount of the postproduction work needed for instructional video is included in the formative evaluation procedures generally applied in instructional design, as described elsewhere in this text. In addition to the formative evaluation procedures, post-production activities for video include editing and distribution.

When creating multi-camera, studio productions, the control and execution of the transition from shot to shot may be considered as a kind of "editing." However, for most video productions, postproduction editing is used to assemble segments, make necessary adjustments to the audio, and add finishing touches such as titles and credits.

Although distribution is a part of the use of any medium, it has particular importance with video because the power of the medium is frequently heavily vested in its distribution potential. Distribution may include the relatively straightforward process of duplicating and mailing videotapes to users, or it may involve the high-tech complexities of an interactive telecourse supported by satellite, microwave, or fiber optic communication systems. A great deal of the interest in "distance education" is found in what can be accomplished through the distribution of video.

*P*roducing Teacher-Based Instruction

One of the most widely used delivery systems for instruction is the human instructor (Geber, 1989). Although instructional designers tend to think of instructor delivery as "just another medium," this is the means of instructional delivery which, until recent years, was the *only* option. Teacher-based instruction still remains in many people's minds the only option for delivery of instruction, with other media being seen as aids. At this point in your training as an instructional designer you are no doubt well beyond this stage of limited thinking.

The traditional view of classroom teaching does not include consideration of instructional design. Indeed, teachers have been planning and conducting instruction for hundreds of years before anyone ever thought of the concepts underlying instructional design. Many people in the field of education are so steeped in these traditional ways of thinking that it is difficult for them to view teacher-based instruction as something that can be a product of the instructional design process. But, as countless examples every day throughout the world can show, the systematic instructional design process can yield more effective, efficient, and appealing teacher-based instruction than traditional techniques.

We have broken down the process of producing teacher-based instruction into two steps: developing instructor guides and training the trainers. Of course, the entire instructional design process is used in producing teacher-based instruction, just as it is used in producing print, computer, or video-based instruction. The two production steps represent the activities that will be unique to designing instruction involving this form of delivery.

Developing Instructor Guides

Instructor guides should contain the material necessary for an instructor to successfully deliver the instruction. The exact nature of the material needed will depend on a number of factors, not the least of which are instructor characteristics such as subject matter knowledge and teaching skills or pedagogical training. For example, inexperienced instructors may need very detailed instructor guides, while experienced instructors may not need such detailed material. Often a full script of a presentation is provided, but it is generally preferable to employ an outline (McLinden, Cummings, & Bond, 1990; Zemke, 1982). Instructor guides are not just plans of presentation, however. Figure 15.9 presents a summary of typical contents of good instructor guides.

Material for both course-level and lesson-level guides is obtained from products of the analysis and strategy phases of the instructional design process. The course title and lesson titles, goals, and purposes are products of the needs assessment; the target audience description comes from the learner assessment; and both course and lesson objectives are a product of the learning task analysis. The facilities needed, equipment needed, materials,

Course-level guides	Lesson-level guides
Course Title	Lesson Title
Course Goal(s)	Lesson Goal
Target Audience	Class roster/name tags
Course Objectives	Lesson Objectives
Course Purpose	Lesson Purpose
Spaces needed	Place of instruction
Equipment needed	Equipment needed
Materials needed	Materials needed
References	References
Schedule	Lesson plan
Synopsis of each lesson	Synopsis of the lesson
	Lesson outline or script (student outcomes and activities, instructor activity)
Time allocation	Time allocation

Figure 15.9: Instructor Guide Contents

references, and the schedule and lesson plans are products of the instructional strategy phase, (specifically, from development of the expanded instructional events).

The lesson plan itself should be thought of as a document describing what the instructor should do or say. Not all teacher-led instruction involves the lecture, and instructional management activities are as important and appropriate for the lesson plan as are lecture notes. An excellent procedure for developing a lesson plan was developed by the United States Air Force for its Academic Instructor School. This form of lesson plan is in three columns. The left-hand column contains an outline of the lesson objectives, called *desired learning outcomes*. This outlines what students will be learning during the lesson. The desired learning outcomes are developed first. Then, for each desired learning outcome, the designer asks, "What do the students need to do to accomplish this learning?" The answers to this question provide the middle column, labeled *student activity*. Activities might be such things as "listens to an explanation of the procedure" or "observes a demonstration of . . ." or "practices the procedure with assistance of a fellow student" or (in a group discussion) "provides a personal example of the principle. . . ." After specifying learner activities, the final step in preparation of the three-column lesson plan is accomplished by asking, "What does the instructor need to do in order to produce the desired student behavior?" The third column is labeled *instructor activity*. In this fashion, the plans for what teachers will say and do are developed out of consideration for the learning task and learner activities. The level of detail of instructor activity may vary from a word-for-word script to a bare outline, and opinions as to what level of detail is best vary widely. The majority opinion, however, seems to favor the outline level, with verbatim script reserved for questions that instructors should ask in discussion lessons.

The three-column lesson plan has strengths in terms of both development and use. As a development tool, it aids the development of instructor activity outlines that are student-centered and that relate to learning objectives. As a classroom tool, having immediate access to intents for student learning and student activity alongside instructor notes helps the instructor direct her efforts productively as the lesson proceeds. An example three-column lesson plan for a lesson in photography is presented in the Extended Example of this chapter.

Training the Trainers

The presence of plans and materials that are suitable for instructor use is not where the production process ends when we are developing instructor-based instruction. Without appropriate training, we may find instructors delivering poor instruction, regardless of the quality of the materials that we have developed.

Although we are predominantly talking about the training of instructors for particular instructional tasks with regard to particular items or systems of instruction, the training of instructors may also include training that involves broader frame of reference, such as training to be a second grade teacher, K-12 language arts teacher, an Air Force instructor, or an IBM mass storage systems instructor. This instructor training, called *teacher education* when directed at preparation for public school teaching positions, is often undervalued. However, there is an important body of pedagogical content to be learned by those who would teach, some of which is illustrated by the need for training trainers in the use of specific instructional units or systems.

When training trainers for particular lessons or courses, it is ideal to allow the trainer to work with the lesson at least twice before being given full responsibility for its delivery. First, the trainer should experience the lesson as a student. Second, the trainer should conduct the lesson with supervision by an experienced trainer. Such a pattern is commonplace in military training as well as in business and industry training.

The training of trainers should emphasize the trainers' gaining experience in the management of student learning rather than "learning what to say." Novice instructors seem generally more concerned with content than they need to be and less concerned with mathemagenics (behaviors that lead to learning) than they need to be. Although well-designed instructor guides go a long way toward prescribing the activities that need to take place, the transition from novice to expert trainer is seen largely in the trainer learning not only the content of the lesson but also the instructional strategies that make the lesson work. This learning should be deeply internalized, of the sort that is generally associated with "self-appropriated" learning.

*T*ime and Cost of Production

The development of instruction is expensive. Just exactly how expensive instructional development is varies with such factors as the organization, the learning tasks, the content, the strategies used, and the media of instruction. In addition to production costs, a large proportion of the cost of instructional development is incurred by the design and evaluation activities described elsewhere in this text.

Time and cost estimates for development of instruction vary from broad rules of thumb to precise formulas. Before looking at either, a major caveat is in order: It all depends. In other words, it's not a good idea to take any of these estimates as a predictor of what it will cost or should cost to develop instruction in a particular organization.

The broadest rule of thumb for development time reported by Lee and Zemke (1987) was 40 hours of development time for each hour of instruction. Figure 15.10 presents two experts' estimates of the development time required to develop the media discussed in this chapter. (The ratios represent the number of hours needed to produce one hour of instruction.)

	Expert A	*Expert B*
Print	100:1	120–345:1
Computer-based training	300:1	160–420:1
Video	200:1	160–345:1
Teacher-led	40–50:1	80–315:1

Figure 15.10: Estimates for Development Time

Another way to look at development time requirements is to categorize the level of instructional sophistication expected or required and make estimates from that. Lee and Zemke (1987) cite a representative of Arthur Andersen & Co. who described a system involving eleven categories based on the presence or absence of training delivery variables. Development of training for a level 11 school, a minimum cost approach, might require as little as 15 hours of development time per hour of instruction, whereas development for a level 1 school, a "Cadillac approach," might require 215 hours of development time per hour of instruction. The factors considered in the various levels included stability (how long the instruction should be valid), size and experience level of faculty, number of participants (students) per year, amount and kind of supporting visuals, and modes of delivery (including discussion, exercises, and content delivery).

Additional variability in development time results from use of one or another particular design approach that is intended to save development time. We have mentioned these "fast track" approaches to instructional design in Chapter 1 and will have more to say about them in the final chapter of this text, Chapter 17.

Development costs may vary even more widely than development time. Some media are just more expensive to develop than others, due to medium-specific factors such as equipment and materials costs. Video is perhaps the most expensive medium to produce. Bergman and Moore (1990) reported a range of $600 to $5,000 per finished minute for video production. Differences in video production costs are attributable to such factors as number of locations used, costs of talent (narrators and actors), music and effects, editing (number of hours spent), equipment used, and time spent in production. Use of "fast track" instructional design approaches can result in cost savings as well as time savings, but development cost savings are more difficult to predict, in a general sense, than development time savings.

Computer-based instruction is also generally regarded as an expensive medium to produce, primarily due to the time it takes to write software. Once the code is developed, physical production and reproduction is relatively inexpensive. Since selection of authoring mode (general purpose language, authoring language, or authoring system) makes such a large difference in CBI development time, the range in time required to author a particular item of CBI software can be quite wide. The diverse range of time and production costs means that project planners and directors must carefully develop budgets for production as a part of the instructional design process.

Summary

In this chapter, we have looked at the production of instructional materials in four different forms: print-based, computer-based, video, and teacher-based. These media comprise the vast majority of instructional delivery approaches in common use. To become truly proficient at production in any of these forms requires specialized and intensive effort; we have provided a general overview of what is involved in the actual production of the materials that are the object and result of our design efforts.

We discussed procedures for producing print-based instruction in a five-step process involving drafting of text and thumbnail illustrations, selecting or designing a grid and text specifications, creation of a dummy, creation of camera-ready copy, and duplication or printing. In discussing development of computer-based instruction, we presented a five-step production process, including (1) development of functional flowcharts; (2) creation of screen designs; (3) creation of pseudo-code; (4) creation of code using general purpose programming languages, special purpose authoring languages, and authoring systems; and (5) testing/revision of software. When we discussed the production of video instruction, we proposed a three-phase view of the process that involves preproduction, production, and postproduction. We also discussed use of storyboard scripts as production planning tools, and we compared the two primary forms of production—studio production and single-camera. In discussing the production of teacher-based instruction, we concentrated on two steps: (1) the development of instructor guides, including the need contents of such guides and an example of a particularly useful format for such guides; and (2) the training of instructors. Finally, we discussed time and cost issues for production, the wide range of time and costs, and the variability being accounted for not only by differences between media but also in differences in production requirements of a particular project.

Job Aid

Forms are included on following pages for teacher/trainer guides (Figure 15.11), CAI screen planning sheets (Figure 15.12), and a storyboard script (Figure 15.13).

Lesson Title: _____

Course: _____

Instructor: _____

Lesson Goal: _____

_____

_____

Terminal Objective: _____

_____

Figure 15.11: Sample Instructor Guide Form

Desired Learning Outcomes: _____

_____

_____

Purpose of Lesson: _____

_____

Equipment Needed: _____

Materials Needed: _____

Time Required: _____

Location: _____

Synopsis of Lesson: _____

Lesson Plan   page no. _____

Desired Learning Outcomes	Student Activity	Instructor Activity
Introduction *(time required: _____)*		
Body *(time required: _____)*		
Conclusion *(time required: _____)*		

Figure 15.11: *Continued*

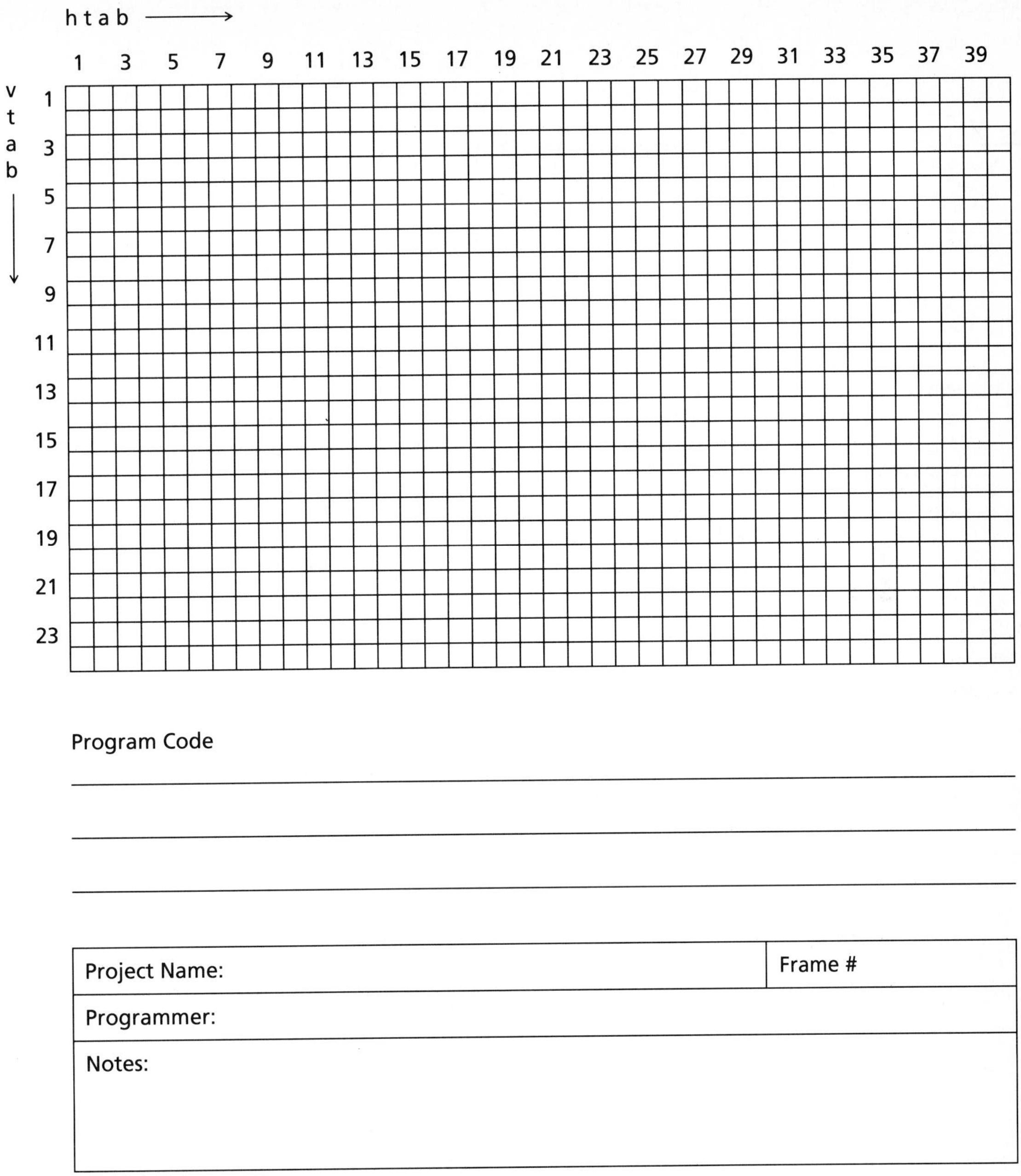

htab ⟶

1　3　5　7　9　11　13　15　17　19　21　23　25　27　29　31　33　35　37　39

v
t
a
b
↓

1
3
5
7
9
11
13
15
17
19
21
23

Program Code

_____

_____

_____

Project Name:	Frame #
Programmer:	
Notes:	

Figure 15.12: Sample CAI Screen Planning Sheet

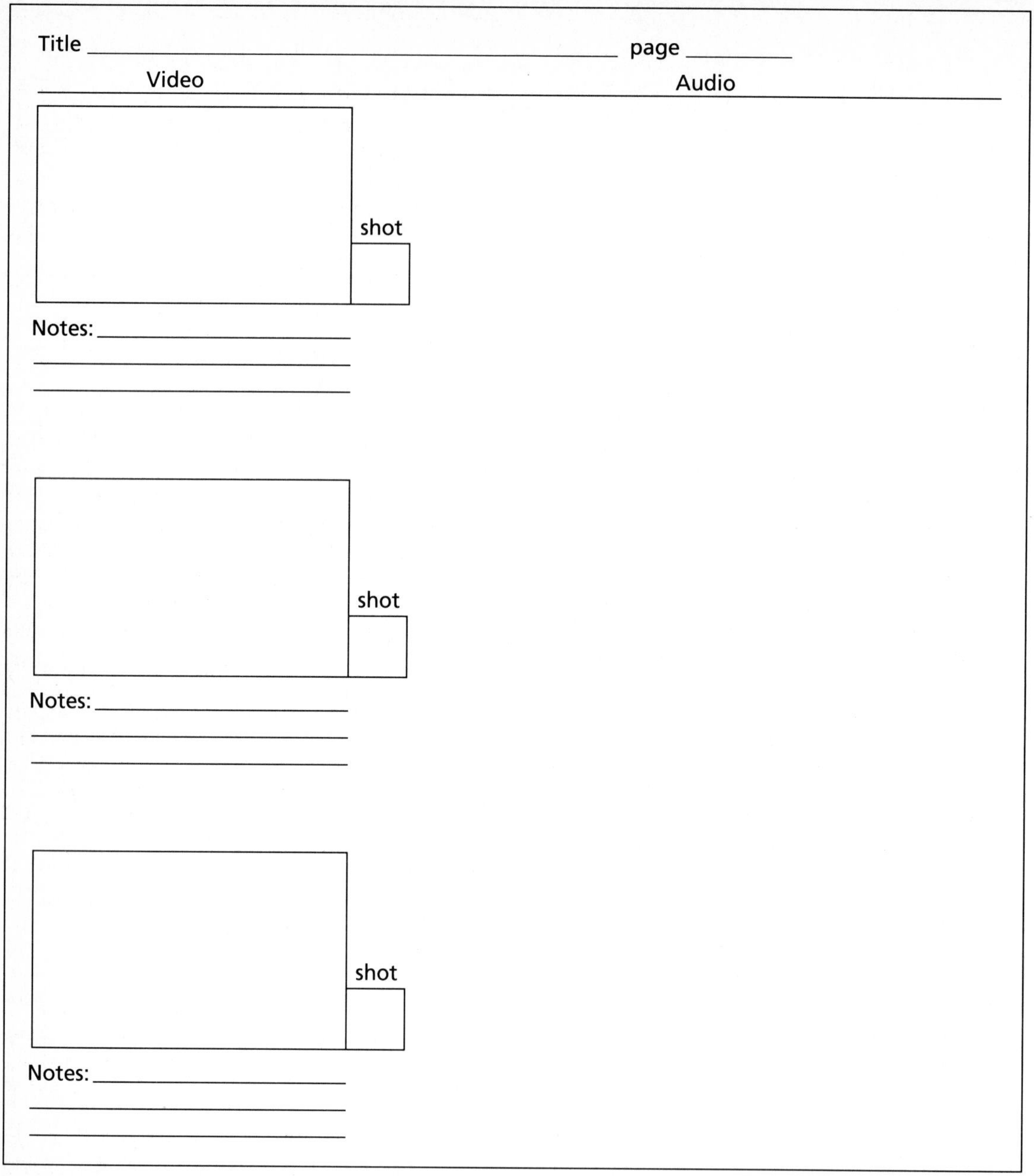

Figure 15.13: Sample Storyboard Script Form

Extended Example

For this chapter, an example lesson plan for an instructor-led lesson on lens characteristics is provided.

Sample Instructor Guide

Lesson Title: Three Characteristics of Lenses

Course: Photography Basics

Instructor: Tillman J. Ragan
Office: ECH Rm. 302 Ph: 325-1521

Lesson Goal: For each student to understand the primary results of using different lens focal lengths.

Terminal Objective: Given a 35mm camera with a zoom lens and the choice of three focal length settings on the lens (28mm, 50mm, and 200mm) representing "wide angle," "normal," and "telephoto" focal lengths, and given a variety of situations and picture goals, the student should be able to select an appropriate focal length and describe the effects of that focal length choice on field of view, perspective, and depth of field in the picture that would result.

Desired Learning Outcomes:

1. Given examples of different lens focal lengths, identify each as wide angle, normal, and telephoto.
2. Given examples of different lens focal lengths, describe the effect of focal length on field of view.
3. Given examples of different lens focal lengths, describe the effect of focal length on perspective.
4. Given examples of different lens focal lengths, describe the effect of focal length on depth of field.

Purpose of Lesson: To assist learners in making better photographs by increasing creative control options offered by selecting lens focal length, either when using a zoom lens or selecting from among different lenses of fixed focal length.

Equipment Needed: Overhead projector and screen; 2×2 slide projector with remote control; 35mm reflex cameras with 28–200mm zoom lenses; development kit.

Materials Needed: Overhead transparency set "Lens Focal Lengths," 35mm slide sets ("Montage of Focal Length Applications," "Examples of Focal Length Characteristics"), unexposed slide film, (one 12-picture roll per 2 students).

Time Required: 2 hours

Location: ECH 231 (classroom with tables and chairs arranged in a seminar fashion) and a courtyard outside the classroom building for exercises.

Synopsis of Lesson: After showing a short montage of good and bad pictures resulting from good and bad selections of lens focal length, the instructor will describe the goal and purpose of the lesson and relate the learning tasks of the lesson to the students' future jobs. The instructor will overview the content of the lesson and describe how the lesson will proceed. In the Body of the lesson, the instructor will describe and illustrate the idea of lens focal length, with student practice at setting and describing different focal lengths. Next, using overhead transparencies to assist in structuring the presentation, the instructor will explain how the three characteristics—field of view, perspective, and depth of field—are affected by lens focal length. The characteristics will be illustrated by 35mm slides taken with the different focal lengths to illustrate each characteristic. A photo assignment exercise will follow in which each student shoots example photos to illustrate the characteristics. The lesson will then include a summary by the instructor—a remotivation emphasizing how the students' new knowledge of lens characteristics can be put to use. The lesson will conclude with a closure.

Following is a lesson plan illustrating the use of the three-column lesson plan in an instructor guide.

Lesson Plan

Desired Learning Outcomes	Student Activity	Instructor Activity
Introduction: 10 min.		
1. Becomes aware that lesson on lens focal length has begun. 2. Becomes interested and curious about using different focal length lenses. 3. Knows what lesson will cover and what will happen during the lesson.	1. Observes instructor beginning lesson. 2. Sees good and poor photographs related to focal length of lens used. 3. Listens to explanation of lesson.	1. Attention: Open lesson. 2. Motivation: Show good and poor photographs resulting from good and poor lens selection. 3. Overview: Lesson main points and how lesson will proceed.
Body: 1 hour, 40 minutes		
	20 minutes	
4. Understands the concept of focal length.	4a. Listens to and observes discussion and examples of focal length. 4b. Sets zoom lens to varying focal lengths and describe resulting images.	4a. Define focal length and provide examples of ''long'' and ''short'' focal length lenses. 4b. Guide practice with cameras. Instruct to: • set to an extreme • aim at a subject • describe • reset to opposite extreme • describe changes
	20 minutes	
5. Is able to describe and predict the result on: • field of view • perspective • depth of field from changes in lens focal length.	5. Listens, observes, and takes notes on the three characteristics. Sets zoom lens to varying focal lengths and describes resulting images, now in terms of field of view, perspective, and depth of field.	5. Describe focal length effect on: • field of view • perspective • depth of field Show and discuss slides illustrating effects. Repeat practice 4b including the three characteristics.
	30 minutes	
6. Is able to select lens focal length to achieve a desired photographic effect.	6. Takes photographs to achieve effects on the three characteristics.	6a. Direct photo assignment exercise: Go outside and take two pictures for each characteristic; one shot for each extreme (6 photos), in teams of two students per team. • process slides • load into slide tray

Desired Learning Outcomes	Student Activity	Instructor Activity
	30 minutes	
6. (continued) Is able to select lens focal length to achieve a desired photographic effect.	6. (continued) Takes photographs to achieve effects on the three characteristics.	6b. Show and lead discussion on how slides illustrate the effects of focal length.

Conclusion: 10 minutes

1. Recalls and consolidates experiences. 2. Realizes applicability of skills learned. 3. Knows that lesson is finished.	1. Listens and recalls. 2. Listens and imagines. 3. Listens.	1. Summary: Review main points of lesson. 2. Remotivation: Describe how students can use their knowledge to improve their pictures. 3. Closure: Remind students of the next lesson, and state that this lesson is finished.

Readings and References

Print

Armbruster, B. B. & Anderson, T. H. (1985). Frames: Structures for informative text. In Jonassen, D.H. (Ed.), *The technology of text, Vol. II*. Englewood Cliffs, NJ: Educational Technology.

Britton, B. K., & Black, J. B. (1985). *Understanding expository prose*. Hillsdale, NJ: Erlbaum.

Duffy, T. M., & Waller, R. (1985). *Designing usable text*. Orlando: Academic Press.

Fry, E. (1977). Fry's readability graph: Clarifications, validity, and extension to level 17. *Journal of Reading, 21*, 242–252.

Gunning, R. (1952). *The technique of clean writing*. New York: McGraw-Hill.

Hartley, J. (1985). *Designing instructional text*, (2nd ed.). New York: Nichols.

Houghton, H. A., & Willows, D. M. (1987). *The psychology of illustration, Vol. 2*. New York: Springer-Verlag.

Jonassen, D. H. (Ed.). (1982). *The technology of text, Vol. I*. Englewood Cliffs, NJ: Educational Technology.

Jonassen, D. H. (Ed.). (1985). *The technology of text, Vol. II*. Englewood Cliffs, NJ: Educational Technology.

Jones, B. F., Friedman, L. B., Tinzman, M., & Cox, B. E. (1984). Content-driven comprehension instruction and assessment: A model for Army training literature. (technical report) Alexandria, VA: Army Research Institute.

Meyer, B. B. (1985). Signaling the structure of text. In Jonassen, D. H. (Ed.), *The technology of text, Vol. II*. Englewood Cliffs, NJ: Educational Technology.

Rye, J. (1982). *Cloze procedure and the teaching of reading*. London: Heinemann Educational.

Smith, P. L., and Tompkins, G. E. (1988). Structured notetaking: A new strategy for content area readers. *Journal of Reading, 32*, 46–53.

Strunk, W., Jr., & White, E. B. (1979). *The elements of style*, (3rd ed.). New York: Macmillan.

Taylor, W. L. (1953). "Cloze procedure": A new tool for measuring readability. *Journalism Quarterly, 30*, 415–433.

Willows, D. M., & Houghton, H. A. (1987). *The psychology of illustration, Vol. 1*. New York: Springer-Verlag.

Computer-Based Instruction

Alessi, S. M., & Trolip, S. R. (1985). *Computer-based instruction: Methods and development*. Englewood Cliffs, NJ: Prentice-Hall.

Criswell, E. L. (1989). *The design of computer based instruction*. New York: Macmillan.

Hannafin, M. J., & Peck, K. L. (1988). *The design, development, and evaluation of instructional software*. New York: Macmillan.

Jonassen, D. H. (Ed.). (1988). *Instructional designs for microcomputer software*. Hillsdale, NJ: Erlbaum.

Myers, D., & Lamb, A. (1990). *HyperCard authoring tools for presentations, tutorials, and information exploration*. Orange, CA: Career Publishing.

Price, R. V. (1991). *Computer-aided instruction: A guide for authors*. Pacific Grove, CA: Brooks/Cole.

Ragan, T. J., & Smith, P. L. (1989). *Programming instructional software*. Englewood Cliffs, NJ: Educational Technology.

Television Instruction

Costa, S. A. (1978). *How to prepare a production budget for film and video tape* (2nd ed.). Blue Ridge Summit, PA: TAB Books.

DeLuca, S. (1990). *Instructional video*. Stoneham, MA: Focal Press.

Kemp, J. E., & Smellie, D. C. (1989). *Planning, producing, and using instructional media,* (6th ed.). New York: Harper & Row.

Zettl, H. (1973). *Sight, sound, motion: Applied media aesthetics*. Belmont, CA: Wadsworth.

Zettl, H. (1976). *Television production handbook* (3rd ed.). Belmont, CA: Wadsworth.

Teacher/Trainer Guides

McLinden, D. J., Cummings, O. W., & Bond, S. C. (1990). A comparison of two formats for an instructor's guide. *Performance & Instruction, 3*(1), 2–13.

Rosenweig, F. (1984). Designing training materials for developing countries. *Performance & Instruction, 23* (5), 26–28.

Zemke, R. (1982) How to write—and recognize—quality instructor manuals. *Training, 19* (3) 32–37.

Management and Budgeting

Bergman, R. E., & Moore, T. V. (1990). *Managing interactive video/multimedia projects*. Englewood Cliffs, NJ: Educational Technology.

Costa, S. (1972). *How to prepare and budget for video and film*. Blue Ridge Summit, PA; TAB Books.

Hannum, W., & Hansen, C. (1989). *Instructional systems development in large organizations*. (See Chapter 11.) Englewood Cliffs, NJ: Educational Technology.

Lee, C., & Zemke, R. (1987). How long does it take? *Training, 24* (6), 75–80.

Posavac, E. J., & Carey, R. G. (1989). *Program evaluation: Methods and case studies* (3rd ed.). (See Chapter 10.) Englewood Cliffs, NJ: Prentice-Hall.

Other References

Geber, B. (1989). Who, how, what. *Training, 26* (10), 49–63.

Langford, M. (1986). *Basic photography* (5th ed.). London: Focal Press.

London, B. (1979). *A short course in photography*. Marblehead, MA: Curtin & London.

Formative and Summative Evaluation

sixteen

Chapter Objectives

At the conclusion of this chapter you should be able to do the following:

- Contrast the purposes of formative and summative evaluation.

- Identify the purposes, procedures, data sources, designer's role, materials, participants, and timing of each of the stages of formative evaluation.

- Compare the procedures, materials, and timing for formative evaluation of different media.

- Display formative evaluation data for each phase.

- Interpret given formative evaluation data.

- Identify the purposes, procedures, data sources, designer's role, materials, participants, and timing of each of the stages of summative evaluation.

Evaluating Instructional Materials

The evaluation of an individual student's performance tells us "whether we're there" with regard to the individual student's learning. After we have evaluated the performance of a group of students, we know whether they have achieved the objectives of instruction. There is yet another kind of evaluation that is critical and essential in the design of instruction. This is the evaluation of the instructional materials. Evaluation of instructional materials occurs during two separate points in the instructional development process for two different purposes. At one point in the design process we evaluate the materials to determine the weakness in the instruction so that revisions can be made to make them more effective and efficient. In this way we know "whether we're there" with regard to the instructional materials, or whether we need to continue the design process. This type of evaluation is called **formative evaluation.** Later, after the materials have been implemented into the instructional contexts for which they were designed, designers may be involved in the process of evaluating the materials in terms of their effectiveness in order to provide data for decision-makers who may adopt or continue to use the materials. This type of evaluation is called **summative evaluation.**

Overview of Formative Evaluation

At the conclusion of the phase in which the instructional strategy is developed, the designer has created prescriptions for instruction. These prescriptions are in the form of outlines (for text-based instruction), storyboards (for video- or slide-tape–based instruction), or frame planning sheets (for computer-based instruction). In any case, the prescriptions show what the instruction will look like and how it will be sequenced. The prescriptions include both the instruction and plans for all the tests that we just described in the previous section. These prescriptions are built upon principles of learning and instruction. Based upon the instructional theory that these principles represent, we hypothesize that the instructional systems they prescribe will instruct effectively. However, instructional theory is not an absolute science: There is still much we do not know about setting up conditions for students to learn. If instructional theory is still incomplete and our interpretations of it are sometimes inaccurate, then it is essential that we "try out" the instruction with representative members of the target audience before using materials with many learners or going through the expense of mass producing the materials. Therefore, formative evaluation is considered to be fundamental to the instructional design process.

Commercial publishers of instructional materials (software or textbooks) are not well known for conducting such formal evaluations. They do send copies of instructional materials to potential teachers/trainers for their opinions, but usually the materials are already in the final form, not in a form in which revisions are possible. At any rate, research indicates that teachers/trainers are not the best sources of information for predicting whether materials will be effective (Rosen, 1968; Rothkopf, 1963). The best source of such information is the learners themselves. Although learners' opinions of the quality of the instruction are important, the key is their learning as a result of the instruction.

Trying out materials with learners can help instructional developers determine where revisions are necessary. As a matter of fact, materials that have been tried out with only one or two representative students and then revised based upon the information gained are substantially more effective than the original instruction. Unfortunately for public education, publishers are often unwilling to commit the time and effort to do such evaluations. This is particularly the case with producers who wish to get their products quickly available for sale. Some states, such as Florida, Texas, and California, are beginning to demand that materials considered for state adoption provide evidence of "learner validation" (i.e., formative evaluation). In business and industry as well, formative evaluation is frequently skipped due to the cost. However, such policies may be shortsighted because more effective training (which frequently results from formative evaluation) can result in more profitable operations in the long run.

An advantage of large-scale projects, for schools or training, is that their budgets may be able to absorb the cost of a fully implemented formative evaluation. When design and development costs can be spread across a large number of courses and learners served by the instruction, the benefits of the instruction make the cost low. The ability to perform a thorough formative evaluation is one example of how an economy of scale can contribute to the quality of instruction.

Not all educational materials are amenable to formative evaluation as we will describe it; however, we believe that all products of systematic instructional design should be. Among those products for which formative evaluation (as we describe it) would not be appropriate would be those materials that were not designed to foster achievement of specified learning goals. Such materials include the traditional textbook that is written as an aid to learning a variety of objectives. Increasingly, textbooks are written with specific learning goals in mind and stated; for those texts, a full formative evaluation is appropriate. For traditional texts, only the first phase of the four that we will describe (expert review) has been traditionally employed by the publishing industry. More and more, particularly with texts intended for the K–12 public school market, texts are being viewed as media of instruction tied to specific learning goals, and such texts should be created and evaluated using instructional design principles and techniques.

Phases of Formative Evaluation

In the following sections we will briefly discuss the procedures of formative evaluation and revision. Four stages of formative evaluation will be described: (1) design reviews, (2) expert reviews, (3) learner validation, and (4) ongoing evaluation. The first two stages are less traditionally considered as part of formative evaluation. Design reviews occur prior to the actual development of any instructional materials. Expert review of materials often occurs after the completion of the materials but prior to their actual use with learners. The next two phases involve the use of the actual instructional materials with learners who represent the target audience.

Design Reviews

The output of each stage of design—goals, learner and context analyses, task analysis, etc.—can all be submitted to formative evaluation in order to make revisions prior to any actual development of materials. These reviews may be conducted as each phase of design is completed. They serve to confirm the accuracy of the design process at each stage. During this phase of formative evaluation the designer is attempting to answer questions such as the following:

- Does the instructional goal reflect a satisfactory response to the problems identified in the needs assessment?
- Do the environment and learner analyses accurately portray these entities?
- Does the task analysis include all the prerequisite skills and knowledge needed to perform the instructional goal, and is the prerequisite nature of these skills and knowledge accurately represented?
- Do the test items and resultant test blueprints reflect reliable and valid measures of the instructional objectives?
- Do the assessment instruments and their related mastery criteria reliably distinguish between competent and incompetent learners?

Goal Review. Goal review confirms that the goals that have been established are: (1) representative of a real instructional need and (2) congruent with the client's expectations. Conducting a formal needs assessment will ensure that the goal meets an instructional need, and having the client (or client's representative) review the instructional goal once it is stated in formal, performance terms will ensure that there is agreement as to the purpose of the instruction.

Review of Environment and Learner Analysis. You will have gained much data as you developed your analysis of the environment and the learners. At the conclusion of these analyses, you will need to review their adequacy. To do so you may wish to collect further information after your original draft in order to confirm or extend your analysis. For example, you may wish to collect survey or aptitude data to confirm your analysis of the targeted learners. For instance, you might wish to give a reading test to sample members of the target audience to confirm your estimates of their reading grade level. Or you might wish to survey managers within the organization to confirm that the attitudes regarding training that you gathered during your analysis of the learning environment are indeed representative of that group.

Review of Task Analysis. The task analysis can be confirmed with a number of techniques. The prerequisite relationship of skills may be confirmed by testing groups of learners who do and do not possess the targeted skills and determining if the learners who can achieve the terminal objective can indeed perform all those listed as subordinate and vice versa. You might refer to White and Gagné (1978) to see the procedure that they followed in order to confirm their learning hierarchies. You might also ask content experts and other instructional designers to review your task analysis for accuracy and completeness.

You may also wish to confirm that the point at which you identified objectives as entry level is accurate. You may assess a sample of your target audience's ability on these entry-level skills in order to confirm the accuracy of your estimates. (You might also want to give a pretest on the skills to be learned.)

Review of Assessment Specifications and Blueprints. Assessment items can be formatively evaluated for their validity by having content and testing experts review the assessment item specifications and blueprints. The reviewers can evaluate the congruence of the objective and the item specifications. They can determine if the type of items outlined by the specifications adequately describes the domain of items that the objective might cover. They can determine if the number of items specified in the item specifications and blueprints is sufficient to adequately sample the range of the domain of the content that the objectives might cover.

The assessment instruments may also be administered to skilled learners prior to the development of the materials in order to determine the practicality and the reliability of the instruments. Traditional statistical tests of reliability often do not work well with instruments developed on a criterion-referenced plan because they often do not have the variability (spread) of scores for the statistics to work. Therefore, methods of reliability analysis based upon "mastery" learning have been developed. One way to assess reliability of a

criterion-referenced test is to determine the consistency of the test in certifying learners as "masters" or "nonmasters." You can refer to Chapter 15 for a brief description of this procedure and Shrock and Coscarelli (1989) for more complete procedures.

Expert Reviews

Before instructional materials are used by learners in the latter stages of formative evaluation, it is often helpful to have materials reviewed by experts: content experts, instructional design experts, content-specific education specialists, or experts on the learners, such as teachers. During one type of expert review—a content review—the designer has a subject matter expert examine the content of the instructional material for accuracy and completeness. For example, if the instructional materials are on the principles of physics, then an expert in physics should review the instruction. An individual who knows the target audience may also be called in to review the materials for their appropriateness. This may involve an examination of the vocabulary, examples, and illustrations that are included. A content-specific educator (in this case a science educator) would also be a good reviewer because she could evaluate the congruence of the presentation of content with current educational theory in the specific content areas. During expert review, depending upon the expertise of the reviewer, the designer is attempting to answer questions such as the following:

- Is the content accurate and up-to-date?
- Does the content present a consistent perspective?
- Are examples, practice exercises, and feedback realistic and accurate?
- Is the pedagogical approach consistent with current instructional theory in the content area?
- Is the instruction appropriate for the target learners?
- Are the instructional strategies consistent with principles of instructional theory?

The materials given to the reviewers at this stage are in draft form. The comments of particular experts should be considered in terms of their expertise. For example, it is not uncommon for content experts to have suggestions regarding the instructional strategy that is used in the materials. While certainly this information should be carefully considered for its value, the expert's advice on the accuracy of the content will be much more valuable. Revisions to eliminate inaccuracies should be made at this time. However, the designer may wish to delay following up on suggestions about instructional strategies until information is obtained on learner performance.

We suggest that the designer divide context experts' comments into three categories: (1) revisions that should be made immediately, (2) questions for which data should be collected during subsequent phases, and (3) suggestions that should be ignored. In the case of items that fall into the second category, the designer should design explicit questions either to ask of the learners during subsequent one-to-one evaluations or to use as particular items on assessment instruments in order to be certain that actual information is gathered regarding the unresolved issue.

Learner Validation

One-To-One Evaluation. During one-to-one evaluation, the designer tries out the instructional materials with two or three members (sometimes more) of the target audience. The purpose of this stage is to determine and rectify any gross problems in the instruction. The types of problems that may be located in this stage are typographical errors, unclear sentences, poor or missing directions, inappropriate examples, unfamiliar vocabulary, mislabeled pages or illustrations, illustrations that do not communicate intent, and frames in incorrect sequences, to name but a few. During one-to-one evaluation the designer is attempting to answer questions such as the following:

- Do the learners understand the instruction?
- Do learners know what to do during the practice and tests?
- Can learners interpret graphics in the text?
- Can the learners read all of the textual material?

The designer sits down with one student at a time and has the student go through the instruction in its draft form, including the tests. This draft form may be draft print materials with hand-drawn illustrations, frame sheets for computer-based instruction, a storyboard for a video presentation, or other drafted materials in a particular medium. It is not typical to use one-to-one evaluation for teacher-mediated instruction, except for any components based on other media.

Designer's Role. The designer's role in one-to-one evaluation is to query the student about any problems that she is having and to clear up these problems by restating the instruction or correcting misconceptions. The designer makes notes in his own copy of the materials about the kinds of problems that the learner encounters and ways to correct these problems. It is a useful practice for the designer to develop a list of questions that she has regarding aspects of the materials: Is certain vocabulary in the instruction familiar to the learner? Is the intent of a particular practice question clear? Does the learner understand a particular explanation? Can the learner understand the use of a particular analogy? If the learner does not comment on these features, the designer can make sure to ask questions regarding them.

Learners' Role. As some learners will be reluctant to criticize the materials, the designer should (1) emphasize that if the learner is having difficulty with the instruction, it is not the learner's fault, but the material's; and (2) ask particular probing questions if the learner does not volunteer problems. Since learners are generally reluctant to make negative comments about materials that they perceive the designer has created, the designer may wish to distance himself from the materials by saying something such as ''I've been asked to try out these materials with learners to see how they work.'' The evaluation of materials is something like a ''tastetest'' of scientific inquiry with learners. Learners used in one-to-one evaluations should represent learners of average, slightly above average, and slightly below average ability. The more verbal the learners tend to be, the better the information that the designer can obtain. It is not uncommon to need to ''prime'' the learners with specific questions. These questions should remind the designer of the issues that are pending regarding the materials. The designer should ask the questions at the ends of sections so as to not interrupt the flow of the learners' processing within a continuous section.

Procedures. One approach that may be useful in conducting one-to-one evaluations is the use of a "read-think-aloud" technique (Smith & Wedman, 1988). When using the read-think-aloud approach, the designer will ask the learner to read and think aloud while interacting with the instructional materials. This approach is particularly appropriate when evaluating instruction that has a print- or computer-based component, but it may also be used when having learners review storyboards for video-mediated instruction. The learner is asked to express aloud any thoughts that are occurring as she reads a particular instructional passage. The learner is not asked to explain these thoughts, only to say them aloud, and then to continue reading orally. These oral utterances can be tape recorded and transcribed, creating a permanent record of the learner's comments. These transcriptions, called *protocols,* provide information not only as to whether the learner can read the materials but also as to what thought processes are occurring within the learner. These thought processes often give clues as to the misconceptions or difficulties that the learner is encountering. As thinking aloud is not a natural action for most learners, we suggest that you demonstrate the procedure and ask the learner to practice the technique before you begin the actual evaluation of the materials.

One way to give learners an idea of the kind of utterances you want is to remind them of how they may talk aloud as they interact with a new computer program or how young children talk aloud as they complete a task. Some learners become very good at this process; others find it impossible to externalize their thought processes. Designers will find that they must frequently prompt learners by saying, "Tell me what you are thinking." If thinking aloud seems to be too great a task for the learner, we suggest that you simply ask the learner to read aloud. Although hearing students read aloud is not as informative as "think alouds," learners' phrasing and misreading of words give some subtle hints regarding their thoughts.

Tests should be included in the one-to-one process, primarily to obtain information as to the learners' ability to respond to the directions and individual items. As the tryout of materials can be rather time-consuming, we often suggest that the tryout of entry-level tests and pretests occur on a day prior to the evaluation of the actual instructional materials. During the administration of the pretests (or even the entry-level tests if your estimate of entry skills is inaccurate), the designer may sense that the learners are becoming frustrated. It is a good idea to construct the tests with the simpler (prerequisite) skills first on the instrument and the more difficult items sequenced later. With this approach, you can determine the point at which the learners' skills fall off. It is still a good idea to encourage the learners to try later items, in case your analysis of prerequisite skills is not correct.

Some of the problems that the learners encounter may be of sufficient magnitude and their revisions may be sufficiently apparent that the designer may make revisions immediately after the evaluation with a single learner. Other problems may appear to be idiosyncratic to the learner, or the designer may have insufficient information as to how to solve the problem. So some designers wait until all one-to-one subjects have completed the instruction. However, at the completion of the one-to-one evaluations it is likely that the designer will revise numerous aspects of the instruction. As one-to-one data are more qualitative than quantitative, we suggest that one-to-one data and the revision decisions based upon them be presented in the form as shown in Figure 16.1.

Displaying and Interpreting One-To-One Data.
We encourage designers to include the source of revision decisions in the "data source" category, as it is important that revisions at this stage come directly from learners' problems. It is also important to tie the revisions to the actual problems that the learners encountered. We rarely include one-to-one posttest scores as data for guiding decisions, as these scores really do not reflect the interactions of the learner and the instruction, but of the learner, the designer, and the instruction. Making decisions based upon the posttest scores, therefore, can be very deceptive.

The designer makes the revisions in the instruction that are indicated by the one-to-one evaluation. The output of this stage of formative evaluation is an instructional lesson that has been revised to eliminate gross problems in the instruction and tests. If problems in instruction were many and the revisions were substantial, then the designer may wish to go through another round of

Objective	Data Source	Information Gained	Revision Decision
G	Pretest	Some students were able to multiply out the numbers greater than 1, obtaining the correct answer while unable to complete the targeted process.	Provide work space on pretest and posttest. Do not count correct where work indicates students have not followed targeted process.
A, B	Pretest/Posttest	Directions to items 1 and 2 are confusing.	Reword directions to read "Circle the letter of the phrase (or number). . . . "
Entry Skill	Student comments on pretest	Students knew what a decimal point was. They felt that asking such an obvious question was confusing. They wondered if I was asking a more complex question.	Students definitely possess this entry skill. Delete this question from entry assessment.
A	S's comments, observations	S1 and S2 had no difficulty with the concept of exponents. S3 had difficulty, but a brief review within the lesson corrected the problem. The concepts of negative and positive exponents were discussed in two separate places in the lesson. S's tended to ignore this discussion.	Instruction should be resequenced and consolidated to produce a short review of the concept of exponents (both negative and positive) at the beginning of the lesson.
All Objectives	S's comments, observations	S's had difficulty separating information and procedures regarding negative exponents from those regarding positive exponents. There was no obvious formatting distinction made in the materials.	Add subheadings "Numbers Greater Than One" and "Numbers Less Than One" to make the two sets of procedures more distinct.

Figure 16.1: Display of One-to-One Data and Interpretation

one-to-one evaluations before proceeding to the next stage. If money or time is not available for further evaluation, the designer has still obtained information that helps eliminate most severe problems. This allows for a product that is substantially more effective than the product prior to the revisions. If time and money are available, the designer should proceed on to the small group evaluation stage. Small group evaluation data provide additional information that may clarify the breadth and severity of any problems that the designer has already found.

Small Group Evaluation

The purpose of this stage of formative evaluation is to check out the efficacy of the revisions made based upon one-to-one data and to see how well the instruction teaches without the designer's intervention. In this phase designers are asking the following questions:

- Do the learners have the entry-level skills that were anticipated?
- If so, did they succeed in the instruction? If they didn't succeed, what revisions are needed?
- If they did not have predicted entry-level skills, did they succeed in the instruction?
- If they did not succeed, what skills were they lacking?
- Did the learners have additional skills that were not predicted?
- How long does it take for the learners to complete the instruction?
- How do the learners feel about the instruction?
- If their feelings are negative, how do these feelings affect their performance?
- What revisions are necessary to improve attitudes toward the instruction?
- Are the revisions made as the result of one-to-one evaluations satisfactory?

In this stage, the designer steps back and observes, supplying help only when problems of such a magnitude arise that students cannot proceed without assistance (an unusual circumstance when revisions based upon one-to-one evaluations have been made). Despite the fact that this evaluation is called "small group," that does not mean that all members of the group must go through the instruction at one time in one room—unless small group activities, such as listening to a lecture or participating in a group discussion, are part of the instructional strategy. The "small group" label indicates how many students will go through the instruction in this stage. Enough students should go through the instruction at this point that the designer can have confidence that the materials have been used with a fairly representative group of students.

Learners' Role. Of course, the more students who participate in the small group evaluation, the more representative the group and the more accurate the data and the consequent revisions will be. We suggest that you use eight to twelve students during this stage. If there are some differences within the target audience in terms of general or specific characteristics that you anticipate might make a difference in the effectiveness, efficiency, or appeal of the instruction, individuals that represent these differences should be included in the small group evaluation. It can be useful to administer a learner analysis questionnaire to obtain general demographic data about the learners participating in the small group evaluation. This questionnaire might assess any initial attitudes or experiences that you think might influence the effectiveness of the instruction.

During this phase, students should sit down with the instruction and go through it as if they were in the real learning environment. They should take any entry-level tests, pretests, or posttests provided. As with one-to-one evaluations, the entry-level tests and pretests may be given on a day prior to the evaluation of the actual instruction, if the designer is worried that the learners will be fatigued by the initial testing and the tryout of the materials. The designer must also be confident that the learners will not "bone up" on the content in the interim.

Designer's Role. In this stage of formative evaluation, the designer is an observer, making notes of any nonverbal cues that may be picked up about the effectiveness or interest level of the instruction and any problems that the learners may volunteer. The designer may assist the learners only in cases in which the instruction cannot proceed without intervention. In cases of group-based instruction it may be useful for the designer to videotape the instruction (after receiving written permission of the participants, of course).

Procedures. This is a good time to address a question that many beginning designers have. You may recall that in Chapter 5 we suggested that the ideal in entry-level tests, pretests, and posttests is that each prerequisite objective is assessed and assessed with sufficient items so that a reliable decision regarding an individual's skill on that objective can be made. We also noted that this thoroughness can result in extremely lengthy assessment instruments and that sometimes these instruments must be shortened for practical purposes. During formative evaluation it is important that you have learners respond to complete instruments assessing all objectives if at all possible.

You may construct shortened forms for actual use when the instruction is implemented. However, it is important during formative evaluation that you gain all the information that you can in order to gain an accurate profile of the effects of the instruction. Hence, comprehensive assessment instruments are critical. Therefore, initial testing may require additional times for administration, and you may feel that you are using an inordinate amount of time in testing. If you become bothered by this, remember that the processes that you use during formative evaluation will ensure good evaluation of the materials. Your procedures for actual instruction might change as a result of this evaluation.

Although lengthy testing may be involved, the procedures for small group evaluation are fairly straightforward. Learners should be informed as to their roles and encouraged to perform at their best level. Initial entry-level tests and pretests should be administered. (Remember: These two initial experiences may occur on days previous to the actual interaction with the instruction.) Learners should then interact with the instruction and receive the posttest and the attitude questionnaire. Then learners should engage in a group debriefing with the designer. The designer may use the attitude opinionnaire as a guide for this discussion or ask more probing questions regarding the learners' feelings toward the instruction. Many designers find that useful information comes from this debriefing because learners are more willing to explain their opinions orally than to laboriously write them. Also, they have a tendency to "piggyback" on each other's ideas, and they are more willing to express critical ideas if they hear peers being critical.

Small group evaluation is conducted with all forms of mediation: print-based texts, prototype computer programs, rough-edited videotapes, and check-disks for interactive video. Small group evaluation may also be conducted with teacher delivery. Particularly in training environments, agencies may have the resources in terms of time, learners, trainers, and facilities to conduct a small group trial with teacher-led instruction. It is useful to have a small group trial with teacher-led training, particularly if the instructional strategy depends heavily on group activities or discussions, or if anything about the instruction is highly complex or problematic. The advantage of limiting the first delivery of teacher-led instruction to a small group is that it allows the teacher to concentrate on the content and delivery, and it limits the possible negative effects of untried instruction to a very small number of learners.

Collecting and Displaying Data. The primary data obtained in small group formative evaluation are the scores on the entry-level test, pretest, practice items, and posttest. In addition, attitude questionnaire data and time data are gathered. The designer uses these data to identify weak spots in the instruction. For example, if the designer finds that all students can perform at mastery level on some of the objectives tested on the pretest, then the instruction can be made more efficient by eliminating the portions of the lesson that address these objectives. If most or all students fail to reach mastery on some of the objectives on the posttest, then the designer can seriously examine both the test items and the instruction that go with those objectives. If time data are well beyond the expected requirements, then the designer may consider dividing the instruction into segments of different sizes. If attitude data indicate a poor motivation level or a bad attitude toward the instruction, additional interest or motivation tactics may be included.

Performance Data. We suggest that the designer collect an assessment of learners' retention and transfer of learning with a parallel form of the posttest because such data may suggest revisions that learners' immediate performance did not indicate. The amount of the delay before the retention test should be dictated by the anticipated length of time that the learners will need to retain the learning before it is used in the next learning context. This may be one day in K–12 situations or several weeks in training environments.

Reducing the data obtained during small group evaluation so that conclusions can be drawn can be something of a task. Performance data can be displayed in two different ways. The first method is use of a chart that displays performance on all tests, listed by objective. The second method involves recording pre and post data on a task analysis diagram. The first method involves displaying learners' mastery of each individual objective on pretest, practice, and posttest (as well as entry-level and delayed posttest if you administered them). Mastery criteria for each objective were developed when you wrote your test specifications. If you abbreviated the number of items or expanded the number of items, you may have to slightly adjust your percentages for mastery from those that appear in the test specifications.

In Figure 16.2 we have included the criteria for mastery performance on pretest, practice, and immediate posttest for an example lesson we evaluated. The figure shows the pretest, practice, and posttest scores for ten students who participated in small group evaluation of instruction on converting numbers into scientific notation. Eight objectives, A through H, were taught in the lesson, with A being the simplest and G and H being the terminal objectives. Here are abbreviated objectives for objectives A–H:

A. Concept of exponent
B. Concept of scientific notation
C. Procedure to convert numbers from standard notation to scientific notation—numbers greater than 1

D. Procedure to convert numbers from standard notation to scientific notation—numbers less than 1
E. Procedure to convert numbers from standard notation to scientific notation—any number
F. Procedure to convert numbers from scientific notation to standard notation—numbers greater than 1
G. Procedure to convert numbers from scientific notation to standard notation—numbers less than 1
H. Procedure to convert numbers from scientific notation to standard notation—any number

The criterion for mastery gives the number of items used to assess the objective and the number of items that must be correct in order for learners to be considered skilled or "masters" in the objective. For example, for a learner to be considered a master on objective H on the pretest, the learner must get five of the six items correct. In addition, the figure indicates what percentage of the ten learners evidenced mastery of the objective. You may find it a bit odd for a mastery level to be indicated on practice items. However, it is impor-

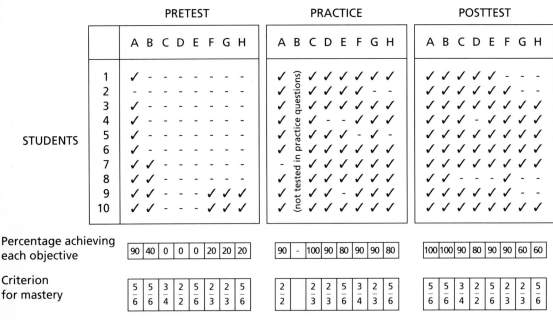

Figure 16.2: Performance Data by Objective Across Tests

tant for us to be able to conclude whether learners were skilled with the objective immediately after instruction on that particular objective. Then from the posttest performance we can determine whether that skill was retained for any period of time.

From the data in Figure 16.2, we can conclude the following:

1. Learners already knew the concept of exponent, as evidenced by objective A on the pretest.

2. Although students 2, 4, and 5 had some difficulty in the practice exercises, overall the students achieved quite well during practice, with at least 80 percent achieving mastery on each objective.

3. Although student 8 had some difficulty throughout the posttest, overall the students' performance was quite good except for objectives G and H. These were the culminating objectives for the lesson. Students' performance fell on these ob-jectives from practice to posttest. It would have been useful to have delayed posttest scores to see if performance fell on other objectives over time.

4. The poor performances of learners 1 and 8 on the posttest may be due to interest factors or prior knowledge factors that should be examined with demographic and opinionnaire data. (The entry-level tests were omitted after four subjects evidenced overwhelming skill during one-to-one trials. Upon reflection, that may not have been a good decision.)

The second method of displaying performance data is to record pretest and posttest data on a task analysis diagram that indicates the prerequisite relationships of objectives (a hierarchy). Figure 16.3 is an example of such a display.

Pretest and posttest data on the hierarchy may indicate where the breakdown in skill occurred. Let us continue to use the example of the scientific

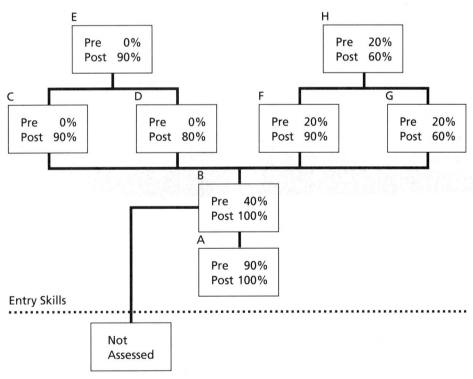

Figure 16.3: Pretest and Posttest Percentages of Learners Mastering Objectives

notation lesson. In this case we conclude that the breakdown in skill occurs in objectives G and H as suggested by the data in Figure 16.2 when placed into the learning hierarchy in Figure 16.3. Since objective G is prerequisite to H, it is highly likely that the poor performance in H is due to the poor performance in G. (The entry-level skill was not assessed during the small group evaluation because the one-to-one evaluations indicated that it was a skill mastered by all learners in the target group.)

Attitude Data.   As we discussed in Chapter 12, learners' attitudes have a critical impact on their learning, so it is important to include a measure-ment of their attitudes in formative evaluation. The attitude opinionnaire also can provide helpful in-formation to explain problems that are evidenced in performance problems on practice and posttests. The format and the vocabulary of the questionnaire will, of course, vary depending upon the charac-teristics of the learners participating in the forma-tive evaluation. For example, with small children the anchors on the questionnaire may be a smiling face, a neutral face, and a frowning face, and the questions may be read to the learners or audio-taped. For adult learners the forms may be quite extensive and the number of anchors larger. Figure 16.4 presents an attitude opinionnaire that may be

---

Directions: Please place a check mark by the phrases below that match your opinion of the "Powers of Ten" unit. Write down any comments you have about any of the questions. Please be candid in your comments. Help me to get the "bugs" out of this lesson.

1. How difficult was this lesson?

     ____ Too easy   ____ About right   ____ Too difficult

     COMMENTS:

2. How was the vocabulary in the lesson?

     ____ Too easy   ____ About right   ____ Too difficult

     COMMENTS:

3. How was the length of the lesson?

     ____ Too long   ____ About right   ____ Too short

     COMMENTS:

4. How were the practice exercises?

     a.____ Too easy   ____ About right   ____ Too difficult

     b.____ Too few   ____ About right   ____ Too many

     COMMENTS:

5. How were the test questions?

     a.____ Too easy   ____ About right   ____ Too difficult

     b.____ Too few   ____ About right   ____ Too many

     COMMENTS:

Figure 16.4: Example Attitude Opinionnaire

6. Did the test questions match the things taught in the lesson?

    ____ No   ____ Some did, but some didn't   ____ Yes
    COMMENTS:

7. How were the directions on the practice items and tests?

    ____ Confusing   ____ O.K.   ____ Very clear
    COMMENT:

8. What did you think about the examples given?

    a. ____ Confusing   ____ O.K.   ____ Very clear
    b. ____ Too few   ____ About right   ____ Too many
    COMMENTS:

9. How did you like the pictures in the lesson?

    a. ____ Weren't needed   ____ O.K.   ____ Very helpful
    b. ____ Distracting   ____ O.K.   ____ Very important
    c. ____ Too silly   ____ O.K.   ____ Very humorous
    COMMENTS:

10. Would you like to receive instruction in this form again?

    ____ No   ____ Maybe   ____ Absolutely
    COMMENTS:

11. Would you recommend this instruction to a friend who wanted to learn about scientific notation?

    ____ No   ____ Maybe   ____ Absolutely
    COMMENTS:

12. How do you like math?

    ____ Hate it   ____ It's O.K.   ____ Love it
    COMMENTS:

13. Would you like to use scientific notation?

    ____ No   ____ Maybe   ____ Sure
    COMMENTS:

14. Do you think you could explain how to use scientific notation to a friend?

    ____ No   ____ Maybe   ____ Sure
    COMMENTS:

modified or used as is in many formative evaluation efforts. (Such a questionnaire should include plenty of room for comments.)

Questionnaire data may be tallied on a clean copy of the form or entered onto a computer-based copy of the form. Comments can be summarized and written in as well. Any related comments from the debriefing may be also added. (You might consider coding these debriefing comments in a separate font or color.)

Time Data. The time required to complete each of the tests and the actual instruction should be recorded as part of small group formative evaluation. If the instruction is individualized, then each individual's time must be recorded. It is often feasible for computer-assisted instruction modules to be programmed so that they gather time data as they are being used, making use of the clock that is built into most computers. If the instruction is group-paced then the total time for the lesson should be recorded, along with each individual's time for completing the tests. Time data may be indicated for each test, the instruction itself, and total learning time. Averages and ranges can be indicated. Figure 16.5 is an example of such a display.

Interpreting Small Group Data. Determining what revisions are needed based upon the data can occasionally be difficult. However, some general

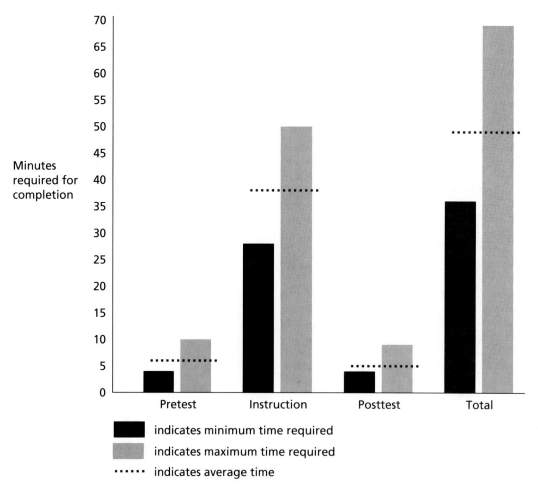

Figure 16.5: Range and Average of Completion Times for Instructional Components

principles that can guide your decisions are described in the following paragraphs.

If performance on practice and posttest for the same objectives are both low, then do the following:

1. First look at the directions and format of items for those objectives to ensure that the vocabulary and intent are clear to the learners. Refer back to any data from the one-to-one evaluations that might provide hints as to problems that exist in practice or tests.

2. If the test directions and item formats are clear, look at the task analysis to determine where the breakdown of skills occurred. Consider whether objectives are mis-sequenced or whether there is a missing prerequisite skill or knowledge. Refer back to one-to-one evaluations to determine any indications of sequence or prerequisite problems.

3. If the above two solutions do not solve the problem, examine the instruction itself. Look for incomplete or ambiguous explanations, examples, practice, or feedback. Consider alternate display modes such as illustrations or other graphics. Review other events of instruction related to deficient objectives. Refer back to one-to-one evaluations for any indications of need for alternate or more complete information.

4. If the previous steps provide no clear solution, refer to the attitude questionnaire data and to the debriefing information for any learners' insights or attitudes that might indicate problems with those particular objectives.

If practice performance is adequate, but posttest performance is low, then do the following:

1. Examine the items assessing deficient objectives on both practice and posttest to ensure that items for both tasks are of the same range of difficulty and level of applicability. Ensure the same weighting of items across these ranges as per the assessment item specifications. If such a problem exists, eliminate it by ensuring that each assessment follows the item specifications.

2. Consider any prompting that may be occurring during practice that is not being presented in the posttest. Either eliminate the prompts or provide some additional practice without the prompts.

3. Consider the feedback that accompanies practice. Determine whether feedback is prompting later responses or being previewed by learners prior to response in the practice. If so, consider adding some practice that does not include feedback. (We do not suggest eliminating feedback from all the items, as feedback is such an integral part of instruction.)

4. Consider adding additional items of practice in later practice sessions in the lesson to encourage retention and automaticity.

5. Consider whether fatigue might have influenced posttest performance. If such a possibility appears likely, consider breaking down the instruction into sections.

6. Consider adding motivational reinforcement comments during feedback.

If practice performance is low and posttest performance is adequate, then do the following:

1. Examine the items assessing deficient objectives on both practice and posttest to ensure that items for both tasks are of the same range of difficulty and level of applicability. Ensure the same weighting of items across these ranges as per the assessment item specifications. If such a problem exists, eliminate it by ensuring that each assessment item follows the item specifications.

2. Consider learners' opinionnaire data and nonverbal behaviors to ensure that any initial frustrations during practice did not produce predictable long-term negative attitudes toward the subject matter or the mode of instructional delivery.

If attitude data is low and posttest performance is adequate, then do the following:

1. Consider the implications for the long-term effects of negative attitudes. If these attitudinal concerns are not an important consideration of the institution or training organization, do nothing.

2. If long-term effects of negative attitudes are of concern, consider specific comments on opinionnaires and debriefing for suggestions for revisions. Only consider those revisions that do not have a negative impact on performance.

3. Consider adding additional motivating and interest-provoking devices, such as relevancy statements, curiosity-provoking scenarios, or relevant human interest stories. (See Chapter 12 for additional suggestions.)

4. If the problems are serious, consider alternate, "easier" media for some segment(s) of the instruction.

The output of the small group stage of evaluation is an instructional lesson that has been revised based upon time, performance, and attitude data from representative members of the target audience. If evaluation has revealed substantial problems, then the designer may choose to conduct another small group evaluation with the revised materials before proceeding on to the field trials.

Field Trials

The purpose of this stage of evaluation is to (1) determine the effectiveness of the revisions made during small group evaluation, (2) ascertain any problems that might arise in the administration of the materials in a real instructional environment, and (3) validate the instruction with a large enough sample of the target audience to make a confident prediction of its effectiveness. The revised instructional materials, including tests, should be used in this stage. Instructional materials should be in a more final form than they were during small group evaluations. While it is optimal to use the complete entry, pretest, and posttest assessment instruments (as well as a possible delayed posttest), the test instruments may have to be abbreviated to include only the major objectives of the instruction. Documentation that prepares the teacher/trainer to integrate the instruction provided in the materials with other instruction in the class (i.e., teacher/trainer guides) should also be included.

Field trials are intended to design revisions that answer questions such as the following:

- Can the instruction be implemented as it was designed?
- What types of administration problems are encountered?
- Does the teacher/trainer guide present the needed information in a form that can be easily used?
- Do the learners have the expected entry-level skills?
- Can the learners attain the objectives of the instruction?
- Are the time estimates for completion of the instruction accurate?
- How do the learners feel about the instruction?
- Are the revisions made as a result of small group evaluations effective?
- How do the teachers/trainers feel about the instruction?
- What changes or adaptations do teachers/trainers make in the instruction?

Learners' and Teachers'/Trainers' Roles. The instructional materials should be tried out with at least 30 students during this stage. In order to obtain information regarding administration problems, which may vary from instructional environment to instructional environment, it is a good idea to conduct field trials in several different instructional sites, such as rural and urban, high and low socioeconomic status, well-funded sites and poorly funded sites, and multiple regions of the country, with approximately 30 learners at each site. Of course, the number and range of sites for field trials depends upon the target audience. If the target audience is local, then the field trial sites should be local. The learners should respond to tests, instruction, and questionnaires.

Teachers and trainers should be involved in the instruction as their role is planned for the actual implementation, whether that role is delivering lectures, managing individualized instruction, or facilitating group activities. Training should be provided to the field trial teachers and trainers. This may include group training sessions, individual consultation, and teacher/trainer manuals. Teachers/trainers will be asked to respond to extensive questionnaires on the actual use of the instruction and any administrative problems associated with the trial of the instruction.

Designer's Role. Quite often the designer is not even present during the field trial stage of formative evaluation, especially if the length of instruction is considerable and there are many field trial sites. It is helpful if the designer can actually observe the trials because it is useful to gather information on whether the instruction has been implemented the way it was designed to be implemented. Such information is especially useful in instruction that has a component of lecture or other group-based activity. If instruction has been changed from its original design, it may affect posttest performance. Sometimes this effect is positive and should be incorporated into the final instruction. Sometimes this effect is deleterious, and it is helpful to know that this effect was not a result of the instruction's design. Fidelity of implementation, or degree of implementation, is also a critical question in summative evaluation, which we will discuss later. If the designer is not present for the actual pilot delivery of instruction, the teacher/trainer questionnaires should try to acquire some information on any changes in the delivery of the instruction.

The designer should coordinate the collection of the data, making the administration of tests and instruction as easy as possible. In addition, the designer analyzes and interprets the data from the field trials and conducts any follow-up data collection, such as interviews that may be needed. The designer may also conduct teacher/trainer training and will create the teacher/trainer manuals.

Data Collection, Display, and Interpretation.
Learners' performance, attitude, and time data may be collected and displayed in the same form that small group data is collected and presented. In addition, information should be gathered from the teacher/trainer regarding the administration of the instruction. Figure 16.6 is an example of a teacher/trainer questionnaire appropriate for field trial data gathering. (Such a questionnaire should include plenty of room for comments.)

We also suggest that within field trials the designer collect data on the degree of implementation of the designed program. In the previous sections we have discussed ways to assess the effects of the instructional program that is being evaluated. Too often designers assume that these effects are the product of the program as defined by the materials

and the teacher/trainer guide rather than the program as implemented. In other words, designers frequently assume that the program is implemented as it was designed to be implemented. This may be a faulty and dangerous assumption. Instead of assuming that the program is being implemented as described, the designer/evaluator should assess the actual level of implementation of the instructional program. This form of evaluation is sometimes called *process evaluation* or evaluation of the *fidelity of implementation*. If an evaluator has a measure of the degree to which the instructional program has been implemented as intended—a description of the program as it actually occurred—then he can be much clearer in determining what revisions in the materials should be made. For example, if one field trial site's data shows an unexpectedly low percentage of learners acquiring the terminal objective of a lesson, it would be very helpful to have information as to whether the lessons were implemented as they were designed. Although we mention this type of data here in the section on field trials, degree of implementation information might also be useful during small group evaluations, and it is certainly necessary for summative evaluations.

To develop an instrument to measure the level of implementation of the instructional program, a clear description of the distinctive features of the program must be developed. In order to assess these features, they must be described in terms of observable features. Instructional designers are often the best people to develop this description because they have developed the program based upon some key principles or theory that they predict will positively affect learning. Fitz-Gibbon and Morris (1975) suggest that the evaluator (designer) develop this list by asking herself, "If a stranger viewed the instructional program in operation, what distinctive features would be seen?" The evaluator must answer the following questions: What specifically would students be doing? How would teachers be acting? What would parents and administrators do? When identifying the key features to be sought, the evaluator will wish to pick out observable manifestations of the instructionally robust features that were built into the instruction. For example, a reading program designer might identify such features as a specific technique for

Directions: Please indicate with a check mark the degree to which you agree with the following statements regarding the administration of the unit "Powers of Ten." Any additional comments you provide will be very helpful in interpreting the results of this questionnaire. Your responses will enable us to improve the quality of this instruction as well as subsequent units. Please be as candid as possible.

Strongly Agree	Agree	Disagree	Strongly Disagree

1. The teacher/trainer guide and the accompanying materials provided all the information that I needed in order to teach the unit.

_____   _____   _____   _____

Comments:

_____

_____

2. All of the materials and equipment that I needed to teach the unit were available to me.

_____   _____   _____   _____

3. The personnel support that I needed to teach the unit was available to me.

_____   _____   _____   _____

4. The facilities that I needed to teach the unit were available to me.

_____   _____   _____   _____

5. The intention and perspective of the instruction was clear to me.

_____   _____   _____   _____

6. The intention and perspective of the instruction was clear to the learners.

_____   _____   _____   _____

7. The time estimates provided in the teacher/trainer guide were accurate for my class(es).

_____   _____   _____   _____

8. My class(es) is very similar to the target audience for the instruction that is described in the teacher/trainer guide.

_____   _____   _____   _____

Figure 16.6: Teacher/Trainer Questionnaire for Field Trials

9. The instruction required adaptation in order to fit my class(es) and this context.

_____   _____   _____   _____

10. The instructional materials were used as described in the teacher/trainer manual.

_____   _____   _____   _____

11. All instructional materials were completed by learners who were present on the days of the instruction.

_____   _____   _____   _____

12. The information that I needed to know was easy to find in the teacher/trainer guide.

_____   _____   _____   _____

13. I found the unit easy to teach.

_____   _____   _____   _____

14. I found the unit interesting to teach.

_____   _____   _____   _____

15. I feel that the students learned from the unit.

_____   _____   _____   _____

16. I would like to teach other units that are designed similarly to this one.

_____   _____   _____   _____

17. I would recommend this unit of instruction to other teachers/trainers.

_____   _____   _____   _____

18. The teacher in-service training prepared me well to teach this unit of instruction.

_____   _____   _____   _____

19. Additional suggestions for improvement of the instruction that are not contained in my previous comments follow:

_____

_____

teaching the blending of sounds when decoding words; this should be manifested by the teacher when teaching and the learners when attempting to decode a word orally. The program might also include a required 1/2 hour of silent reading each day. Another critical feature might be that the learners take a book home each evening and read a minimum of 20 minutes with an adult. The distinctive features may be something that should be *left out* of program as well as features that should be present. For example, a reading program might emphasize the absence of phonics instruction. Since use of phonics is something that is fairly fundamental to many teachers, the assessment of implementation should report the degree to which this prohibition is observed.

A measurement of the degree to which these features are being implemented may be gathered in several ways. It is usually helpful if several measures are used. Extant data, such as teachers' lesson plans, students' papers, notes to and from parents, and administrators' records, may provide evidence of the program's implementation. These data may be examined by an evaluator using a carefully devised checklist that allows the evaluator to note the degree to which the distinctive features of the program are being implemented. One obvious but extremely useful way to measure implementation is through observation of instruction actually occurring. Evaluators may periodically observe classrooms using the instructional program and record observations of the implementation of distinctive program features. Interviews or surveys of students, teachers, parents, and administrators may also yield key information about the implementation of the program. However, this information is subject to the limitations of ''self-report'' data. (People have a tendency to report what they think others wish them to say.)

Analysis and Interpretation of Field Trial Data. Learners' performance, attitude, and time data from field trials can be analyzed and interpreted in a manner very similar to data from small group evaluations. We suggest that the data from each individual class be reviewed, analyzed, and interpreted separately before information is collapsed across separate classes or sites. This will enable the designer to be sensitive to any aberrant groups or patterns that occur with learners from particular regions or backgrounds. Problems that occur

across all sites should be interpreted and revisions should be designed using the principles we suggested in our discussion of small group evaluation. Administrative problems that consistently occur, such as lack of specific equipment or materials, may require revision in the instructional materials, development of alternate mediation, or provision of suggestions for adaptations.

Problems that were idiosyncratic to particular sites should be interpreted in conjunction with the teacher/trainer questionnaire. In addition, such sites may require visits or interviews in order to establish whether the following is true: (1) the learner population actually matched the target description, (2) the instruction was implemented as designed, and (3) additional special problems existed that affected the effectiveness of the instruction. Once this information has been obtained, the designer (in conjunction with the original client or client agency) must determine how representative the aberrant sites are of the actual target audience. This decision will determine whether alternative materials should be constructed to deal with the problems that the learners and/or their teacher/trainers encountered.

Teacher/trainer information should be tallied on a clean copy of the questionnaire. Comments should be summarized on this same form. We suggest that this summarization be done first for individual sites if there are several teachers/trainers in one site. Finally, summarization could be organized by groupings that appear to have similarities in patterns related to the characteristics of the sites. Then, summarization can occur across all sites. Problems that seem to be common across all sites should be addressed. Problems that result from incomplete or inaccurate information in the teacher/trainer guides can be revised. Problems in the instruction itself that seem to have confirmation in learners' attitudes or performance should be addressed in a revision of the instruction. However, these changes should be considered cautiously; the designer must ensure that they are consistent with the strategy designed into the materials and that they specifically address performance or attitude problems. Questions or suggestions that occurred consistently across trial sites but that are deemed inappropriate should be addressed and their inappropriateness diplomatically explained in the teacher/trainer guide or during teacher in-service training or ''train the trainer'' sessions. Implementation data should be carefully examined for consistent nonimplementation of specific features. This nonimplementation should be investigated to determine (1) whether the feature is necessary, (2) why the feature was not implemented, and (3) what instruction was used in place of the missing features.

As with the learners' data, if there are radical differences in responses related to certain types of sites, the designer must consult with the client regarding the centrality of these sites to the target audience.

Ongoing Evaluation

Collection of data for the purpose of revision of that instruction (formative evaluation) should not cease even when the instruction has been implemented in the target systems. Teacher/trainer guides and training on the use of the instruction should include encouragement to take a data-based perspective toward improving the quality of the instruction. To ensure that the revisions teachers make are consistent with the design strategies originally incorporated in the instruction, we suggest that some of the teacher/trainer training time be allocated to pointing out the critical features of the instructional strategies and explaining their importance in the learning process.

Instruction that is mediated in forms other than teachers may be more difficult to revise once the instruction has been implemented due to the expense involved. However, materials that are anticipated to have an extended period of implementation may be revised several times over that period. In some cases these revisions may not be incorporated in the more expensive media, such as an interactive video lesson; however, they will be incorporated in some accompanying media that are less expensive, such as print-based material. On other occasions, the expensive medium itself may be revised in an inexpensive way—such as revising the computer software (rather than the video materials) in an interactive video lesson or changing and re-dubbing the audio track on a video presentation.

Long-term implementation projects should develop methods for gathering effectiveness information into their evaluation plans. Subsequent revisions of the instruction may be dictated by many factors, some of which are changes in the entry-level skills of the targeted learners, changes in the content, and changes in the facilities, equipment, or social mores of the learning context. Some of this data gathering may dovetail with information gathering for summative evaluation, which we will discuss in the next section.

Ongoing evaluation attempts to answer questions similar to the questions addressed in field trials and additional questions that can lead to revisions in the instruction such as the following: Are the revisions made as a result of field trials effective? Do learners' characteristics change over time?

*E*xercises

1. Which stage of the formative evaluation procedure does each of the following statements describe?
   a. Teachers/trainers report on the appropriateness of the documentation that accompanies a package of computer-based instructional software.
   b. Experts in the content area for which a slide-tape set was developed review the materials for accuracy and to ensure that they are up-to-date.
   c. Individual students review the storyboards of an instructional videotape with the designer.
   d. At least 30 students go through the instruction.
   e. The designer only assists students when they encounter severe difficulties.
   f. Students read and think aloud as they interact with written instructional materials.
   g. Test materials are tried out with groups of individuals—some of whom are ''masters'' of the content, and some of whom are not.
   h. Data are collected regarding problems with the instruction after the instruction is implemented in the target contexts.
2. Figure 16.7 shows the data that resulted from a small group evaluation of an instructional package on learning to use Logo, a graphic-based programming language (Cennamo, 1986). Analyze the findings and plan a sequence of actions to plan revisions.
3. Develop a chart that describes the following for each of the six stages of formative evaluation: purpose, stage of development of instruction, role and characteristics of learners, role of designer, and procedures.

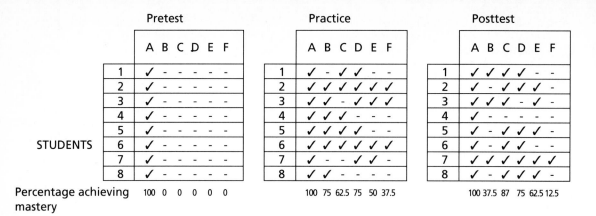

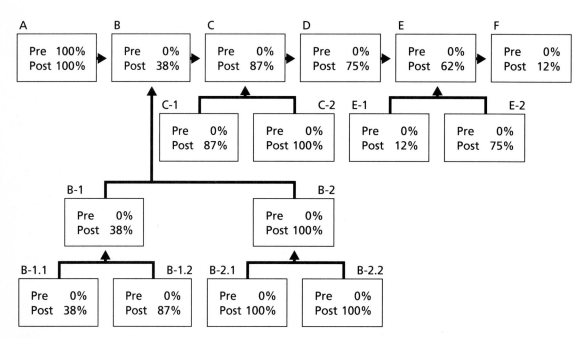

Figure 16.7: Data from Small Group Evaluation

*O*verview of Summative Evaluation

Within the context of instructional design, the purpose of summative evaluation is to collect, analyze, and summarize data to present to decision makers in the client organization so that they can make a judgement regarding the effectiveness, and perhaps appeal and efficiency, of the instruction. This judgement usually leads to decisions regarding continued use of the instruction. There are occasions when the evaluators are also the clients and even the deliverers of the instruction. An example would be a teacher who had developed instruction and after a time collected data in order to decide whether to continue using this instruction. Summative evaluation occurs after the instruction has been implemented into the target contexts.

For systematically designed instruction, often the judgement of effectiveness is criterion referenced and attempts to answer this question: Does the instruction adequately solve the "problem" that was identified in the needs assessment and that resulted in the development of the instructional materials? In such a criterion-referenced evaluation, the criterion of how well the problem must be solved for the instruction to be deemed successful should be established prior to the beginning of the evaluation. Indeed, this criterion should be established in conjunction with the needs assessment, in which the "ideal" attainment is established. These criteria may be stated in terms of payoff from the desired performance of the system, such as "reduction of error rates from 21 percent (in needs assessment terms 'what is' prior to the initiation of the newly designed instruction) to 10 percent or less ('what should be' after the full implementation of the instruction)." Another example would be "reduction in the number of high school dropouts from 42 percent to 20 percent or less."

Sometimes the question is comparative: Which of several programs of instruction best addresses the problem that was identified in the needs assessment? This comparative question may involve comparing the effects of an existing instructional program to those of a newly designed program(s). Even with a comparison of several programs, a summative evaluation following systematic design should refer back to the original needs assessment and identify which of the alternative programs best solves the problem identified in the needs assessment.

More specific questions that may be asked in order to provide grounds for answering whether the problem identified in the needs assessment has been solved include the following:

- Do the learners achieve the objectives of the instruction?
- How do the learners feel about the instruction?
- What are the costs of the instruction?
- How much time does it take for learners to complete the instruction?
- Is the instruction implemented as it was designed?
- What unexpected outcomes result from the instruction?

Alternative Approaches to Summative Evaluation

Currently two approaches to summative evaluation are used in the fields of education and training: objectivism and subjectivism. These two approaches mirror the alternative modes of inquiry that are popular in educational research as well as evaluation. We will briefly discuss these, but we suggest that you read Worthen and Sanders (1987) for a more comprehensive description.

Objectivism relies upon empiricism, answering questions based upon observation and data. The major advantage of an objective evaluation is that the results are replicable, so that trained individuals given the same questions and a similar methodology would gather similar data and draw similar conclusions. An objective evaluation usually employs the scientific method: setting hypotheses, designing an experiment to control extraneous variables, collecting data, and drawing conclusions. In general, such evaluations tend to depend upon the collection of quantitative data. Objective evaluations are often goal-based, focused on determining the degree to which the goals of the instructional program have been obtained. Traditionally, the majority of educational evaluations and evaluation texts have employed an objective basis for evaluation. The major limitation of objective evaluations is that because they are focused upon the goals of the program, they use designs to control extraneous variables, and they examine only a limited number of factors. Therefore, the evaluation may not examine some of the most critical effects of the instructional program, particularly if those effects are from unanticipated sources.

Subjectivism employs expert judgement as the criterion of evaluation. The accuracy of a subjective evaluation depends upon the experience and knowledge of the evaluator(s). Subjective evaluations often employ qualitative methods such as observation and interviews to examine the instructional context. In addition, subjective evaluations are often "goal-free." Goal-free evaluations, as suggested by Scriven (1972), do not start from the goals of the program. Indeed, evaluators employing a goal-free evaluation do not wish to be biased by being informed of the goals of the program. They wish to describe the program and its effects as they perceive it, not as they have been predisposed to perceive it. The advantage of subjective evaluations is that they are more likely than objective evaluations to notice unexpected results of an instructional program. The limitation of a subjective evaluation is that it may not be replicable. The results of the evaluation may be more biased by the idiosyncratic experiences, perspectives, and biases of the individual who conducts the evaluation. An example of a subjective evaluation is Eisner's (1979) educational connoisseurship model. This model employs the tactics of art criticism and literary criticism for evaluating instructional programs.

No evaluation is totally objective or totally subjective; all evaluations fall somewhere on a continuum between the two. Posavac and Carey (1989) suggest that an evaluation may tend toward the subjective end of the continuum if the following factors exist: unclear or complex program goals, disagreement regarding goals and processes of the program, a complex instructional context, or disagreement in perspectives or philosophies among those in or influenced by the instructional context.

As you might expect, summative evaluations of systematically designed instruction tend toward the objective end of the evaluation continuum. Systematic design is consistently based upon the goals of the instructional program. It also depends upon collecting quantifiable data to make decisions, such as revisions as a result of formative evaluation. Therefore, a summative evaluation for a systematically designed program will take a more quantitative, goal-based approach. However, it is often appropriate and desirable to add goal-free and more qualitative aspects to the evaluation in order to examine unexpected outcomes of a program. These unexpected outcomes may be positive, or they may be negative. In any event, findings of subjective evaluation may be of utility in estimating the merit of an instructional program or system from a standpoint somewhat outside the instruction's goals.

Designer's Role in Summative Evaluation. The role of an instructional designer in summative evaluation has been a somewhat controversial issue. Many educators believe that the instructional designer has a strong investment and consequent

bias to find the instruction effective. Therefore, the designer is too biased to give a fair evaluation of the instruction. Others feel that no one knows the instructional program and its potential strengths and weaknesses better than the designer and, therefore, the designer is in the best position to most efficiently design an evaluation that probes deeply into the ultimate effectiveness of the program in its target context.

We feel that it is probably ultimately less problematic to hire an external evaluator to conduct a summative evaluation of an instructional program. However, we do not believe that it is impossible for the designer to obtain an objective evaluation of a program, especially if the evaluation tends toward the objective end of the evaluation continuum. Often an organization is not in a position to hire an external evaluator; therefore, an internal evaluator, even the designer of the program itself, must be used. In such a case, we would strongly recommend a careful and complete documentation of the evaluation procedure so that the measures and procedures employed are known and any biases that may be involved in these procedures and their implementation are open to scrutiny. However, the goal-free part of the evaluation must be conducted by an external evaluator. It is probably beyond the means of any instructional designer to ignore the goals of an instructional program that he designed and conduct an adequate goal-free evaluation.

If designers do not actually direct the summative evaluation, they will be active in providing information to the evaluator. Most of the documentation from context analysis (including needs assessment procedures and conclusions) through learner and task analysis, statement of objectives, assessment item specifications, assessment instruments, and strategy plans should be made available to the evaluator.

Timing of Summative Evaluation. One common error in conducting summative evaluations that causes them to yield fallacious data is conducting the evaluation too early in the implementation of the instructional program. If at all possible, the summative evaluation of a program should not occur in the first implementation of the instructional program. This means that if an instructional program is a year's curriculum, then the program should not be evaluated in its first year. If the program is a six-week training program, then it should not be evaluated in the first six weeks' offering. We suggest this principle because rarely are programs delivered in the first implementation as they were designed to be delivered. Often the teacher/trainer is learning how to deliver the instruction during the first administration.

Procedures for Summative Evaluation

In the following sections we will summarize the steps in completing a goal-based summative evaluation. These steps are similar to procedures recommended by Morris (1978), Popham (1988), and several authors within Borich's (1974) text. We strongly recommend these references (particularly the Morris text) as more complete sources for designers who must design a summative evaluation.

Determine Goals of Evaluation

The foremost activity in this stage of evaluation is to identify the questions that should be answered as a result of the evaluation. These questions will direct all the subsequent procedures. These questions should be identified by the client organization and often may be defined by the requirements of funding agencies or interests of other stakeholders. Here is the list of questions we suggested earlier in the chapter:

- Does implementation of the instruction solve the problem identified in the needs assessment?
- Do the learners achieve the objectives of the instruction?
- How do the learners feel about the instruction?
- What are the costs of the instruction?
- How much time does it take for learners to complete the instruction?
- Is the instruction implemented as it was designed?
- What unexpected outcomes result from the instruction?

Often, more questions are identified than can be economically and efficiently answered. In this case, the evaluators can select the questions to be answered via the evaluation by considering the following issues, which have been adapted from lists by Flagg (1990) and Worthen and Sanders (1987):

- What decisions must be made as a result of the evaluation? Which questions will provide the best information to answer these questions?
- How practical is it to gather the information to answer this question?
- Who wants the answer to this question? Are these individuals key to the future success of the program?
- How critical is the information gained from this question to the continued use of the program?
- How much uncertainty is associated with the answer to this question?

The evaluator and the client organization should agree on the exact nature of the questions prior to advancing to the next steps in the evaluation procedure. This is not to say that as the planning advances additional questions may not be added, priorities changed, or questions clarified. However, in a goal-based evaluation such a clear direction for evaluation is possible.

Select Orientation of Evaluation

As the questions are identified, the evaluator and clients will agree upon the orientation that is most appropriate in answering the evaluation questions. The decisions on orientation will address issues such as the following:

- Will the approach be more goal-based or goal-free?
- If one perspective predominates, will there be aspects of the other orientation?
- Is quantitative or qualitative data appropriate as evidence to answer the questions?
- Will a more experimental or naturalistic approach be used?

Select Design of Evaluation

Evaluation designs describe what data will be collected, when the data should be collected, and under what conditions data should be collected in order to answer the evaluation questions. The evaluation design must be developed in order to allow the client(s) to draw the necessary conclusions and make the necessary decisions. Three issues must be considered in determining what design an evaluation should utilize:

- How much confidence must we have that the instructional program actually caused any effects found in learners' performance or attitudes?
- How important is it that we can generalize the conclusions of the evaluation to learners or contexts not involved in the evaluation?
- How much control can we have over the instructional situation?

The issue of causation is generally termed *internal validity*. There are many things that can cause changes (both positive and negative) in learners' performance and attitude that may have nothing to do with the new instructional program. For example, learners grow older, and this can change their behavior. They may realize that they are part of a study, and this awareness alone can change their effort and performance. Students can be influenced by learning as a result of something that occurs outside the instructional context. If these rival sources of causation are likely, there are ways to organize an evaluation so that these possible effects can be eliminated from consideration. Actually there are many possible rival sources of causation. Most evaluation texts or research design texts will discuss these factors. Or, you might wish to read one of the primary sources on internal validity, Campbell and Stanley (1963).

The issue of generalizability is generally termed *external validity*. Although Campbell and Stanley mention a number of factors that can threaten external validity, there are three threats that are often of particular consideration for systematically designed instructional programs. The first is the effect of pretesting. That is, the pretesting involved in the evaluation context may alert or sensitize the learners in some way that will make the instruction more effective with a pretested group than with students who did not have a pretest. Usually this is not a problem if the instructional program itself is designed to include a similar pretest (as is often the case with systematically designed instruction). The second threat to gener-

alizability is that the learners involved in the evaluation may not be representative of the learners who will use the instruction in the future. In such a situation the learners might perform better, worse, or differently than the students in the evaluation group. The third rival causative factor is that students in the evaluation group may respond differently than students in future implementations because they realize they are in an "experiment." Of these threats, the possible non-representativeness of the learners involved in the evaluation is probably the greatest problem. If in the context of the evaluation this threat is perceived as being a great problem, it can be dealt with in the design of the instruction: The solution is to design instruction so that it is suitable for a wider target audience than originally anticipated.

The issue of control allows the evaluation designer to determine the limits of what can be done with internal and external validity. The two basic ways that the evaluation design can deal with the threats to internal and external validity are comparison groups and randomization. Comparison groups allow us to exclude a number of rival sources of causation because they allow us to compare the performance and attitudes of learners who have experienced the instructional program to the performance and attitudes of learners who have had the same basic experiences with the exception of the instructional program. This is very similar to research studies that employ a research group and a control group.

Randomization allows the evaluator to eliminate threats that may be due to a situation in which the learners who were evaluated were "special" in some way and were—if a control group was employed—"better" (or "worse") than the students in the control group or "better" (or "worse") than students in subsequent "real" implementations of the instructional program. There are two types of randomization. First, students may be randomly *selected* to participate in an evaluation study. Secondly, students may be randomly assigned to receive alternate instructional materials in an evaluation. In some evaluation studies, both forms of randomization may be employed.

Dealing with the three issues of causation, generalizability, and control is a balancing act because there are always trade-offs involved when designing an evaluation that accounts for each issue. Many times in evaluation studies, it is not possible to eliminate all the factors that might threaten internal and external validity. In these cases, the evaluation designer must carefully consider whether the threats are real or only possible. When there are threats that cannot be controlled in the evaluation, they must be acknowledged in a discussion of the limitations of the evaluation in the evaluation report.

In order to systematically employ control groups and randomization, a number of alternative designs have traditionally been employed. We will present only those that have been most commonly employed in evaluations of systematically designed instruction. They vary in terms of whether randomization and control groups are used. In addition, they may vary as to whether a pretest is employed.

Alternative Designs

Instruction ———> Posttest

1. This design is sometimes called the *case study* design. With this design a single group is presented with the instruction, followed by a posttest. This design is limited in that it does not control for threats to conclusions of causality and threats to the ability to generalize. For example, suppose that the performance of the learners is very high. An individual examining such evaluation data might ask, "How do you know that they didn't already know how to perform the tasks on the posttest?" Or, "How do you know that you didn't just have a bright set of learners?" Or, "How do you know that it wasn't the series on television this semester that led to the learning shown on the posttest?" There is no information provided by this design to counter these suspicions. Although this is a weak design, there may be occasions when you have reasons to believe that there are no reasonable threats to drawing conclusions of causality and to generalizing the conclusions to similar groups. In such a case you might use a case study design.

Pretest ———> Instruction ———> Posttest

2. This design is termed the *one-group pretest-posttest* design. You will recognize it as the de-sign that we suggested you use in formative evaluation. In contrast to the case study design, this design can establish that there is an improvement in performance over time. Unfortunately, it cannot establish that the improvement is due to the instruction. It cannot refute the allegation that the learners involved in this study were unusually bright or motivated. In order to counter such rival sources, a control group design must be employed.

G1   Pretest ———> Instruction ———> Posttest
G2   Pretest ————————————————> Posttest
                        or
G1   Pretest ———> Instruction X ———> Posttest
G2   Pretest ———> Instruction Y ———> Posttest

3. This design is termed the *nonequivalent control group* design. The control groups are considered nonequivalent because the study does not employ random assignment of learners to groups. Of the control group designs, this is the one most commonly used because it is quite common to be unable to randomly assign learners to a class for an evaluation study. In this design one group receives the newly designed instruction, and the other group (the control group) receives no related instruction at all. The two groups are pretested. This pretest serves two purposes. First, it allows you to discard the argument that the instructed group performed better because it was somehow sensitized by the pretest. It also allows you to establish some degree of equivalence, even without randomization. If the two groups perform similarly on the pretest, you can at least say that the groups were similar in specific prior knowledge. You cannot conclude that they were similar in other factors that might also impinge on learning and attitudes. The second design (Instruction X and Y) is the design that is often employed when you have a second instructional program that you are comparing in terms of effectiveness. It uses a "comparison" group rather than a "control" group.

G1   Random Assignment ———>
Pretest ———> Instruction ———> Posttest
G2   Random Assignment ———>
Pretest ————————————————> Posttest
                        or

G1   Random Assignment ———>
Pretest ———> Instruction X ———> Posttest
G2   Random Assignment ———>
Pretest ———> Instruction Y ———> Posttest
                    or
G1   Random Assignment ———>
         Instruction ———>   Posttest
G2   Random Assignment ———> Posttest

4. Just as with the nonequivalent groups design, the *pretest-posttest control group* may use a control group or an alternate instruction comparison group. Because it randomly assigns learners to groups, using it is a good argument against the charge that the effectiveness of the newly designed instruction is due to some important differences in the groups whose posttest scores are compared. An alternate form is the *posttest-only control group* design, useful when it is not advisable to use pretests. Perhaps the most powerful as a research design, the posttest-only design has limited usefulness in evaluation of instruction, in which pretests are a regular part of the instructional system.

Pretest —> Pretest —> Pretest —> Instruction —> Posttest —> Posttest —> Posttest

5. The *interrupted time-series* design is often used with a single group when one wants to examine trends prior to and after instruction. Such a design might be extremely useful when examining the ''payoff'' criteria after all learners have received the instruction. For example, you might examine the error rates in a particular job task prior to and following instruction. This design can also be used with a comparison or control group when there are possible rival sources of causation.

Within a single evaluation study more than one design may be employed. Designs may vary for different measurement instruments. For example, a nonequivalent pretest-posttest control group design could be used for learning and attitude outcome measures, and an interrupted time-series design might be used for examining payoff criteria. Of course, the various designs must be compatible with each other. It would not make much sense, for example, to use both a nonequivalent and an equivalent control group design. If you can obtain an equivalent control group, it should be used since it is a more desirable design for supporting conclusions involving causation and generalization.

Design or Select Evaluation Measures

In this section we will describe the particular considerations involved in designing measures of payoff outcomes, learning outcomes, attitude outcomes, level of implementation, and cost effectiveness in evaluation studies. In most evaluation studies the evaluator will plan to have multiple measures of the effectiveness of the instructional program in each of the following categories: payoff, learning, attitude, implementation, and cost. In addition, it is common to also utilize multiple measures within any one category. There are occasions in which an existing standardized test may meet the assessment needs of the evaluation. Often, new measurement instruments must be developed using the principles suggested in Chapter 5.

Payoff Outcomes.   One of the most critical measurements that should occur in evaluation is a measure that allows the evaluator and the client to determine if the problem identified in the needs assessment— the problem that led to the development of the instruction—has been solved. This measure is a measurement of the *payoff* outcomes. Payoff outcomes may be measured in any number of ways, depending upon the problem to be solved. Some examples include the number of errors identified by quality assurance in a manufacturing division, number of dropouts from a high school, number of customer complaints from a service agency, number of National Merit Scholars from a school system, and so forth. Kearsly (1986) lists several factors that may be considered by training agencies as payoff criteria: (1) costs avoided as a result of problems such as overruns, overtime, or employee turnover; (2) increased output in sales/orders, production rate, or number of transactions processed; (3) improved quality, evidenced in customer satisfaction, better safety records, higher success/lower failure rate; and (4) improved efficiency in such things as reduced equipment repair time, faster delivery service, or more customers handled. In many instances, payoff data may be routinely collected and made available as extant data. The task of the evaluator may be to simply identify these data as relevant and obtain access to them. In some cases the evaluator may have to arrange to have the data collected more systematically and more frequently than might be normally the routine.

Learning Outcomes. Principles to consider in developing measures of learning outcomes were discussed thoroughly in Chapter 5. These principles should, of course, be followed when designing assessment instruments for evaluations. In addition, it is critical to have a logical relationship among the payoff outcomes, the goals of the instructional program, and the learning outcomes measured. For example, if through needs assessment and analysis it was established that students' dropping out of a school was related to their inability to read and a reading comprehension program was consequently developed, then the learning outcome that should be measured is reading comprehension ability.

Of course learning outcome measures can take any of the forms suggested in Chapter 5. The instruments developed through the procedures described in that chapter should be used in the development of evaluation instruments for summative evaluation of the instructional program. And the instruments should meet all the criteria of good assessment instruments: reliability, validity, and practicality. The exams used as a part of the actual instruction can be used as data sources in summative evaluation. Two situations might preclude such use. The assessment should reflect the effects of the entire program. Many units and exams of even larger scope assess prerequisite skills in order to provide information for remediation. This thoroughness may limit the adequate (reliable) measurement of the end goal of the program. A special exam may be required to reliably evaluate learners' performance on the terminal objective of the program. A second reason that a special exam may be required would be a situation in which two or more programs with similar but not identical learning goals are being compared for the evaluation. In this case, the assessment instruments for neither of the two (or more) versions may be a fair evaluation of the other program. A separate instrument that reflects the performance reflected in the needs assessment but is not biased toward the particular focus of any of the alternate programs should be developed for the summative evaluation.

Attitudes. Rarely are attitude objectives the primary payoff goals for instructional programs. However, it is not uncommon for attitude outcomes to be clearly related to the payoff criterion. Our previous example of the reading program for school dropouts absolutely must include assessment of attitudes in the evaluation of the program. Even for programs in which attitudes are not so clearly related to goals of the program or to the problem identified in the needs assessment, it is usually critical to evaluate students' attitudes toward the program. In evaluating attitudes toward the program the evaluator may formulate questions that ask about learners' attitudes toward (1) learning, (2) the instructional materials themselves, or (3) the subject matter. When comparing two or more programs in an evaluation, learners' attitudes to the programs may differ significantly enough to influence decisions about the materials. When evaluating a single program, information on the appeal of the instruction should be factored into the decision as to whether the instruction solves the problem identified in the needs assessment. The evaluator should be cautious in planning an evaluation that makes a comparison of pretest and posttest attitudes. Attitudes are slow to change. If the instruction is not lengthy, it is unlikely that a comparison of pre to post attitudes will yield significant and important differences.

Flagg (1990) suggests several indices of appeal that might be considered for assessment in an evaluation: attention, likableness, interest, relevance, familiarity, credibility, acceptability, and excitement (arousal). Although a single evaluation might not examine all of the indices, it is quite possible that the evaluator might plan to examine several of them. These factors might be assessed through self-report interviews, questionnaires, or observation.

Level of Implementation. As suggested in our discussion of field trials, it is extremely useful in both formative and summative evaluation to obtain a measure of the degree to which the instructional program has been implemented as designed. You can see from the careful discussion of evaluation designs that it is important in evaluation to ascribe the effects of an instructional program to the program itself, rather than to some additional source (such as superior students in the sample of students receiving the instructional program). In addition, in drawing the line of causation from the instruction to the results, it is critical to be able to identify the degree to which the description of the program represents what actually occurred during instruction with the new program.

If the instructional program to be evaluated has been systematically designed according to some clearly espoused principles, then the identification of the distinctive features should be fairly easy. Then the evaluator can design the observation, interview, and materials review forms to use when assessing the level of implementation of the program. If two or more programs are being compared in the evaluation, then the features to be evaluated should be those features that are distinctively and critically different in the different programs.

Costs. When evaluators estimate costs during summative evaluation, they usually consider the costs to implement and continue the program. These costs include personnel, facilities, equipment, materials, any other inputs, as well as any inputs required of the students (e.g., calculators, books, lab equipment). For in-service training (training of individuals already on the job) costs also include production time lost from the employees who must be off the job during training. Regardless of whether the materials were developed "in house" (a case in which the costs of design, development, and production must be accounted for) or whether the instruction is purchased, the costs for the instructional program itself are usually considered under the "materials" category.

Most techniques for analyzing costs in relation to effectiveness are devised on a comparative basis. One approach is the "benefits forsaken" comparison (Popham, 1988), in which an evaluator compares the benefits for the cost of a particular program to the hypothesized benefits of other ways in which the money could be spent. Another approach is to compare the relative costs and benefits of two programs. When evaluating systematically designed instruction, comparison programs are sometimes used. The instruction may be compared to a traditional way of presenting the same content or even a new alternative program. However, many times there is no comparison program. The question in such a case is "Will the ultimate outcome of this program be worth the cost?" We will review three types of cost studies recommended by Popham (1988): cost-feasibility, cost-effectiveness, and cost-benefit.

Cost-feasibility is usually stated in terms of the cost for the instructional program per student (or per student hour). Feasibility indices do not consider effectiveness but rather report the cost (or relative costs if two or more programs are being evaluated).

Cost-effectiveness information is usually reported in a ratio of cost for the program divided by some measure of the effectiveness of the program (e.g., per 10 points gain on a standardized exam). Two programs may be compared using a cost-effectiveness ratio if the programs have similar goals and can, therefore, be legitimately measured using the same measure.

The third index for evaluating costs is cost-benefit, which is usually measured in terms of program costs divided by some monetary estimate of the benefits of the program. (Examples would be estimated monetary value in production rate, estimated value of customer satisfaction, or savings because of better safety records due to the new instruction.) The factor evaluated in terms of monetary benefit should be related to the problem identified in the needs assessment (e.g., slow service, employee turnover, or error rate). In public school environments, it is difficult to assess a monetary value to some learning effects, but for certain programs (e.g., programs to reduce dropouts or to reduce drug use) dollar estimates of the benefits of the program might be appropriate.

Collect Data. Once the evaluator has selected the outcomes and other characteristics of the program that should be measured and has selected or developed appropriate measurement instruments, then a plan for the collection of data should be devised. Included in this plan should be appropriate scheduling of data collection periods, which are partially dictated by the evaluation design and partially dictated by the types of payoff and implementation measures desired. Of course, the evaluator must ensure that all policies regarding the collection of information from individuals within the organization are scrupulously followed.

Analyze Data. Data should be analyzed in such a way that it is easy for the client (and other decision makers who will examine the evaluation data) to see how the instructional program affected the problem presented in the needs assessment. In some cases simple descriptive statistics (e.g., means, standard deviations, range, and frequency distributions) may be sufficient to show these effects. In other cases, inferential statistics may be required. It is beyond the scope of this text to discuss inferential statistical analysis. However, we advise caution to the evaluator in cases in which differences in outcomes are found and reported; these may be either differences between two programs or differences from pretest to posttest in a single program. Numerical differences could be due to the effects of programs. However, these differences *may* be due to chance. Inferential statistics allow the evaluator to determine whether differences can be legitimately ascribed to programs rather than chance.

Report Results. Morris (1978) suggests that the summative evaluation report contain the sections outlined below. Instructional design documenta-

tion should provide information for Section 2 (Background). Information needed for the remaining sections can be gleaned by following the suggestions for conducting a summative evaluation as described in this chapter.

1. Summary
2. Background
   - Needs assessment and goal
   - Learner description
   - Context description
   - Description of program
3. Description of evaluation study
   - Purpose of evaluation
   - Evaluation design
   - Outcome measures
   - Implementation measures
   - Cost-effectiveness information
   - Analysis of unintentional outcomes
4. Results
   - Outcomes
   - Implementation
   - Cost-effectiveness information
   - Unintentional outcomes
5. Discussion
   - Causal relationship between program and results
   - Limitations of study
6. Conclusions and recommendations

Summary

During the six stages of formative evaluation, the decisions that were made during the earlier design phases are tested. Problems that learners encounter during instruction are analyzed, and revisions are made. Designers should conduct as many stages of evaluation as possible to ensure a quality product. However, if time and money for evaluation are limited, then evaluation should proceed at the very least through one-to-one evaluation.

Evaluators conduct summative evaluations in order to determine the effectiveness of the instructional program for solving the instructional problem identified in the needs assessment. In conduct-

ing a summative evaluation, the evaluator may assess payoff outcomes, learning outcomes, attitude outcomes, level of implementation of the program, and costs. In addition to goal-based evaluation (which is focused on examining the degree to which the instructional problem is solved), the evaluation may also include an assessment of unintentional outcomes. Such goal-free evaluation uses naturalistic, probing techniques such as non-criterion based observation, interviews, and examination of extant material. Figure 16.8 summarizes key points in this chapter.

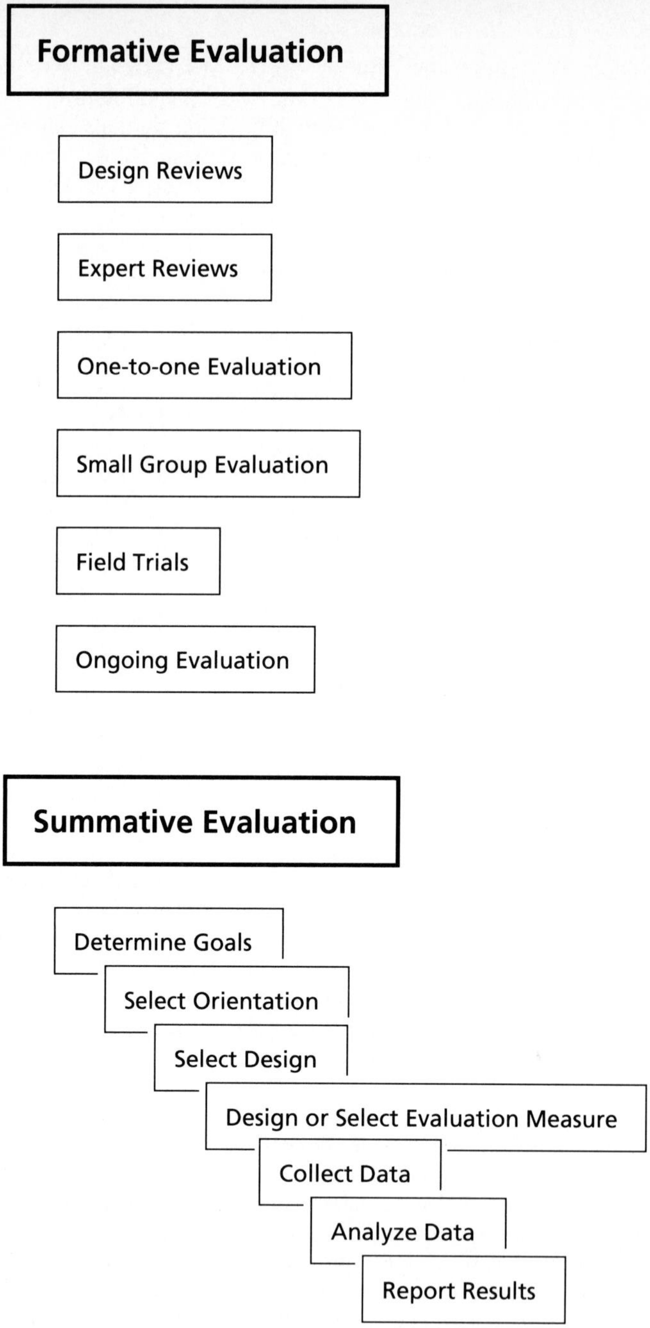

Formative Evaluation

Design Reviews

Expert Reviews

One-to-one Evaluation

Small Group Evaluation

Field Trials

Ongoing Evaluation

Summative Evaluation

Determine Goals

Select Orientation

Select Design

Design or Select Evaluation Measure

Collect Data

Analyze Data

Report Results

Figure 16.8: Summary Diagram for Chapter 16

Job Aid

Formative Evaluation

1. Describe design reviews and resultant revisions.
2. Describe expert reviewers, reviews, comments, and revisions.
3. Describe one-to-one evaluations.
   a. Questions to be answered
   b. Characteristics of materials
   c. Learners' characteristics
   d. Procedures followed
   e. Data gathered, interpretations, and revisions
4. Describe small group evaluations.
   a. Questions to be answered
   b. Characteristics of materials
   c. Learners' characteristics
   d. Procedures followed
   e. Display data gathered
   f. Interpretations and revisions
5. Describe field trials.
   a. Questions to be answered
   b. Characteristics of materials
   c. Characteristics of sites
   d. Characteristics of learners
   e. Characteristics of teachers/trainers
   f. Procedures followed
   g. Display data gathered
   h. Interpretation and revisions
6. Ongoing evaluation
   a. Questions to be answered
   b. Characteristics of sites and learners
   c. Procedures
   d. Time table
   e. Display data gathered
   f. Interpretation and revisions

Extended Example

Formative Evaluation

The Photography Basics course as described earlier in this text was developed and produced in 13 lessons. These lessons were mediated in print, transparencies, teacher, videos, and slide-tape combinations. The course was evaluated during its development in several stages.

Design Reviews. As stated in Chapter 2, the goal of the course—preparing students who are studying education to specify, evaluate, and produce the characteristics of photographs appropriate for delivery via slides, video, print, and computer-based instruction—was reviewed with faculty from a number of universities and with prospective employers to confirm its appropriateness. The description of the learning environment was confirmed with a survey given to Instructional Technology faculty members. The survey included questions about the following: faculty; existing curricula; instructional facilities and hardware; and school, organizational, and community organization and mores. The task analysis and test specifications were reviewed by a team of instructional designers and revised based upon their input. Some empirical validation of the task analysis—the hierarchical relationship among objectives—was conducted by giving a test over the major objectives of the course to students with very diverse backgrounds in photography, following the procedures of White and Gagné (1978). Some additional revisions of the task analysis were made based upon these data.

Expert Reviews. Once the print, video, class outlines, course syllabi, transparency masters, and slides were produced in draft form, they were reviewed by two experts in photography. One was a professor of journalism who teaches a photography class for journalism majors. The other content expert was a photographer for a book publisher. The reviewers had many suggestions regarding the accuracy of content of the course. Many of these suggestions were incorporated in revisions of the course. Many of these suggestions were to include much more detailed information than the designers deemed critical for the targeted competency level of the learners. The design team created a database (which was an annotated bibliography of this information), so that the students could locate sources of more detailed information in these areas and so that this content could be readily located if later revisions of the instruction were necessary.

Learner Validation. In planning the learner-validation portion of the formative evaluation, we had to consider some very serious constraints in conducting such an evaluation. One serious limitation is the lack of resources for funding development of instructional programs in university settings. The other potential limitation is the fact that many of the segments of instruction are teacher-delivered, making one-to-one and small group evaluations of these segments unrealistic. So we decided to conduct one-to-one evaluations of portions of the videos, printed materials, and slide-tapes that we had concerns about and to conduct learner validation of the entire course in a regular course offering during a summer term. The classes in summer are traditionally somewhat smaller, thus making the offering similar to a small group evaluation.

(Notice how a judgement call was required on what amount of formative evaluation was feasible and necessary given the circumstances. Through these Extended Examples we have tried to illustrate the necessity and desirability of such judgement calls rather than slavishly following a procedure or throwing out the whole process because it was not possible to do everything.)

One-to-One Evaluation. During the expert reviews of the storyboards of materials, there were a number of questions among the designers and content experts as to how to most effectively present some concepts and principles, particularly those components selected for delivery via video and slides. The designers prescribed and produced these media in the "leanest" instruction that they could while still being consistent with principles on how to deliver instruction effectively for concepts and rules. For one-to-one evaluation they selected a number of these sections of instruction in

which there was disagreement regarding the most appropriate instructional strategy. For example, there was some discussion as to how to visually represent the concept of "depth of field." This concept was ultimately presented in slides in comparison shots to demonstrate variations in depth of field. There was some discussion as to whether additional descriptive line drawings might clarify the concept or whether to overlay lines onto the photographs themselves. So during the one-to-one evaluations of the slide-tape presentation, the learners were asked to think aloud to ensure that they were interpreting the slides as anticipated. This procedure revealed that the concept was unclear as illustrated and that additional line drawings were required for clarification.

Small Group Evaluation. During the summer delivery of the Photography Basics course, data were collected regarding the effectiveness, efficiency, and appeal of the instruction. The characteristics of this evaluation follow.

1. *Materials:* The materials used in the formative evaluation of the instruction were close to their final forms. Print-based materials were produced with a page-processing software and then laser printed. Video had received its on-line editing. Slides were produced as they were expected to appear in their final form. The designers created a pretest, posttest, and delayed posttest that assessed the objectives on the hierarchy of the task analysis. Practice sheets were developed to assess performance on these same objectives during the instruction.

2. *Participants:* The participants in the formative evaluation were 12 graduate students in the summer offering of the course. Ten of these students were representative of the target audience (instructional technology students), and the remainder were graduate students from other programs. The ten students were considered the evaluation group; however, the performance of the other two students was examined for some indication as to how students from a secondary audience might perform in response to the instruction. Eight of the ten evaluation students were working toward a master's degree in instructional technology (seven from the Generalist

track and one from the Computer Applications track). Two of the students were doctoral students. A preassessment indicated that all students owned cameras, and all but two were automatic cameras. Only one student had received any formal instruction in photography. When asked to rate their knowledge of photography, three checked the rating ''nonexistent,'' four checked ''slim,'' two checked ''some,'' and one checked ''considerable.'' Eight of the students rated their interest in learning photography as ''high,'' and two students rated their interest as ''moderate.'' (Examples of prior knowledge of photography principles are exemplified by pretest scores, which we will soon discuss.)

3. *Procedures:* Students were informed that the course had never been offered in the current format and that additional data would be collected for the purposes of evaluation of the course. They were informed that due to the formative nature of the course, course grades would be Pass/No Pass, as opposed to letter grading, which would have required finer differentiations of grades than might be possible with a trial offering of the course. An extensive pretest and entry-level test was administered on the first two days of class. The course was administered as described in the teacher/trainer manual, which was in its draft form. The instructor noted daily any divergence from the plan prescribed in the manual. Class sessions included lecture/demonstrations, hands-on activities, and viewing of slides and videos. Students viewed the videos and slide-tape presentations as a group; however, copies were available in the learning resource center for repeated viewing. Print-based practice exercises were completed each day. At the conclusion of the semester, in addition to their portfolio of photographs, students completed an extensive final exam, an attitudinal instrument, and a group debriefing, which followed the general format of the attitudinal measure.

4. *Data:* Figure 16.9 shows the performance data for a representative lesson on using the shutter to control exposure and focus. The numbers represent the percentage of students reaching the mastery criterion on the pretest, practice exercises, and posttest. It may seem odd to have

mastery identified in practice exercises, but the data will allow us to determine the state of the learners' knowledge acquisition immediately after receiving instruction on the topic.

Interpretation and Revisions from Performance Data. In order to systematically examine the performance data and make decisions about revisions, the acceptable level of competence on the objectives must be identified. During the development of the test item specifications, the designers identified an 80 percent level of acceptable performance per objective. That is, for the instruction to be deemed effective, following instruction, at least 80 percent of the learners must master each of the objectives, including the terminal (top) objective. The mastery level for each of the objectives was set in the development of the test item specifications, and these same criteria were used for the practice items. These performance data may be interpreted and revision conclusions identified as follows.

1. In general, the performance skills for both the pretest and posttest followed an anticipated pattern, with higher scores at the bottom of the hierarchy and lower scores as the skills became more complex.

2. The learners did not master the entry skill, objective R; however, this did not appear to impede their performance on objectives that were immediately superordinate to it (J and F). Hence, the prerequisite relationship of objective R should be examined. Perhaps it belongs elsewhere in the hierarchy, or perhaps it is a nonessential skill and could be omitted.

3. The skills and knowledge represented by objectives P, O, N, M, L, I, J, K, F, H, and D were mastered. Although practice performance was lower than mastery criterion for objective L (and it was actually lower than their pretest performance), learners must have assimilated the knowledge through overt or covert review because their performance on the posttest was excellent.

4. Objectives E, G, B, C, and A indicate problem areas. It is highly probable that the poor

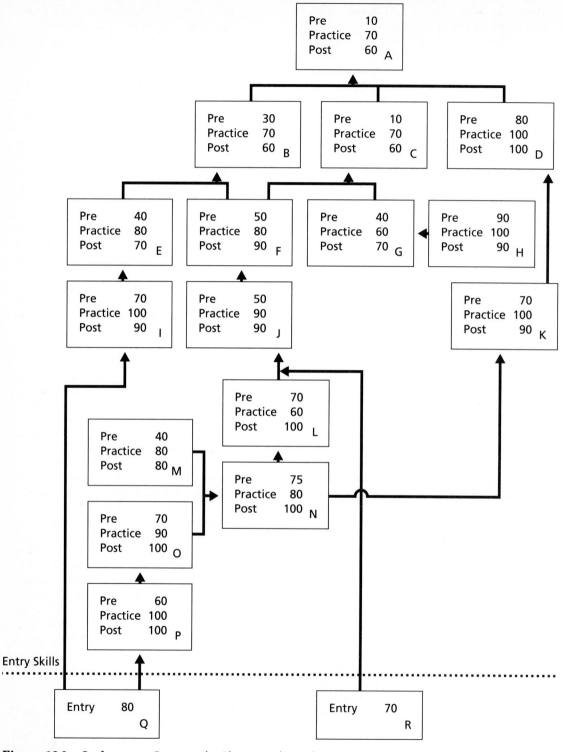

Figure 16.9: Performance Data on the Photography Unit

performance on objective E contributed to the poor performance on B, and that poor performance on objective G contributed to the poor performance on objective C. Further, we could conclude that poor performances on objectives B and C contributed to poor performance on the terminal objective A.

5. Objective E: Although some learners had prior knowledge of the skill represented in objective E, 60 percent of the students clearly needed to acquire the skill. After practice, learners were performing marginally at an acceptable level. However, this performance dropped at the posttest. The designers should first look at the practice and posttest exercises to ensure that the test items were at an equal level of difficulty. If no differences can be identified, then an examination of the amount of practice is appropriate. It is quite likely that some additional practice (perhaps distributed in practice sets later in the lesson for review) would provide sufficient interaction with the principle represented in the objective. This might result in the skill being recalled on the posttest.

6. Objective G: Both the practice and posttest performance were below the criterion level. The designer should examine errors made in the practice items to determine if there are some common misconceptions that the instruction is not addressing. The instruction itself should be reviewed, including the examples and their explanations. Are the examples of the same difficulty level and context as the practice and posttest? Is the explanation of this principle sufficient? Does it include all instructional events, or were some events assumed to be gene.ated by the learners? Were assumptions about the learners' prior knowledge and learning strategies accurate for this objective? Could entry skill R actually be a prerequisite for objective G? Are there other prerequisites for this objective that were not previously considered?

7. Objectives B and C: At this point the designer must examine the performances of learners on practice and posttest items for objectives B, C, and A to determine whether the problems evidenced both in practice and posttest was due to failure to master E and G, or whether there are other problems in the instruction that are evidencing themselves in B and C. It is possible that the problems learners had in B and C were directly a result of their lack of prior knowledge evidenced with their performances on E and G. If this were a self-paced course with many learners available for small group evaluations, we would suggest only revising instruction for objectives E and G and then conducting another small group evaluation to see if problems in B and C were corrected. Since this course is group-paced and infrequently offered, we would recommend that the designer examine the instruction for objectives B and C with the same questions that we listed for objective G and make revisions to the instruction as indicated.

8. Objective A: Performance on objective A is dependent upon prior knowledge from four objectives that were not mastered. We suggest that unless a clear problem in the instruction for objective A is apparent after examining the instruction for E, G, B, and C, the instruction for A be left as is. It is quite probable that revisions in the instruction for these prerequisite objectives would allow the learners to acquire the prior knowledge needed to master objective A. If this is the case, then the instruction on objective A may be sufficient.

Attitude Data. Simple attitude questionnaires were administered at intervals throughout the course. In addition, the questionnaire in Figure 16.10 was administered at the conclusion of the course. Learners were provided a copy of most of this questionnaire at the beginning of the semester and were encouraged to make notes on it as the semester progressed. Some questions were added as a result of comments on the short questionnaires given throughout the semester. The numerical ratings from the 10 students who were representative of the target audience are included. (The comments have been omitted due to space constraints.)

Directions: Please place a check mark by the phrases below that match your opinion of the Photography Basics course. Write down any comments you have about any of the questions. Please be candid in your comments. Help me to get the "bugs" out of this course.

1. How difficult was this course?

__0__ Too easy   __7__ About right   __3__ Too difficult

COMMENTS:

2. Was the terminology used in the course appropriate?

__1__ Too simple   __8__ About right   __1__ Confusing

COMMENTS:

3. Was the scope of the course appropriate to your current and anticipated professional needs?

__1__ Too complex   __7__ About right   __2__ Insufficient information

COMMENTS:

4. How were the practice exercises?

a. __1__ Too easy   __9__ About right   __0__ Too difficult

b. __5__ Too few   __5__ About right   __0__ Too many

COMMENTS:

5. How were the hands-on activities?

a. __0__ Too easy   __9__ About right   __1__ Too difficult

b. __4__ Too few   __5__ About right   __1__ Too many

c. __0__ Too short   __7__ About right   __3__ Too long

COMMENTS:

6. How were the tests?

a. __0__ Too easy   __6__ About right   __4__ Too difficult

b. __0__ Too few   __2__ About right   __8__ Too many

COMMENTS:

7. Did the test questions match the things taught in the lesson?

__0__ No   __1__ Some did, and some didn't   __9__ Yes

COMMENTS:

Figure 16.10: Attitude Questionnaire

8. How were the directions on the practice items and tests?

___1___ Confusing   ___1___ O.K.   ___8___ Very clear

COMMENTS:

9. What did you think about the examples given in the slides and videos?

a. ___0___ Confusing   ___5___ O.K.   ___5___ Very clear

b. ___3___ Too few   ___7___ About right   ___0___ Too many

COMMENTS:

10. How did you like the graphics in the slides and videos?

a. ___0___ Weren't needed   ___1___ O.K.   ___9___ Very helpful

b. ___0___ Distracting   ___2___ O.K.   ___8___ Very important

c. ___1___ Confusing   ___2___ O.K.   ___7___ Very clear

COMMENTS:

11. Would you like to receive instruction in this form again?

___0___ No   ___2___ Maybe   ___8___ Absolutely

COMMENTS:

12. Would you recommend this instruction to a friend who wanted to learn about photography for instructional purposes?

___0___ No   ___2___ Maybe   ___8___ Absolutely

COMMENTS:

13. How do you like photography?

___0___ Hate it   ___4___ It's O.K.   ___6___ Love it

COMMENTS:

14. Do you feel able to prepare photographs for print-based instructional materials?

___0___ No   ___4___ Maybe   ___6___ Sure

COMMENTS:

15. Do you feel able to prepare photographs for video-based instructional materials?

___0___ No   ___5___ Maybe   ___5___ Sure

COMMENTS:

16. Do you feel able to prepare photographs for slides and slide-tape presentations as instructional materials?

  _0_ No   _2_ Maybe   _8_ Sure

COMMENTS:

17. Do you think you could explain to a friend how to produce photographs for instructional materials?

  _0_ No   _4_ Maybe   _6_ Sure

COMMENTS:

18. Many media were used in the course. Were you ever confused as to how the content presented in one medium related to content presented in other media?

  _8_ No   _2_ Occasionally   _0_ Frequently

COMMENTS:

19. Do you feel that you have adequate resources on photography, particularly information in print-based form, to use as reference materials in later courses and after you graduate?

  _6_ No   _3_ Uncertain   _1_ Yes

COMMENTS:

20. Overall, how would you rank this course?

  _6_ Excellent   _3_ Good   _1_ Fair   _0_ Poor

COMMENTS:

21. What concepts or procedures do you feel were covered inadequately or were not presented in the right sequence?

22. What characteristics must learners in this course have in order to be successful in it?

23. Did the syllabus adequately convey the requirements and expectations of the course?

Figure 16.10: *Continued*

Interpretation and Revisions from Attitude Data. These data on student attitudes toward the course, along with written comments and comments volunteered during an oral debriefing following the delivery of the questionnaire, provide some additional suggestions for revisions in the materials and further clarify the performance data.

1. The learners were generally positive about the value of the course and their learning from it.

2. Questionnaire data and comments indicated that the learners were uncomfortable without a "regular" textbook and felt they needed more comprehensive print-based materials.

3. The learners' difficulty on the final exam on the items for objectives E, G, B, C, and A influenced their rankings of the course and lowered their confidence in their ability to transfer what they had learned to job problems.

4. The learners felt they needed additional practice and explanation on objectives E, G, B, and C. They identified omissions in the textual, lecture, and visual materials that caused their difficulties in answering questions on the exam.

5. The learners felt that the slides and videos were key to their learning the content of the course.

6. The learners particularly valued the hands-on activities and had some suggestions for additional activities.

7. As with many formative evaluation groups, the learners felt they were tested too much. They wished that the tests had not been so comprehensive, and they suggested that only the top-level objectives be tested.

Time Data. The course instructor recorded whether the estimate of thirteen 2 1/2-hour lessons that the designers had made as they divided the course was accurate. For each lesson the instructor noted whether more time or less time was needed and estimated the amount of time needed or time to spare. These data are recorded below:

Lesson Number	Amount of additional time needed	Amount of extra time left over
1		45 minutes
2		30 minutes
3		15 minutes
4		45 minutes
5	30 minutes	
6	0	0
7	30 minutes	
8		15 minutes
9	0	0
10	0	0
11	45 minutes	
12	30 minutes	
13	45 minutes	

Interpretation and Revisions. The time data indicate that estimates for the earlier lessons were inaccurate in that they provided more time than was needed. For the later lessons, more time was required. The designers revised the course so that the first four lessons were compacted into three lessons. The extra time was added after lesson 11. Lessons 5 and 7 were examined, and assignments were designed to be assigned prior to these classes. The learners' completion of these assignments prior to the beginning of class would give additional in-class time for lessons 5 and 7.

Summative Evaluation

As discussed in the text, a summative evaluation is not always conducted by the instructional designer. Therefore, we will not be as comprehensive in our example of a summative evaluation as we were with our formative evaluation example. Nevertheless, we will note some points that might be considered if a summative evaluation of the Photography Basics course were to be planned.

1. Background

- Needs assessment and goal
- Learner description
- Context description
- Description of program

This information may be obtained from the descriptions provided in the Extended Example sections in Chapters 2–4.

2. Description of Evaluation Study

Purpose of evaluation. The purpose of the evaluation could be to compare it with alternative photography courses available. However, it is more likely that the evaluation would be comparing the performance of the learners to criteria of acceptable performance.

Evaluation design. If the purpose of the evaluation is to determine whether the learners have learned to a specified criterion, then a one group pretest-posttest design may be sufficient. An evaluation that wishes to establish the superiority of one instructional treatment to another would require a more complex design, such as a pretest-posttest control design.

Outcome measures. Outcome measures would include performance, time, and attitude data. Ideally, the evaluation would also include some measure of delayed performance, either as a delayed posttest or an on-the-job evaluation.

Implementation measures. The evaluation should include an examination of whether the instruction as implemented included key features of the course. These key features would include completion of practice exercises and hands-on activities and viewing of slides and videos. The evaluator should obtain data as to whether segments of instruction were omitted or whether additional information or activities were included.

Cost-effectiveness information. Cost feasibility is the key issue in examining the cost of the program. Much of this feasibility will have been considered in the initial development of the course because a substantial portion of the cost of the course is the development and production of the media used within it. Potential adopters of the program will want to consider whether the achievement of the objectives to the degree that they find in their evaluation is worth the cost of the instructional materials and the cost of the salary for the instructor. This decision may involve consideration of the job market and the centrality of photography skills for the adopters' students.

Analysis of unintentional outcomes. Ideally, the evaluation should include an examination of the impact of the course by an individual who is knowledgeable in the content but not apprised of the specific goals of the course. Such an examination may reveal some desirable effects, such as increased visibility of the program and increased interest in artistic or creative aspects of instruction by the students. It may also reveal undesirable effects, such as a misunderstanding of the goals of the field or an inappropriate allocation of resources.

3. Results

- Outcomes
- Implementation
- Cost-effectiveness information
- Unintentional outcomes

4. Discussion

- Causal relationship between program and results
- Limitations of study

5. Conclusions and Recommendations

The data for items 3, 4, and 5 are not available. However, when examining results and drawing conclusions, the evaluators should be guided by the original purpose of the evaluation. The evaluation questions that were identified as critical should be answered through an examination of the data.

Readings and References

Baker, E. L. (1970). Generalizability of rules for empirical revision. *AV Communication Review, 18*(3), 300–305.

Baker, E. L., & Alkin, M. (1973). Formative evaluation of instructional development. *AV Communication and Review, 21*(4), 389–418.

Borich, G. D. (Ed.). (1974). *Evaluating educational programs and products.* Englewood Cliffs, NJ: Educational Technology Publications.

Cambre, M. A. (1981). Historical overview of formative evaluation of instructional media products. *Educational Communication and Technology Journal, 29* (1), 3–25.

Campbell, D. T., & Stanley, J. C. (1963). *Experimental and quasi-experimental designs for research.* Chicago: Rand McNally.

Cennamo, K. (1986). Report on a beginning logo lesson. Unpublished student project, University of Texas at Austin.

Dick, W., & Carey, L. (1990). *The systematic design of instruction* (3rd ed.). Glenview, IL: Scott, Foresman.

Eisner, E. W. (1979). *The educational imagination: On the design and evaluation of school programs.* New York: Macmillan.

Fitz-Gibbon, C., & Morris, L. L. (1975). Theory-based evaluation. *Evaluation Comment,* Center for the Study of Evaluation, UCLA, *5*(1), 1–4.

Flagg, B. N. (1990). *Formative evaluation for educational technologies.* Hillsdale, NJ: Erlbaum.

Holloway, R. E. (1981). *A methodology for assessing the implementation of educational innovations: Analysis and revision.* Columbia University, Teachers College. National Institute of Education, Washington, D.C., Basic Skills Group. (ERIC Document Reproduction Service No. ED 202 866)

Hughes, A. S., & Keith, J. J. (1980). Teacher perceptions of an innovation and degree of implementation. *Canadian Journal of Education, 5*(2), 43–51.

Kearsley, G. (April 1986). Analyzing the costs and benefits of training: Part 2: Identifying the costs and benefits. *Performance and Instruction, 25*(3), 23–25.

Kimpston, R. D. (1985). Curriculum fidelity and the implementation tasks employed by teachers: A research study. *Journal of Curriculum Studies, 17*(2), 185–195.

Komoski, P. K. (1974). An imbalance of product quantity and instructional quality: The imperative of empiricism. *AV Communication Review, 22*(4), 357–386.

Loucks, S. F. (1983). *Defining fidelity: A Cross-study analysis.* Network of Innovative Schools, Inc., Andover, MA. Paper presented at the Annual Meeting of the American Educational Research Association, Montreal, April 14–15. (ERIC Document Reproduction Service No. ED 249 659)

Morris, L. L. (1978). *Program evaluation kit.* Beverly Hills, CA: Sage Publications.

Popham, W. J. (1988). *Educational evaluation* (2nd ed.). Englewood Cliffs, NJ: Prentice-Hall.

Posavac, E. J., & Carey, R. G. (1989). *Program evaluation: Methods and case studies.* Englewood Cliffs, NJ: Prentice-Hall.

Roitman, D. B., & Mayer, J. P. (1982). *Fidelity and re-invention in the implementation of innovations.* National Science Foundation, Washington, D.C. Paper presented at the Annual Convention of the American Psychological Association, Washington, D.C., August 23–27. (ERIC Document Reproduction Service No. ED 225 058)

Rosen, M. J. (1968). *An experimental design for comparing the effects of instructional media programming procedures: Subjective vs. objective revision procedures.* Final Report. Palo Alto, CA: American Institutes for Research. (ERIC Document Reproduction Service No. ED 025 156)

Rothkopf, E. Z. (1963). Some observations on predicting instructional effectiveness by implementation inspection. *Journal of Programmed Instruction, 2*(2), 19–20.

Scriven, M. (1972). Pros and cons about goal-free evaluation. *Evaluation Comment, 3* (4), 1–4.

Shrock, S. A. & Coscarelli, W. C. C. (1989). *Criterion-referenced test development: Technical and legal guidelines for corporate training.* Reading, MA: Addison-Wesley.

Smith, P. L., & Wedman, J. F. (1988). Read-think-aloud protocols: A new data-source for formative evaluation. *Performance Improvement Quarterly, 1,* 13–22.

Thiagarajan, S. (1978). Instructional product verification: 20 questions and 200 speculations. *Educational Communication and Technology Journal, 26* (2), 133–141.

Wager, J. C. (1983). One-to-one and small group formative evaluation: An examination of two basic formative evaluation procedures. *Performance and Instructional Journal, 22* (5), 5–7.

Weston, C. B. (1986). Formative evaluation of instructional materials: An overview of approaches. *Canadian Journal of Educational Communication, 15*(1), 5–17.

White, R. T. & Gagné, R. M. (1978). Formative evaluation applied to a learning hierarchy. *Contemporary Educational Psychology, 3,* 87–94.

Worthen, B. R., & Sanders, J. R. (1987). *Educational evaluation: Alternative approaches and practical guidelines.* New York: Longman.

Conclusions and Future Directions

seventeen

Chapter Objectives

At the conclusion of this chapter you should be able to do the following:

- Describe and explain the major principles underlying instructional design.

- Given a description of a design situation, determine and explain the degree of precision and formality that would be appropriate to apply in that situation.

- Summarize "fast track" techniques for instructional design.

- Discuss future trends in instructional design practice.

Overview

This chapter has three sections: (1) a summary of the major design principles presented in each chapter of this book, (2) a discussion of the appropriate use of instructional design technology, and (3) a description of what we and others view as future trends in instructional design.

Summary of Major Principles Guiding Instructional Design

Following is a set of major principles that underlie instructional design. These principles are abstracted from the chapters of this text and, as such, represent a summary of the text in principle form.

1. General principles and assumptions that underlie instructional design (ID) are as follows:
- ID is a systematic process (as opposed to a fortuitous, haphazard activity).
- ID has a problem-solving orientation (needs assessment leads to activities directed at improvement of instruction, which in turn lead to evaluation).
- ID is learning and learner centered (as opposed to teacher or medium centered).
- ID has as a goal efficient, effective, and appealing instruction.
- ID insists on congruence among objectives, instruction, and evaluation.
- ID is both theoretic and empirical (as opposed to "intuitive").

2. The design of instruction must be directed by needs and shaped to fit the learning environment.

3. Instructional design must include consideration of the following learner characteristics:
- Likenesses and differences
- Changing and stable characteristics
- Specific prior learning

4. The learning task must be precisely identified and exhaustively analyzed to determine necessary components of learning tasks and their prerequisite skills and knowledge.

5. Assessment of learning is guided by objectives of the instructional system and should em-ploy particular techniques to ensure adequacy of the assessment. Frequently, assessment design involves trade-offs in validity, reliability, and practicality.

6. Instructional strategies can do the following:
- Provide the framework for learning at both micro and macro levels
- Be more generative or more supplantive depending on the task, context, and learners
- Be organized around the expanded instructional events, a framework for instructional strategies

7–13. A fundamental element in the design of instruction is the character of the learning task. Effectiveness of instruction can be improved when instructional strategies are based upon the cognitive demands of different types of learning (using the framework provided by the expanded instructional events).

14. The characteristics of different media, the environments offered by different learner groupings, and the potentials offered by different instructional management strategies interact with task characteristics, learners' characteristics, and the learning context.

15. The translation of specifications into instructional materials is accomplished through production processes, which vary according to the media that will be used to deliver instruction.

16. Evaluation of instruction should be conducted as part of the design/development process (formative) and to estimate the value of completed instruction (summative).

"Appropriate" Instructional Design

An issue that we have alluded to throughout the text but not directly confronted is the level of effort that is required for any particular instructional design project. The issue is illustrated by remarks overheard in the halls: "This instructional design stuff is completely crazy! Classroom teachers (or training designers) can't possibly do all of this! We don't have enough time!"

A friend in the advertising and marketing field shared with us an expression that reflects some harsh realities of projects in either advertising or instruction: "Given three criteria for doing a job—high quality, low cost, and rapid completion of the job—you may have any *two*." In other words, "I can give it to you fast and inexpensively, but it won't be as good; I can give it to you fast and very well done, but it won't be inexpensive; or I can give it to you inexpensively and well done, but it will take a long time." The trade-offs expressed in this wry analysis illustrate the dilemmas often faced by instructional designers who have limited resources and high demands.

E. F. Schumacher (1973) wrote a book called *Small Is Beautiful,* in which he espoused the concept of "appropriate technology." His concern was predominantly with product (hardware) technology, rather than process technology, such as instructional design. However, the principles he advocated can be wisely applied to ID. His suggestion was that when we recommend the employment of a "technology," it may not be wise to export the "highest tech" thing that we have. For instance, to a farming culture that has been using hand implements, a plow may be a more "appropriate" innovation than a tractor.

Leslie Briggs has compared different levels of instructional design sophistication to using automobiles of different costs.[1] He noted that a Cadillac has many desirable attributes and that in some situations, such as transporting heads of state or participating in funeral processions, it is a clear choice (if not *de rigueur*), particularly when compared to a Chevy. However, it is important to recognize, he pointed out, that both the Cadillac and the Chevy will get you there.

The same concept of appropriate technology can apply to the amount of formality and precision used in applying instructional design. Due in large measure, perhaps, to the prescriptive nature and systematic orientation of instructional design, novice designers typically have the idea that all instructional design projects should undergo the same level of rigorous analysis and design effort. The practicality of instructional design itself has been at times called into question by authors in the field for the amount of time and effort that it takes

to employ instructional design principles (e.g., Merrill, Li, & Jones, 1990a, 1990b; Rogoff, 1984; and Rosenberg, 1991). No doubt the student of this text has had similar frustrations over the effort required to fully complete some of the phases of design we have suggested in this text. We would suggest, however, that rather than discard the tools of instructional design when situations make it difficult to use them to their fullest, it is better to learn ways of "tailoring" their application to the situation. This is the basic idea behind "appropriate" design.

The concept of appropriate design speaks to the problem of feasibility and advisability of instructional design in real-world situations. The appropriate design concept suggests that it is not only possible but also advisable to perform design functions at varying levels of effort, depending on available resources, criticality of the task, the level of accountability of the educational or training agency, and expectations/requirements of the client agency. These variances in effort (as enabled by resources) lead to different levels of precision and amount of detail in documentation. The "low road" will include more design tasks "done in your head" but may nonetheless, under certain circumstances, result in completely legitimate, appropriate instructional design. Let's take a closer look at how resources, criticality, accountability, and expectations affect the design process.

Resources. When personnel, physical resources, and time do not allow a full implementation of the procedures described in this text, it is still possible to improve instruction over what would otherwise be used if systematic instructional design were not employed. So, for example, when resources do not allow for a full learning task analysis, it is better to informally reflect on lesson objectives and the kinds of learning that should lead up to them rather than to not be concerned with outcomes at all. And when time does not allow a full four-phase formative evaluation, it is better to try out materials with learners and keep in mind the need for future revision than it is to not be aware of the value of feedback and verification of materials by the learners themselves.

In many cases within the text, we have suggested a few of these less-demanding alternatives, as the following examples illustrate.

---

[1] These comments are from classes that Prof. Briggs taught at Florida State University.

Needs Assessment

For teachers or trainers who are designing instruction for their own classrooms, a needs assessment can be rather informal but is nonetheless important. At the most basic level, such needs assessment can be directed at determining what portions of the curriculum involve learning tasks with which, year after year, a large number of students experience difficulty in learning and for which no readily available instructional solution exists. (Ch. 2, p. 27)

Learner Analysis

How do designers find out about the general characteristics of the target audience? If the designers are developing for their own classrooms, they can observe, talk to, and assess their learners to determine their characteristics. Even then they may wish to conduct some additional research to find out more about the learners. But suppose a designer is developing instruction to be used by learners that he has never met. (Ch. 3, p. 56)

Task Analysis

How can we determine what the information-processing steps are for a particular goal? One of the simplest and most often-used techniques is to simply mentally review the steps that one might go through in completing a task. And often, that is exactly what we do if time is short or the task is simple. (Ch. 4, p. 73)

Instructional Strategy

While these instructional events have been synthesized from a review of research, if you observe master teachers, you may see them including these events whether they have heard of them or not. Teachers probably follow this pattern because they have discovered that students who experience these events tend to learn better than students who do not. (Ch. 6, p. 140)

Instructional Delivery

These media are not by any means necessary to learn intellectual skills. For instance, many generations have been educated without the use of computer-driven interactive video systems. However, one of these alternatives will be the medium of choice in instances where its attributes are needed. In other words, many intellectual skills are readily learned by all learners in the target population through books, handouts, or conventional media. Conventional media should be used when they will work as well as more elaborate technologies. (Ch. 14, p. 347)

Formative Evaluation

Trying out materials with learners can help instructional developers determine where revisions are necessary. As a matter of fact, materials that have been tried out with only one or two representative students and then revised based upon the information gained are substantially more effective than the original instruction. (Ch. 16, p. 388)

If problems in instruction were many and the revisions were substantial, then the designer may wish to go through another round of one-to-one evaluations before proceeding to the next stage. If money or time is not available for further evaluation, the designer has still obtained information that helps eliminate most severe problems. This allows for a product that is substantially more effective than the product prior to the revisions. (Ch. 16, pp. 392–393)

Criticality. The extent to which a task may be deemed "critical" should influence the level of instructional design effort. Among the dimensions of criticality is that of hazard. Instruction for potentially hazardous tasks, such as operating nuclear power plants, parachute packing, controlling air traffic, and providing medical assistance, involves learning skills which, if neglected or improperly performed, can lead to life-threatening consequences for the trainee and/or other people. Our technological society has made it increasingly possible for one person's actions to put not only their own safety in jeopardy but also the safety and welfare of thousands of others. Training for such tasks is a serious business, not to be left to serendipity or happenstance.

Another dimension of criticality is the requirement for homogeneity of outcome. For some critical tasks, everyone must be able to perform at the same level. For example, aircraft mechanics must be predictable in their assembly of engines after tear-down. One aircraft mechanic's skills must be very much like those of the others, whereas a great deal more variability in skill level can be tolerated among graduates of a barber school. Frequently the need for homogeneity of outcome is based on some hazard-related concern, as would be the case with aircraft mechanics. Sometimes the need for homogeneity of outcome is based on other factors, such as management, product quality, or cost-control, as can be seen in the training of fast-food industry employees. For example, it is important to the success of a chain of hamburger restaurants that each restaurant serve hamburgers that consistently represent that chain's product. Training of employees is a major contributor to ensuring that consistency.

Criticality has been considered previously in this text, particularly in the design of assessments:

In life-and-death situations, such as training learners in CPR, training parachute packers, or training employees in safety practices, we should be less willing to make compromises in validity and reliability in order to bow to issues of practicality. Resources should be made available to ensure the most highly reliable and valid instruments possible in such circumstances. In contrast, in cases of informal education, such as a community center course on embroidery, the consequences of incorrect assessment of competence may not have severe consequences for anyone, in which case more radical compromises might be made for the sake of practicality. (Ch. 5, p. 110)

Another dimension of criticality is the centrality of the skill or knowledge to be learned. This aspect appears in public education as well as in training environments. Some skills or knowledge is so central to learning that if it is not acquired, future learning is in jeopardy. An example of such a central feature is acquiring reading comprehension ability in elementary school or being able to apply the concept of "variance" in statistics. These central skills and knowledge may also be difficult to acquire.

Instruction for critical tasks must be designed and conducted with the best that our field has to offer. On the other hand, a great deal of education is conducted in which the exact learning task is not critical. Frequently in such situations, those who deliver the educational experiences are not even concerned about what the learning task at hand is,

much less the criticality of that learning task. Frequently such situations are found in those educational environments that are as much care-taking as they are instructional. And, in educational situations that are more activity-centered, many proceed under vague, changing, or pluralistic goals for learning. This results in a situation in which the tools of instructional design do not fit with the intentions of the organization. In these situations, particular learning tasks are far from being considered as "critical."

Accountability. Related to criticality, accountability has to do with the degree to which the ID developers and the organization delivering the instruction are held seriously accountable for the effects of training, especially poor performance after instruction. There have been situations in which litigation has been instigated against instructional agencies (school systems and training agencies) because the instruction was deemed inadequate. This can lead to serious implications. J. Sample (1989) discusses the issue of liability in "failing to train to standard." After summarizing and illustrating the legal theory behind civil suits involving forms of liability applicable to deficiencies in training (under 43 United States Code (USC), Sec. 1983 and 42 USC, Sec. 1983), Sample provides an eight-step set of recommendations for preventing and limiting liability for failure to train to standard. In summary form, these recommendations are as follows: (1) appropriate job-task analysis; (2) development of appropriate job-related performance measures; (3) modification of selection criteria for hiring personnel who would perform high-liability tasks; (4) use of a standard instructional systems design model to inform and guide the instructional design process; (5) educational units employing certification procedures to document individual competence in high-liability tasks; (6) field supervisors employing qualification procedures on the job shortly after training and at regular intervals thereafter; (7) maintenance of records of training and written documentation of concerns; and (8) the purchase of individual liability insurance (pp. 25–26).

For situations in which the possibility of legal or moral responsibility is high, particularly in cases in which criticality is also a factor, instructional design should be applied precisely and formally documented. Although such care may not avoid legal suits, it will certainly provide information that provides the rationale for decisions that were made in the design process.

Expectations/Requirements of the Client Agency. The expectations and requirements of the client agency for the scale of the instructional design effort vary. Not all client agencies want or need equal effort (and expense) in their instructional design projects. Within a single agency, not all projects will be given the same priority. And priorities for attention to the various phases and facets of the instructional design process will also vary within an organization. For example, organization *A* may be accustomed to spending a great deal of effort on task analysis but relatively little on formative evaluation, while organization *B* may prefer (and find it natural and inevitable) to spend less time on task analysis and more on formative evaluation. Policymakers within the organization have ideas as to the size of effort each project should be given. The wise instructional designer will be sensitive to this reality and not expect that all projects will be given unlimited design and development resources. Not only are we talking about the difference in the amount that can be spent on the production of materials, we are also addressing the question of level of effort in the design *process* itself. There are many occasions when a less ambitious approach will yield completely satisfactory results for the problems and priorities at hand.

What Instructional Designers Actually Do

Which instructional design activities do practicing instructional designers actually incorporate into their systematic design? Wedman and Tessmer (1992) examined this question by surveying 35 practicing instructional designers. Although their data are potentially biased because the majority of the respondents were from one training agency, the findings identify for this group of designers those aspects of design that are deemed ''most appropriate'' to the particular situations in which they most commonly operate. The activities that the respondents ''always'' or ''usually'' performed are listed in the following table:

ID Activity	*Percentage of Respondents*
Write learning objectives	94%
Select media formats	86%
Select instructional strategies	85%
Develop test items	82%
Summative evaluation	75%
Identify types of learning	74%
Determine if need requires instruction	70%
Conduct task analysis	66%
Conduct needs assessment	63%
Assess entry skills	54%
Formative evaluation	49%

It is interesting to note that with the exception of formative evaluation, at least half of the respondents reported doing all of the ID activities that Wedman and Tessmer asked them about in most situations. The three phases of design that we have identified as essential—analysis in the form of objectives (Where are we going?), strategy selection (How will we get there?), and assessment item writing (How will we know when we're there?)—were the most frequently employed aspects of instruction design.

Wedman and Tessmer also asked the respondents for reasons why the ID activities might be eliminated. Surprisingly, the two most frequently cited reasons were not limitations in time and money, but ''decision already made'' and ''considered unnecessary.'' These reasons to omit ID processes were most frequently cited for the following activities: needs assessment, determine if need can be resolved by training, conduct task analysis, assess entry skills, and pilot test. The three activities for which ''not enough time'' was frequently identified as a reason to omit them were needs assessment, task analysis, and formative evaluation. Formative evaluation was the only design activity for which ''cost constraints'' was frequently identified as a reason for omission.

This study was preliminary and descriptive in nature. There is no way to know which factors were considered in determining whether to *include* certain design activity. Also, we do not know to what degree of precision or formality an activity had to be completed for the designers to consider it completed. However, we feel that considering the constraints under which designers frequently operate, it is very encouraging that they are able to include so much design so frequently.

Four Ways to Adapt the ID Process

In the introduction to their study of adapting instructional design practice to the requirements of a situation, Wedman and Tessmer (1990, p. 2) cite their "Practitioner's Lament" with which they represent the practicing instructional designer's quandary:

What do you do
When you have no time
No time to do "model" ID?
Do you skip some steps,
Or water them down,
Combine, or maybe all three?

We have identified four different approaches as techniques for dealing with situations in which full or "traditional" implementation of instructional design practice may not be possible. These approaches involve skipping design tasks, combining design tasks, and "watering down" design tasks in order to meet the requirements and constraints of the situation. Each of these approaches deals in its own way with the question of "appropriate" design (in terms of resources, criticality, and accountability). These approaches are (1) the layers of necessity model, (2) rapid prototyping, (3) windows of opportunity, and (4) use of computer resources to assist the design process.

One model to guide the designer is found in Tessmer and Wedman's "layers of necessity" model (1990; and Wedman & Tessmer, 1991). This model emphasizes performing the design process in multiple layers, with each layer representing a complete cycle of design activity. (This is a kind of elaboration, similar in concept to the Elaboration Model for organizing instruction.) This model proposes five fundamental phases of design: situational assessment, goal analysis, instructional strategy development, materials development, and evaluation and revision. Each of these phases can have multiple and more formal aspects. For example, "situational analysis" may include a formal needs assessment and learner preassessments. De-

sign projects requiring a higher degree of sophistication and care will cascade the process to further layers, with each layer more extensive and elaborated than the previous one. Thus, projects with minimal requirements from a resources and criticality standpoint may be well served by instructional design that produces "good enough for now" instruction. For instruction that requires it, more sophisticated design work is done over time in subsequent design/development efforts. The researchers provided principles for selecting layers—determining what instructional design activities would be engaged in for a given project—in a subsequent paper (Wedman & Tessmer, 1991). The principles reflect the relationships among the factors of load (or costs), payoff, and pressure.

A second approach for an experienced designer to take when money and time are very limited is "rapid prototyping" (Tripp & Bichelmeyer, 1990). Rather than using a layered approach, Tripp and Bichelmeyer recommend an overlapping approach in which the analysis phase overlaps with both the development and formative evaluation phases (see Figure 17.1). In other words, the designer actually begins the design work while conducting the front-end analysis. Overlapping functions illustrated in Figure 17.1 represent the idea that "the analysis of needs and content depends in part upon the knowledge that is gained by actually building and using a prototype instructional system" (Tripp & Bichelmeyer, 1990, p. 35). For an experienced designer who can anticipate the results of much of the analysis, and in cases in which the instructional medium is mutable (such as a computer program), rapid prototyping may be useful. You might recognize that this is an example of "combining steps," a technique Wedman and Tessmer mention in their "Practioner's Lament."

A third approach, which Noel (1991) recommends based upon his experience, is a "windows of opportunity" strategy. He has been involved in a large-scale development of a middle school curriculum for Botswana. As a result of his experiences, he concluded that in such a mega-project in which any designer may enter at any time, it may not be possible to follow through the entire systematic process with all components of the project. Noel recommends looking for "windows of opportunity" in which systematic design procedures are

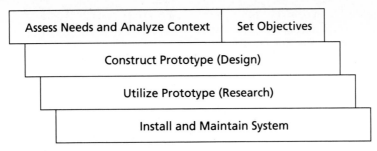

Figure 17.1: Rapid Prototyping ISD Model
Source: Tripp & Bichelmeyer (1990, p. 36)

timely and appropriate. He gave the example of a project in which he was only able to use the instructional design phase of formative evaluation. Since use of the entire instructional design process was not possible in the particular situation, the opportunity was seized to make substantial improvements by using a particular phase of the process as a "tool." Even though Noel's experience was with a rather large-scale project, similar compromises may be made in smaller scale projects in which time and resources are limited. Knowledge of the full instructional design process assists people who need to make such compromises. They are in a good position to (1) predict problems that may occur and (2) develop "work-arounds" for deficiencies resulting from compromises. You might recognize from the "Practioner's Lament" that this is an example of "skipping steps."

A fourth approach is the use of computer resources to assist in the design process. Gayeski (1991) describes many software tools that can be used to assist in the design and development process in various ways. Examples of such systems described by Gayeski include the following: Alberta Research Council and Computer-Based Training Systems, Ltd. computer-assisted course and curriculum development environment; U. S. Air Force Subject Outline Curriculum Resource and Tutoring Expert System (SOCRATES); Courseware, Inc., Computer-Aided Analysis (CAA); U. S. Army Automated Systems Approach to Training (ASAT); Gustafson and Reeves IDioM course development expert system; Omni-Com Associates DesignStation and Content Expert Interviewer (CAI); Automated Test Development

Aid (ATDA); U. S. Army Research Institute Automated Knowledge Acquisition Tool (AKAT); AT&T's Training Delivery Consultant and Training Test Consultant; Sealand & Associates CBT Cost Justification Model; U. S. Navy Authoring Instructional Materials software (AIM); Simulation Design Tool for Training Development (SDTD); Elron Technologies, Inc., Automated Courseware Expert (ACE); and Electronic Vision, Inc., Interactive Video Design Toolkit. An ambitious project in using expert system computer resources to enhance the instructional design process, which is under way as of this writing, is the Utah State University "Second Generation Instructional Research Project" (Merrill, Li, & Jones, 1990a, 1990b). There is insufficient research evidence at this time to conclude for which designers and in which situations such automated tools may be appropriate.

The implications of the adaptations of the instructional design process described above are many and not completely understood at present. There is a clear trend toward improving the efficiency of the overall process. The old expression "All solutions bring new problems" certainly applies to instructional design. Instructional designers must answer the following questions: How will the role of designers change? What knowledge will designers need? Since no one can answer these questions with any certainty, it appears likely that genuine expertise and depth of knowledge of instructional design will become more important in the future. Intelligent decision making in selecting among alternatives such as rapid prototyping or different forms of computer assistance will require a better understanding of in-structural design than that required of the typical designer in day-to-day work that employs conventional means. Furthermore, making good use of the products of alternative approaches to design will require a high degree of instructional design expertise to avoid mistakes on a grander scale than previously thought possible.

*E*xercises A

1. Directions: For each of the following three scenarios involving the development of instruction, consider the level of precision and formality that can/should be employed in the instructional design procedures. Be prepared to discuss your answers.

Scenario 1: You are the instructional designer for a $1.5 million project sponsored by the National Science Foundation to develop a predominantly print-based, tenth-grade general science curriculum for noncollege-bound students. Your time lines indicate a distribution date 36 months after project start-up.

Scenario 2: You are the instructional designer for an in-house project to develop training for managers at a long-distance phone company on legal issues involved in interviewing and hiring. Since there has been some recent new legislation, it is imperative that the employees acquire this knowledge as soon as possible. You have decided to make the instruction via stand-up delivery, with the first class five months after project start-up. Your deliverables are an instructor's guide (including lecture notes and overhead transparency masters), a 10-minute introductory video, a student handbook, and all assessment instruments.

Scenario 3: You are a fourth-grade public school teacher. It is Saturday afternoon and you are developing your lesson plans for next week. You must plan for instruction in reading, language arts, math, social studies, science, art, music, and physical education for the week.

2. What features must instructional planning include in order for you to feel right about considering the planning as reflecting instructional design? List them and provide a rationale for your decision.

*F*uture Directions for Instructional Design

As a form of technology (a *process* technology), instructional design is one area in which we should be able to anticipate particularly rapid and significant change. Whereas distant future estimates are anybody's guess, some near future predictions have a high probability of becoming reality. Having an idea of what to look out for can help the designer keep up with changes and developments in the field. The following paragraphs reflect the incredibly wide array of technical and scientific work in progress. Among the thousands of candidates, we have selected six areas of work that we have reason to believe will yield significant contributions to instructional design in the near future: artificial intelligence, adaptive instruction, interactive technologies, improvements in ID models, performance technologies, and advances in cognitive science and other foundational areas.

Artificial Intelligence (A.I.) and Expert Systems. A number of years ago, Roger Schank observed that of all the potential applications under consideration, including military, construction, medicine, and transportation, it was education—specifically the delivery of instruction—that appeared to have the greatest potential benefit from artificial intelligence (Schank, 1984). The benefit from machine-based mixed-initiative instruction (intelligent tutors) has yet to be felt in any widespread way, despite the fact that some research and development projects have seen successful completion. A primary limitation stems from the amount of time and effort that intelligent tutors and ICAI (intelligent computer-assisted instruction) require. It is likely that developments in A.I. authoring and knowledge bases may make ICAI development a less daunting task. Another application of A.I. techniques that appears to have particularly high promise in instruction is the use of expert systems as instructional designers. It may be more efficient in the short run to employ machine intelligence to help *design* the instruction rather than to *deliver* it. This is due to the wide applicability of an expert system designer, as compared to the more limited utility of an expert system created to teach a particular set of objectives or a subject (Merrill, Li, & Jones, 1990a, 1990b).

Adaptive Instruction. We currently possess the tools to create instruction of a far more dynamically interactive quality than that which is in common application. *Adaptive instruction* is a term used, to describe instruction that changes its delivery based on prior interactions with the learner. The changes that adaptive instruction might supply, in such elements as rate of delivery, examples used, and difficulty of practice, are all elements that our current approach to instructional design supports. Extended with artificial intelligence technology, adaptive instruction can learn from the student. The machine tutor can create a representation of the student's current knowledge and other characteristics by interacting with the student. Producing adaptive instruction, given the design tools as well as the computer technology tools currently available, requires the ambition and commitment to develop. As increasingly ambitious design and development projects are undertaken, completed, and reported, the state of the art will evolve from potentials illustrated by these exemplary efforts.

The cutting edge of current thinking on adaptive instruction can be seen in Winn's (1989) point of view, which would lead instructional designers to rely more heavily on "first principles" of learning and cognition and to make reasoned judgments on such matters as instructional strategy from these principles, while being less concerned (than we have been in the past) with the "how to" steps of a design model or approach. Although Winn's position is a rather extreme one when taken literally (denying, in effect, the possibility of materials such as texts or videos as being useful agents for learning), his argument to increase the use of knowledge from cognitive science is greatly appreciated. (This text has certainly been influenced by Winn's position.)

Interactive Technologies. As of this writing, new interactive technologies such as CD-I (compact disk-interactive) and DVI (digital video interactive) are just beginning to become available for use in instructional delivery. These new technologies—as well as others that involve the marriage of video, computers, and sometimes other media such as telephone systems and print—have enormous promise in increasing the density and processing of digital information to and from visual and auditory materials (Brand, 1988). Al-though interactive technologies are not required to support artificial intelligence and adaptive instruction, the number of instructional medium attributes of materials and experiences that they can support will increase dramatically. Highly realistic simulations, up to and including virtual reality, will be supportable with affordable equipment.

Instructional Design Models. In the future we can expect the models that we employ to guide instructional design to become increasingly powerful and sophisticated. Hannum and Hansen (1989) provide a particularly insightful discussion of changes that may be anticipated with these future developments. Although many of their projections are reflected as reality in this text, not all their points are addressed here. (Also, we do not have any idea as to the extent of impact that this text will have on future practice.) Hannum and Hansen note the following five changes in ID models as ways in which they may be broadened from their original roots in behavioral learning psychology, general systems theory, and audiovisual and communications theory: (1) front-end analysis shaped by anthropological methods; (2) design and delivery shaped by the psychology of perception and cognitive sciences; (3) implementation shaped by market research techniques; (4) evaluation influenced by anthropology and sociology; and (5) design of training programs shaped by job design. Other improvements in instructional design models that are described include the following: (1) development of alterable models; (2) development of iterative rather than linear models, which can model the movement back and forth among phases to revisit those steps that need it based on subsequent decisions; (3) "layered" models within models that elaborate on design procedures; and (4) graduated models, from the ideal to the "quick and dirty" (Hannum & Hansen, 1989).

Performance Technologies. Business and industry in the future may increasingly use the "performance technology" standpoint rather than "instruction" as the umbrella under which instructional design operates. People who practice in this area are often called *performance engineers*. The performance engineer is interested in instruction as only one tool among many alternatives, which can range all the way from provision of job aids and incentives to delivery of psychological or counseling services. For the performance engineer, the central concern is not learning but performance on the job. Learning may or may not be what is needed in a particular situation. This point of view is entirely consistent with our view of instructional design as evidenced in Chapter 2 (especially the section on determining instructional needs). Although it is a somewhat different standpoint, performance technology is not at all contradictory to instructional design as we have described it. In a business or industry that employs a performance technology approach, instructional design will (or should be) the primary area of expertise held by those who—once instruction is determined to be needed—will be the key agents in its development. Thus far, the relevance of performance technology has been restricted to business and industry. The role of agencies such as schools and colleges is fundamentally concerned with learning, and therefore in these environments the performance technology view does not appear to fit. Gilbert's (1978) text is good source of more information on performance technology.

Advances in Cognitive Science. Developments in foundational elements will find their way into application through future generations of instructional design theories, models, and principles. People who are interested in instructional design will stay abreast of new developments in learning, cognition, human information processing, perception, and other specialties that may bear on instruction. Translation of new knowledge about learning, cognition, and other bases into instructional design principles and practice will change what we consider as feasible. Just as we have seen in the past 25 years, in the future we can expect to see science contributing to instruction by making it more efficient, effective, and appealing than ever before.

One of the aspects of cognitive science that has been reflected in Winn's writing and other literature is the constructivist perspective of learning. In essence, this perspective posits that meaning is not resident in the medium that contains the message, but in the learner, who, in interacting with the message, constructs a personal and unique interpretation or meaning. Although few would argue that meaning is not inherent in messages but is

a phenomenon of shared or "negotiated" definitions, researchers are divided on the relevance of this proposition. Some in the field lean increasingly upon generative instructional strategies based upon the constructivist perspective, questioning the efficacy of supplantive strategies (if knowledge is fundamentally constructed, learners should be persons whom we guide to such construction rather than receivers of instructional messages). Others in the field employ the constructivist perspective in a less pervasive fashion, using it to undergird and assist in instances in which a generative strategy has been selected, and to provide a filter and caution when working with supplantive strategies. (This is akin to the way that general semantics has been used for many years as a set of tools to guard against irrational and unhelpful language habits, such as mistaking the map for the territory, mistaking the label for the reality, and overgeneralizing based on labels.) Others reject the constructivist view more or less completely. We find a great deal of stimulating and provocative thought in the constructivist view, and we recommend that instructional design students study it (see Anglin & Belland, 1991 and *Educational Technology*, May and September, 1991).

Other issues that are of current interest, pointing to future directions in the field are (1) supplantive versus generative instructional strategies, (2) instruction in cognitive or learning strategies, and (3) the affective aspects of learning. Each of these issues has been discussed at length previously in this text:

1. Increased maturation of instructional theory is leading us to realize that both supplantive and generative instructional strategies have their place in instruction. We have tried to point this out in the chapters of this text that deal with instructional strategies. (See the discussion of supplantive and generative strategies of instruction in Chapter 6.)

2. A matter of some debate is where to place the emphasis between teaching learners to be better learners on their own—instruction in cognitive strategies or learning strategies—and development of instruction in the areas to be learned. (See Chapter 11 for a discussion of this topic.)

3. The affective aspects of learning is a third area of current and future interest, given our increased recognition of the importance of motivation in learning and our improving tools for designing instruction that is appealing. (Chapter 12 provides a discussion of this issue.)

The six areas described—artificial intelligence, adaptive instruction, interactive technologies, instructional design models, performance technologies, and cognitive science—are not only areas of development for which we can anticipate significant change and contributions to instructional design, but they also are all areas that have a high probability for interconnection and synergy. While we may be somewhat confident that these areas will be key to the future of instructional design, we are less certain as to what will emerge once we mix these elements together.

Instructional design is a "technology" of instruction in the most fundamental sense of the term. Too often we associate *technology* with equipment or with the uses of a class of equipment, such as computer technology. However, a technology consists as much of processes and ideas as it does of things and ways to use them. The history of technology has repeatedly confirmed that as a new and exciting device or system is used and developed, it becomes less and less important compared to the ideas, concepts, models, theories, and new technologies that evolve and emerge as products of its use.

In the past decade, instructional design has been the most powerful and influential "technology" of instruction for the improvement of learning in schools, business and industry, and government/military training, surpassing even popular and widely discussed product technologies such as computers and multimedia learning environments. Just as we can expect continuing advances in computer technology, video, telecommunications, and other media, we will also see advances in process technologies—not only those that may accompany various media but also the more comprehensive, integrative, and process-oriented technology of instructional design.

*E*xercise B

Beginning with the instructional design model presented in Chapter 1 and using the chapter summaries and summary diagrams, construct your own representation of the content of this text. The process of constructing your own summary by incorporating the content of chapters within the framework of the design model can assist your assimilation of the ideas you have studied in this text. It may also improve your recall of the main points, and it should provide you with a graphic organizer to end all graphic organizers!

Summary

This chapter provides three elements to conclude this text: (1) a summary of major principles that guide instructional design, (2) a discussion of "appropriate" design, and (3) a discussion of future developments.

The summary major principles guiding instructional design was a recapitulation of the content of this text, providing the reader with a summary in a different light. The discussion of appropriate design focused upon the proper level

of engagement in design activities. The decision points bearing on that level center around questions of available resources for the design project and criticality of the learning task. The discussion of future developments provided six areas in which we can anticipate significant improvement in the near future: artificial intelligence, adaptive instruction, interactive technologies, improvements in ID models, performance technologies, and advances in cognitive science and other foundational areas.

Readings and References

Anglin, G., & Belland, J. (1991). *Paradigms regained.* Englewood Cliffs, NJ: Educational Technology.

Brand, S. (1988). *The media lab: Inventing the future at M.I.T.* New York: Penguin.

Gayeski, D. M. (1991). Software tools for empowering instructional developers. *Performance Improvement Quarterly, 4*(4), 21–36.

Gilbert, T. (1978). *Human competence: Engineering worthy performance.* New York: McGraw-Hill.

Hannum, W., & Hansen, C. (1989). *Instructional systems development in large organizations.* Englewood Cliffs, NJ: Educational Technology Publications.

Merrill, M. D., Li, Z., & Jones, M. K. (1990a). Limitations of first generation instructional design. *Educational Technology, 30*(1), 7–11.

Merrill, M. D., Li, Z., & Jones, M. K. (1990b). Second generation instructional design. *Educational Technology, 30*(2), 7–14.

Noel, K. (1991, April). *An application of an ISD approach to curriculum development and change in a large-scale educational project: The case of Botswana.* A paper presented at the annual meeting of the American Research Association, Chicago.

Rogoff, R. L. (1984). The training wheel: A simple model for instructional design. *The Magazine of Human Resources Development, 21*(4), 63–64.

Rosenberg, M. (1991, April). *Building bridges to business: Opportunities and challenges for academia.* Address at the annual meeting of the Association for Educational Communications and Technology, Orlando, Florida.

Sample, J. (1989). Civil liability for failure to train to standard. *Educational Technology, 29*(6), 23–26.

Schank, R. (1984). *The cognitive computer: On language, learning, and artificial intelligence.* Reading, MA: Addison-Wesley.

Schumacher, E. F. (1973). *Small is beautiful: Economics as if people mattered.* London: Blond & Briggs.

Tessmer, M., & Wedman, J. F. (1990). A layers of necessity instructional development model. *Educational Technology Research and Development, 38*(2), 77–85.

Tripp, S. D., & Bichelmeyer, B. (1990). Rapid prototyping: An alternative instructional design strategy. *Educational Technology Research and Development, 38*(1), 31–44.

Wedman, J. F., & Tessmer, M. (1990). The "layers of necessity" ID model. *Performance and Instruction, 29*(4), 1–7.

Wedman, J. F. & Tessmer, M. (1991). Adapting instructional design to project circumstance: The layers of necessity model. *Educational Technology, 31*(6), 48–52.

Wedman, J. F., & Tessmer, M. (1992, April). *Instructional designers' decisions and priorities: A layers of necessity study.* Paper presented at the annual conference of the National Society for Performance Improvement, Miami.

Winn, W. (1989). Toward a rational and theoretical basis for educational technology. *Educational Technology Research and Development, 37*(1), 35–46.

author index

Kulik, C. L., 357, 359
Kulik, J. A., 357, 359

Lalik, R. M., 153, 163
Lamb, A., 386
Landa, L. N., 229, 233, 247
Langford, M., 386
Larkin, J. H., 253, 274
Lawson, A. E., 63
Lee, C., 378, 386
Lefcourt, H. M., 49, 62, 359
Lehman, I. J., 109, 136
Leippe, M. R., 324
Leitzman, D. F., 41
Leven, J. R., 189
Levie, W. H., 259, 301, 324
Levin, J. R., 295
Li, Z., 432, 437, 438, 442
Lippert, R. C., 258, 274, 275
Locatis, C. N., 174, 188
Lockhart, R. S., 152, 153, 163
Lohman, D. F., 63
London, B., 386
Loucks, S. F., 429
Low, W. C., 21, 24
Lowenfeld, V., 47, 62
Lowenthal, A., 272

Mager, R. F., 5, 24, 91, 92, 99, 101, 136
Magil, R. A., 327, 329, 331, 341
Maidment, R., 256, 274
Manahan, J., 341
Marcone, S., 231, 247
Martin, B. L., 301, 303, 306, 307, 324
Marzano, R. J., 296
Masia, B. B., 303, 324
Maslow, A. H., 51, 62
Mason, R. G., 324
Massialas, B., 258, 274
Mayer, J. P., 429
Mayer, R. E., 16, 24, 99, 148, 163, 252, 253, 274, 277, 278, 295, 297
McCombs, B. L., 278, 296
McDonald, B. A., 295
McFarland, T. D., 258, 274
McKinnon, J. W., 63
McLinden, D. J., 376, 386
Mehrens, W. A., 109, 136
Meichenbaum, D. M., 281, 296

Merrill, M. D., 67, 99, 191, 211, 327, 341, 432, 437, 438, 442
Merrill, P. F., 99
Meyer, B. J. F., 176, 188, 362, 385
Miller, G. A., 24, 62, 328, 341
Miller, N., 324
Miller, R., 280, 295
Mink, B. P., 352, 359
Mink, O. G., 352, 359
Minsky, M. A., 188
Mitchell, M. C., 247
Molenda, M., 24, 174, 188, 356, 359
Montague, W. E., 296
Moore, C. A., 63
Moore, T. V., 378, 386
Morris, L. L., 136, 403, 411, 417, 429
Murdock, B. B., 24
Murphy, D. A., 277, 278, 281, 295
Myers, C., 41
Myers, D., 386

Nelson, G. D., 148, 163
Newby, A., 296
Newby, T. J., 211, 296, 324, 342
Newel, K. M., 331, 341
Newell, A., 51, 62, 249, 274, 279, 296
Nicholas, J. M., 359
Niles, J. A., 153, 163
Noel, K., 436, 442
Norman, D. A., 158, 163, 277, 296
Norman, G. R., 253, 274
Novak, J. D., 143, 158, 163, 195, 211
Nunnaly, J. C., 303, 324

Oliver, D., 258, 274
Olton, R. M., 249, 272, 294
O'Neil, H. F., 136, 295, 296, 297
Ortony, A., 189
Osborne, R., 153, 163
Owen, K., 352, 359
Owston, R. D., 258, 275
Oxendine, J. B., 327, 341

Paivio, A., 20, 24, 45, 62, 345, 359
Paley, E., 47, 63
Parker, R., 258, 272
Peck, K. L., 370, 386
Peck, S., 163
Penner, P. C., 253, 275

subject index

Moral development, 52
Motivation, 309–316
Motivational design model, 313–314
Motor skills, 326
Multimedia (interactive video) attributes, 348–349

Narrative text structure, 176
Near transfer, 147–148
Needs assessment, 27–30
Negative transfer, 143
Norm-referenced assessment, 103
Normal distribution, 103

Objectives, 141
   conditions of demonstration, 92
   enabling, 88
   performance, 88, 91
   performance standards, 92
   terminal, 88
   terminal behavior, 92
Objectivism, 409
On-job observation, 111
Open skills, 327
Organization, 32, 71
Organizational strategy, 138
Organizers, advance, 195
Organizers, comparative, 195

Paired associate learning, 166
Part practice, 330
Participation, 310
Pattern recognition, 283
Payoff outcomes, 414–415
Pegword technique, 180
Pencil-and-paper tests, 113
Performance engineers, 439
Performance objective, 88, 91
Performance technology, 439
Performance terms (in goal writing), 66
Personalized system of instruction, 357
Persuasion, 302–303
Philosophy (of learning environment), 32
PLAN approach, 356
Practice, 144–146
Prerequisite analysis, 84–88
Prerequisite sequence, 157
Prerequisites, 65
Preview, 142
Primary audience, 43
Principles, 70, 213

Print attributes, 348
Print-based instruction, production of, 362–368
Prior knowledge, 142–143
Prior learning, 54–55
Problem, ill-defined, 250
Problem, well-defined, 250
Problem solving, 70, 80, 94, 249–250
   algorithmic, 249
   assessment, 263
   attention, 261
   cognitive requirements, 250–253
   defined, 249
   deploy attention, 259
   domain specific, 249
   expert versus novice, 253
   feedback, 262
   heuristic, 249
   instructional purpose, 259
   interest and motivation, 259
   learning strategies, 261
   macrostrategies, 253–258
   mental representation, 253
   practice, 261–262
   preview, 259
   prior knowledge, 259–260
   processing information, 260–261
   review, 262
   task analysis, 252–253
   transfer, 262
Problem space, 260–261
Procedural knowledge, 68
Procedural rules, 213
   assessment, 236
   closure, 235–236
   cognitive processes, 226
   complex, 227–228
   conditions supporting, 226–236
   deploy attention, 229
   discovery strategy, 229
   establish purpose, 229
   expository strategy, 229
   feedback, 234–235
   focus attention, 232
   interest and motivation, 229
   learning strategies, 232–233
   practice, 233–234
   preview lesson, 229
   prior knowledge, 230
   process information and examples, 230–232
   remediation, 236